Florilegium Historiale

Wallace K. Ferguson

FLORILEGIUM HISTORIALE

\\\

Essays
presented to
Wallace K. Ferguson

J.G. Rowe W.H. Stockdale

EDITORS

University of Toronto Press
in association with University of Western Ontario

©University of Toronto Press 1971
Printed in Canada by
University of Toronto Press, Toronto and Buffalo
ISBN 8020-1699-5

WALLACE K. FERGUSON

Wallace Klippert Ferguson was born in Peel County, Ontario, on 23 May 1902. His father was a Methodist minister who, before entering the active ministry, taught Hebrew and Patristic Greek. In 1924, Professor Ferguson graduated from the university of Western Ontario with an Honours Bachelor of Arts degree in English and History. He then entered Cornell university as a graduate student and holder of the Andrew Dixon White fellowship in History. His thesis for the Master of Arts degree, under the direction of Carl Becker, was in the field of the French Revolution and was completed in 1925. His first publication, an article on 'The Place of Jansenism in French History,' appeared in 1927. During further graduate work at Cornell under the direction of Preserved Smith, Professor Ferguson began work on one of his life-long interests, the life and works of Desiderius Erasmus. In 1927 Professor Ferguson received the degree of Doctor of Philosophy from Cornell university and spent the next year in Europe on a grant from the Social Science Research Council. This grant enabled him to embody the results of his doctoral research in his first book, *Erasmi Opuscula*, which consisted of an edited collection of the works of Erasmus not included in the Leyden edition of the *Opera Omnia*.

On his return from Europe, Professor Ferguson joined the History department at the Washington Square college of New York university where he remained for twenty-eight years and made a notable contribution to the development of one of the outstanding history departments in North America. In 1956 he returned to the university of Western Ontario to occupy the J. B. Smallman Chair of History and serve as head of the department of history. He is now senior professor of history at the university of Western Ontario.

As a youthful member of the New York university faculty, he began his well-known collaborative work with Geoffrey Bruun, *A Survey of European Civilization*, which was published in 1936. The project was initially suggested by Professor Carl Becker. Professor Ferguson is the author of the first volume of the two-volume work which became and still remains one of the most widely used texts in European history in North America. It has gone through four editions. A Swedish translation appeared in 1938. It is not too much to say that an entire generation of students has used this text. His work on this project stimulated his own interest in problems involving the interpretation of the Renaissance, a field which soon became the one in which he has made his most significant contributions to scholarship. An article on 'Humanist Views of the

Renaissance' appeared in 1939 to be followed (in 1940) by his well-
known essay in the Berkshire series, *The Renaissance*. His interest in the
Renaissance then led to an examination of the historiography of that
period, and he pursued this line of inquiry while on leave as a holder of
a Guggenheim Memorial fellowship in 1939-40. A year spent reading at
the Widener Library and subsequent research resulted in what many
scholars consider to be Professor Ferguson's finest work, *The Renaissance
in Historical Thought: Five Centuries of Interpretation*, published in
1948. Consisting of an exhaustive analysis of varying interpretations of
the Renaissance from the fifteenth to the twentieth centuries, the book
was well received. One scholar has stated that 'there have been few
books since Burckhardt's that can make equal claim to a place at the
elbow of every student working in the field.' Professor Ferguson's interest in the general interpretation of the Renaissance remained strong,
and in 1962 he published *Europe in Transition, 1300-1520*, an interpretive history of western Europe during two crucial centuries, which
one reviewer has characterized as 'a remarkable feat of synthesis and
integration ... probably destined to become as much a bible of graduate
students as the *Renaissance in Historical Thought*.' In addition to the
writings listed above, he has produced many articles of great significance
on the interpretation of his chosen field.

Professor Ferguson's work has not been limited to his considerable
scholarly production. He has been continuously active in service to various societies concerned with historical research and writing. He read a
paper presented at the first meeting of the Renaissance conference of
New England at Brown university in 1939. He served for years as a
member of the Committee on Renaissance Studies of the American Council of Learned Societies. When that committee disbanded in 1952 for
lack of funds, he served as a member of a new body which called itself
the American Committee on Renaissance Studies. It was this body which
took the initiative in the founding of the Renaissance Society of America.
He was a member of the Advisory Board of this society from 1954 until
1965 and served as president of the Renaissance Society, 1965-7 On his
return to Canada in 1956 he was one of the guiding spirits in the formation of the North-Central Renaissance Conference which held its first
meeting in London, Ontario, in April 1960. His activities in other historical societies have been constant and significant. From 1963 to 1967
he served on the council of the American Historical Association. In
1960-1 he was president of the Canadian Historical Association. From

1960 to 1963 he was a member of the Humanities Research Council of Canada. He has served, or is serving, as consultant to various learned journals. For example, from 1956 to 1959 he was on the board of editors of the *Journal of Modern History*, and at present he is on the board of editors of both the *Canadian Journal of History* and the *Dictionary of the History of Ideas*.

Professor Ferguson has been the recipient of many academic honours. The university of Western Ontario awarded him an LL.D. in 1954. He is a fellow of the Royal Society of Canada and in Canada's centennial year (1967) he received the Canada Council Medal. He is also historical co-editor of the Collected Works of Erasmus, in English, to be published by the University of Toronto Press.

His publications and scholarly labours have earned Wallace Ferguson an honoured place in the historiography of the Renaissance. Even so, it is possible that his most significant contribution, albeit an intangible one, has been the unfailing encouragement and support which he has given to countless students and colleagues. The editors hope that this volume of essays contributed by friends and colleagues will serve as fitting testimony to Professor Ferguson's services to the historian's craft during his long and dedicated career.

The editors gratefully acknowledge the assistance and encouragement of their colleagues in the history department of the university of Western Ontario. The publication of this volume has been made possible by the generosity of the university of Western Ontario and the University of Toronto Press. Our special thanks are due to Mrs Louise Weyerman for her careful preparation of the manuscript.

J. G. R.

W. H. S.

CONTENTS

ILLUSTRATIONS

Frontispiece: Wallace K. Ferguson

Between pages 56 and 57

Letter from Erasmus to Wimpfeling, Archives du chapître de St-Thomas,
tome 175, f.6, reproduced with the permission of the Archives et
bibliothèque de la ville de Strasbourg

Between pages 158 and 159

1

Master of the *Epître d'Othéa*, 1405-8, *Atropos-Mors*, Paris, Bibliothèque
nationale, français 606, f.17; reproduced with the permission of the
Bibliothèque nationale

2

Neapolitan, 1361, *Death and a Nobleman*, Naples, Museo della Certosa
di S. Martino; reproduced with the permission of Fratelli Alinari,
Florence, and Art Reference Bureau, New York

3

Francesco Traini, *Death* (detail), Pisa, Camposanto;
reproduced with the permission of Fratelli Alinari, Florence, and
Art Reference Bureau, New York

4

Flemish (Artois), c.1395, *Death and the Pilgrim*, Brussels, Bibliothèque
royale, MS 10176-8, f.112; reproduced with the permission of the
Bibliothèque royale

5

Fourth century B.C., *Thanatos*, London, British Museum; reproduced
with the permission of the Trustees of the British Museum

6

Roman, *Fury* (detail of sarcophagus), Florence, Opera del Duomo;
reproduced with the permission of Fratelli Alinari, Florence,
and Art Reference Bureau, New York

7

Epître Master, *Tisiphone and the family of Athamas*, Paris, Bibliothèque
nationale, français 606, f.10; reproduced with the permission of the
Bibliothèque nationale

Figures 1, 14, and 15 are reproduced with the permission of the Trustees
of the British Museum, London; figures 2-9, 12, and 13 are reproduced
with the permission of the Director of the Royal College of Music,
London; figures 10 and 11 are reproduced with the permission of the
Trustees of the National Portrait Gallery, London

Florilegium Historiale

The
Italian view of
Renaissance Italy

Denys Hay

A me piace abitar la mia contrada,
Visto ho Toscana, Lombardia, Romagna,
    Quel monte che divide e quel che serra
    Italia, e un mare e l'altro che la bagna.   Ariosto, *Satira*, III, 57-60

I must begin this brief essay with an apology for a title which may mislead. 'Renaissance,' as here used, is intended to cover a particular period of time – roughly the period between 1300 and 1550. In what follows I shall not be much concerned with the Italian awareness of the cultural innovations which took place in Italy at this time, a subject which has often been discussed and which forms a significant element of such fundamental books as *The Renaissance in Historical Thought*. My theme is different. I propose to examine the way in which some Italians looked at the geographical area in which they lived, at their *patria* in the largest sense of that term.

For most Italians, *patria* meant, not the entire peninsula, but those narrower localities with which they had immediate sentimental and political ties. Yet, however oblivious in practice to the demands of larger loyalties, literate Italians were forever referring to the land as a whole. It is hard to find a poet or historian, or writer of any kind, who does not offer observations or reflections which might be used to illustrate a view of Italy. During the Risorgimento the scholars who promoted unification ransacked earlier literature to demonstrate that there had always been an Italy. And in the Renaissance they found much material. It was, of course, particularly noticeable in the sources for the late fifteenth and early sixteenth centuries, the years of the French invasion of 1494 and the subsequent Italian wars when 'liberty' was destroyed in Italy and many Italians were conscious of this. There is much recent work on this period, and on the reactions of (for example) Machiavelli and Guicciardini to the tortured choices before them, the safety of Florence against the safety of Italy, and how the individual could survive to influence events in those cruel days.[1] But the contemporary material is nearly all polemical. From Petrarch, in *Italia mia*, to the anguished writers who witnessed the campaigns of Charles VIII, Francis I, and Charles V, the picture of Italy as struggling against barbarism is distorted by immediate political purposes, which in the event were to be frustrated. What I intend to present in the following pages are the opinions of a few Italians who considered the land with no such urgency, who were anxious to display Italy without political overtones, Italy as such and not as an ideal or as a programme.

I shall summon three witnesses: Dante (writing in the early fourteenth century), Flavio Biondo (mid-fifteenth), Leandro Alberti (mid-sixteenth). I shall indicate summarily their varying approaches and then attempt a few conclusions.

By way of preface we should recall the main features of the public scene in Italy during the two hundred and fifty years spanned by the lives of these men. At the beginning of the period, Italy was emerging from the chaos which had engulfed her with the fall of the Hohenstaufen in 1250; at the end, the country was entering the exhausted peace which followed the domination of the peninsula by Spanish armies. In the interval the emperors had lost all effective power and – after residence at Avignon, after the schism, the councils and Luther – so had the popes, save pre-cariously in the states of the Church where they reigned like princes. From a peak of commercial wealth attained in Dante's day, Italian prosperity had generally and steadily declined until in 1550 it was a shadow of what it had been. But these too are the centuries of the Renaissance in Italy, one aspect of which was a heightened understanding of *Italianità,* of the uniqueness and value of Italy. The authors discussed below were not directly concerned to promote such an understanding but their works contributed to its development and reflect changes in cultural emphasis.

The work of Dante is rich in Italian reflections, not least in the *La divina commedia,* where there are many glancing references to the land, both affectionate and contemptuous. In one of his Latin works, the *De vulgari eloquentia* (c. 1305), he deliberately surveyed the scene in a dis-passionate fashion, giving us a personal view of the map of Italy.[2] This work was, of course, intended not as a geographical or chorographical manual, but as a survey of the Romance languages and a guide to writers in 'il bel paese là dove il sì suono.' In the course of his remarkable analysis, the earliest and for ages the only scientific treatise on linguistics, Dante made several observations which reveal his way of apprehending Italy. In reading these portions of the *De vulgari eloquentia* it is important to remember that the author had before him, perhaps literally but most cer-tainly in his mind, a map of the kind associated with Pietro Vesconte.[3] This displayed the peninsula as part of a circular world-map, with Jerusa-lem in the centre and Asia in the top half. Europe was depicted in the lower quarter on the left, separated by the Mediterranean from Africa in the lower quarter on the right. This arrangement – deriving from ancient sources and reflected in the medieval 'T & O' diagrams – meant that Italy was drawn with the Alps at the bottom left and the toe at the upper right.

Dante's references to left and right are accordingly the reverse of later practice.

In discussing the Italian language Dante touches twice on the peninsula as a whole, in chapters ix and x of book I. To illustrate the linguistic variations of Italy he compares:

> the speech of the right side of Italy with that of the left: the Paduans talk differently from the Pisans. Neighbours have different speech: the Milanese differ from the Veronese, the Romans from the Florentines. Even peoples who are of one race are disparate: the Neapolitans and the men of Gaeta, for instance, or the people of Ravenna and those of Faenza.[4]

In a later passage he surveys the peninsula more systematically:

> Italy is divided into two parts, a right side and a left. If you ask about the dividing line I will briefly reply that this is the range of the Appenines, which, like the sloping ridge of a roof,[5] divides the waters running down, channelling them now to one shore and now to the other, as Lucan describes in the second book [of the *Pharsalia*]. The right side drains into the Tyrrhenian sea, the left into the Adriatic. The regions of the right are: Apulia (though not all of it), Rome, the duchy of Spoleto, Tuscany, the March of Genoa. Those of the left are: part of Apulia, the March of Ancona, Romagna, Lombardy, the March of Treviso with Venice. Friuli and Istria thus have to belong to the left of Italy and the Tyrrhenian islands, Sicily and Sardinia, belong to or rather are naturally to be associated with the right of Italy.[6]

Dante goes on to point out that each of these regions had a distinct language; there were at least fourteen. But, in addition to that, in Tuscany, men from Siena spoke differently from those of Arezzo; in Lombardy, the men of Ferrara and those of Piacenza had their own languages. And he refers to an earlier passage in which he had shown that even in a single town there could be more than one vernacular. In Bologna the men of Borgo San Felice, just outside the wall, had a tongue differing from that of the inhabitants of the centre, of 'strada maggiore.'[7] All in all, Dante concludes, 'if one wanted to count the main and the secondary vernaculars of Italy, together with their further divisions, in this small corner of the world the number of linguistic varieties would reach not merely a thousand but even more.'[8]

For centuries no subsequent writer looked at Italy so coolly as Dante did in this extraordinary book. But the realities pointed to in the *De vulgari eloquentia*, like the book itself, were to be ignored. The book, which remained half-finished, was not influential. An Italian translation appeared in 1529 but the Latin original was not published until 1577 when, amid the growing assertiveness of Tuscan, it was felt that Dante's strictures on that species of the vernacular betrayed the cause; it was even argued that the work was not an authentic writing of the poet.[9] Yet Dante's aim had been to advocate a 'courtly' Italian which would unify the land and encourage the fundamental cultural unity he discerned behind all the divisions.

No such ambition lay behind Flavio Biondo's *Italia illustrata*. Biondo, in the papal secretariate from 1434, came from Forlì in the Romagna, and is best known for his *Historiarum ab inclinatione Romanorum imperii decades*, a history of Europe from the fall of Rome to his own day. He also wrote two archaeological works, the *Roma instaurata* and the *Roma triumphans*. The *Italia illustrata* was composed between 1448 and 1453, but it is likely that the author had been collecting materials for some time earlier. It is not a long book, but it is an important one. Dante's description was incidental to his linguistic purposes; Biondo's was the first work expressly devoted to Italy as a whole. It was published (in October 1453) before it was completed, in order to frustrate the circulation of unauthorized copies, and Biondo tinkered with it thereafter almost till his death (in 1463).[10] What was Biondo's purpose in writing this unusual work? The inspiration for it came, it seems, from Alfonso v who asked for a 'description of Italy in which the ancient names were to be related to their modern equivalents.'[11] And this is what Biondo set out to do, basing his account as far as possible on classical authorities, but adding details of men famous for valour and letters so that (in his own words) he provided 'not just a description of Italy ... but a sort of summary of Italian history.'[12]

The book begins with a general discussion of Italy, eschewing praises of the land – which have been sufficiently provided by Vergil, Pliny, and Petrarch – but giving its over-all dimensions. Biondo then writes:

> Italy has a back-bone, the sort we see in fish, and this is the Appenines, a mountain range which begins at the end of the Alps nearest the Tyrrhenian sea, goes straight down towards Ancona and seems about to end there; but it starts off again and goes through the middle of

Italy, ending in Calabria ... Having displayed the site and the size of
Italy, we must now divide up the land and describe in detail the places
in it.[13]

He bemoans the difficulties of this task. Places have changed their names
and Roman Italy is no more. Where of old there were seven hundred cities
the Roman curia now counts only two hundred and sixty-four with bishoprics. Of the ancient regions only one has not significantly changed: ancient Etruria had the same boundaries as modern Tuscany; the other
ancient regions have changed their names and limits several times. He
accordingly divides his survey into eighteen regions (not including the
islands), making use in general of those names best known in his own day.
His regions are: Liguria or the Genoese (p. 295); Etruria (p. 299);
Latium or the Campagna and Maritima of Rome (p. 313); Umbria or the
duchy of Spoleto (p. 328); Picenum or the March of Ancona (p. 334);
Romagna, or Flaminia and Emilia (p. 342); Gallia Cisalpina or Lombardy (p. 356); the Veneto (p. 369); Italia Transpadana or the March of
Treviso (p. 374); Aquileia or Forum Julii (p. 384); Istria (p. 386);
Samnium or the Abbruzzi (p. 389); Old Campania or Terra di Lavoro
(p. 406); Lucania; Apulia (p. 421); Salentini or Terra d'Otranto; Calabria; Brutii.[14] These divisions Biondo derived ultimately from Pliny;[15]
they bore little relation to the political facts of his day, save that Venice –
by the mid-fifteenth century a major territorial power in Italy – was recognized as a separate region, and the existence of the *Regno*, conquered
by his patron Alfonso v, was accepted by Biondo, in grouping at the end
the provinces south of Rome. In fact, not only did Biondo omit the islands,
he also omitted the last four regions, having been disappointed of help
from Neapolitan scholars,[16] so that his survey is very defective.

Biondo begins each description of a region by listing its boundaries,
and then proceeds to deal *seriatim* with towns, castles, rivers. In all this
he follows wherever possible the ancient authorities, and never forgets
that his aim is to relate ancient names with modern. But he regularly inter-
sperses brief indications of scenery and notes the occasions when small
places have momentarily had historical importance. When he discusses
larger towns a succinct account is given of origins, of subsequent history,
of the current situation, including the names of celebrated writers, and of
families who have produced popes. All in all the work is an impressive
attempt to come to terms with the history, geography, and monuments of
divided Italy.

Yet the book is very unbalanced. Apart from the defective treatment of the south of the peninsula and the omission of the islands, the amount of space allocated to the regions of central and northern Italy is hardly what one would expect. The account of the Romagna is the most glaring example of this. It is as long as the sections on Tuscany or Rome and twice as long as the section on the Veneto. But then the Romagna was Biondo's native land. It was the home of the revival of letters and the birth-place of the Italian general Alberigo da Barbiano, whose indigenous militarism seemed to Biondo to point to a happier political future.[17]

The *Italia illustrata* was the first of the chorographical works of the Renaissance, and it deservedly attracted attention.[18] It circulated widely in manuscript form. It was printed at Rome in 1474 and (with other works) by Froben at Basle in 1531. In 1548 Lucio Fauno (who had earlier translated Pius II's abbreviation of the *Decades*) issued an Italian version of the *Roma triumphans* and of the *Italia illustrata* at Venice. This vernacular recension might well have been much to the taste of the public but, in the event, it was to be overtaken by another similar but more elaborate survey, the *Descrittione* of Leandro Alberti.

Leandro Alberti is much less well known than Dante or Biondo. He was born in 1479 and died probably in 1552. He came from Bologna and, though as a Dominican friar and provincial he travelled extensively in Italy, he spent much of his time in his native town. He wrote the history of the town and made a *tavola* of its leading families and he wrote of the great men of the Dominican order.[19] His chief claim to fame, however, was his *Descrittione di tutta Italia*, first printed at Bologna in 1550.[20]

The handsomely printed volume was five times longer than Biondo's but had the same general aim; in the author's words it was 'a work of a geographer, a topographer, and an historian all together.'[21] He began by cataloguing all other descriptions of the peninsula and explained that for moderns it resembled a human leg, beginning with the thickness of the thigh and descending down to the extremity of the foot. 'In fact,' he wrote, 'this seems to me a very helpful concept,' and he or his printer put in the margin at this point. 'Bella simiglianza.'[22] Then he explained that he planned to describe the boundaries of each region, to give the ancient and modern names not only of the regions but of towns, castles, mountains, rivers, lakes, and springs, narrating the marvels of nature, celebrating the famous deeds of those associated with these places; 'in a word I promise to record (as far as I may) the notable and commemorable things of this our Italy.'[23] And then (like Biondo) he urged the difficulties.

Biondo was his immediate model. The eighteen regions of the *Italia illustrata* were broadly followed, though Alberti sometimes defined their boundaries differently and, in all, identified nineteen regions. For the rest his book is more elaborate partly because he could not resist catalogues of ancient authorities. Where Biondo was content with one name, Alberti puts in half a dozen. It was, of course, the case that by the mid-sixteenth century a good many towns and localities had been written about by humanist scholars and topography, particularly in relation to ancient survivals, was establishing itself as a genre. Biondo had pioneered such studies and Alberti was able to make use of a wide range of secondary material which had not existed a century earlier.[24] The larger scale of the work also encouraged more detailed descriptions. These are sometimes extensive and evocative: for example, Lodi, which was discussed in a few lines by Biondo, occupies three pages or so of Alberti and we are told not only of its history but of the cheeses in the market and the irrigation of the countryside.[25] In general a great deal of geographical detail is provided. The *Descrittione* is also easier to follow because, unlike Biondo, Alberti moves systematically down one side of the peninsula and up the other.

There is, however, the same lack of proportion that we have noticed in Biondo though not to so marked an extent. This time the south is fairly discussed but Alberti, like his predecessor, came from Romagna and that province is given elaborate attention; it occupies, in fact, more space than the Campagna. Although under Rome are listed all the emperors and all the popes as well as the main monuments and a potted history, under Bologna there are catalogues of saints, prelates, professors, artists, and so on, in addition to a description of events and buildings.[26] The islands do not figure in the first edition though Alberti explained that he had written about them and if his work was well received, he would add them subsequently.[27] And not all of the recent authorities to which Alberti turned were reliable. He was a victim of the forgeries of his fellow Dominican Annius (Nanni) of Viterbo who died in 1502 and his pages contain many references to the (spurious) writings of Berosus the Chaldaean.

The elaboration and the completeness of the *Descrittione* nevertheless command respect and this was immediately recognized. In 1551 a second edition appeared at Venice[28] and down to 1631 there were a further nine Venetian editions. The promised additional section on the islands appeared in 1561 and in the edition of 1568 each island was accompanied by a map. Two editions of a Latin translation were issued at Cologne in 1566 and 1567, curious tribute to the European appeal of a book which was being used as the *vade mecum* of the northern visitor to Italy. Montaigne ap-

parently had it with him on his celebrated journey,[29] but so had many
other travellers down to the eighteenth century, as one can see from the inscriptions in the surviving copies.[30] Alberti's work is, in fact, a step towards the later guide book, destined to be made otiose only as and when
that new type of travel literature made its appearance with the *Itinerarium
Italiae* of François Schott (1600), another work which in various forms
was to have a long life.[31] But this, as they say, is another story.

What small sustenance can one derive from these sketchy indications? Obviously the map of Italy has been turned the right way up, at least for
those of us accustomed to having the north at the top. Dante's cartography
was necessarily schematic and literary. Biondo and Alberti were looking
at the country much as we look at it: the *portolano* had done its work and
by Alberti's day Italy was rapidly moving into the first great age of systematic cartography. There can be no doubt that Alberti used maps and
that the cartographers of his day and later used his book in making
theirs.[32] The geographical unity of Italy is pronounced and through the
centuries this is reflected in descriptive works.

Yet there are some curious discrepancies. All our witnesses testify to
the Alps being the northern boundary: they had no geographical or historical alternative. Yet, in practice, they neglect the northern fringe of
Italy. Dante said that Trent and Turin were on the frontier but, more surprisingly, also says this of Alessandria.[33] Biondo's discussion of the northern fringe of Lombardy is very scant and, by the time of Alberti, Piedmont,
as he noted, was ruled by the king of France, Henry II, to whom (with his
consort Catherine de' Medici) the *Descrittione* was dedicated.[34] Even
odder is the neglect of the islands. Dante greatly admired the dialect of the
Sicilian nobles of an earlier day, and admitted that Sicily and Sardinia
were part of Italy; but in his survey he was contemptuous of Sardinian
speech and did not mention Corsica.[35] In the *Italia illustrata* Biondo has
no place at all for the islands, and no explanation for their absence. The
work is admittedly defective in its discussion of the southern portions of
the peninsula; it is hard to see how the author could have avoided Sicily
if he had dealt at all adequately with the provinces comprised in the
Regno, though in his request for information in December 1450 he does
not mention the island from which Alfonso V had conquered the main-
land.[36] There are fleeting references to Corsica and Sardinia in connection
with Genoese activity overseas, almost as though they were simple colo-
nies.[37] Alberti's approach to this matter is thus a marked change, for he
firmly states in his introduction[38] that Corsica and Sardinia are part of

Italy and from the start he had included the islands in his survey, although (as we have observed) these sections did not appear in the earlier editions.

What of the images which the three authors invoke to convey a picture of the peninsula? For Dante (and Lucan) the Appenines are, in a curious way, a unifying element in divided Italy. The rain rattles on the tiles and runs off east and west, but one roof shelters the chattering and quarrelling peoples. Biondo likens the structure of the land to a fish with a long spine and Alberti admires this: 'Veramente pare questo Monte un dorso ò sia schiena d'Italia.' [39] But his own preference, as we have seen, is for Italy as a leg; he elaborates the anatomical correspondence at wearisome length.[40] To some degree these inventions reflect the increasing precision of the maps which were available. It was only when representations of the peninsula became fairly accurate that the resemblance to a leg was evident. Alberti's 'bella simiglianza' also suggests the personified maps of Europe which were shortly to be made, such as that in Sebastian Münster's *Cosmographia* (1588).[41]

In more general terms the three texts adduced in these pages underline the peculiar provincialism of Italy. And by 'provincialism' I do not mean the 'Italic' provinces or regions into which the country was divided;[42] I mean those urban units to which real attachment was felt. Dante's analysis is town-based, though sometimes he was thinking also of the *contado*.[43] Biondo, like Alberti, measures the prosperity of the land by the number of its towns. In ancient times, Biondo pointed out, there were 700; Alberti increases this number to 1,166. In Biondo's day there were only 264 and Alberti could count only 300. The view which emerges is one of small urban units, town-based governments, overlaid from time to time (especially in Alberti's discussion) by larger but somehow irrelevant controls.

This impression is encouraged by the arbitrary names of provinces which Biondo adopted and which were carried on and elaborated by Alberti. True, these ancient names were to the taste of classically educated readers, and they had, like the bishoprics of Italy which had boundaries which often still fitted neatly into the old provinces,[44] a kind of permanence amid the perpetual fluctuations of the Italian political scene. Originally, after all, they had to some extent reflected permanent geographical features, not least the Appenines. Yet certain broad political entities were firmly established by the fourteenth century, not least the states of the Church and the kingdom of Sicily. By Biondo's day a large hereditary duchy of Milan might reasonably have figured as a permanent part of his world, though he was writing just after the attempt to establish the Ambrosian republic had failed. And Venice was likewise mistress of the north-eastern provinces. It is not that Biondo or Alberti entirely ignore these features. Biondo (for instance) mentions that the Genoese have really dominated most of Liguria[45] and Alberti writes of the 'great empire and lordship which the gentlemen of Venice have had and still have both by sea and on *terra ferma.*'[46] But they did not see the country organized in such units; they avoided the basic issues of their day. No one concerned with the urgent pressures of politics could have afforded to do this. It is salutary to compare with Biondo his contemporary Pius II who was under no illusions about the state of Italy. This might be illustrated from many of his writings, and not least from the *Commentarii,* but it is displayed most succinctly in his section on the *novitates Italiae* in *De Europa,*[47] written when he was Cardinal Aeneas Sylvius Piccolomini. His chapters are devoted to Genoa, 'mistress and queen of the Ligurians,' Milan, Venice, Mantua, Ferrara, Bologna, Florence, Siena, Rome, Umbria, and the kingdom of Naples – this the longest section in the book.[48] Here again we are presented with towns: but it is those towns which were of general significance in mid-fifteenth century Italian politics. For the foreigners, looking at Italy from outside, the bigger units naturally obtruded; this is evident enough in diplomatic sources, but may be even more tellingly seen in the *History of Italy* compiled by the relatively unenlightened Welsh visitor, William Thomas.[49] Thomas certainly gives the old names of the provinces (he had beside him the *Italia illustrata* of Biondo), but he places them under their present rulers.[50] After reading Alberti it is refreshing to begin Thomas' book with: 'The greatest prince of dominion there at this present time is Charles the Fifth, Emperor of Almain, who for his part hath the realm of Naples and the duchy of Milan.'[51]

Dante's linguistic treatise was designed to promote Italian unity. It is clear also from his other writings, and especially from the *Monarchia,* that this was his aim. However, he accepted political diversities and had no desire that the emperor should obliterate the liberties of Italy. Biondo's *Italia illustrata* is a political morass, perhaps a reflection of the atmosphere of the curia in his day. For Alberti, division has come to stay – or so one feels. His artificial provinces dominate even the index to his work. Each letter of the alphabet is subdivided into nineteen sections, corresponding to each of the *regioni* of the *Descrittione* – a nightmare indeed for the user who did not know which of the ancient territories contained the place about which he sought information. Despite the general confusion Biondo is optimistic; a new day has dawned. This is far from being the sentiment to be distilled from Alberti. In the detailed descriptions of a good many places in the *Descrittione* cheerfulness and pride are evident, but in the introductory section on Italy as a whole he is gloomy enough. 'Evil, envy and unrestrained appetite for power are dominant in Italy and have led her to such misery that from being a lady and a queen she has become worse than a slave girl. One cannot think of this without great grief.'[52] Yet a curious absence of resentment is found in Alberti: he does not revile the French and Spanish barbarians. Biondo had been bitterly critical of the foreign mercenaries of trecento Italy.[53] Alberti accepts a situation which, at the price of foreign occupation, was to give the urban units of the peninsula a peace such as they had not known for three centuries.

Finally one must recognize a steady decline in the originality of the scholarship of the books we have glanced at. Perhaps it is unfair to compare Dante's *De vulgari eloquentia* with the others, for it was a work of rare genius which had few competitors and was, in any case, intended to explore problems to which the geography and history of Italy were in a sense peripheral. Yet his firm and angular Latin, precise and economical, compares favourably with the smooth Latin prose of Biondo, himself no stylist. In turn Biondo's style strikes one as clear and well-structured compared with the flaccid Italian of Alberti, whose sentences limp along with a mixture of Latinizing and vernacular phrases; reading him is a somewhat laborious business. With Alberti one is conscious too that the outpouring of the classical scholarship of the Renaissance can have a stultifying effect. He is besotted with his authorities, and his exposition becomes muscle-bound through over-exercise in name-dropping.

Yet Alberti in Italian was to reach a public infinitely wider than Biondo in Latin. This public was at first largely composed of his own countrymen but, as we have seen, soon the regular visitors to Italy from beyond the Alps were to find him a useful companion. The *Descrittione* overtook the *Italia illustrata*, even in Fauno's Italian version. The *Descrittione* itself, by the end of the sixteenth century, was gradually to be replaced by guide books on the one hand and by more scholarly works on individual towns on the other, a process with which successive publishers of the book strove to cope by revision.[54] Works of this kind, unlike the pilgrim literature of an earlier day, were in constant need of *aggiornamento*, were constantly in danger of becoming obsolete.

In their attempts to convey a total picture of Italy, Biondo and Alberti were thus bound to become outmoded. But one may suspect that in their quiet fashion they (and the men who in different ways were to succeed them – men like Ludovico Guicciardini, Ughelli, Muratori) were to do more by patient description and collection of materials than were the wilder enthusiasts from Dante down to Machiavelli. Biondo and Alberti were also to transmit to the rest of Europe the ambition to describe countries exactly, and to relate the ancient places to the modern names. Both the *Italia illustrata* and the *Descrittione di tutta Italia* have been undeservedly neglected. They expressed an important Italian mood and helped to construct a permanent awareness, at levels deeper than politics and war, of the underlying unity of Italy. They conveyed such an appreciation of Italy among foreign visitors. And they precipated similar national self-consciousness elsewhere.

NOTES

1 A useful recent survey is provided by V. Illardi, 'Italianità,' *Traditio* xii (1956), 339-67.
2 I am grateful to Mr Colin Hardie for a note on the date of the work.
3 See *De vulgari eloquentia* (hereafter DVE), ed. A. Marigo (Florence 1938), pp. 47 and 82, notes: cf. P. Revelli, *L'Italia nella Divina Commedia* (Milan 1922), esp. pp. 59-73 on the 'confini e regioni d'Italia.' For a recent discussion of Dante's geography, see G. Vinay, 'Ricerche sul *De vulgari eloquentia*: iii Apenini devexione clauduntur,' *Giornale storico della litteratura italiana*, cxxxvi (1959), 367-82. I have to thank Professor Cecil Grayson for this reference.
4 DVE, i,ix,4-5 (Marigo, p. 66)
5 Cf. 'Si come neve tra le vive travi/per lo dosso d'Italia si congela ...' *Purg.* xxx. 85-6
6 DVE, i,x,6-7 (Marigo, pp. 80-6)
7 DVE, i,ix,4 (Marigo, p. 66)
8 DVE, i,x,9 (Marigo, p. 88). It is difficult to put neatly into English the phrase 'primas et secundarias et subsecundarias vulgaris Ytalie variationes.'
9 See Marigo's introduction, pp. xliii-xlviii
10 See the account by B. Nogara, *Scritti inediti e rari di Biondo Flavio, Studi e Testi*, 48 (Rome 1927), pp. cxxi-cxxvi; the editor prints, pp. 215-39, some of the later additions. A critical study of the *Italia illustrata*, and an authoritative text, would be welcome.
11 Nogara, *Scritti inediti*, pp. 163-4
12 I quote from the Basel edition of 1531, p. 295
13 *Italia illustrata*, p. 294
14 The places are listed as on p. 293 of *Italia illustrata*, the page references are to the beginnings of the completed sections.

15 *Historia Naturalis*, iii,v,45 – iii,xx. Pliny's description is based on the eleven regions of Augustus. For these, and later modification, see R. Thomsen, *The Italic Regions* (Copenhagen 1947).

16 Nogara, *Scritti inediti*, cxxiv

17 *Italia illustrata*, p. 350. Cf. D. Hay, 'Flavio Biondo and the Middle Ages,' *Proceedings of the British Academy*, xlv (1959), 97-128

18 R. Weiss, 'Lineamenti per una storia degli studi antiquari in Italia,' *Rinascimento*, ix (1960 for 1958), 141-201; see additional note, p. 17

19 A brief life and bibliography by A.L. Redigonda is found in *Dizionario biografico degli italiani*, i (1950) (dbi). A study of Alberti and his *Descrittione* has been undertaken as a doctoral dissertation at Edinburgh by Miss Rosemary Austin, to whom I am obliged for checking the above account. I am also grateful to Dr Esmond de Beer for allowing me to consult his collection of editions of the *Descrittione*.

20 There are two versions of the first pages of the *editio princeps*, one with and one without the engraved portrait of Alberti.

21 Quoted Redigonda, dbi

22 *Descrittione*, p. iii^v

23 *Descrittione*, pp. vi^v-vii

24 R. Weiss, '*Lineamenti*'

25 *Italia illustrata*, p. 362; *Descrittione*, pp. 370^v-3

26 *Descrittione*, pp. 96^v-141, 263-316^v

27 *Ibid.*, p. 469^v. Venice is listed as an island (p. vii^v) but is in fact dealt with in the first edition, pp. 450^v-67^v, as are the 'Isole intorno Vinegia,' pp. 467^v-9

28 This includes in the preliminaries the portrait of Alberti which is found in some issues of the first edition but which was omitted in later reprints. In some of the latter a certain amount of additional material is provided in the text.

29 E.S. de Beer, 'The Development of the Guide-book until the early Nineteenth Century,' *Journal of the British Architectural Association*, 3rd ser., xv (1952), 36n. Dr de Beer has kindly indicated to me a number of parallel passages which are conclusive. Alberti is not referred to by C. Dédéyan, *Essai sur le Journal de Voyage de Montaigne* (Paris, n.d.), whose discussion of 'les sources livresques,' pp. 155-9, is, however, perfunctory.

30 In 1778 W. Minto had a copy of the Venice edition of 1553 with him in Rome. A few years later he urged his executors to give it to the university library at Edinburgh when he died, writing in it: 'This valuable work is very scarce. It is the best Classical Description of Italy. Addison has taken a great many things from it.'

31 See E.S. de Beer, 'François Schott's *Itinerario d'Italia*,' *Library*, 4th ser., xxiii (1942), 57-83

32 R. Almagià, *L'Italia di G.A. Magnini e la cartografia dell' Italia nei secoli* xvi e xvii (Naples 1922)

33 dve, i,xv,8 (Marigo, p. 132); for the limits of the area of 'sì' in Dante, see Vinay's article, note 3 above

34 *Descrittione*, sig.* ij and p. 408
35 DVE, I,xi,7; I,xxii,2,4 (Marigo, pp. 94, 96-8)
36 Nogara, *Scritti inediti*, p. 163: '... ea Italiae pars, quam regnum Siciliae appellamus, in aliquot divisa regiones, Campaniam scilicet veterem, Samnium ... Aprutium, Apuliam, Lucaniam, Calabros, Bruttios et Salentinos.'
37 *Italia illustrata*, p. 298, and Nogara, *Scritti inediti*, p. 229
38 *Descrittione*, p. vi^v
39 *Descrittione*, p. iii; earlier classical 'figures' are listed
40 *Descrittione*, pp. iii^v-iv
41 Reproduced in my *Europe: the Emergence of an Idea* (rev. ed., Edinburgh 1968), frontispiece. But in this Italy appears as an arm, not a leg.
42 In fact, *provincia* is normally used by these writers to mean Italy itself, *regio* or *regione* its larger parts.
43 Cf. Marigo, p. 132n
44 Thomsen, *The Italic Regions*, p. 316; cf. the areas of the *Rationes decimarum* (thirteenth and fourteenth centuries) used in papal taxation in Italy; cf. Revelli, *L'Italia*, p.73.
45 *Italia illustrata*, p. 298
46 *Descrittione*, p. 452^v
47 *Opera Omnia* (Basle 1551), pp. 445-71
48 As it was to prove to be one of the biggest problems of his pontificate. There are a few briefer chapters in the book, which is composed of collections intended to be used in a later expanded form.
49 William Thomas, *The History of Italy* (1549), ed. George B. Parkes, (Ithaca, 1963)
50 *Ibid.*, pp. 16-19
51 *Ibid.*, p. 16
52 *Descrittione*, p. vi
53 *Italia illustrata*, p. 349
54 This is an aspect of the later editions of the *Descrittione* which merits study, though revision does not seem to have been very thorough-going. In the 1558 Venice edition of Fauno's translation of Biondo's work there are 'Annotationi,' sig. HH6-II 3^v.

ADDITIONAL NOTE: Since my essay was written the late Roberto Weiss' *The Renaissance Discovery of Classical Antiquity* has appeared (Oxford 1969). Cf. above, nn. 18 and 24.

Petrarch:
His inner struggles
and the humanistic discovery
of man's nature

————————————————

Hans Baron

Writers have called Petrarch 'the first humanist' or even 'the first modern man,' but very few people seem to have a clear answer when asked how and when Petrarch decisively parted from medieval ways. No doubt, his knowledge of antiquity constantly grew over the years. But was the outlook on life and history that distinguished him from his predecessors the result of a gradual process which continued throughout his life? Should we assume that he only very slowly moved away from the traditions of the Middle Ages and that, as a consequence, he was more detached from medieval values towards the end of his life than he had been during his younger years?

To the modern student, who likes to think in terms of historical continuity, a gradual separation from medieval traditions seems to be the natural assumption and, in fact, this has been taken for granted in much of the writing on Petrarch. But there is another side to this matter, a side which, strangely enough, is often neglected, even though it is closely intertwined with one of the historical priorities with which he is credited: that he was the first modern writer to leave penetrating autobiographical glimpses of his own development. In addition to his correspondence, it is especially the information found in his *De secreto conflictu curarum suarum* – his *Secretum*, 'The Secret Book on the conflict of his restless strivings'–that allows us to see his life through his own eyes. This self-analysis and confession has often been called a counterpart to Augustine's *Confessions*; it certainly tries to be a close parallel to the writing of the church father in its objectives and *forma mentis*. Augustine's aim had been to clarify what we conceive to be his passage from classical, pre-Christian antiquity to a world formed by many of the elements characteristic of medieval thought; he had tried to understand and overcome the sinfulness of a life filled with literary and other solely secular ambitions.

By choosing Augustine's *Confessions* as a guide for his life, Petrarch aimed at a similar conversion; he, too, felt himself to be passing from a phase of full absorption in antiquity to conduct and thought more akin to what he knew had been the Christian outlook since Augustine. When, in 1342-3, about half-way through a life which extended from 1304 to 1374, he reconsidered in his *Secretum*, through the eyes of Augustine, some crucial aspects of his past years, he was already famous for many of the Laura sonnets and, to a smaller circle of friends, for the unfinished Latin epic *Africa*; only one year before, he had been crowned as poet with the laurel on the Roman Capitol. But now he regarded as vain and perilous to his soul the longing for glory and all the other strong passions which

had been the incentives for his own strivings and which still seemed to him
to have been the source of the greatness admired in the ancients.

To Petrarch, therefore, his life, as he saw it when writing the *Secretum*, appeared to be the very opposite of a straight, unbroken journey
toward the world of antiquity and away from what we call the medieval
heritage. Rather, he saw his life as divided into two periods: a time of
great boldness and worldliness in which, like Augustine, he had been nourished solely by the ancient authors and had forgotten his true self because
of too many distractions; and a period of sharper awareness of the insufficiency of such a way of life and of the need for establishing closer
connections with the modes of thought found during the Christian
centuries.

There can be no question that this also remained Petrarch's viewpoint
during the years following the *Secretum*. At the end of his *De vita solitaria* of 1346, he stressed as something new that in this book, 'contrary to
the use of the ancients, whom I am accustomed to follow in so many respects,' he rejoiced in mentioning the name of Christ often; and in the
following year, in his *De otio religioso*, he explained that he had learned
to include the Bible, and especially the psalms, in his readings, and that
this had come about under the influence of Augustine and his *Confessions*.
Until he experienced that influence, he said, he had believed that contact
with the unadorned language of the Bible would be detrimental to his
studies, but slowly he had started to listen to Augustine. 'Thus, in the joyful company of the Holy Scriptures, I now move with awe in an area I had
previously despised, and everything, I find, is different from what I had
presumed.' About six years later, when writing the first draft of his autobiographical *Letter to Posterity*, he found in retrospect that it had become
natural for him to sense in the Bible a 'concealed sweetness,' 'which I
had once scorned' (*quam aliquando contempseram*).[1] This is not to say
that his study of the psalms or any other part of the Bible ever determined
the character of his humanism decisively; it may even be that this influence receded somewhat into the background in later years. But the fact
that Petrarch did experience a change in outlook during the 40s and early
50s is clear from this and similar evidence.

Yet, Petrarch's autobiographical hints have not been taken very seriously by many recent scholars. There has often been a tendency to doubt
the sincerity of the crisis described in the *Secretum*. Given the wide-spread
belief in continuity and the gradualness of change, a relatively sudden
crisis with incisive results, occurring comparatively late in Petrarch's life,

appeared improbable; and suspicion was strengthened by the circumstance that the *Secretum* uses Augustine as a model and guide. Since Petrarch wanted to experience what he admired in Augustine – so it is frequently argued – he may have deceived himself, presenting, in imitation of the experiences of the saint, the misleading picture of a 'conversion.'

These doubts might seem to be confirmed by the testimony, or rather lack of testimony, found in precisely those two works that ought most plainly to reflect a change in Petrarch's attitudes: the collections of his poems (his *Canzoniere*) and his intimate letters (his *Epistolae familiares*). In the sonnets and *canzoni,* irrespective of whether they seem earlier or later than 1342 in origin, the psychological situation never changes essentially; we always meet the same bitter-sweet pain and the same wavering lover. It could be argued that within the carefully delimited area of his love lyrics Petrarch may have changed little throughout his life and yet may have experienced a vital crisis in his relations to antiquity and to the values which he had first embraced; but even in his *Epistolae familiares* we find nothing to indicate any essential change in tone or conviction between the early letters of the 1330s and those of the years which followed the *Secretum.* In fact, the first four books of the *Familiares,* most of whose letters pertain to situations datable before 1342, are imbued with the pessimism and withdrawal and the deep distrust of all human passions characteristic of Petrarch's writings in his later years.

This is nowhere more striking and more puzzling than in Petrarch's famous report on his ascent of Mont Ventoux in 1336, the first letter of the fourth book. Nobody, reading Petrarch's analysis of his reactions to this unprecedented adventure, can doubt that he is face to face with the author known from the *Secretum*; yet the report is said to have been written in 1336, six years before the crisis described in the *Secretum.* Already, in the letter, it is Augustine who teaches Petrarch to realize that his life has been headed in the wrong direction and is in need of total change. This Augustinian impact is fully felt when Petrarch, resting on the mountain top and opening his copy of the *Confessions* at random, chances upon the warning that in admiring high mountains and wide vistas man is prone to sin by forgetting to take care of himself. The complaint of the letter that 'men neglect the noble heritage within themselves by becoming lost in curiosity about the distracting variety of things and in their efforts to discover outside of themselves what they ought to have

sought in their inner lives'[2] has exact counterparts in the *Secretum*. There
is undoubtedly already a sense of crisis and conversion in the letter. For
instance, while Petrarch's companion in the enterprise, his beloved
younger brother Gherardo, who took vows in a Carthusian monastery a
year after the *Secretum*, climbs straight and rapidly up to the summit,
Petrarch's own indecision in not choosing a direct but arduous route
makes him waste a part of the day wandering aimlessly in the valleys surrounding the summit; the Augustine of the *Secretum* would have reprimanded Petrarch for this. And, just as in the *Secretum*, Petrarch muses on
his way about the struggle of two wills, the one debasing and the other
uplifting, that has been going on within him for a number of years. Reading this account makes it, indeed, almost impossible to accept Petrarch's
claim that not until the early 40s did a crisis in his convictions take place.

Almost, but not completely impossible. For, thanks to the revolutionary results of the criticism of the *Familiares* achieved during the last few
decades, a completely different explanation of the enigma has emerged.
This rests upon the surprising, but today no longer questionable, discovery that the apparent harbingers in Petrarch's pre-*Secretum* letters of
his later thinking were added – as forgeries, if one wants to call it so – to
the text of the letters about a decade after the *Secretum*.[3] During the early
years of the 50s, Petrarch prepared his letters of the 30s and 40s for in-
clusion in the carefully constructed book edition of the *Epistolae familiares* and, as we now know in great detail, did a thorough job of revising,
rewriting, and sometimes inventing entire paragraphs and even entire
letters that had never been sent to their alleged recipients. He did so where-
ever he wished to round out the portrait of himself for those years in
which his correspondence had still been sparse, and the result was a continuous intrusion of all the worries and irritations of his mature years
into the letters of his youth.

In other words, the apparent uniformity of spirit between Petrarch's
early letters and his post-*Secretum* correspondence is deceptive. The process of alteration and falsification can nowhere be better traced than in
Petrarch's report of his ascent of Mont Ventoux. For instance, the paragraph in which Gherardo's straight climb to the summit is contrasted to
Petrarch's wavering in the valleys must have been written after Gherardo
had taken the Carthusian vows. By the same token, all the other symbolism of the letter – the struggle of the two wills in Petrarch and his musings
on the greatness of the human soul which dwarfs the mountain's height –
belongs by necessity to the time when similar ideas are widely reflected in

his writings: that is, the aftermath of the *Secretum* crisis. Also, it must give us pause that we cannot find any trace of the letter during the 30s and 40s, although other early letters of Petrarch to the same recipient and other friends in Naples were systematically collected long before their revision for the *Epistola familiaris*. Moreover, the person to whom the letter was allegedly sent – Fra Dionigi da Borgo San Sepolcro – was presumably not in Naples but in Avignon during 1336, and, consequently, too near to Petrarch to receive letters from him at that time. The unavoidable conclusion from all these observations is that the text, as handed down to us in the *Epistola familiaris*, IV, 1, can never have existed as an independent letter: it is an expression of Petrarch's mind about a decade after the *Secretum*.

The problem which we have to face is not whether a letter like the *Epistola familiaris*, IV, 1, reflects Petrarch's reactions of later years, but how we can be certain that a piece of writing which is in every trait a product of the 40s and 50s in fact rests upon an actual experience of Petrarch's earlier years. Since, in describing his ascent of the Alpine peak, Petrarch had in mind an ancient example, as he himself relates – the ascent of Mount Haemus in Thracia by King Philip of Macedonia, an episode Petrarch knew from the geographer Pomponius Mela and from a detailed account by Livy – there seems to be no a priori guarantee that Petrarch was ever on the mountain. His beautiful and striking letter might be nothing but a feat of imitation and consummate literary art.

This very negative postscript to the triumphs of modern criticism has, indeed, been strongly advocated in recent years,[4] and it is evident that, if this suspicion were the last word, our estimate and understanding of Petrarch's humanism would be essentially affected. For, ever since the emergence of the Burckhardtian conception of the Renaissance, a new inquisitiveness and fresh desire to see the world – the *multa videndi ardor*[5] that drove young Petrarch to journeys through all European countries and to the first ascent of a summit of the Alps – have been part of our idea of the period. It would indeed greatly matter if we had to consider one of the earliest and most moving manifestations of the new longing for 'discovery of the world' to be a piece of mere fiction and rhetoric. It would also change the image of Petrarch as a humanist and as a human being if we had to accept that one of the allegedly powerful experiences which he describes as a source of delight, anxiety, and inner struggle was nothing but a literary invention.

In coming to this frontier of modern Petrarchian research, we should, however, remember that it is difficult to judge the nature of any literary work without considering all the circumstances of its author's life at the time when it was written. If we assume that Petrarch's ascent of Mont Ventoux was pure fiction there are a number of questions which will have to be answered. Petrarch's companion in the venture, so the letter of the early 50s reports, was his beloved brother Gherardo; accompanied by two servants, they shared the toil and experience of that day. God and Gherardo are called as witnesses to the fact that, when Petrarch opened Augustine's *Confessions* on the mountain top, he did, in truth, chance upon the words that put his curiosity and enjoyment of the magnificent vista in a dubious light and, for the remainder of the day, turned his eyes inward. By the early 50s, Gherardo had long been leading not only the life of a Carthusian monk, but also one that Petrarch had reason to regard as saintly (in a letter of about 1352 he tells us of Gherardo's self-sacrificing courage during a plague),[6] and the two brothers during those years were in personal contact. They met in 1347, and in 1352 Petrarch tried to see Gherardo again in his monastery at Montrieux, but was forced to return before reaching it since the roads were closed or unsafe. When he finally visited his brother in 1353, they talked about Augustine's *Confessions*; for Gherardo asked Petrarch to send him a copy as a gift.[7] Given these personal contacts at the time when the letter was written, and Petrarch's reverence for Gherardo's saintly figure, is it probable, or even believable, that Petrarch would have professed the veracity of his Mont Ventoux story by calling on the name of God and his brother, had he and Gherardo never set foot on the mountain? Furthermore, would Petrarch have unhesitatingly described himself as doing something new and unheard of, if any inquiry by his readers might have brought out that he was bragging about something he had not done?

Even if he was not afraid of these consequences, how could he have described in detail the vista from a mountain never climbed by anyone known to him, unless he had himself been at the top? After reaching the summit, so he tells us in the letter, he looked for the Pyrenees in the west because, according to his geographical knowledge, no obstacle lay in the way; yet human eyesight proved insufficient. 'But I could see with the utmost clarity on the right the mountains of the region around Lyons, and to the left the bay of Marseilles and the waters that lash the shore of Aigues Mortes, although all these places are so far away that it requires a journey of several days to reach them. Under our very eyes flowed the

Rhone.'[8] Unless another source for these details can be found, it seems impossible that a panorama traced with so much sense of geographic location and visibility could have been described by a writer who had never been on this or any other high mountain peak. It is also important in this connection to note that Petrarch's report of bright moonlight which, during the following night allowed him to make the descent long after the sun had set, has been found to accord with the actual astronomical conditions on 26 April 1336, the alleged day of the venture.[9]

Finally, even though it is true that for a number of details in his descriptions Petrarch imitates Livy's story of King Philip's visit to Mount Haemus, the motivation for his adventure has no model but is entirely his own and allows for specific questions as to whether the aim of his account does not also presuppose an actual mountain expedition. According to Livy,[10] King Philip had decided to climb Mount Haemus with a small troop of soldiers because he wished to verify the correctness of a popular story according to which both the Caspian and Black seas, as well as the Alps, could be seen from the top of Haemus; for such a panoramic view would help him to plan the strategy for his imminent war against Rome. Petrarch, on the other hand, begins his letter with the assertion that his sole motive for the ascent had been a 'passionate longing to see a place of such unusual height' (*sola videndi insignem loci altitudinem cupiditate ductus*); and in the course of his letter it becomes clear that, when writing his account during the 50s, he looked back upon that desire as the 'excusable' passion of a young man (*excusabile ... in iuvene ...*) that had in it a strain of sinfulness from which allegedly – the real topic of the letter – he had tried to free himself already on that occasion. In other words, when writing the letter in the early 50s, he discerned in the Mont Ventoux adventure the same youthful passion that had made him travel through many lands and that later, in his *Letter to Posterity*, would be similarly described as *multa videndi ardor ac studium*.[11]

During the 40s and 50s one often finds, indeed, the same procedure in Petrarch's various reactions to the *affectus* that had once propelled him in his youth. He became accustomed to reiterating the pattern first worked out in the *Secretum*, where he had systematically surveyed his former passions and had found in his love and in the thirst for glory the two most perilous drives of his nature, which had to be limited and subjected to higher aims. Now, it is clearly a prerequisite for the reasoning pursued in the *Secretum* that the longings of his younger years, as re-examined in that book, had been real and, in fact, had surfaced on certain still-remembered occasions; otherwise there would have been no sense in working out the diagnoses and prescriptions set forth there. Petrarch's procedure is identical in dealing with his youthful curiosity to see the world – the passionate desire that is the driving force behind the experience described in *Epistola familiaris*, IV, 1. To renew old memories in order to reassure himself that a stronger will had formed within him is precisely what we would expect of Petrarch during the decades that followed the *Secretum*. In those years it was natural for him in his writings to recall actual experiences of his youth and to reconsider them in the light of the deeper insight he had gained. It is against this background that the Mont Ventoux story and the problem of its truthfulness must be placed.

Therefore, far from leading to unqualified scepticism regarding the foundations of our knowledge of Petrarch's pre-*Secretum* years, the recent trenchant criticism of the credibility of his letters has made it easier for us to free the information on his early years from possible later adulterations. Once we can reliably distinguish earlier and later stages and harmonize the testimony of the sources with Petrarch's own assertions on the course of his inner life, it will no longer be so difficult to discern the successive trends, or patterns of change, in his development.

Admittedly, until now there have been only a few, scattered attempts to build something new on the foundations reconstructed by recent scholarship. Too often the continued discoveries of later interpolations in vital letters and other writings have discouraged efforts to follow up the leads given by Petrarch himself. Yet one may dare to predict that in the years ahead an approach more in harmony with Petrarch's own view of changes in his conduct and convictions will become a necessity and a growing challenge. On the pages which follow, I will try to give an idea, sketchy though it may be, of the kind of picture that is likely to emerge.[12]

A review of the intellectual world of Petrarch's youth must begin with a description of his vision of ancient Rome. Here, doubtless, was his first deviation from medieval ways.

Among the authentic letters from the early period of Petrarch's life is one – written a few years before his ascent of Mont Ventoux – in which Pompey is reprimanded for having allowed Caesar to escape after his defeat at Dyrrachium. Pompey's failure to destroy Caesar, so the letter argues, caused all the subsequent evils that befell Rome: the slaughter of so many citizens, the death of Cato which brought Roman *libertas* to an end, and, indirectly, all the misery of the world down to the present day.[13]

It would be difficult, or even impossible, to find any comparable judgment in the whole of medieval writing. For, as the founder of the divinely
appointed, universal empire in which the Middle Ages believed, Caesar
had a secure and central place in the historical views of medieval writers.
Why did young Petrarch dare to judge differently? His motive did not
stem from any republican convictions. Already at the time when his implied criticism of Caesar was written, Petrarch had begun to dream of a
strong saviour, a tyrant-monarch who could bring peace to Italy[14] – a
hope which in later years was replaced by republican ideals only during
the brief episode of Cola di Rienzo's Roman revolution. But when contem-
plating ancient Rome, Petrarch, from the very first, felt magnetically
attracted by the *virtus Romana* of the republican period.

In another early letter we read: though many great men have been of
the opinion that those states are the happiest which are governed by one
just ruler, it cannot be denied that the Roman state grew much more under
the rule of many citizens than under that of a single head. It seems, therefore, the letter concludes, that the authorities and historical *experientia*
contradict one another.[15]

The use of the word *experientia* is remarkable in this context. Petrarch
liked to contrast the superiority of *experientia* gained in actual life with
the bookishness of mere studies;[16] the relation he had formed to the history of republican Rome must have had for him the immediacy of one of
those experiences in his life that made him revolt against medieval authority and precedent. He followed this historical *experientia* when, in 1339
during his first stay in the Vaucluse, he drew a picture of ancient Rome in
the first books of his *Africa*, the epic which he wrote as a *poeta historicus*,
as he put it in his coronation oration.

The crucial aspect of the new conception of ancient Rome in the
Africa is a shift of attention away from those events that had been dearest
to medieval writers. For the author of the *Africa*, the struggle between
Scipio Africanus the Elder and Hannibal, and the final victory of the
virtus of republican Rome in the battle with Carthage at Zama, have replaced in significance Caesar's foundation of the imperial monarchy and
the rule of the Emperor Augustus under whom Christ was born. In the
Africa, the story of Roman liberty begins with the exclusion of Tarquinius
Superbus, the last king, from the Ciceronian heaven of the great Romans
and with his banishment to the inferno, while the author notes that
Tarquinius' tyranny was not futile historically because it caused the
ardent desire for liberty to grow in Roman hearts. Lucrezia and the elder
Brutus appear as Roman heroes of that period; with them 'the freedom of

our era begins' – the freedom of Scipio's days. In a dream of Scipio's, the
later course of Roman history unfolds itself in a striking historical panorama. For the time of the republic the spotlight falls on Pompey, whereas Caesar is harshly criticized: he, the greatest of conquerors, could have
been the happiest of men, had he known how to limit his passion for
power; but 'the wretched man could not,' overwhelmed as he was by the
ambition 'to lay claim to all power for one ruler, thereby setting an evil
example for others.' He plundered the public treasury; he imposed new
orders on the helpless senate; 'he turned his ever-victorious hands against
the flesh and blood of his own commonwealth and stained his triumphs
over foreign enemies with the blood of citizens.'[17]

One is again struck by the boldness with which what the Middle Ages
considered the landmarks of history are here overthrown. Petrarch was of
course not the first to learn from ancient sources – Sallustius, Lucanus,
and certain passages of Cicero – that the Roman dominion over the world
had been built up under the republic. But whereas almost every medieval
writer had eventually judged the republican period to be a mere preparation for the imperial and Christian era,[18] Petrarch, in the *Africa*, above
all admires the state of mind – the psychological force – responsible
for Rome's ascendancy: the *virtus Romana* under the republic. It is the
normal human condition, we read in the epic, that only a very few men do
not flinch from danger, pain, and death; but, by 'one of the greatest of all
miracles,' Rome by the time of Scipio the Elder had succeeded in making
that rare attitude a common occurrence: every army of Roman citizens
showed a readiness *pro libertate tuenda / recta fronte mori*.[19] Here republican liberty has become an indispensable condition for the greatness of
Rome, though what Petrarch admires is not so much the republic's free
constitution as the dedication and military prowess of her citizens.

During the same years in which these new historical views appeared in
the *Africa*, a distinct note of independence from traditional standards
entered into various judgments of Petrarch on the way of life of his
friends and on the values he cherished for himself. His comments on contemplation and the active life were at times the very opposite of his consistent praise of the *vita contemplativa* in the decades after the *Secretum*,
when he was working on his *De vita solitaria*.

In 1339, Petrarch became personally acquainted with a French prince
– Humbert, the lord of the Dauphiné – who did not wish to be a lord, for
he valued more highly a solitary and even monastic life, and eventually
resolved to cede the Dauphiné to the French king. To Petrarch in 1339,

this intention appeared in an entirely negative light. Anyone could see, so he wrote to the Dauphin, that a decisive conflagration was about to break out between France and England (it was the time of the beginning of the Hundred Years' war). Was not the land of every prince in Europe in danger of being drawn into the whirlpool of events? In such a time a man had to prove his virtue and make himself worthy of a good name. Countless examples from antiquity preached persistence in one's task and warned against shirking hard work. 'Return to your responsibility!' When the world trembles, it is not the time to wish for sleep![20]

The tone as well as the content of this admonition make it unlike anything later written by the author of the *De vita solitaria*; and the same tone is found in Petrarch's reaction to a similar situation, which aroused his feelings still more strongly. A Genoese friend destined for a political career had decided after long consideration to enter a monastery. As long as we are young, Petrarch told him, we should live for our *patria*. You are not born for yourself; your country has a right to make her demands on you, as Plato teaches; and does not Cicero, in his *Somnium Scipionis*, say that a heavenly reward awaits those who have helped to preserve and strengthen their country, and that nothing is more agreeable to God than a life spent in the *civitas*? The step contemplated by his friend should not be taken before 'a man's longings and passions have abated with increasing age.' Do not believe, says the Petrarch of the 1330s, that this advice is contradicted by the preference of many philosophers and church fathers for the *vita contemplativa*. Does not even Plotinus teach 'that man can attain felicity not only through the virtues of purification and those of the mind already purified, but also along the path of the *politicae virtutes*?' And although in the gospels Mary Magdalene is said to have chosen the best part, is not Martha also praised?[21]

But what, then, of Petrarch himself? It will perhaps be said that the hermit of the Vaucluse did not heed the advice he gave to his friends. Yet, when at that time he spoke about the life of a writer and poet, the values which he extolled were very different from the ideals he was to defend six or seven years later, when the *De vita solitaria* was conceived. When, in 1341, he interrupted his Alpine retreat to be crowned as a poet on the Roman Capitol, the oration he gave on that occasion reveals quite strikingly his innermost thoughts. At this most impressive moment of his life, standing on the height of the Capitoline hill, dressed in a purple cloak, a gift of King Robert of Anjou, the poet laureate began his oration by quoting from Virgil's *Georgics*: 'But a sweet longing urges me upward over the lonely slopes of Parnassus' (*Sed me Parnassi deserta per ardua/dulcis raptat amor*). This reference to a poet's impulses he then turned into the general psychological comment that 'without loving effort, profound joy, and rapture' no work of the spirit will reach its goal.[22]

What followed was an oration not merely on the poet's thirst for glory, but on the right and necessity of human passion. His argument was based on the fourth book of Cicero's *Tusculanae disputationes*, the same work which for many centuries had been among the most influential sources of that Stoic doctrine which in the name of reason calls for the suppression of all *affectiones* and passions. In the nineteenth chapter of the fourth book of the *Tusculans*, one of the doctrines refuted by Cicero is the belief that *affectiones* might work as a positive force, as spurs to virtue and action. Anger, Cicero reports, is thought by the Peripatetic school to stimulate fortitude. Themistocles' unique gifts and energies are believed to have developed because envy of the glory of Miltiades did not allow him to rest; and some have argued that without a 'burning longing' (*flagrans cupiditas*) philosophy would not have advanced, and the earth would not have been explored by eager travellers.

To the author of the *Tusculanae disputationes* all this had been partial or false teaching, interesting merely because it revealed the innate longing of all men for immortal fame and, therefore, provided an argument to prove the existence of immortality. To Petrarch, in 1341, the examples referred to in the *Tusculans* bore evidence of the justification and necessity of great passion and of the striving after glory. They show, says Petrarch in his oration, that even among sages and philosophers hardly anyone will be found who is not spurred on by thirst for glory. Many great minds have admitted this motivation. Did not Cicero himself say that no man is willing to make a great effort and face danger 'unless he may hope for glory as a kind of reward?' and did not Ovid express the opinion that 'excellence grows when it is praised' and that 'the thought of glory is a powerful spur?' Was Virgil not convinced that *amor patriae* and an immense desire for praise are strong aids to success (*Vicit amor patriae laudumque immensa cupido*)? The conclusion, as the speaker on the Capitol is not ashamed to confess, is 'that the desire for glory is innate not merely in ordinary men, but to the greatest degree in those who have wisdom and excellence.'[23]

Let us try to place the outlook of the young Petrarch in historical perspective. When we recall the themes and values that were to come to the fore in humanistic literature after 1400, especially in quattrocento Florence, the Petrarch of those pre-*Secretum* years may be called a harbinger of the quattrocento. We can describe the most creative trends of thought in early Renaissance Florence in terms very similar to those which have emerged from our analysis: a rediscovery of the *Respublica Romana* and a critique of the imperial monarchy; a positive and sympathetic attitude toward the *vita activa politica*; and, finally, the rise of a new psychology, beginning with a fresh evaluation of passion and the desire for glory.

Yet, if the guiding ideas are similar, their scope and function were to be totally different two or three generations after Petrarch, when citizens of Renaissance city republics looked upon life in the *Respublica Romana* as a model for their own day and they themselves led lives of political commitment like citizens of Athens and Rome. For Petrarch there were few bridges from the new values and the inspiration he found in the Roman past to his own way of life. He was a secular cleric who had taken the minor vows, lived on prebends, and was in constant intellectual exchange with other clerics whose minds were formed as much by a common piety as by their common classical studies. In time he became suspicious of what Virgil, Ovid, and his own personal experience were teaching him – that a poet's passion can be a needed incentive. During the latter part of his life, after he had returned from papal Avignon and from his solitary refuge in the Alpine valley of the Vaucluse to Italy, he was to attach himself to the north Italian tyrant courts and eschew the life of a citizen in the city republic of his Florentine ancestors. Increasingly he came to feel, as Dante had, that peace for a divided and war-devastated Italy could be expected only from the rulers of the *Sacrum imperium*, the successors to Rome's imperial monarchy; eventually he found himself in close personal affiliation with Emperor Charles IV.

It must be apparent that from this world of Petrarch to the intellectual world of the quattrocento there could be no continuous evolution or direct transition. If the historical discoveries and newly affirmed values of the young Petrarch were to be fruitful in his own time, they had to be garbed in a way that could be understood and appreciated by his still half-medieval age. Once Petrarch had experienced his change of heart, it resulted in effect in a building of bridges and a striving for reconciliations, even if this caused an attenuation, and sometimes the loss, of his original thrust. The full historical significance of Petrarch's thinking, therefore, does not emerge until we are equally aware of these two basic facts: that from his earliest years he was original enough to play the decisive role in the crea-

tion of a new humanistic view of man, but that he also became aware before long of the wide gulf between the religious mood of his age and some
of the values which he extolled and in the second half of his life worked
ceaselessly on some kind of synthesis.

That this process included a frequent wavering, a never-ending *dissi-
dium mentis*, is an observation of more than merely psychological import.
However little Petrarch was as yet able to question medieval standards in
principle, his vacillation and inner struggles were the result of his inability and unwillingness to give up the new attitudes and values, once he
had made them his own. In order to understand the work he produced
during the second half of his life, one must never forget that soon
after the coronation of 1341 Saul became Paul and, consequently, often
contradicted outright the bold assertions he had formerly made; but in
spite of his retractions he never fully reverted to the traditional ways.

The ambivalent attitude toward his own innovations and discoveries
started with the *Secretum*. As the 'Secret book on the conflict of his restless
strivings' indicates, almost immediately after his return from the loud
celebrations on the Roman Capitol to the peaceful Alpine mountains and
the valley of the Vaucluse, he began to reassess his life according to the
choices described in Augustine's *Confessions*: between a brilliant career
in letters, and a life of spiritual concentration leading to God. As he now
saw it, unless he could overcome the longings and passions which had
once already driven him away from his Alpine retreat to the turmoil of
his coronation in Rome and to estrangement from his true self, he would
be lost, as Augustine would have been lost had he not found the strength
to renounce his ambitions. But almost simultaneously Petrarch also realized to what extent the very essence of his being was ingrained with those
longings and passions. Out of this conflict emerged a searching account *de
conflictu curarum suarum*, which examined all his unruly passions one
by one and allowed the reader to see that, although many of the trends of
Petrarch's youth had been reversed – so many, indeed, that in the manuscripts the *Secretum* is often entitled *De contemptu mundi* – some of the
yearnings of his earlier years proved unyielding to the warnings attributed to Augustine.

What, then, were the *passiones* that had made Petrarch restless and did
not allow him to elevate his thoughts? As Augustine's interrogations
bring out, none of the ordinary vices of envy, anger, avarice, pride of
body or of talent were so strong in Petrarch that they could be the latent
cause of his lack of inner peace. But when his probing reaches the point[24]

where Augustine calls the two strongest emotions of Petrarch's past years, his love for Laura and his thirst for glory, 'chains' to be thrown off, Petrarch's devoted obedience to his master comes to an end. 'You want to deprive me of my most beautiful concern; you want to cast gloom upon the bright side of my soul,' Petrarch complains: 'it is the most noble kind of passion that you condemn.' His love for Laura had made him turn away from lowly pleasures; it had spurred him on to his literary work and to his love of fame. Any virtue he may possess has become stronger through his love. Yet is not this love one of the emotions that have estranged him from God? In the end Petrarch admits: all reasoning that love of a human being may lead a man to love of God is a delusion, because this 'reverses the natural order' (*pervertit ordinem*). The progress of man is from God to his creatures, not vice versa: 'There are few things in the world that make man forget God more quickly than an attachment to earthly beings.'[25]

There remains as the ultimate stronghold of Petrarch's defence (his 'last sickness,' as he makes Augustine call it) his 'striving, beyond all rational measure, for glory and the immortality of his name.' Petrarch admits that this desire exceeds due measure in him. 'Nonetheless, nothing will succeed in turning my thoughts away from this desire.' The truism of the philosophers that the earth, the only arena for our glory, is no more than a tiny speck of dust offers no help. 'I do not want to become a god,' Petrarch replies; 'as a mortal man I am asking only for mortal goods.' 'To my mind, as long as we are on this earth we should aspire to a glory which we can hope to achieve ... Of a higher kind of glory or honour we shall partake in the future, in heaven ... Is it not a well-ordered course for men to look to earthly things above all while we are on earth, and leave eternal things to the existence to come?' But again Petrarch finally has to admit that, with arguments of this sort, he is treading a path on which many have lost their God and salvation. At last he listens humbly to his master's teachings – but only until Augustine draws from them the inescapable conclusion: if, then, you wish your mind to be unburdened and free for divine things, give up your unending work on the *Africa* and the biographies of the *De viris illustribus*, the fruits of your ambition; 'be free again, be yourself entirely, and prepare for the day of your death!'[26]

This is the climax, but also the turning point of the discussion. Petrarch shrinks back: 'What, then, should I do? Should I interrupt and abandon my labours? ... How can I calmly forsake a half-finished work on which I have spent so much time and effort!' 'Should I not rather hurry on even more urgently than before in order to complete these works with God's help, so that subsequently, with a free mind, I shall be able to devote myself to higher things? ... I certainly can see that it would be a safer journey if I devoted my life to the one thought that is needed and chose the direct way to salvation. But I feel unable to restrain the longings of my heart ... I will engage in my work with double dedication, to turn to the greater task as soon as the first is completed.' Even Augustine must acquiesce in the end. 'May it so be,' the dialogue concludes, 'since it cannot be otherwise. Humbly I implore God ... to guide your fumbling steps onto solid ground.'[27]

How strong these longings actually were we know from Petrarch's subsequent accounts of the course of his literary labours. The ambivalence which in the *Secretum* he discerns in his very devotion to his work would never cease to stir his conscience, as some of his later letters testify. After his return to Italy, when he made ambitious plans at Milan to resume his work on the many books he had begun in the Vaucluse, he begged an intimate friend not to mistake this programme for a product of vanity. 'You know my heart, you understand that I would be ashamed rather than considering it a glory if at my age I had ambitions other than the care of my soul. But I am convinced that what I am aiming at is something that will also profit my soul.' And in another letter of those years he further tried to fathom his *affectus*. 'I swear, neither ambition nor greed are driving me, but my [accustomed] labourious leisure and an insatiable thirst for letters, which, I foresee, will never leave me until my last breath.'[28] It was, indeed, near the end of his life that he put down the most moving apology for the passion which even his firm will to learn from Augustine had been unable to suppress. In the year before Petrarch's death, Boccaccio entreated his friend and master to allow himself to rest at that late hour of his life, and to leave something for younger men to do. The old man replied that he appreciated the affection that prompted the thought, but 'I should surely die the sooner if I followed your advice. Continued work and exertion are the nourishment of my mind. The moment I began to relax and rest, I should cease to live ... Do you not know that passage from Ecclesiasticus "When man has finished his research he is but at the beginning, and when he rests then does he labour"? To me it seems as if I had but begun ... If in the meanwhile the end, which certainly cannot be far off, should come, ... I desire that death should find me reading and writing – or, if it pleases Christ, praying and in tears.'[29]

To return to the *Secretum*, it is important to realize that the outcome of its psychological search is not simply, as has often been asserted, recognition of the power of the human desire for glory. Attempts to vindicate *cupiditas gloriae* were to continue through Petrarch's later life, as we will presently observe; but the major result of his self-interrogation in the *Secretum* is the discovery that not only this *affectus* but also another passion that contradicted the demand of Augustine and the Stoics for cool, philosophic disengagement from life had been a necessary incentive for his literary activities, and that this passion, the creative drive, was giving deeper meaning to his striving for 'glory.'

It is also essential to realize that these apologies for the ceaseless activity of intellectual labour are unmistakably by the same pen that, during the 1330s, had written praises of the *virtus Romana* in the *Africa*. In spite of all the changes brought about by Petrarch's crisis at the time of the *Secretum*, deep down in his heart there had survived an assent to the right and to the psychological necessity of creative passion.

This does not mean that profound changes had not occurred and that there had not been serious curtailments of the bold vision of life and history found in Petrarch's younger years. Even apart from the *De remediis utriusque fortunae*, the work of his old age, in which a bitterly pessimistic view of man's nature defied the values he had once upheld, one can point to many occasions on which the Petrarch of the 40s, 50s, and 60s reacted in accord with medieval traditions and came into open conflict with what, as a daring young humanist, he had previously said. Indeed, it is through such a comparison that the historical place of the *De vita solitaria*, the major document of Petrarch's later humanism, can be best understood.[30]

Let us once more recall how the young humanist had evaluated life and its goals on different occasions. He had censured Humbert of the Dauphiné for giving up his princely position in order to lead a life of religious withdrawal. Petrarch, at that time, had insisted that in the gospels Martha was not despised when Mary Magdalene was praised, that Cicero's *Somnium Scipionis* calls the life in the *civitates* the most agreeable to God, and that Plotinus had taught that man can attain felicity not only through the spiritual virtues, but also through the *virtutes politicae*.

In the *De vita solitaria*, Pope Celestine v, who had given up the papal see in order to lead a hermit's life and who, in Dante's *Divina Commedia*, had been relegated to the circle of those *animae tristes* who had lived 'without ignominy and without praise,' is glorified as a saintly teacher of the solitary life. If others 'were made apostles, saints, and friends of God' for giving up lowly positions or secular kingdoms, how greatly must we admire the man who 'scorned the papacy, than which there is no loftier station.' This was, to be sure, the renunciation of a saintly soul, but Petrarch's evaluation of the event is couched in such secular and psychological terms that comparison with his youthful reaction to decisions by others to renounce worldly careers and enter monastic orders does not seem farfetched. For the description of Celestine's abdication, in the *De vita solitaria*, reads like the story of the escape of a follower of Petrarch's solitary life from a golden prison. The former pope left his office 'with good cheer and with signs of spiritual joy in his eyes ... his freedom restored at last, looking not as if he had withdrawn his shoulder from a flattering burden, but his neck from the fatal axe ... In truth, he was returning from toil to rest, from insane disputations to divine intercourse; he was leaving the city and, in his imagination, was ascending ... a mountain: rugged and steep, I admit, but from which he had a smooth path to heaven.'[31]

Elsewhere in the *De vita solitaria* the story of Martha and Mary is again recalled. Some people, Petrarch now says, stress the fact that Martha, who did not follow Mary's flight to a desert cave and spiritual solitude, 'is nevertheless a saint.' The author of the *De vita solitaria* replies: 'I do not deny it, but surely Mary is much holier.' The deeper meaning of the story of the two sisters 'leaves no room for doubt that the contemplative life was placed before the active life in Christ's judgment and should be preferred by his faithful whenever there is a choice.'[32] As for the recognition in ancient literature of the values of the *vita politica*, the *De vita solitaria* gives the following reply to Aristotle's saying that only a beast or a god could live outside human society: he, Petrarch, wished, indeed, to become a 'godlike man' (*divinus vir*). And what else was to be learned from Plotinus but that the virtues of the *vita politica* are the lowest in the entire scale of human perfection? The higher virtues will be acquired by 'those who leave the *civitates* behind, live in leisure, and become true philosophers' as men who have conquered their passions.[33]

This new love of contemplation deeply affects the second book of the *De vita solitaria*, which in its substance is a series of historical biographies. After a long pageant of saints, philosophers, and poets has demonstrated that all of them owed their best to the *vita solitaria*, statesmen and citizens are made the objects of severe criticism. Those of this group who interest Petrarch as human beings are men in public careers on whom the conflict between the two ways of life has left a special mark. There is Augustus, who always longed to become free eventually of his exalted position and spend his old age as a private citizen, but could never bring himself to give up the splendours of his high office. His life testifies to the almost unsurmountable obstacles that arise once a man has become enmeshed in the responsibilities of public life. He may, of course, have hesitated out of fear of dangers that might have menaced him in private life, or out of a sense of obligation toward the senate and the people. But, 'perhaps he was troubled by a natural human weakness. For, to one standing at fortune's peak as lord and ruler of the world, the descent to the humble and lowly position he desired must have appeared extremely abrupt ... and so he stuck to his place and never descended from it until his death.'[34]

Diocletian 'did what Augustus had desired to do,' thus setting the greatest and most moving example to the world. Precisely because he was the first Roman emperor to demand ceremonial worship as a god, he finally 'grew weary of the turbulent court and the costly encumbrance of troops of attendants and of general servility, suddenly changed his mind, and felt a strong desire to be alone, poor, and free and to escape by swimming from the sea of imperial cares into the heaven of a humbler life, naked like a pilot from a great shipwreck.' It is the same gesture that had attracted Petrarch to Saint Celestine; Petrarch draws the parallel himself: 'We admire Celestine, although that holy man did for the sake of an eternal life what the great sinner Diocletian had done for the sake of the ... uncertain remainder of his old age, when out of longing for the utmost peace of mind he accepted the lot of a private citizen.'[35]

The two figures who stand at opposite poles, and in the condemnation or approval of whom the central issue of the *De vita solitaria* comes to a head, are Cicero, the philosopher who chose the political life, and Scipio the Elder, the statesman and general who returned to a life of leisure.

Petrarch's denunciation of Cicero, after he had come to know him as a Roman citizen and statesman, is a crucial clue to the changes in Petrarch's outlook on life. In 1345, not long after the *Secretum* crisis, he had his first opportunity to gain intimate knowledge of Cicero's personality, thanks to the discovery of one of the collections of Cicero's correspondence, the *Epistolae ad Atticum*. As a result, he strongly disapproved of Cicero's conduct and way of life. His criticism allows us to see that by that time both his attitude toward the *Respublica Romana* and his evaluation of the active life had moved away from the persuasions of his youth, and that the two changes were inseparable. Gone was the admiration and sympathy for those who had made themselves champions of the *Respublica Romana* in the period of the civil wars, the breakdown of republican institutions, and the rise of Caesar. During the 30s, as we have seen, this sympathy had been so strong that Petrarch had become convinced that the course of Roman history would have changed for the better had Pompey, after his victory at Dyrrachium, annihilated Caesar and his army; and in the first books of the *Africa* Petrarch had bitterly condemned Caesar as the destroyer of the republic. In contrast, his reaction to the *Epistolae ad Atticum* in 1345 is based on the claim that if Cicero had been a truly wise man he would have 'withdrawn from the civil wars once liberty was extinguished and the Republic buried and mourned.'[36] Those times no longer called for freedom, but for Caesar's famed 'clemency.' The Ciceros and Catos ought to have been content to accept it. It is true that a few years later, during the late 40s, we find a certain resurgence of Petrarch's sympathies for Caesar's adversaries when he looked for a while with hope upon Cola di Rienzo's audacious efforts to re-establish a republic in papal Rome. But after Rienzo's failure, he finally renounced his former scorn of Caesar and applause for the last defenders of the *Respublica Romana*. In the end he even resumed Augustine's reproof that the ultimate motive of Cato and Brutus had been their striving for empty glory.[37]

At the heart of these changes in Petrarch's attitude after the *Secretum* crisis was his increasing trust in the *vita solitaria* as the supreme standard: the truly wise man, concerned with intellectual and spiritual matters, should not become ensnared in distracting political struggles, as had happened to the Roman defenders of the *Respublica*. As early as 1345 Petrarch's major criticism of Cicero ran: 'what I find lacking in your life is perseverance, a striving for quietude such as is becoming to a philosopher's profession.' 'Why did you involve yourself in so many contentions and useless quarrels and forsake the calm so becoming to your age, your position, and the vicissitudes of your life? What vain splendour of fame drove you ... to a death unworthy of a sage? ... Oh, how much more fitting it would have been had you, philosopher that you were, grown old in rural surroundings, ... meditating upon eternal life, ... and not aspiring to consular *fasces* and military triumphs ...!'[38]

According to the *De vita solitaria*, Cicero emerges in his life and work as an historic witness – a witness despite himself – to the truth that those engaged in the pursuits of the spirit must, as Plotinus teaches, shun distracting involvement in politics and the active life. When the breakdown of the republic sent Cicero, champion of the *vita activa politica*, into enforced leisure and he took advantage of it for his literary work, he did so unwillingly. But the new way of life proved its worth. 'It transformed the greatest of orators into a great philosopher, and there is not a student who does not know how magnificently Latin studies were enriched by this circumstance.' Cicero himself was forced to concede the beneficial influence of his new environment. Although he still 'affirmed that the active life is more profitable to the state, which in a measure even I will not deny, he admitted that the retired life is safer and easier, less burdensome and vexatious than other modes of life, and therefore he not only sanctioned it for those who have some good reason for embracing it, but especially commended it to those who excel in intellect and learning.' Cicero began to be reconciled to his retirement, in which he accomplished much more than he had been able to achieve in all the occupations of his busy life before the downfall of the republic. He learned in his solitude to be 'sufficient unto himself ... It was solitude that caused this man's mind to open out; moreover – this is the strange and wonderful thing – it was a solitude obnoxious to him. What, one may think, would it not have accomplished had he desired it, or, how much should we not long for that which brings such great benefit even to one who is unwilling to endure it?'[39]

The evident bias in such sentences notwithstanding, there is a keen, personal interest in this endeavour to grasp the meaning of Cicero's fate. One ventures to think that nothing like it had yet been seen before the time when Petrarch passed through the successive phases of his development and experienced the struggle of opposing values in his life as well as through the medium of his humanistic and historical imagination. The same thing may be said of his pictures of the real hero of the *De vita solitaria*, Scipio Africanus the Elder, and of the man who continued his work, his namesake, Scipio Africanus the Younger. As the incomparable representatives of the spirit which animated Rome before the coming of Caesar and the rise of imperial monarchy, these two historical figures kept open for Petrarch access to the world of the *Respublica Romana* even at the time when his appraisal of Caesar and of the last defenders of the republic had radically and irreversibly changed.

The two Africani who, for the author of the *Africa*, were the great military and political leaders of Rome, had been vividly pictured by Valerius Maximus in the *otium* which, after their victories, they had led on their estates by the sea. Thanks to their twofold distinction, they could become the supreme models for the *De vita solitaria*. They alone among the great men of public affairs, so Petrarch thought, knew how to lead a perfect life with friends in nature when, after the exertions of the wars, they showed themselves to be 'as much lovers of solitude as of virtue.'

'What a wonderful spectacle, transcending the pomp and sceptres of all kings, to see such men, saviours of the state, liberators of the citizens, defenders of Italy ..., their task successfully performed, ... their bodyguard left in Rome, ... strolling alone, at leisure, ... over the hills and along the shore, often picking up little shells or sea pebbles ...' What this happy solitude meant in the lives of the two great leaders, we know from Scipio the Elder's 'magnificent dictum, worthy of a great and wise man:' 'that he was never less at leisure than in his leisure, and never less lonely than in his solitude.'[40]

The picture of the *otium* of the two Scipios is the climax of the *De vita solitaria*. 'The virtue of Scipio's aphorism,' comments Petrarch, 'is that it conveys in a few words what I have in mind. I mean ... a leisure that is neither idle nor profitless ... I do not allow the intellect to lie fallow except that it may revive and become more fertile by a period of rest.' He would, says Petrarch, 'make this wonderful saying of the great general fully my own' and even sharpen its expression: 'I would assert that I was always at leisure except in my leisure, always lonely except in my solitude.'[41]

Next to the criticism of Cicero, Petrarch's continued admiration for Scipio the Elder provides the best clue for understanding the extent and limit of the changes in his outlook and evaluations. In his youth, Scipio had been to him the symbol of the vigour and driving force in the political existence of Roman citizens. Even when the values of the *vita politica* had faded from Petrarch's own philosophy of life, his old vision of the *virtus* of the *civis Romanus*, still focused on Scipio, continued to mould and nourish the ideal of the ceaseless activity of the mind. This was one of the enduring links between the world of the young Petrarch and the world of the post-*Secretum* humanist. Along this road some of the ideas of the young pioneer were carried on in disguise, despite the profound changes in Petrarch's outlook.

The truth of this observation becomes evident when it is realized that in the image of Scipio still another element of Petrarch's early bold persuasions survived: the recognition that a desire for glory is necessary. But this compels us to step beyond the confines of the *De vita solitaria*.

As early as the *Africa*, Petrarch had associated Scipio with the ideas on glory so boldly proclaimed in his oration on the Roman Capitol. According to ancient accounts, Scipio, when being crowned after victory, had the poet Ennius, herald of his deeds, crowned with the same laurel.

The *Africa* celebrates their close companionship and Ennius' role in the making of Scipio's glory.

Thanks to the preservation of three consecutive versions of Petrarch's *Life of Scipio*, one of the major biographies in his *De viris illustribus*, we can trace the continuance and ever stronger defence of the *gloriae cupiditas* as a trait of Petrarch's image of Scipio from the early days of his work on the *Africa* through his later life.[42] Although the philosophical doctrines increasingly upheld by Petrarch after the *Secretum* were bound to throw deep shadows over all *affectus*, each return of Petrarch to Scipio's biography produced a more elaborate and positive analysis of the *gloriae cupiditas* – perhaps just because only by making this one, crucial exception could Petrarch submit to the demand of 'ataraxy' and the repression of all passions that he conceded theoretically in most of his later works.

In the first version of the *Vita Scipionis*, written several years before the *Secretum*, passionate longing for glory is claimed to have been one of the springs of Scipio's greatness, and the claim is couched in terms very similar to the defence of the poet's irrepressible striving for fame in the coronation oration. In that first version of the *Vita Scipionis* one of the episodes from Scipio's life runs: As the historians tell us, Scipio recklessly exposed himself and the fate of Rome in a small, unarmed vessel, in order to reach the shores of Africa more quickly. That, says Petrarch, was certainly indefensible before the judgment seat of cool reason; yet 'the boundless hope and ardour in the heart of one who strove for the highest goal took Scipio through all perils. It made him think of nothing but true glory and of the end of the war as he had conceived it.'[43]

In revising this account, at about the time the *Secretum* was written (to be exact, between 1341 and 1343), Petrarch must have felt provoked by the Augustinian reproach that the Romans' great deeds had been the result, not of the often praised *virtutes Romanae*, but rather of their *gloriae desiderium*. Although this is true, Petrarch says in an insertion made at that time, one should not forget Cicero's observations that hardly any man would greatly exert himself or expose himself to danger if he did not expect glory as his reward, and that the *gloriae cupiditas* has ineradicable roots in noble minds, and especially in those of great generals.[44] Petrarch undoubtedly had in mind two passages of the *De officiis* (I, 19, 65 and I, 22, 74), yet he was actually turning a Ciceronian warning against the dangers of *cupiditas gloriae* into acceptance of this desire—exactly as in his coronation oration he used the *Tusculans* to reconstruct and

make his own the Peripatetic defence of passion that had been denounced
in Cicero's discussion. What the Ciceronian phrase in the *De officiis* to
which Petrarch alluded actually averred was that 'greatness of the spirit
places moral relevance ... not in glory but in conduct ... Yet it is the lofti-
est spirits that are most easily tempted by a passion for glory to commit
acts of injustice. But here we are on slippery ground, for scarcely a man
will be found who, after taking hardship and danger upon himself, does
not wish for glory as his natural reward.'[45] The Petrarch of the early 40s,
then, who glossed over the unmistakable moral disapproval in Cicero's
words, using them unconcernedly in the defence of Scipio's *gloriae cupiditas*, was, on this one score at least, in spite of all his Augustinian leanings, still the man who on the Roman Capitol had delivered the
oration on the creative passions of the poet.

His feelings had not changed when he expanded the *Vita* of his beloved Scipio into an almost book-length biography during the 50s, at the
time when in his *De remediis* he made his final effort to work out a moral
philosophy resting on man's freedom from violent emotions. Like a strong
magnet, his portrait of Scipio now drew into its field every statement of
the ancient authors acclaiming the thirst for glory. For instance, Petrarch
quotes the scene from Livy in which young Scipio, after his victories in
Spain, competes for command of the army in Africa while frankly admitting his aims and ambitions. By unconsciously expanding the meaning of
the words used by Scipio in Livy, Petrarch makes Scipio confess 'that it
was his goal to aspire to both virtue and glory, and not only to equal the
fame won by the great men of the past, but to surpass it.' To this, says
Petrarch, he wished to add another precious dictum of Scipio, namely,
'that the desire for glory has its objective beyond our lifetime, since it is
above all concerned not with our coevals, but with the opinion of posterity, and that therefore in great and excellent minds there is inborn a desire
to compare themselves and to contend for fame not only with contemporaries but with the illustrious of all ages.'[46]

At this point, if Petrarch had still been of the same mind as the youthful speaker on the Roman Capitol, he would have stopped; but not so the
writer who had gone through the crisis of the *Secretum*. The Petrarch of
the 50s, while acknowledging the necessity of Scipio's 'passion' as a psychological stimulus, nevertheless believed that the higher goals of life
could not permit the soul to be disturbed by any kind of violent emotion.
So he was forced, in his mature view of life, to give some recognition to
the partial validity of the two conflicting evaluations. In its third version,

the *Vita Scipionis* quotes a dictum from Valerius Maximus more challenging than any classical citation previously employed: 'no kind of human humility is so great that it could never be touched by the sweetness of glory.' Petrarch comments that with this quotation he does not wish to suggest that virtue should not be followed for its own sake; and yet, to look upon glory merely as an ornament of good deeds, not as a goal and reward – 'how much more easily this is done by word than by deed!'[47]

The less Petrarch is able to solve this human dilemma by means of definitions, the dearer Scipio becomes to him. For Scipio, through no fault of his own, embodied in his life not only the rise to greatness caused by the thirst for glory but also the misery which (as Petrarch now knew) inevitably follows the satisfaction of this *cupiditas*, as it does that of every passion. When telling of the envy and ingratitude of Scipio's fellow citizens, which caused the saviour of Rome to die a lonely death away from the city he had saved, Petrarch sets down the bitter but proud words: If you have won a name by pursuing the path of virtue, trust virtue and God alone; do not trust glory! 'For glory is nothing solid; it is like a shadow or a fleeting breath of air,' changeable as the crowd on whose lips your fame must rely. The same *gloria* which had spurred Scipio on to greatness also made him envied and odious to his fellow citizens. '*O vere difficilis ars vivendi!*' 'And thus, unfortunate Scipio, all your denial of pleasure, your readiness to accept danger and death have been in vain.' Those for whom you have done all this and more, 'will envy, reject, hate, and finally expel you from the land which you have saved. But no: Blessed Scipio! You have done your duty with magnanimity; wretched are those who neglected theirs!'[48]

We do not know exactly when this final version of the *Vita Scipionis* was written, but at least eleven, and possibly many more, years had passed since Petrarch's inner crisis at the time of the *Secretum*. From the authorities whom he now recognized he had learned to say: Trust virtue and God alone, do not trust glory! Yet, just as in the days of the coronation oration and the beginning of his work on the *Africa,* he still felt that the *desiderium gloriae* was a stimulus without which the striving for virtue and for God could not be powerful enough. Even great and good men, he was convinced, must be propelled by this natural goad; but they will have to pay for their strivings with tears; they will not receive happiness and peace from them. The young Petrarch's bold defence of powerful emotion as a necessary spur for the heroic mind had thus withstood all changes in his philosophy of life; but it had lost some of its positive overtones in the adaptation to a more traditional, religious view. In this respect, Petrarch was now far removed from that bold confidence in the strong inborn drives of human nature which had characterized his youth and which, after 1400, would become an article of faith for the early Renaissance.

It has seemed best to describe the changes which took place in Petrarch's life by basing our understanding of his views of man and history partly on the observation of his literary and historical imagination. Indeed, since he was not a philosopher concerned primarily with the clarity and consistency of his definitions of ethical maxims, he cannot be fully comprehended unless the picture of his humanistic outlook is made to include the biographical and autobiographical imagery of his works – his changing representations of those whom he considered the great leaders of antiquity, as well as his own spiritual portrait, which he drew and redrew under the impress of successive experiences. If one gives this dimension of Petrarch's humanism due emphasis, as we have tried, and thus arrives at a clearer picture of the growth and retrenchment in his development, one also becomes better prepared to judge his place in the Weltanschauung of the Renaissance. For, because of the fundamental differences in the various periods in his life, even a general estimate of the historical role of Petrarch's work must concentrate on the successive changes in his imagination and thought before one can attempt to define his place in the transition from the Middle Ages to the Renaissance.

The ideas of Petrarch's youth, as we have come to recognize, show a strong kinship with the outlook of the early quattrocento. Even for that phase of his life, however, the conventional notion of Petrarch as the 'harbinger' or even 'father' of Renaissance humanism proves to be too vague. Since Petrarch did not continue the trend of his early years beyond middle age, and since neither the *Africa* nor the coronation oration were among the works still widely read after 1400, we ought at least to add that the outlook of the young Petrarch on life and history was a prelude rather than the basic factor in the rise of the ideas of the quattrocento. The true historical relationship is that some of the key ideas that came to the fore after 1400, first in Florence and subsequently in many places in quattrocento Italy, had already been touched upon by Petrarch in his early years, but that they could not have gained currency and maturity had not Florentine citizens, living under unique political conditions around 1400, given humanism a changed place in the society of the Renaissance and on this different basis produced a new civic outlook and education. In other words, since Petrarch's early ideas, at the time of the conception of the *Africa*, had sprung from a rediscovery of the world of Roman citizens, the fruit could ripen only when citizens of Renaissance city states who, in their own lives, were near enough to the values and conditions of ancient citizens took over the intellectual work that Petrarch had left half done.

A second consideration must focus on the structure of Petrarch's humanism during the latter part of his life. One symbol of this period is Petrarch's Cicero: the quattrocento would base its ideals of conduct and culture on the same Cicero, Roman statesman and citizen, whom Petrarch during the second half of his life so bitterly denounced. No judgment of Petrarch's historical place is, therefore, adequate which does not take into account the fact that many of the ideas he held in his later years did not lead on to the world of the quattrocento. Petrarch's Scipio, on the other hand, reveals a different dimension of Petrarch's post-*Secretum* outlook. The impact of young Petrarch's psychological discoveries of the power of strong emotional drives had not been lost; besides the *gloriae cupiditas*, attributed to Scipio, one recalls Petrarch's inability to subordinate his passionate urge to do creative work to the demands of Augustinian and Stoic teaching. The observation that many *affectus* are ambivalent – helpful to virtue, yet not justifiable in the light of the laws laid down by philosophy and religion – remained an integral part of the synthesis established with tradition in Petrarch's later years. We probably should look upon this synthesis as one of those powerful but, after the late trecento, soon abandoned efforts to accommodate the new with the old that are characteristic of the century of transition which had opened with Dante.

Petrarch's later – and more mature – writings are, however, not merely of interest as documents of the trecento struggles and efforts at conciliation. His *conflictus curarum suarum* transcends the level of late medieval doctrinal conflicts. In his hands, that *conflictus* has developed into an analysis of human nature by an already truly humanistic mind; it is relevant beyond the disputes of Petrarch's century. There is something distinctly 'modern' in his understanding of the necessity, fraught with inevitable tragic consequences, of Scipio's *desiderium gloriae* – a grasp of the reality of life. In the realm of Petrarch's historical ideas, his return from the *Respublica Romana* to profound admiration of Caesar does not result in a mere revival of the medieval vision of the *Sacrum Imperium*; it also opens the road to the modern discovery of Caesar's personality and greatness as a statesman and general. This interest in man as man and this deliverance from mere tradition are also obvious and have often been noted in the independence from conventional and ceremonial forms in Petrarch's relations with friends as well as with princes and emperors. Almost everywhere in his letters and works, even where the answers to his problems are still 'medieval,' the problems themselves are usually already those of the humanists of the Renaissance.

In other words: however indispensable it is to pursue the historical analysis of thought here proposed – to understand that the work of Petrarch in his youth, although a unique prelude to things to come, did not lead directly to the Renaissance ideas of the quattrocento, and that his own final view of life represents one of the great semi-medieval syntheses characteristic of the trecento – nonetheless there is also some lasting truth in the old claim that Petrarch with his basic human traits and sensitivity to new values was 'the first modern man.'

NOTES

* This essay, based on studies still in progress, is an amplification of an address read before the first North-Central Renaissance Conference in London, Ontario during April 1960. Wallace K. Ferguson, the founder of this conference and its guiding spirit, was responsible for its programme. The text of my address, brought up to date, enlarged, and provided with source references, is now printed for the first time. For the critical problems involved in the approach to Petrarch offered here, consult the chapter 'The Evolution of Petrarch's Thought: Reflections on the State of Petrarch Studies' in my *From Petrarch to Leonardo Bruni: Studies in Humanistic and Political Literature* (Chicago 1968).

1 For a fuller appraisal of this and other evidence for Petrarch's change of attitude toward the Bible, see Baron, *From Petrarch to Leonardo Bruni*, pp. 41-4.

2 '... michi ... in silentio cogitanti quanta mortalibus consilii esset inopia, qui, nobilissima sui parte neglecta, diffundantur in plurima et inanibus spectaculis evanescant, quod intus inveniri poterat, querentes extrinsecus.' *Epistola familiaris*, IV, 1.

3 On this revolution in Petrarch criticism and the role played in it by G. Billanovich, in particular regarding the letter on Petrarch's ascent of Mont Ventoux, cf. Baron, *From Petrarch to Leonardo Bruni*, pp. 15-23. Billanovich's reinterpretation of the letter is found in his *Petrarca Letterato, I: Lo Scrittoio del Petrarca* (Rome 1947), pp. 192 ff., and in his essay 'Petrarca e il Ventoso' (i.e., Ventoux), *Italia Medioevale e Umanistica*, IX (1966), 389-401.

4 Radical scepticism is the ultimate advice of Billanovich's latest and most comprehensive discussion of *Ep. fam.*, IV, 1, where the alleged discourage-

ment of the climbers by an old shepherd—very possibly fictive, because it is
a traditional literary motif – is used as a yardstick in the pronouncement
of the fictitiousness of Petrarch's vow in the name of God and his brother
and of his assertion that he had climbed the mountain in a year which,
according to various indications, must be 1336. As Billanovich says, 'Tito
Livio e Pomponio Mela persuasero il Petrarca a immaginare la grande
ascensione.' See 'Petrarca e il Ventoso,' pp. 392 f., 396, 401.

5 *Ep. fam.*, III, 2 (probably 1333, according to E. H. Wilkins, *Petrarch's Correspondence* [Padua 1960]. This manual is always followed wherever no
source or reason for the dating of Petrarch's letters is adduced).

6 *Ep. fam.*, XVI, 2, which relates how two Carthusian priors told Petrarch the
story of a monk at Montrieux, Gherardo, who during the plague, unlike his
prior who fled, stayed in order to take care of all his stricken thirty companions until they died and to bury them – a report continued until the
speakers suddenly became aware of Petrarch's likeness to Gherardo and
exclaimed: 'O felix fratris pietate!'

7 On Petrarch's visits to Montrieux and his love and respect for his brother
shown on those occasions, cf. E.H. Wilkins, *Life of Petrarch* (Chicago
1961), pp. 117, 121 f., 125.

8 'Limes ille Galliarum et Hispanie, Pireneus vertex, inde non cernitur, nullius quem sciam obicis interventu, sed sola fragilitate mortalis visus; Lug-
dunensis autem provincie montes ad dexteram, ad levam vero Massilie
fretum et quod Aquas Mortuas verberat, aliquot dierum spatio distantia,
preclarissime videbantur; Rodanus ipse sub oculis nostris erat.' *Ep fam.*,
IV, 1.

9 See P. Guiton, 'Il Petrarca al Ventoux,' *Club Alpino Italiano, Rivista
Mensile*, LVI (1937), 191 ff. Consideration should also be given to the fact
that several other early letters which, in the light of the criticism applied
to *Ep. fam.*, IV, 1, seem to be products of a later period, have been more or
less convincingly shown to include immediate reactions to personal experiences of Petrarch's youth – evidence that these reports on Petrarch's life
cannot be regarded as entirely fictitious. Cf. for the letters *Ep. fam.*, I, 3-6
and IV, 3: Baron, *From Petrarch to Leonardo Bruni*, pp. 19-22.

10 Livy, XL, 21-2

11 *Posteritati*, ed. P.G. Ricci in *Francesco Petrarca: Prose* (vol. 7 of *La Letteratura Italiana: Storia e Testi* [Milan 1955]), p. 10

12 Initial concentration on the most characteristic features is needed to
make one aware of the successive changes in Petrarch's thought, but one
must not lose sight of the fact that, even in the model case of *Ep. fam.*,
IV, 1, reality is more complicated than it would seem from an over-all
view of the periods of his development. Though it is true that the pervad-
ing symbolism and spirituality of this letter place it with certainty in the
time in which Petrarch had begun to review his past and his studies, this
does not mean that Augustine and his *Confessions* had never troubled his
conscience before the *Secretum* crisis. The naming of God and his brother
as witnesses in the scene in which he opens the *Confessions* on the moun-

tain top suggests the actuality not only of a mountain ascent, but also of Petrarch's carrying a copy of the *Confessions* during his wanderings in 1336, six years before the *Secretum*; and we have other information that the pocket-size copy of the *Confessions*, used on Ventoux according to the letter, was Petrarch's constant companion in those early years. Moreover, three years before 1336 a list of Petrarch's favoured books had placed Augustine, represented by the *Confessions* and three other works, as sole Christian author beside the ancient classics. (Cf. Baron, *From Petrarch to Leonardo Bruni*, p.47). Therefore, an exhaustive analysis of Petrarch's mind would have to trace the role of Augustine as a counterweight to the classicizing tendency in Petrarch's studies from a very early date and emphasize that the 'conversion' after 1340 could hardly have occurred if his readings had not long given a place to Augustine and the Augustinian teachings. But this does not diminish the validity of the contention that, at the time of the *Secretum*, the character of Petrarch's Humanism changed. Before the 1340s, the Augustinian strain had come to the fore on certain provocative occasions, such as the day on the mountain peak, but it had not influenced his literary work or changed the balance of his 'favoured' books. Consequently, although the knowledge of this early strain is indispensable for understanding why and how the later changes came about, the first step must be the clear discernment of the diversity of Petrarch's attitude toward life and antiquity in his early and later years.

Another point which can on the whole be ignored in an over-all view of Petrarch's work is the frequent observation that his 'Augustine' is not a true mirror of the church father, but represents a mixture of an Augustinian state of mind and a kind of Stoic rationalism which in some respects is the very opposite to Christian piety. Although important for judging the historical place of Petrarch's 'Augustinianism,' the nature of this mixture is not a direct concern in a confrontation of Petrarch's later views with his pre-*Secretum* outlook because the Stoic strain found in his Augustinianism is as far removed from the ideas of the pre-*Secretum* period as is the genuine Augustinian attitude.

13 'Magnus Pompeius ad Dyrachium victor Iulium Cesarem prope captum dum retinere posset, abire permisit ...; ex qua mox in Thesalia calamitas publica, et in Egipto ducis ipsius mors miserabilis consecuta est, et in Africa Catonis simul ac libertatis interitus, et in Hispania tristis reliquiarum strages, et Rome spoliatum erarium, oppresse leges ...; postremo, inde usque in seculum nostrum tantorum series malorum ...' *Ep. fam.*, III, 3 (1333).

14 *Epistolae metricae*, I, 3 (1333) expresses the hope 'fors impia bella/cessabunt, subitum pigeat dum cernere regem.' *Ep. fam.*, III, 7 (1339, possibly 1342) : 'Certainly, in our present political situation ... there remains absolutely no doubt that monarchy is the best form of government ...'; see my *Humanistic and Political Literature in Florence and Venice at the Beginning of the Quattrocento* (Cambridge, Mass. 1955), pp. 25 f.

15 'Ita pugnare simul autoritas et experientia videntur.' *Ep. fam.*, III, 7

16 See the examples in K. Heitmann, *Fortuna und Virtus: Eine Studie zu Petrarcas Lebensweisheit* (Cologne 1958), pp. 109 f.

17 '... Quam turpiter omnia calcat/Ambitus! Ut totum imperium sibi vindicet unus!/Primus et exemplum reliquis, spolietque superbus/Aerarium, miserosque novo legat ordine patres.' *Africa*, II, 149 ff. (the quoted lines, 235 ff.).

18 Even the exception represented by Ptolemy of Lucca is not a full exception; see my *Crisis of the Early Italian Renaissance* (rev. ed., Princeton 1966), p. 57.

19 *Africa*, III, 631 ff.; IV, 9 ff.

20 '... neglectum hactenus ad officium redi! Mundo enim tremente dormire, nescio quid morti similius quam sopori est.' *Ep. fam.*, III, 10 (1339), the concluding words.

21 '... constetque, iuxta Plotini sententiam, non purgatoriis modo purgatique iam animi, sed politicis quoque virtutibus beatum fieri. Ut enim aliquid more nostrorum loquar, actuosa Marthe solicitudo non spernitur, quamvis sublimior contemplatio sit Marie.' *Ep. fam.*, III, 12 (apparently about 1340, according to E.H. Wilkins, *Petrarch's Eight Years in Milan* [Cambridge, Mass. 1958], p. 237).

22 Petrarch's coronation oration, ed. A. Hortis in *Scritti inediti di Francesco Petrarca* (Trieste 1874), pp. 311 f. There is an English translation of the oration in E.H. Wilkins, *Studies in the Life and Works of Petrarch* (Cambridge, Mass. 1955), pp. 300-13.

23 Coronation oration, Hortis, *Scritti inediti*, pp. 318 ff.

24 *Secretum*, ed. E. Carrara in *Francesco Petrarca: Prose*, p. 130 (all future references to the *Secretum* are to this edition)

25 *Secretum*, pp. 130, 132, 148, 154, 160

26 'Mortalibus utor pro mortalibus ...' 'Itaque istum esse ordinem, ut mortalium rerum inter mortales prima sit cura; transitoriis eterna succedant, quod ex his ad illa sit ordinatissimus progressus.' *Secretum*, pp. 188 ff., 196 ff., 198, 200 ff.

27 *Secretum*, pp. 206, 214

28 *Ep. fam.*, XXI, 12 (1359, according to Wilkins, *Petrarch's Eight Years*, pp. 199 ff.) and *Ep. fam.*, XIX, 16 (1357, *ibid.*, pp. 138 ff.)

29 '... labor iugis, et intentio pabulum animi mei sunt, cum quiescere coepero atque lentescere, mox et vivere desinam.' 'An tu forsitan non Ecclesiasticum illud audisti: Cum consumaverit homo, tunc incipiet, et cum quieverit, tunc operabitur. Equidem nunc coepisse mihi videor ... Si haec inter vitae finis adveniat, qui certe iam longinquus esse non potest, ... opto ut legentem, aut scribentem, vel si Christo placuerit orantem, vel plorantem mors inveniat.' *Seniles*, XVII (XVI), 2 (1373); in *Opera Omnia* (Basel 1581), p. 968.

30 Here I must once more remind the reader of the difference between an exhaustive analysis of Petrarch's work and an elaboration of the phases of his development. The latter need not take into consideration the fact that the ideas of successive periods sometimes overlap or coexist in later phases.

The *De remediis* is a case in point. Written late in Petrarch's life, this work nonetheless attempts to reconcile the severity of the Stoic teachings, to which Petrarch had definitely adhered by that time, with the psychological view of human nature characteristic of his earlier years. In a measure, the observation that even in this most systematic statement of his Stoic convictions his doubts and struggles were effective enough to modify his final views is one of the strongest testimonies to the profundity of those doubts and struggles. But in order to form a clear and simple concept of the difference between the ideas dominating Petrarch's writings from the *Secretum* and his previous views of Antiquity and the nature of man, the *De vita solitaria* and some of his biographical works provide more useful texts than the not always consistent discussion of philosophical doctrines in the *De remediis*.

31 *De vita solitaria*, ed. G. Martellotti, in *Francesco Petrarca: Prose*, pp. 340-2 (all future references to *De vita solitaria* are to this edition). Translations in the text, here and in the next few pages, partly follow *The Life of Solitude by Francis Petrarch*, trans. J. Zeitlin (Urbana, Illinois 1924).

32 *De vita solitaria*, pp. 502-4

33 *Ibid.*, pp. 578-80

34 *Ibid.*, pp. 542-4

35 *Ibid.*, pp. 544-6

36 'Neque tamen in vita tua quicquam preter constantiam requiro, et philosophice professioni debitum quietis studium et a civilibus bellis fugam, extincta libertate ac sepulta iam et complorata republica.' *Ep. fam.*, XXIV, 4 (1345). For the historical place of this attack and its contrast to the understanding of Cicero's motivation during the early Renaissance, see Baron, *Crisis of the Early Italian Renaissance*, pp. 121 ff., and Baron, 'Cicero and the Roman Civic Spirit in the Middle Ages and the Early Renaissance,' *Bulletin of the John Rylands Library*, XXII (1938), revised and enlarged in *Lordship and Community in Medieval Europe*, ed. F.L. Cheyette (New York 1968).

37 For Petrarch's condemnation of Brutus and Cato in later years, see Baron, *From Petrarch to Leonardo Bruni*, pp. 38 f.

38 Concluding *Ep. fam.*, XXIV, 3: "Ah quanto satius fuerat philosopho presertim in tranquillo rure senuisse, de perpetua illa, ut ipse quodam scribis loco, non de hac iam exigua vita cogitantem, nullos habuisse fasces, nullis triumphis inhiasse, nullos inflasse tibi animum Catilinas.'

39 *De vita solitaria*, pp. 534-8

40 *Ibid.*, pp. 550-2

41 *Ibid.*, pp. 554-6 and 586-8

42 The sequence of the three versions was established by G. Martellotti, who has published them in his *Francesco Petrarca: La Vita di Scipione L'Africano* (Milan 1954).

43 'Sed immensa spes ardorque animi ad summa tendentis per circumfusa pericula nullius, preter veram et excelsam gloriam et quem mente con-

ceperat belli exitum, rerum memorem trahebat.' *De Publio Cornelio Scipione Africano* (earliest version, ed. Martellotti), p. 172.

44 'Huic tamen illud Ciceronis annectam: quod "vix invenitur qui laboribus susceptis periculisque aditis non quasi mercedem rerum gestarum desideret gloriam"; et hec glorie cupiditas, ut ait idem, "in magnis animis et ingeniis plerunque contingit, eoque magis si sunt ad rem militarem apti, cupidi bellorum gerendorum." ' *De Publio Cornelio Scipione Africano* (second version, ed. Martellotti), pp. 211 f.

45 'Vera autem et sapiens animi magnitudo honestum illud ... in factis positum, non in gloria iudicat ... Facillime autem ad res iniustas impellitur, ut quisque altissimo animo est, gloriae cupiditate; qui locus est sane lubricus, quod vix invenitur, qui laboribus susceptis periculisque aditis non quasi mercedem rerum gestarum desideret gloriam.' *De officiis*, I, 19, 65.

46 'Verbumque illud altissimum adiecit, desiderium glorie ultra vite tempus extendi, ... ideoque naturaliter inesse magnis et excellentibus animis, ut non modo cum coevis sed cum omnium seculorum viris se comparent, cum omnibus de claritate contendant: dictum omnibus semper qui in altum nituntur memorabile.' *De Publio Cornelio Scipione Africano Maiore* (final version, ed. Martellotti), pp. 147 f. To be compared with Livy, XXVIII, 43, 5-8, a text of which Petrarch actually gives a paraphrase; but the words 'Verbumque illud altissimum adiecit,' 'ideoque naturaliter inesse magnis et excellentibus animis,' 'dictum omnibus semper qui in altum nituntur memorabile' have no equivalent in Livy.

47 '... aliquanto difficilius re contemni quam verbo nemo michi quoque negaverit.' *De Publio Cornelio Scipione Africano Maiore* (final version, ed. Martellotti), p. 133.

48 *Ibid.*, pp. 151, 153, 155

A little-known
letter of Erasmus,
and the date of
his encounter with Reuchlin

Paul Oskar Kristeller

Allen's monumental edition of Erasmus' correspondence, completed and supplied with indices after his death, rests on such a solid foundation that the chances of finding additional letters are very slight indeed.[1] The editors of the new critical edition of Erasmus' works, sponsored by the Netherlands' Academy of Sciences, have rightly decided not to undertake a new edition of this part of Erasmus' work. However, it might be well to plan at least a small supplement to Allen. I have noticed more than once in my own research that he failed to utilize a number of manuscripts of Erasmus letters that were derivative or at least not autograph, and that might still yield some interesting variants, or at least some interesting data for the diffusion of these letters. In rare instances, we may thus hit upon some new letters addressed to Erasmus,[2] or even upon an additional letter of Erasmus himself.

Several years ago, I had occasion to scan the printed inventory of the archives of St-Thomas in Strasbourg and I found listed there a letter from Erasmus to Wimpfeling.[3] Upon my request, I received a description and a microfilm of the letter,[4] and was able to ascertain that the letter was not included in Allen's collection. I had to wait for a suitable occasion before I was ready to study and to publish the letter.[5]

The letter is clearly not an autograph,[6] but was written by a German scribe of the period. Hence it is not surprising to find occasional errors in it. However, there is no reason to doubt that it is an original letter.[7] Apart from the content, which is perfectly genuine, the single sheet shows traces of having been folded, and the address appears on the outside of the folio, as is customary. Rather unusual is the fact that the text of the letter begins with a greeting formula that is grammatically connected with the address on the outside. Hence the page that contains the text of the letter must be considered as the verso page of the sheet, while the address is on the recto.

The letter is addressed to Jacob Wimpfeling and his literary society in Strasbourg.[8] Jacob Wimpfeling (1450-1528), the well-known Alsatian humanist, lived for many years in Strasbourg. Around 1510 he founded there a literary society, probably after the model of Celtis (*sodalitas litteraria* or, as it is called here by Erasmus, *litterarium sodalitium*). When Erasmus, on his way to Basel, passed through Strasbourg in August 1514 he was received with great honours by Wimpfeling and the literary society, and this episode, solemnly recorded in subsequent letters of Wimpfeling and Erasmus, marks the most famous event in the history of the society and also the beginning of Erasmus' close friendship with Wimpfeling.[9] Their later correspondence is rather scanty, but Wimpfeling is frequently mentioned in Erasmus' correspondence with others, and they probably met on several occasions. When Wimpfeling died, Erasmus paid a warm tribute to him in a letter to a mutual friend.[10] The new letter is another testimony of this friendship, and it also tells us that Erasmus was received by the Strasbourg circle on another occasion when he was on his way to Mainz and England. We learn at the end of the letter that his friends footed Erasmus' hotel bill, as we know they did on other occasions.[11]

The largest part of the letter is taken up by an account of two misfortunes that befell Erasmus during his journey. A part of his money was stolen, and he had an attack of fever. He tells us that his money supply consisted of sixty-six gold coins including two nobles, some crowns and ducats, one florin, and one Philip's guilder.[12] Later he says that more than twenty-two florins were stolen (it is not clear whether they include the two nobles which he noticed first to be missing) and that he was left with forty-eight gold coins. This means that he must originally have carried at least seventy gold coins and, unless a specialist in numismatics comes up with a better explanation, we must conclude that something is wrong with Erasmus' arithmetic or with that of his scribe. I must leave to historians of medicine the diagnosis of Erasmus' illness. He was always of frail health, and it may not be a coincidence that he had been sitting near a German stove (hypocaustion or hypocaustum) of which he was to complain more than once in his later years.[13]

Of greater interest are Erasmus' comments on the persons to whom he spoke during his journey. Above all, he reports that he has just met Reuchlin, and adds a few words of praise which are by no means unique, but are a welcome addition to our knowledge of the relations between the two great scholars.[14] Their encounter had been known from letters of Hutten and Crotus, and from a much later letter of Erasmus to Wolsey,[15] but our letter provides the first direct testimony from Erasmus himself, written shortly after the event.

Erasmus also mentions having met Nicolaus Gerbellius, probably for the first time, and has some words of high praise for him.[16] Since Gerbellius was to take up residence in Strasbourg before long, this may have been intended as an introduction for him to Erasmus' friends in Strasbourg.[17] Beatus Rhenanus, with whom Erasmus had been in close touch since he came to Basel, is mentioned incidentally, but there is no indication that he was present.[18] Finally, Erasmus mentions as present two publishers, Matthias Schürer of Strasbourg and Wolfgang Lachner of Basel. Both of them are well known for the production of their presses, and for their close association with Erasmus. Lachner was the father-in-law and business partner of Johannes Froben, Erasmus' friend and chief publisher in Basel.[19]

The letter is undated, and it remains to be seen when and from where it was written. I am inclined to think that the letter was written and sent from Frankfurt. It has been previously inferred that on one of his trips between Basel and England Erasmus visited the Frankfurt book fair, and that his only meeting with Reuchlin took place on that occasion.[20] The fact that our letter mentions two booksellers as present and that Erasmus speaks of his plan to buy books is best explained within the context of the book fair. This also accounts for the statement that Lachner refuses to sell here (*hic*) his second edition of the *Proverbia* (the *Adagia*) as long as the first edition is not yet sold out.[21] If we infer, as has been assumed by others, that Erasmus travelled from Strasbourg to Frankfurt in the company of Schürer and Lachner,[22] we may easily conclude that our letter was taken from Frankfurt to Strasbourg by Lachner or Schürer, and more probably by the latter, after Erasmus had left for England.[23] Erasmus states that the letter was written shortly before his departure.

The most serious question concerning our letter is the date which we should assign to it. The firmest basis for dating it is the fact that it was written during a journey that took Erasmus from Strasbourg via Mainz to England. Among Erasmus' trips to England, only two took him through Strasbourg: his journey from Italy in 1509, and his journey from Basel in 1515.[24] The former date is to be excluded, for it would force us, on the basis of our letter, to predate Erasmus' close connections with Basel and Strasbourg by several years, and also to postulate an earlier meeting with Reuchlin for which there is no other evidence. However, if we date our letter in the spring of 1515, everything seems to fall in line. The close relations with Basel and Strasbourg had been established the year before, and the meeting with Reuchlin turns out to be the one attested before, though less directly, that can now be more surely assigned to the spring of 1515.[25]

The new letter makes a rather modest contribution to Erasmus' biography. Yet it supplements our information about his personal relations with several friends, especially Reuchlin, and it belongs to a period of his life for which only a small part of his correspondence has been preserved.

Strasbourg, Archives et bibliothèque de la ville

Archives du chapître de St-Thomas

tome 175, f.6

D. Jacobo Wimphelingo reliquoque litterario sodalitio Argentorati[26] [f.6ᵛ] Salutem plurimam. Eodem die geminum michi vulnus inflixit genius aliquis malus. Maguntie recensueram pecuniole mee summan ut scirem si quid intercidisset (nam territus rumore de nave direpta reieceram in ocreas) : reperi sexaginta sex aureos inter quos nobiles duo, coronati aliquot sole insignes et ducati, minimus omnium florenus aureus excepto Philippeo unico. Erat hypocaustion adherens cubiculo michi proprium in quo fabulamur[27] ad multam usque noctem una cum Schurerio ac ceteris aliquot amiculis. Omnibus digressis crumena inibi relicta pergo cubitum.[28] Mane nihil etiam suspicans[29] mali de novo visum est recensere summam qui scirem quantum liceret in libros coemendos decidere. Mox ex promptu video deesse duos nobiles. Ilico tetigit[30] animum, percenseo, reperio deesse super viginti duos florenos aureos. Reliquerat enim fur ille quadraginta octo aureos, civilis scilicet et minore contentus portione. Ea res non adeo vulneraverat[31] animum meum, ita me deus amet, ut nec summam cutem aliqua mesticia perstrinxerit.[32] Optabam ut eo incommodo totius itineris infelicitas foret expiata. Verum gravius successit malum. Sub noctem lassitudo quedam oborta[33] instantis morbi[34] signa dedit. Ceno parcissime. Eo cubitum. Mox tanta me febris corripit ut in vita non senserim graviorem. Ea perseverat in octavam usque sequentis diei. Sudatum est supra modum. Halitus et urina nihil aliud erat quam merus ignis. Credo ni sudor accessisset, capitale malum futurum fuisse. Verum nunc eo sum statu ut bene sperem. Nec tamen me poenitet huius itineris per quod mihi contigit Reuchlinum complecti, quem hominem profecto non iam suspicio tantum ob eximiam eruditionem, verum etiam unice amo ob raram quandam civilitatem morumque iucunditatem. Complexi sumus, imo complures horas frui licuit Gerbellio nostro cuius lingua, mores, eruditio sic fatiunt ad meum ingenium, ut nullius consuetudine iam annis aliquot eque sim delectatus. Nec est de quo michi maiora polliceor quam de Beato Rhenano et Gerbellio. Lachnerus hic noluit divendere nova Proverbia quo vetera prius extrudat, vos e Basilea petatis oportet. Hec scripsi raptim iam ad iter accinctus. Reliqua cognoscetis[35] ex Anglia. Habeo gratiam quod vestra benignitate discesserim immunis e diversorio. Id tametsi mihi iam non est novum, tamen studio in me vestro maiorem in

Erasmus, letter to Wimpfeling
Archives du chapître St-Thomas, tome 175, f.6

Erasmus Roterodamus

modum delector. Bene valete omnes, quibus ut uni scribo, quo indissolu-
bili necessitudinis vinculo cohereatis omnes.

Erasmus Roterodamus

To Jacob Wimpfeling and the other members of the Strasbourg literary
circle cordial greetings. On one and the same day, an evil genius inflicted
a double wound on me. At Mainz, I had recounted my money in order to
know if something had been lost. For I had been frightened by rumours
that a ship had been plundered, and hence had put my money into my
boots. I found 66 gold pieces including two nobles, some crowns with the
sign of the sun and ducats, the smallest of all being a gold florin except for
a single Philip's guilder. There was a stove next to my bedroom that belonged to me. There we chatted deep into the night with Schürer and some
other young friends. When all had departed, I left my purse there and
went to bed. In the morning, I suspected no evil, but decided to recount my
money so that I should know how much I may be permitted to spend on
purchasing books. Immediately I see that the two nobles were missing.
This struck my mind, I count again, and find that more than 22 gold florins were missing. For that thief had left me 48 gold pieces, being very
kind and satisfied with the smaller part of the total. So may God love me,
this matter did not hurt my mind to the point that it did not even scratch
my skin with any sadness. I wish the bad luck of this journey had been ex-
piated by this misfortune. Yet a more serious evil followed. At night a
feeling of fatigue overcame me that indicated an impending illness. I eat
sparingly for supper and go to bed. Soon a stronger fever seizes me than
I had ever experienced in my life. It lasted to the eighth hour of the next
day. I perspired excessively, my breath and urine were like fire. I think it
would have been a deadly illness if the sweat had not come. Yet now I am
in such a state that I am hopeful of an early recovery. Yet I do not regret
this journey which enabled me to embrace Reuchlin, a man whom I not
only respect for his great learning, but also uniquely love for his civilized
and pleasant manners. I also embraced, or rather enjoyed for several
hours, our Gerbellius whose talk, manners, and learning are so much to
my taste that for some years I have not been as much pleased with any-
body's company. Of nobody I entertain greater expectations than of
Beatus Rhenanus and of Gerbellius. Lachner did not want to sell here the
new edition of the *Adagia* so that he may dispose first of the old edition.
You must order it from Basel. I am writing in a hurry because I am ready

for my journey. You will hear the rest from England. I am grateful because, thanks to your generosity, I left the inn without charge. This is no longer new to me, and I am increasingly pleased by your thoughtfulness towards me. Keep well, all of you. I write to you all as to one person, since you are all tied together by the unbreakable bond of friendship.

Erasmus of Rotterdam

NOTES

1 *Opus Epistolarum Desiderii Erasmi*, ed. P.S. Allen et al. (Oxford 1906-58), 12 vols. The collection includes 3,141 letters, not counting some addenda. See my review of the index volume, *Renaissance News*, xiv (1961), 14-17. References to this edition will be to letter numbers.

2 P. O. Kristeller, 'Two Unpublished Letters to Erasmus,' *Renaissance News*, xiv (1961), 6-14

3 *Inventaire des archives du Chapître de St-Thomas de Strasbourg* (Strasbourg 1937), c. 286: Tome 175. Recueil factice. Varia ecclesiastica x, no. 3, f.6. Erasmus Roterodamus Jacobo Wimpfelingo. The Latin text is reproduced on p. 56, followed by an English translation.

4 I am indebted to M. Ph. Dollinger of the Archives et Bibliothèque municipale in Strasbourg for the information and microfilm he kindly supplied to me. I am also indebted, for bibliographical information and suggestions, to Professors Roland H. Bainton, Raymond de Roover, and Lewis W. Spitz, to Mr Henry Grunthal of the American Numismatic Society, and to Mrs Marianne Salloch.

5 This text and note may be considered as an appendix to *Erasmi Opuscula: A Supplement to the Opera Omnia*, ed. Wallace K. Ferguson (The Hague 1933). The letter was published once before, as I have been informed by Professor Otto Herding of Freiburg, in *Das Narrenschiff von Dr. Sebastian Brant*, ed. A. W. Strobel (Quedlinburg and Leipzig 1839), pp. 80-1. The editor failed to indicate his manuscript source. In the notes to my transcription of the letter s indicates Strobel and m indicates the manuscript.

6 I have not seen the letter, but have compared an enlarged photoprint made from the microfilm with specimens of Erasmus' known handwriting. See *The Poems of Desiderius Erasmus*, Cornelis Reedijk, ed., with introduction and notes (Leiden 1956), plate facing p. 356; G. Mentz, *Handschriften der Reformationszeit* (Bonn 1912), plate 1. I do not accept as an autograph the specimen given by O. Clemen, *Handschriftenproben der Reformationszeit* (Zwickau 1911), no. 18.

7 Many original letters of Renaissance scholars are not autograph. See P.O. Kristeller, "Some Original Letters and Autograph Manuscripts of Marsilio

Ficino,' in *Studi di bibliografia e di storia in onore di Tammaro De Marinis* (Verona 1964), III, 5-33. As we shall see, the circumstances under which the new Erasmus letter was written gave him ample opportunity to dictate it to a German scribe. This may also account for some of the slight errors in the text.

8 On Wimpfeling and his Strasbourg literary society, see P.A. Wiskowatoff, *Jacob Wimpheling* (Berlin 1867) ; Bernhard Schwarz, *Jacob Wimpheling* (Gotha 1875) ; Charles Schmidt, *Histoire littéraire de l'Alsace* ... (Paris 1879; repr. Nieuwkoop 1966), I, 1-188; Joseph Knepper, *Jakob Wimpfeling* (Freiburg 1902) ; Lewis W. Spitz, *The Religious Renaissance of the German Humanists* (Cambridge, Mass. 1963), pp. 41-60; Otto Herding, 'Der elsaessische Humanist Jakob Wimpfeling und seine Erziehungsschrift "Adolescentia," *Zeitschrift für Württembergische Landesgeschichte*, XXII (1963), pp. 1-18; *Adolescentia*, ed. O. Herding (vol. I of *Jacobi Wimpfelingi Opera selecta* [Munich 1965]).

9 Allen, 302 (II, 7-9, Wimpfeling to Erasmus, Strasbourg, 1 September 1514) and 305 (II, 17-24, Erasmus to Wimpfeling, Basel, 21 September 1514). There is an earlier letter from Wimpfeling to Erasmus, dated 19 August 1511 (Allen, 224, I, 462-5).

10 Erasmus to Joh. Vlatten, Basel, 24 January 1529 (Allen, 2088, VIII, 19-20)

11 In a letter written to Nicolaus Gerbellius from Louvain on 20 October 1518, after another passing visit in Strasbourg, Erasmus sends his greetings and thanks to the members of the *sodalitas*, 'qui solita sua benignitate in diversorio me immunem esse voluerunt' (Allen, 883, III, 420-1).

12 The noble was a typically English coin, but it was also struck in the Low Countries (F. Friedensburg. *Münzkunde und Geldgeschichte der Einzelstaaten des Mittelalters und der neueren Zeit* [Munich and Berlin 1926], p. 58; 66-7). It is probable that Erasmus' English friends had sent him a part of his travel money. The *coronati sole insignes* are French *écus de soleil*. The Philip's guilder was a coin struck by Philip the Handsome of Austria and Burgundy in the Low Countries. Cf. H. Enno Van Gelder and Marcel Hoc, *Les Monnaies des Pays-Bas bourguignons et espagnols, 1434-1713* (Amsterdam 1960), pp. 35 and 76.

13 'ad nidorem hypocaustorum aegrotare coepimus' (letter to Matthaeus Schinner, Basel, 14 December 1521, Allen 1248, III, 509, with Allen's note that refers to several other passages). 'Non abhorret animus a visendo Friburgo ante brumam; sed deterrent hypocausta et vina' (letter to Conrad Heresbach, Basel, 18 October 1522, Allen, 1316, V, 133).

14 See p. 56, line 23 of letter: 'Nec tamen ... iucunditatem.'

15 In a letter written from Mainz on 13 June 1515, Hutten writes to Jacobus Fuch: 'Nundinis praeterea cum esse Francofordii illum (sc. Erasmum) et simul Capnionem ac Hermannum Buschium intellexisset (sc. Itelvolfus de Lapide), cupidissime eo concessit' (Ulrichi Hutteni ... *Opera*, ed. E. Boecking [Leipzig 1859], I, 43-4, no. 26). Crotus wrote to Mutianus from Fulda on 11 June 1515: 'Reuchlinus et Buschius obmutuerunt illo loquente (sc. Erasmo) anno praecedente Moguntiae teste Hutheno meo.'

(Der Briefwechsel des Mutianus Rufus, ed. C. Krause [Kassel 1885],
p. 599, no. 533). Erasmus in a letter to Wolsey, written from Antwerp on
15 May 1519, merely says: 'Cum Reuchlino semel dumtaxat congressus
sum Francfordiae.' (Allen 967, III, 589). In his note, Allen rightly questions the testimony of Crotus as to the place and date of the meeting, and
insists, correcting an earlier statement of his, that the meeting took place
in Frankfurt in March or April 1515. This date is accepted in a recent
study by Manfred Krebs who connects the meeting with the book fair
('Reuchlins Beziehungen zu Erasmus von Rotterdam,' in *Johannes
Reuchlin, 1455-1522, Festgabe seiner Vaterstadt* ... [Pforzheim 1955], pp.
139-55, at p. 145). Ludwig Geiger *(Johann Reuchlin* [Leipzig 1871, repr.
Nieuwkoop 1964], p. 337) says that the meeting took place in Frankfurt,
but dates it in the spring of 1514 when Erasmus was on his way from
England to Basel. Our letter clearly confirms Allen's and Krebs' view that
Erasmus was on his way to England when he met Reuchlin.

16 For Gerbellius (1485-1560), see A. Buechle, *Der Humanist Nikolaus
Gerbel aus Pforzheim* (progr. Durlach 1886) ; C. Varrentrapp, 'Nicolaus
Gerbel: Ein Beitrag zur Geschichte des wissenschaftlichen Lebens in
Strassburg im 16. Jahrhundert,' in *Strassburger Festschrift zur 46.
Versammlung deutscher Philologen und Schulmänner* (Strasbourg 1901),
221-38; W. Horning, *Der Humanist Dr. Nikolaus Gerbel* (Strasbourg,
1918) ; P. Merker, *Der Verfasser des Eccius dedolatus* (Halle 1923).
Gerbellius settled in Strasbourg before 8 August 1515 (Allen, 343, III,
121-2), and visited Basel in September (Allen, 358, II, 148).

17 In a letter to Ottomarus Luscinius, sent from Basel on 31 December 1515,
Beatus Rhenanus lists Gerbellius among the prominent members of the
Strasbourg literary society *(literariae sodalitatis proceribus,* see *Briefwechsel des Beatus Rhenanus,* ed. A. Horawitz and K. Hartfelder [Leipzig
1886], no. 54, pp. 80-1).

18 For Beatus Rhenanus (1485-1547), see Allen and Horawitz-Hartfelder,
passim. When Erasmus arrived in Basel, Beatus Rhenanus was among the
few persons whom he had informed in advance and who came to see him
immediately (Allen, 305, II, 22).

19 For Schürer (1470-1520) see: Charles Schmidt, *Répertoire bibliographi-
que strasbourgeois* (Strasbourg 1896, repr. Baden-Baden 1963), vol. 8;
François Ritter, *Histoire le l'imprimerie alsacienne* (Strasbourg and Paris
1955), pp. 160-70. He came to Strasbourg in 1501 and had his own printing press from 1508 until 1519. He printed many works of Erasmus, several of them for the first time. For Lachner (c1465-1518) : J. Stockmeyer
and B. Reber, *Beiträge zur Basler Buchdruckergeschichte* (Basel 1840),
pp. 86-7; Ch. W. Heckethorn, *The Printers of Basle* (London 1897), p.
87; R. Wackernagel, *Geschichte der Stadt Basel* (Basel 1924), III, 167-8.
Lachner came to Basel in 1488. He is often mentioned in Erasmus' correspondence.

20 See above, note 15

21 The first edition of the *Adagia* published in Basel by Froben appeared in

1513, the second, in 1515. See F. van der Haeghen, *Bibiotheca Erasmiana* (Ghent 1893, repr. Nieuwkoop 1961) pp. 1-8. The *Adagia* are frequently referred to as *Proverbia*.

22 Allen, II, 67

23 In a letter dated from Basel, 17 April 1515, Beatus Rhenanus complains that a letter from Erasmus had not reached him because he did not send it through Lachner; if he sent it through Schürer, it will arrive with great delay since Schürer is careless (Allen, 328, II, 62-5). On 30 April 1515, Rhenanus complains again that he had not received the letter Erasmus had sent to him from Frankfurt, and that he had not heard from Schürer (Allen, 330, II, 65-6).

24 On Erasmus' itinerary, see Allen; Preserved Smith, *Erasmus* (New York 1923), p. 59; G. Marc'hadour, *L'Univers de Thomas More: Chronologie critique de More, Erasme et leur époque* (Paris 1963).

25 On 7 March Erasmus was still in Basel (Allen, 325); on 13 April he was in St. Omer (327), and on 7 May he had arrived in London (332). According to Allen's system, our letter should be numbered 326a.

26 D. Jacobo ... Argentorati *in fine posuit* s (for apparatus, see n. 5)

27 fabulamus s

28 cubiculum s

29 suspirans s

30 tetegit M

31 vulneraerat M

32 perstrinxerat s

33 om. s

34 morbi(?) M

35 cognoscatis s

De modis disputandi:

The apologetic works of Erasmus

Myron P. Gilmore

In the summer of 1504 Erasmus found in the Premonstratensian monastery of Parc near Louvain a manuscript of Lorenzo Valla's *In novum Testamentum ... adnotationes*. When he returned to Paris a few months later he took lodgings with Christopher Fisher, an English friend in the papal service, who persuaded him to publish the manuscript. This edition of Valla's *Annotations*, printed by Badius, appeared in Paris on 13 April 1505 with a preface by Erasmus in the form of a letter to his host.[1]

In this dedicatory epistle he confesses that he relies on his friend's encouragement and approbation against anticipated criticism of the publication because Valla is well known to have been a dangerous fellow who attacked practically everyone. He dared to criticize authorities. 'An unworthy crime indeed,' says Erasmus, 'as if Aristotle had not rejected almost everything in his predecessors and as if Brutus had not condemned the entire style of Cicero ... Jerome that of Augustine ... and, most recently, Filelfo that of Quintilian. What of the fact that Pliny did not believe his book had pleased a friend unless he knew that some things in it had displeased him? So far is it from being a vice that, in the field of literary studies, it is very much to be desired that there be dissension and conflict which Hesiod tells us is most useful to mortals.'[2] Here Erasmus refers to the opening of the *Works and Days* in which Hesiod proclaims that there are not one but two kinds of strife or *Eris* in the world; one is wholesome in its effects and stirs men up to creative activity, while the other is destructive and produces cruel war.[3] According to Erasmus in this preface, disputes between scholars are of the first kind. Erasmus himself welcomes criticism of his ideas and prefers the critic who condemns to the friend who applauds. 'If the critic is right I learn something, if wrong, I am stimulated to a more vivid defence of the truth.'[4] The only reservation in this defence of criticism is that it must not degenerate into anger and wrangling.

Such were the views of Erasmus in the early years of the sixteenth century before he had become the most famous scholar of his generation and before the religious revolution had altered the very assumptions on which intellectual exchanges were based.

Sixteen years later the prospect of scholarly controversy was less appealing. In the preface to his reply to Stunica's criticisms of the edition of the *New Testament*, Erasmus apologizes to the reader. 'Who is so idle as to take pleasure in reading disputes of this kind?' Valla comes to his mind again but this time not to be defended for his controversies. 'Lorenzo

Valla,' he says, 'was a man of undeniable erudition and eloquence who had gladiatorial fights with Poggio. We read today his *Elegantiae* and nothing is more cold than the things they waxed so hot about. When I contemplate the brevity of life and how little remains to me, how much I regret wasting time on these trivialities, not to speak of the fact that when we engage in or are engaged in quarrels of this kind we lose the tranquility of a Christian soul, we lose the pleasure and a good part of the fruit of our studies and many people are alienated from literature altogether.'[5]

The same distaste for polemics was registered at length in the *Catalogus lucubrationum*, the first version of which was written for John Botzheim in January 1523. No less than twelve pages in the Allen edition of this important document are devoted to the description of the apologetic works. Erasmus begins this section by recalling that he had been wont to boast that no one was ever wounded by his pen whether in jest or in earnest. It was always his vow that his literary encounters should be without bloodshed, but he was defeated by two circumstances: He was most hatefully attacked in print by those from whom he had never deserved ill and whom it was no advantage to have overcome or even to have had as adversaries; in other words, people for whom he had contempt. So, constrained by necessity, he describes these works in as few words as possible. When he has counted them all up, '*Me miserum*,' he says, 'let them be the eighth volume and they will just fill an entire volume.'[6]

When Erasmus wrote to Botzheim there were still many more apologies and vindications to come. In the end, the apologetical works fill almost the whole of the last two volumes of the Leclerc edition of 1706 and amount to a total of nearly forty treatises of varying length, not including the many letters which would enter into the same category.

In view of the fact that Erasmus seems to have let almost no occasion go by without responding to his critics and that he always did so with verve and in detail, giving as good as or better than he had received, it is difficult to take seriously his protestations of reluctance to enter into these combats. They gave ample scope for the irony and invective of which Erasmus was a master and from the point of view of both style and content they deserve as a whole more attention than they have commonly received from Erasmus' biographers. Although it is obviously impossible to enter into detail on all these apologia, this essay will attempt to analyze the various types of attack to which Erasmus was subjected and to consider how far his responses help us to understand more precisely his religious position in the last decades of his life.

Although, as we have seen, Erasmus himself suggested that his apologetic works fell into two classes, those provoked by the attacks of treacherous friends and those written against ignorant enemies, this too summary division fails to take into account more subtle differences arising from his varied feelings towards his opponents and his sensitivity to certain kinds of criticism. In the period before he began to feel trapped by the controversies of the Reformation there is a group of apologetic writings in which Erasmus replies in a friendly way to his critics, maintaining the standards which he had recommended in the preface to the edition of Valla in 1505.

The *epistola apologetica* written to Martin Dorp in May 1515 might indeed seem a practical application of Erasmus' earlier precepts on how a debate should be conducted. Dorp was a philosopher and theologian, later rector of the university of Louvain, whose relations with Erasmus continued to be friendly in spite of the hostile judgments of the Louvain faculty of theology. In September 1514 Dorp had written to Erasmus deploring the *Praise of Folly*, commending the edition of St Jerome, but advising against the publication of the edition and translation of the *New Testament* which Erasmus was preparing.[7] Erasmus' reply declared in the most fulsome terms, and perhaps not without irony, his high opinion of Dorp's judgment, learning, and taste. He is so far from being offended by the criticisms that Dorp is even dearer to him than he was before. Dorp may even be called a celestial genius and his approval is to be sought above that of a thousand others.[8] In this period Erasmus could still write, 'No one is so much my enemy that I would not like to bring him back into friendship if possible.'[9] Defending the *Moria*, he declares that he had presented the principles of Christian life simply and directly in the *Enchiridion militis christiani*, whereas in the *Moria* he had done the same thing but *sub specie lusus*.[10] He points out Dorp's inconsistency in approving of the edition of St Jerome which is execrated by those who disapprove of the *Moria*. As for the new edition of the *New Testament*, he maintains that it is clear to all that errors of translation and interpretation have crept in since the time of Jerome's translation. He is able to cite Valla and the *Commentaries on St Paul* by Lefèvre d'Étaples in support of the necessity of a return to a purer text.[11] The tone throughout remains a mixture of rational persuasion and friendly admonition. One characteristic may be noted which was to recur in many of Erasmus' apologies – the prolixity of his reply. In this case he writes an epistle of over nine hundred lines to answer one of one hundred and sixty-five. He leaves the impression that he is carried away by his own eloquence in defence of his position and is anxious to leave no detail undefended.

A year and a half later, and still before the bitter polemics that followed the Reformation, comes the controversy with the same Lefèvre whose *Commentaries* he had cited against Dorp. A friend had shown him the passage in which the French scholar had condemned Erasmus for his note on Hebrews 2:7, 'Thou hast made him a little lower than the angels.' This verse was a quotation from the eighth psalm where the original Hebrew of the Old Testament had 'God' in place of 'angels.' The author of the Epistle to the Hebrews had taken 'angels' from the Greek Septuagint translation of the Psalms where it had been mistranslated. Erasmus considered that, although it was an error, it was one made by the author of the Epistle to the Hebrews and so should be allowed to stand. Lefèvre maintained that not only was it wrong, as a mistranslation, but it was impious to describe Christ as 'lower than the angels,' and in consequence he accused Erasmus of impiety.[12] In his *Apologia* Erasmus undertakes to show that there is nothing impious in describing Christ as lower than the angels since he took on human nature and was crucified on the cross.[13] Throughout Erasmus' argument there is a tone of sadness and disappointment, missing from the exchange with Dorp. He continues to use complimentary vocatives in addressing Lefèvre but could have wished that the latter had presented his case in a more friendly fashion and in a less prolix disputation. This last charge may cause some astonishment in view of the fact that Erasmus expanded his *Apologia* to thirty-three folio columns against the twelve of his opponent. Nor is Lefèvre spared some Erasmian irony: Erasmus assures him that he does not doubt that, whether Lefèvre took up this matter on his own judgment or on that of another, he has done so sincerely.[14]

In another vindication two years later he remonstrated with Latomus on his opposition, expressed in the *Dialogue*, to the teaching of the three languages, Latin, Greek, and Hebrew. The trilingual college at Louvain had been established by the will of Jerome Busleyden in 1517 and became a centre of the new learning in the Low Countries. Erasmus had its success very much at heart and was dismayed by the opposition the new establishment encountered in the faculty of theology. In his remonstrance he speaks of an old friendship which he has done nothing to break. He was reluctant to take up the issue but constrained to do so by the urging of friends.[15]

In the same year, 1519, he directed to the students of the faculty of theology at Louvain an *Apology for his Declamation on Matrimony,* repudiating the imputation of heresy which he hears has been made against him by a Carmelite orator. In this work his tone becomes a little more pleading, certainly far less direct and ironic. He protests that his works have never harmed anyone. He notes that it is easy to make accusations of heresy and that no one from Cyprian to Gerson, including Augustine and Thomas Aquinas, has escaped. 'He who undertakes to censure the work of another ought first to be sure he understands the argument deeply, second that he acts under the influence of reason rather than emotion, and finally that he is mindful of the Christian tradition lest an unjust condemnation fall on him. Who has ever written with such circumspection that he pleases everybody, especially when we consider the great variety of opinions to be found in even a small group of people?'[16]

In the group of works written in 1519 Erasmus still, on the whole, follows the principles he had set down in 1505 for the conduct of scholarly controversy. In his defence he employs above all the rhetoric of persuasion with an almost rhythmic alteration between remonstrance and compliment.

A very different style characterizes a second group of replies to his critics – those for whom Eramus felt nothing but contempt, with whom it was no honour to have been engaged. These were especially the scholars who had criticized his *Annotations on the New Testament.*

In the second edition of the *Novum Instrumentum* (Basel 1519), Erasmus had altered the Latin text of the gospel of St John 1:1, from *In principio erat verbum* to *In principio erat sermo,* and defended this change in his note on this text.[17] This proposed emendation of the Vulgate was immediately attacked in Brussels and in London and Erasmus at once launched a characteristic counterattack in the form of an open letter to pious and just readers. The first edition contained a short preface afterwards removed.[18] Erasmus describes in colourful language the reports he has received of the denunciations against him by ignorant preachers. These critics are now said to 'rave' and 'babble.' Words like *debacchari* and *deblaterare* are now used to describe the lectures and writings of those who oppose him.[19] They are motivated by a *diabolica malitia.*

Among these 'malicious' opponents in 1520 was Edward Lee, the future archbishop of York. Lee had had a humanistic education and had become acquainted with Erasmus in 1515 at Louvain where he had come to study Greek. On hearing that Erasmus was preparing a new edition and

translation of the *New Testament* Lee circulated in manuscript some suggested critical notes, perhaps motivated by the hope of gaining fame for
himself as a participant in the great enterprise. In the second edition of
1519 Erasmus neglected some of Lee's criticisms and refuted others, caus-
ing Lee to put out a stronger attack on Erasmus' biblical scholarship.[20]

Erasmus immediately responded to Lee's annotations on the gospels
and epistles with a series of spirited and contemptuous replies which were
published in 1520. In the preface he recounts that his friends had been of
diverse opinions on whether so unworthy an attack should be answered at
all. It seems foolish to refute with care what has only to be read to be refuted. 'If I were free,' Erasmus exclaims, "to enumerate how many times
Lee understands neither what he censures nor what he says, how many
times he falsifies what I have neither said nor thought, how many times he
condemns with outrageous language what has been admirably said, how
many times he twists the expressions of authors in a way to misrepresent
their sense, how many times he writes the grossest absurdities in his zeal
for finding fault, how many times with incredible arrogance he tries to
explain things he does not precisely understand, how many tragedies he
stirs up without cause, O Immortal God, how many indexes would be
needed!'[21]

Here we see how Erasmus' sensitivity to any criticism leads him into
exaggerated rhetoric designed to demolish completely an enemy hardly
worthy of such artillery. The preface concludes by declaring that it is
many years since Erasmus read a book from which he learned less and in
which he is more rebuked. He begs the reader that if he finds anything that
pleases him in the book to give credit for it to Britain as a whole; if he
finds anything to condemn to attribute it to Lee alone. Since Britain has
many men of remarkable honesty, learning, and faith, it would be unjust
to judge a whole people from the nature of one man.[22]

In spite of his protestations in this preface that he could not and
should not spend much time in answering Lee, Erasmus devoted what
amounted to one hundred and sixty folio columns in the Leyden edition of
the *Opera omnia* to the detailed refutation of Lee's notes on the *New Testament*. The modern reader can only agree with Erasmus' own sentiment
on the waste of time *talibus naeniis refellendis*.

Another controversy arising out of the *Annotations on the New Testament* was still more protracted. This was begun by the Spanish theologian,
Diego Lopez Zuniga or Stunica. Stunica belonged to a noble Spanish
family whose members had played a considerable part in political and

ecclesiastical life. He himself had received an education at Cardinal Ximenes' new university of Alcalà and he had participated in the preparation of the *Complutensian Polyglot*. He had therefore some grounds for supposing himself a qualified Biblical scholar. When the first edition of Erasmus' *New Testament* appeared he prepared some critical notes against it, but their publication was apparently forbidden by Cardinal Ximenes. However, after the death of the cardinal, Stunica went ahead with the publication and prefaced his notes with some very disparaging comments on Erasmus in which he accused him of seeking additional fame by turning from profane to sacred texts and undertaking an edition and translation for which he had no proper qualifications.[23]

Erasmus heard about this publication before he had received it and wrote to a friend on 2 August 1520 that another Lee had appeared in Spain. 'A certain Stunica has written a virulent attack against both Lefèvre and me. The Cardinal had forbidden it but after his death Stunica has poured forth his poison. I have not yet seen the book but let them beware lest it fall into my hands.'[24] We have almost the impression that he is eagerly and confidently awaiting another combat which will give him the opportunity to crush yet another aspiring scholar who has had the impudence to attack his learning. We are already very far from the Erasmus who preferred the critic who condemned to the friend who applauded.

Indeed, when the book did come to his hand he lost no time in discharging a blast against it. This *Apologia* was published in Louvain in September 1521 and consisted of a detailed refutation of each of Stunica's annotations prefaced by a general attack on Stunica's learning and motivation. The preface is filled with a display of literary allusions and exaggerated metaphors which do little credit to Erasmus' sense of modesty or restraint. For example, Stunica's hope for a victory is compared to that of envious women who disfigure the countenance of others in the hope that they themselves will seem beautiful.[25]

Stunica immediately replied in kind with a work entitled *Erasmi Roterodami blasphemiae et impietates*, published in Rome in 1522. For the next two years the opponents continued to exchange vituperative attacks, four more coming from the pen of Stunica and three from that of Erasmus.[26] In the end, improbably enough, Stunica became more favourably inclined toward Erasmus. In 1527, whether from counsels of prudence or effects of exhaustion, he proposed to send his criticisms of the fourth edition of Erasmus' *New Testament* to Erasmus directly instead of publishing them, but he died before he could accomplish this intention.[27]

While Erasmus was still involved in the controversy with Stunica, he was attacked from the very citadel of orthodoxy, the faculty of theology of the university of Paris, represented by its syndic, Noel Bédier or Beda. Already in 1523 this faculty had condemned Erasmus' *New Testament* as superfluous.[28] Now in 1524 Beda began the examination of Erasmus' *Paraphrase on St Luke*, as well as a number of other Erasmian works. The resulting criticisms were circulated in manuscript and Erasmus replied to Beda on 25 April 1525 taking a disarmingly receptive view of the corrections which had been suggested. He professed to be not at all offended and hoped that Beda would continue his work with the rest of the *Paraphrases* and with the *Annotations*. He desired nothing so much as to have removed from his books anything which was in error or offensive.[29] When Beda proceeded to publish his censure, Erasmus changed his tone and brought out successively his *Elenchus in Natalis Beddae censuras erroneas* and his *Supputatio errorum in censuras Beddae*, published at Basel in 1527. The *Elenchus* begins with the statement that if Beda had been more sincere he would not have brought out his censures and would have saved himself from manifest lies and evident calumnies. The *Supputatio* catalogues one hundred and eighty-one empty charges or lies, three hundred and ten calumnies, and forty-seven blasphemies, and, Erasmus adds, this is to omit many examples of ignorance and stupidity. The whole refutation of Beda amounts to more than two hundred and fifty folio columns.[30]

The cause of Beda and the faculty of theology was taken up by Petrus Sutor against whose *Debacchationes* Erasmus wrote another long apology dedicated to Jean de Selve, first president of the parlement de Paris.[31] By this dedication he probably hoped to secure the protection of this powerful magistrate against the Sorbonne theologians.

The Parisian charges were echoed and enlarged in Spain where the monks of Salamanca took up Stunica's indictment of Erasmus and, basing themselves not only on the *New Testament* but on many other works, found Erasmus guilty of attacks on the Trinity, the divinity of Christ, the sacraments, the cult of the Virgin, and the proper use of ceremonies, and in general accused him of being an arch-heretic against whom they invoked the intervention of the ecclesiastical authorities. Erasmus answered them with weary contempt.[32] These were among the opponents whom, as he said in his *Catalogus*, 'non pulchrum erat vincere.'

A third group of Erasmus' polemical works is composed of his exchanges with his protestant opponents. Some of these involved the tragic rupture of earlier friendships, which gave to these controversies a poignant quality altogether lacking in the attacks and counterattacks on such figures as Stunica and the Spanish monks.

Ulrich von Hutten was one of the younger generation in Germany who had rallied to the defence of Reuchlin against his condemnation by the Dominicans. As one of the authors of the *Epistolae obscurorum virorum* he had been praised by Erasmus who was regarded by Hutten and his contemporaries as the chief inspiration for the attack on obscurantism. After the revolutionary events of 1517-21, however, Hutten made of Luther's protest a focus for a German nationalist revolt against the tyranny of Rome. This Erasmus could not accept and relations between them became strained, finally reaching a crisis when Hutten journeyed to Basel in the winter of 1521-2 and sought an interview with Erasmus which was denied. In a letter to a friend Erasmus afterwards asserted that what had been proposed was only a visit of courtesy, and it was refused because he could not bear to be in a room with an over-heated stove whereas Hutten, in his then debilitated condition, could not be without one.[33] It is certain, however, that Hutten took this refusal as a mortal insult inspired by Erasmus' fear of being associated with one whose views might compromise him with Rome. Hutten retired to Zurich and published his *Expostulatio cum Erasmo*.[34] In the most violent language this work condemned Erasmus as a trimmer who had denied his earlier encouragement to the revolutionaries because of fears for his own safety and position. Upon receiving a copy of Hutten's attack, Erasmus devoted six days in July 1523 to writing a refutation characteristically twice as long as Hutten's attack. The *Spongia adversus aspergines Hutteni* was published at the end of August, its appearance coinciding with Hutten's death on 29 August. Erasmus later admitted that whatever favour his tract might have received was lost by this circumstance which imputed to him a vicious enmity toward a man who could no longer reply. He declared in the preface to the second edition that if he had foreseen Hutten's death he would have either not replied at all or replied in a different way. Some things were intended for Hutten's eyes alone and it is doubtful if he ever saw the tract.[35] This latter admission is interesting as an indication of the personal quality of many of Erasmus' apologia: although directed to the interested public, they had often the character of a private debate.

The *Spongia* is frequently referred to as one of Erasmus' most violent compositions. In fact, although it certainly has the tone of an impassioned and at times indignant defence, it is far less violent than the attack which provoked it, and it contains moving and eloquent passages on Erasmus' sense of his own position in the midst of tragic conflict. In particular he distinguishes, more clearly than in many other works, between attacks on abuses and attacks on the true uses of institutions and doctrines. Particularly noteworthy is his definition of the church and his allegiance to it.[36] He challenges Hutten to admit that the church of Rome is the true church and none the less so because of a multitude of abuses. He allows that the bishop of Rome has the first place among metropolitans while denying that he has ever defended unjust papal usurpation of powers.

The great public debate with Luther began in the following year with the publication of Erasmus' *De libero arbitrio* in September 1524. Erasmus had long been urged to write against Luther by those of his friends who were eager to keep him in the Roman allegiance. The colloquy *Inquisitio de fide* may represent a version of a first attempt to define his position.[37] His decision to centre his most important tract against Luther on the freedom of the will clarified the divergence between the humanist tradition and Luther's interpretation of Christian imperatives. Erasmus produced a modest volume, temperate in tone, founded on an examination of the meaning of scriptural texts but lacking an understanding of the problem in theological terms. Luther replied with the *De servo arbitrio*, published a little more than a year later, in December 1525. Erasmus did not receive a copy until February of 1526 and then wrote, against time, the first *Hyperaspistes* to have it ready for the spring book fair in Leipzig. The second book followed a year later. The tone of these treatises is that of a dignified and reasoned exposition of Erasmus' general views. If to the modern critic it appears all too clear that he was incapable of understanding Luther's thought on grace and justification, he could nevertheless write an eloquent manifesto in defence of positions which he had consistently held all his life. The second *Hyperaspistes*, in particular, contains passages, which, as Renaudet has said, make it 'un des plus beau livres de la renaissance.'[38] Although Erasmus was irritated by the violence of Luther's reply, he avoided the kind of vituperation and irony which he had adopted in his quarrels with Beda or the Spanish monks, as if in recognition of the seriousness of the debate. In his peroration he prayed that the spirit of Christian charity would produce the unity which he felt to be such an essential quality of Christian civilization.[39]

In his debates with Luther Erasmus was confronting a figure who dominated the European scene. A much less prominent opponent, who had been a friend and disciple, gives us a more intimate glimpse of the tragedy of the controversies of Erasmus' later years. Gerard Geldenhauer – or, in Latin, Noviomagus – was a young Dutch humanist who had come to study at Louvain in 1514 and had accepted completely the intellectual leadership of Erasmus.[40] In 1525 the abbot of Middelburg, in whose service he then was, sent him on a mission to Wittenberg; whether because of his experience in the capital of the Lutheran movement or because of other influences, he repudiated Rome and accepted the Reformation. Marrying in 1527, he established himself in Strasbourg and accepted the principles of the reformers in that city. In 1529 he published some excerpts from Erasmus' *Apologia against the Spanish monks* with comments of his own on the persecution of heretics, and this elicited from Erasmus, who felt he had been misrepresented, an angry indictment. In this work Erasmus defends the view that by divine dispensation heresies have been permitted to exist in the church in order that the truth might shine more brightly in contrast with error.[41] In the end, in spite of their disaccord on Geldenhauer's unauthorized use of Erasmus' writings, the former returned to a just estimate of the greatness of his teacher's services in his lives of Agricola and Wessel in 1536.[42]

In spite of the bitterness of controversy there is, in many of Erasmus' writings against the protestants, some sense of respect for his adversaries. However, towards another group of critics, the last we shall consider, his attitude was still more uncompromising. These are the men who by education, position, and convergence of interest should have supported the Erasmian programme. Instead, they turned against it and did everything they could to undermine Erasmus' position at Rome. Their betrayal was more bitter to Erasmus than were the attacks of ignorant traditionalists or avowed adversaries. In the last decade of his life he had to defend himself against his two most powerful enemies within the church, Girolamo Aleander and Alberto Pio, prince of Carpi. In 1507 Aleander had been Erasmus' close friend and roommate at the Aldine establishment in Venice when Erasmus was producing the second and greatly enlarged edition of his *Adagia*. Alberto Pio, nephew of the great Pico della Mirandola, had been the patron of Aldus and had provided the means for establishing the famous press in Venice.[43]

As early as 1525 Erasmus had received word that the prince of Carpi was talking against him in the highest circles in Rome.[44] In September 1526 he wrote to a friend, Simon Pistorius, that he had received two pamphlets written against him in Rome, one by the prince of Carpi and one anonymous one which Erasmus believed was by Aleander.[45] At that point neither was printed and the one by Aleander remained unpublished, but was circulated in manuscript. Erasmus referred to it in a letter to Thomas More on 30 March 1527.[46] Strangely enough, considering his readiness to reply to criticism from almost any quarter, Erasmus never wrote a direct response to this attack. It may be that he felt it was unnecessary to answer it as the pamphlet remained in manuscript and the author officially anonymous. It may be that he hesitated to attack openly one who by now occupied so powerful a position in the hierarchy. Although the tract was circulated in several copies, as we can see from the letters of Erasmus, it was long supposed that no copy survived. However, in 1948 Professor Eugenio Massa discovered in the Bibliothèque nationale in Paris a manuscript which he identified as the lost *Racha* written by Aleander against Erasmus.[47]

The title is taken from the Hebrew word which appears in Matthew 5: 22. One of the author's aims had been to expose Erasmus' ignorance of Hebrew on the basis of his annotation of this text in his *Novum Instrumentum*. Erasmus had translated *racha* as *cerebro carens* or *vacuus* and contributed a long discussion of the use of this obscure Hebrew term of abuse in the Old Testament, with reference also to its interpretation by Jerome and Augustine.[48] Aleander refutes Erasmus' interpretation and gives a learned one of his own in which he brings out other examples of Erasmus' ignorance of Hebrew.[49] However, he goes far beyond the question of Erasmus' competence in Hebrew philology. He has nothing but contempt for Erasmus' methods. He declares that those who resort to puerile grammatical explanations destroy all understanding of divinity. The Saxon and German heretics have been armed as if from a Trojan horse by one who denies the divinity of Christ and defends the Arians.[50] In a passionate peroration the author demands how the world can endure these things, why this scoffer of the church and the evangel is not removed by God? His works have been corrected and censured time and time again. The common errors of men Aleander can bear, but not impiety and contempt for sacred things. Erasmus is the first after John Hus to stir up the seas to their depth. He is responsible for the Reformation.[51]

Such charges as these, which Erasmus was quickest to resent when they were made openly and in print, he answered on this occasion very obliquely. Professor Massa has traced, in the annotations to the relevant texts in the successive editions of the *New Testament* and in letters to friends, Erasmus' repudiation of Aleander's attack.[52] In these scattered fragments we have an example – perhaps the only example in all of Erasmus' controversies – of a hidden polemic which he carried on for years, full of resentment against his old friends, but which he was perhaps afraid of bringing into the open.

The conflict with Alberto Pio was the opposite of that with Aleander in that it involved Erasmus in one of the most public as well as one of the most bitter denunciations of his career. The prince of Carpi in his earlier career had won the admiration of humanist scholars for his support of Aldus Manutius and for his patronage of arts and letters in his little principality. He had had a distinguished career as a diplomat, first serving as the orator of the emperor at the papal court and then, on the accession of Charles v, switching his allegiance to the king of France. The defeat of the French in Italy cost him his principality of Carpi and he was a refugee at the papal court when he began to occupy himself with Erasmus.

When Erasmus heard that Alberto Pio and Aleander were talking against him at the papal court he decided to attempt a direct appeal to the former. In a letter filled with flattering references, he reports that he has heard that the prince of Carpi has put it about the college of cardinals that Erasmus is neither a philosopher nor a theologian. 'Quite true,' says Erasmus, 'I have never written on theology except for my treatise of the freedom of the will which was written at the urging of others. I have never given any support to a faction not recognized by the Roman church. This attitude you would not wholly despise if you knew the disposition of men in these parts and the tumults I might have created. I have only fought the battle for a better education intended to serve the glory of Christ and not the restoration of paganism.'[53]

This letter did not allay the suspicions of the prince of Carpi who composed a long reply to it, dated 15 May 1526, which reached Erasmus simultaneously with Aleander's *Racha* in the autumn of 1526.[54] For the time being the work remained in manuscript, and perhaps Erasmus hoped that, like the *Racha*, it would not be printed. However, the sack of Rome in the spring of 1527 caused Alberto Pio to flee from the papal states; by the following winter he was in Paris under the protection of the French king and Erasmus heard that he was preparing his manuscript for the press. In a not very convincing appeal Erasmus wrote to Alberto Pio that he had not replied earlier because he had not known how to reach him after the sack of Rome. He urged him to withdraw or at least to mitigate his charges.[55] The appeal arrived too late and Alberto's *Responsio paraenetica* was published in Paris.[56]

The work begins disarmingly. Alberto recognizes Erasmus' great services to learning and remembers having seen him in the house of Aldus in Venice, in the company of Thomas Linacre. Then he says that although Erasmus has done much for the cause of literature he has neglected the study of theology. He has circulated false historical ideas on the primitive church and has in fact so many points in common with Luther that one may say that either Erasmus Lutherizes or Luther Erasmusizes. It is really Erasmus who is responsible for the two most pernicious principles of Lutheranism, namely, the exaggeration of scripture at the expense of tradition and the exaggeration of private judgment against authority.[57]

Erasmus was stimulated by this to write a reply of eighty octavo pages in ten days, to have it ready for the spring book fair at Frankfurt. Though he still preserves some of the amenities his tone becomes more bitter: the times are such that under every stone is found a sleeping scorpion. Although he confesses that he has written certain things which he now regrets, he firmly repudiates the charge of being in any way responsible for Luther. He has tried to do what he could to restore Christian piety and the prince of Carpi should have done the same instead of listening to unfounded complaints about Erasmus. It was not Erasmus' business to drive Luther off the stage – this should have been done by those, of whom Alberto was one, who sat in the orchestra; Erasmus was always a spectator in the gallery.[58]

The prince of Carpi was very irritated by this reply. He was deeply convinced of the truth of his charges of Erasmus' complicity with Luther and he also felt that they had been too lightly dismissed. He resented Erasmus' ironical tone. Consequently, he set about the preparation of a counterattack which he intended to be so complete that his opponent would be overwhelmed and would be moved to public recantation. He began work on this treatise in March 1529 when Erasmus' *Responsio* was published and he continued until his death in January 1531. In his last days he assumed the Franciscan habit in which he was buried, which provided Erasmus with the opportunity to satirize the piety of his enemy in the colloquy 'The Seraphic Funeral.' The Italian humanist Franciscus Floridus Sabinus, who had been a member of Alberto's household, saw the treatise through the press after his patron's death, contributing a poem of his own in the form of a dialogue between the book and the reader in which the book deplores the death of the author who has had to leave it in an unpolished state.[59]

This work is designed on an ample scale with a documentation intended to illustrate the whole history of the controversy. Book I reprints the original letter of Erasmus to Alberto Pio with the latter's reply. Book II reprints Erasmus' *Responsio* with detailed marginal comments by Alberto. This gives it the effect of a dialogue in which the characters and convictions of the two opponents are sharply brought out.

> ERASMUS: I regret that my unpolished letter was given to the world without my consent.
> ALBERTO: You yourself brought about its publication nor were you at all upset by it since it is a very elegant composition.[60]
> ERASMUS: I admit to hating revision of my works.
> ALBERTO: I have always known that there are some who edit their books before they write them and write them before they are conceived.
> ERASMUS [defending the *Moria*]: I have heard from my friends that Leo X himself took pleasure in reading this work.
> ALBERTO: I know that he did not approve of it although he enjoyed some of the jokes.[62]

The detailed comments on Erasmus' *Responsio* are followed by a preface to the twenty-one books which examine Erasmus' ideas in detail. In this preface Alberto shows that he has made a serious study of Erasmus' works. He admits that he had not read many of them at the time the controversy began but he has now gone into them thoroughly. The result of his study is to confirm his conviction that Erasmus is fundamentally responsible for many of Luther's ideas. In documenting this conviction he has not been moved by malice toward a man who he recognizes has done great service to the cause of literature; he has acted only because of his zeal for the Catholic faith.[63]

The twenty-one books which compose the remainder of the volume take up in detail Erasmus' writings and attempt to prove that his views are heretical or have influenced heresies on a wide variety of institutions and doctrines of the church. Their titles are as follows: Book III, *The Moria*; IV, *Fasting*; V, *Monasticism*; VI, *Ceremonies*; VII, *Adornment of Churches*; VIII, *Images of Saints*; IX, *Relics and the Cult of the Virgin*; X, *Scholastic Theology*; XI, *Authority of Scripture*; XII, *The Trinity and Arianism*; XIII, *Priests and Bishops*; XIV, *Primacy of St. Peter and the*

Power of the Pope; xv, *Ecclesiastical Constitutions and Laws*; xvi, *Chastity and Other Vows*; xvii, *Celibacy*; xviii, *Matrimony*; xix, *The Sacra-
ment of Confession*; xx, *Faith and Works*; xxi, *The Just War*; xxii,
Oaths; xxiii, *Mendicancy*. The work is ill-organized and shows evidence
of the unfinished state in which Alberto left it. As a whole, however, it
constitutes the most complete contemporary exposition of the thesis that
Erasmus had prepared the way for the Reformation. In the conclusion
Alberto again expresses the hope that Erasmus will recant and that in the
future he will write nothing but what is proper.[64]

In spite of the fact that Alberto had been removed from the scene, the
posthumous publication of his book provoked Erasmus to a rapidly executed counterblast. It was published by Froben in Basel in June of 1531
and by the next month was already in the hand of an Italian friend who
wrote remonstrating with Erasmus for the violence of his attack on a man
who was dead and whose last years had been full of misfortune.[65] The remonstrance had some justification for in this *Apologia* Erasmus no longer
observed any amenities; it is one of the most savage compositions he ever
wrote. One of his few concessions was to suggest, in the title to the first
edition, that the prince of Carpi, senile and moribund, had been suborned
by others into writing his calumnies.[66]

For once Erasmus is content to write a reply briefer than the attack
which had provoked it. The violence and bitterness of his tone are, however, unrestrained. He opens by declaring that his opponent has ingeni-
ously escaped through death but, like the bee, leaving his sting behind.
Although he admits that it is wrong to write against the dead, how else in
this case can Erasmus protect his reputation from slander? Erasmus
charges that the prince has produced a hodge-podge; he has pieced together misunderstood and misrepresented selections from Erasmus' work.
His indictment is full of lies and furthermore is not even the work of
Alberto himself as he has had help and encouragement from other enemies.[67]

Alberto's marginal comments on the *Responsio* Erasmus regards as
not less false than the rest of the book. He answers them *seriatim* and so
the acrimonious dialogue is continued, leading Erasmus to many reveal-
ing assertions on the nature of the church, on history, and on the degeneration of human institutions.[68]

The remainder of the *Apologia* takes up Alberto's preface and the
topics presented in his twenty-one other books. The margins of the pas-

sages from Alberto reprinted in Erasmus' text are liberally sprinkled with 'lie!' and 'false citation!' Perhaps the most interesting section is the justification of the *Moria*. Here Erasmus is able to score heavily by pointing out that the prince of Carpi was unable to understand how the speeches of Folly should be interpreted. Interspersed in this part of the defence are such interesting autobiographical passages as the description of Erasmus' association with Greek scholars at the Aldine establishment in Venice in 1508.[69] He had earlier been charged by Alberto with misrepresenting this episode in his career.

The final peroration is a passionate denial of the charges which the prince of Carpi has brought against him. He welcomes the prayer that in the future he may utter only what is proper but will in turn himself pray that Alberto find in the next world more justice than he has shown to Erasmus. What is Erasmus to recant? Certainly not the propositions formulated by Pio and put into Erasmus' mouth; despoiling priests, condemning monasticism, abrogating the authority of scripture, condemning ceremonies, reviving the Epicureans, and many other absurdities. 'It would be a new kind of recantation if, yielding to men who are delirious with the vice of slandering, I became my own accuser. Nay, rather, let them recant who furnish us with an example of the devil, openly and shamelessly fastening libels of this kind on those who do not deserve them, and, through such sordid actions, either seek fame or promise themselves vindication and victory as if Christ were dead and had no care of his church.'[70]

Even this apology did not give Erasmus the last word against the prince of Carpi. Alberto Pio found a defender in the person of Juan Gines de Sepulveda who later became the historiographer of Charles v and Philip ii. As a young man he had come into close association with Alberto when Cardinal Ximenes had sent him to Bologna. Erasmus had erroneously believed that Sepulveda had had a large part in helping to compose Alberto's treatise. Sepulveda now wrote against Erasmus an *Antapologia* in favour of Alberto. He had no difficulty in proving that he could have had no part in Alberto's work in Paris. Sepulveda kept his tone moderate and courteous. He is grieved because Erasmus has not used that charity which he has so often preached. He still thinks Erasmus the foremost scholar of his age although he regrets his violence. Sepulveda sent him a copy of the *Antapologia*, saying that he had written it not in wrath but as a duty.[71]

It is pleasant to record that this time Erasmus reacted in a manner in keeping with the spirit which Sepulveda had hoped he stood for. He replied that Sepulveda had shown an attitude worthy of one who served both Christ and the muses. He added wearily: 'I do not see what can come from answering such attacks except more strife of which there is already enough in the world. Therefore I think it more advisable not to reply.'[72]

This brief survey of some of the types of apologia which Erasmus produced to refute his critics gives us a view of the range of possibilities which he found in this type of formal defence. No doubt he much preferred as a mode of expression the dialogue, which he had adopted for the *Colloquies* and the *Ciceronianus*, but when it came to defending his work and his influence he was ready enough to resort to a less subtle argumentation. The apologetic works which fill the last two volumes of the Leiden edition of the *Opera* have in common the fact that they are almost all longer than the attacks which evoked them. They are also characteristically filled with digressions. Much as Erasmus protested that he hated being involved in these polemics and that they were a sad waste of time, reading these works leaves the impression that at least on many occasions he really loved the battle and enjoyed his verbal triumphs over his enemies. In spite of the fact that many of them were composed in great haste – eight days, ten days, a month – he was unable to omit the slightest point on which he might score against his opponent as if some compulsion led him to protest too much – against Lee, against the Spanish monks, against Hutten.

As a body of Erasmian prose these works offer a most interesting study in style. We have seen examples ranging from straightforward exposition, through friendly persuasion, petulant remonstrance, irony, diatribe, to invective. The varieties of rhetorical devices indicate how much Erasmus had absorbed of the classical and Renaissance traditions on the uses of rhetoric. Against some of his critics Erasmian eloquence was more than half the battle. In the adjectives used to describe such opponents as Hutten and Alberto Pio he shows himself to be a worthy heir of the literary gladiators of quattrocento Italy. His extraordinary knowledge of classical literature and the fact that he had compiled the *Adages* gave him an inexhaustible armoury of weapons in the form of the apt literary allusion. Many of his metaphors, such as the one in which he describes Alberto as seated in the orchestra while Erasmus had only a place in the gallery, recall the stage and the changes of scenery which Erasmus had used in the *Ciceronianus* to illustrate his sense of the difference between historical epochs. They seem to anticipate lines of Shakespeare on the world as a stage.

In addition to their interest for the student of Erasmus' style, the apologiae serve to define with greater precision his religious position in the last decade of his life. They confirm the fact that, in his own eyes and in the view of many of his contemporaries, he remained loyal to Rome. In the polemic with Hutten, and in both the first and second *Hyperaspistes,* there are eloquent passages on his definition of the church. A multitude of evils, he says to Hutten, does not bring it about that the church of Rome is any less the true church.[73] Similarly, on the power of the pope, on monasticism, on the sacraments, on ceremonies, and on all the other matters which became the subject of Alberto Pio's cumulative attack on him, we can find formulations which clarify his position. These texts deserve more careful study than they have yet been given by any of Erasmus' biographers.

The wordy polemic with Alberto Pio, prince of Carpi, has a particular importance and a particular dramatic significance. Here there emerge already, by 1531, the two contrasting theses on the origins of the Reformation which were to have a great and undeserved fortune in historiography. Alberto Pio maintained with great conviction that the works of Erasmus had led directly to Luther's attack on the church, while Erasmus maintained with equal conviction that abuses in institutions and doctrine were the cause of the religious revolt. Erasmus thus paradoxically supplied generations of protestant historians with an untenable thesis while his opponent, in attacking Erasmus' historical ideas, was already formulating the basic propositions of the Counter Reformation.

By the time we reach the conflict between Erasmus and Alberto Pio it is clear that Erasmus has moved far from the position, enunciated in 1505, that the critic who condemns is more welcome than the friend who applauds. Much as he may have enjoyed some of his polemical exchanges, his mood in the last years of his life is most accurately conveyed in his letter to Sepulveda, 'There is already enough strife in the world – it is more advisable not to reply.' In his most despairing moments he could exclaim that the slanders of Alberto showed that he lived in an age when Christ had ceased to care for his church. In the great changes of the climate of opinion imposed by the religious revolution, Erasmus could no longer say that he welcomed a variety of opinions from which the truth would emerge. As far as his personal position was concerned, he found

that he could not tolerate certain criticisms. Nevertheless he never invoked
the authority of either church or state for the silencing of his enemies but
preferred to rely on the strength of his own arguments. He continued to
believe in the possibility and the eventual necessity of an accord reached
on the basis of what was essential in the evangel, leaving aside what was
indifferent and unimportant.

In spite of the intractability with which he conducted many of his
polemics and his increasing reluctance to endure the attacks of many of
his critics in his later years, it was this sense of the possibility of accord
which represented the essential heritage of Erasmian thought in the sixteenth century. It had a great and diverse influence on such figures as
Marguerite de Navarre, Rabelais, Bonaventure des Periers, Castellion,
Montaigne, and the Bodin of the *Heptaplomeres*. It may be argued that
this heritage was less important than considerations of *realpolitik* in
achieving the degree of practical toleration which was gained in the sixteenth century, but it has nevertheless remained one of the precious
sources of our conception of liberty of conscience in the modern world.

NOTES

1 P.S. Allen, ed., *Opus Epistolarum Des. Erasmi Roterodami* (Oxford 1906-
   58), I, 406-12. This work will hereafter be cited as Allen with reference to
   volume and page and, in the case of the text of letters, to lines.
2 Allen, I, 408, lines 45-55: 'Ausus est Laurentius in authoribus aliquot voc-
   ulam taxare. Indignum facinus! quasi vero non omnia poene in omnibus
   repraehenderit Aristoteles, quasi non totam Ciceronis dictionem contemp-
   serit Brutus, Maronis ac Livii Caligula, Senecae Fabius atque Aulus
   Gellius. Augustini Rufinique Hyeronimus, postremo Quintiliani Philelphus. Quid quod Plinius non credit librum suum amico placuisse, nisi
   cognoverit quaedam displicuisse? Adeo vicio danda non est, ut etiam vehementer optanda sit ista in studiis dissensio conflictatioque quam Hesiodus
   utilissimam esse mortalibus scripsit, modo ne in rabiem exeat et citra
   convicia consistat.'
3 Hesiod, *Works and Days* (Loeb ed.), lines 11-26
4 Allen, I, 408, lines 55-61: 'Mihi quidem sano non gratior sit amicus
   applausor quam vel inimicus repraehensor ... Etenim si vere repraehendit
   discedo doctior; sin falso, tamen acuor, extimulor, expergefio, reddor
   attentior, cautiorque, animor ad defensionem veri.'
5 Clericus, ed., *Desiderii Erasmi Roterodami opera omnia* (Leyden
   1703-6) IX, c. 283. This work will hereafter be cited as LB with reference
   to volume and column. 'Quis enim adeo feriatus est ut huiusmodi rixas
   libeat legere? ... Fervebant olim Laurentii Vallae hominis (quod negari

non potest) eruditi ac facundi cum Poggio digladationes. Huius elegan-
tias pene solas habemus in manibus neque quicquam magis hodie friget
apud nos quam in quo illi tum maxime calebant. Quoties autem contem-
plor animo quam brevis ac fugax sit haec vita, deinde quam huius exigua
portio mihi supersit, vehementer molestum est in huiusmodi naeniis rei
cum multo omnium pretiosissimae, tum irreperabilis facere jacturam; ut
interim omittam quod dum huiusmodi rixis invicem incessimus et inces-
simur perit illa tranquillitas animi Christiani perit dulcedo studiorum
perit et fructus bona pars, compluribus ab his studiis alienatis.'

6 Allen, I, 21-33; 41, lines 11-12: 'Octavum occupent Apologiae. Me Miserum! et hae iustum volumen efficient.'
7 Dorp's letter is published in Allen, II, 11-16.
8 Allen, II, 91, lines 18-21: 'Vehementer enim cupio quicquid ago te approb-
ante fieri cuius ingenio pene coelesti cuius eruditioni singulari, cuius
iudicio longe acerrimo tantum tribuo ut malim unius Dorpii quam mille
caeterorum calculis approbari.'
9 Allen, II, 93, lines 71-2: 'Praeterea nullus est tam inimicus quem non
optem si fieri possit in amicum redire.'
10 Allen, II, 93, lines 87-93: 'In Enchiridio simpliciter Christianae vita forman
tradidimus. In libello de principis institutione palam admonemus quibus
rebus principem oporteat esse instructum. In Panegyrico sub laudis
praetextu hoc ipsum tamen agimus oblique quod illic egimus aperta
fronte. Nec aliud agitur in Moria sub specie lusus quam actum est in
Enchiridio.'
11 Allen, II, 109-12
12 Erasmus' annotation on the passage, Lefèvre's comment on it, and
Erasmus' reply are printed in LB, IX, cc. 17-80. I acknowledge with grati-
tude the corrections supplied by Professor Roland Bainton to my account
of this controversy as presented in a paper read at the ACLS meeting in
Baltimore, 21 January 1967.
13 LB, IX, c. 33 DEF
14 LB, IX, c. 17: "Neque enim quicquam addubito quin tu sive tuopte iudicio
negotium hoc sumpseris, sive alieno impilsu susceperis, simplici pruoque
animo id feceris.'
15 LB, IX, cc. 79-106
16 LB, IX, c. 110 E: 'Opinor in libris meis nihil esse quo quispiam deterior
reddi possit. Hominem me esse fateor. Animum iuvandae pietatis cupidum
praestiti, eventum polliceri non possum. Candidum et aequum lectorem
ubique postulo, qui si desit, nec in Cypriano, nec in Hilario, nec in
Hieronymo, nec in Ambrosio, nec in Augustino, nec in Scoto, nec in
Thomas, nec in Petro Lombardo, nec in Gersone: ut finiam in nullo neque
veterum, neque recentium aberit, quod ad haeresis crimen trahi possit.
Ut ne commemorem interim quod Lactantium, quod Poggium, ac Pon-
tanum etiam taciti legimus. Porro qui alienorum voluminum se facit
censorem, primum hoc agere debeut rem penitus intelligat: deinde ut
rationem, non affectum habeat in consilio; nec enim iudicat livor, nec

simplices oculos habet odium aut ira. Postremo meminerit Christianae civiltatis, ne vices iniqui judicii in ipsum aliquando recidant. Quis enim mortalium unquam omnibus horis sapuit? Quis tam circumspecte scripsit ut ubique placeret omnibus praesertim cum inter paucos etiam tanta sit sententiarum varietas?'

17 Allen, IV, 194. For Erasmus' defence, see LB, VI, cc. 335-6

18 Allen, IV, 195

19 LB, IX, c. 111: 'Is [the anonymus preacher] Londini in urbe totius Angliae celeberrima, in loco totius urbis celeberrimo, nimirum in coemeterio divi Pauli professus se dicturum de charitate christiana, subito totius caritatis oblitus coepit impotenter debacchari in Novum Testamentum a me versum ... Lutetiae non dissimilem huic fuisse tumultum ex amicorum litteris cognovi. Eadem blaterantur passim apud mulierculas apud negotiatores apud primores aulicos ... [c. 122] ... laedere cuivis facile est: laedere immerentem turpissimum est etiam apud improbos: porro laedere bene-merentem diabolicae cuisudam malitiae est.'

20 Allen, III, 203

21 LB, IX, cc. 123-4: 'Denique stultum videtur, accurate vellet refellere, quod attente legisse refeuisse sit. Nam si mihi liberet numerare, quoties non intelligit neque quod reprehendit, neque quod loquitur: quoties palam calumniatur, quae nec dixi nec sensi: quoties atrocibus verbis exagitat, quod optime dictum est: quoties Auctorum verba ad calumniandum detorquet in diversum sensum: quoties aviditate carbendi scribit absurdis-sima: quoties miro supercilio docere conatur ea quae prorsus non intel-ligit: quoties tragoedias excitat, ubi nihil est causae; Deum immortalem, quot et quales mihi nascerentur elenchi ..."

22 LB, IX, cc. 125-6: 'De opere Lei nihil adhuc pronuntio, praeter illud unum, quod multis annis nullum legi librum unde minus didicerim, cum tamen objurger passim. Sed quicquid inter legendum tibi veniet in mentem, optime lector, etiam atque etiam te rogo, ut si quid placet, imputes toti Brittaniae: si quid displicet, in unum Leum conjicias. Nam cum ea gens habeat tam multos insigni prudentia, probitate, modestia, doctrina, fide-que praeditos, iniquum fuerit, ex unius hominis ingenio totam aestimare gentem ...'

23 For a summary of the controversy, see Allen, IV, 621-2

24 Allen, IV, 320, lines 2-6: 'Habet et Hispania Leum alterum. Zunega quidam edidit librum, ut audio, satis virulentum adversus Fabrum ac me. Vetuerat Card. Toletanus defunctus, Eo mortuo prodidit sua venena. Opus nondum vidi. Id caveant ne liber veniat in manus meas.'

25 LB, IX, c. 288: '... non dissimilis quibusdam stulte invidis mulierculis, quae faciem aliarum deturpant, sperantes fore ut sic demeum formosae videan-tur ipsae.'

26 Bibliography in Allen, IV, 622

27 Juan Gines de Sepulveda, *Antapologia pro Alberto Pio Principi Carpensi in Erasmum Roterodamum* (vol. 4 of Sepulveda's *Opera* [Madrid 1780], cap. 3).

28 Allen, VI, 65

29 Allen, VI, 67, lines 2-6: '... qua quidem diligentia tua adeo non sum offensus, ut vehementer optem te idem facere in reliquas Paraphrases sed praecipue in Annotationes meas. Nihil enim malim quam e libris meis tolli quicquid inest vel erroris vel offendiculi.'

30 The *Elenchus* in LB, IX, cc. 495-514. It begins: 'Si Natalis Bedda tantum sinceris pectori habuisset erga me quantum gerebam erga ipsum non ita praecipitasset suas censuras, ea re melius consuluisset, tum utriusque nostrum honori, tum studiorum utilitati, tum theologici nominis dignitati. Saltem a manifestis mendaciis et evidentis calumniis temperasset.' The *Supputatio* occupies cc. 515-702.

31 LB, IX, cc. 739-812. On Sutor see Allen, VI, 132n

32 LB, IX, cc. 1015-94

33 Allen, V, 220, lines 689-96.

34 Published July 1523 at Strasburg

35 Preface to the second edition of the *Spongia*, Allen, V, 335, lines 1-6: 'Hutteni decessus gratiae nonnihil detraxit nostrae Spongiae, si tamen huiusmodi libellorum ulla est gratia. Nam si praescissem, aut non respondissem aut respondissem aliter; nunc quaedam insunt quae solus Huttenus erat intellecturus. Cui Spongiam nondum arbitror fuisse perlectam: quod tamen affirmavere quidam, siquidem Huttenus periit vigesimo nono die mensis Augusti, atque eodem ferme tempore Frobenius Spongiam finiit quo ille vitam.'

36 LB, X, c. 1654 E: 'Primum opinor fatebitur Romae esse ecclesiam: nam multitudo malorum non efficit, quo minus sit Ecclesia. Alioqui nullas haberemus Ecclesias. Et arbitro esse Orthodoxam: nam si qui mixti sunt impii, tamen in bonis manet Ecclesia. Huic autem Ecclesiae dabit opinor Episcopum. Eum patietur esse Metropolitanum, posteaquam tot sunt Archiepiscopi in his Regionibus, in quibus nullus unquam fuit Apostolus, cum Roma habeat et Petrum et Paulum, duos sine controversia summos. Iam inter Metropolitanos, quid absurdi sit, si primus locus detur Pontifici Romano? nam hanc tantam potestatem, quam sibi seculis aliquot usurparunt, nulles audivit me defendentem.'

37 See Craig Thompson, ed., *Inquisitio de fide: a Colloquy of 1524* (New Haven 1950), introduction.

38 A. Renaudet, *Erasme et l'Italie* (Geneva 1954), p. 174

39 The two books *Diatribae Hyperaspistes* are in LB, X, cc. 1249-1572. The second book concludes: 'Nec enim arbitror quenquam esse tam iniquum, ut aequum videri postulet, tantam habendam esse mihi rationem differentium, ut in horum gratiam ad calumniam, quae me vocabat in manifestum famae vitaeque discrimen, debuerim esse mutus: praesertim reclamante conscientia, cui scrupum profecto praedurum injecissem, si passus fuissem simplices, mei nominis fuco deceptos in eam pertrahi sententiam, quam ipse non ausim profiteri, quia mihi nondum persuasi. Meo sum officio functus, reddidi facti mei rationem populo. Quod superest, precor ut Dominus nos omnes faciat unanimes in doctrina sana et caritate non ficta.'

40 Allen, II, 379

41 LB, X, c. 1584 C: 'Ita Dominus interdum permittit exsistere schismata et haereses in Ecclesia sua, ut suorum et exerceat patientiam et erudiat imperitiam. Quis enim nescit Ecclesiam per haereses fuisse vehementer et corroboratam et illustratam?'

42 Allen, II, 379

43 On Aleander, see J. Paquier, *Jerome Aléandre de sa naissance à la fin de son séjour à Brindes* (Paris 1899), and on Alberto Pio, H. Semper, F.O. Schultz, and W. Barth, *Ein Fürstensitz der Renaissance* (Dresden 1882). Also Allen, I, 502 and VI, 200.

44 Allen VI, 77, lines 38-41

45 Allen, VI, 403, lines 129-34

46 Allen, VII, 12, line 248

47 Eugenio Massa, 'Intorno ad Erasmo: una polemica che si credeva perduta,' in *Classical, Mediaeval and Renaissance Essays in Honor of Berthold Louis Ullman*, ed. Charles Henderson, Jr. (Rome 1964), II, 435-55. On the meaning of *Racha* see H.L. Strack and P. Billerbeck, *Kommentar zum Neuen Testament aus Talmud und Midrasch* (Munich 1922), I, 278-9.

48 LB, VI, c. 29

49 Bibl. nat. ms. Paris lat. 3461, ff. 6v-11v

50 Paris lat. 3461, f. 6r

51 Paris lat. 3461, f 17v: 'Dixi castigatissima opera eademque emendatissima esse sua, quippe quae et tot eruditissimi viri adversus eius inscritiam scribentes toties castigaverint et ipse errorum copia convictus, multo mortalium risu toties repugnare et emendare coactus est ... affectusque hominum et communes culpas ferre facile possum: homines enim sumus: impietatem, haereses, sacrarum rerum contemptum atque irrisiones ferre non possum ... quid in eum animadvertatis qui primus omnium post Johanem Hus maria diu tranquilissima ab imo turbavit: primo fluctus commovit, tempestatem excussit, Carolstadios Melanchthones et id genus monstra peperit.'

52 Massa, 'Interno ad Erasmo'

53 Allen, VI, 201-3, especially lines 57-68: 'Quumque hinc theologi quidam odio bonarum litterarum nullum non moverent lapidem quo me in factionem, ut ipsi putabant, iamiam damnandam protruderent, hinc Lutherani blanditiis, technis, denique minis et conviciis idem hoc agerent, licet consilio diverso quam theologi, tamen hactenus digitum latum dimoveri non potui, ut ab Ecclesiae Romanae societate discederem. Hunc animum non omnino contemneres si nosses tot regionum nostratium animos, si principum consilia; si scires quos tumultus excitare potuissem, si me ducem huius negocii voluissem profiteri. Sed ego malui me nudum et inermem utriusque partis iaculis exponere quan ullum porrigere digitum factioni quam non agnoscit Ecclesia Romana ... Principio erat bellum cum linguis ac Latinis litteris. His ego hactenus favi, ut admissae ornarent iuvarentque recepta studia, non ut veteres professores de Ponte, quod aiunt, deiicerent; et servirent gloriae Christi, non ut veterum Paganismum nobis revocarent.'

54 See note 45 above
55 Allen, VII, 544-5
56 The full title is *Alberti Pii Carporum comitis illustrissimi ad Erasmi Roterodami expostulationem responsio accurata et paraenetica Martini Lutheri et asseclarum eius haeresim vesanam magnis argumentis et iustis rationibus confutans.*
57 *Responsio,* ff. 11v-29r
58 LB, IX, c. 1118 C: 'Ubi vero scripsi Lutheranae tragoediae prologum mihi fuisse non injucundum? Scripsi non omnino displicuisse, sed ita non displicuisse ut tamen reclamarem, imo scripsi mihi nunquam placuisse. Qui namque fieri potuit ut reclamarem, si placeret? Sed spectatorem me praebui, verum cum tot hominum millibus, qui taciti spectabant, cum ego protinus reclamarim. Hominen e proscenio depellere non erat meum, sed eorum qui spectabant ex orchestra. Inter hos tu, mi Alberte, sedebas, cui tanto maior aderat cohibendi mali facultas, cui tutum erat facere, quod alioqui cum vitae periculo faciendum scribis et profecto pie scribis.'
59 The full title of the work is *Alberti Pii Carporum illustrissimi et viri longe doctissimi praeter praefationem et operis conclusionem tres et viginti libri in locos lucubrationum variarum D. Erasmi Roterodami quos censet ab eo recognoscendos et retractandos.* (Ascensius, Paris 1531). Hereafter cited as XXIII *libri.*
60 XXIII *libri,* f. xlciir
61 XXIII *libri,* f. xlixr
62 XXIII *libri,* f. lvv
63 XXIII *libri,* ff. lxviiiv – lxixr
64 XXIII *libri,* f. 193r
65 Allen, IX, 305
66 The title of the first edition as given in Allen, VI, 200, is *Apologia, adversus rhapsodias calumniosarum querimoniarum Alberto Pii quondam Carporum principis quem et senem et moribundum et ad quidvis potius accomodum homines quidam male auspicati ad hanc illiberalem fabulam agendam suborarunt.* I have not seen a copy of this edition. A second edition, of which there is a copy in the Vatican Library, was produced on 5 January 1532 with the title *Ultima apologia adversus rapsodias calumniosarum querimoniarum Alberto Pii quondam Carporum comitis illustrissimi nuper diligentissime excussa.* The Apology is printed in LB, IX, cc. 1123-6 under the title *Apologia brevis ad viginti quatuor libros Alberti Pii quondam Carporum comitis.* The editor, Leclerc, by counting the conclusion as an extra book, had converted Alberto's twenty-three books into twenty-four.
67 LB, IX, cc. 1123-5
68 LB, IX, c. 1128 B
69 LB, IX, c. 1137 A-F
70 LB, IX, c. 1196 B-D: 'Novum palinodiae genus, si hominibus calumniandi morbo delirantibus morem gerens ipse mei fiam sycophanta. Quin ipsi canunt palinodiam qui nobis referunt exemplum Diaboli palam et impu-

denter huiusmodi calumnias impingentes immerenti et ex factis tam
illiberalibus aut venantur famam aut sibi promittunt vindictam et victor-
iam perinde quasi Christus esset mortuus nec ullam haberet Ecclesiae
suae curam.'
71 On Sepulveda see Allen, x, 3-4
72 Allen, x, 83, lines 4-8: 'Sentio te quorundam affectibus inservivisse sed
    iste animus dignus erat qui Musis tantum et Christo serviret. Et reciproca-
    tione talium libellorum non video quid nasci possit praeter dissidia quor-
    um in mundo plus satis est. Itaque consultius arbitror non respondere.'
73 LB, x, c. 1654

Jacques Lefèvre d'Étaples
and the medieval Christian mystics

Eugene F. Rice, jr

Over three hundred editions of works written or edited by Lefèvre d'Étaples appeared between the publication of his first book in 1492 – paraphrases of Aristotle's works on natural philosophy – and the eclipse of his fame in the decade after his death in 1536.[1] Contemporaries usually praised him for restoring true philosophy, especially that of Aristotle.[2] But after the appearance of the *Quincuplex psalterium* (1509) and his commentaries on the Pauline epistles (1512), they often called him 'theologian' as well as 'philosopher,' although he had no theological degree and never studied for one in a theological faculty. When the young Bugenhagen asked Murmellius in 1512 who were the greatest living philosophers and theologians, Murmellius wrote back: 'In my opinion, the two theologians and philosophers of our age who most nearly approach the level of the ancients are Gianfrancesco Pico, count of Mirandola [nephew of the more famous Pico][3] ... and Jacques Lefèvre d'Étaples, who has written commentaries on several books of Aristotle, on the songs of David and Paul's epistles. To these two I will add Charles de Bovelles and Johann Reuchlin; while in eloquence and translation from the Greek Erasmus holds the palm.'[4] Perhaps Lefèvre's contemporary reputation is best summed up in the notice of him in the first supplement (written by a Frenchman in 1512) to Trithemius' biographical dictionary, a reference book used by every literate person in the first part of the sixteenth century. Here we learn that Lefèvre restored the liberal arts to their antique splendour; that he freed every part of philosophy from the fog of barbarous sophistry; that he was the first of the Gauls (like Cicero among the Romans) to join a previously rude and unpolished philosophy with eloquence; that he gave himself heart and soul to the study of divine things, helping the professional theologians by restoring, emending, explaining, and publishing scriptural and theological texts.[5]

Testimonia like these suggest the pattern of Lefèvre's intellectual interests: the philosophy (especially the moral philosophy) of Aristotle; biblical and more particularly New Testament scholarship; patristic literature; and the visionary and speculative theology of ancient and medieval Christian mysticism. To these should be added a serious interest in mathematics. Lefèvre built these interests into a consistent scholarly and educational programme. In 1506 he wrote:

For knowledge of natural philosophy, for knowledge of ethics, politics and economics, drink from the fountain of a purified Aristotle ... Those who wish to set themselves a higher end and a happier leisure will prepare themselves by studying Aristotle's *Metaphysics*, which deals with first and supramundane philosophy. Turn from this to a reverent reading of Scripture, guided by Cyprian, Hilary, Origen, Jerome, Augustine, Chrysostom, Athanasius, Nazianzen, John of Damascus and other fathers. Once these studies have purified the mind and disciplined the senses (and provided one has extirpated vice and leads a suitable and upright life), then the generous mind may aspire to scale gradually the heights of contemplation, instructed by Nicholas of Cusa and the divine Dionysius and others like them.[6]

Knowledge of the mystics and of medieval mystical theology played an important role, in Lefèvre's view, in this ascent from sense experience to the heights of contemplation.

In order to make works of contemplative mysticism available to a larger public, Lefèvre and his collaborator Josse Clichtove published an impressive list of texts, many of them for the first time: the *Visio Wettini*, written down by Hatto, abbot of Reichenau, at the beginning of the ninth century; several works by Hugh and Richard of Saint-Victor; the *De claustro animae* of Hugues le Foulois and a book of the same title by Guillaume d'Auvergne; the most important works of three visionary nuns of the twelfth and thirteenth centuries – Elizabeth of Schönau's *Visiones*, Hildegard of Bingen's *Scivias*, and the *Liber specialis gratiae* by Mechthild of Hackenborn; the *Liber visionum* of Robert of Uzès, a little-known Dominican prophet who died in 1296; seven works by Ramon Lull; Ruysbroeck's *De ornatu spiritualium nuptiarum*; and the *Contemplationes idiotae* of Raymundus Jordanus.[7] Closely related to these publications were editions of the Dionysian corpus and the *Opera omnia* of Nicholas of Cusa.

By a number of early sixteenth-century standards the propriety, orthodoxy, or style of several of these works was not impeccable. Some people, for example, doubted that any trust could be put in the revelations of women. Earlier condemnations and the reservations of hostile contemporaries raised more serious doubts about the inspiration and orthodoxy of Lull and Ruysbroeck. Neither the vernacular nor the Latinity of any mystic of the Gothic age conformed to humanist canons of eloquence. Lefèvre had to justify the mystics before he praised them.

Lefèvre defended the visions of Elizabeth of Schönau, Hildegard of Bingen, and Mechthild of Hackenborn (and defined his own matter-of-fact conception of the mystical experience) by an appeal to what he thought was patristic authority, proving the possibility and antiquity of female revelations from two texts of St Jerome, both spurious. The first – an apocryphal letter to Paula and Eustochium, on the assumption of the Virgin, written by the Carolingian author Paschasius Radbertus – describes Paula's vision of the Christ child. What Paula saw, Lefèvre suggested, more recent holy women could see too. The second text, from Pseudo-Jerome's *Regula monacharum,* describes one of Jerome's own visions. Since he wrote it down for nuns, the evidence is again designed to show that, from the earliest days of the church, God granted visionary experiences to women, and especially to nuns. 'Although I am full of weakness, abject, vile, and still living in the body, I have often heard the angelic choirs and for a week at a time seen nothing but divine things. Having looked upon the future life for many days, I returned to the body and wept. What happiness I had there, what unspeakable joy I felt, the most blessed Trinity is witness (for I saw the Trinity, though with what sight I know not), as are also witnesses the blessed spirits present there.'[8]

Paula's vision was a simple *visio sine extasi*; Jerome's was an ecstatic vision, *visio cum fortibus extasibus.* Lefèvre defined *extasis* as a certain removal of the mind and its separation from the body (*recessus quidam mentis et quaedam a corpore avocatio*). Separated from matter in this manner, the mind perceives spiritual sights, visions which come to the good from good spirits, but to the wicked and curious from evil ones, the one lower than nature, the other supranatural. Illness causes a third variety of ecstasy. It is against nature rather than above or below nature, a form of madness, the *lipothymia* of the medical writers. Of these three varieties of ecstasy the first is better than health; the second is worse than illness; while the third is simply a human sickness.[9] Lefèvre attributed the first form of visionary ecstasy to Elizabeth of Schönau and Mechthild of Hackenborn (he considered Hildegard's holy visions to have always been *citra omnem extasim*). He reminded his readers that angels and the Holy Spirit, not men, had given all three women their visions, and attacked the 'proud audacity and audacious pride' of their detractors. 'Will they deny such revelations,' he asked 'because they themselves have never experienced them? Will the owl dispute with the eagle about the radiance of the sun and moles deny the beauty of the day?'[10]

To establish the possibility, propriety, and antiquity of female visions was an easy task; to defend the orthodoxy of Lull and Ruysbroeck was more difficult.

Since Ramon Lull's death, Lullism and Lullists had been under attack. The leading persecutor had been Nicholas Eymeric, fourteenth-century Dominican inquisitor for Aragon, who described him in his *Directorium inquisitorum* as a heretic, an ignoramus, and a necromancer. In 1376 he produced a bull from Gregory XI (probably a forgery), containing one hundred propositions condemned as heretical, and persuaded the king of Aragon to prohibit Lullian teaching in his kingdom. By the beginning of the fifteenth century, however, supporters of Lull's doctrine had turned the tide: in March 1419 Martin V declared the bull a forgery, while in later years Sixtus IV, Innocent VIII, and Leo X all praised the Lullian art.[11]

In 1516 Alfonso of Aragon, archbishop of Saragossa and Valencia, sent his physician, Juan de Vera, to make inquiries at the university of Paris about the orthodoxy of Lull's teaching, probably moved by pressure, on the one side from Lull's Aragonese and Catalonian adherents, already lobbying for canonization (they were to manage beatification early in the seventeenth century) and, on the other, from detractors whose suspicions had been rearoused by the publication of Eymeric's *Directorium inquisitorum* in Barcelona in 1503. Juan de Vera extracted a formal testimonial in favour of Lull from several professors at the university. On 11 October 1516, the following members of the faculty appeared before two notaries: the celebrated John Major of the college of Montaigu, Major's students the brothers Luis and Antonio Coronel, fellows of the Sorbonne and professors of theology, and Juan de Quintana, bachelor of theology and fellow and prior of the Sorbonne. They testified under oath that in this present year (1516) a 'certain Albert' (whom I have not been able to identify) lectured publicly at the convent of the Mathurins on Lull's *ars*; that he attracted many hearers who praised his lectures; and that many books by Lull were to be found in the libraries of the Sorbonne and of the Paris Charterhouse.[12]

Juan de Vera begged Lefèvre also for a letter. He supplied it by dedicating to Alfonso of Aragon a book containing two of Lull's works, the *Liber proverbiorum* and the *Arbor philosophiae amoris*. He wrote, in a prefatory epistle to the archbishop, dated 25 December 1516:

I and my colleagues have the same opinion of Lull as the Romans, Venetians, Germans and your own countrymen, all of whom print, read and admire his works, all of whom attend public lectures on them and approve what they have heard. Here too, at this most famous university of Paris, his works are printed, while those who have knowledge of his arts lecture on them publicly and privately. Only last year, the year of our Lord 1515, the noble doctor of theology, Bernardo Lavinheta,[13] lectured on them to an enthusiastic audience. Moreover, our libraries, especially those of the Sorbonne, that noblest home of famous theologians and public theological debate, and of the abbey of Saint-Victor have many of his works. The Carthusians, located just outside Paris, have an unusually fine collection, and these holy men read Lull's works constantly, gathering from them fruits of piety, lend them generously, and allow them to be printed. And how often have we not heard the authority of the Roman pontiff defend and approve them? How can we not approve what has been approved by the head of our faith? But we are told that sometimes our own masters and doctors of the university of Paris have not approved of Lull. If this be true, then it happened in that period when the university was dominated by the followers of Averroës, who was first a Moslem, then a Christian, then an impious apostate. Ramon Lull struggled valiantly against him and his followers in disputations and in writing. Finally truth overcame hatred. For now the impious Arab lies prostrate and Lull is rightly seen as the pious victor. The Arab, rejecting all law, fought for the devil; Lull, accepting the law of eternal life, fought for Christ.[14]

Ruysbroeck's orthodoxy had been questioned by a more embarrassing antagonist: Jean Gerson, who had succeeded Pierre d'Ailly as chancellor of the university of Paris in 1395 and whom Lefèvre respected as a 'man of piety and weighty authority, with the mind of a monk under the garb of a secular priest.' Gerson, Lefèvre admitted, 'attacked certain of Ruysbroeck's doctrines as erroneous.'[15] The phrase is correct but vague. Gerson, in a letter to the Carthusian monk Barthélemy Clantier (winter 1398-9), had criticized Ruysbroeck for specific, important doctrinal deviation: for writing that the human soul in a state of perfect contemplation of God is formally identified with the divine essence, absorbed in the divine essence, lost in the abyss of divine being.[16] But Lefèvre had not read the principal documents in this controversy (although they were available to him in a manuscript in the library of the monastery of Saint-Victor, where he was a frequent visitor, and in the six editions of Gerson's works published before 1512). His real source was the notice of Ruysbroeck in Trithemius' *De scriptoribus ecclesiasticis*. So his defence lacks precision if not bite. Only one authority blames Ruysbroeck; a host of holy men defend him. Lefèvre cited one: Thomas à Kempis. Gerson wrote secular literature, that is, works suitable for the secular clergy; Ruysbroeck wrote spiritual literature. Both are good and to be read, one in the world, the other in the cloister. In any case, Gerson must have read the *De ornatu* in a corrupt manuscript or in an inaccurate translation.[17]

Gerson also posed the problem of style. Lefèvre, following Trithemius, believed that Gerson had judged Ruysbroeck *parum litteratus*. On this point his information was not simply vague but wrong. What Gerson said was that some people believed that the *De ornatu* had been written by an *idiota sine litteris* directly under the miraculous inspiration of God. To this Gerson replied that it was precisely its style that proved the book's human origin. The writing is neither *sordidus* nor *abjectus* (Quintillian, *Institutio oratoria*, II, 12, 7), but shows a proud and cunning art: its rhythmically accented prose is highly rhetorical, it quotes the profane poets and philosophers, it is, in short, humanly rather than divinely eloquent.[18] Lefèvre, a humanist who admired the medieval mystics, wanted to have it both ways: to show that they were eloquent, even when they wrote in the vernacular; but to show also (for he shared Gerson's premises) that they were *idiotae* whose eloquence was of God, not of man.

He warned his colleagues on the faculty of arts and his patrons at court and among the magistrates of the parlement of Paris not to have what St Paul called 'delicate ears' (2 Timothy 4:3-4). To be sure, he himself sometimes quietly rewrote a text. For example, he revised Hildegard of Bingen and Lull's *Liber de laudibus beatissimae virginis Mariae* (*stilum aliquantulum erexi*) in an effort to bring them into line with humanist taste, just as he had 'tempered the style' of the vulgate of the *Organon* and as his student Beatus Rhenanus had 'elevated the style' of the medieval translation of Nemesius of Emesa, 'lest its rustic barbarity put the reader off.'[19] More commonly his defence was historical. He admitted that the contemplative and visionary works he published had been written in a barbarous age when men 'spoke Gothic rather than Latin'; but he argued that by the decayed standards of their own age they were remarkably eloquent. Thus competent judges considered Ruysbroeck, for his time (*pro illa tempestate*), elegant and copious.[20] Clichtove used the same argument. 'Because of the admirable suavity of his style,' he wrote of Hugh of Saint-Victor, 'he was called in his own day a second Augustine.'[21] Sometimes, as in the case of Lull, Lefèvre shifted ground and acknowledged that the style of an admired author's books was inadequate to express the beauty of their contents. But the man who reads Lull with 'spiritual eyes' and 'spiritual ears' will find nothing barbarous. On the contrary, his rusticity of style has positive religious value. It proved to Lefèvre, who exaggerated Lull's literary simplicity and ignorance, that he was an authentic *idiota illitteratus* and that his books were written under the direct inspiration of God, the result of a *superna infusio*, vehicles of the Christian folly that defeats the wisdom of the world.[22]

Most commonly of all, Lefèvre distinguished between human and divine eloquence. To criticize books of contemplation because their style is barbarous is to miss the point that a 'humble Christian style' is the only one appropriate to divine theology and supramundane philosophy. The orator will judge a book like the *Contemplationes idiotae*, for example, to be without eloquence. But the book savours more of God than of the world and its humble, pure, and Christian style does not lack divine eloquence.[23] Nicholas of Cusa is eloquent; but his eloquence is Christian not forensic, catholic not rhetorical. Divine eloquence is simple, bare, and modest. It prefers intelligibility to ornament and what Lefèvre calls theatrical pomp (*theatralis pompa*). It is superior to secular eloquence.[24] Properly read, therefore, a twelfth-century mystic is more usefully eloquent than a contemporary Ciceronian.

Having justified the mystics, Lefèvre praised them. 'May the most merciful God,' he exclaimed, 'open the eyes of the men of our age so they may recognize books that are truly good.' Illumined by the light of Christ, although he was otherwise unlearned (an *idiota*), the pious hermit Ramon Lull defeated the wise men of this world and for love of him did not flinch from martyrdom. He possessed a marvellous fecundity of intellect, he never turned his mind from the eternal lover, and his books lift the minds of his readers to divine things.[25] The book of *Contemplationes* written by a 'certain pious and holy man, who called himself by no other name than Idiota' is pious and *religiosus*. It teaches the reader to 'bestir himself, to distrust himself, and to put his confidence in God and not in himself,' and these three things are the same as the Dionysian ascent to God by illumination, purgation, and perfection.[26] Dionysius himself is a *tuba divina*; Nicholas of Cusa a 'divine man,' supreme and most fruitful in every discipline pertaining to the contemplative life, a treasury of *altae et sublimes theoreses*.[27] Elizabeth of Schönau is a holy fountain of spiritual consolation, for she 'well conveys the power of the Holy Spirit and reproduces angelic discourse in the simplicity and purity of her holy visions'; and, although, in Lefèvre's opinion, Hildegard of Bingen from time to time

introduced something of herself into her visions, they also are 'pious, edi-
fying, and a consolation of pious minds.'[28]

Lefèvre's general attitude then to the varied and representative collection of mystical texts he published was one of the warmest admiration.
Such books illuminate, purge, and perfect. They edify. Their Christian
eloquence raises the mind to divine things. They provoke sympathetic
readers to inner reformation and renewal and train them in contemplation. Clearly they represented for Lefèvre a peculiarly desirable pattern
of Christian thought and conduct, ideal models of Christian piety. What,
more specifically, were the virtues he and his friends saw in this piety?

To begin with, the mystics help us to understand scripture better. They
explain its mystical sense (*mysticus sensus*). When we read the parable
of the man who sold all his possessions in order to buy the treasure hidden in a field, we should understand 'hidden treasure' to mean the *abstrusa
scripta* of holy fathers 'who have explained for us the hidden meanings
of holy scripture,' which are more valuable than gold, silver, and precious
stones. The divine writings are often beyond the capacity of our understanding; so we must particularly prize works by ancient fathers 'in
which that treasure is opened for us and the mysteries of divine scripture
uncovered.'[29] Among these *patres antiqui* are St Bernard and Hugh of
Saint-Victor, both equally celebrated for the holiness of their lives and
their 'exceptional knowledge of divine things.' In the preface to a volume
of commentaries on the Old and New Testaments by Richard of Saint-
Victor (he attributed them to Hugh of Saint-Victor), Josse Clichtove
made explicit the exegetical virtues of the mystics. Hugh reveals the high
mysteries of the faith hidden under the historical narrative of the Bible:
his spiritual interpretation is a *mystica intelligentia* of the text. At the
same time, it is 'so accommodated to persons, things, and places that one
finds no violence done to the text, no forced meaning, and nothing
added.'[30] Clichtove believed the theology of the mystics to be as simple,
clear, pure, and spiritual as that of the church fathers, a holy rhetoric
humbly serving the text of scripture. His terminology itself forced the
comparison, for the phrase *patres antiqui* at once ranged Bernard and the
Victorines in the patristic tradition and suggested that their works too
were to be preferred to the logical knots, empty disputations, and arro-
gant theological *scientia* of the scholastics. The fathers wrote no summas;
neither did the mystics.

A second virtue of the mystics, in the opinion of Lefèvre and his circle, was their preoccupation with the moral life and with moral instruction. Clichtove summed up the contents of the *Opera* of St Bernard: 'You will find nothing here but what illuminates the difficulties of sacred scripture or thunderingly chastizes vice and pressingly invites to virtue.'[31] It is the virtue of the several allegorical rivers that Hugh of Saint-Victor conjures up from the single historical fountain of scripture to water parched minds and encourage them to bear a harvest of good works. 'Aristotle says in the *Ethics* that words are very powerful in provoking men, especially well-born boys, to throw off their torpor and do good deeds. If fugitive human speech can accomplish so much, how much more effective must we not consider books which join moral precepts with the piety of our most holy religion.'[32] The books Clichtove had in mind were Hugh of Saint-Victor's *Seven Gifts of the Holy Spirit, On the Education of Novices, In Praise of Charity, The Manner of Prayer*, and a commentary on the *Pater Noster*. Lefèvre argued that two things properly form our lives: knowledge of general moral principles and specific rules for directing our actions and intentions to their proper end. Study of moral philosophy gives the first; mystical works, like those of Lull, are especially useful sources of the second.[33]

Closely related to the contribution of mystical literature *ad sancte instituendam formandamque vitam* was its support of the freedom of the will. Lefèvre was impressed by how the mystics, like the Greek fathers, confirmed and legitimized his own view of moral freedom, a harmony of New Testament teaching and the opening chapters of the third book of the *Ethics*, especially chapter 7 where Aristotle said that it is in our power to do good or evil acts, that 'being good or vicious characters is [therefore] in our power,' and that man is the 'originator or generator,' the *principium*, 'of his actions as he is the generator of his children.' The nature of his soul, said Dionysius, makes man a free being without a master;[34] while in the *De visione Dei* Cusanus praised human nature because man can augment or diminish, amplify or restrict his receptivity to God's grace by the exercise of his free will (*libera voluntas*).[35] Ruysbroeck's *De ornatu* listed common assumptions of the tradition: that because man is free to accept or reject grace he actively co-operates by spiritual exercises in his ascension to the divine vision; that the human soul is a kingdom whose king is free will, for the will is free by nature and is even freer by grace; that a mortal man in this life can actually lose his identity in the divine and achieve union, however briefly, with the One; that man in this life is capable of a kind of deification: can become, as Cusanus put it, in the famous chapter 'De homine' of the *De coniecturis*, a mortal god: 'For man is a god, but not absolutely; he is a human god ... The boundaries of the human enclose God and the whole universe as potential objects. So man can be a human god or god in human fashion; he can be a human angel, a human beast, a human bear or lion or anything else. In his own manner [*suo modo*] man is potentially capable of becoming all things.'[36]

It is appropriate that the most elaborate discussion of moral freedom in Lefèvre's works should occur among the scholia to his edition of the *Corpus Dionysiacum*. God in his goodness has given man a great gift: free will (*liberam nobis fecerit voluntatis potestatem*). Certain nominalist theologians of the fourteenth and fifteenth centuries had asserted that man is predestined. Lefèvre's scholium is an attack on these *idiotae* (the word is now pejorative). He agreed with them that there is a 'book of life' in which is written the name of every man predestined for salvation. But he insisted that human actions on earth could change the book of life in heaven. There are men who do not participate in the archetypal and exemplary virtues – *primordialis bonitas, primordialis amor*, and the like – which comprise the word of God and his wisdom. They are wicked, full of hate, disobedient, corrupt, unjust, cruel, avaricious, improvident, and foolish. But any one of them, if he is penitent and humbly asks God to grant him goodness and perfection of living (God whose very nature it is to pity, to hold out his hand to the fallen, to admit the reprobate to the grace of reconciliation), then this man becomes a 'son of reconciliation,' seeks to be good, obeys the divine commands, and participates according to his capacity in the other divine *paradigmata* of the virtues. This man, who before his change of heart had been predestined to damnation, is now predestined to salvation and his name is written in the book of life. Conversely, those predestined to salvation in the book of life can repeat the fall of Adam. 'Then our names are crossed out; but nevertheless will again be found there if we try to rise once more; and we can rise (though not of ourselves). God raises us, for He encourages those who have fallen and is the strength of those who remain firm, and the virtue of those who try to rise again.'[37]

Mystical works not only instruct the will and stimulate individual reformation; Lefèvre also believed they could help reform the monastic clergy. From the beginning an important reason why Lefèvre searched out and published mystical texts was his conviction that their assumptions and values were the same as the monks' and that knowledge of them would help recall the monastic clergy to its vocation. Union with the One, he wrote to a Carthusian novice, is true contemplation and the sweetest fruit of the contemplative life. The purpose of monastic life is the same: it rejects the world and embraces the otherworldly, deserts multiplicity and cleaves to the One. Books like the *De ornatu* arouse beginners, teach them the end of monastic life, and spur them on to fruitful contemplation.[38] Clichtove dedicated works of Hugh of Saint-Victor, Guillaume d'Auvergne's *De claustro animae,* and the *De claustro animae* of Hugues de Fouilloy to Jacques d'Amboise, bishop of Clermont and abbot of Cluny and the great Norman house of Jumièges. Jacques d'Amboise decorated the choir of Cluny with tapestries representing the first four abbots, gave Jumièges richly carved choir stalls, and tried pertinaciously to reform both houses. Clichtove's dedications were meant to support the reform of Cluny. They reflect his belief that repeated reading of such works produces spiritual fruits: holiness of life and contemplation of God.[39] But perhaps the noblest contemporary embodiment of the union of mystical piety and monastic reform was John Mombaer of Brussels, who was both a successful monastic reformer in the region around Paris and the author of the *Rosary of Spiritual Exercises*, a book that was to link the *devotio moderna* and Loyola. Badius Ascensius published a new edition of it in 1510 on Lefèvre's recommendation.[40]

However, what Lefèvre seems to have valued most in the mystics was not so much their Christian eloquence, nor their interpretations of scripture, nor their concern for regeneration (*nova regeneratio in Deo per Dei filium*) and personal reformation (*reformatio*),[41] their moral fervour and defence of free will, nor even their usefulness in reforming monastic life and piety. He admired Dionysius, the Victorines, Lull, and Cusanus above all because they helped him shape and clarify his own theory of knowledge, his conception of what the best philosophy and theology should be like and the relation that should obtain between them.

In his commentary on Richard of Saint-Victor's *De Trinitate* (1510), Lefèvre made his clearest statement about how human beings know God. An ascending hierarchy of cognitive types corresponds to the hierarchy of the great chain of being: inanimate matter, plants, animals, men, angels, and God. Rocks exist; plants live. Animals, men, angels, and God not only exist and live: they also know; and each knows in a manner appropriate to itself. Sensible knowledge is proper to animals; rational knowledge is proper to men; intellectual knowledge is proper to angels. Just as man is higher in the scale of being than animals, but lower than the angels, so reason (*ratio*), the cognitive faculty appropriate to him, occupies a middle place between the senses and imagination of beasts and the properly angelic faculty of intellect (*intellectus*). Above the intellect is a fourth faculty of knowledge, *mens*. This mode of knowing is appropriate to God, 'although,' Lefèvre remarks, 'I prefer to say that God is beyond all intellect and even *mens*.'[42]

The median position of man between animals and angels is reflected in the diversity of his cognitive faculties and the complexity of his mental operations. For although his appropriate faculty is reason, he shares sense and imagination with brutes and intellect with angels. He can therefore know in three different ways: by sense, by reason, and by intellect. The way of sense is below his natural capacity; the way of reason is precisely adequate to it; the way of intellect is above it. These three distinct and ascending ways of knowing yield three corresponding types of knowledge: experience, ratiocination, and intellection. The object of experience is sensible particulars; and experience is the beginning of knowledge, its lowest mode as sense is the lowest cognitive faculty. It may be likened to a hunting dog who leaps toward its prey at the sound of the hunter's horn. The object of intellection is divine and eternal things, archetypes in the mind of God. The *intellectus* knows the archetypal truth, that *prima veritas* of which all other truths are reflected vestiges. Intellection is the end of knowledge and may be compared to the hunter, who sees from afar the prize to be captured. Ratiocination, like reason itself, is median. It is knowledge of universals abstracted from sense experience, a median vestige of the *prima veritas*. It should be compared to the dog pursuing its quarry by smell, a sense superior to hearing but inferior to sight.

The pursuit of divine things by sense and imagination leads to idolatry and error. Only reason and intellect are capable of knowledge distinct from mere opinion. Reason, whose characteristic disciplines are logic and mathematics, must judge, correct, and refine the images of sense. It is equally necessary that the intellect, the faculty of intuition and vision, judge, refine, correct, and pass beyond the images of reason to an area where those who think they see are blind and those who know they do not see behold something of the truth, where ignorance is more highly prized than knowledge.[43]

In the pagan mysticism of the neo-Platonists a psychology based on the distinction of reason and intellect, similarly defined, was an integral part of a properly and exclusively philosophical system, that is, a system ignorant of the Christian dualisms of grace and nature, faith and reason. Lefèvre, like Cusanus, transformed the problem by identifying intellection with faith: *fides igitur [est] apud theologos quod intellectus principiorum apud philosophos.*[44] Reason, he argued (and the argument is almost a paraphrase of Cusanus), yields a human knowledge of divine things, intellect an illuminated knowledge of them. Reason combats the shadows of error by its own natural light; in intellection the 'greater light,' that is, the light of divine illumination, floods the lesser light of reason. In this context the hierarchical function of the cognitive faculties takes on a new meaning, and Lefèvre's vocabulary registers the shift. Imagination supplements the senses; reason supplements the imagination; and faith supplements reason. Intellection is that mode of knowing in which faith corrects, organizes, and certifies the data supplied by reason. Each act of intellectual cognition is an amalgam of faith and reason. The *prima veritas* is the word of God and the divine light. It illuminates the intellect as the sun's light illuminates the world. Faith therefore yields the highest certainty of any kind of knowledge; while reason, although its knowledge of divine things is inadequate, is autonomous and natural. Its inadequacy is compensated for by intellection, which can know invisible and eternal things. But intellect can know none of these things naturally; for in intellectual cognition faith is the *principium* of all further knowledge; and as the *prima veritas* of the divine mind is the archetype of faith (*fides archetypa*), so is faith the first truth of the human mind (*prima mentis nostrae veritas*).[45] Lefèvre's virtue is to preserve the autonomy of reason and its co-operative, though diminished role, in reaching truth while simultaneously fusing faith and reason in intellectual cognition and opening the mind to the regular penetration of the divine light – and ultimately opening it to the mystical vision of divine things, and even, in exceptional cases, to ecstasy.

Lefèvre was not himself a mystic. He recorded no visions for us; his mind apparently never deserted his flesh in ecstasy. But he found in the mystical tradition valuable examples of a Christian piety appropriate, in his view, to the needs and aspirations of his time: simple, clear, pure, eloquent, closely tied to scripture, unobscured by what he considered empty sophistry, morally instructive, warmly emotional. Mystical assumptions coloured his idea of liberty and influenced his theory of knowledge. He repeatedly cited the mystics' silence as the exemplar of the highest form of contemplation. The relation of his own thought to the mystical tradition, however, was never a simple one, and it changed a good deal with time. The following curious passage, from a letter of 1501, illustrates the difficulty: 'Aristotle is supreme in rational philosophy. Parmenides, Anaxagoras, Heraclitus and Pythagoras in intellectual ... Aristotle is the life of learning; Pythagoras the death of learning, which is superior to life. It rightly follows that Pythagoras taught by keeping silent, Aristotle by talking, but silence is act and speech privation. In St Paul and Dionysius there is much silence; in Cusanus also and in the ὁμοουσίῳ of Victorinus; in Aristotle there is very little silence and many voices; but silence speaks and utterance says nothing and the best words are simple silence.'[46]

Are pagans then capable of intellection? Is there a rational and intellectual philosophy, natural and gentile, which we should distinguish from a Christian theology also divided into two parts, rational and intellectual? How should we understand the position Lefèvre assigns to the pre-Socratics? How much weight should we attach to the praise of silence and his implied interpretation of it as a negative theology? How exactly do the Christian mystics fit into this esoteric scheme? One thing at least is clear. Lefèvre would not have written the passage this way ten years later. For he soon qualified his enthusiasm for the pre-Socratics. He had already warned his readers to distinguish Plato (who may be safely studied) from Timaeus and Parmenides (who are often mistaken);[47] and in his commentary on the *Politics* (1506) he lashed the Pythagoreans: 'Nothing is more vain and empty than those who call themselves Pythagoreans ... Read Irenaeus and you will find that the Pythagoreans were the most vicious opponents of the Christian religion.'[48] And to a visiting Italian about 1511 he emphasized that he was not an Aristotelian (and still less a Platonist) but was a Christian only.[49] Aristotle remained his admired guide in rational philosophy but, once he had firmly linked *fides* and *intellectus* in his commentary on Richard of Saint-Victor's *De Trinitate* (1510), he looked for models of silent intellection only among Christians, especially the early fathers of the church and the mystics. Finally, in his old age, even the towering figures of Dionysius and Cusanus receded. The psalms, gospels, and Paul became virtually the sole objects of his study. For many years Lefèvre joined philosophy to piety by progressing from the natural and moral philosophy of Aristotle, through bibical texts and their patristic exegesis, to the speculative and visionary mysticism of the masters of the contemplative life. The last Aristotelian

edition with which he was associated appeared in 1518. He published
his last edition of a medieval mystic in 1519. Thereafter he was an
evangelical reformer.

APPENDIX

The Medieval Mystical Works edited by
Jacques Lefèvre d'Étaples and Josse Clichtove

I

*Hic continentur libri Remundi pij eremite. Primo. Liber de laudibus
beatissime virginis marie: qui et ars intentionum Apellari potest. Secundo.
Libellus de natali pueri paruuli. Tertio. Clericus Remundi. Quarto. Phantasticus Remundi.* Paris, Guy Marchant for himself and Jean Petit, 6 April
1499. fol. Edited by Lefèvre d'Étaples (Dietrich Reichling, *Appendices
ad Hainii-Copingeri Repertorium bibliographicvm* [Monachii 1905-11],
3686; Louis Polain, *Catalogue des livres imprimés au quinzième siècle
des bibliothèques de Belgique* [Bruxelles 1932], 3310; Frederick R. Goff,
*Incunabula in American Libraries: A Third Census of Fifteenth-Century
Books Recorded in North American Collections* [New York 1964], L 390;
Elíes Rogent and Estanislau Duràn, *Bibliografía de les impressions Lul-
lianes* [Barcelona 1927], pp. 20-2, no 24). There exists a second printing: Paris, Guy Marchant for Jean Petit, dated 10 April 1499 (W. A.
Copinger, *Supplement to Hain's Repertorium bibliographicum* [London
1895-1902], 10327*; Polain, 3310 A; Goff, L 391; Rogent and Duràn,
pp. 22-3, no. 25).

The volume contains four works by Ramon Lull.

  1 *Liber de laudibus beatissimae virginis Mariae*, written in Rome c.
1290. Catalan text in *Obres de Ramon Lull*, ed. S. Galmés, vol. x (Palma
de Mallorca 1915); the only published Latin text is that of Lefèvre's edition. See Littré and Hauréau, in *Histoire littéraire de la France* (HLF),
XXIX (Paris 1885), p. 257, no. 81; E. Allison Peers, *Ramon Lull: A Biography* (London 1929), pp. 228-31; J. Avinyó, *Les obres autèntiques del
beat Ramon Lull* (Barcelona 1935), p. 103, no. 42; E. W. Platzeck,
Raimund Lull: Sein Leben, seine Werke (Düsseldorf, 1962-4), II, p. 23*,
no. 60.

2 *Liber de natali pueri parvuli Christi Jesu,* planned on Christmas night 1310, written in Paris in January 1311, and dedicated to Philip the Fair. The richly illuminated manuscript that Lull presented to the king is in the Bibliothèque nationale (Par. lat. 3323). Lefèvre did not use this manuscript, and his text differs from it considerably; in particular it omits the last four pages of the original. Marianus Mueller reproduced Lefèvre's text in *Wissenschaft und Weisheit,* III-IV (1936-7). See HLF, XXIX, no. 53, pp. 237-40; Peers, pp. 348-50; Avinyó, p. 249, no. 157; Platzeck, II, p. 61*, no. 187.

3 *Liber clericorum,* an elementary catechism for ignorant clerics dedicated to the 'venerable university of Paris, and principally to its chancellor, rector, dean and other chief members.' The Latin version was finished at Pisa in May 1308. The Catalan original is lost. Latin text (reproducing Lefèvre's) in *Obres,* ed. M. Obrador i Bennassar (Palma 1906), I, 295-386. See HLF, XXIX, pp. 255-6, no. 78; Peers, p. 355; C. Ottaviano, *L'Ars compendiosa de R. Lulle avec une étude sur la bibliographie et le Fond ambrosien de Lulle* (Paris 1930), p. 66, no. 117; Avinyó, p. 216, no. 126; Platzeck, II, p. 51*, no. 150.

4 *Phantasticus* or *Disputatio Raymundi phantastici et Petri clerici,* written in September 1311 while Lull was on his way to the Council of Vienne. Latin text ed. Marianus Mueller in *Wissenschaft und Weisheit,* II (1935), 311-24 (based on Lefèvre's text). See HLF, XXIX, pp. 240-1, no. 54; Peers, pp. 356-8; Ottaviano, p. 76, no. 158; Avinyó, p. 259, no. 170; Platzeck, II, p. 67*, no. 210.

Lefèvre's is the first edition of all four works. He does not indicate where he found the manuscripts, though he probably used copies from one or another of the three excellent collections of Lull's works in Paris in the late fifteenth and early sixteenth centuries: those in the libraries of the Sorbonne and of the monasteries of Saint-Victor and Vauvert, the Paris Charterhouse. In 1311 Thomas le Miesier, a canon of Arras, prepared a catalogue of works by Lull in the library of the Carthusians. It lists one hundred and twenty-three books (Par. lat. 15450, ff. 88ʳ-89ᵛ). Lull's will, made at Mallorca in 1313, specified other books to be sent to the Carthusians. See Delisle, *Le Cabinet des manuscrits de la Bibliothèque nationale* (Paris 1874-81), III, 69, 76, 114; Ramon de Alós y de Dou, *Los catálogos lulianos. Contribución al estudio de la obra de Ramón Lull* (Barcelona 1918); and J. Tarré, 'Los códices lulianos de la Biblioteca Nacional de París,' *Analecta sacra Tarraconensia,* XIV (1941), 155-74.

II

Contenta. Primum volumen Contemplationum Remundi duos libros continens. Libellus Blaquerne de amico et amato. Paris, Guy Marchant for Jean Petit, 10 December 1505. fol. Edited by Lefèvre d'Étaples. (Cambridge, University Library; Chicago, Newberry; London, BM; New York, NYPL; Oxford, Bodleian; Paris, BN. Georg Wolfgang Franz Panzer, *Annales typographici ab artis inventae origine ad annum 1536.* [Norimbergae, 1793-1803], VII, 514, no. 121; Rogent and Duràn, pp. 32-3, no. 35.)

The volume contains two works by Ramon Lull.

1 *Liber contemplationis in Deum* (c. 1272), Lull's first important work. Catalan text in *Obres*, ed. M. Obrador i Bennassar (Palma, 1906-14), vols. II-VIII; Latin text in *Opera*, ed. Salzinger, vols. IX and X. See HLF, XXIX, pp. 220-35, no. 48; J.-H. Probst, *Caractère et origine des idées du bienheureux Raymond Lull* (Toulouse 1912), pp. 98-101; Peers, pp. 45-81; Avinyó, pp. 26-35, no. 3; Platzeck, p. 3*, no. 2.

The *Liber contemplationis*, says Lull, is 'an art whereby man may learn to love Thee' (*Obres*, VII, 130), an art of almost a million words, in three hundred and sixty-six chapters and five books, in remembrance of the five wounds of Christ on the cross. Lefèvre acquired the manuscript in 1491 under the following circumstances (sig. a, iᵛ) : 'Fluxerunt anni supra quattuordecim (narratione paulo longiore utar), erat mihi tunc aureus obolus paene inutilis, venit ad me quidam Galliae Narbonensis mihi apprime notus et amicus, librum tenens, quem protinus erat venditioni expositurus; laborarat enim adversa valitudine et inopia premebatur. Viso titulo de contemplatione scilicet quae fit in Deo, rapior ilico libri legendi desiderio; obulum aureum (qui mihi tunc aderat) illi praetendo, ut si vellet acciperet, etiam a me non accepto libro, lectionem tamen requirenti. Ille vero (quae sua erat modestia) voluit ut librum caperem et sublacrimabatur pariter. Sic enim librum caro prosequebatur affectu. Ego vero illa intentione cepi, ut non minus immo etiam magis illi quam mihi liber esset usui; unum et ipse plurimum gaudere coepit quod necessitate compulsus tandem in alterius manus illum non consignasset. Incessit illi cupido (membris nondum satis ex morbo solidatis) patrios invisere lares, et quae fortuna circa eum postmodum acciderit me latet. Liber itaque apud me mansit et plurimam mihi attulit consolationem; et paene ad hoc pertraxit, ut demisso mundo Deum in solitudine quaererem; et forsitan felix si tractum secutus executioni demandassem.'

Lefèvre published the first volume, books I and II, of the *Liber contemplationis.* Their subject, with much digression and repetition, is the divine attributes and certain aspects of the creation. He dedicated the book to Gabriel, a Carthusian novice at Vauvert, because the Carthusians had lost the first volume of their own copy, given to them by Lull himself: "Et quod ad te potius scripserim causa haec est: quia apud sanctae conversationis vestrae Parisiacam domum secundum contemplationis volumen habetur tres reliquos libros continens, ex dono eiusdem pii viri dum adhuc ageret in humanis (colebat enim apprime caelibes illius tempestatis viros sacrosque recessus et frequentissime Cartusiorum solitudines), primum autem volumen vobis deerat, sic apud vos (quibus contemplativa vita propria est) invenient qui desiderabunt integrum contemplationum opus' (sig. a, iᵛ). The missing volume is now in the Bibliothèque nationale (Par. lat. 3448 A) and is inscribed as follows: 'Ego Raymundus Lul do librum istum conventui fratrum de Cartusia.' Below this is another note: 'Hoc est primum volumen Meditationum magistri Raymundi, quod ipse dedit fratribus et domui Vallis Viridis prope Parisiis, cum duobus aliis sequentibus voluminibus istius tractatus, anno gratiae MCC nonagesimo octavo.'

2 *Libellus Blaquernae de amico et amato,* written in Montpellier c.1283. Catalan text in *Obres,* ed. S. Galmés (Palma 1914), IX, 379-433. The only published Latin text is that of Lefèvre's edition. English translation by Peers, *Book of the Lover and the Beloved* (2nd ed. London 1946); German translation by L. Klaiber (Olten 1948). See HLF, XXIX, pp. 252-5, no. 76; Peers, *Lull,* pp. 178-91; J.-H. Probst, 'L'Amour mystique dans l'Amic e Amat de Ramon Lull,' *Arxius de l'Institut de Ciències* (Barcelona 1917), IV, 292-322; Avinyó, pp. 79-88, no. 31; Platzeck, II, p. 16*, no. 44g. Lefèvre copied the work in 1500 in Padua at the Benedictine monastery of Santa Giustina. The manuscript he transcribed was a Latin translation made during Lull's lifetime and which Lull himself had given in 1298 to Doge Pietro Gradenigo. It is now in the Marciana. Lefèvre's is the first edition.

III

In Hoc Libro Contenta Opera Hvgonis De Sancto Victore. De institutione nouitiorum. De operibus trium dierum. De arra anime. De laude charitatis. De modo orandi. Duplex expositio orationis dominice. De quinque septenis. De septem donis spiritus sancti. Paris, Henri Estienne, 12 October 1506. 4°. Edited by Josse Clichtove and dedicated to Jacques d'Amboise, bishop of Clermont and abbot of Cluny. (Boston, Simmons College; London, BM; Oxford, Bodleian; Panzer, VII, 521, no. 175; A. A. Renouard, *Annales de l'imprimerie des Estienne* [2nd ed. Paris 1843], p. 3, no. 1.)

The volume contains the following works by Hugh (and Richard) of Saint-Victor.

1 *De institutione novitiorum* (ed. 1506 ff. 2^r-22^v) = *De institutione novitiorum liber* (ed. Migne, PL, CLXXVI, cc. 925-52).

2 *De operibus trium dierum* (ff. 23^r-43^v) = *Eruditionis Didascalicae libri septem*, book VII (PL, CLXXVI, cc. 811-38).

3 *De arra animae* (ff. 44^r-58^r) = *Soliloquium de arrha animae* (PL, CLXXVI, cc. 951-70).

4 *In laudem charitatis* (ff. 58^v-63^r) = *De laude charitatis* (PL, CLXXVI, cc. 969-76).

5 *De modo orandi* (ff. 63^r-71^r) = *De modo orandi* (PL, CLXXVI, cc. 977-88.)

6 *Duplex expositio orationis dominice*. (a) *De Oratione Dominica secundum Matthaeum et de septem petitionibus in ea contentis* (ff. 71^v-76^r) = *Allegoriae in Novum Testamentum libros novem complectentes*, book II, ch. 2 (PL, CLXXV, cc. 767-74; cf. J. Chatillon, 'Le contenu, l'authenticité et la date du *Liber exceptionum* et des *Sermones centum* de Richard de Saint-Victor,' *Revue du moyen âge latin*, IV (1948), 43-4, no 37: the manuscript evidence makes it clear that this text is an integral part of the *Allegoriae* and should therefore be assigned to Richard of Saint-Victor rather than to Hugh). (b) *Expositio secunda* (ff. 76^r-87^r) = *Allegoriae*, II, chs. 3-14 (PL, CLXXV, cc. 774-89).

7 *De quinque Septenis* (ff. 87^v-91^r) = *De quinque septenis seu septenariis opusculum*, chs. 1-4 (PL, CLXXV, cc. 405-10).

8 *De septem donis spiritus sancti* (ff. 91^v-95^v) = *De quinque septenis*, ch. 5 (PL, CLXXV, cc. 410-14).

See J.-B. Hauréau, *Les œuvres de Hughes de Saint-Victor* (Paris 1886), pp. 35-7; Roger Baron, *Science et sagesse chez Hughes de Saint-Victor* (Paris 1957), pp. xix, xxiv; D. Van Den Eynde, *Essai sur la successsion et la date des écrits de Hughes de Saint-Victor* (Rome 1960), pp. 26, 31, 65-9, 113-15, 149-50, 154, 163-6.

IV

Contenta. Guilhelmus Parisiensis de Claustro Anime. Hugonis de sancto victore de Claustro Anime libri quatuor. Paris, Henri Estienne, 10 September 1507. 4°. Edited by Clichtove and dedicated to Jacques d'Amboise (London, BM; Panzer, VII, 525, no. 211; A. A. Renouard, *Estienne*, p. 5, no. 3).

The volume contains two works of medieval monastic piety.

1 Guillaume d'Auvergne, *De claustro animae* (c. 1240). Clichtove's is the *editio princeps* and the only printed edition. See N. Valois, *Guillaume d'Auvergne, évêque de Paris, 1228-1249* (Paris 1880), pp. 169-70, and I. Kramp, 'Des Wilhelm von Auvergne "Magisterium divinale",' *Gregorianum*, II (1921), 185-7.

2 A treatise, *De claustro animae*, which Clichtove attributed to Hugh of Saint-Victor (copyists were already assigning it to Hugh in the twelfth century), but which is in reality by Hugues de Fouilloy, prior of Saint-Laurent-au-Bois. Text in Migne, PL, CLXXVI, cc. 1017-1182. See Hauréau, *Les œuvres de Hugues de Saint-Victor*, 155-64, and H. Peltier, 'Hugues de Fouilloy, chanoine régulier, prieur de Saint-Laurent-au-Bois,' *Revue du moyen âge latin*, II (1946), 25-44. The work had already been published in Cologne in 1504 correctly ascribed to Hugues de Fouilloy: *Tractatus de claustro anime, domini Hugonis Folietini, sancti Petri Corbiensis canonici, in quo non solum pericula secularium: sed etiam spiritualium abusiones personarum perstringuntur* (London, BM; Paris, BN; Panzer, VI, 354, no. 69).

V

Melliflui deuotique doctoris sancti Bernardi abbatis Clareuallensis. Cisterciensis ordinis opus preclarum suos complectens sermones de tempore, de sanctis, et super cantica canticorum. Aliosque plures eius sermones et sententias nusquam hactenus impressas. Eiusdem insuper epistolas, ceteraque vniuersa eius opuscula. Domini quoque Gilleberti abbatis de Hoilandia in Anglia prelibati Ordinis super cantica sermones. Omnia secundum seriem hic inferius annotatam collocata, vigilanter et accurate super vetustissima Clareuallis exemplaria apprime correcta. Paris, André Bocard for Jean Petit, 31 March 1508. fol. (Munich; Sélestat; Panzer, VII, 530, no. 257; L. Janauschek, *Bibliographia Bernardina* [Hildesheim 1959], pp. 90-2, no. 350.)

Because Clichtove contributed a complimentary preface to this collection of the works of St Bernard, bibliographers have often credited him with editing the volume. But, as the colophon makes clear, editorial work was the responsibility of Cistercian monks at the abbey of Clairvaux:

'Deuoti mellifluique doctoris diui Bernardi Clareuallis abbatis seraphica scripta diligentissime cum archetypis bibliothecae Clareuallis a quibusdam eiusdem domus monachis emendata.' According to a letter from Badius Ascencius to Mathurin de Cangey, monk of Clairvaux, dated 24 December 1507, Mathurin was the principal editor: 'Tua siquidem unius opera et accuratione divinae devotissimi Bernardi lucubrationes sub uno codice propediem in vestitu prosilient deaurato.' (P. Renouard, *Bibliographie des impressions et des œuvres de Josse Badius Ascensius, imprimeur et humaniste 1462-1535* [Paris 1908], III, 124-5.)

Many subsequent editions of Bernard's works copied this of 1508, the earliest of which are Paris, Bertold Rembolt for Jean Petit, 30 June 1513 (Columbia; Holy Cross; London, BM; Janauschek, pp. 98-9, no. 379); Lyons, Jean Cleyn, April 1515 (London, BM; Baudrier, *Bibliographie lyonnaise*, XII, 290-1; Janauschek, pp. 101-2, no. 388); Paris, Bertold Rembolt for Jean Petit, 4 July 1517 (London, BM; Oxford, Bodleian; Janauschek, pp. 106-7, no. 402); Lyons, Jean Cleyn, 19 July 1520 (Paris, BN; Baudrier, XII, 303-9; Janauschek, pp. 111-12, no. 422).

VI

Egregii Patris Et Clari theologi Ricardi quondam deuoti coenobitae sancti victoria iuxta muros parisienses de superdiuina Trinitate theologicum opus Hexade librorum distinctum Et Captivm xv Decadibvs. Adivnctus Est Commentarivs artificio Analytico: metaphysicam et humani sensus transcendentem apicem, sed rationali modo complectens intelligentiam, quod opus ad dei trini honorem & piarum mentium exercitationem Foeliciter Prodeat In Lvcem. Paris, Henri Estienne, 19 July 1510. 4°. Edited by Lefèvre and dedicated to Louis Pinelle, professor of theology and chancellor of the university of Paris. (Cambridge, University Library; Paris, BN, BSHPF; Sélestat; Panzer, VII, 547, no. 399; A. A. Renouard, *Estienne*, p. 7, no. 2).

This volume contains the *De Trinitate* of Richard of Saint-Victor (c. 1165) and Lefèvre's commentary on it. Critical edition of Richard's text by Jean Ribailler (Paris 1958); French translation by Father Gaston Salet (Paris 1959). Lefèvre's is the first edition. Some fifty manuscripts are known, but the one which Lefèvre used has disappeared. The principal variants of Lefèvre's text are noticed in Ribailler's apparatus. Lefèvre used only the one manscript in preparing his edition, occasionally correcting readings that seemed to him defective. A table at the end of the volume lists these corrections. Cf. A.-M Ethier, *Le 'De Trinitate' de Richard de Saint-Victor, Publications de l'Institute d'études médiévales d'Ottawa* (Paris and Ottawa 1939) and the bibliography in G. Dumeige, *Richard de Saint-Victor et l'idée chrétienne de l'amour* (Paris 1952), 170-85. According to the colophon, Lefèvre wrote his commentary on the *De Trinitate* at Saint-Germain-des-Prés in 1510.

VII

Rosetum exercitiorum spiritualium et sacrarum meditationum: in quo etiam habetur materia predicabilis per totius anni circulum Recognitum penitus et auctum multis. Praesertim primo et vltimo titulis: per ipsius authorem (qui dum vita manebat temporalis nominari noluit). Uenerabilem Patrem Joannem Mauburnum: natione Bruxellensi. Uita autem et professione regularem seu Canonicum ex institutione diui patris Augustini: cuius obseruantissimam egit vitam prius in celeberrimo cenobio Montis sancte Agnetis Traiectensis diocesis, Deinde in Francia in regali abbatia diui Seuerini iuxta castrum Nantonis: in qua regularem (que multis retro annis penitus corruerat) restituit disciplinam. Postremo in Liuriacensi monasterio in quo cum (expulsis inde irreformatis moribus) Canonici regularisque obseruationis viros colocasset: cum eisque aliquanto tempore vixisset Abbatis functus officio honorifice sepultus est. Paris, Josse Badius Ascensius for Jean Petit and Jean Scabelerius, 13 August 1510. fol. Edited by Josse Bade and dedicated to Jean Saulay, a canon of Notre-Dame de Paris. (London, BM; Oxford, Bodleian; P. Renouard, *Badius*, III, 80-82.)

For the *Rosetum exercitiorum spiritualium* of Jean Mombaer of Brussels, see Pierre Debongnie, *Jean Mombaer de Bruxelles, abbé de Livry, ses écrits et ses réformes* (Louvain 1927) and Johannes Donndorf, *Das Rosetum des Johannes Mauburnus* (Halle 1929). Badius' edition is the third, preceded by one in 1494 (Hain-Copinger, 13995) and a second edited by Johannes Speyser and published by Jakob von Pfortzheim in Basel in 1504 (Hain-Copinger, 13996). Debongnie, pp. 306-8, offers a useful concordance to the three editions. The edition of 1510 is clearly described by Donndorf, pp. 4-6. As he tells the reader on the title page and in his preface, Badius included new material written by Mombaer himself in the last days of his life.

Badius published the *Rosetum* in part because Lefèvre had recommended it to him so highly: 'Rosetum ... impressimus ... tum quod viri

egregii longe circumspectiore quam nos simus iudicio praediti (inter quos
te [Saulay] et Fabrum nostrum Stapulensem non minus pietate quam
litteratura praeditos reponimus) opus ipsum tantopere commendarunt,
tam ob auctoris sanctitatem et zelum in omnes Christianos quam ob doctrinae eius integritatem atque suavitatem' (sig. aa, i^v).

VIII

*Deuoti et venerabilis patris Ioannis Rusberi presbyteri, canonici ob-
seruantiae beati Augustini, de ornatu spiritualium nuptiarum libri tres.
Primus de ornatu vitae moralis et activae. Secundus de ornatu vitae spiri-
tualis et affectivae. Tertius de ornatu vitae superessentialis et contemplativae.* Paris, Henri Estienne, 3 August 1512. 4°. (Cambridge, University Library; Harvard; London, BM; Oxford, Bodleian; Paris, BN; Panzer, VII, 566, no. 562; A. A. Renouard, *Estienne*, p. 11, no. 4.)

The volume contains Lefèvre's edition of Jan van Ruysbroeck's *Die
gheestelike Brulocht* (c.1350) in the Latin translation of Willem Jordaens
(c.1360). Two manuscripts of this translation are known: Brussels, Bibl.
roy., no. 2384 and Paris, Bibl. Mazarine, no. 921. Lefèvre's is the first
edition. He used a manuscript very similar to that in the Mazarine, a
fifteenth-century manuscript formerly in the library of the abbey of
Saint-Victor. Critical edition of the Dutch text in Ruysbroeck, *Werken*,
vol. I, ed. J. B. Poukens and L. Reypens (Malines and Amsterdam 1932);
Lefèvre's remains the only edition of the Jordaens translation. English
translation by Eric Colledge (London 1952). See A. Auger, *Étude sur les
mystiques des Pays-Bas au Moyen Age: Mémoires couronnés par l'Aca-
démie royale de Belgique*, XLVI (1892), 187, and André Combes, *Essai
sur la critique de Ruysbroeck par Gerson* (Paris 1945), I, 68-70, 75-82,
114-18, 135-233.

IX

*Liber trium virorum & trium spiritualium virginum. Hermae Liber vnus.
Vguetini Liber vnus. F. Roberti Libri duo. Hildegardis Sciuias Libri tres.
Elizabeth virginis Libri sex. Mechtildis virgi. Libri quinque.* Paris, Henri
Estienne for himself and Jean de Brie, 30 May 1513. fol. Edited by
Lefèvre and dedicated to Adelheid von Ottenstein, abbess of the Benedic-
tine convent of Rupertsberg near Bingen (diocese of Mainz). (Cambridge
University Library; Edinburgh, University Library; London, BM; Mu-

nich; Oxford, Bodleian; Paris, BN; Sélestat; University of Illinois; Vienna; Panzer, VIII, 6, no. 649; A. A. Renouard, *Estienne*, p. 14, no. 2.)

The volume is a collection of visionary works by three holy men and three holy virgins.

1 The Shepherd of Hermas, whom Lefèvre, following Origen and Jerome, identified with the disciple of Paul mentioned in Romans 16:14, dates from the middle of the second century. References in J. Quasten, *Initiation aux Pères de l'église*, trans. J. Laporte (Paris 1955) I, 107-22; B. Altaner, *Patrologie* (5th ed. Freiburg-im-Breisgau 1958), 69-71; the editions of Molly Whittaker (Berlin 1956) and R. Joly (Paris 1958) ; and Stanislas Giet, *Hermas et les Pasteurs* (Paris 1963). The Shepherd was known in the west in two Latin translations, the *versio vulgata*, which possibly dates from the second century (*Hermae Pastor. Veterem Latinam interpretationem e codicibus edidit Adolphus Hilgenfeld* [Leipzig 1873], and C. H. Turner, 'The Shepherd of Hermas and the Problem of His Text,' *Journal of Theological Studies*, XXI [1920], 199-209) and the later *versio Palatina*. Cf. J. T. Muckle, 'Greek Works Translated Directly into Latin before 1350,' *Mediaeval Studies*, IV (1942), 37. Lefèvre published the *versio vulgata*. His edition is the first. The Greek text appeared only in 1856 after the discovery on Mount Athos of a fourteenth-century manuscript.

2 *Libellus de visione Uguetini monachi*. Lefèvre got his erroneous information about 'Uguetinus' from the incipit of his manuscript: 'Visio Uguetini prius canonici, postea monachi, quam ostendit illi Deus per angelum et quam nos fratres eius ipso narrante scripsimus, servi sancti Vicentii Metensis' (f. 17ʳ; cf. Migne, PL, CV, c. 771 A). The work is in reality the *Visio Wettini*, written down by Hatto, abbot of Reichenau, before 806 when he became bishop of Basel. Lefèvre's is the first edition. Critical edition by E. Dümmler in *Monumenta Germaniae Historica, Poetae Latini aevi Carolini*, II (Berlin 1884), 267-75.

3 *Liber Sermonum Domini Ihesu Christi quos locutus est in servo suo* and *Liber visionum quas dedit videre dominus Ihesus servo suo*, two short works by the Dominican mystic Robert of Uzès (died 1296). Lefèvre prefaced the *Liber visionum* with the following remarks (f. 24ᵛ) : 'Sequens liber visionum factus est a docto fratre Roberto maxima pro parte ante religionis ingressum. Et ideo ordine prior; nihil tamen referat si posterior legatur, nam etiam continet quae edificare possint non pauca, et utiles sunt non parum spiritum intelligentibus visiones.' See *Scriptores Ordinis*

praedicatorum notis historicis et criticis illustrati, eds. Fr Jacobus Quétif
and Fr Jacobus Echard. (Parisius 1910-14), I, 449-50 and Ulysse Cheva-
lier, *Répertoire des sources historiques du moyen âge: Bio-bibliographie*
(Paris 1905-7), II, 4011.) Lefèvre says nothing about the provenance
of the manuscript. Renaudet, p. 602, n. 3, conjectured plausibly that he
found the works of Robert of Uzès and the *Visio Wettini* in Metz during
his trip to Germany in the summer of 1510.

4 The *Scivias* of Hildegard of Bingen (1098-1179). Lefèvre's edition is
the first. His text is reproduced in Migne, PL, CXCVII, cc. 383-738. There is
no critical edition yet. Lefèvre found a manuscript of the *Scivias* in the
convent of Rupertsberg during his trip to Germany in the summer of 1510.
He reported to Beatus Rhenanus in a letter datel from Saint-Germain-des-
Prés, 24 June 1511, that he had had the manuscript copied, but that publication was delayed because the copyist had omitted parts of the text; in
the meantime, another friend, Kilian Westhausen of Mainz, was restoring
the missing passages (A. Horawitz and Karl Hartfelder, *Die Briefwechsel des Beatus Rhenanus* [Leipzig 1886], p. 38: 'Superiori anno Aquis-
granum profectus sum ... incidi in monasterium virginum beatae Hildegardis, de qua alias ad te scripseram. Comperi profecto libros devoti
pectoris, copia mihi facta est ad utilitatem postérorum. Verum aliquid
exemplari defuit, unde factum est, ut nihil adhuc ex officina emitti potuerit.
Exspecto in dies ex vicinia illa Quilianum nostrum, qui resartiet quae
desunt.') See Jacques Christophe, *Sainte Hildegarde* (Paris 1942); Bertha Widmer, *Heilsordnung und Zeitgeschehen in der Mystik Hildegards
von Bingen* (Basel 1955), pp. 217-86; and M. Scrader and A. Führkötter,
Die Echtheit des Schrifttums der heiligen Hildegard von Bingen (Cologne 1956), pp. 17, 185-92.

5 Selected works of Elizabeth of Schönau (1129-64). Lefèvre published
the following: (a) *Visiones* (ff. 119ʳ-129ʳ) = *Die Visionen der hl. Elisabeth sowie die Schriften der Äbte. Ekbert und Emecho von Schönau*, ed.
F. W. E. Roth (2nd ed. Brünn 1886), pp. 1-15, i.e., Lefèvre published only
book I of Roth's edition, divided this text into two books, and omitted
books II and III; (b) *Liber viarum Dei* (ff. 129ʳ-138ᵛ) = ed. Roth, pp. 88-
122; (c) *Visio Elizabeth ... quam vidit in Sconaugiensi coenobio de as-
sumptione virginis Mariae matris domini* (ff. 138ᵛ-9ʳ) = *Visiones*, book
II, chs. 31 and 32, ed. Roth, pp. 53-5; (d) *Liber revelationum Eliz. de
sacro exercitu virginum Coloniensium* (ff. 139ʳ-43ʳ) = ed. Roth, pp. 123-
35; (e) *Epistolae* (ff. 143ʳ-6ʳ) = ed. Roth, eps. 1-17; (f) Ekbert, *De
Obitu Eliz. virginis* (ff. 146ʳ-50ᵛ) = ed. Roth, pp. 263-77. Lefèvre's

source for the letters and Ekbert's *De obitu* was possibly a German manuscript, perhaps called to his attention during his visit to Rupertsberg and Johannesberg. For Elizabeth's other works he used a fifteenth-century manuscript of the same family as Par. lat. 2873, a twelfth-century codex very close to Lefèvre's printed text. See Roth, pp. l-li; E. Krebs, in W. Stammler, *Die deutsche Literatur des Mittelalters: Verfasserlexikon* (Berlin 1933-43), I, 554-6; and Kurt Köster, 'Elisabeth von Schönau: Werk und Wirking im Spiegel der mittelalterlichen handschriftlichen Ueberlieferung.' *Archiv für mittelrheinische Kirchengeschichte,* III (1951), 243-315.

6 *Liber specialis gratiae* by Mechthild of Hackenborn (1241-99). Critical edition by the Benedictines of Solemes, *Revelationes Gertrudianae ac Mechtildianae,* II. *Sanctae Mechtildis virginis ordinis sancti Benedicti Liber specialis gratiae* (Paris 1877), pp. 5-369. Lefèvre's edition followed a German translation published in Leipzig in 1503 and an excellent Latin text published in Würzburg in 1510. He knew neither edition. His own text of books I-IV is faithful to the best manuscripts. Book V is badly mutilated. Books VI and VII were not in the manuscript he used and therefore do not appear in his edition. Despite a careful search, Lefèvre was unable to identify Mechthild, so he wrote Beatus Rhenanus asking him to question the sisters of convents near him (Horawitz-Hartfelder, p. 38). He incorporated the results of these inquiries in his introduction (sig. a, ii^r) ; 'Mechtildis quae fuerit, facta diligenti multaque indagine, neutiquam adhuc agnoscere valui quaenam ea fuerit, cuius religionis, et in quo coenobio diversata. Scripsit tamen ad me Beatus Rhenanus, quem super ea re epistolio consulueram, intellexisse se eam fuisse Germanam et circa montes Rhetios habitasse vergento ad Elvetios, unamque de filiabus alicuius comitum fuisse, atque in ills locis coli memoriam eius et sacrum obtinere sacellum. Arbitror eam ordinis beati Bernardi fuisse.' Actually Mechthild of Hackeborn was a nun at the Cistercian convent of Helfta, and among her sisters were the celebrated mystics Gertrud of Helfta and Mechthild of Magdeburg. Cf. E. Krebs, in Stammler, III, 321-3.

X

Haec Accvrata Recognitio Trivm Volvminvm, Opervm Clariss. P. Nicolai Cvsae Card. Ex Officina Ascensiana Recenter Emissa Est. Cvivs Vniversalem Indicem, Proxime Seqvens Pagina Monstrat. Paris, Badius Ascensius, 1514, 3 vols. fol. The second volume is dated 23 August 1514.

Edited by Lefèvre and dedicated to Denis Briçonnet, bishop of Toulon
(20 December 1497-1514) then of Saint-Malo (18 August 1514-35).
(Cambridge, University Library; Cornell; Munich; New York, Union
Theological Seminary (vol. II) ; Rome, Vaticana; Sélestat; P. Renouard,
Badius, II, 356-7. Photographic reprint, Frankfurt-am-Main, Minerva
G.m.b.H., 1962.)

Lefèvre's edition of the *opera omnia* of Nicholas of Cusa is in three volumes: the first contains philosophical and theological works; the second
theological and mathematical works; the third the *De concordantia
catholica*. All of the works in the first volume and several in the second
had already appeared in earlier editions: Strasbourg, Martin Flach
(c.1488) (Hain-Copinger, 5893, Polain, 2814) and Milan (Cortemag-
giore), Benedictus Dolcibelli, 1502 (ed. P. Wilpert, *Nikolaus von Kues.
Werke. Neuausgabe des Strassburger Drucks von 1488* [Berlin 1967],
I, pp. vi-ix. For these works the Strasbourg edition was Lefèvre's only
source. Of the remaining treatises Lefèvre's edition is the first. He had
been collecting material for this remarkable edition since at least 1507.
On sig. aa, iii[v] he thanked the many friends who had found and copied
manuscripts for him: Beatus Rhenanus, the Carthusian monk Gregor
Reisch, Jan Schilling of Cracow, Pierre Meriele, Joannes Brosgoicus,
Reuchlin, Jacob Faber of Deventer, Toussaint Vassier, monk of Livry,
Nicolaus Moravus, and Gaspar and Kilian Westhausen of Mainz. Michael
Hummelberg helped Lefèvre with the editorial work; Michael Pontanus
and Ludovicus Fidelis read the proofs.

XI

*Prouerbia Raemundi. Philosophia amoris eiusdem. Iodoci Badii qui im-
pressit tetrastichon.*
　　Est cibus hic animi purgati pneumate sacro
　　　Coctus in eximii pectore syluicolae.
　　Qui quoniam radios detraxit ab aethere mundos:
　　　Ab radiis mundis nobile nomen habet.
Paris, Badius Ascensius, 13 December 1516. 4°. Edited by Lefèvre and
dedicated to Alfonso of Aragon, archbishop of Saragossa (14 August
1478-24 February 1520) and Valencia (23 January 1512-20). (Oxford,
Bodleian; New York, Hispanic Society of America; Paris, BN; Rome,
Vaticana; P. Renouard, *Badius*, III, 48; Rogent-Duràn, p. 59, n.62).

The volume contains two works by Ramon Lull.
　1 *Liber Proverbiorum*, written in Rome in 1296. Catalan text in *Obres*

de Ramon Lull, ed. Galmés, xiv (Palma 1928), pp. 1-324; Latin text in *Opera*, ed. Salzinger, vi, 283-413. See Peers, *Lull*, pp. 273-4; Avinyó, pp. 134-6, no. 63; Platzeck, ii, pp. 30*-31*, no. 81.

2 *Arbor philosophiae amoris*, written in Paris in 1298 and dedicated to Philip iv of France. Catalan text in *Obres*, xviii (Palma 1935), 67-227; Latin text in *Opera*, ed. Salzinger, vi, 159-224. See Peers, *Lull*, pp. 279-87; Avinyó, pp. 146-9, no. 69; Platzeck, ii, p. 33* no. 88. Lefèvre's is the first edition of the Latin text of the *Arbor philosophiae amoris*. The *Proverbia* had already appeared in Barcelona in 1493 (Rogent-Duràn, pp. 18-19, no. 20) and in Venice in 1507 (Rogent-Duràn, p. 36, no. 37). Jean Chapelain, principal physician of Louise of Savoy, sent Lefèvre the *Proverbia*, while the manuscript of the *Philosophia amoris* came from the library of the Paris Carthusians (sig. a, ii^v).

Hvgonis De sancto victore Allegoriarum in vtrunque testamentum libri decem, Paris, Henri Estienne, 10 October 1517. 4°. Edited by Josse Clichtove. (Harvard; Paris, bn; Mazarine; Yale; Panzer, viii, 39, no. 944; A. A. Renouard, *Estienne*, p. 19, no. 1).

The volume contains the *Allegoriae in Vetus et Novum Testamentum*, which correspond to Richard of Saint-Victor's *Liber exceptionum*, part ii, books i-ix and xi-xiv (ed. Jean Chatillon [Paris 1958], pp. 222-372, 439-517). Part i of the *Liber exceptionum* (1155-62) is a universal history; part ii is a treatise on the spiritual and figurative senses – allegorical, tropological, and anagogical – of the historical books of the Old Testament and of the four gospels. For the attribution and contents of the work and for Clichtove's interesting editorial procedures, see Chatillon's introduction, esp. pp. 53-7. A special apparatus usefully notes the principal variants of Clichtove's text. Clichtove himself attributed the work to Hugh rather than Richard of Saint-Victor, no doubt under the influence of a tradition still vigorously defended by the monks of the abbey of Saint-Victor in the early sixteenth century. There is in the Bibliothèque de l'Arsenal a twelfth-century manuscript of the *Liber exceptionum* formerly in the library of Saint-Victor (ms. 266 a, ff. 1-140). On the upper margin of f. 1, a later, probably thirteenth-century hand has added: 'Liber exceptionum magistri Hugonis de Sancto Victore.' The same codex contains a table of contents in the hand of Claude de Grandrue, the librarian of Saint-Victor who catalogued the libary in 1513-14. The table begins: 'Tabula hic contentorum. Liber exceptionum magistri Hugonis de Sancto Victore continens duas partes principales.' Another manuscript from

Saint-Victor reflects the same tradition of attribution: Par. lat. 14504, which the catalogue of Claude de Grandrue also assigns to Hugh (Par. lat. 14767, f. 102ʳ). Cf. Chatillon, 'Le contenu, l'authenticité et la date du *Liber exceptionum* et des *Sermones centum* de Richard de Saint-Victor,' *Revue du moyen âge latin*, IV (1948), 31-2. Clichtove's edition is the first.

XIII

Contemplationes Idiotae. De amore divino. De Virgine Maria. De vera patientia. De continuo conflictu carnis et animae. De innocentia perdita. De morte. Paris, Henri Estienne, August 1519. 4°. Edited by Lefèvre and dedicated to Michel Briçonnet, bishop of Nîmes (7 January 1514 – 3 August 1554). (Chicago, Newberry; Edinburgh, University Library; London, BM; Paris, BN; University of Pennsylvania; Panzer, VIII, p. 55, no. 1091; A. A. Renouard, *Estienne*, p. 22, no. 10).

The *Contemplationes* were very popular in the sixteenth and seventeenth centuries, and Lefèvre's first edition was frequently reprinted. The following editions depend directly on that of 1519 and include Lefèvre's dedicatory epistle:

1 Paris, *Simon de Colines*, 1530, 16°. (Paris, Arsenal; Philippe Renouard, *Bibliographie des éditions de Simon de Colines,1520-1546* [Paris 1894], 161).

2 Paris, Simon de Colines, 1535. 16°. (Harvard; Paris, BSHPF; P. Renouard, *Colines*, 253).

3 Antwerp, Joannes Grapheus for Joannes Steels, 1535. 16°. (London, BM; W. Nijhoff and M. E. Kronenberg, *Nederlandsche bibliographie van 1500 tot 1540* ['s Gravenhage 1923-], no. 1228).

4 Antwerp, Joannes Grapheus for Joannes steels, 1536. 16°. (Oxford, Bodleian; Nijhoff-Kronenberg, no. 3270).

5 Paris, Jean Bignon for Pierre Regnault, 25 April 1538. 16°. (Paris, BN, BSHPF).

6 Paris, Olivier Mallard for Galliot Du Pré and Jean de Roigny, 1538. 16°. (Edinburgh, National Library of Scotland).

7 Antwerp, Joannes Grapheus for Joannes Steels, 1539. 16°. (Nijhoff-Kronenberg, no. 1229).

8 Lyons, Thibaud Payen, 1542. 16°, (Baudrier, IV, 226).

9 Lyons, Thibaud Payen, 1545. 16°. (Paris, BN).

10 Lyons, Thibaud Payen, 1546. 16°. (Baudrier, IV, 234).

11 Antwerp, Joannes Steels, 1546. 16°. (Cambridge, University Library).

12 Lyons, Thibaud Payen, 1546. 16°. (Baudrier, IV, 237. The colophon reads M.D. XLVI, the title page 1547.)

In the sixteenth century 'Idiota' was generally thought to have lived in the ninth century or earlier, and it was not until the middle of the seventeenth century that Théophile Raynaud discovered a manuscript of the works which identified their author as Raymundus Jordanus, a canon regular of St Augustine, prior to the house of his order in Uzès in 1381, and afterwards abbot of the monastery of Selles-sur-Cher in the diocese of Bourges. As the supposed work of a reasonably early Christian writer, the *Contemplationes* found a place in Johannes Heroldt, *Orthodoxographa* (Basel 1555), J. J. Grynaeus, *Monumenta S. Patrum Orthodoxographa* (Basel 1569), in the various editions of La Bigne, *Bibliotheca veterum Patrum*, and in several editions of works by St. Augustine. In August 1518 Guillaume Briçonnet, bishop of Meaux, translated the section of the work entitled *De virgine Maria: Les contemplations faictes a lhonneur et louenge de la tressacree vierge Marie, par quelque deuote personne qui sest voulu nommer Lidiote, translatees par leuesque de Meaux, le xiii. Aoust. M.D. xix.*, [Paris, Henri Estienne, 1519] (Paris, BSHPF; P. Renouard, *Colines*, p. 421; A. Endrès, 'Les débuts de l'imprimerie à Meaux,' *Positions luthériennes*, XII (1964), 101-5). Briçonnet later translated part three of the *Contemplationes, de vera patientia*; for in a letter to Marguerite d'Angoulême dated 22 December 1521 (Paris, BN ms. n. acq. fr. 11495, f. 83)ᵛ he refers to *L'ydyot de vraye patience* which he has lately sent her – information kindly given me by Mr. Henry Heller of the University of Manitoba. A complete French translation appeared in 1538, a Dutch translation by Jan van Alen was published by Willem Vorsterman in Antwerp in 1535 and a Spanish translation by F. Diez de Frias in 1536. There was an English translation in 1662. See the *Catholic Encyclopedia*, VII (1910), 635, and the introduction by Father de Boissieu to his French translation (Saint-Maximin, Var, 1923) and that of Emilo Piovesan to his Italian translation of part I of the *Contemplationes, De amore divino* (Florence 1954).

NOTES

1 The fundamental work on Lefèvre remains Augustin Renaudet, *Préréforme et humanisme à Paris pendant les premières guerres d'Italie (1494-*

1517) (2nd ed. Paris 1953). Among recent studies see: E. Ph. Gold-
schmidt, *Medieval Texts and Their First Appearance in Print*, Supplement to the Bibliographical Society's *Transactions*, XVI (London 1943),
52-7; V. Carrière, 'Lefèvre d'Étaples à l'Université de Paris,' *Etudes
historiques dediées à la mémoire de M. Roger Rodière* (Arras 1947),
107-20; R. Wiriath, 'Les Rapports de Josse Bade Ascensius avec Erasme
et Lefèvre d'Etaples,' *Bibliothèque d'Humanisme et Renaissance*, XI
(1949), 66-71; A.E. Tyler [Elizabeth Armstrong], 'Jacques Lefèvre
d'Etaples and Henri Estienne the Elder, 1502-1520,' *The French Mind:
Studies in Honour of Gustave Rudler* (Oxford 1952), 17-33; M. Villain,
'Le Message biblique de Lefèvre d'Etaples,' *Recherches de science
religieuse*, XL (1952) *(Mélanges Jules Lebreton)* II, 243-59; D.P. Walker,
'The "Prisca Theologia" in France,' *Journal of the Warburg and Courtauld Institutes*, XVII (1954), 204-59; J. Dagens, 'Humanisme et Evan-
gelisme chez Lefèvre d'Etaples,' *Courants religieux et humanisme à la fin
du XV e et au début du XVIe siècle*, colloque de Strasbourg, 9-11 mai 1957
(Paris 1959), 121-34; C. Vasoli, 'Jacques Lefèvre d'Etaples e le origini
del "Fabrismo,"' *Rinascimento*, x (1959), 221-54; R.J. Lovy, *Les Origines
de la réforme française, Meaux, 1518-1546* (Paris 1959) ; Jean Boisset,
'Les "Hecatonomies" de Lefèvre d'Etaples,' *Revue philosophique de la
France et de l'Étranger*, CL (1960), 237-40; J.W. Brush, 'Lefèvre
d'Etaples: Three Phases of his Life and Work,' *Reformation Studies:
Essays in Honor of Roland H. Bainton*, ed. Franklin H. Littell (Richmond,
Va., 1962), 117-28; C. Louise Salley, 'Jacques Lefèvre d'Etaples: Heir of
the Dutch Reformers of the Fifteenth Century,' *The Dawn of Modern
Civilization: Studies in Renaissance, Reformation and Other Topics Presented to Honour Albert Hyma*, ed. Kenneth A. Strand (Ann Arbor,
Mich., 1962), 73-124; E.F. Rice, 'The Humanist Idea of Christian
Antiquity: Jacques Lefèvre d'Etaples and his Circle,' *Studies in the Renaissance*, IX (1962), 126-60; H. de Lubac, 'Les Humanistes chrétiens du
xve-xvie siècle et l'herméneutique traditionelle,' *Archivio di filosofia*, 1-2
(1963), 173-82; *Epistres et Euangiles pour les cinquante et deux sep-
maines de lan*, reproduced in facsimile with introduction, bibliographical
note, and appendices by M.A. Screech, *Travaux d'Humanisme et Renaissance*, LXIII (Geneva), 1964; A.H.T. Levi, 'Humanist Reform in Sixteenth
Century France,' *The Heythrop Journal*, VI (1965), 447-64.

2 *The Correspondence of Sir Thomas More*, ed. Elizabeth Rogers (Princeton 1947), p. 36

3 See now Charles Schmitt, *Gianfrancesco Pico della Mirandola (1469-
1533) and his Critique of Aristotle* (The Hague 1967)

4 *Dr. Johannes Bugenhagens Briefwechsel*, ed. O. Vogt (Stettin 1888), p. 6

5 *De scriptoribus ecclesiasticis* (Paris, Berthold Rembolt for himself and
Jean Petit, 16 October 1512), ff. CCXV^v-CCXVI^v

6 *Politicorum libri octo*, ed. Lefèvre d'Etaples (Paris, Henri Estienne,
5 August 1506), ff. 123^v-4^r

7 See Appendix for a description of these editions. The Roman numerals
used below refer to the volumes listed there.

8 IX, sig. a, i^r; Migne, PL. XXX, cc. 122D-3A and 414B. Cf. C. Lambot, in *Revue bénédictine*, XLVI (1934), 265-82

9 IX, sig. a, i^v

10 IX, sig. a, i^r

11 See Menendez y Pelayo, *Historia de los heterodoxos españoles* (Madrid 1917), III, 278-89; Joan Avinyó, *Història del Lulisme* (Barcelona 1925), pp. 343 ff.; E. Allison Peers, *Ramon Lull: A Biography* (London 1929), pp. 378-85; Thomás and Joaquín Carreras y Artau, *Historia de la filosofia española* (Madrid 1943), II, 31-44.

12 Jaume Custurer, *Disertaciones historicas del culto inmemorial del B. Raymundo Lulio* (Mallorca 1700), disert. II, cap. 7, p. 451. For Juan de Quintana and Luis and Antonio Coronel see R.G. Villoslada, *La Universidad de Paris durante los estudios de Francisco de Vitoria O.P.* (Rome 1938), pp. 386-90, 413, 429.

13 On the Franciscan friar Bernardus de Lavinheta, a zealous Lullist who appears to have spent much of his life in the order's Lyons house, see Georg W.F. Panzer, *Annales typographici ab artis inventae origine ad annum 1536* (Norimbergae 1793-1803), VI, 376, no. 258; *Dictionnaire de théologie catholique*, IX (1926), cc. 36-7; Elíes Rogent and Estanislau Duràn, *Bibliografía de les impressions Lul.lianes* (Barcelona 1927), pp. 59-62, 71-2, 103, 117-18, 144-5; Carreras y Artau, II, 209-14; Frances Yates, 'The Art of Ramon Lull,' *Journal of the Warburg and Courtauld Institutes*, XVII (1954), 166.

14 XI, sig. a, i^v

15 VIII, sig. a, ij^r

16 Gerson, *Epistola prima ad fratrem Bartholomaeum*, ed. André Combes, *Essai sur la critique de Ruysbroeck par Gerson* (Paris 1945), I, 618-19: 'Ponit autem tertia pars libri praefati quod anima perfecte contemplans Deum, non solum videt eum per claritatem quae est divina essentia, sed est ipsamet claritas divina. Imaginatur enim, sicut scripta sonant, quod anima tunc desinit esse in illa existentia quam prius habuit in proprio genere, et convertitur seu transformatur et absorbetur in esse divinum et in illud esse ideale defluit quod habuit ab aeterno in essentia divina. De quo esse dicit Johannes in evangelio: quod factum est in ipso vita erat, et hoc esse ponit auctor iste causam nostrae existentiae temporalis, et esse unum cum eo secundum essentialem existentiam. Addit quod perditur anima contemplantis in esse tali divino abyssali, ita ut reperibilis non sit ab aliqua creatura.' Cf. Melline d'Asbeck, *Documents relatifs à Ruysbroeck* (Paris 1928), pp. 26-64.

17 VIII, sig. a, ij^r

18 Gerson, *Epistola ad fratrem Bartholomaeum*, ed. Combes, *Essai*, p. 617: 'Ceterum stilus ipse libri non sordidus est nec abjectus. Certe tamen induci nequeo credere librum ipsum fuisse conflatum per os idiotae, quasi per miraculum. Stilus enim ipse magis sapit et redolet humanam eloquentiam quam divinam: nam et poetarum verba, ut Terentii et Boetii, et philosophorum sententiae, et orationis cursus ostendunt palam illic studiosam industriam, et diligentiae laborem diuturnum praecessisse.'

19 *Libri Logicorvm ad archetypos recogniti*, ed. Lefèvre d'Etaples (Paris, Wolfgang Hopyl and Henri Estienne, 17 October 1503), sig. a, iᵛ; A. Horowitz and K. Hartfelder, *Briefwechsel des Beatus Rhenanus* (Leipzig 1886), p. 44. Cf. E.F. Rice, in *Studies in the Renaissance*, IX (1962), 129-31

20 VIII, sig. a, ijʳ

21 XII, sig. a, iiᵛ; cf. v, f. 22ᵛ

22 I, sig. a, iᵛ. Lull was self-educated, not uneducated; and although he wrote most of his books in Catalan, he knew Latin well enough to lecture in it and to write several works directly in that language. See S. Bové, Ramon Lull y la llengua llatina,' *Boletin de Real Academia de Buenas Artes de Barcelona*, XIII (1915-16), 65-88.

23 XIII, sig. a, iᵛ-a, ijʳ

24 X, sig. aa, ii,ʳ⁻ᵛ

25 XI, sig. a, i,ᵛ

26 XIII, sig. a, iᵛ–a, ii,ʳ

27 Pseudo-Dionysius, *Opera*, ed. Lefèvre d'Etaples (Paris, Johann Higman and Wolfgang Hopyl, 6 February 1498/9), f. 49ᵛ; x, sig. aa, iiʳ.

28 IX, title pageᵛ

29 v, f. 22ᵛ

30 XII, sig. a, iiᵛ

31 v, f. 22ᵛ

32 III, sig. a, iᵛ

33 I, sig. a, iᵛ: 'Cum duo sint quae vitam nostram rectissime instituunt, universalium scilicet cognitio (quam morales disciplinae pariunt) et operandi modus, qui ordinata operatione comparatur, pauciores profecto invenimus qui singularia ad operandum pandant quam qui recte universalia coniectent. Neque id quidem ab re evenit; nam singularia ad infinitatem devergunt, universalia vero se colligunt ad unitatem. Et cum utrumque ad sancte et beate vivendum necessarium sit, modus tamen operandi (ut qui vicinius ipsam operationem dirigit in qua nostra salus summaque perfectio sita est) praecellere videtur. Unde iure evenit ut hi libri in pretio haberi debeant, qui quae rara et necessaria sunt utiliter monstrant; cuiusmodi revera librum unum pii eremitae Raemundi animadverti, qui operandi modum monstrat, operandi dico, laudandi, orandi, et intentionem finemque dirigendi, quae ad sancte instituendam formandamque vitam unicuique necessaria sunt.'

34 *De cael hier.*, XV, 3 (Migne, PG. III, c. 329 D; ed. René Roques [Paris 1958], p. 173)

35 *Nikolaus von Cues: Werke, Neuausgabe des Strassburger Drucks von 1488*, ed. P. Wilpert (Berlin 1967), I, p. 296

36 *Ibid.*, I, p. 173; Ruysbroeck, *Opera Omnia*, ed. and trans. L. Surius (Cologne, heirs of Johann Quentel, March 1552), pp. 318, 305-6, 352

37 Pseudo-Dionysius, *Opera*, ff. 66ᵛ-8ᵛ. '... tunc nostra nomina deleta sunt (et sponsus aeternus nescit nos), et nichilominus tamen semper scripta si nobis resurgere sit curae, et possumus (ex se enim potest nullus) sed deus

est erector, et qui post casum firmat, et stantium et resurgentium fortitudo et virtus' (f. 67ʳ). Like Erasmus, Lefèvre believed it was especially dangerous to attack free will in front of the young because it would undermine morals.

38 VIII, sig. a, iᵛ: 'Cum omnis particularium religionum status, carissime Raemunde, sit quaedam mundi fuga et ad extramundana accessio, sit multorum et dividuorum derelictio et ad unum adhaesio, tantum igitur quaeque veritatis habet quantum extramundanis et illi uni quod est super omne unum haeret. In qua unione et haerentia vera consistit contemplatio et dulcissimus contemplativae vitae fructus ... Et nullam esse puto particularem religionem in qua etiam non sint aut fuerint aliqui qui nonnihil huius dulcedinis perceperint, et maxime quae magis solitariae, abstractae, arctae sunt ... Quapropter et libros contemplativorum virorum vel maxime amant, non quod libri contemplativos faciant maxime perfectiores, sed praeparant et incitant incipientes; Deus autem cetera complet. Nam altiori modo contemplativos radius caelestis efficit et divina quaedam congressio.'

39 III, sig. a, iᵛ

40 Appendix, VII

41 *Contenta In Hoc Volvmine. Pimander. Mercurij Trismegisti liber de de (sic) sapientia et potestate dei. Asclepius. Eiusdem Mercurij liber de voluntate diuina. Item Crater Hermetis A Lazarelo Septempedano* (Paris, Henri Estienne, 1 April 1505), f. 36ʳ

42 VI, ff. 19ᵛ-20ʳ: 'Quia gradus quibus ab imis ad summa ascendere solemus haec sunt: esse, vita, sensus, ratio, intellectus, mens. Esse infimum locum tenet, vita ei proximum, sensus supra vitam, ratio supra sensum, intellectus supra rationem, mens vero supra intellectum. Lapis est, planta vivit, animal sentit, homo ratiocinatur, angelus intelligit, mens autem iugiter Deo haeret ... Malim igitur ipsum [Deum] potius dicere intellectualem quam rationalem, et potius super intellectualem quam intellectualem, super intellectum et super mentem quam intellectum aut mentem.'

43 VI, sig. a, iᵛ-a, ii ʳ; ff. 5ʳ⁻ᵛ; 7ʳ⁻ᵛ; 8ʳ

44 VI, f. 5ʳ

45 VI, ff. 7ʳ⁻ᵛ: 'Tribus cognoscendi vires perfici: sensu, imaginatione, intellectu; et tres esse earum cognoscendi modos: experientiam, ratiocinationem, et fidem ... sic experientia cognitionum initium est, infimum tenens cognitionis modum ut sensus quidam; fides summum ut intellectus; ratiocinatio medium ut imaginatio. Experientia sensibilium singularium est et ultimorum cognoscibilium; fides intelligibilium primorum et summorum. Nam obiectum eius prima veritas, humane humana et divine divina, ut experientia ultimorum veritatis vestigiorum, ratiocinatio mediorum ab universalibus et cognoscibilibus mentis humanae suffragium quaerens. Et fides maxime divina lumen est animorum et primae veritatis infulgentia. Quo fit ut nullus sit fide superior cognoscendi modus, quam si qui non capiunt, non aliter fidei iniuria id obtingit quam diurne lucis iniuria si ipsa non capitur ab oculo nycteridis.' Cf. x, sig. aa, iiᵛ: 'Enimvero tripli-

cem comperio theologiam: primam et summam, intellectualem; secundam
et mediam, rationalem; tertiam ac infimam, sensualem ac imaginariam.
Prima in pace veritatem indagat; secunda aperto Marte rationis via ex
veris falsum expugnat; tertia in insidiis ex quibuslibet etiam falsis verum
oppugnare nititur. In prima lux maior minorem offundit; in secunda
lumen tenebris opponitur; in tertia tenebrae lumini. Prima in silentio
docet; secunda in sermonis modestia; tertia in multiloquio perstrepit.
Prima sursum habitans, si quando demittit oculu, id facit, ut ex imis
rursum sibi reparet ascensum; secunda, alis rationis fulta, media luminis
inhabitat loca; tertia, quasi humi repens, obscuritatibus involvitur et
variis obruitur phantasmatum tenebris. Primae lucis immensitas tenebrae,
cuius ignoratio potior est scientia; secundae finitum lumen lumen est,
cuius scientia praecipua possessio; tertiae tenebrae lumen apparent, est-
que huius partis opinio, scientia et multo magis illa ignoratione deterior.'
46 Carolus Bovillus, *In artem oppositorum introductio* (Paris, Wolfgang
   Hopyl, 24 December 1501), sig. a i^v-a, ii^r: 'In rationali valuit Aristoteles,
   in intellectuali forte Parmenides, Anaxagoras, Heraclitus et Pythagoras ...
   Ergo si ita est, Aristoteles studiorum vita est, Pythagoras autem studiorum
   mors, vita superior; hinc rite docuit hic tacendo, ille vero loquendo, sed
   silentium actus est et vox privatio. Et ut tibi et multis hac in parte prosim,
   in Paulo et Dionysio multum silentium, deinde in Cusa et Victorini
   ὁμοουσίω, in Aristotle autem silentii perparum, vocum multum, nam silentium dicit et tacet voces, siquidem voces diceret, simpliciter taceret.' Cf.
   R. Klibansky, 'Plato's Parmenides in the Middle Ages.' *Mediaeval and
   Renaissance Studies*, I (1941-3), 281-9; Victorinus Afer, *De ὁμοουσίω
   recipiendo* (Migne, PL, VIII, cc. 1137-49) and P. Séjourné, in *Dictionnaire de théologie catholique*, XV, 2 (1950), cc. 2887-954.
47 Pseudo-Dionysius, *Opera*, f. 77^r
48 *Politicorum libri octo*, f. 98^r
49 Renaudet, *Préréforme et humanisme*, p. 620, n. 6

'By little and little':
The early Tudor humanists
on the development of man

Arthur B. Ferguson

Most Renaissance scholars would nowadays agree that humanism derived its distinctive character and made its distinctive contribution to Renaissance culture less through any absolute originality than through the new uses to which it put old ideas, less through its study of the classics as such, than through the new questions it asked of them, less through any preoccupation with the past, classical or whatever, than through an intense preoccupation with the present and its problems. However, the full import of this near truism seems not as yet fully appreciated. Failure to understand its implications has done much to perpetuate that interpretive smog which still appears to hang over Renaissance studies, especially when viewed from a distance.

An interesting case in point is the use the English humanists made of classical speculation on the early career of man on earth. Although their references to such accounts may at first glance seem little more than examples of the pious cribbing from the classics for which their kind has on occasion been criticized, closer examination will reveal that they have been placed in a context which gives them fresh meaning. In the context of social analysis and reform this borrowed anthropology became a useful point of departure for any examination of society and one especially valued in an age peculiarly preoccupied with origins. Or, to put it another way, it provided a vanishing point logically necessary to a gradually clarifying temporal perspective in which the fact of social development could become more clearly recognizable. In this sense it becomes one aspect of that deepening sense of history which was becoming so important a part of humanist thought – this even though it told nothing provable about the beginnings and early history of civilization. It also throws considerable light on the early history of progressivist thought.

Perhaps it is in relation to this latter problem that the humanist anthropology becomes most immediately pertinent. The notion of progress continues to haunt the modern mind even in this age of disillusionment.[1] Indeed, because of our very disenchantment with it, we have tended to criticize the idea rather than to forget it or relegate it to the inactive file of intellectual history. Some have even turned upon the idea with amazing venom, finding in it not the natural product of the scientific revolution but a debased form of Christian eschatology and Jewish messianism – in short, a heresy to be extirpated.[2] Meanwhile, the older interpretation still stands as a sort of secular orthodoxy, largely as Bury established it. However, neither the Baconians nor those who find the idea of progress a Judaeo-Christian heresy have done much to clarify the nature of Renaissance thought: to throw light, that is, on a period that might reasonably be supposed to tell something about the emergence of an idea so characteristic of the modern mind. The former have tended to underrate and at times misconstrue the role of humanism in this respect, and the latter tend to leave the humanists in a sort of trackless waste that extends pretty much from Joachim of Flora to the heavenly city of the eighteenth-century philosophers. Despite the element of truth in both interpretations, they share a common weakness; a tendency to leave unexplained those shifts in intellectual climate which were essential to the eventual germination of new ideas. It is to this process of changing attitudes and emphasis that the English humanists made a significant contribution.

The history of humanism in pre-Elizabethan England is more than the story of a new scholarship, fundamental as that was to Renaissance thought. It is also – and herein lies its peculiar character – the story of how this new learning was applied in the pursuit of socially desirable ends. For by the time humanism reached England it had already accomplished much of its pioneer work in the area of scholarship and had to a large extent outgrown its preoccupation with form. What impressed Englishmen of the first half of the sixteenth century was not so much the actual content of classical learning as the applicability of the example and precept it afforded to contemporary life, not so much the rules of rhetoric as its adaptability for use as a tool of persuasion in the interests of policy. Theirs was of course a Christian humanism in the best Erasmian sense of the term; and, since their work coincided more or less with religious upheaval, it often tended to be drawn into the special service of ecclesiastical controversy. But throughout the period it retained a distinctly secular aspect. The writings of men like Thomas Starkey, for example, or Sir Thomas Smith, reveal a willingness to explore secular affairs as an area peculiarly and legitimately open to rational analysis and susceptible to reform through constructive policy. To a much greater extent than their predecessors, the social critics of medieval England, they were able to see beyond the moral nature of man to his creative potential and to reinterpret the traditional and ostensibly static concept of the organic commonwealth in terms of the causal forces actually operating within it. Despite the depressing evidence presented by unchristian warfare among Christian peoples and social changes which could be, and frequently were, interpreted as decay within the divinely ordained scheme of things, these men were able to think with some degree of consistency in terms of social development.[3]

It was, therefore, only natural that some of them – in particular, those who undertook a more or less systematic critique of their society – should elect to begin their investigation from what they considered a solid basis in moral philosophy and history – which is to say in man's creative potential and in the history of his actual progress from simple and barbarous beginnings to a civilized state. Naturally, too, given their educational background and prejudices, these writers sought both, but especially the latter, in the writings of classical antiquity. On the spiritual life and on all ethical considerations related to it they relied largely on their Christian heritage, with, of course, gratefully accepted assistance from the many compatible elements in pagan philosophy. But, on the necessarily speculative history of early man, they found what they believed to be a more coherent account in classical literature than in the scriptures, though they recognized no irreconcilable conflict between the two. In other words, they found in classical tradition a theme peculiarly adaptable to their own reforming purposes, for it implied that man's rise to civilized status was a natural process depending on the ability of the human mind to adjust to, and eventually to shape, its environment.[4] They could have found others. The ancients differed widely as to the earliest condition of man: was it idyllic or wretched, innocent or beastly, a Golden Age or very like what moderns call the Stone Age? They differed also about man's subsequent development: was it good or bad, progressing or degenerating, or was it caught in a hopeless series of recurrent cycles? Renaissance readers could and did find classical support for a variety of theories. The humanists of early Tudor England who attempted to analyze their society in the name of the 'very and true commonweal' in fact chose only one. With remarkable consistency they chose to believe, with Aristotle, perhaps, or Lucretius or Vitruvius or, still more likely, Cicero (the immediate source of so widespread an idea is unimportant), that man was originally a cave dweller who gradually adapted himself to the exigencies of his mundane existence and eventually was able to construct social institutions and cultivate the arts of civilized life. By the same token, although they were by no means uniformly happy with the results of this process, they did manage to avoid the pessimistic implications inherent in the notion of a past Age of Gold and in the prospect of a recurrent round of growth and decay. What interested them in the more progressive accounts – or rather in the progressive aspects of these versions, for they conveniently ignored the promise of ultimate disintegration usually appended to even the most glowing rehearsal of past achievements – was that mankind had apparently used its natural endowments in the past in order to do what these critics now hoped to do, namely, create a better society; and then, as now, it had been up to man himself whether the results of his efforts would be good or bad.

The humanist reformer was not, it is true, much given to looking far ahead. The perspective of the past was not yet so compelling as to prompt speculation into the distant future. The 'commonwealth men' thought they already knew what a true commonwealth should be, and it was not too different from their own society, intelligently reformed. Even the imaginary society of Utopia existed in the present. Indeed, there is much in the so-called commonwealth literature to indicate that reform could still mean merely the restoration of an ideal *status quo ante*. But the discussion of constructive policy, increasingly characteristic of that literature by the mid-century, belied the conservative implications in the traditional concept of the 'commonweal.' The spirit had already outstripped the letter.

What sustained this qualified optimism, what in fact determined the humanist's approach to both present problems and past achievements, was his deep and stubborn faith in the educability of man. Despite the discouraging evidence of events, he clung to the happy assumption that, although man had in him the potentiality for evil as well as good, the good could always be induced by proper education and by that quality of right thinking which it made possible. If there is characteristic exaggeration in Erasmus' epigram, *homines non nascuntur sed finguntur*, and if this to him carried no necessarily optimistic implications, that statement did bear within it an implied environmentalism which could well open the way to a developmental view of man's earthly history. Now it is just this dawning awareness of the possibilities inherent in the interaction of environment and the creative intellect that gives fresh meaning to the humanist's borrowed anthropology.

Two writers in particular wrote at sufficient length on these matters to make possible analysis in some depth. Though hardly an evenly matched pair, their thought followed roughly parallel paths. One was Thomas Starkey, the Englishman trained in Italy and drawn with others of similar background into the service of the Tudor state in that critical period marked by Thomas Cromwell's ascendancy. For the other I must beg to have recourse to the unwritten law of Tudor studies which allows the researcher to make use of those fortunate and influential visitors who found the England of Henry VIII, for a while at least, a congenial place in which to work. Juan Luis Vives, like Erasmus and Polydore Vergil, spent several of his most creative years in England and left there an intellectual legacy which has not in his case been fully explored but which must surely have been rich.

In his *Dialogue between Cardinal Pole and Thomas Lupset*[5] Starkey set out to determine what were the characteristics necessary for a true commonwealth and what had to be done in England to achieve those desiderata. It was a typically humanist dialogue concerning a typical humanist problem, one involving the application of intelligence to the achievement of a society compatible with the natural dignity of man. And, with an equally characteristic desire to trace problems to their origins, Starkey saw it as one continuously facing man ever since the beginning of his life on earth.

Those beginnings were poor indeed. 'Stories many and diverse' tell of a time when man lived 'without city or town, law or religion,' when he 'wandered abroad in the wild fields and woods none other wise than you see now brute beasts to do,' when he was 'led and drawn without reason and rule by frail fantasy and inordinate affects.' From this unfortunate condition he was rescued by 'certain men of great wit and policy' who 'with perfit eloquence and high philosophy' persuaded him to leave his rude life and to realize the higher perfection inherent in his nature. The process of building cities and especially of creating laws took time, 'for it was not possible suddenly to enact law and policy to bring such a rude multitude to perfit civility.' But, in the long run, men were brought 'by little and little' to 'this civility which you now see established and set in all well-ruled cities and towns.'[6]

This process had, it would appear, been an essentially intellectual one, brought about largely by the leadership and inventive genius of great minds. In another passage Starkey refers to the example of Plato, Lycurgus, and Solon 'by whose wisdom and policy divers cities, countries and nations were brought to civil order and politic life.'[7] He would appear, in fact, to be looking to some agency like Polydore Vergil's 'inventors' or More's King Utopus,[8] any of whom were capable of making some catastrophic change in the direction of human life. Starkey, however, is not content simply to name inventors; nor is he willing to follow the Euhemeristic shortcut[9] to which many Renaissance minds had recourse in their effort to establish the origin of customs and the arts. Civil order and politic life had been achieved only 'by "little and little" and in large part by adjustment to circumstances.' The human intellect, he believed, was an instrument both potentially creative and uniquely sensitive to its environment.

In support of this conviction he again returned to ancient thought. Man's mind is hindered by no inborn obstacle from recognizing and solving practical problems and profiting by education. For 'after the sentence of Aristotle, the mind of man first of itself is as a clean and pure table, wherein is nothing painted or carved, but of itself apt and indifferent to receive all manner of pictures and image.' True, it has an inborn conscience which will react appropriately to external stimuli whether of evil or good; but it is for all practical purposes open to that training which embodies a knowledge of the good, a knowledge from which virtuous action will ultimately stem. And if it is argued that reason and the will are both subject to 'strong opinion' and 'persuasion,' surely 'diligent instruction and wise counsel may at last in long time restore the will out of such captivity.'[10] So it is that the truly learned, and hence virtuous, man occupies a very important place in society. He is, in fact, the agent by which society achieves its true objective. For 'hither tendeth all prudence and policy; to bring the whole country to quietness and civility, that every man, and so the whole, may at the last attain to such perfection as by nature is to the dignity of man due.'[11]

Mind, then, is the moving force in society. When properly conditioned, it is capable of realizing the potential for good inherent in man's nature. It is capable of so ordering things as to approximate more and more to that perfection to which man is by his nature inclined. Yet it is also the product of its environment. This is the conclusion toward which Starkey's borrowed epistemology impelled him. It is also related to his sense of historical relativism. Although all men at all times are subject to the uniformities of natural law, variations in place and time bring about varying responses in the form of custom and civil law. That law 'taketh effect of the opinion of man; it resteth wholly in his consent and varieth according to place and time, insomuch that in diverse time and place contrary laws are both good and convenient to the politic life.'[12]

Starkey shared the teleological bent of the Aristotelian tradition, with its sense of universal becoming. Indeed, it penetrated his thought and goes far toward explaining this sense of development. Man, like all creatures, he saw striving to achieve the end inherent in his nature. But Starkey did not believe that man was bound to succeed; for there were subrational tendencies in his nature which had always to be kept in check. That some degree of success was likely, however, Starkey seems to have held as an article of faith, faith in the dignity and rational capacity of man.

Of the two opposing myths from which most classical estimates of the life of primitive man emerged, Starkey clearly preferred the Promethean over that of the Golden Age. For a moment his interlocutors do toy with the question whether civilization has after all been a boon, only to drop it for the duration of the discussion. His mind had little room for the romantics' picture of an original age of innocent simplicity. The human race had progressed from origins no sane person would wish to return to, and it had done so only slowly and by hard work.

How long that process would continue into the future is quite another matter. Characteristically, he seems to have given it little thought. Like the rest of the more socially oriented of the early Tudor humanists, he was concerned primarily with the present and its problems. He had a vision of what a true commonwealth should be and it was not so very different from the England he knew or, at any rate, what it might be with some rational, but hardly radical, changes. He may, indeed, have thought that the 'right ordering of a common weal' might one day conceivably achieve its purpose. Traditional values, quite characteristic of medieval thought, still existed in Starkey's mind along with apparently incompatible attitudes more characteristically modern. In one and the same breath he can refer to 'quietness and civility' as the end of policy – desiderata more suitable to the traditional and basically static notion of the 'body politic,' which he also accepts without question, than to the modern idea of the state – and to the process by which society may in time achieve the perfection inherent in human nature.[13]

Perhaps, if asked, he would have followed his classical authorities by admitting the likelihood of cyclical decline following any period of growth. It was, after all, an idea almost inevitable among humanist scholars whose concept of historical periods depended to a large extent on their sense of having taken up where the ancients had left off and having rescued culture from the long slump of the 'middle' age. Or he could have had recourse to some application to worldly affairs of the Christian story. As it is, he did neither. He had none of the instincts of the prophet, nor did he see any reason for making imminent Christian eschatology. His concern was with the present and its problems, and he had come to see those problems in the perspective of past achievement. But the possibility of decline lay always implicit in his idea of human nature: man could always be diverted from good by evil 'affects.' It was therefore up to man himself whether he allowed this to happen or followed that 'sparkle' of the divine in him toward the realization of his human potential.

It will, I believe, be possible to see Starkey's ideas in the right perspective if we set them side by side with the more mature and more fully articulated thought of Vives. There may well have been a more than coincidental relationship between them, though the generally parallel lines their thinking followed could merely reflect much that was by the twenties and thirties in the common domain of northern humanism. Certainly Vives showed the same sense of public duty which animated so many of the scholars of early Tudor England, even if he did not share their insularity. He did not hesitate to offer advice to Henry VIII on matters of state. Indeed he appears to have offered it once too often and had as a consequence to leave England. During the six years of his stay there (1522-8) he became well known in the circle of English humanists. He wrote parts of his influential treatise on education during that period. And his treatise on poor relief, written in 1526 for the city fathers of Bruges, was translated by William Marshall and became the model for the latter's 'policy paper' on the subject.[14] Although the reforming ideas of the English humanists of this period are usually spoken of as Erasmian – and rightly so if considered in the broadest meaning of Christian humanism – in their more specific analysis of society they might more accurately be called Vivesian.

Like Starkey, Vives considered man's development from an uncivil to a civil state as a distinctly human achievement – within, of course, the limits prescribed by the will and purposes of the Creator. Like Starkey, too, Vives grounded his idea of man in the epistemology of a Christianized Aristotelianism. The senses are the doorway to knowledge. The arts and civilized society are born of experience, ordered by reason: 'whatever is in the arts was in nature first ... Therefore, the first observers who hoped that something could be brought into some art are the first discoverers of the arts ... Experience through various applications has made art.'[15] Like Starkey, he saw in man's ability to profit by experience, to turn knowledge to useful ends, a virtually inexhaustible potential,[16] provided of course that it be directed by that sense of right and wrong somehow embedded in the mind even before it was subjected to the impact of sense perception. Man was, in short, quite capable of adjusting to and of remaking his environment. His nature might be fixed in the divine act of creation, but his society could change and, in one way or another, develop.

On the actual process of development Vives is much clearer than Starkey. Although they both recognized that it had been slow, a matter of 'by little and little,' and essentially the work of man himself, Vives was more specific in his reconstruction of man's early efforts to adjust to his environment and to satisfy his basic needs.[17] Starting with the natural desire for self-preservation, Vives pictures man gradually finding the foods most suitable for him and avoiding, where possible, the diseases to which his flesh was prone, discovering how to protect his body by clothing and the shelter of caves, and later constructing 'huts and tents' of bits of wood and branches of trees. At the same time family affection led him from the common life of the cave to a separate and scattered exist- ence over the open plain. But the need for mutual assistance necessitated the formation of villages. The disputes unavoidable in such communities required a judicial and law-making agency and the need for common protection required military defence. 'Changes in these conditions were brought about in the course of time according to opportunities; daily business brought men together, and speech bound them to move as close- ly as possible amongst one another in an indivisible perpetual society.'[18]

The conditions of an emerging culture became in themselves circum- stances promoting further growth. The development of speech made pos- sible communication in public which in turn permitted minds to 'reveal themselves,' thus providing the conditions necessary for rational action and the exercise of 'practical wisdom' – that agency, so dear to the heart of the humanist reformer, which is 'like a rudder for guiding a ship' and embraces 'all the humanities.'[19] To this process of communication the art of writing made a further contribution, absolutely vital to the trans- mission of knowledge. Esdras realized that the law, to be maintained in- tact, would have to be written; the Druids, by failing to recognize this fact, left only a fragmentary and garbled tradition.[20]

In the course of its unfolding, the mind passed from necessities to conveniences, especially at times of peace and quietness which Vives held to be essential to cultural growth.[21] At this point it becomes apparent that something more than the instinct to preserve life and property has been at work. Curiosity, the pleasure of discovery, has become a positive ele- ment capable of creating the superstructure of knowledge through which man comes to understand himself and the universe and in which he finds the means most suited to the growth of his 'practical wisdom.' Though potentially dangerous, always likely to feed pride as well as wisdom, to foster a tendency toward the short-cut of magic as well as rational investigation, this pleasure possessed an even greater potential for good. It was in any event a progressive element. It was 'constantly increasing, since some things seemed to follow from the finding of others.'[22] The arts, 'never either perfect or pure, not even in their beginnings,' evolved gradually by way of cumulative experience and intelligent reflection thereupon: 'from a number of separate experiments the mind gathered a universal law,' which was then handed down and combined with newly discovered data by 'men of great and distinguished intellect.'[23] Curiosity and the desire for knowledge could not of course transcend the limitations of local circumstance. The Chaldeans and Egyptians owed their early knowledge of the stars to the fact that they lived on plains and under clear skies. And the development of navigation by the canny Phoenicians illustrated that the prospect of profit could be a great stimulus.[24]

It is interesting to notice that Vives places the emergence of religion rather late in this process of cultural evolution. In the course of time certain wise men began to realize that the 'onrush of mental energy' which had produced the arts of civilized life must have some still more remote, still higher goal, one beyond the range of the 'small lamp' afforded the human mind. In short, man needed God.[25] Religion thus completed what the arts could not. Careful as Vives had been to keep philosophy from, as he said, leaping across to theology,[26] he was above all else a Christian humanist, and the 'reasons' he sought in nature could, he knew, lead him so far and no farther. But it is also important that he recognized in that distance traversable by reason in nature the measure of a virtually unlimited opportunity for the free and legitimate activity of the creative intellect.

As Vives reconstructs the early history of man it becomes apparent how far he has gone, not only beyond his contemporaries but beyond his classical sources, especially in his appreciation of the psychological and environmental conditions which directed the evolution of societies and cultures. There is, moreover, little in his reconstruction to indicate that dependence upon the sudden contributions of 'inventors,' either human or demigod, which preoccupied Polydore Vergil and robbed his treatise *De inventoribus rerum* of much of its anthropological value. Indeed Vives allowed even less room than Starkey to catastrophic creativity. He gave, it is true, due credit to 'great minds,' to Hippocrates, for example, for distilling rules from experience, to Aristotle for organizing data and clarifying thought;[27] but he also recognized that the achievements of civilization had involved a gradual adjustment to the circumstances of life, an intelligent exploitation of the opportunities they afforded, and an exploration, equally gradual, of the powers of speech and writing. Even the contribution of an Aristotle or an Hippocrates is the result of the patient building upon foundations laid by others. Nor was he impressed by the reputation commonly enjoyed in his own day by the ancient writers. Much as he admired Aristotle, he was quite prepared to find him deficient in comparison to modern scholarship.[28] Why, he asks in effect, should we expect the definitive from such a pioneer, *nam nulla ars simul et inventa est, et absoluta?*[29]

Indeed his study of both ancient and modern achievements had convinced him that his own contemporaries were unduly humble. He deplored their tendency to look upon the ancients as supermen or demigods and themselves as mere men. And he rejected the venerable cliché that modern men were at best but dwarfs standing upon the shoulders of giants.[30] They were, he asserted, just as capable as the men of antiquity, and, all things considered, they could, by applying themselves with comparable diligence, render better judgments on matters of life and nature than Aristotle, Plato, or any other of the ancients.[31]

The problem was, of course, this very matter of diligence. Basically Vives was proud of man's ancient achievements and optimistic regarding his abilities. There was no place in his thought for the widespread notion that all nature was decaying and sinking like all organisms into unavoidable senescence. Such pessimism was foreign to the nature of most of these dealers in reform through the application of 'practical wisdom.' But man was his own master in all this, and human nature had in it the potentiality for both success and failure. Modern men could outstrip the ancients, but it would take self-discipline and hard work, the kind of hard work that had in fact gone into the making of civil society in the first place. This is the burden of his treatise *De causis corruptorum artium*. The arts have suffered at the hands of men who, through indolence, ignorance, avarice, or false pride – those evil 'affects' which Starkey also feared – have taken short-cuts to learning.[32] The ancients themselves have been shabbily used by these pseudo-scholars with their everlasting *compendia* and *florilegia*.[33] The history of culture, Vives recognized, had in fact been far from one of steady improvement. The barbarians, for example, had ushered in a long period of decline.[34] Vives remained nevertheless optimistic. The treatise concerning the corruption of the arts must be balanced – as Vives asuredly meant it to be – by the companion treatise *De tradendis disciplinis* which proclaimed the educability of man and reconstructed his actual rise from humble beginnings. The human race had obviously had its ups and downs; but Vives seems to have regarded them neither as inevitable nor, more remarkably, as evidence of the kind of cyclical recurrence which had so frequently clouded the long-term prospects of mankind in the writings of antiquity.

Optimism, even the wary optimism of Vives and Starkey, did not always accompany a naturalistic anthropology in the humanist thought of this period. It was, after all, a period marked by eruptions within the Christian world which bade fair to destroy what was left of the ideal of a unified Christendom and which must have been discouraging indeed to the Christian humanist.[35] It took a sturdy mind to see beyond the confusion of the present into the long perspective of history without reading into the past the discouragement of the moment. It must have been especially difficult for Vives who, like Erasmus, considered himself a citizen of the republic of letters and who was therefore bound to be sensitive to things that affected all of Christendom.[36] Starkey, whose vision was more nearly limited to the problems of the island kingdom, no doubt escaped some of this difficulty. Be that as it may, the fact remains that both men managed to preserve a certain humane equanimity in the face of disaster, actual or potential, real or imagined. Erasmus, on the other hand, saw no reason to view the development of man with anything like the same degree of optimism. Yet, and this is significant, he used much the same evidence for the pre-history of society and interpreted it in similarly naturalistic terms.

No doubt following the somewhat equivocal speculations of Lucretius, Erasmus also had recourse to the picture of pre-civilized man living in caves and as yet barely differentiated, except for the divine spark within him, from the brute beasts. But he found the idea far from reassuring. Still less was he tempted to make it the starting point for any general analysis of society. His thought was not historically oriented to the same extent as that of either Vives or Starkey.[37] His approach to the problems of society, trenchant as it was and at times bitter, was that of the satirist rather than the analyst or the devisor of policy. Still less was it that of the historian. Although his faith in the educability of man prevented him from taking a uniformly gloomy view of the course of history, one contemporary problem sent him back to the birth of civilization in an effort to explain how man, with all his creative capacity, had managed to use his talents to such miserable effect. What depressed him was, of course, the spectacle of Christian princes fighting each other and for reasons quite incompatible with the *philosophia Christi*. And he believed man's bellicose propensities were rooted in the very process by which he adjusted to natural circumstances and progressed thereby from primitive barbarism to a more sophisticated existence.

He pictured man at first having to fight for his life against beasts, a fact which gave a peculiar prestige to the best fighter.[38] From fighting beasts to fighting other men was an easy and natural step. Similarly, 'in process of time,' combat of man against man evolved into group combat in which 'many assembled to take part together, either as affinity, or as neighborhood, or kindred bound them.' Somewhere along the line arms more sophisticated than sticks and stones were devised 'by ingenious craft.' Finally, 'by little and little' (the phrase is the seemingly inevitable choice of the Tudor translator), it came about that cities and whole countries became embroiled in warfare to such an extent that they gave to that 'manifest madness' a certain legality of custom. Thus, while accepting without question the fact of man's development, Erasmus had the insight to recognize that in particular instances that development could be pernicious in its end product. Where the race was to go in the future he does not suggest; but we may assume that he retained some of that stubborn optimism in the face of discouraging fact which in any age keeps the educator and the satirist in business.

Of the other writers directly or indirectly associated with that reforming, 'applied' humanism which was so characteristic of early Tudor England, less need be said. Most of them shared the attitude toward man and his development more fully articulated by Starkey and Vives. John Colet is, however, an enlightening exception, as, in a very different way, is Polydore Vergil. Keen as was his sense of history, Colet could exercise it only within the scheme of the history of salvation. Whereas Vives, for example, took the fall of man for granted as the beginning of his 'natural' history,[39] Colet could not avoid its implications which, he was convinced, permeated all history and prevented any meaningful interpretation of human development in terms of adaptation to natural environment. After the sin of Adam, nature constituted a fallen estate. The law of nature itself was a corrupt law, and those laws which emanated from it, the law of nations and civil law, retained the stigma of a 'tainted and impaired nature.' Only the grace of God and the historical event of Christ's advent promised any escape from this 'general depravity.'[40] This no doubt remained the attitude of many whose concerns were, like Colet's, primarily with the reform of religion. But the context within which the progressivist elements of classical thought enjoyed a new life and a fresh interpretation was that not of religious but of social reform.

Lack of such a setting for his investigation of the beginnings of civilized life may help explain the somewhat paradoxical position of Polydore Vergil in this respect. A practising historian and a pioneer of a sort in the comparative study of cultures, he shared and abetted the appetite of his contemporaries for origins, and he collected a vast amount of material on the 'first begetters of things.' Yet he failed to place the evidence derived from his classical authors in any working relationship with the concerns of the present.[41] His willingness to be content once he had discovered in ancient literature the inventor, real or mythical, of an art or a custom serves to highlight the fact that others subordinated such data to the process by which man 'by little and little' achieved a sophisticated culture. Certainly he had far less understanding than Thomas More or Vives of the psychological and environmental factors which caused men to invent or which made different peoples at different times adopt similar beliefs.[42] His view of what he apparently considered the golden age of invention, that early era in which history shades off into myth, remains oddly static. Only when he comes to deal with religion, and more particularly with that of his own pre-Reformation church, does he reveal any understanding of cultural processes. Then, for example, he is on occasion able to see significant similarities between Christian and pagan practices and to suggest that one derived from the other.[43] Otherwise he remains every inch the scholarly antiquarian, the collector of *curiosa*, recording with a minimum of comment the fruits of his wide reading among the 'authors.' It comes, therefore, as no surprise to find that his essentially positivistic mind left little room for any philosophy of history more penetrating than that which he stated in his *Anglica historia* when he remarked that 'all things human do ebb and flow so that nothing is so certain as uncertainty itself and continual change either into better or worse.'[44]

Thomas More is quite another matter. Although he did not, in *Utopia*, make direct use of classical theories about primitive man, that work, which did so much to create the very context of social concern in which subsequent English commentators laboured, bears the distinct suggestion of just that gradual rise from humble beginnings to a condition of relative civilization, just that creative solution to natural problems which was implied in the borrowed anthropology of his contemporaries – this even though the actual constitution of the Utopian state had been the work of a single law-giver, a creative intellect like Starkey's Lycurgus or Solon. The Utopians were 'exceedingly apt in the invention of the arts which promote the advantage and convenience of life,' and their chronicles tell of striking advances, most notably in architecture. They were also quick to make use of an imported scholarship and the principles of printing and paper-making which visiting travellers described for them.[45] What their very early state had been, More does not say; but no one who, like himself, had read Vespucci's reports of his voyages to the new world would have nourished any romantic illusions about the life of primitive peoples.[46]

Sir Thomas Elyot, on the other hand, resorted directly to the familiar classical account of the origin and development of civilization. He did so within the more particular context of educational reform. This did not, of course, seriously restrict the scope of his thought, for, as we have seen, the assumption of man's educability underlay the entire structure of humanist thought in England at this period. It may, however, help to explain a special emphasis in his reference to the beginnings of civil society. Whereas Vives traced those beginnings to the gradual response of man to his environment and Starkey assigned the creative role to philosophers and law-givers while retaining the concept of 'by little and little,' Elyot gives credit rather summarily to 'orators' and follows classical mythology by giving specific credit to 'Mercurius ... or some other man.'[47] Although he may not have given as much thought to this subject as either Vives or Starkey (his reference to the primitive life of man is both standard and perfunctory), he no doubt had reason for this emphasis on orators. Since he was, in the *Governor* (1531), dealing with the basic problem of education for citizenship, it was only natural that he should give a high place to the arts of persuasion. Moreover, to him, as to his fellow humanists, rhetoric meant more than a mere competence in speech and writing. It was the medium through which knowledge informs wisdom and makes it possible for wisdom, in turn, to accomplish its social purpose.

This is clearly how the more or less professional rhetoricians among the humanists visualized their function in society and in the history of man. Thomas Wilson, the best of the rhetoricians of Tudor England, considered men of eloquence, capable of interpreting the dictates of reason, to have been the divinely appointed agents by whose ministrations mankind, after the fall, was brought from the familiar state of quasi-bestial nature to 'society.' The task had been difficult; but 'after a certain space' the power of eloquence and reason made 'of wild, sober: of fools, wise: and of beasts, men.'[48] It becomes apparent, however, that, although Wilson made the customary use of classical anthropology, he used it within a quite different setting. Not only was he thinking, like his fellow humanists, of the potential existing in the art of rhetoric for creating a reasonable society, he was also thinking of the process of civilization as an episode within the theological history of man, a restoration by God's grace rather than adjustment of man to his natural environment. Reason and the eloquence that interprets it were there all the time, ready for men appointed by God for the purpose to set them to work.

Whether or not Vives and Starkey would have gone this far with Wilson – without denying its truth, they would have found his theological view of history, in this context, somewhat beside the point – they would have agreed with him and with Elyot about the importance of rhetoric as a factor in social development.[49] The humanists naturally enough tended to create the founders of civilization in their own image and to interpret the development of society as a process of intellectual leadership and 'counsel.' But some of them, especially Vives, were able to go one step beyond to those basic material and psychological factors which they knew had to precede the more sophisticated stage of eloquence and persuasion.

It was, no doubt, as rhetoricians, broadly considered, that in so many humanist writings throughout the century poets received credit for inspiring and even for shaping civilized life. This is clearly how Stephen Hawes, earlier in the century, saw them. In his semi-humanist, semichivalric allegory of the aristocratic education he credited 'poets' with re-establishing justice and government after the collapse of the Roman empire had left people in a state of barbarism and anarchy.[50] But in one persistent tradition, stemming apparently from Horace's *Ars poetica*, poets as such were given a place of primacy as the founders of civilization. This was especially true among those later scholars who in the age of Elizabethan literary efflorescence undertook with understandable enthusiasm to defend poetry against its more literal-minded detractors and to establish its English rules.[51] Vives had also recognized the historical or, more accurately, the anthropological, significance of poetry. As a cultural force he seems to have considered it prior to rhetoric, primitive in the fullest sense. It was the medium through which Moses spoke to God, David to the Israelites, and the pagans to their deities.[52] But he does not follow the Horatian myth: Amphion and Orpheus were to him bona fide poets among the 'gentiles'; but we look in vain for any reference to

the former building cities with stones that came at the sound of his harp
or to the latter assembling the wild beasts to listen to his music as an example to a rude and savage people. To Vives, poetry was a form of expression peculiarly suited to the transmission of those things, legends or
revealed religion, which are not suited to rational or historical expression; and as such it was no doubt older in the cultural process.

The history of language served as an object lesson in cultural development especially pertinent to the humanist mind. Committed though they
were to classical studies, the Tudor humanists were coming more and
more to rely on the vernacular for the kind of didactic and persuasive
writing in which they placed so much confidence. But, to become an efficient and graceful instrument of expression, the English of their day
clearly needed reform. Hence, for example, Wilson's concern for an English rhetoric. But, on a more immediately practical level, it was apparent
that even the reading of English was seriously hampered by the chaotic
state of its orthography. This was no doubt peculiarly irritating to the
classicists who were accustomed to a rigid standard of spelling in Latin
and Greek. It should therefore come as no surprise that spelling reform
became a subject of discussion among these reform-minded scholars, nor
that this more pedestrian problem should once again prompt consideration of man's development.

Sir Thomas Smith, whose scholarly and public-spirited mind had
encompassed much larger problems of social change, was among the first
to suggest a scheme of orthographic reform, and in his *De recta et emendata linguae Anglicae scriptione dialogus* (published in 1567, but apparently written in 1542)[53] he anchored his argument in the usual story of
man's gradual rise from artless and uncivilized (if innocent) beginnings.
Nor was this a mere figure of speech, a 'state of nature' cliché
brought in for rhetorical effect. It was apparent to Smith's historical
sense and important to his argument for reform that mankind had gone
through a long process of fitting symbols to the natural sounds of the
voice. Early societies recognized the importance of this process by sin-
gling out and deifying the 'inventors' of letters. But Smith knew that the
process had been gradual. Moreover, speculation of this sort was easily
reinforced by what could be traced within the period of written records
and in the history of modern languages. And it all helped him override
the opposition of those who would make custom sacred and reform impious. Not the least of the uses to which the favourite anthropological
speculation of the humanists could be put was to support that new sense

of relativity becoming apparent in the socially oriented pamphlets of the mid-century.

Insofar as it depended upon the peculiar conjunction of classical anthropology and social reform, the humanist vision of man's achievements and potentialities did not live long beyond the mid-century. However, that is not to say that it found no other source of nourishment and perished accordingly, or that classical anthropology did not continue after a fashion to inspire progressivist, as well as more pessimistic, ruminations concerning man's earthly sojourn. One simply misses the confidence with which a Starkey or a Vives placed his own vision of a reasonable society in juxtaposition with one particularly congenial theme in ancient thought.

Actually, conditions after the mid-century were *not* always conducive to such an outlook. For one thing, religious controversies continued to take their toll of that naturalism, largely inspired by classical learning, which had hitherto been able to live in a curiously symbiotic relationship with the Christian humanism of an earlier generation. Not that it disappeared, nor was it in some quarters seriously weakened: a moderate realism was after all a permanent contribution of Renaissance thought. It is simply that scholars now tended to worry about discrepancies between their pagan and biblical sources which earlier humanists had taken pretty much in their stride. We have already seen how Thomas Wilson, writing in the first years of Elizabeth's reign, found it necessary to combine the familiar classical account of early man with the Christian doctrine of the fall – not, as Vives had been able to do, in such a way as to leave the postlapsarian state the virtually unchallenged preserve of rational investigation, but so as to leave man in the active custody of providence. The result was a hybrid statement, part speculative anthropology, part *Heilsgeschichte*, which quite failed to convey the idea of man's ability to adapt to his environment as a factor in his social development. A few years earlier, Thomas Lanquet had encountered similar difficulties with the 'ethnic' philosophers. In his *Epitome of the Chronicles* (1549) he is concerned about what he clearly believed to be irreconcilably discrepant sources.[54] He takes pains to refute the pagan philosophers, yet he is obviously fascinated by their account of the origin and development of man. He is drawn to their naturalism, yet unable to make the kind of historical interpretation which had permitted even the profoundly religious Dean Colet to picture Moses as a poet presenting the story of creation as a 'high and noble fiction,' suitable for the minds of the simple rustics with whom he had to deal in those days.[55] Protestant bibliolatry maintained at times a paradoxical connection with rationalism – witness the long-continued efforts of sober and erudite minds to rationalize the legend of Noah or to fit the primitive societies of the new world into the biblical scheme.[56] The end result was once and for all to separate myth and historical fact; but that was not to be for a long time. Meanwhile, the book of Genesis continued to assert its priority at the expense of more naturalistic speculation, thereby restricting the area within which such reconstructions could be made with impunity.

Protestant polemic no doubt contributed to that strain of pessimism which, even when little more than a *fin de siècle* lament over the mutability of life, did much to counteract any optimistic faith in man's potentiality for rational and constructive action. With no Joachim at hand to bring Christian eschatology somehow within the projected scheme of world history, the millenarian who contemplated history in terms of the book of Revelation, or for that matter the prophecies of Daniel, could easily conclude that his own were indeed the 'last days.'[57]

There were, to be sure, other reasons for Renaissance pessimism – at least among Elizabethan intellectuals.[58] In science and philosophy as well as in religion, the old certainties were by the end of the century coming more and more to be called into question; and, in the world of affairs, those overreachers of Marlovian cast were finding fortune's wheel more often than not impossible to turn with their own hands. The resulting climate undoubtedly encouraged gloomy thoughts, or at best arcadian dreams of a past golden age; and it was unquestionably easy to see the history of civilized man as a retrograde process, or at best a record of mere flux.

But life in Elizabethan England could be exciting as well as sobering, prodigal of opportunity as well as prey to apparently meaningless vicissitudes. The fashionable mood of pessimism probably infected *belles lettres* more than the writings of those who, like the early Tudor pamphleteers, were addressing themselves to the practical problems of their age. The problems had changed. 'Practical' men of the new age were concerned less with social reform than with technological developments and the rumours of a new astronomy, with the discovery of new lands and peoples, and with the demands of a vernacular literature at last coming of age. And there is ample evidence that they met these problems with enthusiasm and, in the area of invention and knowledge of the physical world, with a refreshing sense of having already overtaken the ancients.[59] In this atmosphere the anthropology of the early Tudor humanists remains in spirit, if not always in fact, in its traditional classical form. We need not take seriously the repeated revival by men of letters of the notion that poets were the 'founders' of civil society; yet we recognize the progressivist implications even of this now-hackneyed Horatian convention when repeated in the context of a developing language and literature. When, however, a scientist of the stature of William Gilbert[60] reverts to a broader, more characteristic form of the classical tradition, with all that it implied of human creativity, we can only conclude that the tradition itself retained real meaning.

It is above all in their increasing grasp of the processes by which society undergoes change that the Elizabethans reveal their kinship with the humanists of the earlier period. To the end of the century, and long after, formal historiography remained preoccupied with *res gestae*; but in the progress of investigation a few – Stowe and Camden are conspicuous examples – managed to achieve some feeling for the character of societies and cultures, for the relationship between them, and for the processes of development observable within them. Jewel and Whitgift found it intellectually satisfying, as well as politically useful, to treat the church as a developing institution, in all but the essentials of faith subject to the changing circumstances of time and place. Others, like Hakluyt, who made no pretence to writing history as such, were impelled by the discovery of a new world and the economic opportunities it offered to carry forward something of that feeling for the importance of economic factors in social change which had begun to be recognized by such earlier observers as Sir Thomas Smith. And the spectacle of savage peoples who did not fit into traditional systems of cosmography raised questions which, even though not as yet answerable, were pregnant with developmental implications. If, as might be expected, the new sense of history proved more effective in illuminating the past than in charting the future, if these men of the later sixteenth century were little more given than their predecessors to projecting the possibility of improvement into the indefinite future, if, indeed, many of them fell back upon the concept of cyclical growth and decay in the life history of cultures,[61] there is little question but that the century had, for good or ill, brought English thought decisively closer to the modern idea of progress.

The humanist heritage was far from being depleted in Elizabethan England; nor, despite the changing circumstances, was it being expended on projects far removed from those contemplated by its founders. The heirs of the early Tudor pamphleteers, those who explored the practical problems of their society, carried forward many of their predecessors' most profound assumptions concerning the secular sojourn of man. Without always feeling it necessary to begin with speculation borrowed from the ancient world, they continued to recognize that man had indeed developed through the ages, that his development had been originally in response to his natural environment, that the nature of his response was in turn dictated, for better or worse, by the potentialities inherent in his own nature, potentialities given him by God but his alone to realize, and that he could exercise his creative capacity to an appreciable extent in the task of shaping his own environment. Above all, the humanists bequeathed a sense of history – of history considered not primarily as the memory of great deeds or the source of useful examples, but as process. Perhaps, indeed, it is here that they made their most characteristic contribution, however indirect, to those attitudes which were prerequisite to the emergence of the modern idea of progress. If these tendencies do not constitute the dominant theme of the late sixteenth century, they are sufficiently apparent to make the outcome of the ensuing quarrel of the ancients and moderns, when viewed in the hindsight of history, seem a foregone conclusion. They might also caution us against accepting without qualification any interpretation of the idea of progress which minimizes the contribution made to its origins by Renaissance humanism.

NOTES

1 There is by now a vast literature on the subject. Reference to most pertinent items may be found in the recent article by W. Warren Ungar, 'Modern Views of the Origins of the Idea of Progress,' *Journal of the History of Ideas*, xxviii (January-March 1967), 55-70.
2 *Ibid.* Note especially the work of Löwith, Vogelin, Niehbur, and Bailie.
3 This interpretation is developed more fully in Arthur B. Ferguson, *The Articulate Citizen and the English Renaissance* (Durham, N.C. 1965).
4 For ancient thought on this and related subjects, see A.O. Lovejoy and George Boas, *Primitivism and Related Ideas in Antiquity* (Baltimore 1935).
5 Ed. K.M. Burton (London 1948). Much of the following analysis of Starkey's thought was originally made for the related purposes of my *Articulate Citizen*.
6 *Dialogue*, p. 60. Starkey's 'by little and little' renders the spirit, and perhaps intentionally, of Lucretius' *minutatim* in the well-known passage from the latter's *De rerum natura*, book v.
7 *Ibid.*, pp. 21-2

8 On both More and Polydore see below. Cf. the unashamedly eclectic answer made by William Baldwin to the question who 'invented' philosophy and 'in what nation' (a question, which, incidentally, he categorized as 'more curious than necessary') : *A Treatise of morall phylosophie* (London 1547) STC 1253, chap. I; see also chap. III.
9 For a discussion of Renaissance Euhemerism see J. Seznec, *La Survivance des dieux antiques* (London 1940)
10 *Dialogue*, pp. 42-4
11 *Ibid.*, p. 26
12 *Ibid.*, p. 33; cf. pp. 28-9
13 *Ibid.*, p. 26
14 Vives, *De Subventione Pauperum*, in *Some Early Tracts on Poor Relief* ed. F.R. Salter (London 1926). Marshall's translation is also reprinted in this collection. G.R. Elton, 'An Early Tudor Poor Law,' *Economic History Review*, 2nd ser., VI (August 1953), 55-67.
15 *Vives: On Education (De tradenis disciplinis* [1531]) trans. Foster Watson (Cambridge 1913), p. 20
16 This was already the theme of his earlier *Fabula de homine* (1518), *Opera omnia* (Valentia 1783), IV, 3-8. Cf. Marcia L. Colish, 'The Mime of God: Vives on the Nature of Man,' *Journal of the History of Ideas*, XXIII (January-March 1962), 3-20
17 *De causis corruptarum artium* (1531), *Opera*, VI, 8
18 *On Education*, p. 14
19 *Ibid.*, pp. 14-15
20 *De causis*, pp. 9-11
21 The attitude of Vives toward peace and war is analyzed in R.P. Adams, *The Better Part of Valor* (Seattle 1962).
22 *On Education*, p. 16
23 *Ibid.*, p. 2; cf. *De causis*, pp. 16-17
24 *De causis*, pp. 14-16. It is tempting to think that Vives may have helped Starkey achieve his awareness of cultural diversity and his sense of historical relativism: see *ibid.*, pp. 43-4, 46-7.
25 *On Education*, p. 2
26 *Ibid.*, preface
27 *Ibid.*, p. 20
28 *De causis*, book I, chap. 5
29 *Ibid.*, p. 124
30 *Ibid.*, p. 39
31 *Ibid.*, pp. 6-7
32 *Ibid.*, book I, chap. 3; see also chaps. 6 and 10
33 *Ibid.*, book I, chap. 10
34 *Ibid.*, pp. 43-4
35 See Adams for a study of the humanist reaction to the problem of war in this period.
36 See, for example, his letters to Pope Adrian VI (1522) and Henry VIII (1525), and his treatise *De concordia et discordia* (1529), all in *Opera*, V.
37 On Erasmus' historical thought, see P.G. Bietenholz, *History and Biog-*

raphy in the Work of Erasmus of Rotterdam (Geneva 1966) ; Myron P. Gilmore, '*Fides et Eruditio:* Erasmus and the Study of History,' in *Humanists and Jurists: Six Studies in the Renaissance* (Cambridge, Mass. 1963)

38 The following analysis is based on *Erasmus against War*, ed. J.W. Mackail (Boston 1907), a sixteenth-century translation of *Dulce bellum inexpertis*, pp. 18-23. Cf. Erasmus, *The Complaint of Peace*, ed. W.J. Hutten (New York 1946), pp. 10-13.

39 *De causis*, p. 181

40 *Exposition of St. Paul's Epistle to the Romans* in *Opuscula quaedam theologica*, ed. and trans. J.H. Lupton (London 1876) pp. 134-40; cf. p. 162

41 On Polydore and the *De inventoribus rerum* see Denys Hay, *Polydore Vergil: Renaissance Historian and Man of Letters* (Oxford 1962), especially chap. 3. The first three books of the *De inventoribus* were published before Polydore's arrival in England in 1502 and the additional five books in 1521. It is consequently not very surprising that he should have missed some of the ferment among English social critics which had only really begun by the latter date. In this connection, too, it is worth noticing that whatever sense of change there is in the finished work is apparent in the last five books.

42 Hay, *Polydore Vergil*, pp. 63-4; 77-8; 135-6

43 *An Abridgement of the notable worke of Polidore Vergile*, trans. Thomas Langley, (London 1546), stc 24654, book v, chap. 1

44 *Polydore Vergil's English History*, ed. Sir Henry Ellis (Camden Society, 1st Series, xxxvi, 1846), i, 307

45 *Utopia*, in *The Complete Works of Saint Thomas More*, ed. Edward Surtz and J.H. Hexter (New Haven 1965), iv, pp. 121-3, 179-85

46 *The Letters of Amerigo Vespucci*, ed. and trans. C.R. Markham (The Hakluyt Society, no. 90, 1894). That these reports are probably not authentic is beside the point.

47 *The Boke Named the Gouernour* (1531), ed. H.H.S. Croft (London 1880), i, 117.

48 *The Art of Rhetorique* (1560), ed. G.H. Mair (London 1909), preface

49 See, for example, *De causis*, pp. 152-3, where Vives states that rhetoric is essential to the discharge of justice. The reader will recall Starkey's emphasis on 'men of great wit and policy' who 'with perfit eloquence and high philosophy' persuaded men to forsake their rude ways. Cf. William Forrest, *Pleasant Poesye of Princelie Practise* (1548), ed., in extract, S.S. Herrtage (Early English Texts Society, e.s., no. 32, 1878), stanzas 1-7.

50 *The Pastime of Pleasure*, ed. W.E. Mead (Early English Texts Society, o.s. no. 173, 1928), lines 876-96; cf. 246-52

51 A few examples: George Puttenham, *The Arte of English Poesie* (1589, though parts apparently written considerably earlier), ed. G.D. Willcock and A. Walker (Cambridge 1936), book ii, chap. 3, p. 6; Thomas Lodge, *Defence of Poetry* (1579), ed. Gregory Smith, *Elizabethan Critical Essays* (Oxford 1904), i, 73-5; William Webbe, *A Discourse of English Poetrie*

(1586), ed. E. Arber (Westminster 1895), pp. 21-2, cf. 38 ff.; Philip Sidney, *An Apologie for Poetrie* (1583), ed. Albert Feuillearat, *Works* (Cambridge 1912-26), III, p. 4; Henry Peacham, *The Garden of Eloquence*, ed. W. Crane (Gainsville, Fla. 1954), dedicatory epistle to 1593 ed. Peacham identifies 'orators' with Horace's reference to Orpheus as the founder of culture, and rationalizes the story of the beasts coming to the sound of his harp as an allegory of man's own rise, through 'the mighty power of wisdom, and prudent art of persuasion,' to a state befitting mankind.

52 *De causis*, pp. 93-4

53 Ed. Otto Deibel (Halle 1913), see especially the introductory dialogue. On Smith, see Mary Dewar, *Sir Thomas Smith: A Tudor Intellectual in Office* (London 1964). John Hart was interested in the same problem and was familiar with Smith's work; but, although he shared Smith's naturalistic approach to the subject of orthography, he did not concern himself with the early history or the speculative pre-history of letters. See B.A. Danielsson, *John Hart's Works on English Orthography and Pronunciation* (Stockholm 1955).

54 *An Epitome of Chronicles* (London 1549), STC 15217, sigs. Aiii-Bi

55 *Letters to Radulphus on the Mosaic Account of Creation*, in *Opuscula*, pp. 8-9, 23-8

56 On the former subject, see D.C. Allen, *The Legend of Noah: Renaissance Rationalism in Art, Science, and Letters* (Urbana 1963), and on the latter, Margaret T. Hodgen, *Early Anthropology in the Sixteenth and Seventeenth Centuries* (Philadelphia 1964), especially chap. 6. It is interesting also to notice how the more or less sceptical mind of Ralcigh became, in the *History of the World* (1614), inextricably entangled in the problem of rationalizing the biblical narrative, with, however, brief reflections of both the anti-primitivist strain in classical anthropology and the new data flowing into England from the newly discovered lands. See, for example, book I, chap. 9, pars. 1-2; II, 6, 4; V, 1, 4.

57 E.L. Tuvenson, *Millenium and Utopia* (Berkeley 1949), especially chap. 2

58 Renaissance pessimism has been written about a great deal, no doubt in part because the Elizabethan men of letters wrote about it a great deal. Among more recent treatments, see D.C. Allen, 'The Degeneration of Man and Renaissance Pessimism,' *Studies in Philosophy*, XXXV (1938), 202-27; A. Williams, 'A Note on Pessimism in the Renaissance,' *ibid.*, XXXVI (1939), 243-6; H. Weisinger, 'Ideas of History in the Renaissance,' *Journal of the History of Ideas*, VI (October 1945), 415-35; V. Harris, *All Coherence Gone* (Chicago 1949); R. Chapman, 'Fortune and Mutability in Elizabethan Literature,' *Cambridge Journal*, V (March 1952) 374-82; Anthony Esler, *The Aspiring Mind of the Elizabethan Younger Generation* (Durham, N.C. 1966), pp. 227 ff.

59 E.g., the reflections on the cumulative character of physical knowledge and the possibility of continual contribution to it to be found in the writings of such men of the last half of the sixteenth century as Best, Borough,

Bostocke, Dee, Digges, Eden, Hakluyt, Jaggard, Norman, and Recorde.
See also F.R. Johnson, *Astronomical Thought in Renaissance England*
(Baltimore 1937), especially p. 296; R.F. Jones, *Ancients and Moderns*
(2nd ed. Berkeley 1961) chap. 1, and cf. Hans Baron, 'The *Querelle* of
Ancients and Moderns as a Problem for Renaissance Scholarship,'
Journal of the History of Ideas, xx (January 1959), 3-22.

60 *De Magnete* (1600), ed. S.P. Thompson, *William Gilbert ... on the Magnet*
(Gilbert Club, London, 1900), pp. 1-2

61 Indeed, the cyclical interpretations of history which are in this period best
exemplified by Bodin and LeRoy, but which tinged much English writing
too, were far more likely to foster those attitudes essential to the development of the modern idea of progress than any version of the Christian
story then likely to be accepted, despite its linear, teleological character.

Atropos-Mors:

Observations on a rare early humanist image

Millard Meiss

Between 1400 and 1402 Christine de Pisan wrote the *Epître d'Othéa*, in which a goddess bearing this strange name instructs the youthful Hector of Troy, probably an allusion to the author's own son.[1] The one hundred chapters are devoted to ancient history and to myth, which Christine explains historically and interprets morally and spiritually, with many references to the Bible and to the church fathers. In this way, she said, the legends yielded 'leur grans secrez soulz couverture de fable.'[2] For this manual of mythology Christine had prepared herself, to use her own phrase, by 'un chemin de long estude.' The *Epître d'Othéa* was her first major work, and it proved to be her most popular. Over forty manuscripts of the fifteenth century alone have been identified,[3] and the text was printed in Paris about 1499-1500.[4]

The earliest fully illustrated manuscript, Bibliothèque nationale français 606, is also the most beautiful. Illuminated c. 1405-8, it composed part of an edition of the collected writing of Christine that was acquired by the duke of Berry.[5] Among the four or more illuminators responsible for the miniatures one is outstanding in France and indeed in Europe at that time. I have named him the Epître Master after this cycle.[6] Christine, who supervised the production of manuscripts of her writings for the Valois princes, must herself have chosen the Epître Master as her illuminator for this manuscript. She employed him also slightly earlier for the illustration of three copies of her *Mutacion de Fortune*. The choice was not insignificant. The writer, born in Venice the daughter of an Italian astrologer who moved to the court of Charles V, was associated with the group of early French humanists, all of whom looked with great admiration to Petrarch and Boccaccio. Christine was especially interested in Boccaccio's Latin texts, two of which were indeed translated into French just as Christine wrote the *Epître*.[7] The Epître Master, in turn, was a close student of Lombard painting.

In the miniatures near the beginning of the text seven planets appear in the sky above the persons whom they influenced. Christine here communicated astrological ideas which were no doubt inspired initially by her father. The design of planet above, 'children' below, was maintained in many other miniatures in the manuscript that represent mythological figures or personifications of virtues. Among all these celestial apparitions, Death, 'whom the poets call Atropos,' is the most memorable (figure 1). Christine's description, written next to the miniature in chapter XXXIV, is brief:

Ayes a toute heure regard
A Atropos et a son dart
Qui fiert et nespargne nul ame ...
Les poetes appellerent la mort Atropos ...

In the miniature a swarthy woman in a dun dress soars on a ragged cloud. She brandishes a large arrow, her unkempt black hair falling over her bare shoulder. Her décolletage exposes a rather bony frame and a sagging breast. With vigour and skill she exercises her fateful power. Her action as well as her attributes associate her more with the traditional representation of Death than of Atropos. In Roman art Atropos, an ideal personification, often reads her fateful words from a *rotulus*. In conformity with ideas held in antiquity and in the Middle Ages about death, Christine's Atropos strikes, not the weak and the aged, but the young and the powerful, especially kings, bishops, popes.[8] The painter has given to these victims, despite their high station, little of the strength with which he has endowed the embodiment of their fate. Atropos may be unkempt but she is determined, and she aims one arrow at the pope while keeping three others in reserve in her left hand. She moves indeed within an extraordinary geometric design. The lowering cloud sustains her and introduces a balancing diagonal. The bundle of darts provides order as well as a promise of continued effective action. The pendant breast, one of the most conspicuous verticals in a mobile field, seems, therefore, to acquire a special though puzzling significance.

The idea of Death's preference for the strong rather than the weak had been dramatically represented during the preceding century in the famous fresco of the *Triumph of Death* in the Camposanto in Pisa, painted by Francesco Traini,[9] and it was communicated in 1361 by a relief, little known, in the Museo di San Martino in Naples (figure 2). In the relief the victim tries in vain to buy his freedom. The personification of death assumes the skeletal form that had become conventional in the *trecento* and that persisted, indeed, in the art of later centuries.[10] Mors is a skeleton in the Giottesque allegory of chastity in the lower church at Assisi and in several representations of the 'Triumph of Death.' When in these compositions Death is equestrian there may be an allusion to the rider of the Apocalypse.[11] Death assumed the form of a skeleton hurling a lance in a French miniature which entered the duke of Berry's collection shortly after the *Epître d'Othéa*.[12]

A very few personifications of death in the late Middle Ages depart from this skeletal image, which stresses the Christian conception of the corruptibility of the body. One of these is the famous old woman in black who, wielding a scythe, flies to the attack in Traini's fresco in the Camposanto (figure 3). Her finger- and toe-nails have grown to the size of predacious talons.[13] Death is conceived of as an old woman also by Guillaume de Digulleville in his *Pèlerinage de vie humaine,* composed in 1330-1 and revised in 1355.[14] The menacing figure comes to the bedside of the pilgrim, bearing a scythe and a coffin.

Quant en l'enfermerie fu
Et une piece y oi ieu
Soutainement et en seursant
Une vieille qui estoit haut
Montee sur mon lit ...
Une faus en sa main tenoit.
Et i sarclis de fust portoit ...[15]

The illustrations of this passage conform with the text, except that the woman is not tall (figure 4). Like Atropos, she is entirely human, without even the avian talons of the flying figure in Pisa. There, however, the similarity ends, for *la vieille,* her head bound in a kerchief, looks like a crabbed ancient gravekeeper. Atropos on the other hand is neither old nor bent. Indeed, with her high forehead and regular features, she has a spirited and even noble bearing.

Atropos is an exceptional figure in the work of the Epître Master. The drawing, the structure, the pattern of drapery folds, the large geometric design, all suggest a *trecento* model, although I cannot point to it. The personification of death as a dignified human being rather than a grinning skeleton seems to reflect ancient ideas, ideas that were studied by the early Italian humanists and their followers in the circle of Christine de Pisan in Paris. Though the skeleton was represented in antiquity as a *memento mori,*[16] in personifications the Greeks and Romans affirmed the value of life − or especially − in death. Thanatos was a handsome, winged young man (figure 5), and the Fates were rendered no less ideal than other women.

Among the Romans Mors assumed a female form. According to Horace she flies on black wings, and Statius described her as the daughter of Night who chooses those most worthy of life.[17] Boccaccio quoted this passage in his *De genealogiis deorum,* on which he worked during the third quarter of the fourteenth century. Mors, he said, is given other names, the first of which is Atropos.[18] When Christine referred to the 'poets' who stated this fact, she may have had Boccaccio in mind.[19] In his *Trionfi*, written at approximately the same time as the *Genealogiae*, Petrarch singles out 'pontefici, regnanti, e 'mperadori' as the victims of Death, who is a woman wrapped in a black dress:

> ed una donna involta in veste negra.
> Con un furor, qual io non so se mai
> al tempo de'giganti fosse a Flegra,
> si mosse ...[20]

The two pictorial representations of Death that approximate to these ancient conceptions revived by Boccaccio and Petrarch are the fresco in Pisa and the miniature in the *Epître d'Othéa*. Traini's *Morte*, probably painted somewhat earlier than the composition of the two relevant texts,[21] corresponds with Petrarch's image of a woman in black, whereas *Atropos* resembles the literary tradition more closely because she is completely a woman.

The figure of Atropos, so unusual and so compelling, is distinguished by one attribute that appears to be unique. A common connotation of a bared breast – mercy – can scarcely be intended here. Does the pendant shape, together with the rather prominent ribs, indicate age? Remembering Death's *furor*, emphasized especially by Petrarch, and keeping in mind the long, disheveled hair of our figure, we may ask whether to Atropos-Mors are added attributes of a Fury. In antiquity the Furies were sometimes represented with a bared breast and long, wild hair (figure 6),[22] but for the bared breast I have not found a written tradition, which would have been more accessible than monuments in the late fourteenth century. Though the Furies have little place in medieval art they appear, nude and tearing their breasts, in illustrations of canto IX of Dante's *Commedia*. It is interesting that, in fr. 606, the Fury Tisiphone appears seven folios before Atropos (figure 7). The miniature tells a story that Christine had in large part taken from the *Ovide moralisé*. Standing possessively at the gate of the palace of King Athamas, this forceful and dramatic figure releases a pair of serpents that drive him mad. His wife Ino already lies dead, and he kills his two children. *Tisiphone* is a kind of sister of *Atropos*, a more furious sister, we might say, darker and wilder. Her brown dress, however, shows no signs of a similar décolletage, though we are left uncertain because of her averted position.

The proximity of Tisiphone in the manuscript of the *Epître* would of course not be relevant if what we have assumed to be the *trecento* model of *Atropos* showed all the attributes of the figure by the Epître Master. In such circumstances there is another image that would not be relevant either, although it appears in a poem that Christine knew very well. In a gruesome passage in the *Roman de la rose* devoted to the Three Fates, Atropos, who cuts the thread of life, throws corpses to Cerberus and also suckles him to satisfy his insatiable appetite (figure 8).[23] She offers him three breasts, one for each of his heads. The feeding is thus perfectly economical, but only as a consequence of a gross anatomical distortion.

The miniature by the Epître Master, together with the entire cycle in fr. 606, was copied shortly afterward in a manuscript illuminated for the queen of France by the Cité des dames workshop.[24] One would have expected that these two miniatures, the earliest illustrations of Christine's chapter on Atropos, would have established a pictorial tradition. It was abandoned, however, in some of the best illustrations in the later fifteenth century. They regressed, so to speak, from the mythological figure to the widely diffused Christian image of the skeleton (figures 9, 10).[25] A similar abandonment of the classical personification occurred even in the illustration of Petrarch's *Triumphus mortis*, one of the probable sources, we have seen, of Christine's figure. This part of Petrarch's poem, like the cycle as a whole, began to be illustrated in Italy about the middle of the fifteenth century. The representations appeared in manuscripts of the text as well as in paintings independent of it. Some depictions of the Triumph of Death, including the earliest, such as Pesellino's (figure 11), show a woman in a dark dress, her hair streaming out behind her. However, she is not entirely a living woman; her head is hollow-eyed and skeletal. Petrarch's 'donna involta in veste negra' was not, to be sure, forgotten in later art, and in his *Iconologia* Ripa described *Morte* as a 'donna pallida ... vestita di nero, secondo il parlar dei Poeti ...' From the beginning, however, this personification yielded to the image of the body partly decayed or reduced entirely to bones.[26] Even followers of the great antiquarian, Mantegna, preferred the skeleton (figure 12).[27]

In the *Roman de la rose*, too, the ubiquitous skeleton sometimes supplanted the three-breasted Atropos described in the poem (figure 13). Brandishing spears above a victim, the skeleton accompanies the verses devoted to the Three Fates, but it is more closely related to the rubric above it: 'O chascun le deffende fort / Contre Atropos ce est la mort.'[28]

The skeleton took precedence over images of Atropos or Death as a woman in other contexts as well. In the seventeenth century Bernini established it firmly in the history of the tomb.[29] In the early sixteenth century in France and the Netherlands, however, there was one peculiar and interesting innovation, which Müntz and d'Essling noticed long ago.[30] In cycles of Triumphs derived from Petrarch's and accompanied by inscriptions taken from various sources, the Three Fates replaced the skeleton. The Sisters, or Atropos alone, sometimes ride in the usual chariot drawn by bulls; they may also, in accordance with the sequence of Petrarch's poem, conquer Chastity (*Mors vincit pudicitiam*). Chastity even may lie underfoot, in medieval fashion (figure 14).[31]

The *Epître d'Othéa* was published in Paris shortly before the appearance of this series of representations, but the woodcut for the chapter on Atropos showed no figure of Fate. She has been replaced by a skeleton (figure 10), in conformity with the general preference of the time and the later fifteenth-century illustration of this chapter (figure 9). Such 'regressions' only highlight the little triumph of restoration brought about by early French humanism, Christine, and the Epître Master. Recognition of this restoration of the classical tradition is due whether she or her painter invented the image of Atropos-Mors or whether, as I suppose, they had the wit to find it in the new repertory of late *trecento* painting.

NOTES

1 G. Mombello, 'Per un' edizione critica dell' "Epistre Othea" di Christine de Pizan,' *Studi francesi*, VIII (1964), 401 ff.

2 Lines 80-2

3 Mombello, 'Per un' edizione'

4 By Philippe Pigouchet under the misleading title *Les cent histoires de Troye*. Another edition appeared about 1530. Christine's *Fais d'armes* and *Livre des trois vertus* were printed in 1488 and 1497, respectively.

5 Ed. M. Roy, *Œuvres poétiques de Christine de Pisan* (Paris 1886), I, xxii; F. Lecoy, 'Ballades de Christine de Pisan,' in *Fin du moyen âge et Renaissance: Mélanges de philologie française offerts à Robert Guiette* (Antwerp 1961), pp. 107-14; Mombello, 'Per un' edizione,' p. 108 ff.; M. Meiss, *French Painting in the Time of Jean de Berry: The Late XIV Century and the Patronage of the Duke* (London 1967), pp. 300, 313

6 Meiss, *French Painting*, pp. 299 ff., 358. See also J. Porcher in 'Paris, Bibliothèque nationale,' *Les manuscrits à peintures en France du XIIIe au XVIe siècle* (Paris 1955), p. 76

7 *De mulieribus claris* and *De casibus virorum illustrium*. Cf. Meiss, *French Painting*, pp. 4, 302

8 See, for instance, Statius, *Thebaid*, VIII, 376, quoted by E. Dobbert, 'Der Triumph des Todes im Camposanto zu Pisa,' *Repertorium für Kunstwissenschaft*, IV (1881), 27 f.

9 M. Meiss, *Painting in Florence and Siena after the Black Death*, (Princeton 1951 and New York 1964), fig. 85

10 For some examples see, for instance, E. Panofsky, 'Mors Vitae Testimonium,' in *Studien zur Toskanischen Kunst: Festschrift L.H. Heydenreich* (Munich 1964), p. 221 ff. For the Neapolitan relief, which is an ex-voto of Franceschino di Brignale, see G. Doria, *Il Museo e la Certosa di S. Martino* (Naples 1964), p. 97.

11 Apocalypse 6:8. For the fresco in Assisi see B. Kleinschmidt, *Die Basilika San Francesco in Assisi* (Berlin 1926), II, fig. 128. For equestrian skeletons see M. Meiss, 'The Problem of Francesco Traini,' *Art Bulletin*, XV (1933), 169; R. van Marle, *Iconographie de l'art profane au moyen-âge et à la Renaissance et la décoration des demeures* (The Hague 1931-2), II, figs. 402, 405; L. Guerry, *Le Thème du 'Triomphe de la Mort' dans la peinture italienne* (Paris 1950).

12 Meiss, *French Painting*, fig. 643

13 The fingernails, as well as other parts of the figure, are repainted, but the feet and the toenails are original.

14 E. Faral, in *Histoire littéraire de la France*, XXXIX (1962), 10 ff.

15 Cf. *Pèlerinage*, ed. J.J. Stürzinger (Roxburghe Club, London, 1893), lines 13417 ff. In a second poem by Digulleville, *Pèlerinage de l'âme*, Death is, on the contrary, a skeleton (cf. Paris, Bibliothèque nationale, fr. 823, f. 95).

16 See the cups reproduced by M.I. Rostovtsev, *Social and Economic History of the Roman Empire* (2nd ed. rev. P.M. Fraser, Oxford 1957), I, pl. 7. For this reference I am indebted to James F. Gilliam.

17 Horace, *Satirae*, II, 1, 57; Statius, *Thebaid*, VIII, 376. For these passages, and similar ones in Greek and Roman literature, see Dobbert, 'Der Triumph des Todes,' p. 26 ff., and Roscher, *Ausführliches Lexikon der griechischen und römischen Mythologie*, s.v. *Mors*. An ivory of the fourth century in the British Museum represents both Death and Sleep as winged women (O. Dalton, *Catalogue of the Ivory Carvings of the Christian Era ... in the British Museum* [London 1909], no. 1).

18 Bk. I, s.v. 'Mors'

19 P-G-C Campbell, 'L'Épître d'Othéa,' *Étude sur les sources de Christine de Pisan* (Paris 1924), p. 124, is not certain that Christine knew the *Genealogiae*. In two respects, however, her account of Perseus accords with his and not with the verse *Ovide*, her common source. Perseus rides Pegasus when delivering Andromeda and Persia is said to be named after him.

20 'And a woman shrouded in a dress of black,/With fury such as had perchance been seen/When giants raged in the Phlegraean vale,/Came near ...' (trans. E.H. Wilkins, *The Triumphs of Petrarch* [Chicago 1962], p. 54). It should be added that E. Pellegrin (see n.31) has not been able to identify a copy of Petrarch's text in French libraries around 1400.

1 Master of the *Epître d'Othéa*, 1405-8, *Atropos-Mors*, Paris,
Bibliothèque nationale, français 606, f.17

2 Neapolitan, 1361, *Death and a Nobleman*, Naples, Museo della
Certosa di S. Martino

3 Francesco Traini, *Death* (detail), Pisa, Camposanto

4 Flemish (Artois), c.1395, *Death and the Pilgrim*, Brussels, Bibliothèque royale, MS 10176-8, f.112

5 Fourth century B.C., *Thanatos*, London, British Museum

6 Roman, *Fury* (detail of a sarcophagus), Florence, Opera del Duomo

7 *Epître* Master, *Tisiphone and the family of Athamas*, Paris, Bibliothèque nationale, français 606, f.10

8 French, c.1425, *Atropos and Cerberus*, Valencia, Biblioteca de la
Universidad, MS 1372, f.134

9 Circle of L. Liedet, 1461, *Atropos*, Brussels, Bibliothèque royale,
MS 9392, f.37ᵛ

10 Woodcut, 1499-1500, *Atropos,* in *Les cent histoires de Troye,*
Paris 1499-1500, Pigouchet

11 Pesellino, *Triumph of Death*, Boston, Isabella Stewart Gardner Museum

12 Follower of Mantegna, *Triumph of Death*

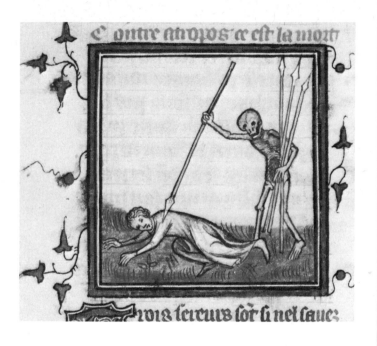

13 French, c.1365, *Atropos*, New York, Morgan Library,
M 132, f.140ᵛ

14 French, early sixteenth century, *Triumph of Death*, Paris,
Bibliothèque de l'Arsenal, MS 5066, f.6

21 The fresco in Pisa is not precisely dated by external evidence (cf. M. Meiss, 'Alesso di Andrea,' in 'Atti del Congresso giottesco 1967' [in press], with references to opinions ranging from c. 1330-70). Petrarch and Boccaccio were at work on their respective texts during the third quarter of the century. Death in British Museum, MS Cotton Tiberius c. VI, f. 6ᵛ of the eleventh century, has sometimes been described as a woman but the figure is bearded (F. Wormald, 'An English Eleventh-Century Psalter with Pictures: British Museum, Cotton MS Tiberius c. VI,' *Walpole Society*, XXXVIII [1960-2] pl. 2).

22 (C.) A. Rosenberg, *Der Erynien* (Berlin 1874); G. Pauly-Wissowa, *Real-Enzyclopädie der classischen Altertumswissenschaft*, supp. vol. VIII (1956), p. 13 ff.

23 See lines 19805 ff. *(Roman de la rose*, ed. E. Langlois, [Paris 1924], V, p. 17). The image of Atropos suckling Cerberus is described as 'inventive, frightful, and frightening' by R. Tuve, *Allegorical Imagery* (Princeton 1966), p. 271.

24 British Museum, MS Harl. 4431, f. 111

25 See also the late fifteenth-century miniature, Oxford, Bodl. 421, f. 29ᵛ (F. Saxl and H. Meier, *Catalogue of Astrological and Mythological Illuminated Manuscripts of the Latin Middle Ages*, ed. H. Bober [London 1953], III, pt. 1, p. 301)

26 For the representation of an emaciated woman in the third quarter of the fifteenth century, see Prince d'Essling and E. Müntz, *Pétrarque* (Paris 1902) pp. 1, 139, 173, 189, 191

27 On the substitution of the skeleton for Petrarch's woman in black see *ibid.*, p. 118 ff. Also Van Marle, *Iconographie de l'art profane*, II, pp. 124 ff., 361 ff., 397, figs. 135, 138, 153; G. Carandente, *I Trionfi nel Primo Rinascimento* (Turin 1963), fig. 31; P. Schubring, *Cassoni* (Leipzig 1923), pp. 357, 407, figs. 215, 578, 582; Essling and Müntz, *Pétrarque*, pp. 151, 165 f., 187, 197, 201, 227

28 New York, Morgan Library, M 132, f. 140ᵛ. A skeleton, riding a horse, again illustrates the same passage in the *Roman de la rose* in Bodleian Library, MS Douce 195, f. 141ᵛ, datable about 1470 (cf. Saxl and Meier, *Catalogue*, III, p. 355).

29 E. Mâle, *L'Art religieux après le Concile de Trente* (Paris 1932), p. 204 ff., esp. p. 225. Also Panofsky, 'Mors Vitae Testimonium'

30 d'Essling and Müntz, *Pétrarque*, pp. 118, 209, 211

31 *Ibid.*, pp. 202 ff., 271, and E. Pellegrin, 'Les manuscrits de Pétrarque dans les bibliothèques de France,' *Italia medioevale e umanistica*, VII (1964), 422 f.

A music book for
Anne Boleyn*

Edward E. Lowinsky

Manuscripts of sacred music of the Renaissance fall into various categories. Some of them, like the famed series of codices of the Sistine chapel, were written for use by the entire church; others, like the parchment choirbooks of Jena, with their magnificent illuminations from the workshop of the famous Alamire, were done for a court chapel; many manuscripts, of more modest appearance and written on paper, were executed for city churches.

Among the most interesting manuscripts are those which do not come under the category of church music pure and simple, but contain an admixture of contemporaneous Latin texts alluding, directly or by biblical metaphor, to current events. Here we encounter one of the most intriguing types of manuscripts, individual creations of a clearly definable cultural-political centre with their own biographies, whose secrets must be ferreted out by a close study of their musical, textual, and visual aspects. In addition to their intrinsic significance, they assume importance as documents of cultural, religious, and political history.

Such a manuscript is the choirbook 1070 of the Royal College of Music in London.[1] Although it contains only one secular motet – but at an important place, the opening of the manuscript – analysis of the texts, together with other evidence, sheds new light on one of the darkest chapters of Tudor history. It is a strange and difficult manuscript with a confusing multitude of variegated, and at times conflicting, evidence. We shall do well to proceed cautiously from a description to the weighing and interpreting of the visual, textual, and musical evidence.

CONTENTS OF THE MANUSCRIPT

The choirbook consists of thirty-nine Latin motets – most of them written on liturgical texts – and three French chansons. Only two composers are named: 'Josquin,' as author of the famous Passion motet, *Huc me sydereo*, and 'Jac. Obreth' for a three-part setting of the Marian antiphon, *Alma Redemptoris Mater*. W. Barclay Squire listed a number of other authors.[2] A postcard to Barclay Squire from the late Albert Smijers, dated 1 June 1922, is attached to the manuscript and enumerates ten works as certainly, and one as probably, attributable to Josquin.[3] Barclay Squire suggested composers for four additional works, one erroneously.[4] Systematic comparison with the motet repertoire of the period has yielded further results: in addition to the ten works by Josquin, there are nine motets by Mouton, three each by Brumel and Compère, two by Antoine de Févin, and one each by Obrecht, Thérache, and Claudin de Sermisy. The authors of twelve compositions – ten motets and two chansons – remain anonymous; of these, eight are *unica*. This song book is an anthology of compositions by the finest composers of Franco-Flemish origin. A number of them – Josquin, Mouton, Compère, Févin, and Sermisy – served, in one position or another, at the French court under Louis XII and François I.

The repertory of the manuscript points to a period of about 1500 to 1515. A number of the compositions were written before 1500, and several, particularly the chansons which appear in the later layers of the manuscript, may have been composed after 1515. If the manuscript originated in France, the main part might have been written about 1515. When we compare it with the Medici Codex of 1518,[5] for example, we would have to place it considerably earlier on two counts: it does not contain works by the younger composers such as La Fage, Richafort, De Silva, Willaert, and Festa; and among its ten motets by Josquin (d. 1521) there is not a single late work, or even a work of Josquin's maturity, such as the *Déploration d'Ockeghem* of about 1496 or the setting of psalm 50, *Miserere mei, Deus*. With the single exception of the *Ave Maria gratia plena ... Virgo serena*, all works seem to predate the period of maturity which one might assume to begin at about 1495, or a few years earlier. Leaving the three chansons out of consideration for the moment, the youngest motet composer is Antoine de Févin, who is assumed to have been born about 1473 and who died at the end of 1511 or in the beginning of 1512. Nor do we encounter any of the 'modern' works of Mouton (d. 1522) contained in the Medici Codex.

However, if our manuscript originated in England – and we shall prove this to be the case – it might well have been written considerably later, since it takes time for the repertory of one national centre to migrate to and establish itself in another. Here it is essential to point out that there were sources of French music in England prior to our manuscript. One of them is the beautiful illuminated parchment manuscript Royal 8 G VII, written for Henry VIII and Catherine of Aragon at about 1520, containing an almost exclusively Franco-Flemish repertory of motets by such composers as Josquin, La Rue, Mouton, Févin, Isaac, Verbonet, and Thérache, in addition to one obscure German composer and five anonymi. Another source is the magnificently illuminated MS Pepys 1760 in Magdalene College, Cambridge, which has four concordances with our manuscript. The collation of Thérache's *Verbum bonum et suave* in the Medici Codex has shown[6] that the scribe of our manuscript used either the Pepys manuscript itself (and this seems the more likely case, in view of the common mistakes) or the source that served as model for the scribe of the Pepys manuscript. Other motets concordant with the latter source, such as numbers 40 and 41, have enough (but by no means all) variant readings in common with it to sustain the belief in a relationship between the two sources.[7]

The Pepys manuscript has variously been claimed to have been written for Henry VII,[8] his oldest son Arthur,[9] or Henry VIII as prince of Wales.[10] The coat of arms on the first folio could belong to Henry VII or Henry VIII, but the miniature that headed the third composition is now missing. According to a catalogue of 1697,[11] the book was made 'in the time of King Hen. VII for the then Prince of Wales; being the Prince's Original Book, elegantly prickt and illuminated with his Figure in Miniature.' If the manuscript was written for Arthur, it would have to be dated before 1502, since Arthur died in April of that year. Since Prince Henry ceased to hold the title, Prince of Wales, on the death of his father, either of the other attributions would place the writing of the manuscript before 1509. Neither Henry VII nor Prince Arthur are known for their love of music; Henry VIII, on the other hand, was a music enthusiast. Moreover, study of the repertory makes a dating after 1509 mandatory. Among its fifty-one compositions, the manuscript contains twenty-two works by Antoine de Févin (c 1473-1511), one motet by Richafort (whose first compositions otherwise appear in 1518 and 1519), and one chanson by 'Hyllayre' (Penet), who was born in 1501,[12] was a choirboy in the chapel of Louis XII in 1513, and in the service of Leo X from 1514 to 1522, and whose first composition – he must have been precocious – was published by Petrucci in 1514.

I believe that the manuscript was written for the young King Henry VIII and his wife, Catherine of Aragon, in 1516, and for the following reasons.

The source is one of the most luxurious parchment manuscripts of the time and well suited to be given to a king and a queen.

The coat of arms is that of a king, not of a prince; it could have been that of Henry VII or Henry VIII.

With its preponderance of works by Févin, it might well be an anthology of his compositions upon his relatively early death.

The half-dozen chansons by Févin on the jealous husband[13] would make excellent sense in a manuscript dedicated to a happy young couple – the husband giving good-natured warning to his wife of how jealous he is.

The great number of Marian motets (seventeen out of twenty-four) appearing under the heading *in laudem celestis regine* favours the assumption that the manuscript was written upon the birth of Mary on 18 February 1516, an event whose significance for the parents must be measured in terms of the death of five previous children, including Prince Henry, who lived barely two months. Mary's birth was indeed an event to be celebrated and memorialized in a manuscript in which the highest arts of musician and illuminator were joined.

Thus MS 1070 is not an isolated source of French music at the time of the Tudors; it exists in company with at least two splendid parchment manuscripts whose repertory is not only French but also intimately related in the choice of composers.

DESCRIPTION OF THE MANUSCRIPT

Written on rather thin paper, not of the finest quality, and consisting of 268 pages, MS 1070 measures 28.5 x 19 cm. While it is in the ordinary choirbook format, its size, smaller than most choirbooks,[14] would put it into the category of a quarto book.[15] There are two numberings, one in folios, the other in pages, both in pencil by modern hands. At each end there are two flyleaves of different paper. The modern binding, brown leather pasted over cardboard, is worn and scratched. The spine reads: 'MOTETS. / 16TH CENT.' Pasted on the inside cover is the following printed notice (a clipping from a catalogue?) : 'Antiphonarium, *Manuscript with coloured ornamental initial letters, and music noted,* XVIth century, folio.'

Folio 1 consists of blank staves; the paper is yellowed. Folios 1 and 2 have been cut on the inner margin and pasted to a different paper. The same is true for the last two folios. Perhaps the manuscript remained unbound for a long time, during which the outer folios became loose.

The staves for the whole manuscript were ruled beforehand in brown ink between two guidelines in red ink. There are also red-ink guidelines for the text. On every page, from 1 to 204, spaces were left for initials in all parts. From pages 205 to 264, space was left only for soprano and alto initials; on pages 265 to 268 no space was left for initials.

Pages 1 to 204 carry eleven staves, pages 205 to 268 only nine. Page 204 is more yellowed and soiled than the surrounding pages. It is the end of a gathering; perhaps the remainder, with its different staff arrangement, was joined at a later time.

Two main hands and two subsidiary hands can be distinguished. Some variation within these hands may be the result of differences of pens or the mood of the writer. The first main hand, responsible for the text from pages 1 to 204 (with the exception of pages 44, 156, 173, 184-5, and 188), conforms in general to what has been described as a 'bastard hand' that had its probable origin in fifteenth-century France[16] (see the opening folio, on figure 2). The second main hand, less formal and more cursive, completed pages 44, 156, 173, and 188 – left blank by the first scribe – and continued on pages 206 to 225 and 234 to 263 (see figure 3, with the beginning of the anonymous four-part motet *Popule meus*). A different, more fluent and modern hand is responsible for pages 184 to 185[17] and 266 to 267 (see figure 4, containing the anonymous three-part chanson *Gentilz galans compaingnons*). A fourth hand wrote pages 226 to 229 (see figure 5, containing the anonymous four-part chanson *Venes regres*).

Neither the hands responsible for the music nor those that wrote the words – they may be the same – are of a high calligraphic calibre. They are hands of professionals, but not of the first order. Nor is the manuscript written with particular care. It contains an unusual number of corrections. Sometimes the first scribe was careless and did not break off all voices at the same measure at the end of the page. The second scribe corrected these mistakes by striking out the text and music at the bottom of a folio and transferring them to the top of the next folio;[18] the reverse also happens.[19] The corrections, made at times by the hand that wrote the original text, at times by another, are entered unceremoniously, without any attempt to cover up the mistakes made; wrong notes, wrong words are simply struck out; the corrections are plainly visible as such. The first scribe apparently did not proofread his work. The manuscript appears to have been used in performance, on which occasion the errors must have been discovered and amended. Such use is also indicated by accidentals that were added later; the original accidentals occupy a full space; those added later appear crowded between the notes. The text is missing on whole pages.[20] The manuscript is marred in places by spots, smudges, and tears at the lower ends of the pages.

Irregularities also appear in the structure of the manuscript. Altogether there are seventeen layers, mostly consisting of eight folios each. Exceptions are one layer with six folios, three layers with seven folios, and three layers with nine folios. The order of the manuscript as presently preserved is set out in the table following. It would seem that the order of the fascicles was disturbed, and that when the second scribe got the manuscript he found some pages missing. Thus, he had to complete pages 44,

Gathering	Number of folios	Page numbers	Blank pages	Hands
1	6	1-12	1	1
2	7	13-26		1
3	8	27-42	42	1
4	8	43-58	43, 45	1 (p. 44 = hand 2)
5	8	59-74		1
6	8	75-90	76-9	1
7	8	91-106	92-3	1
8	7	107-120		1
9	8	121-136	124-5	1
10	9	137-154	146-54	1
11	8	155-170	155	1 (p. 156 = hand 2)
12	8	171-186	182-3, 186	1 (p 173 = hand 2; pp. 184-185 = hand 3)
13	9	187-204	187	1 (p. 188 = hand 2)
14	7	205-218	205	2
15	8	219-234	230-3	2 (pp. 226-229 = hand 4)
16	9	235-252		2
17	8	253-268	264-5, 268	2 (pp. 266-267 = hand 3)

156, 173, and 188, and added the last four fascicles.

Some of the irregularities in the gatherings can be explained. In layer 2 one folio is missing between pages 12 and 13, with a resulting loss of music. In layer 8 one folio is cut out after page 112, but without loss of music. In layer 13 one folio (pages 189-90) was glued in later. Layer 2 shows that a folio could be removed without physical evidence of its having been taken out. The same may be true for layers 10, 14, and 16. In layer 10 pages 146 to 155 are blank; it is possible that a blank folio has been removed. Another possibility exists in the case of layer 14. Page 204 shows the beginning of a large work by Josquin with three *partes*. Since only the first page (soprano and tenor) is notated, one whole gathering (plus one folio) may be missing.

The same paper has been used throughout, except for the last folio. The watermark is an ornamental M that appears sideways, as happens in quarto format (see note 15 above), in which position it looks like a lyre (see figure 6A). How unhelpful watermarks can be as a guide to dating a manuscript is evident in the present case. The paper of MS 1070 bears a watermark that Briquet (no. 8418)[21] variously assigns to Paris, 1493; Paris, 1505-10; Arras, 1505-21; Troyes, 1509-16; Lisieux to 1515; Pays

Bas, 1495. In the words of Hilary Jenkinson, 'the student should remember, however, that watermarks (since paper may lie long in stock) are unsafe as an indication of any date except the *a quo*.'[22]

The last folio has a different watermark, a hand with a star on top and a cuff below (see figure 6B). There is a large variety of such watermarks. The closest to that in MS 1070 is the hand with open fingers, cuff, and five-part star. Briquet lists it as number 10794 for Ingolstadt, 1532; Avignon and Carpentras, 1555; Pau, 1545; and Navarrieux, 1547. The only safe conclusion to be drawn is that the paper of the last folio is of later origin than that of the rest of the manuscript.[23]

The most interesting visual aspect of the manuscript is the elaborate coloured initials painted on pages 2 to 41. That the remainder of the manuscript was intended to be similarly decorated, is demonstrated by the spaces left free for initials. A typical choirbook, MS 1070 divides every folio into four fields, with soprano and tenor on the verso and alto and bass on the recto page. Each voice part is graced with coloured illustrations, whether or not an initial is needed. At the beginning of a composition the illustrations fuse with the shape of the initial (see figure 2), but on the succeeding pages, as the composition continues, illustrations appear without functioning as letters (see figures 7, 8, 9, and 12). The initials and pseudo-initials are in irregularly drawn rectangles of blue and red on the white paper. The red and blue watercolours are often faded. The objects of the illuminations are traditional: foliage and flowers, berries and seed corns alternate with grotesque heads, fantastic animals, and monsters, or with graceful birds and mermaids, and medallions of attractive women (see figure 7). The objects are not always clearly separated. In the traditional fantastic style of illustration, leaves turn into fish; shoots emerging from a stem on top and bottom meet in the head of a fair youth; branches and flowers become a monster's head with tongue outstretched.

It is particularly in the field of the grotesque and monstrous that the illuminator gives free reign to his fancy. A two-legged, thick, snake-like animal with short wings turning its long curled tail and goat-like head upward to the surrounding flowers; a mermaid with flowing hair in half-figure, the lower part of her body encased in a shell-like structure, raising her arms shoulder high; a two-headed, two-legged monster with a quadruped's body surrounded by flowers; a helmeted man with a fishtail, beating a bush with a branch; a griffin-like creature with a barrel for, or affixed to, its lower body; a wild man's crowned head with tongue sticking out (see figures 7 and 8) – these fantastic visions appear in the innocent company of flowers, fruits, plants, leaves, and acorns.

Novel as the individual image may be, its patterns go back over six hundred years and longer. The Codex Vossianus in the Bodleian Library, from the early tenth century, has initials showing the biting heads of fantastic animals joined by a human head emerging from a horn embedded in the mouth of a mythical horned animal.[24] Similar fanciful creatures and combinations of creatures with foliage or ornamental scrolls occur in manuscripts of the eighth and ninth centuries.[25] The late twelfth-century Westminster psalter at the British Museum shows an initial Q with the two curved lines of the letter filled with seed corns (a figure which occurs throughout MS 1070) of proportionally increasing and diminishing sizes, birds in the outer rim, and the tail of the Q ending in a long-necked, fantastic animal's head spitting out long sprays of floral shoots.[26] In particular, the models for animals – real, fancied, and monstrous – were to be found in bestiaries. The early Christian gnostics drew on classical myth and fable for stories of animals, real or fancied, to which they applied their favourite method of allegorical interpretation. We have found illustrated bestiaries from as early as the tenth century.[27] Even the colour scheme used in the initials of MS 1070 has models in the twelfth century, at which time manuscripts appear in which 'the smaller initials were sometimes coloured plain red or blue, and decorated with fine pen flourishes in the same colours.'[28]

Compared with the great art of the past, the quality of the coloured initials in our manuscript is modest indeed. It suggests the hand of a skilful, but by no means first-rate, professional. Two experts in Renaissance illumination, who briefly examined the manuscript, confirmed the 'provincial' character of the initials and placed them at the end of the fifteenth or the beginning of the sixteenth century.[29] The British Museum has a book of hours from the end of the fifteenth century (MS Add. 15216) which shows certain formal similarities to MS 1070. In addition to full-page illuminations in a rather primitive Flemish style, it has initials in rectangles, on blue or red, and with gold (instead of the white of our manuscript). Models were also available in the initials of printed books. French incunabula, especially, favour initials in the form of rectangles and with foliage, flowers, birds, animals, and grotesques similar to those in our manuscript.[30]

ORIGIN OF THE MANUSCRIPT

Barclay Squire, in his description of the manuscript, pointed to an inscription on page 157: 'M^{ris} A. Bolleyne nowe thus,'[31] followed by three minims with upright stems and a *longa* with downward stem (see figure 13). This inscription has been noted several times since, but no one has been able to make any sense of it, to explain the meaning of the notes, or to connect the name in any logical fashion with the manuscript.

I believe that this inscription, written in a clearly contemporaneous English script, is the clue to the origin of the manuscript. It at least proves that the manuscript was in English hands, and presumably in England, in the sixteenth century. Another note, on the last page of the book, says: 'This MSS is about 250 years old,' below which another hand wrote in explanation, 'that is the year 1540.' If we may assume the two notes to be close in time of origin, both would have been written in about 1790, which would prove that the manuscript remained in England and that in England there were people expert enough to date the manuscript fairly accurately – as we shall see later. Robert William Haynes – perhaps the same man who published, together with H. G. Stevens, *A Catalogue of Modern Law Books* (1865) – probably acquired the manuscript from an English bookdealer (who was perhaps the source of the clipping mentioned earlier).

I shall now attempt to show that the manuscript was written for Anne Boleyn after she had been crowned queen of England. To build the needed foundation for this thesis, an account of the relationship between Henry VIII and Anne as well as of Henry's divorce of Catherine of Aragon is indispensable.

The relationship between Henry and Anne began in 1526.[32] At the outset, the king, who had had an affair with Anne's sister Mary some years earlier, was no more serious about Anne.[33] But Anne decided to play for higher stakes. Either she would be queen, or she would not be Henry's. The king was not accustomed to resistance. His passion was kindled by Anne's aloofness. Finding Anne unbending, the king made a solemn promise to divorce Catherine and make Anne his queen. But he had not counted on the dilatory tactics of the pope, the opposition of Charles V, nephew of his wife, and last but not least, the quiet, unyielding firmness of Catherine of Aragon, who, in the midst of adversity, remained dignified, strong, and resourceful.

Henry called on the best theologians of his realm and abroad to pronounce his marriage unlawful on the grounds that Catherine had been the wife of his older brother Arthur before her marriage to Henry. The case was to be based on Leviticus 20:21: 'And if a man shall take his brother's wife, it is an unclean thing: he hath uncovered his brother's nakedness; they shall be childless.' Henry took the view that Catherine and he had been living in sin. Was not the terrible fate which had befallen them — deprived of one child after another (there were seven children, three sons among them, of whom only Mary survived) — God's visitation upon Henry for his disregard of the divine commandment? The struggle to obtain the pope's approval was long, tedious, and fruitless. In 1534, after years of diplomatic wrangling, the pope pronounced sentence against Henry, who then took the fateful step which he had long threatened: he separated the church of England from the church of Rome, had himself declared supreme head of the English church, and forced his subjects to take an oath to him under the Act of Supremacy. The conflict convulsed England; it cost the lives of two of her greatest sons, Bishop John Fisher and Thomas More, who refused to take the oath.

What of Henry's and Anne's relationship during the long years of controversy? The general opinion is that Anne kept Henry waiting from 1526 to 1532 — a view hard to accept in light of our knowledge of Henry's character and temperament and the moral climate of his court. A number of events combine to render this opinion doubtful. On 9 December 1529, in a banquet given at court, Anne took the place of the queen; in May 1530 Henry went riding, 'Anne sitting on the pillion of his horse'; in August 1531 Catherine was definitely banished from court, and in October she left for the Moor; a few days later Anne Boleyn made her entrance at court, receiving the homage due to a future queen. One year later Anne was created marchioness of Pembroke; the title was made hereditary to all male issue, the words 'lawfully begotten' ordinarily inserted in patents of creation being omitted. In October 1532, when Henry went to meet François I at Calais, Anne accompanied the king. Finally, on 25 January 1533, Anne was secretly married to Henry, while the divorce proceedings in Rome were still dragging on. It was a desperate step to take, for the marriage entered into would have to be interpreted as bigamy according to civil as well as canon law — unless, of course, Henry's point of view prevailed, and it had yet to be legally established. Only one reason could have moved the king to so unconventional a procedure: Anne was with child. Now events followed in swift order;

Thomas Cranmer, one-time chaplain of the Boleyn family,[34] who had long sided with the king and Anne, was consecrated archbishop of Canterbury in December 1532; on 10 May 1533, he opened his court of inquiry into the validity of Henry's marriage with Catherine and on 23 May he pronounced the marriage null and void; on 1 June Anne Boleyn was crowned queen of England. On 7 September 1533, Anne gave birth to Elizabeth.

There is no doubt about Henry's passionate sincerity in his desire for a male heir to the English throne. Catherine's failure to give him a son and the catastrophic series of infant deaths and miscarriages with which she was plagued weighed heavily on his mind. When Anne, too, failed to give Henry a son, and when she also suffered a miscarriage, Henry's disappointment could not have been keener. But the marriage did not go well for other reasons.

Anne Boleyn, on her father's side, had come from the wealthy merchant class, and on her mother's side from the lower nobility. Unlike Catherine, who was of Spanish royal blood, she was neither born nor educated to be a queen. The long years of embarrassing uncertainty, the growing ambiguity of her position at court, the resistance of the pope, of the emperor, of Catherine herself who, for a long time, continued to preside at court as queen, the development of factions for and against her, her unpopularity among the common people, all of these would have been hard to bear for the strongest character and the most serene temperament. Anne had neither. When she finally became queen, she showed herself imperious, haughty, and *intrigante*. She could not help but make numerous enemies. Worst of all, she was unable to cope with the king. Henry, an ardent lover first and then an indifferent husband, was to her a man to master or to quarrel with. Henry would tolerate neither.

Catherine, in all her unyielding strength, had had one quality that disarmed Henry. He, who was thoroughly indoctrinated in the mystique of the divine origin of kingship, found in her a woman who was deeply convinced of the king's divine mission. She never forgot that, wrong though Henry the man could be, he was always the king ordained by God's grace to occupy the throne of England. Anne was quite incapable of conceiving of her relationship with Henry in such terms. She quarreled violently with Henry when the king, only one and a half years after their marriage, began to look for greener pastures.

Two years after the marriage, Henry, already paying court to Jane Seymour, thought of a means to rid himself of Anne. He left the plotting to Thomas Cromwell, Wolsey's successor, who shortly cooked up a stew of such horrendous accusations as to render any defence illusory. Anne was charged with having committed adultery with a whole roster of men, among whom were a musician, some nobles, and her own brother. Her trial was a mockery of justice and a European scandal. Melanchthon voiced a common sentiment when he pronounced Anne 'regina magis accusata quam convicta adulterii.'[35] A few days after her trial, only three years after her coronation, Anne and her reputed lovers were beheaded at the Tower of London.

M^{ris} A Bolleyne nowe thus   ━   ♭♭♭ 𝄆   ━

Let us have another look at this mysterious inscription (page 157 of MS 1070, see figure 13). Would it not seem that it refers to Anne's death? 'Mistress Anne Boleyn,' once so proud and upright, has now fallen into the dust. 'Now thus' was Thomas Boleyn's motto.[36] Perhaps the three notes with stems going upward were meant to point to her three years as queen of England. Perhaps the minims were intended to indicate how fast they had passed by, while the *longa* with its stem downward was to be a sign of the end that had come in a catastrophic reversal of fate.[37] The *longa*, because it is always used as the final note of a piece, denotes the end. The crucial question is this: what has the inscription to do with the manuscript? Let us begin at the beginning.

The manuscript opens with a work not to be found in any other source (see figure 2). It is a four-part setting of a poem in the lesser Sapphic metre:

Forte si dulci Stigium boantem	With sweet-voiced song,
Cerberum cantu modulatus Orpheus	Well timed, did Orpheus
	Mute roaring Cerberus,
Strinxit et caecos fidibus seorsum Tendere manes.	With lutes drew on The blinded spirits.
Ergo maiori reputetur arte	With greater art
Mortuum Christus veniens Olimpo	Came Christ, consider, from Olympus.
Lazarum qui una tenebris reverti Voce coegit.	By one word, dead Lazarus He forced to part From ghostly shades.

Quippe sanato precibus sororum	Since Lazarus
Lazaro plures supero tonanti	By sisters' prayers grew whole,
Perfidi credunt animis ovantes	Sure, many heal their disbelief,
Esse beatis.	In Heaven's Thund'rer trust,
	To join the blessed souls.
Pallas Actaea memoratur arce	By th'Actaean mount
Laeta Junoni Samos est tributa	Is Pallas recalled. To Juno was
Equoris divus Tenedo beatur	Glad Samos giv'n. Holy Gades of
Hercule Gades.	smooth waves
	Hercules from Tyneros' ground
	Did joyful make.
Edua totus requiescit urbe	Each man calléd
Viribus sacris modulis vocatus	By sacred songs his powers restores
Lazarus summa potiturque sede	In Haedui-town, and more, lays
In paradiso.	hold
	On him in seat exalt'd,
	On Laz'rus in Paradise.
Nos ubi Christum varia precemur	With diverse praise
Laude vel carum dociles amicum	Let us who hope to learn implore
Reddat ut nobis facilem magistrum	Him there: Christ for us as loving
Omnipotentem.	friend procure
Amen.	An easy master
	The Omnipotent. Amen.[38]

(The final 'Amen' of the composition clearly does not belong to the poem. Its addition vitiates the structure of the Sapphic ode. It must have been added by the composer for the purpose of creating a well-rounded musical ending.)

Neither the author of the poem nor the composer of the music is known. Nor have I found the text set by any other composer. Unquestionably, it is a neo-Latin ode written in the most artful humanistic fashion of the day. In the words of Professor Morrison, 'it was not meant to be understood; rather, to leave the impression of inscrutable learning.' The main idea, the comparison between Orpheus and Christ, is ingenious: if Orpheus enjoys fame for having tamed with his music the monsters of the underworld, how much more art does not Christ show in recalling dead Lazarus to life! The implication seems clear: whereas Orpheus – what-

ever the reason – did not succeed in recalling Euridice from the shades of
the underworld, Christ, with one command of the divine voice, revived
the dead. Great is the power of Orpheus, but Christ alone can raise the
dead, and – by allegorical implication – give eternal life.[39]

Now this is a chief tenet of the Reformation. The worship of Christ
replaced the veneration of Mary. Only Christ can forgive, only he can
give immortality. Lazarus' resurrection was a popular theme of Reformation drama.[40] Anne Boleyn, vexed by the unyielding resistance of the
Roman Catholic church to the dissolution of Henry's marriage to Catherine of Aragon, turned more and more to the Protestants.

The second part of the poem introduces Pallas, Juno, and Hercules,
connecting them with Christ and Lazarus in that strangely syncretistic
style adopted by humanists bent upon creating a new fusion of Greek
mythology and Christian religion.

Can the Sapphic ode be placed with any hope of accuracy? Its classical metre, its polished if highly artificial verse, and its mixture of Christian and pagan figures recall the spirit of the festivities in honour of
Anne's coronation – an event described by various chroniclers in colourful detail.[41] The festivities and processions began on Thursday, 29 May
1533; they lasted till Whitsuntide, Sunday, 1 June, the day of the coronation. The king had sent letters to the mayor and the council of the city
of London, requesting them 'to make preparacion aswell to fetche her
grace from Grenewyche to the Tower by water as to see the citie ordered
and garnished with pageauntes in places accustomed, for the honor of
her grace.' The mayor commanded all guilds 'to prepare barges and to
garnishe them, not alonely with their banners accustomed, but also to
decke theim with Targettes by the sides of the barges ... and every barge to
have mynstrelsie.' The mayor's barge 'was garnished with many goodly
banners and stremers, and richely covered, In which barge were Shalmes
[shawms], Shagbushes [sackbuts], and divers other instrumentes, which
continually made a goodly armony.' 'On the left hand of the Maior was
another Foyst, in the whiche was a mount and on the same stode a white
Fawcon crouned upon a rote of golde environed with white roses and red,
whiche was the Quenes devise: about whiche mount satte virgyns singyng
and plaiying swetely.'

The classical humanistic tone of the festivities was manifest in the
pageants prepared for Anne as she was conveyed through London.[42] The
chronicler reports the route that Anne's entourage took and describes
every stop on the way. Thus he tells how

she roade into Gracious church corner, where was a costly and mar-
vailous connyng pageaunt made by the marchauntes of the Stylyarde
[Steelyard], for there was the mount Pernasus with the fountayne of
Helycon, which was of white Marble and iiii. streames without pype
did rise an ell hye and mette together in a litle cuppe above the fountain, which fountain ranne aboundantly Racked Rennishe wyne til
night. On the mountaine satte Appollo and at his fete satte Calliope,
and on every syde of the mountain satte iiii. Muses plaiyng on severall
swete instrumentes, and at their feete Epigrammes and Poyses [poe-
sies] were written in golden letters in the whiche every Muse accordy-
ing to her propertie praysed the Quene.

Some pageants acted out a scene. At Leaden Hall there was

a goodly pageaunt with a type [cupola] and a heavenly roffe, and
under the type was a rote of golde set on a litle mountaine environed
with red roses and white, out of the type came doune a Fawcon all
white and sate upon the rote, and incontinent came doune an Angell
with great melody and set a close croune of golde on the Fawcons
head ...

[The queen] passed a lytell further, and at the lesser condyt was a
costly and a ryche pagent, where as was goodly armonye of musyke
and other mynstrels, with syngyng: and within that pagent was fyve
costly seates, wherin was set these fyve personages, that is to wete
Juno, Pallas, Mercury, and Venus, and Parys havyng a balle of
golde[43] presentyng it to her grace with certayne verses of great honour, and chyldren syngyng a balade to her grace, & prayse to all her
ladyes ...[44]

Pallas and Juno in the second part of the poem are very appropriate
for the pageant at Anne's coronation. The omission of Venus and substitution of Hercules for Paris might be the result of Christ's presence in
the initial portion of the poem. Pallas and Juno represent goddesses of
virtue; Hercules was celebrated throughout the Renaissance for his
choosing duty over pleasure, *Virtus* over *Voluptas*.[45] All in all, the opening motet, with its fusion of humanistic and Reformed ideas and with its
echo of the pageants from her coronation, fits well in a manuscript written
for Anne Boleyn.

Latin verses and orations as well as English ones greeted the queen
wherever she stopped in the coronation processions. Manuscript Royal 18

A LXIV in the British Museum contains 'a copie of divers and sundry verses as well in Latin as in Englishe devised and made partely by Jhon Leland and partely by Nicholas Vuedale.' John Leland (1506-52, antiquary) wrote only Latin verse; Nicholas Udall (1505-56, headmaster at Eton and author of the first English comedy, *Ralph Roister Doister*), wrote both Latin and English verses for the occasion.[46] In these recitations Anne is compared to famous ancient queens and to goddesses. It goes without saying that she is made to outshine them all in beauty, wisdom, and virtue.

How one would wish to have a similar book containing the music performed! Many of the verses must have been sung; the chroniclers say so, but we are not told which ones, and we do not have the music. Our poem on Orpheus and Lazarus is not among the verses in the Royal manuscript and it was certainly not written by Leland or Udall. For, in comparison to its highflown contrivance, their most ornate Latin style is almost sober. Nevertheless, it might well have been performed, indoors or outdoors, during the long-drawn-out festivities.

The second composition, Josquin's famous *Memor esto verbi tui* (verses 49 to 64 of psalm 118), is also fitting in a choirbook for Henry's second wife. Glareanus tells us that Josquin composed the work in order to remind Louis XII of a promise made and that it did indeed have the desired effect.[47] The work enjoyed a certain vogue at the court of Henry VIII. The Venetian ambassador to England, Nicolo Sagudino, reported in a letter of 17 May 1517 that Dionisio Memo, the Venetian organist whom Henry made his chaplain to keep him at his court, set a beautiful four-part composition on the words '*Memor esto verbi tui*' and played it for the king on the organ, placing the text in his hands. 'Surely,' added the ambassador, 'his wish will be fulfilled.'[48] Since we know of no compositions by Memo, it is most likely that he played his own keyboard arrangement of Josquin's work. To assign the second place in the manuscript to this famous work may be interpreted as an allusion to the king's word of honour that he would marry Anne Boleyn. What could be more pertinent than the opening lines, 'Remember your word to your servant, with which you gave me hope. It comforted me in my humble station ...' ? All the world now knew that the king had indeed kept his word.

Quite logically, the manuscript continues with a setting of psalm 116: 'Praise the Lord, all ye nations: praise him, all ye people, for his merciful kindness is great toward us: and the truth of the Lord endureth for ever.'

The next work is crucial for an understanding of the precise historical background of the manuscript. It is the gospel for the nuptial mass, whose text comes from Matthew 19:3-6:

> The Pharisees also came unto him, tempting him and saying unto him. Is it lawful for a man to put away his wife for every cause? And he answered and said unto them, Have ye not read, that he which made them at the beginning made them male and female, and said, For this cause shall a man leave father and mother, and shall cleave to his wife: and they twain shall be one flesh? Wherefore they are no more twain but one flesh. What therefore God hath joined together, let no man put asunder.

At first blush one might well feel that were this manuscript written for Anne, then surely a setting of Christ's words against divorce would not figure in it, since Anne's elevation was the result of Henry's divorce from Catherine of Aragon. But Henry's, and of course Anne's, position on this matter was that there was no divorce since there had been no lawful marriage.[49] Henry and Catherine had lived in sin and only now had Henry entered into a legitimate marriage. To Cardinal Campeggio, the papal legate sent by Clement VII to England to try the divorce case, Henry had said (according to Campeggio) 'that he wished nothing except a declaration whether his marriage was valid or not, always presuming it was not, and I think that an angel descending from heaven could not persuade him otherwise.'[50] For these reasons, to include in a choirbook for Anne Boleyn a setting of the gospel for the nuptial mass was not only flattery of a kind that Anne would appreciate, it was also a most devastating blow against Catherine and her supporters. The motet was inserted to bear witness that the sanctity of marriage was a concept valid only for the union of Henry and Anne.

The next work, made up of a number of biblical passages, warrants particular attention. Study of other contemporary manuscripts, and notably the Medici Codex, has led to the formulation of the following principle: 'When a composer of this era chooses the text for a single composition from many disparate parts of the Bible, when he thus constructs a text that occurs neither in the liturgy nor anywhere else, he obviously wishes to say, this is a unique text; it fits a unique situation; look into the sources of the text and you may find the key to its meaning.'[51] The

following list gives the text of the motet in the left-hand column and its
sources in the right-hand column.

Ps. 150:1 Laudate Dominum in sanctis eius	Laudate Deum in sanctis eius et audiatur
Ps. 117:15 vox exsultationis et salutis in tabernaculis iustorum	vox exsultationis et salutis in tabernaculis iustorum
Ps. 6:10 Exaudivit Dominus deprecationem meam	Quoniam deprecationem eorum exaudivit Dominus,
Ps. 20:2 Domine, in virtute tua laetabitur rex, et super salutare tuum exsultabit vehementer	in cuius virtute rex exsultavit vehementer
I Kings 2:1 quia laetata sum in salutari tuo	et ego laetata sum in salutari suo.
Ps. 115:18 vota mea Domino reddam in conspectu omnis populi eius	Igitur vota mea reddam Domino, in conspectu sanctorum eius.
Ps. 21:25 et, cum clamarem ad eum, exaudivit me.	Quia, cum clamarem ad eum, exaudivit vocem meam.
Ps. 15:9 Propter hoc laetatum est cor meum, et exsultavit lingua mea, insuper et caro mea requiescet in spe.	Propter hoc laetabitur cor meum, et exsultabit lingua mea, insuper et caro mea quae refloruit requiescet in spe
Ps. 27:7 et refloruit caro mea	
Ps. 22:6 Et misericordia tua subsequetur me	misericordiae quae subsequetur me
Ps. 21:32 Adnuntiabitur Domino generatio ventura, et adnuntiabunt caeli iustitiam eius.	dum annuntiabitur generatio ventura, tunc annuntiabunt caeli iusticiam eius.
Ps. 146:1 Laudate Dominum, quoniam bonus est psalmus, Deo nostro sit iucunda decoraque laudatio.	Laudate ergo Dominum, quoniam bonus est psalmus, Deo nostro sit iucunda decoraque laudatio.

Superficially, the text of the fifth motet yields no information of special
significance. It is another 'Praise the Lord' text, seemingly a psalm, but in
reality freely varied verses gathered from a number of different psalms,
starting with the first line of psalm 150, the psalm in praise of the Lord

and of music. The lines from psalm 117 are particularly fitting for a day of exultation, containing as they do the words 'This is the day which the Lord hath made; we will rejoice and be glad in it.' The next psalm recounts the psalmist's sufferings and persecutions, but 'the Lord hath heard the voice of my weeping. The Lord hath heard my supplication.'

The author of this psalm *mélange* changes singular to plural, adds a word here, omits another there, and takes all sorts of liberties. But the origin of the lines can always be traced. The next line, although appearing in a relative clause, comes from psalm 20, the psalm exalting the king who is blessed by the Lord: 'The king shall joy in thy strength, O Lord: and in thy salvation how greatly shall he rejoice! Thou hast given him his heart's desire, and hast not withholden the request of his lips.' And as if to indicate what the king's desire was, comes now a line surprising in the use of the feminine gender, quite extraordinary in the psalms. 'And I have rejoiced,' sings the woman, 'in his salvation.' But who is the woman? And, if the psalms do not speak in the feminine gender, where does the passage come from? Chapter 1 of the first book of Samuel (or, as the Vulgate says, *Liber primus Samuelis quem nos 'primum Regum' dicimus*) recounts the story of Elkanah and Hannah who were childless. Hannah went to the temple to sacrifice 'in bitterness of soul,' weeping and praying, and to ask that the Lord give her 'a man child.' Hannah's prayer was heard; she gave birth to a son and called him Samuel, and when he was weaned she took him to the temple to dedicate him to the Lord's service. The second chapter begins with the words, 'And Hannah prayed, and said, My heart rejoiceth in the Lord, mine horn is exalted in the Lord: my mouth is enlarged over mine enemies; because [and these are the words paraphrased in our text, *laetata sum in salutari tuo*] I rejoice in thy salvation.'

The biblical reference becomes more pointed if we recall that the Latin text speaks not of 'Hannah,' but of 'Anna.' A more pertinent reference to Anne's situation could hardly be devised. Moreover, by changing *in salutari tuo* to *in salutari suo* – with *suo* referring to the king – the compiler of the text has cleverly tied together God, king, and Anne. It seems hardly necessary to examine the sources of the remaining lines of the text; they all come from psalms, as demonstrated in our comparative survey. But it must be granted that the text writer, by taking all lines save one from the psalms, showed great cunning in directing the curious to the book of Samuel where he would find the name of Anna. Biblical passages in which a woman speaks to God are rare; the Vulgate has only one pas-

sage in which the words *laetata sum* occur. This rendered it easier for the
sixteenth-century reader to discover the hidden reference. And the reference was not only to Anne; it highlighted the one issue that all people, no
matter what their political or religious bias, could plainly see: the king's
desperate desire for a male heir, a desire that Catherine had been incapable of fulfilling.

That the author of this motet is Mouton, the French court composer,
who died in 1522, would seem to demolish our whole theory, were it not
that Mouton served Louis XII, who was married to Anne of Brittany. Their
marriage was afflicted by a series of frustrations similar to those of Henry
and Catherine.[52] Their wish for a son was never fulfilled. The selection of
Mouton's motet by the editor of Anne Boleyn's choirbook may be regarded as evidence that his contemporaries indeed knew how to read and
interpret the text of a psalm *mélange*. What was written for Anne of
Brittany and Louis XII fitted Anne Boleyn and Henry VIII to perfection.

In the light of the foregoing, it will scarcely be considered a coincidence that the next motet deals with the nativity. Mouton's motet features
the dialogue of the shepherds: 'Noel, whom do you see in the stable?'
'Jesus, of a Virgin born' – a renewed, strengthened allusion in biblical
cloth to the desired birth of a son.

The text of the seventh motet is puzzlesome:

O salve genitrix Virgo	Hail, sweetest Virgin Mother,
dulcissima salve. Salve	hail. Hail, Mary, who holds
quae superum sceptra Maria	the sceptre of the heavens.
tenes. Et ipsa rosas	You outshine the roses and
vincis et omne iubar. Ad	all radiance. To you we
te clamamus, soboles	call, children of pitiable
miserabilis Evae quos	Eve whom, driven from our own
propria pulsos vallis	[home = Paradise], the bitter
acerba locat.	valley [of tears] houses.

It sounds like a familiar Marian prayer, but all efforts to trace it have
been futile. The text is made up of thoughts and phrases which occur in
other Marian texts.[53] Every word, or at least every thought, can be found
in older Marian prose or poetry save one: *et ipsa rosas vincis*. In medieval poetry Mary is often likened to a rose or a lily, but she is not said to
excel, to outshine, to conquer the roses. The closest analogue that one can
find in Marian hymns is the phrase that probably served as model: *quae*

solis rotam vincit decore ac lumine (who excels the wheel of the sun's chariot in splendour and radiance). This image occurs in the fourth-century Christmas hymn by Prudentius, *O sola magnarum urbium*.[54] But Anne Boleyn, having won the king's heart, may well be said to have conquered the roses, symbol of the Tudor family. The phrase was probably smuggled in by the writer in one of those substitutions of an earthly woman for Mary that were so much a habit of the period.[55]

The first seven works of MS 1070, three of which are *unica*, were obviously planned with special care to mark the choirbook as written for and dedicated to Anne Boleyn after her coronation. But the great number of Marian texts and prayers to holy women characterize the book as one intended for a woman: twenty-two out of thirty-nine works consist of such motets.

The sacred repertory of the manuscript ends fittingly with a prayer to the Holy Trinity: Févin's famous *Sancta Trinitas*, which appears in fifteen other sources. It is preceded by a prayer to St Renatus, patron saint of expectant mothers, set by Mouton. Originally written for Anne of Brittany and Louis XII, it was adapted for Catherine and Henry in MS Royal 8 G VII of the British Museum. In MS 1070 the name Anna did not need to be changed, and the name Ludovicus was not changed. Nevertheless, the presence of this prayer for progeny at such a prominent place is another piece of evidence supporting the presumed destination of the codex for Anne Boleyn.

The same holds for the two chansons that appear in the midst of the Latin motets in the portion of the manuscript written by the second scribe. The two compositions express perfectly the two poles of Anne's life: love's triumph and tragedy. The first one, Claudin de Sermisy's famous *Jouyssance vous donneray mon amy*, is the kind of song that Anne may have sung to the accompaniment of the lute for Henry's pleasure. We quote it in Gustave Reese's elegant translation:

> Joy, dearest lover, thine shall be,
> And I shall lead thee tenderly
> Where hope would have thee seek thy pleasure;
> Alive I shall not part from thee,
> And still when death has come to me
> My soul its memories shall treasure.[56]

The second chanson is one we could well picture Anne singing while held in the Tower of London:

Come regrets, come all to my heart,
Come swiftly, let none of you depart;
Come care, come sorrow, and come tears,
Come all that oppresses a lover's heart.

The evidence so far adduced that the manuscript was written for Anne
Boleyn adds up to no more than possibility, perhaps probability. The
manuscript, however, offers more than that; it contains tangible, that is,
visual proof that it was indeed so intended. On pages 28 and 29 occurs the
ending of the gospel for the nuptial mass, with the words, *Itaque iam non
sunt duo sed una caro. Quod ergo Deus coniunxit homo non separet.*
These two pages are decorated with four drawings worthy of study.
Among the botanic, zoological, and anthropoid fantasies, two portrait-
like paintings of women stand out (see figure 9). They are neither large
enough nor skilfully enough drawn to serve for comparisons with real
portraits. But it is fair to say that the head on the upper right has some
similarity to Catherine of Aragon (see figure 10), and the one on the
lower left to Anne Boleyn (see figure 11), who was described as wearing
her hair loose at the festivities preceding the coronation,[57] and who had
long, oval, graceful features in contrast to Catherine's strong roundish
face with the hair done up and covered by a headdress, as she appears in
portraits. But if this is admittedly no more than a reasonable guess, there
is nothing uncertain about the attributes appearing to the side of each
woman. To the left of the supposed Catherine is the pomegranate, Catherine's badge,[58] and to the right of the supposed Anne is the falcon, her
heraldic bird that was prominently featured in the chroniclers' reports of
the coronation festivities quoted earlier.
    If the presence of Catherine in Anne's manuscript is surprising, it
cannot cast doubt on the destination of the manuscript to Anne Boleyn. In
a manuscript destined for Queen Catherine we would not expect to find
the device of her husband's mistress; but two other illuminations provide
an answer to what Catherine's likeness and heraldic badge are doing in
Anne's choirbook. On page 22 there is a falcon pecking at a pomegranate,
and on page 4, in the opening work of the codex, there is another falcon,
wings spread and beak opened, furiously attacking a pomegranate (see
figure 12). The Tudor rose in the upper initial asserts its dominance over
and protection of the falcon – and supports the argument for the English
origin of the manuscript.
    When we consider that it took six long years before Anne reached her

goal and became Henry's wife and queen of England, we can imagine how bitter the enmity between the two women had become – particularly on the part of Anne, who was deemed to be the illegitimate intruder and upstart, not, like Catherine, of royal blood, nor even of noble origin. No doubt Anne took immense pride in her eventual victory over Catherine of Aragon; the visual presentation of Catherine's defeat in symbolic form would have sweetened her taste of victory.

Slowly, some of the puzzling features of the Royal College manuscript become comprehensible. The codex must have been in the process of being written when Anne was tried, sentenced, and executed – proceedings that were completed with indecent haste. Anne was arrested on 2 May 1536; she appeared before her tribunal on 15 May, was sentenced to death, and executed on 19 May. On that same day Henry obtained a special licence from Cranmer to marry Jane Seymour; the wedding ceremony took place on 30 May, only eleven days later.[59]

This sequence of events explains the fragmentary character of the manuscript, never properly completed, containing works with voices missing, missing text, notes without stems, and with only forty of its two hundred and sixty-eight pages decorated, although spaces for decoration were left. It is a reflection of the broken life of Anne Boleyn. Scarcely having had time to enjoy the queenship she had so ardently desired, thwarted in her hopes to win Henry's permanent affection, frustrated in her dreams of giving England a male heir to the throne, she was cut down in the prime of her life.

ANNE BOLEYN

History takes still more from those who have lost everything and gives yet more to those who have taken everything. For its sweeping judgments acquit the unjust and dismiss the pleas of their victims.

Maurice Merleau-Ponty

The assumption that Anne Boleyn was the dedicatee of Royal College MS 1070 raises a few questions. How do we explain the almost exclusively French character of the repertory? Was she musical enough to appreciate so sophisticated an anthology of the most distinguished contrapuntal music of her time? What sort of person, what kind of woman was she? Unfortunately, the student of Anne's personality, her education, her talents and attainments in literature, music, or any other field of humanistic

and artistic endeavour is confronted with two difficulties: the meagreness
of sources and their contradictory nature, and the partisanship that even
today obstructs an objective assessment of her character and her abilities.

Garrett Mattingly, in his famous biography of Catherine of Aragon,
sums up his judgment in one sentence: 'Anne's education had been partly
in France, but she spoke no better French than many a court lady, and
time has left us no record of any special skill of hers in music or dancing,
of any erudition above the common, or any taste in poetry or the arts.' The
only thing uncommon that he sees in her is that, 'having started the king
in pursuit, she had calculation and dexterity and nerve enough to continue
to evade him.'[60] Geoffrey Parmiter, in a recent book, states the common
opinion: 'The secret of the fascination which Anne Boleyn had for Henry
puzzled the king's contemporaries and has remained a puzzle ever since.'[61]
And like Mattingly and other writers, he quotes the description of Anne
given by a Venetian ambassador in 1532: 'Madame Anne is not one of the
handsomest women in the world; she is of middling stature, swarthy com-
plexion, long neck, wide mouth, bosom not too much raised, and in effect
has nothing but the English king's great appetite, and her eyes, which are
black and beautiful.'[62] Why this appraisal of Anne should have been so
generally and uncritically accepted is a mystery. For one thing, the animus against Henry in this statement is so manifest that the gentleman's
objectivity, although never challenged, should indeed be placed in doubt.
For another, comparison of a Venetian and a northern painting of Venus
should furnish sufficient proof that the feminine ideals of north and south
differed widely. Finally, the only other contemporary eyewitness of
Anne's figure whose testimony we have – Henry himself – is on record as
having been enamoured of her 'prety dukkys' – and Henry was something
of a connoisseur in such matters.[63]

Suffice it to say that Anne had many admirers before Henry began
noticing her and that the most famous of them, Thomas Wyatt – a handsome man, as Holbein's portrait shows – a man of talent and of taste, and
the finest poet at Henry's court, had been ardently in love with her.[64]

The most attractive women excel not so much in beauty as in charm.
Grace, wit, vivaciousness, repartee, and talent often attract sophisticated
men more than statuesque beauty of the type the Venetian gentleman
might have preferred. All of these Anne seems to have possessed in rich
measure. Surely, the years spent at the court of Queen Claude of France in
the most formative period of her life made her an accomplished lady of
the world, capable of holding her own in the highest company.

Anne has to be seen in relation to the woman to whom Henry had been married for eighteen years; Catherine was Spanish-educated and was trained from childhood for the serious responsibilities of queenship. She was equally well versed in household duties, the Latin classics, and the church fathers. A woman of great learning, staid, calm, serious, of strong moral character, and deeply religious, she was forty-two years of age when the king's affair with Anne began, six years older than Henry and, exhausted by an endless cycle of pregnancies and miscarriages, withdrawing more and more into religious devotion. Is it really so puzzling that Henry succumbed to the youthful charm of Anne? Moreover, the king was a passionate lover of music and a talented musician.[65] And so was Anne. One of the earliest sources testifying to Anne's musical talents and education in general is a 'Letter containing the criminal trial brought against the Queen Anne Boleyn of England'[66] written in French verse by 'Carles, almoner of the dauphin,' Lancelot de Carles, bishop of Riez,[67] known for blazons and sacred poetry, who died in 1568, 'assez âgé.'[68] As two manuscripts in the French Bibliothèque nationale show (MSS fr. 1742 and 2370), the poem was written within two weeks of Anne's death, under its immediate impact; both sources give the date of 2 June 1536.[69] It was published nine years later, when its author was almoner of the dauphin Henri, son of François I.

What an effect the news of Queen Anne's execution must have had upon the French court! Old memories of the young lady in the circle of Queen Claude were revived, impressions and stories exchanged, and endless was the gossip about her terrible fate. The poetic letter is a reflection of all that. The interest was increased by the personal connection between the dauphin and Anne's father. Sir Thomas Boleyn, in the name of Henry VIII, had officiated as godfather for François' son, Henri, who had been given his name in honour of the English king.[70] There is thus an indirect bond between the writer, the dauphin, and Anne Boleyn. Certainly, the 'Monsigneur' whom the author addresses in the poem is the dauphin, who is named in the title as the author's master. The dauphin's mistress was Diane de Poitiers, lady-in-waiting at Queen Claude's court at the same time as Anne Boleyn, and but a few years older than her.[71]

Carles, in writing the poem on Anne, commanded an excellent tradition. He had at his disposal the personal recollections, of members of the court, of Anne Boleyn as a young girl growing into womanhood and the vivid impressions that Anne made during her visit with Henry in 1532. Moreover, François and the dauphin had close personal and political ties with Henry. The bias in favour of the English king, shown particularly in the account of Anne's 'crimes,' excludes the possibility of any attempt at flattery toward Anne's memory. The failure of Anne's biographers to consider these connections is responsible for the sparse attention given to this poem, which certainly must be considered a central source for the appreciation of Anne's personality and education.[72]

The poem recalls how 'Anne Boullant' came to France in the train of Mary Tudor, the political objective of whose marriage with Louis XII is stated baldly: 'to seal the alliance of the two kings.' Anne, continues the writer, put all her mind to imitating the ladies of honour and to learning French; as a result, when Mary returned to England (upon the death of Louis XII), Anne was retained by Queen Claude. Her education was so successful that anyone judging from her bearing and her manners would have thought her to be not English, but rather of the finest French extraction. She was a good singer, an accomplished dancer, and a fine conversationalist. She played the lute and other instruments to chase away melancholy thoughts. Beyond the virtues and exquisite graces which she had happily acquired in France, she was beautiful and had an elegant figure. She had the most enchanting eyes and knew how to use them to advantage, keeping them quiet at times, sending them off at others as secret messengers of her heart. The elegant French verses speak better for themselves:

> Or Monseigneur, ie croy que bien sçavez
> Et de long temps la cognoissance avez
> Que Anne Boullant premierement sortit
> De ce pays quand Marie en partit
> Pour s'en aller trouver le Roy en France
> Pour accomplir des deux Roys l'aliance.
> En ce temps la Boullant, qui ieune estoit
> Venuë en France, saigement escoutoit
> Dames d'honneur s'efforçant d'inciter
> Tous ses espritz a bien les imiter
> Et employa ses sens de tel couraige
> Qu'a peu de temps elle apprint le langaige
> Apres que fut Marie revenuë
> En ce pays, elle fut retenuë
> Par Claude qui puis apres succeda
> Ou tellement ses graces amenda

Que ne l'eussiez oncques iugée Angloise
En ses façons, mais née fine Françoise:
Elle sçavoit bien chanter, & dancer
Et ses propos saigement adiancer
Sonner de lucz, & daultres instrumens
Pour divertir les tristes pensemens,
Oultre ses biens, & graces tant exquises
Qu'avoit en France heureusement acquises
Elle estoit belle, & de taille elegante
Estoit des yeulx au cheoir plus attirante
Lesquelz sçavoit bien conduire a propoz
En les tenant quelque fois a repoz
Aulcunesfois envoioyent en messaige
Porter du coeur le secret tesmoignage.

Notwithstanding the great tragedy that had befallen the young queen, notwithstanding the terrible crimes she was accused of – and which the poem presents as facts – the author's pride in her French education is unlimited; for it is to that and nothing else that he ascribes her ascent to the English throne:

O que tenuë elle estoit a l'honneur
De France, qui luy causoit ce bonheur:
O quel honneur, quelle obligation
Elle debuoit à la perfection
De ceulx de qui elle apprint tant de biens
Qui l'ont depuis faicte Royne des siens.

A 'Traicte de Dame Anne Boullan Iadis Royne d'Angleterre par ung gentillome françoys,'[73] dated 1601, seems a fragmentary poetic paraphrase of Carles' *Epistre*, as a few lines will show:

Elle savoit tres bien sur toute autre princesse
fort bien lart de danser, ayant aussi ladresse
de bien jouer du lut, et autres instruments
pour chasser de son ame les tristes pansements.

Anne's musical and linguistic talents were not denied even by her detractors. 'The life of Kinge Henrie the 8th from his fallinge in love with Anne Bulloyen to the death of Queene Katherine his wife,'[74] is vehemently critical of Henry and of Anne, but admits that the latter 'was then in the

prime of her youth, of ffaire countenance and of plausible quallities for
such a one to delight in. Ffor shee could play upon an Instrument, dance,
etc., and had her Lattyn and ffrench tongue.'

In the Royal collection at the British Museum there are few manuscripts which belonged to Anne Boleyn. One reason for this scarcity is
certainly the shortness of her reign, another, her catastrophic end which
would have made advisable the destruction of books conspicuously
marked as having been written for and dedicated to her. The small number surviving are all rather modest books and usually in poor condition.[75]
Because of their scarcity what they tell us of her is all the more important.

Compared with the sumptuous book of hours of Henry VIII,[76] Anne's
book of epistles and gospels[77] is simple to the point of austerity, the only
illuminations being a now-faded crucifixion scene and decorated initials.
The exhortations are in English, but the gospels and epistles are rendered
in French. The manuscript is a testimony to Anne's religious leanings.
The Reformers did away with Latin Bibles and prayer books, rendering
the scriptures as well as prayers in the vernacular.[78] They also objected to
the idolatrous use of pictures in churches and in books. In an unsigned
dedication the author confesses to be attached to the marchioness not only
by 'your frendly dealynges, with so divers and sondry benifites' but also
by 'the perpetuall bond of blood,' and he reveals that it was 'by your com-
mandement I have adventuryd to do this.' On folio 4, carrying the initial E
enclosing Anne's armorial bearings, there is this message of a distinctly
Reformed ring: 'And let us realize that it is time to arouse ourselves from
slumber, for now our salvation is closer than we had thought.'[79]

Another modest paper manuscript dated 1530 (new style) contains,
in the second half, with a separate pagination, a French treatise on the art
of letter writing with this dedication: 'A noble et excellente Dame ma
dame Anne de Rochefort.'[80] The dedication, signed by a certain Loys du
Brun, says, in part:

When I consider the great affection and complete inclination that you
hold toward the French tongue, it does not surprise me that one never
finds you without some French book in your hand, according to the
season, containing some useful and necessary instruction to teach the
right way to all virtues, such as translations of the Holy Scriptures
approved and filled with all good doctrines or, likewise, of other
books of yours by learned men offering salutary remedies for this
mortal life and consolations for the immortal soul. And principally,

last Lent and the one before last (as I then conversed with you at that magnificent, excellent, and triumphant court) I always saw you reading the salutary letters of St. Paul that contain the complete teaching and rule of good living according to the best moral principles ...

Letter writing was a literary genre in the Renaissance; many books of letters and on letter writing were published. The gift should have been welcome to Anne. In her new social position, as Lady Rochford, she needed more than ever to know the etiquette of writing to men of all stations.[81]

A few years later, after Anne's coronation, François I presented Henry and Anne, or perhaps Anne alone, with a delightful little book for Lenten reading, *Le Pasteur évangelique*, a poem in 490 ten-syllable lines.[82] The poem is made up of biblical passages on 'the good shepherd,' rendered in French rhymes and cleverly connected into a continuous whole. The Latin passages used are quoted in the margins and are taken mostly from the four gospels, St Paul's epistles, and the psalms. This graceful small book on vellum with lovely golden initials on a blue ground (sometimes reversed, with blue letters on a gold ground) reveals its provenance in speaking of 'Françoys nostre roy,' of his three sons, and his sister, 'la precieuse et bonne Marguerite'; it shows its destination by ending with a eulogy of Henry VIII and an address to Anne. The manuscript bears Anne's coat of arms and beneath it her device, a silver falcon, crowned, holding a sceptre, and standing on the stump of a tree, with bare roots (see figure 1). The poem ends with a wish to Anne that she may bear Henry a son, the living image of his father, and see him grow up to manhood:

> O ma dame Anne, O royne incomparable
> Ce bon pasteur qui vous a aggréable
> Vous doint ung filz qui soit lymaige vifve
> Du Roy son pere quil surcroisse et vive
> Tant que vous deux le puissiez veoir en lage
> Que lhomme doibt ou iamais estre saige.

I discovered, accidentally, that the author of *Le Bon pasteur* is none other than Clément Marot.[83] Since Marot's name does not occur, whereas François' name is prominently mentioned, it seems reasonable to assume that it was not Marot but the French king who presented the elegant manuscript. The special form of the poem had its origin in its special purpose.

Clément Marot is not the only French poet who addressed Anne Boleyn. Nicolas Bourbon (Nicolaus Borbonius), a friend of Marot and, like him, of Reformed conviction, but apparently unknown to Anne's biographers, addressed a number of neo-Latin poems[84] to the queen, to Henry,[85] to Henry and Anne,[86] to Thomas Cromwell,[87] to various other English noblemen,[88] to his former English disciples,[89] and even to London and the Thames.[90] His Latin renderings of Marot's French verses testify to the friendship between the two poets.[91] There is no biography of Borbonius,[92] but a study of his poems reveals that he spent a short time, one or two years at the most, in England as tutor to young English noblemen, and close to the court. A poem addressed to Thomas Cranmer is dated 1535;[93] another one directed to the French ambassador in England bears the same date.[94]

A number of poems dedicated to François I indicate that Borbonius had been imprisoned in France.[95] From poems addressed to Anne Boleyn, it is evident that he was set free through her intervention. While still in prison he addressed these distichs to her:

> Shut up in this dark prison, wretched, I lie.
> None is there who could help me, none who would
> dare, save you, O Queen: you can, noblest
> mistress, and you dare, as one whom the King,
> whom God himself loves.[96]

In another poem, directed to Anna, queen of England, he writes:

> For no crime, under false indictment by some, and due to their rancour, I was shut up in prison ... when your compassion from far away was mindful of me, O Anne, and snatched the afflicted one from the grip of evil. Otherwise I would still languish, chained, in the darkness of death, miserable.[97]

Borbonius was known for his pro-Lutheran sentiments.[98] That his imprisonment was the result of his heretical convictions has long been surmised,[99] but a further hypothesis is in order. The same event that forced Marot to flee to Ferrara must have caused Borbonius' imprisonment and subsequent flight to England.

For the student of Anne Boleyn in search of testimony on her character, convictions, and intellectual qualities, this is a precious addition to the scarce biographical material available. It is the second case in which Anne personally intervened in behalf of a man persecuted for reasons of faith.[100] It shows her as a woman of generous impulses who used her high position to aid victims of repression in the confrontation between the old and the new faith. It confirms existing evidence of her own pro-Lutheran feelings. It suggests that her ties to France's poets were close and intimate. Finally, the numerous poems addressed to her by Borbonius argue in favour of a fine humanistic education and a good command of Latin, for it is unlikely that a poet would write for a patron unable to understand the language in which he was writing.

The contemporary sources investigated lead to the following conclusions: in the most formative years of her youth Anne Boleyn stayed at the French court, became fluent in the French tongue and versed in French manners. There she acquired the French taste for elegance and sophistication, for literature and the arts. Above all, she became an accomplished singer and lutanist, tried her hand also at other instruments, and heard at the French court the finest and most highly developed music of the age; indeed, she may well have had the opportunity to meet the great Josquin and Mouton as well as other famous musicians at the French court.[101] That she should be the recipient of a book of French music containing music chiefly by Josquin and Mouton and some other French court composers is entirely in keeping with her tastes, talents, and her French education. French books and poems were written for her and dedicated to her. Nothing illustrates better the general view of her than the remarks made by Mary of Hungary, writing to her brother Ferdinand on the occasion of Anne's death: 'I hope the English will not do much against us now, as we are free from his lady, *who was a good Frenchwoman*' (italics mine).[102]

That 'a good Frenchwoman' should be the recipient of a musical manuscript written on French paper, decorated with initials reminiscent of French style, and containing a repertory of the finest French music is not to be wondered at.[103]

THE DONOR OR EDITOR OF THE MANUSCRIPT

While offering no direct clue to the donor or editor (or perhaps donor-editor), several aspects of the manuscript are unusual enough to prompt some speculation on his identity. Although written for a queen, the manuscript was copied on paper of mediocre quality. The manuscript is in a strangely fragmentary condition: whole voice parts are missing, certain works have no text, and the notes in others lack stems. A great number of corrections have been made without any effort to conceal them: passages are struck out on one page and are added on another, and text is crossed out and corrected. Above all, the initials cover only forty pages, not quite one-sixth of the whole. Neither the initials, interesting and skilful though they are, nor the writing of music and text was done by highly trained professionals. The colours of the decorations are of poor quality and now faded. Although written sometime between 1533 and 1536, the manuscript would appear to be much older if judged by its repertory, handwriting, initials, and paper. The donor obviously did not have access to the most modern musical repertory, the most up-to-date illustrators, or the finest scribes. Hence he produced in the mid-1530s a manuscript that might for the most part have been written twenty-five to thirty years earlier.

For all of these reasons we must rule out the possibility (otherwise so tempting, especially because of the content) that the manuscript was written at the French court and donated by François I to Anne on the occasion of her coronation or shortly thereafter.[104] When François presented Anne with *Le Pasteur évangelique,* he did so in a precious little volume written on vellum with gold initials on blue ground – the colours being still as fresh as if the book had been done yesterday. No other court would send a completely French repertory. Nor would a nobleman wish to offer the queen of England anything but the most precious book done by the finest professionals available.

Hence we must look for a donor from the lower ranks of the citizenry, well versed in music, someone aware of Anne's particular taste for French music – a taste widely shared at the Tudor court – possibly a person connected with the court.

The records of the time offer us an almost ideal candidate in the person of Mark Smeton, the musician whose testimony confirmed the sentence on Anne Boleyn. Unfortunately, Mark Smeton is a shadowy figure, for whose life, character, and talents, documents are even harder to come by than for Anne Boleyn. The one outstanding and clearly documented fact is that Mark, as he is called in the documents, was the only one of the five men accused of having committed adultery with the queen who confessed – a confession generally thought to have been obtained by intimidation and torture.[105]

Mark was of humble origins. Contemporary documents call him variously a musician, a virginal player or player on the spinet, an organist, a gentleman of the king's privy chamber. He was all of these. Fortunately, the privy purse chamber expense accounts have been preserved for the years 1529 to 1532.[106] They testify to Mark's having been a gentleman in the king's privy chamber as early as 1529.[107] The editor of these accounts observes that Mark 'was wholly supported at the king's expense, and ... it may be consequently inferred, was one of his favourite minions.'[108] Regular payments are made for his hose, shoes, shirts, and bonnets, and every Easter and Christmas he is the recipient of a special reward. He usually appears in these accounts together with 'young master Weston,' lutanist, 'the two Guillams' (instrumentalists, one of them a player on the rebec),[109] sometimes with 'the childe that waytes on Philip.' Philip is the Netherlander Philip van Wilder who emigrated to London and appears as early as 1526 at the court. He was the leading musician of the king's privy chamber[110] and in charge of the king's chamber music. That Mark Smeton served under him is shown by the difference in payments made to Philip and Mark. For example, on 28 December 1530 Mark received a reward of 20 shillings, Philip of 40.[111] But Mark must have improved his standing in the king's estimation considerably, to judge by the reward that he received on 6 October 1532, to wit, the sum of 3 pounds, 6 shillings, and 8 pence.[112] The date is of considerable interest, for it was in the beginning of October that Henry and Anne had started on their trip toward Calais where Henry was to meet François.[113] Mark was not the only musician in the royal party; according to the privy purse accounts, Pero, the king's minstrel, Nowell, another minstrel, and, most important of all, 'Philip of the privy chamber,' Philip van Wilder,[114] also accompanied Henry and Anne to Calais.

Unfortunately, no privy purse accounts survive from the years 1533 to 1536, so we cannot study Mark's rise in the royal esteem. That he must have been in the limelight may be fathomed from the maliciously ambiguous distichs of Borbonius in which the poet castigates Mark for his lack of restraint in singing his songs:

> You, Mark, maker of poor songs, by reciting them to me more than is right, make them worse. Let us grant that they are good, but by so assiduously singing them you achieve displeasure and render them tedious. Anything overdone is unwelcome; it is an old saying that even honey, if taken too much, becomes bitter.[115]

The sardonic tone that Borbonius permits himself in this poem is perhaps a reflection of Mark's low birth. In another poem Mark is accused of greed, and a rather crude pun on his name reveals that he was of slender figure – information that agrees with his reputation as a 'deft dancer': 'Curb your hunger for riches, check your thirst for gain, or you will be asked, Mark, why you are so meagre.'[116] That Mark, working his way up from grinding poverty, should have become eager to gather riches is understandable.

But could Mark Smeton have afforded a gift which, though modest by royal standards, nevertheless cost money? There are several answers to this, the first found in a list of prisoners in the Tower which was drawn up in May 1536, detailing the charges of their maintenance; to this was appended a note: 'Lady Anne, Lord Rocheford, Sir Francis Weston, Master Hen. Norrys, Sir Wm. Bruton [Brereton], and Markes Smeton. These persons had lands and goods sufficient of their own.'[117] These prisoners, therefore, did not have to be maintained at the state's expense. Mark is the only one in this company who lacks a title, but obviously he did not lack funds.

In the second place, the production of a handwritten book at that time was not too expensive. The duke of Norfolk in February 1482 paid a local chapelmaster 14 shillings and 4 pence for 'a song-booke and iiij amtemys [anthems]'[118] and Fayrfax received twenty pounds upon presentation of a music book to the king on New Year's; this was, in the opinion of John Stevens, 'far more than the copying can have been worth commercially.'[119] Surely, the donor of MS 1070 counted on a similarly generous reward. The example of Fayrfax demonstrates furthermore that it was perfectly proper for a court musician to present a musical manuscript in homage to king or queen. As John Stevens reminds us: 'The service which above all others conferred honour, even if not permanent status, was waiting on the king in the privy chamber. Had Mark Smeton not been of the chamber, he could hardly have been described as "gentylman." '[120]

But, we must now ask, was Mark Smeton enough of a musician to bring together an anthology of music such as is represented in our manuscript? To this question the fact that he was a virginalist and an organist can provide an answer. For a keyboard player was one of the best trained musicians at the time. He had to know how to read and write a tablature and how to read a score, and the great polyphonic literature of the time set for voices was the repertory from which he constantly drew his pieces to play, to arrange, to ornament.[121] Nor should we forget that Mark Smeton must have been an extraordinarily talented musician and performer to please so great a connoisseur as Henry, who was no mean performer himself[122] and who had known such great keyboard virtuosi as the Venetian, Dionisio Memo, mentioned earlier. Mark Smeton should well have been able to oversee the making of the anthology of French music for Anne Boleyn, indeed to have a decisive hand in the selection of the works themselves. With the excellent musicians in the Chapel Royal as well as in the king's

1 MS Royal 16 E XIII f.1ᵛ Anne Boleyn's crest

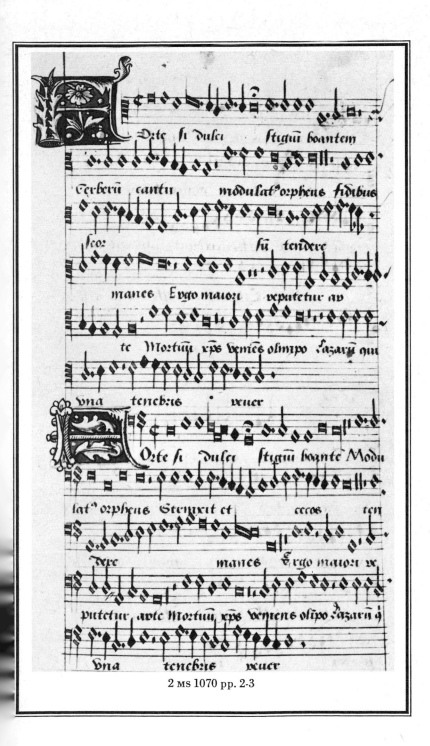

2 мs 1070 pp. 2-3

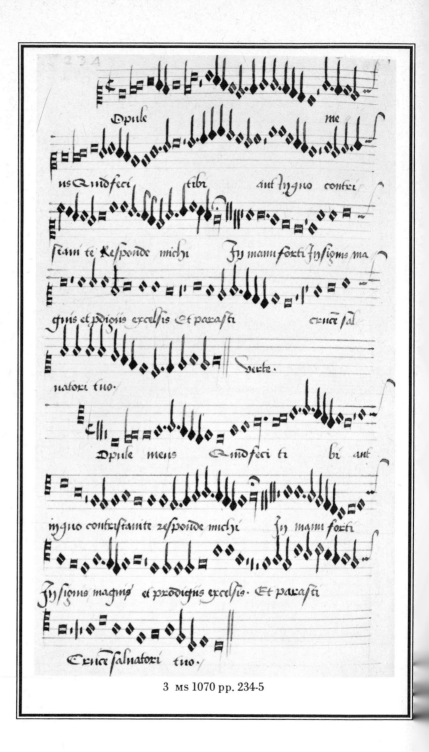

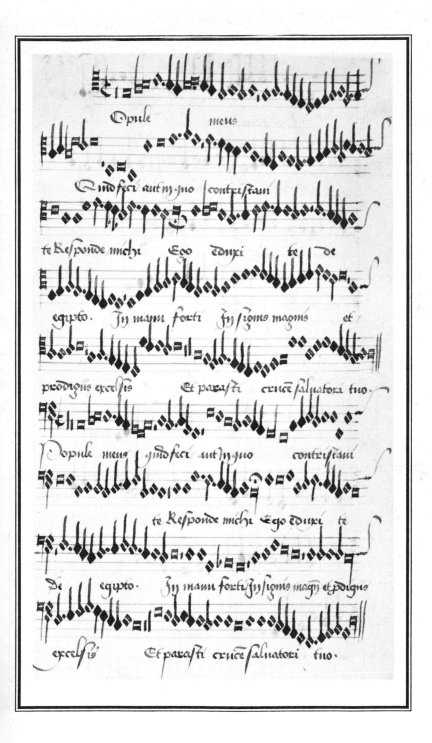

4 ms 1070 pp. 266-7

5 ms 1070 pp. 228-9

6A ms 1070 first watermark

6B MS 1070 second watermark

7 ms 1070 pp. 8-9

9 ms 1070 pp. 28-9

10 Catherine of Aragon

11 Anne Boleyn

12 ms 1070 pp. 4-5

13 ms 1070, detail of p. 157

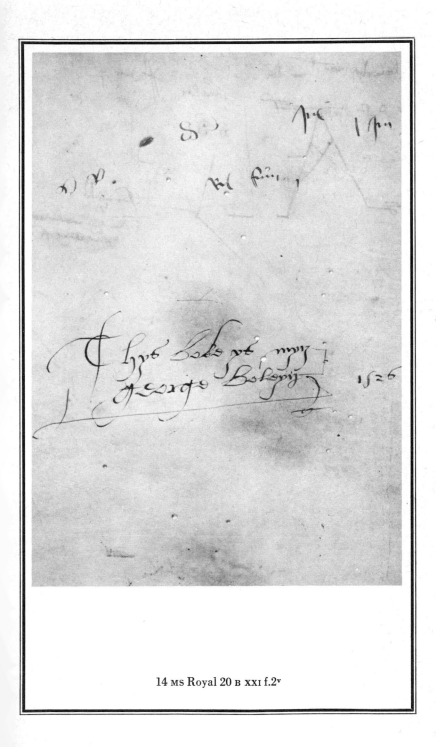

14 MS Royal 20 B XXI f.2ᵛ

q̃ se noltet oultce en feu
En peaulx aunes ltoute sa cuve
Pour bourra fair ceste cytouire
En unfondant les langues males
Cap ll stet bien que tous les masles
Estes poulas joye r kyros
Atant smevan mo propos
Jusqua tant que plus sauge bieugne
que ceste matie sonstienne
Je croy que jamais finer
Ne sera ne deffunne
Cap bdnal est lamour du monde
Anavoir trop y abonde
plus nen dirap ceste fois
A dieu bons bdmal je men bois

A moy n ayau n

privy chamber, he had no lack of advisers and helpers, should he have needed any. Since Mark accompanied Henry and Anne on their trip to France in 1532, he heard French music[123] and had occasion to speak to French musicians[124] and to take French musical manuscripts home with him.

If Mark was the person largely responsible for assembling and editing the manuscript, it would explain not only the modest appearance of our source but also its curiously incomplete character. For, normally, the death of the recipient while the manuscript was in the process of being written would be no reason for the editor and donor (who was perhaps the main scribe) not to have finished so valuable a musical anthology and destined it for a different purpose. But if the original editor died himself, then it is easy to understand why the manuscript should have remained so incomplete, why several different hands should have followed the first hand that wrote the largest portion of it, why its original character as a motet manuscript seems to have been forgotten when, toward the end, a few chansons were added, and why the artist responsible for the initials discontinued his work.

The assumption that Mark Smeton was the donor-editor and perhaps principal scribe of MS 1070 is aided by a curious Latin inscription on page 232, which has no music. It reads: 'Tuo te pede metire. Nosce teipsum ut noris quam sit tibi curta suppellex. (Measure yourself by your own rule; know yourself so that you be aware of how poorly you are furnished.)' Enigmatic as these lines sound, they explain themselves by the context from which they are drawn. *Tuo te pede metire* comes from the last line of Horace's seventh epistle, book one, and *noris quam sit tibi curta suppellex* is the last line of the fourth Satire of Persius.

Horace's seventh epistle tells the story of poor, hardworking Vulteius Mena who accepts from rich Philippus a lovely farm, half gift, half loan. Content before with a few humble friends, a hearth of his own, and the games in the campus after work, he now 'just about kills himself / Fixing *this* and trying out *that*, and ages rapidly / From his love of possession.' Finally, in desperation, he betakes himself to Philippus and beseeches him: 'Give me back my former life!' Horace ends with this moral:

> As soon as one's seen
> How the life he left behind surpasses the one
> He gained by giving it up, he ought to go home
> In time to become again what he ought to have been.
> The best rule by which to measure ourselves is: OUR OWN.[125]

Persius' fourth satire harps on precisely the same theme.
It ends with these lines:

If ...

... your few scruples forsake you
At the mere sight of money, if you'll follow your phallus
Into anything and try any sharp trick to milk
The market, it's pointless to offer the populace
Your ears thirsting for praise. Reject all that is not
Yourself. Let the mob have back what it gave you. Live in
Your own house and learn what a bare lodging it is.[126]

The story of Vulteius Mena is a fitting parable for Mark Smeton; its
moral and the exhortation from Persius read like an appropriate epitaph
on the life of the unfortunate musician. They agree remarkably well with
the satiric lines that Nicolaus Borbonius dedicated to Mark. They also
agree admirably with the account given by George Cavendish, Wolsey's
gentleman-usher and biographer, in which Mark is made to say the very
words from our presumed 'epitaph': 'knew not myself.' Here is the poem:

My father a carpenter, and laboured with his hand
With the swett of his face he purchast his lyvyng
For small was his *rent,* much lesse was his land;
My mother in a cottage used dayly spynnyng
Loo in what mysery was my begynnyng
Till that gentle prynce, kyng of this realme
Toke me de stercore et origens pauperem

And being but a boy clame upp the hygh stage
That bred was of naught, and brought to felicite
Knew not myself, waxt proud in my corage
Dysdayned my father, and wold not him see,
Wherfore nowe Fortune by hir mutabilitie
Hathe made so cruelly hir power for to stretch
For my presumption, to dye like a wretch.[127]

The contemporaneous accounts reflect what must have been the common opinion at the time: that Mark, of humble origins, aspiring to the
court of the king, overreached himself and came to fall through his own
hubris.

There is one final aspect of the manuscript that favours the hypothesis
of Mark Smeton's editorship. The manuscript looks as if it had remained

in the hands of musicians. This is clear not only from the many entries of pieces by new hands, but also from the corrections that bespeak performance and consequent detection of errors. Moreover, one can distinguish between the original accidentals and those entered later, presumably in the course of performance. If Mark Smeton was the editor and perhaps main scribe of the manuscript, then, upon his death, the unfinished music book would quite logically have remained in the hands of his fellow musicians at the court.

However that may be, I hope that I have established with a fair degree of certainty that MS 1070 of the Royal College of Music in London is not only a repertory of sixteenth-century music, but one of the most fascinating historical documents of the time of Henry VIII, and that it was specifically written for Anne Boleyn whose personality, distorted by controversy, slanted by partisanship, obscured by loss and destruction of evidence, is illuminated in it by an art that she practised and appreciated with enthusiasm and talent, as did the king her husband, and Mark Smeton, her reputed lover. Thus, MS 1070 of the Royal College of Music in London brings together Henry VIII, Anne Boleyn, and Mark Smeton in a relationship whose mystery promises to defy certain and permanent solution. It is a melancholy commentary on a tragic episode, but its artistic content transcends the frailty of human entanglement and transmutes the discord of conflicting passions into the permanent harmony of great art.

POSTSCRIPT

A return visit to London allowed me to examine British Museum MS Royal 20 B XXI which, according to Patricia Thomson,[128] bears the handwriting of Mark Smeton:

> The manuscript is a fifteenth-century book of French poetry, containing Jean Le Fèvre's 'Les Lamentations de Matheolus' and 'Le Livre de Leesce.' The former is a translation of a satire on women and marriage, the latter an original poem with the alternative title 'Le Resolu en Mariage' – reading matter, incidentally, of some interest to Anne's group ...
>
> [Anne's brother, Lord] Rochford, who probably acquired the book on one of his many visits to France, has inscribed 'Thys boke ys myn George Boleyn 1526' [see figure 14] before the text (f.2ᵛ). We may conjecture that he either gave or lent it to Smeaton, who has writ-

ten 'A moy m marc S' [see figure 15] at the end of the text (f.98ʳ) ...
[Wyatt's] name is the last to crop up ... on the back fly-leaves (ff. 99ᵛ
and 100ʳ), and these also bear a variety of mottos and proverbs in
Latin, French, Spanish, and Italian ... Possibly he inherited the book.

The inscription 'a moy m marc S' would suggest that George Boleyn
gave rather than lent the book to Mark. Both the inscription and the
language in which the book is written point to Mark's command of French
– significant because of the French character of MS 1070. The important
thing, in view of the possibility that Mark was the principal scribe of MS
1070, is the handwriting. We cannot be too careful in comparing the chief
hand in our manuscript and the hand of Mark's signature. We must remember that hands of the sixteenth century followed traditional patterns,
that the same hand occasionally uses different characters for the same
letter, that signatures often deviate from the ordinary hand of the writer
(in particular, the flourishes and ornaments that ordinarily go with a
signature must be disregarded), and that a signature does not offer a
large enough repertory of letters for comparison. But after these warnings have been properly taken note of, a comparison must nevertheless be
made.

The letters of Mark's signature may be compared with letters on some
of the pages that appear in our illustrations from MS 1070. We choose
page 2 (see figure 2) and note the similarities between

1 the *m* of *marc* and that of *mortuum* (line 5);

2 the *o* of *moy* and the *o* of *modulatus* (line 2), *olimpo* (line 6), *mortuum* (line 10);

3 the *ar* of *marc* and that of *arte* (lines 5 and 10);

4 the *c* of *marc* and that of *cristus* (line 5);

5 after making due account for the size and ornaments of the *S* in
S(meton) expressing (like the flourish in *marc*) the writer's pride in his
name and person, we can detect the basic relationship between that letter
and the *S* in *Strinxit* (line 8; see the same word on line 8 of page 3).

In addition to these, the capital *A* with which the signature begins can
be found in pages 58 (last line), 62 (lines 4 and 8), 95 (line 1) and so
forth. The *y* of *moy* can be found in the word *alleluya* in various places of
the manuscript: pp. 164 (line 5 and last line), 165 (lines 4, 5, and last)
and so forth.

The following conclusions may be drawn:

1 The only signature of Mark Smeton known to survive shows the same
general script as does the principal hand responsible for writing the text

of MS 1070, which palaeographers characterize as a 'bastard hand' originating in fifteenth-century France. It suffices to compare it with the signature of George Boleyn to observe how entirely different a script that two men, so close in time, place, and age, use.

2 There is nothing in the lettering of Mark's signature that would rule out the possibility that he was indeed the main scribe of MS 1070, but much to support it.

These observations find an unexpected corroboration in a remark made by Lodovico Guicciardini in his chronicle of European history from 1529 to 1560, in which he recounts the events leading to the death of Anne Boleyn.[129] Here Mark is referred to as 'Marco Fiammingo suo sonatore' (Mark, the Fleming, her [keyboard] player). Guicciardini, who traveled widely in the Netherlands and lived for a long time in Antwerp, was in a good position to know, if he called Mark Smeton a Fleming. Mark's original name may have been de Smet or de Smedt.[130] In England he may have changed it to Smeton (sometimes written as Smeaton), a name that goes back to the tenth century.[131]

The Flemish origin of Mark Smeton would explain Mark's command of French, his French hand, and, last but not least, his acquaintance with the repertory of Franco-Flemish music of about 1500-20. Indeed, one may well consider the possibility that Mark came to England in the company of the Fleming Philip van Wilder, under whose direction he later performed his duties as 'gentylman' of the king's privy chamber.

Patricia Thomson points to Thomas Wyatt, the last proprietor of the book, according to the inscriptions of mottoes and proverbs carrying his name. One of the proverbs in French, a translation of the Italian, as Thomson shows, is the following: 'qui asne est et cerff cuyde bien estre/a sallir une fosse on le puyt bien cognostre' which she translates as: 'He who is an ass, and thinks himself a hind,/on leaping the ditch will realize the truth.'[132]

Miss Thomson makes a fairly good case that
'Asne' is Anne, who thought herself, and was thought to be, a hind. As such she had appeared in Wyatt's 'Who so list to hount, I knowe where is an hynde.' At that time, *c*. 1527, she had been elevated by Caesar-Henry. Now, in due course, she has fallen. The illusion is shattered. Anne is, in the long run, no hind, but – true to her name – 'asne.' Such would be the epitaph of Wyatt, or of one of his friends, on his old idol.[133]

I am unable to believe, however, that Thomas Wyatt could write so

unfeeling, indeed so cynical, an epitaph on his former love, and on a
fallen queen. The man who watched the execution of Anne and her friends
'from a window of the Tower,' the man who wrote on these events, 'These
blodye dayes haue brokyn my hart,'[134] could not have referred to Anne
as the ass who fancied herself a hind. When one leafs through the manuscript and sees Wyatt's name and inscriptions follow directly upon the
signature of Mark Smeton, one feels rather that Wyatt was commenting
upon the rise and fall of Mark Smeton – an interpretation borne out by
Borbonius' poems and by the inscriptions found in MS 1070 that we likewise related to Mark. It conforms to the rank-conscious attitude of the
time that the common target of mockery and derision was the humble
figure of Mark Smeton, son of a carpenter.

APPENDIX I

Catalogue by Bonnie J. Blackburn

SIGLA OF MANUSCRIPTS USED IN THE CATALOGUE

Barc. 454	Barcelona, Biblioteca Central, MS 454
Berg. 1209	Bergamo, Istituto Musicale 'G. Donizetti,' MS 1209 D
Berl. 40021	Berlin, Staatsbibliothek, Mus. MS 40021 (now in Tübingen, Universitätsbibliothek)
Bol. Q19	Bologna, Civico Museo Bibliografico Musicale, MS Q 19
Bol. Q27	Bologna, Civico Museo Bibliografico Musicale, MS Q 27
Bol. SPetr. XXXVIII	Bologna, Archivio Musicale di San Petronio, MS A. XXXVIII
Cambrai 124	Cambrai, Bibliothèque Municipale, MS 124 (125-128)
Cambridge 1760	Cambridge, Magdalene College, MS Pepys 1760
Cop. 1848	Copenhagen, Kongelige Bibliotek, MS 1848
Cop. 1872	Copenhagen, Kongelige Bibliotek, MS Gl. kg. samling 1872
Cop. 1873	Copenhagen, Kongelige Bibliotek, MS Gl. kg. samling 1873

Cort. 95-6	Cortona, Biblioteca Comunale, MS 95-96
Flor. 11	Florence, Archivio del Duomo, MS 11
Flor. 58	Florence, Biblioteca Nazionale Centrale, MS Magl. XIX, 58
Flor. 2794	Florence, Biblioteca Riccardiana, MS 2794
Friuli 59	Friuli, Museo Archeologico di Cividale, MS 59
London 2037	London, Royal College of Music, MS 2037
London 8GVII	London, British Museum, MS Royal 8 G VII
Mad. 607	Madrid, Biblioteca Medinaceli, MS 607
Milan 2267	Milan, Archivio del Duomo, MS 2267
Milan 2268	Milan, Archivio del Duomo, MS 2268
Milan 2269	Milan, Archivio del Duomo, MS 2269
Mod. III	Modena, Archivio Capitolare, Codex III
Mod. IX	Modena, Archivio Capitolare, Codex IX
Mun. 41	Munich, Bayerische Staatsbibliothek, MS 41
Nur. 83795	Nuremberg, Germanisches Museum, MS 83795
Pad. A17	Padua, Biblioteca Capitolare, MS A 17
Pad. D27	Padua, Biblioteca Capitolare, MS D 27
Paris 1817	Paris, Bibliothèque Nationale, MS f. fr. 1817
Reg. AR876	Regensburg, Proske-Bibliothek, MS A.R. 876
Reg. AR891/92	Regensburg, Proske-Bibliothek, MS A.R. 891/92
Reg. AR893	Regensburg, Proske-Bibliothek, MS A.R. 893
Reg. AR940/41	Regensburg, Proske-Bibliothek, MS A.R. 940/41
Rome Chigi	Rome, Biblioteca Vaticana, Chigiana C. VIII. 234
Rome CS42	Rome, Biblioteca Vaticana, Cappella Sistina, MS 42
Rome CS44	Rome, Biblioteca Vaticana, Cappella Sistina, MS 44
Rome CS46	Rome, Biblioteca Vaticana, Cappella Sistina, MS 46
Rome CS76	Rome, Biblioteca Vaticana, Cappella Sistina, MS 76
Rome CS77	Rome, Biblioteca Vaticana, Cappella Sistina, MS 77
Rome Pal. lat. 1976-79	Rome, Biblioteca Vaticana, Palatini latini MS 1976-1979
Rome Pal. lat. 1980-81	Rome, Biblioteca Vaticana, Palatini latini MS 1980-1981
Rome Vallic.	Rome, Biblioteca Vallicelliana, Vall. s. Borr. E. II. 55-60
Seg	Segovia, Catedral, MS without number
Speciálnik	Hradcek-Kralové, Museum, Speciálnik Codex
St Gall 462	St Gall, Stiftsbibliothek, MS 462
St Gall 463	St Gall, Stiftsbibliothek, MS 463

Toledo 13	Toledo, Biblioteca Capitolar, MS 13
Tournai	Tournai, Chapitre de la Cathédrale, Missal
Ver. DCCLX	Verona, Archivio Capitolare, MS DCCLX
Vienna 15941	Vienna, Oesterreichische Nationalbibliothek, MS 15941
Vienna 18825	Vienna, Oesterreichische Nationalbibliothek, MS 18825
Vienna 15500	Vienna, Oesterreichische Nationalbibliothek, MS suppl. mus. 15500

ABBREVIATIONS FOR PRINTS USED IN THE CATALOGUE

1502[1]	Petrucci, Motetti A
1504[1]	Petrucci, Motetti C
1512[1]	Oeglin, Liederbuch
1514[1]	Petrucci, Motetti de la Corona, L. I
1519[1]	Petrucci, Motetti de la Corona, L. II
1521[3]	Antico, Motetti L. I
[1521][4]	Antico, Motetti L. II
1521[5]	Antico, Motetti L. IV
[1521][6]	Antico?, Motetti e canzone L. I
[c.1521][7]	Antico?, Motetti et carmina gallica
1526[1]	Giunta, Motetti de la Corona, L. I
1526[2]	Giunta, Motetti de la Corona, L. II
[c.1528][5]	Attaingnant, Trente et deux chansons musicales
1529[1]	Attaingnant, XII. Motetz musicaulx
1534[3]	Attaingnant, Liber primus quinque et viginti musicales quatuor vocum motetos
1537[1]	Grapheus (Formschneider), Novum et insigne opus musicum
1553[2]	Du Chemin, Liber primus collectorum modulorum
1555[10]	Montanus & Neuber, Secundus tomus Evangeliorum
1559[2]	Montanus & Neuber, Tertia pars magni operis musici
Mouton 1555	Le Roy & Ballard, Joannis Mouton Sameracensis musici praestantissimi, selecti aliquot moduli

OTHER ABBREVIATIONS USED IN THE CATALOGUE

A.H.	*Analecta Hymnica*, ed. G. M. Dreves and C. Blume (55 vols.; Leipzig 1886-1922)

Ant. Sar.	*Antiphonale Sarisburiense*, ed. W. H. Frere (n.p., n.d.)
L.A.	*Liber Antiphonarius* ... (Rome 1912)
L.R.	*Liber Responsorialis* (Solesmes 1895)
L.U.	*Liber Usualis* (Tournai-New York 1956)
Proc.	*Processionale Monasticum* (Solesmes 1893)
V.P.	*Variae Preces* (Solesmes 1901)
Chev.	Ulysse Chevalier, *Repertorium Hymnologicum* ... (6 vols.; Louvain, 1892-1919)
Mone	F. J. Mone, *Lateinische Hymnen des Mittelalters* (3 vols.; Freiburg im Breisgau 1853-5)
Att.	A. Smijers, ed., *Treize livres de motets parus chez Pierre Attaingnant* (13 vols.; Paris 1934-63)
Finscher	Ludwig Finscher, ed., *Loyset Compère Opera Omnia,* IV (Rome: American Institute of Musicology 1961)
Lowinsky	Edward E. Lowinsky, *The Medici Codex of 1518* (3 vols.; *Monuments of Renaissance Music,* III-V; Chicago 1968)
Smijers	A. Smijers, ed., *Werken van Josquin des Prés* (Amsterdam-Leipzig 1921-)

N.B. The spelling of the texts follows the manuscript

CATALOGUE OF LONDON, ROYAL COLLEGE OF MUSIC, MS 1070

	1 Forte si dulci stigium boantem (2.p., Palas actea) pp. 2-9	2 Memor esto verbi tui servo tuo (2.p., Porcio mea) pp. 10-19	3 Laudate dominum omnes gentes pp. 20-3
Text and use	Contemporary humanistic poem (see above, pp. 172-3)	Ps. 118:49-64 (Zain)	Ps. 116 (complete), with Gloria Patri
Voices	4	4	4
Composer		[Josquin]	
Concordances	None	See Smijers	None
Remarks		Published in Smijers, Motetten, Bundel VI, p. 3. Incomplete; one folio missing between pp. 12 and 13	

	4	5	6
Text and use	In illo tempore accesserunt ad Jesum (2.p., Propter hoc dimittet) pp. 24-9 Matthew 19:3-6; Gospel in nuptial mass, L.U. 1291	Laudate deum in sanctis eius, et audiatur vox (2.p., Quia cum clamarem) pp. 30-5 Psalm melange and paraphrase (see above, pp. 178-9)	Queramus cum pastoribus verbum incarnatum (2.p., Ubi pascas ubi cubes) pp. 36-41 Motet for the Nativity
Voices	4	4	4
Composer	[Mouton]	[Mouton]	[Mouton]
Concordances	Bol. Q19, f.98ᵛ (P. Molu) ; Reg. AR940/41, no.48 (Anon.) ; St Gall 463, no.130 (Petrus Moulu) ; Vienna 15941, f.87; [c1521]⁷, f.11ᵛ (Anon.) ; 1537¹, no.50; 1559², no. 17; Mouton 1555, f.2	Pad. A17, f.31ᵛ (Anon.) ; Vienna 15941, f.68ᵛ ; Vienna 15500, f.279ᵛ (Anon.) ; 1514¹, f.6ᵛ ; 1526¹, f.6ᵛ ; Mouton 1555, f.12	Bol. SPetr xxxviii, f.19ᵛ (Anon.) ; Flor. 11, f.30ᵛ (Anon.) ; Mad. 607, p.82; Mod. III, f.161ᵛ (Anon.) ; Pad. D27, f.105 (Anon.) ; Rome cs46, f.34ᵛ ; Rome cs77, f.4ᵛ (Anon.) ; St Gall 463, no. 142; 1521³, f.11ᵛ; [c1521]⁷, f.9ᵛ (Anon.) ; 1529¹, f.9ᵛ; 1553², f.14ᵛ ; 1559², no.15; Mouton 1555, f.6
Remarks		Incomplete; one folio missing in the *secunda pars*, between pp. 34 and 35	

	7	8	9
	O salve genitrix virgo dulcissima salve p. 44	Stabat mater dolorosa (2.p., Eya mater) pp. 46-53	Mittit ad virginem (2.p., Accede nuncia) pp. 54-61
Text and use	See above, pp. 180-1	Sequence for the Feast of the Seven Dolors of the BVM, 15 September, L.U. 1634ᵛ	Sequence for the Annunciation, 25 March, V.P. 133
Voices	[4]	5	4
Composer		[Josquin]	[Josquin]
Concordances	None	To the concordances listed in Smijers, add: Cop. 1872, f.4ᵛ (Anon.); Cop. 1873, no.37 (Anon.); Reg. AR891/92, no.32	See Smijers
Remarks	Incomplete; s and T only	Published in Smijers, Motetten, Bundel VIII, p. 51	Published in Smijers, Motetten, Bundel I, p. 14

207

	10 Ave maria gratia plena ... virgo serena pp. 62-5	11 Fer pietatis opem miseris mater pietatis pp. 66-7	12 Tota pulcra es amica mea et macula non est in te pp. 68-9
Text and use	Opening line from the sequence for the Annunciation, V.P. 46; remainder from hymn *Ave cuius conceptio*, Mone II, 5	Prayer to the BVM	Song of Songs 4:7
Voices	4	4	4
Composer	[Josquin]		[Mouton]
Concordances	To the concordances listed in Smijers, add: Berl. 40021, f.51ᵛ (Anon., with text 'Verbum incarnatum'; Mod. IX, f.73ᵛ; Mun. 41, f.226ᵛ (Anon., *a 6*); Nur. 83795, f.166ᵛ (T), 124ᵛ (B) (Anon.); Seg., f.83ᵛ; Speciálník, p. 64 (Anon.)	None	[1521][6], f.11
Remarks	Published in Smijers, *Motetten*, Bundel I, p. 1		

208

	13 Sub tuum presidium confugimus pp. 70-1	14 Verbum bonum et suave pp. 72-5	15 Maria magdalene et altera maria pp. 80-3
Text and use	Antiphon in honor of the BVM, L.U. 1861	Sequence for the Epiphany, v.P. 94	Compilation of biblical phrases, for Easter Sunday
Voices	4	4	4
Composer	[Brumel]	[Thérache]	
Concordances	Cambridge 1760, f.17ᵛ; Flor. 58, f.88ᵛ; [1521]⁶, f.10	See Lowinsky, *Medici Codex*, III, 145	None
Remarks		Published in Lowinsky, *Medici Codex*, IV, no.12	

	Tempus meum est ut revertar ad eum (2.p., Viri galilei aspicientes) pp. 84-91	Sancti dei omnes orate pro nobis (2.p., Criste audi nos) pp. 94-101	Bona dies per orbem lucessit (2.p., Pax vobis ego sum) pp. 102-9
Text and use	Not identical with the responsory, L.R. 101	Magnificat antiphon at Vespers, Common of two or more martyrs, L.U. 1160 ('Gaudent ... in aeternum') ; Versus and response at Vespers, Feast of All Saints, 1 November, L.U. 1721 ('Laetamini ... recti corde') ; Prayer, in the *Horae nostrae Dominae secundum usum Romanae Ecclesiae* of c.1490 (Zwickauer Facsimiledrucke, no.22) ('Infirmitatem ... intercessione averte') ; the *secunda pars* consists of portions taken from the Litany for Holy Saturday, L.U. 776v and 776FF	The *l.p.* is a rhymed text about the Resurrection; the *2.p.* begins with the antiphon *Pax vobis* (L.U. 1702) but continues differently
Voices	4	4	4
Composer	[A. de Févin]	[Mouton]	
Concordances	Mod. IX, f.84^v; Reg. AR876, no.4: Rome cs44, f.87^v (Anon.) ; Rome Pal. lat. 1976-9, f.80^v (Anon.) ; Vienna 18825, f.23^v; 1514^4, f.12; 1526^5, f.12; 1555^{10}, no.10	To the concordances listed in Smijers, add: Friuli 59, f.64^v (Anon.) ; Rome cs76, f.158^v ; Mouton 1555, f.7	None
Remarks		Published in Smijers, *Motetten*, Bundel xx, p. 27; Paul Kast, ed., *Jean Mouton: Fünf Motetten (Das Chorwerk 76)*, p. 15	

	19	20	21
	In illo tempore maria magdalene (2.p., Dic nobis maria) pp. 110-15	Regina celi letare (2.p., Resurrexit sicut dixit) pp. 116-23	Preter rerum seriem (2.p., Virtus sancti spiritus) pp. 126-35
Text and use	Combination of texts for Easter: beginning of Gospel, Mark 16:1, L.U. 781 ('In illo tempore ... Jesum') ; variant of Offertory for Easter Monday, L.U. 787 ('Angelus Domini ... alleluia') ; two strophes from Easter sequence, *Victimae paschali laudes*, L.U. 780 ('Dic nobis Maria ... resurgentis') ; variant of versus of responsory *Christus resurgens*, Proc. 66 ('Dicant nunc Judaei ... alleluia') ; verse 8 of Easter hymn *O filii et filiae*, L.U. 1875 ('Vide, Thoma ... alleluia')	Antiphon in honor of the BVM, Sundays at Compline, L.U. 275	Sequence for the Nativity, A.H. 20, no.53
Voices	4	4	6
Composer	[Mouton]		[Josquin]
Concordances	Berg. 1209, f.85ᵛ; Bol. Q19, f.63ᵛ; Cambrai 124, f.102ᵛ (Anon.) ; London 2037, f.37ᵛ; Mod. RX, f.80ᵛ; Mun. 41, f.238ᵛ (Anon., a 6) ; Pad. A17, f.50ᵛ (Anon.) ; Ver. DCCLX, f.10ᵛ (Josquin) ; Vienna 18825, f.14ᵛ; 1521⁵, f.8; [c.1521]ᵀ, f.17 (Anon.) ; 1529¹, f.6ᵛ	Ver. DCCLX, f.80ᵛ (Anon.)	To the concordances listed in Smijers, add: Cop. 1872, f.87ᵛ; Flor. 11, f.39ᵛ (Anon.) ; Rome Vallic, no.50
Remarks			Published in Smijers, *Motetten*, Bundel VII, p. 21

	22 Virgo salutiferi (2.p., Tu potis es prime; 3.p., Nunc celi regina) pp. 136-43	23 [Gaude Barbara beata, summe pollens; 2.p., Gaude quia meruisti] pp. 144-5	24 Paranymphus salutat virginem intemeratam (2.p., Ecce virgo decora) pp. 156-9
Text and use	Humanistic poem by Ercole Strozzi (see Lowinsky, *Medici Codex*, III, 199-200)	Sequence in honor of St Barbara, virgin and martyr, 4 December, Chev. 6711	The first three words come from the sequence, Mone II, 37, but the text continues differently
Voices	5	4	4
Composer	[Josquin]	[Mouton]	[Compère]
Concordances	See Lowinsky, *Medici Codex*, III, 199	Cambrai 124, f.1^r (Anon.); Cort. 95-6 and Paris 1817, f.70^v (Anon.); Flor. 58, f.163^v; Friuli 59, f.59^v (Anon.); Mad. 607, p. 6; Rome Pal. lat. 1980-1, f.65^v (Anon.); 1514^1, f.2; 1526^1, f.2	Berg. 1209, f.76^v; Pad. A17, f.111^v (Anon.); 1512^1, no.47 (Anon.); [1521]^4, f.15
Remarks	Published in Att. IV, p. 138; Smijers. *Motetten*, Bundel VII, p. 42; Lowinsky, *Medici Codex*, IV, no.42. Canonic voices missing in *1.p.*; most of text missing	Incomplete; only half the *1.p.* was written, without stems and without text	Published in Finscher, IV, 39-40

	25	26	27
Text and use	Profitentes unitatem veneremur trinitatem (2.p., Digne loqui de personis) pp. 160-5	O genitrix gloriosa, mater dei spetiosa (2.p., Maria mater gratie) pp. 166-9	O virgo virginum quomodo fiet istud (2.p., Filie Jerusalem) pp. 170-3
	Nine verses of the sequence in honor of the Trinity, followed by the Gloria Patri, Benedicamus, Alleluia, and Amen; A.H. 54, p. 249	The *prima pars* is made up of a gathering of various phrases in honour of the BVM; the *secunda pars* consists of the second strophe of the hymn *Memento salutis auctor*, L.A., App., 46, with four interpolated lines, and the first two strophes of the hymn *O gloriosa Domina*, L.A., App., 46	Antiphon to the Magnificat, Feast of the Expectation of Birth of the BVM, 18 December, L.A. [115], Proc. 246
Voices	4	4	4
Composer	[Compère]	[Compère]	
Concordances	Friuli 59, f.66ᵛ (Anon.) ; Rome cs42, f.141; 1504¹, f.23 (Anon.)	Cop. 1848, p. 286 (Richafort) ; Flor. 2794, f.9ᵛ (Anon.) ; Milan 2267, f.51ᵛ (1.p. only, Anon.) ; Milan 2268, f.36ᵛ (2.p. only, Anon.) ; Milan 2269, f.149ᵛ (2.p. only, Anon.) ; Rome, cs46, f.98ᵛ ; 1502¹, f.4ᵛ (Anon.)	None
Remarks	Published in Finscher, IV, 41-4	Published in Finscher, IV, 29	

	28	29	30
	[Maria virgo semper laetare; 2.p., Te laudant angeli] pp. 174-81	Sicut lilium inter spinas pp. 184-5	Que est ista que processit (2.p., Et sicut dies verni) pp. 188-91
Text and use	Antiphon in honor of the BVM, Proc. 258 ('Maria Virgo ... Salvatorem'); antiphon for the Annunciation, Proc. 148 ('Virgo Verbo ... regem'); responsory for the Annunciation, Proc. 146 ('Gaude Maria ... mundo'); first part of responsory for the Nativity, Ant. Sar. 49 ('Te laudant angeli ... baiulasti'); antiphon, Proc. 252 ('Beata es ... Christum')	Song of Songs 2:2; Antiphon, Feast of the Purity of the BVM, 17 October, L.A. [207]	Responsory, Feasts of the BVM, L.R. 253
Voices	4	4	4
Composer	[Mouton]	[Brumel]	[Brumel]
Concordances	1519[1], no.20; 1526[2], no.20; 1534[3], no.10 (Gascongne)	See Lowinsky, *Medici Codex*, III, 138	Flor. 58, f.86v; [1521][6], f.11v
Remarks	Published in Att. I, p. 82; no text appears in MS 1070	Published in Lowinsky, *Medici Codex*, IV, no.7	

	31	32	33
Text and use	Liber generationis (2.p., Salomon autem; 3.p., Et post transmigrationem) pp. 192-203 Matthew 1:1-16; Gospel for the Nativity of the BVM, 8 September, L.U. 1624	Factum est autem cum baptizaretur p. 204 Luke 3:21-38; Genealogy of Christ, following ninth lection and responsory at Epiphany	Gabrielem archangelum scimus divinitus (2.p., Gloria patri) pp. 206-13 Versus of the responsory for the Annunciation, *Gaude Maria Virgo, cunctas haereses*, Proc. 146
Voices	4	4	3
Composer	[Josquin]	[Josquin]	
Concordances	See Smijers	See Smijers	None
Remarks	Published in Smijers, *Motetten*, Bundel III, p. 59	Published in Smijers, *Motetten*, Bundel III, p. 70. Incomplete; half of I.p. of s and T only.	Probably the 2.p. of a motet *Gaude Maria Virgo, cunctas haereses*

	34	35	36
Text and use	Alma redemptoris mater (2.p., Ex stella maris; 3.p., Tu que genuisti; 4.p., Virgo prius; 5.p., Sumens illud ave) pp. 214-25 Antiphon in honour of the BVM, Sundays at Compline, L.U. 273	Jouyssance vous donneray pp. 226-7 Chanson by Clément Marot	Venes regres venes tous pp. 228-9
Voices	3	4	4
Composer	Jac. obreth	[Claudin]	
Concordances	None	See Howard M. Brown, *Music in the French Secular Theatre, 1400-1550* (Cambridge, Mass., 1963), p. 245, no.232i	[c.1528][5], f.9v (Anon.)*
Remarks	Published in J. Wolf, *Werken van Jacob Obrecht, Motetten*, Bundel IV, p. 157	Published in G. Reese, *Music in the Renaissance* (rev. ed.; New York, 1959), p. 292	*I owe this concordance to the courtesy of Professor Lawrence F. Bernstein of the University of Chicago.

216

	37	38	39
Text and use	Popule meus quid feci tibi (2.*p.*, Ego eduxi te mare rubrum; 3.*p.*, Ego eduxi te per desertum; 4.*p.*, Quid ultra debui) pp. 234-41 Variant version of the Improperii, L.U. 737	Huc me sydereo (2.*p.*, Felle sitim) pp. 242-9 Humanistic poem by Mapheus Vegius (see Lowinsky, 'Josquin des Prez and Ascanio Sforza,' *Il duomo di Milano: Congresso Internationale, Atti,* ed. M.I. Gatti Perer (2 vols. Milan 1969), II, p. 18 Nur. 83795, f.147 (T), f.104(B)	Homo quidam fecit cenam (2.*p.*, Venite comedite) pp. 250-5 Responsory in honour of the Blessed Sacrament, L.U. 1856
Voices	4	6	5
Composer		Josquin	[Josquin]
Concordances	Nur. 83795, f.104(B) (Anon.)	To the concordances listed in Smijers, add: Cop. 1872, f.71ᵛ (Anon.); Reg. AR893, no.43	See Smijers
Remarks		Published in Smijers, *Motetten,* Bundel vi, p. 11; first alto missing in MS 1070	Published in Smijers, *Motetten,* Bundel v, p. 147

	40	41	42
	Adiutorium nostrum in nomine domini pp. 256-9	Sancta trinitas unus deus pp. 260-3	Gentilz galans compaingnons pp. 266-7
Text and use	Prayer to St Renatus, patron saint of expectant mothers, asking for a child for Louis XII and Anne of Brittany	Prayer to the Trinity (*Heures à l'usaige de Romme*, Paris, P. Pigouchet, 1497, f.i6)	
Voices	4	4	3
Composer	[Mouton]	[A. de Févin]	
Concordances	Cambridge 1760, f.23v (A. de Févin); London 8cvii, f.4v (Anon.); Rome Pal. lat. 1976-9, f.9v (Anon.); 1514[1], f.13; 1526[1], f.13. In the two latter sources this motet occurs as the 2.p. of Mouton's *Caeleste beneficium*.	Barc. 454, f.176v; Bol. q27, Pt. II, f.10v (Anon.); Cambrai 124, f.11B (Anon.); Cambridge 1760, f.19v; Friuli 59, f.83v (Anon.); London 8cvii, f.12v (Anon.); Mod. ix, f.88v; Pad. A17, f.82v (Anon.); Rome Chigi, f.79v; St Gall 462, f.110v (Anon.); Toledo 13, f.25v; Tournai, f.14v (Anon.); Ver. dcclx, f.50v (Anon.); 1514[1], f.9; 1526[1], f.9	See Brown, *Music in the French Secular Theatre*, p. 221, no.140d
Remarks		There is also a version for six voices (two added by Arnoldus de Bruck). Jachet wrote an 8-part motet on the same text, borrowing Févin's superius (see Lowinsky, 'A newly discovered sixteenth-century motet manuscript', *Journal of the American Musicological Society*, III (1950), 220 and 224)	

APPENDIX II

Thematic catalogue of *unica*

The following catalogue includes numbers 20, 36, 37, and 42, which are not *unica* but for which no composer is known.

20 Regina celi letare

2.p. Resurrexit sicut dixit

27 O virgo virginum

2.p. Filie Jerusalem

33 Gabrielem archangelum

2.p. Gloria patri

Jac. obreth

34 Alma redemptoris mater

2.p. Et stella maris

3.p. Tu que genuisti

4.p. Virgo prius

5.p. Sumens illud ave

36 Venes regres venes tous

37 Populе meus quid feci tibi

2. Ego eduxi te mare rubrum

3. Ego eduxi te per desertum

4. Quid ultra debui facere

42 Gentilz galans compaingnons

NOTES

* I am greatly indebted to Oliver Davies, reference librarian, and Richard Townend, assistant to the reference librarian, of the Royal College of Music, for granting me every consideration during my stay in London for the study of the manuscript. Moreover, Mr Townend answered my written inquiries with unfailing courtesy and promptness. Mr Davies obtained permission for me to have the manuscript transferred to the British Museum for comparison with other manuscripts of the period; Dr C.E. Wright, deputy keeper of manuscripts at the British Museum, allowed me to use the manuscript in the students' room of the British Museum, a true scholar's paradise. The staff of the department of manuscripts at the British Museum are beyond praise.

    I owe a particular debt of gratitude to my research assistant, Miss Bonnie J. Blackburn, who aided me in bibliographical questions. She discovered the relationship between the French Neo-Latin poet Nicolaus Borbonius (Nicolas Bourbon) and the English court. The catalogue, based on my index of sixteenth-century motets, is her work.

    I consider the present study only a preliminary investigation.

1 The manuscript has never been the subject of detailed study. However, James R. Braithwaite, in his unpublished dissertation, 'The Introduction of Franco-Netherlandish Manuscripts to Early Tudor England: The Motet Repertory' (Boston University 1967), has discussed it, together with other Franco-Flemish manuscripts in England. Mr. Braithwaite has not had the opportunity to study the manuscript in the original, and I have not been able to make use of his description and analysis. I nevertheless wish to thank him for the kindness with which he placed the relevant portions of his dissertation and part of his correspondence with the librarian of the Royal College of Music at my disposal.

    The manuscript originally formed part of the library of the Sacred Harmonic Society of London, founded in 1832 as an organization of musical amateurs dedicated to the performance of sacred choral music (see Grove's *Dictionary of Music and Musicians* [5th ed. London 1954-61], VII, pp. 350-1). MS 1070 is listed in the *Catalogue of the Library of the Sacred Harmonic Society* (rev. ed. London 1872), pp. 200-1, under the number 1721 as a 'Collection of Latin Hymns, Psalms, &c. for three, four, five, and six voices (each part being written separately, but on the same folio).' It offers as date: 'written about the 16th century' and it adds that it was 'presented [in 1854] to the Society by Mr. R.W. Haynes.' On page xviii, under 'Donors to the Library,' occurs the name 'Haynes, Mr. Robert William.' In 1883 the manuscript, together with the library of the society, was transferred to and became the property of the Royal College of Music. The numbers 157 and 760A found on the verso of the first flyleaf are old catalogue and shelf numbers of the Royal College of Music.

2 In his unpublished 'Catalogue of the Manuscripts in the Library of the

Royal College of Music, with additions by Rupert Erlebach' (1931),
pp. 302-4

3 The probable ascription to Josquin of *In illo tempore* (p. 110) is superseded by the evidence of other sources that attribute the work to Mouton.

4 The chanson *Jouyssance vous donneray* is by Claudin de Sermisy, not
Gombert.

5 *The Medici Codex of 1518: A Choirbook of Motets Dedicated to Lorenzo
de' Medici, Duke of Urbino*, ed. Edward E. Lowinsky (*Monuments of Renaissance Music*, III-V; Chicago 1968).

6 *Ibid.*, III, pp. 146-7

7 We must remember that nos. 40 and 41 were written by the second scribe–
about which more presently.

8 Bernard Kahmann, 'Ueber Inhalt und Herkunft der Handschrift Cambridge Pepys 1760,' *Bericht über den internationalen musikwissenschaft-
lichen Kongress Hamburg 1956* (Kassel 1957), pp. 126-8. Kahmann refers
to the title of the manuscript, 'Henry VII's Music Book,' and to the coat of
arms. That title, however, was added when the manuscript was rebound
at the end of the seventeenth century.

9 A. Tillman Merritt, 'A Chanson Sequence by Févin,' *Essays on Music in
Honor of Archibald Thompson Davison* (Cambridge, Mass. 1957), pp.
91-9. Merritt, on the basis of M.R. James, *Bibliotheca Pepysiana: A Descriptive Catalogue of the Library of Samuel Pepys, Part III, Mediaeval
Manuscripts* (London 1923), pp. 36-8, ascribes the anthology to the ownership of the 'then Prince of Wales, Arthur, son of Henry VII' – a view
shared by Frank Ll. Harrison *(Music in Medieval Britain* [London 1958],
p. 340) and John Stevens *(Music at the Court of Henry VIII* [*Musica Britannica*, XVIII; London 1962], p. 108, n. 83, and p. 109, n. 99), who points
out that two compositions in the manuscript edited by him (Add. 31922)
agree almost note for note with the versions in the Pepys manuscript.

10 Howard M. Brown, 'The Genesis of a Style: The Parisian Chanson, 1500-
1530,' *Chanson and Madrigal 1480-1530*, ed. James Haar (Cambridge,
Mass., 1964), p. 5. Brown believes that the manuscript was 'the property
of Henry VIII of England' but was written for Henry when he was prince
of Wales.

11 Edward Bernard, *Catalogi Librorum Manuscriptorum Angliae et Hiber-
niae in unum collecti* (Oxford 1697), II, p. 209, no. 6806.87. Whoever described the manuscript in 1697 was not an expert, for he claimed that the
manuscript contained music of 'the most Eminent Masters, English and
Forrein,' whereas its contents are purely French.

12 See Fasquelle's *Encyclopédie de la Musique* (1961), III, pp. 405-6. The
name 'Perrichon' in the *tabula* that Merritt (probably following the M.R.
James catalogue) believes to be that of the composer, belongs to the chanson text instead, which runs, 'Il m'est advis que je voys perrichon.' 'Perrichon' is a woman's name. The name given to the composer over the composition is Hyllaire – Hilaire Penet – and this is corroborated by other
sources.

13 See Merritt, 'A Chanson Sequence by Févin,' *loc. cit.*
14 The Medici Codex, for example, measures 42 x 27.5 cm. (see the facsimile edition in vol. v of *Monuments of Renaissance Music*).
15 Heinrich Besseler, in his article 'Chorbuch' in *Die Musik in Geschichte und Gegenwart*, II, cc. 1332-49; 1336, characterizes choirbooks of this size as Quarthandschriften. In addition, the sideways position of the watermark (of which later), with the chain-lines running horizontally, places the manuscript in the category of quarto (see Ronald B. McKerrow, *An Introduction to Bibliography* [Oxford 1962], pp. 166-7).
16 Hilary Jenkinson, *The Later Court Hands in England from the Fifteenth to the Seventeenth Century* (Cambridge 1927), chap. 10, pp. 47 ff. (cf. also his 'alphabet no. 1' of 'Bastard Hand: c. 1432'). The closeness to a French bastard hand can be studied in *tabula* 49 of Joachim Kirchner's *Scriptura Gothica Libraria* (Munich and Vienna 1966). The sample 'probably' comes from Paris, is written in the year 1406, and is characterized as 'Bastarda Gallica.'
17 A facsimile of these two pages, containing Brumel's *Sicut lilium*, is given in Lowinsky, *The Medici Codex*, III, p. 139.
18 See pp. 72 and 74, tenor and soprano; pp. 106 and 108, soprano
19 See pp. 106 and 108, where a portion of the tenor on p. 108 is moved back to p. 106; likewise a portion of the alto on p. 109 is moved back to p. 107
20 See pp. 136, 138-45, 174-81. On pages 144-5 a new motet begins without text. The work is incomplete and so is the notation: stems are missing, which suggests a most curious practice: not writing the stems with the note heads but adding them later.
21 C.M. Briquet, *Les Filigranes: Dictionnaire historique des marques du papier* (Paris 1907)
22 Jenkinson, *The Later Court Hands*, p. 22
23 There are other manuscripts of English origin using paper with similar watermarks. Stephen D. Tuttle, in his study on 'Watermarks in Certain Manuscript Collections of English Keyboard Music' (*Essays on Music in Honor of Archibald Thompson Davison* [Cambridge, Mass. 1957], pp. 147-58; 149), has described and traced the watermarks in MS Royal Appendix 56 in the British Museum, 'one of the oldest existing collections of English keyboard music,' and a slightly different one in Royal Appendix 58. Tuttle writes concerning the watermark: 'It has not been identified.' Surely this was an oversight, for Briquet describes whole families of this watermark under the numbers 10779, 10794, 10795, 11222, 11419, 11426, 11429, and 11452. John Ward has dated Royal Appendix 58 as after 1540 (see his 'Sources de la musique pour le clavier en Angleterre' in *La Musique instrumentale de la Renaissance*, ed. Jean Jacquot [Paris 1955], pp. 225-36; 226; see also his 'The Lute Music of MS Royal Appendix 58' in *Journal of the American Musicological Society*, XIII [1960], 117-25). MS Royal App. 58 is of further interest for the present inquiry because it contains a selection of French chansons published by Attaingnant between 1528 and 1532 *(ibid.*, p. 117, n. 2). A watermark very close to that of MS 1070 occurs in

the title page of the first English music print, *In this boke ar conteynd. XX. songes*, dated 1530 (RISM 1530[6]), and containing chiefly English songs by, among others, Cornysh, Taverner, and Fayrfax. All of this confirms what is known from other sources, that England, in the sixteenth century, imported its paper from France, in particular from Normandy and Brittany (see Allan H. Stevenson, 'Watermarks are Twins,' *Studies in Bibliography*, IV [1951-2], 57-91; 59).

24 See O. Elfrida Saunders, *English Illumination* (Florence 1928), I, plates 22d, e

25 *Ibid.*, I, plate 22a, showing the initial B in a long circular ornamental figure with a duck's head on one end from Bede's Cassiodorus, Durham Cathedral Library, 8th century; plate 22b, showing the initial H with a biting fish's head entwined in leaves and scrolls from Aldhelm, *De Virginitate*, Lambeth Palace Library, 9th century.

26 *Ibid.*, I, plate 56

27 *Ibid.*, I, chap. 4, pp. 45 ff., 'Bestiaries'

28 *Ibid.*, p. 51

29 Professor L.M.J. Delaissé, author of *A Century of Dutch Manuscript Illumination* (Berkeley 1968) and other books on illuminations, and Miss Janet Backhouse, assistant keeper of manuscripts at the British Museum in London. The latter remarked also on the provincial and derivative aspect of the decorations that showed French rather than Flemish character but might have been done by an English craftsman who had trained himself on French models. I wish to thank both scholars for their kindness.

30 [Abraham Horodisch], *Initials from French Incunabula, with 1011 Reproductions* with an introduction by Hellmut Lehmann-Haupt (New York 1948); see for example, nos. 47, 68, 70, 74, 80, 81, 109, 364, all of which come from Parisian printers between 1494 and 1499

31 In the *Catalogue of the Library of the Sacred Harmonic Society* the following remark occurs: 'The name "Mrⁱˢ A. Bolleyne" is written on one leaf.'

32 Paul Friedmann, *Anne Boleyn: A Chapter of English History, 1527-1536* (London 1884). This book is the fundamental work on Anne Boleyn. To this day it is unexcelled in the thoroughness of its documentation and the solidity of its conclusions. It is the main basis of the following presentation.

33 This is evident from one of a number of his love letters to Anne, written in French and now preserved in the Vatican archives, in which he writes:'but if you please to do the duty of a true and loyal mistress, and to give up yourself, body and heart, to me ... I promise you that not only the name shall be given you, but also that I will take you for my mistress, casting off all others that are in competition with you, out of my thoughts and affection, and serving you only.' See G-A Crapelet, *Lettres de Henry VIII à Anne Boleyn, publiées d'après les originaux de la Bibliothèque du Vatican* (2nd ed.; Paris 1835); both the original French text and the translation are found on pp. 110-13.

34 See Friedmann, *Anne Boleyn*, I, pp. 105 and 174; Garrett Mattingly, *Catherine of Aragon* (London 1950), p. 253; about Dr. Cranmer's secret mar-

riage to a young Lutheran woman in Germany, see Friedmann, *ibid.* I, p. 177, and Mattingly, *ibid.*, p. 254.

35 In a letter to Joachim Camerarius of June 1536 in which he called Anne's execution a 'casus tragicus' (see Henry Ellis, *Original Letters Illustrative of English History* [2nd ed.; London 1825], II, p. 66).

36 I am indebted to Mr Frank Tirro, a member of my doctoral seminar, for calling my attention to this motto; see James E. Doyle, *The Official Baronage of England* (3 vols, London 1886), III, p. 681.

37 Sir Jack Westrup, who chaired the meeting of the Royal Musical Association on 23 October 1969 at which I read a paper on the present manuscript, made the witty observation that the *longa* also looked like an axe.

38 I am greatly indebted to Karl Morrison, professor of history at the university of Chicago, for the English rendering of the poem, in which he succeeded in infusing the same tone of arcane wisdom as the original. He was aided in parts by an ingenious prose translation made by Professors Bonner Mitchell and Elbion de Lima of the university of Missouri on the occasion of the performance of the work during my lecture there on the present manuscript. Both translations had to take liberties to wring some sense out of the text. I quote the prose translation of the last two verses, where the two renderings show the greatest divergence: 'Hercules in two-columned Gibralter rests his holy forces; Lazarus, called by a harmonious song, enjoys a high place in Paradise, where we ask Christ as our dear friend and omnipotent master, with varied praise, that he make us meek.'

39 According to an old tradition fostered in particular by Clement of Alexandria, Orpheus 'was a prototype of Christ ... Christ is the New Orpheus because he brings the salvation which the old Orpheus failed to realize.' This tradition, which is reflected in representations of Christ as Orpheus in catacombs and mosaics, in stone tablets and engravings, was transmitted to the middle ages and found its poetic climax in the anonymous fourteenth-century poem *Sir Orfeo*. I am greatly indebted to Professor Michael Masi of Loyola University for bringing this connection to my attention and for permitting me to quote from his study on 'The Christian Music of *Sir Orfeo*' in advance of publication.

40 See Hugo Holstein, *Die Reformation im Spiegelbilde der dramatischen Litteratur des sechzehnten Jahrhunderts* (Halle 1886), pp. 58, 138-40, 144; see also Edward E. Lowinsky, *Secret Chromatic Art in the Netherlands Motet* (New York 1946), pp. 119-20.

Professor Morrison has drawn my attention to another important element in the interpretation of the poem. Edua is the Latin name for the French town of Autun, which has an eleventh-century cathedral dedicated to St Lazare. Further research established that St Lazarus was the 'legendary bishop of Aix-en-Province.' He was the brother of St Mary Magdalene and St Martha; these three were said to have been 'placed by the heathens in a rudderless boat' together with some friends. Angels guided their boat to France (see George Kaftal, *Iconography of the Saints in Tuscan Painting* [Florence 1952], cc. 625, 720). The connection with France is signifi-

cant. The composer surely must be sought in France. The composition is a
work of the purest Josquin imitation which flourished during his life and
after his death. The motet will be published in the *Proceedings of the
Royal Musical Association,* together with a greatly condensed version of
the present study.

41 *The noble tryumphaunt coronacyon of quene Anne, wyfe unto the moost
noble kynge Henry the VIII* (London [1533]) ; 'The receivyng, conveiyng
and coronacion of quene Anne wife to the high and mightie prince kyng
Henry the eight,' in Edward Hall, *Henry VIII,* ed. Charles Whibley (London 1904), II, pp. 229-42. The following account of the coronation festivities is taken from the latter source.

42 There were no pageants at all for the festivities in honour of the marriage
of Henry VIII and Catherine of Aragon in 1509; in 1511 three pageants
were prepared for their entry at Coventry, none having any reference to
ancient mythology. The first time that the classical element enters in
English pageants is on the occasion of Charles v's visit to London in 1522,
when the story of Jason and Medea was presented in reference to the order
of the Golden Fleece, which was adopted by the Drapers as a trade symbol
(see Robert Withington, *English Pageantry, An Historical Outline*
[Cambridge, Mass., 1918], I, p. 176).

In France the classical tone and figures and scenes from antiquity had
appeared in the beginning of the sixteenth century. The model and inspiration for the festivities in honour of Anne seem to have been the celebrations in Rouen one year earlier, in 1532, in honour of Queen Eleanor. They
comprised 'les chars de Mercure, de Junon, de Pallas, traînés par des serpents, des paons, par les Muses et suivis d'une foule de divinités à pied ou
à cheval' (see Josèphe Chartrou, *Les Entrées solenneles et triomphales à
la Renaissance (1484-1551)* [Paris 1928], p. 82). Among a multitude of
figures from Greek antiquity, 'Apollon, la harpe à la main, conduit les
Muses attelées au char de Pallas' *(ibid.,* p. 83).

43 The motif was favoured at Henry's court. In an inventory of the king's
jewels of 1532, mention is made of 'a cup of gold, called the Dream of
Paris, having on the cover the images of Paris, Jupiter, Venus, Pallas and
Juno, and Paris' horse, garnished with 19 diamonds ...' (see *Letters and
Papers, Foreign and Domestic, of the Reign of Henry VIII,* ed. James
Gairdner, V [1880], no. 1799, p. 738).

44 *The noble tryumphaunt coronacyon,* ff. 4v-5

45 See Erwin Panofsky, *Hercules am Scheidewege (Studien der Bibliothek
Warburg,* XVIII [Leipzig 1930]).

46 These poems have been reprinted several times; the best edition is the one
by Frederick J. Furnivall, *Ballads from Manuscript, Volume I: Ballads
on the Condition of England in Henry VIII's and Edward VI's Reigns ...*
(London 1868-72), I, pp. 364-401. For further samples of Leland's poetry
and a fine appreciation of the poet, see Leicester Bradner, *Musae Anglicanae: A History of Anglo-Latin Poetry, 1500-1925* (The Modern Language Association of America General Series, X [New York 1940; repr.
1966])

47 See Helmuth Osthoff, *Josquin Desprez* (Tutzing 1962-5), I, p. 41

48 See Otto Kinkeldey, *Orgel und Klavier in der Musik des 16. Jahrhunderts* (Leipzig 1910), p. 103

49 Hall's chronicle has the king say that 'the docters of the universities ... have determined the mariage to be voyde, and detestable before God' (Hall, *Henry VIII*, II, p. 209).

50 Mattingly, *Catherine of Aragon*, p. 196

51 Lowinsky, *The Medici Codex*, III, p. 46. We are speaking of an heuristic principle, of course. For the habit of gathering texts from various sources had become quite prevalent in the pre-Tridentine era. Not every text so assembled can be regarded as containing a special message of a political or personal character. Texts relating to one single event or religious occasion and culled from related sources constitute perfectly ordinary phenomena at the time. But those texts in particular that are put together from *disparate* biblical sources are worthy of close attention.

52 Anne of Brittany, first wedded to Charles VIII, bore him three sons and one daughter, all of whom died in childhood or shortly after birth. By Louis XII Anne had two sons, both still-born; but two daughters, Claude and Renée, lived (see Helen J. Sanborn, *Anne of Brittany* [Boston 1917]).

53 *Salve* is the favourite form for greeting Mary; it occurs notably in the *Salve regina*, but also in *Salve sancta parens* and other Marian prayers. *Genitrix* usually occurs in the phrase *Dei genitrix* found in various antiphons *(Sub tuum praesidium* and elsewhere) ; *dulcis* and *digna* are frequently attributed to Mary; the notion that Mary holds the sceptre of the heavens is inherent in the idea of Mary's queenship, *Regina caeli*. The phrase *ad te clamamus soboles miserabilis Evae* is a variation of the *ad te clamamus, exsules, filii Hevae* of the *Salve regina*, the *vallis acerba* a variant of the *in hac lacrimarum valle* of the same antiphon.

54 For the full text of the hymn, see the *Liber usualis* (Tournai 1956), p. 456 (at lauds of the feast of the epiphany of our Lord). For a slightly different version of the text, see Clemens Blume, *Unsere liturgischen Lieder: Das Hymnar der altchristlichen Kirche* (Regensburg 1932), p. 201.

55 See Lowinsky, *The Medici Codex*, III, p. 221

56 *Music in the Renaissance* (rev. ed. New York 1959), p. 292

57 Hall, *Henry VIII*, II, p. 233

58 See Mattingly, *Catherine of Aragon*, p. 316, n. 2. The opening page of MS Royal 8 G VII in the British Museum shows Henry's coat of arms together with the Tudor rose and the pomegranate. A woodcut of 1509 of the coronation of Henry and Catherine shows Henry sitting under a gigantic Tudor rose and Catherine under a huge pomegranate. The woodcut belongs to the university library of Cambridge and is reproduced by G.W.O. Woodward in *King Henry VIII: An Illustrated Biography* (London 1967), p. 6.

59 Not one day later as most histories report; see A.F. Pollard, *Henry VIII* (London 1925), p. 346.

60 *Catherine of Aragon*, p. 181

61 Geoffrey de C. Parmiter, *The King's Great Matter: A Study of Anglo-Papal Relations, 1527-1534* (London 1967), p. 9

62 *Ibid.*, p. 10
63 Crapelet, *Lettres de Henri VIII*, pp. 138-40. For a facsimile, translitera-
   tion, and modern rendition of the same letter, see G.W.O. Woodward, *King
   Henry VIII*, p. 14.
64 There has been a long debate on whether Anne had been Wyatt's mistress.
   Wyatt's last biographer and editor of his poems, Kenneth Muir, thinks so
   (see the chapter on 'Wyatt and Anne Boleyn,' in his *Life and Letters of
   Thomas Wyatt* [Liverpool 1963], pp. 13-37, which combines full documentation with an incisive analysis of Wyatt's poems). Patricia Thomson,
   in her *Sir Thomas Wyatt and his Background* (London 1964; see particularly chap. 2 on 'Courtly Love,' pp. 10-45), gives the documents, poems,
   and Muir's interpretation of them an independent and critical reading.
   While certain that Wyatt was in love with Anne and that Anne responded
   to Wyatt's suit, she does not commit herself on the question of how far the
   relationship went (pp. 28-9). Wyatt is said to have informed the privy
   council (according to other sources, Henry himself) 'that his former mistress was not a suitable wife for the King' (Kenneth Muir, *Collected
   Poems of Sir Thomas Wyatt* [London 1949], p. x; *ibid.*, *Life and Letters*,
   pp. 17 ff.).
65 See John Stevens, *Music and Poetry in the Early Tudor Court* (London
   1961), *passim*; see also the same author's *Music at the Court of Henry
   VIII* (Musica Britannica, XVIII [London 1962]), containing almost three
   dozen compositions by the king himself.
66 *Epistre contenant le procès criminel faict a l'encontre de la royne Anne
   Boullant d'Angleterre. Par Carles Aulmosnier de Monsieur le Daulphin.
   On les vend à Lyon, près nostre Dame de Confort. M.D. XLV.*
   Copy in the British Museum.
67 Friedmann, *Anne Boleyn*, I, p. 40, n. 1, says that this poem was 'ascribed to
   Lancelot de Carles, to Marot and to Crispin de Milherve,' and that it was
   printed by 'Charles ausmonier de Mr. le Dauphin.' He misread the title,
   from which it is clear that the name is 'Carles,' not 'Charles,' and that it
   refers to the author, not the printer.
68 See Arthur Tilley, *The Literature of the French Renaissance* (New York
   1959), I, pp. 89, 319
69 See Friedmann, *Anne Boleyn*, II, p. 317
70 See Julia Pardoe, *The Court and Reign of Francis the First, King of
   France* (London 1887), I, p. 333
71 Friedmann has shown that Anne was born in 1502 or 1503, not in 1507, as
   commonly assumed, and that it was she, and not her sister Mary, who accompanied Mary Tudor to France when she went there in 1514 to marry
   the elderly Louis XII (*Anne Boleyn*, I, p. 39; in II, app. A, pp. 315-22, the
   author erroneously changes this date to 1503-4). J.H. Round, *The Early
   Life of Anne Boleyn* (London 1886), p. 12 f., discovered additional evidence for Friedmann's assumption and placed Anne's birthdate in the year
   1501. On Mary Tudor in France, see the account given by Lowinsky in *The
   Medici Codex*, III, pp. 43-7.

72 Marvin H. Albert, in his recent book on *The Divorce: A Re-Examination by an American Writer of the Great Tudor Controversy* (London 1966), p. 82, refers to 'an enthusiastic account of the young Anne Boleyn ... written by a member of the French court, Viscount Chateaubriant' whom he quotes as saying: 'She possessed a great talent for poetry, and when she sang, like a second Orpheus, she would have made bears and wolves attentive ... Besides singing like a siren, accompanying herself on the lute, she harped better than King David, and handled cleverly both flute and rebec.' We should have loved to have contemporaneous testimony to Anne's being regarded as 'a second Orpheus.' But Albert quotes no source. With some effort his report could be traced to the *Mémoires de Messire Jean de Laval, Comte de Châteaubriant. Écrits par lui-même, en 1538, et publiés pour la première fois; avec un Avant-propos* (Impression spéciale, faite pour la Bibliomaniac Society, 1868). In the *avant-propos* the nameless editor reveals (a) that he never saw the manuscript that he is publishing; (b) that all he owned was the transcription sent to him by a friend; (c) that the friend never finished the transcription; (d) that the original was never found; (e) that it was up to the reader to judge whether the memoirs were apocryphal.

   History should not be written on the quicksand of unseen and unidentified sources. The memoirs are a *chronique scandaleuse* of an entirely fictitious origin, in which the twelve-year-old Anne, on her voyage to France, is made to seduce a sailor, etc., etc. In attenuation of Albert's naïveté, it may be surmised that he never saw the memoirs but copied the passage from A. Strickland, *Lives of the Queens* (1842), IV, p. 168, as did the usually more circumspect John Stevens, who quotes the same passage, adding: 'from memoirs of Viscount Chateaubriant, courtier of Francis I' (*Music and Poetry*, p. 293, n. 78; see also p. 280). This is an instructive example of how myths are generated.

73 London, BM, MS Egerton 2403, a small book on paper containing 51 leaves. The larger part is in English and contains 'The sad Complaint of Mary Queen of Scotts who was beheaded in England in the reign of Queen Elizabeth' and some religious poems. The manuscript belonged to or was written by Thomas Wenman. The above-named 'traicté' begins on f. 50^v.

74 London, BM, MS Sloane 2495. The catalogue of Sloane manuscripts gives no description of this manuscript beyond dating it as of the seventeenth century.

75 The one exception is the collection of grants made by Henry to Anne from the year 1532 on. It comes, not from the royal library, but from the Harley collection and carries the number 303. It seems as if Anne, after having been crowned queen of England, had this collection of grants to her and her heirs copied and bound in one volume. On the spine of the book is written: *Cartae concessae Annae, Marchionissae Penbrocheae 1532-3*. It contains seven grants, written in the best chancellery Latin, dating from 1 September 1532 to 1 March 1533. The act creating her marchioness of Pembroke is the first of the documents, decorated with a brilliantly coloured

initial showing a crowned falcon in silver – now darkened – standing on a golden tree stump with bare roots, and the letter H in gold with blue shading, the continuation of the name 'Henricus' likewise in gold. There are special grants concerning the annuity of one thousand pounds, the lands and manors given to her in perpetuity, and, the most curious of all, document two, granting her pre-eminence *stando sedendo eundo* before all marchionesses of the realm.

76 London, BM, MS King's 9; vellum, 303 folios, magnificently illuminated throughout.

77 'The Pistellis and Gospelles for the LII Sundayes in the yere in French. With an exhortation to each, in English, Translated for Anne Boleyn, Marchioness of Pembroke,' London, BM, MS Harley 6561, written on vellum, 202 folios. Most of the headings, written in blue, have disappeared and the book is waterstained. Since Anne is called marchioness of Pembroke – and the initials A P can be found throughout – the manuscript must have been written between September 1532, when she was created marchioness, and 1 June 1533, the date of her coronation.

78 In a letter to Thomas Cromwell Anne Boleyn asks that 'Richard Herman marchaunte and citizen of Antwerpe in Brabant [who] was in the tyme of the late lorde Cardynall put and expelled frome his fredome and felowshipe of and in the Englishe house there ... for that he dyd ... helpe to the settyng forthe of the New Testamente in Englisshe ... [be] restored to his pristine fredome ... and the soner at this oure requeste ...' Henry Ellis, who published this letter in his *Original Letters*, II, pp. 45-6, remarks: 'From the following Letter, if from no other source' (the present manuscript was unknown to him) 'it may be gathered that Anne Boleyn favoured the dissemination of the Scriptures in the vulgar tongue. Her own copy of Tyndal's translation of "The Newe Testament, imprinted at Antwerp by Marten Emperowr, Anno M. D. xxxiiii." is still extant among the Books bequeathed, in 1799, to the British Museum, by the rev. Clayton Mordaunt Cracherode. It is upon vellum, illuminated. Upon the gilding of the leaves, in a red letter, are the words ANNA REGINA ANGLIAE.'

79 'Et sachons ce, qu'il est temps de nous lever de somne: car maintenant nostre salut est plus prochain, que quant nous l'avons cuyde.'

80 London, BM, MS Royal 20 B XVII, quarto, 46 folios. At the end (f. 46) we find the following note: 'Escript a Londres le sixiesme None de Janvier en lan Mille v^e vingt neufz.'

81 Her own letters were published by Mary Anne Everett Wood, *Letters of Royal and Illustrious Ladies of Great Britain* (London 1846), II, nos. 7, 18, 19, 23, 76, 77, 78, 79.

82 London, BM, MS Royal 16 E XIII, 15 folios

83 Having only a few excerpts of the poem from the manuscript at the British Museum at my disposal, I am not in a position to say more than this: The *Oeuvres Complètes de Clément Marot*, ed. Pierre Jannet (Paris 1873), I, pp. 74-86, contain as no. VIII, the 'Sermon du bon pasteur et du maulvais,' which begins with the same lines as *Le Pasteur évangelique* but with signi-

ficant variant readings. It does not contain either the lines about François
I, his children and his sister, or the eulogy on Henry VIII and the final
address to Queen Anne. A thorough comparison between the printed and
the written versions should be interesting, the more so since the manuscript seems to be unknown to students of Marot; it is not mentioned in
C.A. Mayer, *Bibliographie des œuvres de Clément Marot*: I, *Manuscrits*
(Geneva 1954). Marot's authorship makes it possible to date the manuscript as having been written between 1 June 1533 (the date of Anne's
coronation) and 18 October 1534, the day when the Reformers put up pla-
cards throughout Paris condemning the celebration of the mass as a 'hor-
rible, great, and insufferable abuse.' They nailed a poster at the door of
the king's bed chamber. The king, previously tolerant, now erupted in terrible anger and had some two hundred persons arrested, of whom twenty-
four were burned. All those compromised as being known to favour the
Reform, among them Marot, had to flee France. Marot sought refuge in
Ferrara under the protection of the Reform-minded duchess, Rénee of
France. See *The New Cambridge Modern History* (Cambridge 1958), II,
p. 220; for a detailed account see Pierre Champion, *L'Envers de la tapis-
serie: Le règne de François Ier* (Paris 1935), pp. 210-19. What impact this
event made upon French letters has been described by Tilley, *Literature
of French Renaissance*, I, pp. 26-9. Presumably, the poem was written,
copied, illuminated, and sent to England shortly after Anne's coronation.

84 See *Nicolai Borbonii Vandoperani Lingonensis, Nugarum libri octo*
   (Basel 1540). The first edition appeared in 1533, the second revised and
   augmented edition in Paris in 1538. The Basel edition appears to be a
   reprint of the 1538 edition.
85 *Ibid.*, L. IV, p. 260: *Britanniae laus*
86 *Ibid.*, L. VII, p. 425, *Regi ac Reginae*; see also the eulogy of Henry and
   Anne in the letter to Lucio Stella, introductory to L. VI, pp. 326-46; 342
87 *Ibid.*, L. IV, p. 260, *Ad D. Thomam Cramoëllum*; L. V, p. 296, *Ad Th.
   Cramoëllum Anglum virum clariss*
88 *Ibid.*, L. IV, p. 261, *Ad D. Ioan. Dudlaeum & D. Henr. Cnevetum Britannos,
   nobileis viros*
89 *Ibid.*, L. V, p. 295, *D.H. Careo, H. Noresio, Th. Harvaeo, meis olim apud
   Britannos discipulis*. It is a loving memento, written after his return to
   France, and addressed to his disciples, 'whom the King and his wife, the
   Queen, had committed to my care.'
90 *Ibid.*, L. IV, p. 262, *De urbe Londino & Thamesi fluvio*
91 *Ibid.*, L. V, p. 305, *Ex vulgari carmine Clem. Maroti iocus.; Ibid.*, p. 308,
   De passere mortuo Lampadis puellae, ex vulg. Maroti
92 A Latin dissertation on Borbonius by G. Carré seems not to be available
   in the United States. Sidney Lee, *The French Renaissance in England: An
   Account of the Literary Relations of England and France in the Sixteenth
   Century* (Oxford 1910), p. 44, speaking about Frenchmen in England who
   taught French to children of the nobility, writes: 'Among other French
   tutors in Tudor England was Nicolas Bourbon, a protégé of Queen Anne

Boleyn. He was a humanist of wide repute, whose friends included Rabelais and Marot. From Bourbon, Robert Dudley, Earl of Leicester, with his brothers and their kinsfolk learnt French as children. Bourbon mingled with leaders of the reforming party while in England during Henry VIII's reign, and eulogized in facile epigrams Cromwell and Cranmer, while he discourteously taunted Sir Thomas More with his lowly origin and the resemblance of his surname to the Greek word for "fool." On re-settling in France, Bourbon abandoned the church of the Reformers and re-entered the orthodox fold, but his humanist sympathy and reputation knew no decay, and distinguished him in both camps.' For a well-balanced appreciation of Borbonius' talent and his writings, see D. Murarasu, *La poésie néo-latine et la renaissance des lettres antiques en France (1500-1549)* (Paris 1928), pp. 83-99.

93 *Nicolai Borbonii*, L. VI, p. 357, *Ad Thomam Crammarum Cantuariensem antistitem, quem invitat ad rusticandum. Scripsit in Anglia, anno Christi, M.D. XXXV* (two other poems to Cranmer occur in L. VII, pp. 392 and 393)

94 *Ibid.*, L. VII, p. 397: *Ad And. Castronovanum Tarb. praesulem, Christianissimique Galliae Regis, apud Britannos oratorem, Anno Christi 1535*

95 *Ibid.*, L. VII, p. 419, *Ad Franciscum Regem*; L. VIII, p. 459, *Ad eundem Regem*. The latter poem contains the following lines: 'Effugi auxilio vincula dura tuo./Insontem quamvis, me in carcere livor habebat:/Iamque neci dandus, more nocentis, eram.'

96 *Ibid.*, L. VII, p. 418, *Ad reginam*. 'Pauper in hoc iaceo tenebroso carcere clausus:/Nemo est qui possit ferre vel ausit opem:/Te praeter, regina: potes nympha optima, & audes:/Ut quam rex, ut quam diligit ipse Deus.'

97 *Ibid.*, L. VII, p. 428, *Ad Annam Angliae Reginam*. 'Nullius sceleris caussa, set crimine falso/Quorundam, atque odio, carcere clausus eram/ ...' 'Cum tua me extremo pietas respexit ab orbe,/Adflictum eripiens omnibus, Anna, malis./Quod ni evenisset, tenebris ego vinctus in illis/Languerem infelix, & retinerer adhuc.'

98 Ferdinand Buisson, in his work on *Sébastien Castellion* (Paris 1892), I. pp. 54 ff. and 80 ff., has shown how certain strongly pro-Lutheran poems found in the first edition of 1533 were replaced by innocuous, if not orthodox, verses in the later editions of 1538 and 1540. See also H. Hauser, 'De l'humanisme et de la Réforme en France, 1512-1552,' *Revue historique*, LXIV (1897), 258-97, 282n.

99 Buisson, *Sébastien Castellion*, I, p. 81

100 See note 78

101 John Hawkins, *A General History of the Science and Practice of Music* (London 1853; repr. 1963), p. 335, writes that 'Anne Boleyn, a lively and well accomplished young woman, and who had lived some years in France, doted on the compositions of Jusquin and Mouton, and had collections of them made for the private practice of herself and her maiden companions.' Regrettably, Hawkins gives no indication of the source of his information. One wonders whether he knew MS 1070 and realized that it was written for Anne Boleyn. Percy M. Young, *A History of British Music* (London 1967),

p. 92, believes that 'encouragement to cultivate the Flemish style ... came from Anne Boleyn, whose favourite composers were said to have been Josquin des Prés and his pupil Jean Mouton.' Young likewise fails to give any documentation and he does not refer to Hawkins' *History*.

102 *Letters and Papers*, x (1887), no. 965, p. 401
103 The question remains why the manuscript contained no composition in honour of Anne Boleyn. While seemingly structured predominantly in layers of eight folios, the manuscript begins with a layer of six folios. There is a good possibility that the first layer was intended to have eight folios and that the missing two folios either were saved for the end, as was often the case, because they would contain the most precious miniature (probably with a coat of arms) or were done but removed from the manuscript when Anne Boleyn was executed.
104 A comparison between our illustrations and the facsimile volume of the *Medici Codex of 1518* (Monuments of Renaissance Music, v), written at the French court, will prove the point.
105 Friedmann, *Anne Boleyn*, II, pp. 347-8
106 Nicholas Harris Nicolas, *The Privy Purse Expences of King Henry the Eighth, from November MDXXIX, to December MDXXXII* (London 1827)
107 They give the lie to the *Spanish Chronicle of King Henry VIII of England*, trans. M.A. Sharp Hume (London 1889), pp. 55 ff., where Anne Boleyn, 'soon after the death of the sainted Queen Katharine,' is said to have engaged Mark 'who was one of the prettiest monochord players and deftest dancers in the land.' This would place the beginning of Mark's service at the court after 7 January 1536, the day of Catherine's death, and it would put him among Anne's servants – things still considered possible by such recent and critical writers as Patricia Thomson (*Sir Thomas Wyatt*, p. 40), who was unaware that Mark appears in the privy purse accounts.
108 Nicolas, *The Privy Purse*, p. 336
109 See Stevens, *Music and Poetry*, p. 308
110 *Ibid.*, p. 307
111 Nicolas, *The Privy Purse*, p. 100
112 *Ibid.*, p. 262
113 'The royal party set out, going by river to Gravesend and then proceeding to a house of Sir Thomas Cheyne, the king's favourite and a great friend of Anne' (Friedmann, *Anne Boleyn*, I, p. 169). The privy purse accounts of 7 October mention a payment 'in Rewarde to a servant of Maister Cheneys for bringing fesaunts to the king' (Nicolas, *The Privy Purse*, p. 265). This shows that on 7 October the king and Anne were certainly at the house of Sir Thomas Cheyne. There is a good possibility therefore that the king's party had arrived at Sir Thomas' estate on the evening of 6 October and that Mark received the generous reward for entertaining the noble company with his playing on the virginals.
114 He was paid 4 pounds, 13 shillings, and 4 pence 'in rewarde' on 10 November (*ibid.*, p. 271).
115 *Nicolai Borbonii*, L. II, p. 112, *In Marcum:* 'Tu, qui, Marce, facis mala

carmina, saepius aequo/Illa mihi recitans, deteriora facis:/Ut bona sint,
demus, tamen assiduè illa canendo,/Efficis ut mala sint, displiceantque
magis./Omne quod est nimium, ingratum est: sententia prisca est,/Si
nimium sumas mellis, amaror erit.' That this poem is directed to Mark
Smeton and that Borbonius was familiar with Mark is certain not only
from his relations with the court in general, and from the contents of the
poem, but specifically from his poems to other gentlemen of the privy
chamber, such as Henry Knevet (L. VIII, p. 461, *In seipsum, ad Henricum
Cnevetum Anglum*; see also n. 88 above) or Norris and Cary (L. VIII, p.
440, *Literae, seu eruditio, quid ad Noresium et Careum pueros egregios*;
see also n. 89 above). Another charming poem, addressed *Noresio amico*,
occurs in L. VIII, p. 494. A physician by the name of Mark, also disliked by
Borbonius, is carefully distinguished by the heading *In Marcum medicum
malum* (L. V, p. 312).

116 'Tu vel opum compesce famem, lucrumque sitire/Desine; vel cur sis qua-
erere, Marce, macer.' This distich, under the heading *In Marcum*, occurs
in Janus Gruterus, *Delitiae C. Poetarum Gallorum* (Paris 1609), on p. 770
of the section of vol. I devoted to Borbonius, pp. 766-93. Two other poems
In Marcum avarum are printed in *Nugae*, L. I, p. 27, and L. II, p. 99.

117 *Letters and Papers*, XII, pt. 2 (1891), no. 181, p. 60

118 Stevens, *Music and Poetry*, pp. 309-10

119 *Ibid.*, p. 310

120 *Ibid.*, p. 318

121 One glance at some of the great repertories of keyboard music now available in modern editions shows their immense indebtedness to the vocal
polyphony of their respective periods. It may suffice to mention *Das Bux-
heimer Orgelbuch* (ed. Bertha Antonia Wallner in *Das Erbe Deutscher
Musik*, XXXVII-XXXIX [Kassel 1958-9]), or the sixteenth-century tablature
of Johannes of Lublin (ed. John Reeves White in *Corpus of Early Keyboard Music*, ed. by Willi Apel [American Institute of Musicology
1964-7]).

122 Stevens, *Music and Poetry*, pp. 275 ff.

123 The privy purse accounts record a payment on 26 October 'to the syngers
of the frenche kings pryvay Chambre in Rewarde' (Nicolas, *The Privy
Purse*, p. 268) and another one on 28 October 'to the singers of the Cardy-
nalle de larena' (*ibid.*, p. 269).

124 Patricia Thomson (*Sir Thomas Wyatt*, pp. 39-40) speaks about a French
book inscribed by Mark Smeton. It is the Royal MS 20 B XXI in the British
Museum, 'a fifteenth-century book of French poetry, containing Jean Le
Fèvre's "Les Lamentations de Matheolus" and "Le Livre de Leesce."
This interesting bit of evidence renders it very likely that Mark knew
French (see Postscript, pp. 197-200).

125 See Smith Palmer Bovie, *The Satires and Epistles of Horace: A Modern
English Verse Translation* (Chicago 1959), pp. 183-7

126 *The Satires of Persius*, trans. W.S. Merwin (Bloomington, Indiana, 1961),

pp. 79-81. The preceding 'Know thyself' goes back to Thales and Plato, and has been varied by Cicero and many modern writers from Chaucer on.

127 Quoted in Nicolas, *The Privy Purse*, p. 336

128 See note 124

129 I am indebted to Miss Bonnie J. Blackburn for the valuable reference to the *Commentarii di Lodovico Guicciardini Delle cose più memorabili seguite in Europa: specialmente in questi paesi bassi; dalla pace di Cambrai, del M.D.XXIX, insino à tutto l'Anno M.D.LX.* (Venice 1565), p. 20.

130 See Gustave van Hoorebeke, *Etudes sur l'origine des noms patronymiques flamands* (Brussels 1876), p. 259

131 See Henry Harrison, *Surnames of the United Kingdom: A Concise Etymological Dictionary* (2 vols, London 1918), II, p. 168.

132 *Sir Thomas Wyatt*, p. 41

133 *Ibid.*

134 For the complete poem, see *ibid.*, p. 42

The enlargement of
the great council of Venice

Frederic C. Lane

A crucial step in forming the basic governmental structure of the long-lived republic of Venice was the law of 1297 reforming the great council in a manner which is commonly called 'the Closing' (*la Serrata del Consiglio*) and is generally regarded as a triumph of an oligarchy over the people, of aristocratic over popular sovereignty. It will be here maintained, in contrast, that an aristocrary was in practical and unchallenged control in 1297, that there was in Venice at that time no class conflict between commoners and nobles, and that the so-called closing was in fact a widening of the ruling class in a fashion designed successfully to moderate the strife of factions. A restrictive policy was adopted a decade or two later, to be sure, but it was directed more against recent immigrants than against commoners. It found expression in considerable xenophobia and in heightened concern with determining who was really Venetian and who was not. It was part of the 'protectionist' movement which in 1302 repealed the liberal measures in commercial policy taken during the second Genoese war and which culminated in the institution, through the *Officiales de Navigantibus* in 1324, of restrictions on capital investment overseas. This tightening of restrictions, both politically and economically, came only after the membership of the great council had been widened by Doge Pietro Gradenigo.

I THE CHRONICLES

The interpretation of the reform of 1297 as a move to shut commoners out of the great council has no support in the oldest chronicles which report the admission of new families to the council at about that date. There are no Venetian chronicles written by contemporaries describing the life of the city between 1280 and 1320, nothing comparable to the accounts provided by Villani for Florence and Mussato for Padua. Andrea Dandolo, who about 1350 wrote the chronicle which was accepted by his countrymen as authoritative, terminated his full account, his *Chronica per extensum descripta*, in 1280. His *Chronica brevis* extended the story some decades, but the entries in the surviving copies are brief and of uncertain origin. Its only mention of a change in the great council refers not to closing but to the opposite. Referring to Doge Pietro Gradenigo, whom everyone regards as the leader in the reform, it says: 'This Doge with his Council ordered that some commoners be admitted to the Great Council.'[1] Almost as early, perhaps earlier, is the account in the Giustinian chronicle. It too describes not a closing but an opening and it associates this with the arrival of refugees from the Levant after the fall of Acre in 1291. It reads: 'In January 1303, at the time of this doge [Pietro Gradenigo], the Lord Doge and other nobles determined to make [members] of the Great Council of the Venetians many descendants of Syrians who had escaped from Acre and its neighbourhood and had come to Venice to live and also many Venetian commoners who had conducted themselves bravely in the above mentioned war with Genoa [that of 1294-8].'[2]

Neither the Dandolo nor the Giustinian chronicle report directly the law of 1297 which changed the procedure in choosing members of the great council; the passages quoted merely refer to the use made of the procedure by the doge and his council.[3] No reference by any chronicler to the change of procedure in choosing members of the great council can be surely dated before 1400, but the Trevisana chronicle contains two accounts, one of which may come from the Nicolò Trevisan who died in 1369 and wrote some sections.[4] Its description of the change in procedures emphasizes that the new law assured continued membership to those already members and made provision for choosing new members when the doge and his council wished. The narrative is interrupted to list two hundred and fifteen names of persons voted on as candidates and adds that there were many who came later and, by claiming descent from someone once a member, secured admission. Then, after recounting the war of Ferrara, it lists fifteen names of families which had been considered nobles at Constantinople and were made part of the great council in Venice and ten names of similar families from Acre.[5]

While a number of families which had ranked as commoners were being made members of the great council – thus in effect moving up into the ranks of the nobility, since membership soon became the criterion of nobility – other commoners failed to receive that kind of recognition and were disgruntled at being passed over. Right after their reports of additions to the great council, the chroniclers report that a commoner named Marin Bocco or Bocconus conspired to kill the doge and was hanged with fellow conspirators. None of the earliest chronicles attribute his action to political principles, but the Trevisana chronicle, after first reporting Boccono's conspiracy without reference to any motive, refers to it again when reviewing the background of the greater conspiracy in 1310 and then connects Boccono's conspiracy with the general discontent with Doge Gradenigo, saying that Boccono resented being excluded from the great council, resented the election of the doge by the nobles only, and felt Gradenigo to be unworthy.[6]

It is in connection with its description of the much more important conspiracy of Bajamonte Tiepolo in 1310 that the Trevisana chronicle gives what seems to be the earliest general view of the policy of Doge Gradenigo and of a political programme opposed to it. The policy of the doge is stated in the following somewhat ambiguous language:

> He wished to reform the Great Council, into which he wished to admit a larger number of families, so that they might be recognized as noble and equal to the others, and not that a few families [only] should be the chief and most revered of the city, taking away [at the same time, however] from the citizens and the common people the way that they used to have of being admitted to the Great Council. And the root of this innovation was the hate which he had towards the common people who before his election had acclaimed Doge Messer Jacomo Tiepolo ... and continued after his election to show their preference for the house of Tiepolo.[7]

This statement, written as early as two generations after the event, is the first to provide a basis for considering that the reform of 1297 was directed against 'the people' (*popolari*). It is noteworthy that it is equally explicit in saying that Doge Gradenigo desired to raise some of the commoners up to the same level as the already noble families.

Attribution to the conspirators of 1310 of an opposing policy appears in the speeches which the chronicler puts in their mouths. It is far from a clear programme, being interlarded with denunciation of the war then going on against the pope over Ferrara. Bajamonte Tiepolo is reported to have said that he and his associates were slighted whereas honours had been given to others who 'have nothing of manhood but the appearance nor of Venetian but the name.' That jibe may express hostility to Gradenigo's readiness to admit refugees from the east to the great council or it may refer to the election of the Dalmatian, Count Doimo of Veglia, to the ducal council. Tiepolo's Quirini allies had opposed this election as illegal, perhaps because they did not consider the count a real Venetian, but it had been put through by the dominant faction. The other leading conspirator, Marco Quirini, is reported to have said that Gradenigo was ruining the city in many ways, one of which was 'to close the *Maggior Consiglio* and prevent valiant and good commoners from arriving at the rights of the nobles of Venice,' which would, he said, lessen their devotion to the city and prevent immigration of foreigners, except those who came just to make money.[8]

Although the Trevisana chronicle thus provides some basis for considering the opponents of Gradenigo as champions of excluded commoners, it also contains a suggestion of opposition to nobles who were considered not really Venetian and indicates that the main causes of the conspiracy were personal animosities, the war of Ferrara, the papal interdict, and the accompanying defeats and property losses of the Venetians. To this chronicler, as to Piero Giustinian and the contemporary chroniclers of other Italian cities, it was primarily an uprising attempted by Venetian Guelfs.[9] Venetian historians have generally boasted that Venice never suffered from the rivalry of Guelf and Ghibelline and the accompanying feuds which weakened Genoa and most Italian cities. But the war of Ferrara, 1309-11, did produce temporarily just such a split among Venetian leading families. The Tiepolo, the Badoer, and a very important branch of the Querini had all voted against the decisions which had brought on the war with the pope over Venice's efforts to gain Ferrara and, when the papal nuncio threatened excommunication, Jacopo Querini had been the chief spokesman in the great council in favour of obeying the pope. At one point during the uprising adherents of Tiepolo went around demanding of all they met whether they were Guelf or Ghibelline and beating up those not willing to declare themselves Guelf. At least, that was the charge on which they were condemned.[10]

As in other cities, the 'Guelfs' of Venice had their personal grievances against those they called 'Ghibellines' and were moved more by these factional hates than by devotion to the papacy or any general principle. The grandfather and great-grandfather of Bajamonte Tiepolo had been doges and his father was the Jacopo Tiepolo who had been the popular candidate for the dogeship when the nobles had elected Pietro Gradenigo. The obvious reason for the nobles' opposition to Jacopo Tiepolo's election was that it might seem to give that family an hereditary claim to the office. Jacopo, a man of restrained ambition, withdrew from Venice to avoid a disturbance. His son Bajamonte was of a different temper, the kind of man who justified the fear of giving too much prestige to one family. When castellan at Modon he had entertained in princely fashion and claimed that that justified his illegal appropriation of funds there, an act for which he was condemned to a heavy fine.[11] According to the Trevisan chronicle, the affront to his honour figured largely in the grievances which he voiced in the discussions among the conspirators.[12]

Even more important in initiating the conspiracy was Marco Querini, a brother of the Jacopo Querini who had pleaded for obedience to the pope, and the father-in-law of Bajamonte Tiepolo. Marco Querini was bitter particularly because he was blamed, unjustly he felt, for a defeat when in command at Ferrara. He and his relatives, supported by the Badoer, had, in opposing the election of Count Doimo to the ducal council, quarreled violently with the Giustiniana (who were relatives of the count), and Michiel even coming to blows in the council chamber. These Querini were also at odds with the Morosini family, which was in high favour and allied by marriage to the king of Hungary. A Morosini who was serving as a *signore di notte* tried, at the Rialto, to search a Querini to see if he was violating the law against concealed weapons, and was tripped up and humiliated. Others of the same branch of the Querini, known as those of the Big House ('Cà Mazor'), had a quarrel with a Dandolo who, when serving as state's attorney, had been zealous in prosecuting one of them on the charge of committing an outrage against a Jew in Negroponte.[13]

The third leader among the conspirators, Badoero Badoer, had large estates in Paduan territory and could almost be considered one of the Paduan Guelfs.[14]

The more careful later chroniclers of Venice followed the Trevisan account of the reasons for the Tiepolo conspiracy almost word for word even as late as the sixteenth century.[15] On the other hand, the Trevisana's report of Gradenigo's resentment against 'the people' for the popular acclaim given Jacopo Tiepolo, and its reference to Querini's criticism of the doge's reform of the great council, seem to have been taken up and elaborated by some later writers, but they may have had independent sources for a tradition of popular opposition to Gradenigo.[16] When in the fifteenth century a humanist, Marcantonio Sabellico, undertook to write a history of Venice he put into Venetian history echoes of the history of republican Rome and interpreted the dogeship of Piero Gradenigo in terms of a conflict between patricians and plebeians.[17]

In so doing the humanist was adopting the attitude which the Venetian nobility itself was adopting in the fifteenth century. By that time membership in the great council and nobility were identical. After the first decades of the fourteenth century practically no new families were added except for the admission in 1382, by extraordinary action, of thirty families in recognition of their services during the war of Chioggia.[18] Further additions were refused. A proposal was made, to be sure, in 1403 by two of the *capi* of the *Quarantia*, Pietro Arimondo and Pietro Miani, to add to the great council a worthy family of native-born commoners whenever one of the noble families died out. The proposal was killed by the ducal council.[19] The rejection of this reform proposal of 1403 symbolizes a definitive change in the nature of the Venetian aristocracy. Earlier it had been a body which had readily absorbed new families; thereafter for more than two hundred years it was a closed caste fearful lest the admission of new men destroy its solidarity. During the fifteenth and sixteenth centuries the Venetian nobility showed unwillingness to share with new families the honour and power of their status, and they read this sentiment back into the events of 1280 to 1320.

II OTHER CONSIDERATIONS

The traditions recorded in the chronicles convincingly portray a split within the nobility at the beginning of the fourteenth century. On the one side, dominating the councils, were the Gradenigo, the Dandolo, the Morosini, the Giustiniani, and the Michiel; on the other the Tiepolo, the Querini di Cà Mazor, the Barozzi, and the Badoer.[20] If the conspirators had succeeded in seizing the piazza and the palace many more might have come forward to join them, for many stayed home while the issue was in doubt and the streets dangerous.[21]

The common people also were divided. Not only do the chroniclers say so explicitly but such is the necessary inference from the events they record. Bajamonte Tiepolo had behind him the great popularity of his grandfather, Lorenzo Tiepolo, an admiral and war hero, who had married a daughter of Boemondo di Brienne, king of Serbia and Rascia.[22] In spite of his chivalric tastes he was on good relations with the Venetian guilds. Some historians have assumed that Bajamonte Tiepolo and the Querini di Cà Mazor also catered to the guilds and had guild support in their conspiracy.[23] But there is no evidence to that effect. Murano, the glass-making centre, is said to have been on the side of Tiepolo in 1310[24] while Chioggia and Torcello, shipping and fishing centres, supported the doge, but the only way in which any guild figures in the early accounts of the uprising is in the report of vigorous fighting by the painters' guild on the side of Gradenigo.[25]

In the 1260s and 1270s guilds had presented a political problem. They represented craftsmen and local shopkeepers; there was at Venice no guild of merchants engaged in foreign trade, nothing comparable to the Calimala of Florence, for wholesale traders were in such firm control of the Venetian government that they had no need of a separate organization. Also there was no guild of judges and notaries, so important at Padua. The seamen, the largest occupational group, also had no guild of their own, not at least until very much later, although in 1255 they were regulated by a new maritime code which required them to take an oath to report to the authorities any violations of the maritime statutes.[26] But among the shipyard workers and in some other building trades there were guilds which had many of the functions of trade unions, and even more powerful were the guilds which functioned like trade associations of manufacturers. Among the earliest and most important of these latter were the goldsmiths or jewellers, the iron smiths, the tailors, the apothecaries, the hemp spinners, and the dyers.[27] Compared to the merchant aristocracy, they represented a new and different kind of well-to-do businessmen.

When the guilds first developed out of religious fraternities, the ruling class placed no obstacle in the way of their formation but subjected them to regulation by officials called the *giustizieri* who had been created to have charge of weights, measures, and market regulation generally. They forbad the tailors in 1219 and the jewellers in 1233 to form price-fixing cartels.[28] In 1264-5 more sweeping prohibitions show that subversive activities in the guilds were feared in that decade.[29] It was a time of political danger. The first Genoese war was inflicting commercial losses even though Venice was winning the big battles. There are reports of a tax riot in 1265 of such violence that the doge, Renier Zeno, pretended to give in to the rioters, although he later hunted out and hanged the leaders, including one named Niccolo Bocco. At about the same time the antagonism between Dandolos and Tiepolos became so violent that Lorenzo Tiepolo was injured in the piazza by Giovanni Dandolo or one of his partisans. Commoners showed a tendency to line up either with the Dandolo or with the Tiepolo by displaying the arms of the faction which they favoured. To prevent such generalizing of factional alignment a law was passed forbidding commoners to display the arms of any noble house.[30] There is no direct evidence that guilds were actively involved in this family fight but the law forbidding them to form any covenants against the honour of the doge and commune showed that the rulers feared lest they become involved.

The danger was dissipated mainly through the leadership of Lorenzo Tiepolo. His dogeship, 1268-75, was a period of reconciliation. He was persuaded to patch up his quarrel with Giovanni Dandolo.[31] To the guilds Lorenzo made it clear that the laws passed during the latter years of his

predecessor would not be used to destroy their organizations. His acceptance of the festival reception given him and the dogeressa by the guilds
symbolized recognition of the guilds as an integral and honoured part of
Venetian society, but lacking in political power.[32]

This position of the guilds was crystallized by the official revision of
guild statutes which was effected under Doge Lorenzo Tiepolo. Between
October and December 1271, at least eleven more guild statutes were
added to the twelve which had been approved earlier. These statutes all
included the anti-sedition law of 1265, but they left the guilds considerable self-government: the choice of their own *gastaldi*, two meetings a
year at which they could suggest changes in their statutes for approval
by the *giustizieri*, settlement by their own officials of disputes and violations involving minor sums, and freedom in making their own arrangements about the fraternal and devotional activity of their *scuole*.[33] Some
guilds, like the masons, were even permitted to strike or boycott an em-
ployer who failed to pay masters their due.[34] This combination of subor-
dination and limited self-government was to continue to be their status for
the next five hundred years.

If any guildsmen were dissatisfied with this subordinate status it was
probably the rich members of those guilds which were trade associations
of employers. It has been noted that, at Padua, where the guilds were
represented in the governing councils from the 1280s on, the shopkeepers
and craftsmen of the *popolo minuto* did not rise through their guilds to
be leaders of the republic; they were content to leave political leadership
to other sections of the Paduan population, primarily to the lawyers.[35]
And at Florence, where guilds became the all-important political con-
stituencies, the small tradesmen and craftsmen did not compete for leadership with the old ruling class; the threats in the early fourteenth century
came from its own divisions or from the ambitions of newly rich merchants of large affairs.[36] It is likely that any challenge from guildsmen to
the Venetian ruling class came also from some of those who may be
characterized as the new rich.

In the last years of Lorenzo's dogeship a plot against the government
is reported as well as a new law against conspiracies, but there is no reason to connect this with the guilds.[37] Indeed it seems more likely that
Tiepolo felt he could rely on the guilds and thought of summoning them
to arms if necessary. But such an action would have given them political
importance and it is significant that, in the revision of the ducal oath at
his death (it was revised afresh for each new doge), the doge was forbid-

den to summon to arms the guilds or their *gastaldi* without the express approval of the ducal council.[38]

The next doge, Jacopo Contarini, continued Lorenzi Tiepolo's policy of reconciliation. The guilds were neither abolished nor further restricted; on the contrary, their statutes were reaffirmed in 1278 by the *giustizieri* who collected them all into one register or codex.[39] The doge issued pardons to persons who had been exiled or had fled in fear after the tax riot of 1265 and persuaded many to return, in spite of the fact that another conspiracy had been discovered at the beginning of his term.[40] That plot of 1275 is the last conspiracy reported until the effort in 1299 or 1300 of the disgruntled commoner Marino Bocco or Boccono, apparently of the same family as the leader condemned for the tax riot of 1265.[41] But there is no evidence connecting either affair with the guilds, and it seems a far-fetched supposition, in view of the way in which the status of the guilds had been clarified in the meantime, to assign to 1299 or 1300 the kind of situation implied by the anti-subversion law of 1265. The guilds as a whole seem to have been passive, while some of their members were probably on Gradenigo's side, some on the other.

Among the commoners who supported Doge Gradenigo were, naturally enough, those who under his programme had received permanent membership in the great council and who had thus been raised into the nobility, since the old line between commoners and nobles disappeared during the next generation and a new line took its place dividing those not members of the great council from those who were and were therefore considered nobles. After the suppression of the Tiepolo conspiracy some additional families of commoners were admitted to the council in reward for their support during the crisis.[42] The size of the great council increased from less than 400 prior to 1297 to more than 1,100 by 1320.[43]

To many Italian cities of the fourteenth century the rise of *il popolo* meant primarily the admission to the ruling class, not of humble craftsmen and shopkeepers, but of newly rich merchants. In Venice that process had been going on for a long time without producing civil war.[44] The old rich were sufficiently willing to extend political participation to the newly rich that the latter did not have to ally with craftsmen guilds in order to fight their way to a share of public office. The enlargement of the great council under doge Gradenigo merely continued the penetration of the new men into the ranks of the ruling class.

Perhaps the most convincing evidence of the lack of any class feeling pitting commoners and nobles against each other as self-conscious classes appears in the distribution of commands in the war with Genoa which was in progress from 1294-9. Whereas the fleet which suffered a crushing defeat at Curzola in 1298 was commanded by a representative of what is considered the conservative wing of the nobility, a son of the late doge, Giovanni Dandolo, the naval hero of the war from Venice's point of view had the suggestively humble name of Domenigo Schiavo.[45] In 1262, many years earlier, the Venetians when outfitting a fleet had begun to place a noble called the *sopracomito* in command of each galley above the *comito*, formerly the top post and one that continued to be filled by a commoner.[46] But in 1299, after the great defeat at the hand of the Genoese, the *sopracomiti* appointed on the galleys that Venice then armed to show the flag of San Marco in daring raids were commoners.[47] Such a reliance on commoners in posts of crucial military importance argues against class antagonism at that level.

Another sign of the lack of antagonism between commoners as such and nobles as such is the role given to both by the leading chroniclers. Martino da Canale, writing in the middle of the thirteenth century, constantly praised the knightly qualities of the Venetian nobles but sings the praise also of the people. Andrea Dandolo in the mid-fourteenth century emphasized the role which the commoners as well as the nobles had had in crucial moments of early Venetian history, such as in the choice of the first doge. All Venice's traditions placed the fount of authority with the people, meaning the whole community, but Dandolo went even beyond his sources in specifying the participation of the commoners (*plebei*).[48] If he had exaggerated the role of the people in the events of his own time, one might discount it by arguing that he and fellow nobles wished to keep them unaware of how completely real power had passed into the hands of an hereditary aristocracy. But he had no such motive for emphasizing the role of the common people at the turning points of Venetian history centuries earlier.

Of course there were conflicts between various interest groups in Venice, some arising from individual ambitions and hatreds and some from conflicting economic interests. Economic difficulties resulting from what might be called class struggle are evident in the first decade of the fourteenth century, particularly in the fleets. Seamen were losing status as fighting men and were being subjected to harsher discipline. Many of them were being imprisoned for debt and then let out of jail in order to work off their debts on the galleys. A sharper line was developing between shipowners on the one hand and sailors and oarsmen on the other. Travelling merchants, who had been a numerous part of a ship's company and had shared authority with the captain, became less important with the use of commercial techniques favourable to resident merchants. All these developments created a widening gap between the mass of seafarers and the well-to-do merchant shipowners.[49] But there had never been any question of admitting ordinary seamen to the great council. That certainly was not the issue in 1297 or 1310. There was a social change going on which accentuated differences between a lower and an upper class in the navy and merchant marine, but its upper class contained both nobles and commoners. The reform of 1297 concerned the distribution of power and functions within this upper class.

Commoners and nobles were not two classes economically distinct.[50] It is an anachronism to consider a rivalry between nobles and commoners the key to the political development of that period and even more of an anachronism to assign to the one party an aristocratic ideology and to the other a more democratic ideology.[51] The political ideals which affected action, so far as any did, were the beliefs current generally in Venice: that those in power held their power as representatives of the community, that tyranny was the pressing and dangerous evil to be avoided, and that the seed-bed of tyranny was the conflicts of factions. Quite secondary was the form of government, whether a rule by one man, or by a few, or by the many; although it may be significant that the only Venetian to write a treatise on government in that period, Fra Paolino, simplified Aristotle's description of the six forms of government by saying that the three perverted forms were government by a tyrant, by the rich, and by the poor, and that the three good forms were rule by one man alone, by a few men of virtue, and by the many who were rich.[52] The essentials were peace and the rule of law. On that the influential political thinkers of the time, such as Thomas Aquinas, Dante Alighieri, Tolomeo of Lucca, and Marsiglio of Padua all agreed. They put less stress on class struggles than had Aristotle, from whom they took so much, and they pointed to factionalism as the danger that was destroying peace and creating tyranny in one Italian city after another.[53] The Venetian concern with the evils of factionalism are evident in a resolution voted to be read before each balloting in the great council. It bound every member when voting on nominations to vote for the best man and not aid their friends and injure their enemies.[54] The system perfected in 1268 of electing the doge through a long series of committees chosen partially by lot was specifically designed to confuse and moderate factional rivalries.[55] There are no grounds for believing that Pietro Gradenigo and his colleagues were ideologues whose actions were guided by political doctrines, but in so far as they combined their self-interest with general political thinking, their frame of reference was probably not the superiority of the will of an aristocracy over the will of the people but the importance and the difficulties of preserving the peace of the city (as well as their own power) through moderating and controlling factionalism.

This view of the state of affairs is quite compatible as far as it goes with Roberto Cessi's interpretation of the so-called *serrata* as a mere technical administrative reform. After a lifetime of unrivalled familiarity with Venetian records, Cessi expounded the view that the aristocracy was firmly in the saddle long before 1280 and its position was not seriously threatened at the end of the century by any popular movement.[56] The problem in the 1280s and 1290s was merely that of finding for the great council a membership adapted to its functions. It had become in effect the supreme legislative body. Also it elected a growing number of officials and elected the members of the councils which had taken over the deliberative functions it had formerly exercised. Three other such councils were of prime importance: the ducal council of six plus the doge; the Forty – the *Quarantia*; and the sixty who composed the nucleus of what was to be called the senate (then called the *Consilium rogatorum* or *Consiglio dei pregadi*). All three met and voted with the great council in approving new legislation. Also there were at least a hundred other officials, the state attorneys (*Avvogadori di comun*), the treasurers (*Camerlinghi*), etc., who were chosen by and met with the great council. The election of one hundred members in addition to all these *ex officio* members required in the 1270s a total of over four hundred selections. Then the number fell until in 1295 it was only 257, for by that time, as Cessi explains it, the new offices and councils were stabilized. He attributes the earlier large number of elections to the great council to the fact that many of those originally named to the great council were elected to other posts so as to become *ex officio* members. When that happened, other men were nominated to take their places as ordinary members. After the number of new offices and councils was stabilized, there was less need for new elections. There then developed a conflict between elective and hereditary principles. On the one hand tradition required that the membership in a council which had such wide general authority as the great council should be elective. That way it better represented the whole community, as it should according to the ascending theory on which the Venetians based their sense of legitimacy. On the other hand, tradition also required that certain families be represented and that men who had held high office be included.

To evaluate the technical or administrative problem and its possible implications it is necessary to inquire how the members of the great council were chosen before 1297 and how many of them there were. The procedure in choosing members seems surprisingly casual and uncertain in view of its importance. According to the general Venetian practice, what we loosely call election consisted of two parts: a first part that we would call nomination (although they called it *electio*) and a second part consisting of the approval or testing of the nomination (*approbatio*). In the early days, nominations were made by the ducal council, later generally by committees chosen by lot, and the nominating committees were ordered to conclude their nominations the same day they were named, before leaving the palace.[57] Obviously they were not supposed to consult friends but to use their individual judgment. Each member of a nominating committee was recorded as the proposer or guarantor of those whom he had suggested and who had been accepted by his colleagues.[58] For such positions as the very powerful ducal councillors, there were at least two nominating committees; they each submitted a name or list of names to the great council, and its vote approving one list or name constituted the real election.[59] However, in the thirteenth century there was only one slate nominated for the great council, and this list of a hundred men (or in some years one hundred and fifty), and subsequent lists of needed replacements, if voted on at all in the great council, seems to have been voted on as a whole. Practically speaking, the nominating committee did the electing, as is often true in a club or any society with by-laws that provide for a nominating committee and for no other way to make nominations.

The committees which made nominations for the great council were *ad hoc* committees. One, composed of men called electors for the year, was chosen in September to name one hundred regular members to serve for the ensuing twelve months. After the newly chosen great council met, new nominating committees were formed to serve for a half-year and to make additional nominations when the doge and his council said they were needed. Cessi implies that additional nominations were made only to the extent that the men named in the original one hundred were subsequently chosen for one of the positions which made them *ex officio* members.[60] If that was the case, then there was a positive correlation between the number nominated and the number serving, although the totals would not be the same since many *ex officio* members would be named to the other offices directly and not appear on the lists of nominees for the great council.[61] But there were probably other reasons also for new nominations. One was to replace men who had died or were hopelessly ill. Another may have been to replace those who resigned or refused to serve.[62] Being a member of the council may have seemed a burden to some men for they were then subject to fines for failure to attend certain sessions.[63] As a general principle, no Venetian citizen was free to indulge his taste for idleness; all were obliged to serve in any office to which they were named, or lose political rights and pay heavy fines, *unless* excused by the doge and his council. A man who had undertaken obligations with a view to a trading voyage would be excused.[64] Many of the original hundred nominated by the electors may have been thus excused so that there was a large need for substitutes, especially in periods when trade was booming. In that case the number nominated would not indicate the number serving and tells little about the size of the council. Indeed, surviving records of the number voting on important occasions and the number nominated shows little correlation between the two figures. A well-attended meeting of the great council before 1297 consisted of about three hundred: the one hundred regular members; the forty of the *Quarantia*, and the sixty of the senate; and about one hundred who had rights of attendance because of their office and were also in Venice and free to attend.[65]

The committees making nominations for the great council were small. The electors of the year consisted of at most twelve, more often three or four. To give to just three or four men the power to choose the membership of the supreme council would have been very unsettling if their power had really been arbitrary, that is, if they had not been limited in their choices – as were the censors of ancient Rome in the naming of senators – by some well-established customs. The electors were chosen from different *sestieri*, to be sure, and named men from their *sestieri*, but in addition there must have been an understanding concerning some leading families that had to be represented. On the other hand, there must have been an area of doubt also. Commoners as well as nobles were included in the great council; there was as yet no legal distinction between the political rights of the men called nobles and those called commoners.[66] The return of partially Venetian families from Romania and the crusaders' states in the late thirteenth century increased the uncertainties.

The declining number of selections about 1290 must have intensified concern about whom the electors of the year would include and whom they would leave out.

The uncertainty of the situation was all the greater because of the manner in which the electors of the year were chosen. As in the choice of other nominating committees, an element of chance was involved. The doge and his council named the electors, but in accordance with a system which rotated the function among experienced council members, giving a turn to men from each of thirty-odd election districts, the *trentacie*.[67] The 'electors' thus named had to be approved by a vote of the great council.[68] In 1293 only three of the four named were approved but they were authorized to go ahead and make the nominations, which, as has been explained, amounted to election.[69] Whether this somewhat haphazard system should be continued was a constantly open question, for the council ordinarily voted every September a new resolution to determine how the membership for the ensuing year would be chosen: whether by the traditional method just described, or with a different number of electors, or with electors differently chosen, or with the nominees of the electors subject to approval one by one by another council such as the *Quarantia*.[70] These uncertainties invited a reform that would stabilize the way of choosing the great council.

There can be no doubt that, as Cessi emphasized, there was a need to give the great council a membership appropriate to its functions. The existing uncertainty was also a good reason for reforming the rules determining its membership. But the way the problem was solved was sure to affect the interests and ambitions of all the groups competing for power and wealth within the society. The number of resolutions defeated and the provisional character of the first steps approved, not to mention the subsequent conspiracies, suggest that behind the provisions concerning procedure and machinery there were bitter conflicts for power.

Giorgio Cracco has recently made a new analysis of the economic interests of various groups associated with different aspects of Venetian policy. His delineation of the various interest groups is far superior to the old-fashioned simple contrast between 'nobles' and 'the people.' He makes clear that the line between nobles and commoners was not clearcut, and not the same as that between rich and poor, nor that between old Venetian families and new families. He does not hesitate to speak of 'popoli nobili.'[71] But he depicts a vigorous class struggle against what he

calls the *grandi* or *magnati*. They were Gradenigo's party and consisted
of the families which had been rich and powerful in 1172 and had maintained their wealth and power ever since. Cracco believes that their leadership or control was threatened at the end of the thirteenth century
because trade was becoming less profitable. The *grandi* could ride out the
depressions but the middle class of traders could not, and they sought
compensation by striving all the harder for political power which would
enable them to enjoy the perquisites of office holding. Gradenigo's party
triumphed over its opponents, Cracco says, and assured its own continued dominance by buying off a section of the middle class, the *borghesia*
of old Venetian families. It did so in 1297 by giving them membership in
the great council and thus access to political offices from which those not
in the great council were excluded.[72]

It would be hard to document Cracco's analysis of the economic situation, but there is at least evidence that office holding was becoming more
popular and this may well have been one of the considerations which
made reform of the great council urgent. This pressure, which Cracco
chooses to call class struggle, seems to me only one of several factors
involved.

III THE COURSE OF EVENTS

Among these factors, the following fears operating within the ruling
class seem to me important in determining the course of events: (1) the
fear of being excluded from political positions by a hostile faction; (2)
the fear that factional fighting would weaken the republic and lead to
tyranny; (3) the fear of foreigners as competitors for honours, jobs, and
trade.

At the beginning of the efforts to reform the great council the fear of
being excluded was most important. Four unsuccessful proposals for
changing the rules concerning its membership were made, three in 1286
and one in 1296. Why were they defeated? None of them so far as we
know made any provision for enlarging the size of the great council. All
of them would have made the choices of the electors of the year subject
one by one to a subsequent vote, either by the ducal council or the *Quarantia*, or the great council itself, or some combination of these councils,
except that one proposal, that of 5 October 1286, would have excepted
from the need of such approval those nominated who had a paternal ancestor who had been a member of some Venetian council. The fate of this

resolution of 5 October 1286 is the only one fully recorded. It was opposed by the doge, Giovanni Dandolo, and was defeated by a relatively small vote: eighty-two noes, forty-eight in favour, and ten neutral, only one hundred and forty altogether.[73] This vote is generally considered a rejection of an open avowal of the principle of heredity, although that principle was already largely followed in practice and the proposed law provided for exceptions. But why were other proposals which made no mention of ancestry also defeated or abandoned? The answer lies, I believe, in the fact that none gave any assurance, even to members of old and noble Venetian families, that they would be included in the great council in the future. What they all had in common was this: While leaving limited the number to be chosen by the electors of the year, these proposals made the nominations more subject than before to subsequent rejection by some council.[74] A faction controlling the council in question could have rejected members of hostile factions. The defeated reforms would have lessened the elements of chance and rotation which entered in the existing method of selection through the way the electors of the year were chosen, and in doing so would have made it easier for a party or faction to monopolize power and offices.

Although there were some commoners and some new men among the members of the great council when those votes were taken, they were a distinct minority. Most of the votes which defeated proposals for reform in those years must have been cast by nobles and members of old families. It is easy to imagine why they should have voted against reducing the element of chance in the selection of the membership and against increasing the possibility that a faction in control could exclude opposing factions from the great council and thus from any effective participation in political life. Nobles would be even more sensitive to fear of exclusion than commoners since they had more to lose, in honour and pride, even if not in wealth, if excluded. They could see in many other Italian cities, most notably in Genoa and Florence, seizures of power by one faction after another, each using its period of power to try to exclude permanently its opponents. It is true that at Venice the nobles, atlhough they had indulged in violent family quarrels in earlier centuries, had since 1172 shown remarkable restraint in their rivalries and a willingness to subordinate family pride and ambition to communal patriotism in a way which aroused the envious admiration of contemporaries. But there were signs that the hundred years of restraint were coming to an end, as indeed was shortly to be proved true by the conspiracy of Bajamonte Tiepolo and Marco

Querini. Not only the rivalry of Dandolo and Tiepolo factions but also
the events which Venetian nobles could see elsewhere in Italy at the end
of the thirteenth century make it reasonable to suppose that many feared
exclusion from all honours and offices by some ambitious clique which,
having gained control, would resolve to complete and perpetuate its
power.

If they had such fears, they were allayed by the reform which was
passed in February 1297. That law assured that everyone who had been a
member during the last four years could apply for membership on 29
September next and if he could then obtain as many as twelve favourable
votes out of the forty of the *Quarantia* he would be a member of the great
council. This opened the way to an indefinite increase in the size of the
council. The law said nothing whatever about ancestry, but once the principle of perpetual membership was established it might have been expected to be extended from father to son.

The law of February 1297 also provided for the election to the council
for the next year of men not members during the previous four years.
They were to be chosen by three electors when the latter were called on to
do so by the doge and his council, and would then be voted on one by one
in the *Quarantia* and considered approved if they received twelve votes.
Final clauses made it very difficult legally to change the operation of the
law in any way before September 1298, and required that it be reconsidered at the beginning of that year.[75]

Just what happened during these next two years, or between February
1297 and 1300, is difficult to determine in detail. The documentary records,
the surviving minutes of the great council for those years, are fragmentary
and confusing and may have been so even at the time.[76] Venice was in the
middle of the second Genoese war, which was approaching its disastrous
climax. Large fleets were being outfitted every year from 1296 to 1299.
When the membership of the council was renewed in September 1297
many people who counted, or thought they ought to, may have been away
with the fleets. In 1298, on 6 or 8 September, came the stunning defeat at
Curzola in which Venetian dead were numbered at seven thousand and
the prisoners were said to be even more numerous.[77] Since there is no hint
of any rebellion in those years, one may assume that Doge Gradenigo's
leadership was being accepted and that defeat caused the Venetians to
subordinate factional ambitions in order to preserve their commune and
its power against the threat of utter defeat by the Genoese rival. Under
these circumstances the sequence of events described in the Trevisan
chronicle seems likely. It says that when the new system introduced by

the law of February 1297 went into effect in September of that year, many applied and the proceedings became disorderly and full of controversy. As a result the doge decided to waive the annual balloting on those already members and make membership in the great council legally and formally permanent, so that on 11 September 1298 (which would have been during the week after the disastrous defeat) the great council voted that thereafter all who were members should continue to be members for life without any further voting.[78] This making permanent of membership in 1298 is what is called the 'Serar' or 'Serata' by Trevisan and later chroniclers who repeated his account.[79] Rather than translate it as the 'Closing' which implies exclusion or locking out, it would be better to translate it as the 'Locking in' of the great council, reassuring, in a moment of national emergency, all members already in the ruling class that they would not be left out in the future.

No law of exactly that kind is to be found in the surviving minutes of the great council. Indeed, all the records of decisions taken in September 1298 and September 1299 concerning the great council are in other than regular form.[80] These irregular entries say only that the law of February 1297 should be renewed.[81] Nowhere is there a law stating that members of the great council should continue to be members as long as they lived.[82] Yet it seems clear that that was what was decided in September 1298, just as the Trevisana chronicle reported. Technically, legally, their names had to be submitted each year to the *Quarantia* but, from 1298 on, the re-election of all those already members was a mere formality; the real action was on the addition of new names, either of young nobles who had reached the appropriate age or of men whose fathers were not or had not been in the council. It may seem surprising that the most basic right of the Venetian nobles was not spelled out in law, but there have been other instances when what was recorded in the minutes and what was settled in people's minds were different. Although as a legal technicality, yearly approval by the *Quarantia* was needed, after 1298 it was understood by those who formed the *Quarantia* and by all others concerned that membership in the great council was for life and was hereditary, and they voted accordingly.[83]

A general understanding concerning the election to the great council of persons not already members was not reached so quickly. The only distinction made in the law of 1297 between old members and new members was that the names of the former came before the *Quarantia* automatically, whereas the names of new men had to be proposed by three electors who were called on by the doge and his council to nominate new members. Under the law of 1297 both old and new men required only twelve votes from the *Quarantia*, but in September 1299 it was required that all those nominated by the electors for the great council or the senate must be voted on one by one in the *Quarantia* and receive a majority in their favour.[84] The next year, 1300, the doge and council were forbidden to propose new names to the electors without the approval of the *Quarantia*.[85]

Such laws, placing the approval of new members more and more firmly in the hands of the *Quarantia*, provided the means of excluding new members who did not belong to old families. There was no mention of ancestry in the laws of 1297-1300 concerning the great council. Indeed, after the resounding defeat in 1286 of the proposal for a distinction on the basis of ancestry, ancestry was not specifically mentioned again in rules regarding membership in the great council until 1323.[86] But the Trevisana chronicle says that the vote on 11 September 1298 meant that 'all those *families* [italics mine] who were already admitted to the great council should continue to be so without having to be voted on each year.'[87] Certainly that was the effect and it may have been the effect intended. Control over the *Quarantia* was assured to the old families by a vote, in December 1298, that no one could be elected to the *Quarantia* unless he or his ancestors had been members of the great council.[88] Thus the hereditary principle, which was to become basic for the great council, but which was not yet openly avowed, was applied to the composition of the *Quarantia* at the same time as the *Quarantia* was being placed in a position to apply it in approving nominations for other councils.

In the war years, however, and in the first years after the war, the expansive and liberal aspects of the reform of 1297 prevailed. The early chronicles all agree that in those years Doge Gradenigo was the leader in a substantial enlargement of the Venetian ruling class, both through the acceptance of refugees from the Levant and by the addition of commoners to the great council. We have seen that the texts of the laws do not exclude that possibility, and that something of that kind was going on is implied by the law of 1300 cited above, which limited the initiative of the doge and his council regarding additions.

Doge Gradenigo's leadership in this enlargement of the great council is easily reconciled with the hatred he is said to have had for the common people who had shouted for Jacopo Tiepolo as doge at the time of his own election. Strengthening of the great council by enlarging it may well have seemed to him the best way to diminish the influence on the government of the city mob and of the general assembly of all citizens, called the *arengo* or *concio*, which he may have considered little better than a street mob. Indeed, the *parlementum*, a general assembly in the main square, or possibly the main church, was traditionally considered in the Italian communes to be an expression of the sovereign people. In Venice, also, since the Venetians firmly held that the powers of the doge and all the councils derived from the community as a whole, a popular assembly in boats or in the piazza of San Marco had been treated as the ultimate authority. Although, since 1172 it had been regulated and managed by committees headed by the ducal council, the *arengo* was called to give approval to basic laws and to the choice of doge made by the authoritative nominating committee.[89] The way in which the general assembly in other cities was packed or purged by the violence of factions, gave Doge Gradenigo good grounds for fearing that the same might happen at Venice – and to his disadvantage, considering the popularity of the Tiepolos.[90]

He did in fact succeed in strengthening the great council and in preventing factional fighting at Venice from becoming as severe as it might have been. Permanent membership in a council of unlimited size assured the existing leading families that they would not be excluded from the pleasures and perquisites of political office. Enough new families, or families on the edge of belonging to the old upper class, were added so that family rivalries were moderated by the sheer number of the families involved.[91] The reforms obviously did not stop all such rivalries. At Venice as elsewhere it was a severe crisis in its external affairs, the war with the pope over Ferrara, which led one faction to attempt to seize power by open violence. But only a relatively small number of families were implicated in the conspiracy of 1310 and a relatively small number sent into exile. How they were prevented from forming any such government-in-exile or group of *fuorusciti*, as did the parties driven out of Genoa or Florence, is another story. Another story also is the gradual process by which the Venetian popular assembly (the *arengo*) faded into significance long before it was finally abolished altogether in 1423. There were no struggles, no recorded protests, over its passing. The great council had already for years taken over its function as the ultimate representative of the sovereign community.

Long before that stage in Venice's constitutional development the restrictive aspect of the reform of 1297 had become dominant. Prior to the reform of 1297, many persons not members of the great council were elected to various offices and, after being thus known and honoured, were

named by the electors to be regular members of the great council. Gradually it was required of one office after another that its holder be a member
of the great council. It was made obligatory for senators in 1311.[92] Meanwhile, the naming of new men by the electors lapsed, with the result that,
after the admission of the commoners who were rewarded for their support during the conspiracy of 1310, practically no new families were admitted until the war of Chioggia about seventy years later. Election by
the great council, through the process called *grazia*, was made extremely
difficult, requiring in 1328 approval by five out of six ducal councillors,
thirty of the *Quarantia*, including their three *Capi*, and two-thirds of the
great council itself.[93] The importance of ancestry was implicitly recognized in the provisions of 1315 for registering births, nominally in order
to prove the age of the applicant and his legitimate birth,[94] and was explicitly recognized in the resolution of 1323 declaring that a father's or
forefather's membership in the great council was the essential for admission.[95] All those who could prove such parentage by proper registration at
birth in what came to be called the 'Golden Book' could become members of the council automatically at twenty-five, without needing any vote
of approval. Thirty were chosen by lot and admitted at twenty. All of the
twenty-year-olds were formally certified as members of the nobility by
being accepted at the drawing of lots, having proved their parentage.[96]

A more restrictive commercial policy went hand in hand with the
tightening of the restrictions of membership in the great council. Restrictions on the trade of foreigners at Venice had been repealed during the
second Genoese war. From 1302, when trade was picking up again after
the war and there was less need of foreigners and foreign capital to keep
the wares moving, restrictions were restored.[97] At the same time officials
called the *Provveditori di Comun*, who had been created at the end of the
war to increase revenue and who were elected by the *Quarantia*, were
especially charged with preventing any defrauding of the customs.[98] That
gave them occasion to inquire as to who was a Venetian and who was
really a foreigner. In enforcing the collection of tolls levied on foreigners
they questioned the Venetian citizenship of some long-time residents of
Venice, seizing the wares of one man who had been paying taxes at Venice
for thirty-four years.[99] The proceedings of the *Provveditori di Comun*
made proof of ancestry very important in one connection, while the
policy of the *Quarantia* regarding membership in the great council was
heightening its importance in another connection.

Stricter enforcement led to modification of the previous rules concerning naturalization.[100] In 1305 naturalization was permitted of those who had lived in Venice or Venetian dominions and paid taxes to Venice for twenty-five years. If they had been there for ten years, they were to be permitted to stay and could acquire full citizenship rights fifteen years later. Meanwhile they could practise the craft or local trade by which they lived.[101] Guided by these rules, the *Provveditori* busied themselves over the next decade in determining who should have the right to trade as Venetian and who should not.[102]

While 'foreign' was thus being carefully defined, hostility to the competition of foreign merchants and capital was expressed in laws forbidding Venetians to conclude partnerships with foreigners or to act as 'fronts' handling their wares for them.[103] Imports to Venice by foreigners from many regions were almost entirely forbidden, especially from the eastern Mediterranean.[104] The climax of what has been called the protectionist movement was reached in 1324 with the creation of the *Officiales de Navigantibus*. These officials were charged with punishing by confiscation of merchandise any Venetian who imported from the Levant wares of a total value higher than the amount of his own wealth as assessed at the office through which the republic levied the forced loans used for emergency finance.[105] This was a way of preventing Venetians of limited funds from acting as stand-ins for foreigners or from borrowing foreign capital. This purpose was plainly referred to in connection with its enforcement.[106]

To be sure, the *Officiales de Navigantibus* were in existence only a few years. There were waves of reaction to the policy of commercial restriction and the tight financial policy which accompanied it. A striking evidence of the xenophobic, inquisitorial interest in ancestry and of a reaction against that spirit is the *relazione* of Marco Minotto, *bailo* in Constantinople about 1320, and himself unquestionably a member of a distinguished noble family. He begins by remarking that some of those in positions of authority go to extremes in demanding proof of Venetian citizenship of all who present themselves as Venetian, inquiring not only about their fathers but their grandfathers and great-grandfathers until, says Minotto, they make him wonder whether he himself could meet the formal tests of proving himself Venetian; 'although not everyone knows whose son I am and who my father was ... yet I have always passed as Venetian wherever I went.' He contrasts the policy of the Genoese, who, he says, 'accept all readily regardless of who their father was, even those who were Venetian in person and in possessions.' Therefore, he says, 'in

Romania we continually grow smaller and the Genoese increase constantly because not only many Venetians but also Greeks have turned Genoese, when they see that they cannot enjoy the privileges and exercise the rights which their fathers and forefathers had had [as Venetians], so let your Excellency make provision in this matter for the good, honour, welfare, and utility of our commune and of the merchants who operate in Romania, because those who are many are more feared than those who are few ...'[107]

A less rigorous policy in deciding who was Venetian would no doubt have made the Venetians more numerous. That dictum could have been applied to the Venetian political community in Venice as well as to the commercial communities overseas. But comparisons with Genoa, which Minotto's report itself suggests, raises doubts whether it would have made Venice stronger at that time. Genoa was more open and made naturalization easier, and Genoa was repeatedly crippled politically by civil war. Florentines also attributed their excessive factionalism to diversity of origin in the population. The belief was voiced by Villani[108] and by Dante in the famous lines:

> Sempre la confusion de le persone
> Principio fu del mal della cittade
> Come del vostro il cibo che s'appone.
> *Paradiso*, XVI, 67-9

Fear of factions and fear of foreigners gradually fused at Venice. Hostility to foreigners and recent immigrants found expression in commercial policy and in closing the doors of political life against new men. The concern with factional rivalries, after working in favour of the increase of the membership of the great council between 1297 and 1310, became thereafter a reason for refusing any new admissions which might dilute the homogeneity of Venice's governing class.

Looked at with the advantages of hindsight, Doge Pietro Gradenigo's reform must be considered extraordinarily successful. At a time when other Italian communes were being torn by factions, Venice acquired a structure of government relatively able to resist that evil. Its base was the great council as enlarged by Gradenigo. This council was gradually accepted as sovereign, displacing in that role the general assembly of the people, a body much more easily manoeuvred by factions. By admitting to the Venetian nobility a certain number of refugees from the collapsing Latin states in the Levant, by admitting also a certain number of old Venetian families not hitherto considered noble, and above all by assuring continued membership in the great council to nearly all those who were already part of the ruling class, broadly defined, his reforms moderated the fierceness of political rivalries.

NOTES

1 Andrea Dandolo, *Chronica Brevis,* in L. Muratori, *Rerum Italicarum Scriptores* (old edition, hereinafter referred to as *RISS (1),* xii [Milan 1728]), c. 409. This sentence appears also in the copy in Paris, Bibl. nat., ms Latin 5875, f. 179ᵛ. It does not appear in the edition by Ester Pastorello, in L. Muratori, *Rerum Italicarum Scriptores* (new edition, hereinafter referred to as *RISS(2)*), xii, 1 (Città di Castello 1938), p. 370. On the nature of the several texts and of the additions they contain, see Pastorello's introduction, pp. 333-42, and Heinrich Kretschmayr, *Geschichte von Venedig* (Gotha 1920), ii, p. 537.

2 'In 1303 mese Januario istius ducis tempore multas proles Surianorum quae de Acon et illis partibus evaserant, et Venetiis habitare venerant, ac etiam multos populares Venetos, qui in guerra Januensi supradetta se gesserant confidenter, dominus dux et alii nobiles de maiori Venetiarum consilio facere statuerunt.' London, bm, ms Kings 148, f. 89, and similarly in Paris, Bibl. nat., mss Latin 5877, f. 29. Two manuscripts at Venice, Biblioteca Nazionale Marciana, ms Latin, Cl. x, cod. 36a, f. cxx and cod. 237, f. 60, contain a somewhat similar but slightly shortened passage which also states that some commoners were added to the great council. These manuscripts at the Marciana are the basis of Roberto Cessi and Fanny Bennato, eds., *Venetiarum Historia vulgo Petro Justiniano Justiniani filio adjudicata* (Deputazione di Storia Patria per le Venezie, *Monumenti Storici,* n.s., xviii [Venice 1964], cited hereafter as *Venetiarum Historia*). The passage cited is p. 205. Dandolo's *Chronica brevis* also refers to the arrival of refugees; indeed, it does so in the sentence immediately preceding that quoted above. Additions to the Venetian nobility after the fall of Acre are also mentioned by the anonymous chronicle of about 1400, Marciana, Cl. vii, cod. 2034, f. 198-9.

This article was essentially finished before I had the benefit of the studies of Antonio Carile, now published: *La cronachistica veneziana (secoli xiii-xvi) di fronte alla spartizione della Romania nel 1204, con una appendice di P.R.-J. Loenertz* (Fondazione Giorgio Gini, Centro di Cultura a Civiltà, Studi xxv, Florence: Olschki, 1969). Very generously, Dr Carile placed a typescript of his book at my disposal in 1968. That enabled me to supplement my earlier research, which had included examining the copies of the Giustinian chronicle in London and Paris, but I have not taken full advantage of his Herculean labour in comparing hundreds of chronicles to go through an equal number comparing what they say about 1297. Loenertz moved in that direction studying a different theme: R.J. Loenertz, 'Menego Schiavo, esclave, corsaire, seigneur d'Ion (1296-1310),' *Studi veneziani (già Bollettino dell'Istituto di Storia della Società e della*

Stato Veneziano of the Fondazione Giorgio Cini), ix (1967), 315-38. My
interpretation is strengthened by Dr Carile's arguments for believing that
the Latin ms Kings 148 in London and Latin ms 5877 in Paris are copies
of the chronicle of Piero Giustinian who lived about 1350. He identifies
as of different provenance the manuscript published by Cessi and Bennato
under the title *Venetiarum Historia*, above cited.

With Dr Carile's guidance, I examined without finding any reference to
changes in the great council at the end of the thirteenth century a group
of manuscripts which he calls family A and which derived from a composition of about the same time as the *Chronica brevis* of Andrea Dandolo
and the chronicle of Piero Giustinian: namely, Museo Civico Correr, Venice, P.D., 392c; Staatsbibliotek, Munich, Latin 14621 on microfilm at the
Istituto di Storia della Società e dello Stato of the Fondazione Giorgio
Cini; Bibl. Naz. Marciana, Venice, Cl. x, cod. 136 (3026) ; and A volgare,
Marciana, ms Ital., Cl. vii, cod. 38 (8748). Similarly I examined some
manuscripts of what Dr Carile calls family B, which are derived from the
chronicle of Enrico Dandolo composed about 1360, namely: Museo Civico
Correr, Cod. Cicogna 3423 (2831) and Bibl. Ambrosiana, Milan, н 85 inf.,
using the microfilm at the Fondazione Giorgio Cini, Venice.

S. Collodo, 'Temi e caratteri della cronichistica veneziana in volgare del
Tre-Quattrocento (Enrico Dandolo),' *Studi veneziani*, ix (1967), 127-51,
a survey of the political themes treated in the vernacular chronicles of the
mid-fourteenth century, reports no comments on any 'serrata' in 1297.

3 As pointed out by Margarete Merores, 'Der grosse Rat von Venedig und
die sogenannte Serrata von Jahre 1297,' *Vierteljahrschrift für Sozial- und
Wirtschaftsgeschichte*, xxi (1928), 82.

4 Nicolò Trevisan, *Cronaca di Venezia, continuata da altro autore sino all
'anno 1585*, Venice, Bibl. Naz. Marciana, ms Ital., Cl. vii, cod. 519 (Coll
8438), f. 86ᵛ. On its author, see Vittorio Lazzarini, *Marino Faliero* (Florence 1963), p. 98, and in *Nuovo archivio veneto*, xiii (1897), 8. The manuscript is a sixteenth-century copy which embodies Nicolò Trevisan's account of the Falieri conspiracy and the Cretan rebellion, matters about
which he wrote from personal knowledge having been a member of the
Council of Ten. Other parts are copied from other authors or chronicles,
see Heinrich Kretschmayr. *Geschichte von Venedig*, ii, p. 540; Carile, 'La
chronachistica,' pp. 138-46, and 'Note di chronachistica veneziana: Piero
Giustinian e Nicolo Trevisan,' *Studi veneziani*, ix (1967), 119-25.

The reform of 1297 is described twice. The first description (f.86) gives
in the vernacular an accurate summary of the law and then the text in
Latin, followed by the list of members approved, a list which the author
says he copied from chancery records omitting some names which he
found too faint to read. Some are marked with a cross, some not, and the
author expresses doubt whether the cross meant that those without it
were not approved. Then he says (f. 88) that the voting by the *Quarantia*
as provided by the law went on year after year until the time of Doge
Foscari (on the significance of such ballotting see below, note 83). This
first description is obviously the result of research which was made after

Francesco Foscari became Doge in 1423, as Merores noted: '*Der grosse Rat*,' p. 83.

The second description of the reform of 1297, of which Merores took no notice apparently, is inserted in a later point in the Trevisan chronicle, f. 89ʳ, after a relatively terse account of the Tiepolo conspiracy as a part of an elaborate explanation of that conspiracy. It not only elaborates on the first account but in part contradicts it for, after again summarizing the content of the law, it says that on 11 September 1298 'fu statuito ne mazor conseio che nell' avenir el mazor conseio dovesse continuar estar come alora se atrovava, coie tutte quelle famigie che allora si trovavano esser admese nel mazor conseio doveseno continuar *senza la solitta balotatione* che si facevano da San Michiel' (italics mine). This contradiction shows that the second account must have been derived from a different source than the first account. It is followed by speeches of the conspirators and a full second account of the fighting on the day of the revolt. It is this second account, ff. 89ʳ-92, which may be thought to reflect a tradition, perhaps oral, perhaps written down much earlier.

Of the earliest fifteenth-century chronicles, that at the Museo Civico Correr, Cicogna, 2413, gives lists of old and new houses and says that the purpose of the *serrata* was to distinguish clearly 'gentiluomini' from others. Somewhat resembling Trevisan's account but differing by mistakes in important details is that in the Marciana, MS Ital., Cl. VII, cod. 2043, which says that the annual ballotting on membership of the great council continues 'until today' ('in fina al d d'anchur') (f. 199, cf. 198ʳ).

5 Trevisan *Cronaca*, ff. 86-8. The *Venetiarum Historia* notes in its list of noble families, pp. 255-76, some, such as the Pisani, p. 270, of whom it says that they had been *populares* and were made members of the great council at the time of Doge Gradenigo.

6 Trevisan *Cronaca*, f. 88ʳ and 90; *Venetiarum Historia*, p. 205; Dandolo, *Chronica Brevis, RISS(1)*, c. 409

7 ' ... ebe animo de reformar el gran consegio nelqual volse admeter mazor numero di famigie che fuseno reconosute nobele et equale a le altre et non che poche famiglie esser dovesero le principale de la citta et piu reveride, tolendo alli citadini et populari il modo che avevano di esser admese nel maggior cons[ei]o ; e la radice di tal novita era l'odio ch'el portava alli populari, li qualli avanti la eletione sua avevano chiamado Doge Messer Jacomo Tiepolo ...' Trevisan *Cronaca*, f. 89ʳ.

8 *Ibid.*, ff. 90-1

9 *Chronicon Giustiniani*, MS Kings 148, f. 91, and *Venetiarum Historia*, p. 208-10; Cf. Dandolo, *Chronica Brevis, RISS(1)*, c. 410; Giovanni Villani, *Cronica*, ed. Francesco G. Dragmani (Florence 1845), II, 147-8; Albertino Mussatto, in *De gestis italicorum post mortem Henrici VII Cesaris*, in *RISS(1)*, x (1727), c. 583.

10 *Historia Veneziana di Gio. Giacomo Caroldo, Secretario dell ecc. Consiglio di X*, (Museo Civico, Gradenigo 78, f. 432, and in the copy at the Marciana, MS Ital., Cl. VII, cod. 128a, coll. 8639, f. 148). Although writing in the sixteenth century, Caroldo had access to the records of the Council of Ten,

as well as to earlier chronicles. *Venetiarum Historia*, p. 209, says the rebels aimed to kill all 'nobilibus gebelinis.'

11 *Cassiere della Bolla Ducale: Garzie – Novus Liber* (1299-1305), ed. Elena Favaro, in *Fonti per la Storia di Venezia*, Ser. I, *Archivi pubblici* (Venice: Comitato per la Pubblicazione delle fonti relative alla storia di Venezia, 1962), pp. 24, 55.

12 Trevisan, *Cronaca*, f. 91

13 *Ibid.*, f. 90; S. Romanin, *Storia documentata di Venezia* (2nd ed. Venice 1912-31), III, pp. 15-31

14 J.K. Hyde, *Padua in the Age of Dante* (Manchester and New York 1966), pp. 58, 79, 202, 234-5, 252

15 For example, Caroldo, *Historia*, Bibl. Marciana, MS Ital., Cl. VII, cod. 128a, f. 141^r, repeats the Trevisan *Cronaca*, Marciana, Coll. 8438, f. 89^r

16 Merores, '*Der grosse Rat*,' p. 83, said that the idea of a 'serrata' comes from the chronicle of Donato Contarini. The copy of Vienna, Nazional Biblioteca, no. 6260, Fond Foscarini (consulted on the microfilm at the Fondazione Giorgio Cini) does indeed contain this interpretation, f. 110, and a reference in the same paragraph to the election of Francesco Foscari dates its composition as mid-fifteenth century. In the copy in the Bibl. Naz. Marciana of what is also called the chronicle of Donato Contarini (Ital. Cl. VII, cod. 95, ff. 91-2) the treatment is quite different.

17 Marco Antonio Sabellico, *Dell' Historia Venitiana libri xxxiii* (Venice 1678), pp. 148, 154, 156-7.

18 Romanin, *Storia documentata*, III, pp. 300-1

19 Archivio di Stato di Venezia (ASV), Notatorio di Collegio, reg. 3, f. 110^r, item 399

20 *Venetiarum Historia*, pp. 208-9 BM, MS Kings 148, f. 91; Romanin, *Storia documentata*, III, p. 36n; Dandolo, *Chronica Brevis, RISS(2)*, p. 371. Because some members of a family were involved does not mean, however, that all its members were implicated in the conspiracy of 1310.

21 At the first meeting of the great council after the rebellion, on 17 June, only 377 attended; Romanin, *Storia documentata*, III, *pp.* 35-6. The membership at that time was over 900 and the relatively small vote on the decree exiling Bajamonte Tiepolo may have encouraged him and other conspirators to continue to plot in exile. Cristoforo Tentori, *Saggio sulla storia civile, politica, ecclesiastica e sulla corografia topografica degli stati della repubblica di Venezia* (Venice 1785-90), V, pp. 162, 218-20.

22 Merores, '*Der grosse Rat*,' 95, and Andrea da Mosto, *I Dogi di Venezia* (Milan 1960), pp. 90-2.

23 Götz Freiherr von Pölnitz, *Venedig* (Munich 1951), pp. 211-12; Gino Luzzatto, *Storia economica di Venezia dall' xi al xvi secolo* (Venezia: Centro internazionale delle arti e del costume, 1961), pp. 117-18

24 *Venetiarum Historia*, p. 209

25 Romanin, *Storia documentata*, III, pp. 33-4

26 *Gli statuti maritimi veneziani fin al 1255*, eds. R. Predelli and Adolfo Sacerdoti (Venice 1903) and in the *Nuovo Archivio veneto*, n.s., IV and V, *Statuto del R. Zeno*, cap. xl. A Scuolo di San Nicolo di Marineri existed in

the seventeenth century, see ASV, Cinque Savii, n.s., busta 91; Prov. all'-Armar, busta 10, ff. 85-91, and Bibl. Naz. Marciana, MS Ital., Cl. IV, cod. 300 (Coll. 5305), sect. 5.

27 *I capitolari delle arti veneziani sottoposte alla Giustizia e poi alla Giustizia Vecchia dalle origine al MCCCXXX*, ed. Giovanni Monticolo, in *Fonti per la Storia di Italia*, 26-28 (Rome 1896-1914), I

28 Gunnar Mickwitz, *Die Kartellfunctionen der Zünfte und ihre Bedeutung bei der Entstehung des Zunftwesens* (Societas scientiarum Fennica, *Commentationes humanarum litterarum*, VIII, 3 [Helsingsfors 1936]), p. 33; Monticolo, *I capitolari*, I, pp. 12-13 and 119-20

29 *Ibid.*, II, p. 23, and repeated in other *capitolari*. Whereas the earlier prohibitions of 'conspirationem' concerned prices and purchases or sales (*ibid.*, I, p. 119), that of 1265 threatened those guilty of 'aliquod ordinamentum vel compagnia seu comilitatem aut conspirationem per sacramentum vel per fidanciam aut per aliquam aliam promissionem contra honorem domini ducis et eius consilio ac comunis Veneciarum seu contra aliquam personam' and required anyone knowing of such to reveal it at once to the doge.

30 Andrea Dandolo, *Chronica per extensum descripta* (hereinafter referred to as *Chronica*), *RISS(2)*, p. 314; *Venetiarum historia*, p. 176; Marino Sanuto, *Vitae ducum venetorum, RISS(1)*, XXII, c. 564

31 Dandolo, *Chronica, RISS(2)*, p. 316; Sanuto, *Vitae*, cc. 565-6

32 The festivals are elaborately described in Martino da Canale, *Cronaca veneta*, eds. Filippo Luigi Polidori and Giovanni Galvani, *Archivio storico italiano*, VIII (1845), pp. 605-27, and are mentioned in *Venetiarum historia*, p. 179.

33 *I capitolari* includes many regulations, for example the rules of 1222 for the *numeratori di tegoli* and those of 1229 concerning kilns making bricks, applying to men who had no guild, that is, no organized association with its own officers. In some cases, for example that of the bowmakers before 1300, the existence of a guild is doubtful; but the indications are that the following eleven guilds had their statutes approved in the last three months of 1271: the furriers, tanners, shoemakers, house carpenters, ship carpenters, caulkers, masons, mercers, coopers, ironsmiths, and painters; and that of the regulations approved earlier those for the following twelve applied to organized guilds: the tailors, the jacketmakers, the fishmongers, the hemp spinners and rope makers, the goldsmiths and jewellers, the apothecaries and retailers of spices, the dyers, the hoopmakers, the glassworkers, the barber surgeons and physicians, the sellers of oil and salt meats, and the silk weavers. At least a dozen other guilds were approved soon after 1271. The butchers, the bakers, and the woollen-cloth makers were not subject to the *Giustizieri Vecchi*; consequently the dates at which they became organized guilds cannot be determined from the statutes printed by Monticolo. A bakers' guild supervised by the *Ufficiali al Frumento* existed at least as early as 1333; ASV, Arti, buste 445-6, Arte dei Pistori.

34 *I capitolari*. II, pp. 285, 295

35 J.K. Hyde, *Padua in the Age of Dante*, pp. 178-81, 212-13, 216, 243-51
36 Marvin B. Becker, 'An Essay on the "Novi Cives" and Florentine Politics,' *Medieval Studies*, xxiv (1962), 37-50; *Florence in Transition* (Baltimore 1967), i, 17-18, 26-7, 45-6
37 Dandolo, *Chronica, RISS(2)*, p. 321; *Venetiarum historia*, p. 183; Sanuto, *Vitae*, c. 567; in ms Marciana, Ital. Cl. vii, cod. 800. f. 139; *Deliberazioni del Maggior Consiglio di Venezia*, ed. R. Cessi in *Atti delle assemblee con-stitutionali italiane dal medio evo al 1831* (published by the R. Accademia dei Lincei, series iii, section i, vol. ii [Bologna 1931]), p. 65, 6 Dec. 1274.
38 *I capitolari*, ii, i, pp. xxvi-xxvii
39 *Ibid.*, i, introduction. Von Pölnitz, *Venedig*, p. 211, mistakenly speaks of 'Auflösung der Zünfte and Bruderschaften.' Giorgio Cracco, *Società e stato nel medioevo veneziano* (Civiltà veneziana: *Studi*, 22, Firenze; Olschki, for the Fondazione Giorgio Cini, 1967), pp. 247, 292, opines that the form in which statutes were codified in 1278 restricted the guilds so severely that those issued under Lorenzo Tiepolo must have been altered in being copied into the new codex. He apparently believes Lorenzo Tiepolo was so closely allied with the guilds that he would not have permitted the restrictive leg-islation passed by the great council in the 1260s to be written in their stat-utes. Cracco bases this opinion on two kinds of evidence. (1) He cites a sentence from Sanuto's *Vitae* written more than two centuries later which, however, says only that Lorenzo Tiepolo promises the people to let them form craft guilds ('promise al popolo tutte le scuole de suoi mestieri las-ciar fare' in *RISS(1)*, xxii, c. 565, and Marciana ms, Ital. Cl. vii, cod. 800, f. 130ᵛ). The surviving form of the statutes is not inconsistent with such a promise. (2) Cracco finds strange the way in which the laws of the 1260s to restrict the political activities of guilds are in some cases tacked on separately instead of being integrated with other provisions. But it was common in guild statutes and in the statutes governing various offices to add the texts of laws passed after an earlier codification had been made. The way the provisions of the 1260s are introduced into some statutes, such as those of the barbers or the sellers of oils and fats, merely indicates that these trades had compiled by-laws of their own for their guilds before 1265, perhaps before they were given statutes officially approved by the *giustizieri*. What Cracco regards as a contradiction in the case of the bar-bers is not really a contradiction; it only implies that in an early form the by-laws had provided that members could be fined for not attending meet-ings called by the *gastaldo* and that in 1265 the government, without changing the earlier provisions giving him power to fine those absent with-out cause, limited the number of meetings the *gastaldo* could call. *I capito-lari*, ii, pp. 42, 48. In the statutes of the ironsmiths, approved under Lorenzo Tiepolo, the provisions concerning number of meetings and the fines for non-attendance are combined in the one chapter, chap. 34.
40 Sanuto, *Vitae*, cc. 570, 571; Dandolo, *Chronica, RISS(2)*, p. 325
41 Sanuto, *Vitae*, c. 581, calls it the conspiracy of Marion Bocco, Giovanni Baldovino, and Michele Juda, and misdates it 1299. He says they conspired because they were left out of the great council. On Baldovino or Baldvino,

see Vittorio Lazzarini, 'Aneddoti della congiura Quirini-Tiepolo,' *Nuovo archivio veneto*, x (1895), 85-9. The recurrence of the names Bocco and Baldovino in revolts almost a generation apart indicates a handful of plebeian (popular) families in which there was a tradition of discontent and rebellion, but I know of no evidence of a link between them and any guild. Giorgio Cracco, *Società e stato*, p. 340, although he depicts a political alliance of the guilds and Lorenzo Tiepolo, indicates that the guilds were politically inactive in 1310.

42 On the size of the great council see below, note 65

43 Merores, 'Der grosse Rat,' 90; *Deliberazioni*, I, xiii-xvi; Kretschmayr, *Geschichte von Venedig*, II, p. 72

44 Margarete Merores, 'Der venezianische Adel,' *Vierteljahrschrift für Sozial and Wirtschaftsgeschichte*, XIX (1926), 193-237; Gino Luzzatto, 'Les activités économiques du patriciat vénitien (X-XIV siècles),' in his *Studi di storia economica veneziana* (Padua 1954), pp. 125-66. Cracco, *Società e stato*, chap. 1, and part I of chap. 2. An extreme example of the social mobility at Venice in the twelfth century is given in Claude Cahen, 'Le commerce anatolien au début du XIII⁰ siècle,' in *Mélanges d'histoire du Moyen Age dédiés à la mémoire de Louis Halphen* (Paris 1951), pp. 100-1: Zaccaria Stanairio was descended from a Dalmatian slave who was freed in 1125 and became a commercial agent. His son was a mate and sailing master, and Zaccaria, the grandson, became rich enough to ally himself by marriage with a Trevisan who was a councillor of the patriarch of Constantinople.

45 *Venetiarum historia*, pp. 201, 203-4: Trevisan, *Cronaca*, ff. 85ᵗ, 86; Camillo Manfroni, *Storia della marina italiana dal trattato di Ninfeo alla caduta di Costantinopoli* (Livorno 1902), I, p. 215; R.J. Loenertz, 'Menego Schiavo,' in *Studi veneziani*, XI (1967), 315-18

46 Alathea Weil, *The Navy of Venice* (London 1910), p. 167; Dandolo, *Chronica, RISS(2)*, p. 311; Camillo Manfroni, 'Cenni sugli ordinamenti della marina italiana nel Medioevo,' *Rivista marittima*, XXI, 4, (1898), pp. 465-89

47 *Chronicon Giustiniani*, BM, MS Kings 148, ff. 88ᵛ; Trevisan, *Cronaca* (Marciana Coll. 8438), f. 86

48 Dandolo, *Chronica, RISS(2)*, pp. 105-6, 139, 259; F.C. Lane, *Venice and History* (Baltimore 1966), p. 308. Cracco, *Società e stato*, pp. 408-36, recognizes the role that Dandolo gave the commoners, but finds it quite subordinate to the role that he gave the doges. He agrees that Dandolo is far from expressing any class feeling between commoners and nobles, but believes that Dandolo, reacting in 1350 against the bad government of the *grandi*, hoped for an all-powerful doge, a *signore*.

49 F.C. Lane, 'The Crossbow in the Nautical Revolution of the Middle Ages,' in *Economy, Society, and Government in Medieval Italy: Essays in Memory of Robert L. Reynolds*, ed. David Herlihy *et al.* (Kent, Ohio 1969), pp. 161-71, and *idem*, 'Venetian Seamen in the Nautical Revolution of the Middle Ages,' in 'Venezia e il Levante fino al 1500,' to be published by the Fondazione Cini; *idem*, 'Venetian Merchant Galleys, 1300-1334: Private

and Communal Operation,' in *Speculum* XXXVII (1963), 198, and in *Venice and History*, pp. 219-20.
50 Merores, 'Der venezianische Adel,' 202-6, 224-8, and 'Der grosse Rat,' 64-71, 89-98; and 'Der venezianische Steuerkataster von 1379,' *Viertel-jahrschrift für Sozial- und Wirtschaftsgeschichte*, XVI (1922), 416-17; Gino Luzzatto, *Storia economica di Venezia* (Venice 1961,) pp. 24-9, 79-93; 127-35, and especially p. 130.
51 Giuseppe Maranini, *La costituzione di Venezia dalle origine alla serrata de Maggior Consiglio* (Venice 1927; in a later printing [Rome 1932] it is vol. I of *La costituzione di Venezia* and is here so cited, although I used the 1927 printing). Maranini's basic interests were those of a constitutional lawyer, and his account seems to me distorted by his attributing to oppos-ing parties constitutional conceptions of aristocratic or popular sovereign-ty. See pp. 174-6, 182-3. He ignores the extent to which 'populus' was used in early centuries to mean the whole community or the whole laity (p. 192), and he does not even attempt to distinguish occasions when it refers to the poor and occasions when it refers to the new rich. 'Popolare' seems to mean for him primarily what expresses the will of the people rather than the will of the aristocracy, and the existence of such a will as a con-stitutional principle is implied by his account. But in the reports of early chronicles the only recorded instance of a conflict between the will of the people and the will of their natural leaders (as Maranini himself calls the aristocracy, p. 354), is the refusal of the nobles to elect Jacopo Tiepolo doge. In recounting that episode Maranini suggests that a Tiepolo popular party was stirring up the people and ignores the fact that the only evi-dence about it is to the effect that Jacopo, instead of arousing supporters, withdrew from the city. He considers Giovanni Dandolo a leader of an anti-popular party, ignoring that fact that, as doge, he was the opponent of the restrictive reform proposed in 1297 (*ibid.*, pp. 332-43). On the other hand, Maranini emphasized, as I would, that Doge Gradenigo favoured a broad aristocracy, not a narrow oligarchy. See *idem, La costituzione di Venezia dopo la serrata del Maggior Consiglio* (Venice 1931), p. 8. (In the Rome 1932 reprinting it is: vol. II of *La costituzione di Venezia.*) Moreover, there is much that is appealing in his formulation: 'Altrove l'aristocrazia dei primi arrivati si difendeva come classe, e fu vinta. A Venezia si difese come Stato, e vinse in pieno la sua battaglia,' *La costituzione di Venezia*, I, p. 326. But this formula should be interpreted to allow for the readiness of the aristocracy during many centuries to admit new families, as shown by Merores in the articles above cited.
52 Fra Paolino Minorita, *Trattato de Regimine Rectoris*, ed. Adolfo Mussa-fia (Vienna and Florence 1868), chap. 67
53 F.C. Lane, 'Medieval Political Ideas and the Venetian Constitution,' in *Venice and History*, pp. 285-308
54 *Deliberazioni*, II, p. 87
55 Vettor Sandi, *Principii di storia civili della Repubblica di Venezia*, I (Ven-ice 1758-72), II, pp. 631-2
56 Robert Cessi, *Storia della Repubblica di Venezia* (Milan and Messina

1946), I, pp. 265-70; *Deliberazioni,* I, pp. xi-xix. Merores, after the most thorough analysis of the sources yet made, also concluded that the nobles were in unchallenged control and the so-called *serrata* was of secondary importance. She even went so far as to conclude that the line between noble and commoner was clearly drawn on the basis of membership in the great council in the mid-thirteenth century and that the reform of 1297 merely formalized standards of nobility already established in practice and custom, 'Der grosse Rat,' 61, 88, 108.

57 *Deliberazioni,* I, pp. 263, 264; II, pp. 88-101, 225; III, pp. 244-5, 349-50; Enrico Besta, 'Intorno a due opere recenti sulla costituzione e sulla politica veneziana del medio evo,' *Nuovo archivio veneto,* n.s., XIV (1897), 207-9; Sandi, *Principii di Storia,* II, I, pp. 278-9

58 For example, Romanin, *Storia documentata,* III, p. 26, n.2; *Deliberazioni,* I, pp. 342-61; II, p. 89

59 At least after 1274, *Deliberazioni,* II, p. 93

60 *Deliberazioni,* I, pp. xii, 269, 341; III, pp. 9, 14, 51, 84, 85, 123, 125, 156, 365. Merores, 'Der grosse Rat,' 70, implies that the nominating committee (*electores*) had some freedom to use their discretion in naming members beyond the 100 which they were directed to name by the resolution creating the committee. Also, it is not clear that the doge and his council, who decided when additional nominations were needed, were necessarily limited by the occurrence of vacancies on the original list of 100.

61 Sandi, *Principii di Storia,* I, II. p. 701. A long list of officials with *ex officio* membership in the great council is given by Besta, as cited in *Nuovo archivio veneto,* n.s., XIV (1897), 204-6, but Besta, 202-3, expressed doubt about the reasons for choosing additional members during the year.

62 Giovanni Antonio Muazzo, 'Del antico governo della Repubblica di Venezia: Discorso historico-politico,' MS of which there are many copies, in Bibl. Naz. Marciana, MS Ital., Class VII, cod. 966 (7831) and in Biblioteca Correr at the Museo Civico, MS Cicogna 2000, f. 46; Tentori, *Saggio,* V, p. 162

63 *Deliberazioni,* II, p. 83; Merores. 'Der grosse Rat,' 79, says that before 1297 membership may have been considered by the busy businessman as merely a burdensome duty.

64 Vittorio Lazzarini, 'Obbligo di assumere publici uffici,' *Archivio veneto,* ser. 5, XIX (1936), 184-98

65 Figures on the number voting on important occasions are given in the same manuscript from which Cessi published the names of the nominees, Marciana, MS Ital., Cl. VII, cod. 551. It says (f. 149r) that the number voting in 1275 was 275 although 577 nominees are listed for that year; in 1276 (ff. 149-50), 300 although 444 nominees were listed, by Cessi's count; in 1277 (f. 161r), 268, 307, 292, and 304 voting although 465 nominees listed; in 1278 (f. 162r, 167), 251 and 236 voting although 435 nominated; in 1283-4 (ff. 200-5), 220, 260, 277, 278, 316, and 344 voting. The number nominated in 1282 was 336; in 1293, 332; whereas in 1283-92 it is not recorded. In 1295 the number nominated had fallen to 257. In 1296 the record is incomplete; only 107 are recorded. *Deliberazioni,* I, p. xv.

Maranini, *La costituzione di Venezia,* I, pp. 345, 350, says there were 366 voting in October 1286 and 588 voting in February 1297 (our style, 1296 Venetian style), a surprisingly large number in view of the lists published by Cessi. For these figures Maranini cites a 'Liber Fractus.' The only volume with that name mentioned in current catalogues and indices of the archive or in Cessi's description of the records of the great council contains neither folios nor dates corresponding to Maranini's references. A 'Liber Fractus' existing in the archives of the Avvogaria di Comun overlapping Bifrons and Cerberus is mentioned by Maximilian Claar, *Die Entwicklung der venetianischen Verfassung von Einsetzung bis zur Schliessung der grossen Rat (1172-1297)*, (Munich 1895), p. 149n. Maranini cited the same passages Claar had cited. Tentori, *Saggio*, ff. 172-3, also refers to a 'Liber Fractus dell' Avogaria' when he in fact is citing what is now called Zanetta, *copia*. Unless another volume called 'Fractus' can be found, all Maranini's references to 'Liber Fractus' are suspect. Merores, 'Der grosse Rat,' 34n, refers to Maranini's 'erfundene Zitate.'

Consistent with the large numbers he mentions as voting is Maranini's interpretation of a law concerning *ex officio* members passed 20 March 1288. He interpreted it to mean that all who had held certain offices were thereafter *ex officio* members of the great council for life. But the law as he prints it, *La costituzione di Venezia*, I, pp. 217, citing Bifrons, par. 38, is different from the text printed by Cessi (*Deliberazioni*, III, p. 200) citing Zanetta. Maranini reads 'sine quod eligantur' where Cessi reads 'usque ad sanctam Michaelem secundum quod eligantur.' In the context, Cessi's reading gives certain officials a year of *ex officio* membership in the great council the year after they retired.

66 Romanin, *Storia documentata*, II, p. 341; Roberto Cessi, *Le origini del ducato veneziano* (Naples 1951), p. 329

67 The sixty-odd Venetian parishes (*contrade*) were grouped into thirty districts, mostly of two parishes each. Canale, *Cronaca*, pp. 566-7, 572. These *trentacie* had served as election districts since the beginning of the thirteenth century. *Deliberazioni*, I, p. 263, and G. Cassandro, 'Concetto e struttura dello stato veneziano,' *Bergamum*, LVIII, 2 (1964), 37-42, a good brief summary. Exactly what rules the doge and his council were expected to follow in nominating the electors is not known, but it is possible that they had sufficient latitude, first in making up the list to be gone through, and then in deciding which members were at a given moment ineligible for one reason or another, e.g., absence, parentage, or debts, so that a clique which wished to perpetuate itself at all cost and which had control of the ducal council could, by using the electors of the year in much the way the Medici in Florence used the *Accoppiatori*, pack the great council and other councils and magistracies with their partisans. One advantage of the reform put through by Gradenigo was that it made impossible a narrowing of the ruling class by such methods.

68 *Deliberazioni*, I, pp. ix-xii; II, pp. 97, 100, 225; III, pp. 9, 156, 244-5, 365

69 *Ibid.*, III, p. 350

70 *Ibid.*, I, pp. ix-xii; II, p. 225; III, pp. 9, 14, 51, 84, 123, 156, 184-5, 349-50,

365. See also Besta as cited in *Nuovo archivio veneto*, n.s., xiv (1897), 201-2.

71 Cracco, *Società e stato*, pp. 104-11. But after showing how imprecise was the meaning of *nobile*, he continues to use *popolare* in opposition to *aristocratici*, as on pp. 120-1; and continues to call the Tiepolo *popolare* after three generations had held the highest offices.

72 *Ibid.*, pp. 337-50

73 Changes were proposed in 1286 on three days. On 3 October it was voted that those chosen by the electors for the senate and the great council should be voted on one by one and must be approved by a majority of the *Quarantia*. Two days later, on the 5th, there was a new motion which would have set up a different procedure. It provided that anyone who did not have a paternal ancestor who had been a member of the great council could not become a member unless approved by a majority of the ducal council and the great council. Opposing that proposal was a motion supported by the doge the content of which is reported only as 'stare firmi ad morem consuetum.' The doge's motion was that passed, 'de stare firmi.' On 17 October it was moved that the men nominated for the great council by the electors must be approved by majorities in the ducal council, the senate, and the *Quarantia*. This was defeated as it was again voted 'de stare firmi, or 'stare firmum.' *Deliberazioni*, iii, pp. 156-7; asv, Maggior Consiglio, Deliberazioni, Juna-Zanetta-Pilosus, f. 81. Although Cracco, *Società e stato*, p. 332, refers to the motion passed 3 October as valid thereafter, I believe it was repealed by the votes on 5 and 17 October to stand by customary procedure. This rather obvious interpretation is confirmed by the lack of any reference to approval of the nominees one by one in the resolution governing the electors passed in September 1287 (*Deliberazioni*, iii, pp. 184-5) in 1293 (*ibid.*, iii, pp. 349-50), in 1294 (*ibid.*, iii, p. 365) and 1296 (Marciana, ms Ital. Cl. vii, cod. 551, f. 235 and 252^t).

74 The fourth defeated proposal was made 6 March 1296 and defeated by a motion to 'stare firmi.' The content of the motion is not given; that it was the same as the motion defeated 5 and 17 October in 1286 is mere assumption. *Deliberazioni*, iii, p. 396.

75 *Deliberazioni*, iii, pp. 417-18; Besta, in *Nuovo archivio veneto*, xiv, (1897), 216-18

76 Cessi, in printing the volume of minutes called Liber Pilosus, noted that the register was incomplete (*mutili*) and that it can be partly completed from the Liber Cerberus of asv, Avvogaria di Comun. *Deliberazioni*, iii, pp. v-vi. The *copia* of Pilosus in asv, Maggior Consiglio, Deliberazioni, shows that some of the gaps were there centuries ago but some additional record of resolutions can be found in the Marciana ms, Ital. Cl. vii, cod. 551, in the copies embodied in the work of Muazzo, cited above, n. 62, and in the Gradenigo ms, busta 112 at the Biblioteca Correr in the Museo Civico, Venice. See below, n. 82. Maranini, *La costituzione di Venezia*, i, p. 345, cites the register Fractus for this period but the only register of that name in the present guides to the archives contains nothing beyond 1282

and no folios of the high numbers cited by Maranini. The only explanation for his references seems to be that he used late copies and confused their references to their source.

77 Manfroni, *Storia*, I, pp. 207-14; Romanin, *Storia documentata*, II, p. 335; Georg Caro, *Genua und die Machte am Mittelmeer* (Halle 1895-99), II, pp. 248-53

78 Trevisan chronicle (Marciana, 8438), ff. 89ᵗ-90, in his second account: 'tutte quele famigie che alhora si trovavano esser admese nel mazor conseio doveseno continuar senza la solitta balotatione che si faceva da San michel et cusi se principio,' Repeated almost word for word by Gian Jacopo Caroldo, 'Historia di Venetia,' MS, Bibl. Naz. Marciana, Ital. Cl. VII, cod. 128a (8639), f. 141ᵗ.

79 *Ibid.*, and Sanuto, *Vitae, RISSI(1)*. XXII, 581, 583, 584

80 In the original record, ASV, Maggior Consiglio, Deliberazioni, Pilosus, f. 211, the law of September 1298 appears only as a footnote to the law of February 1297. In the authoritative record of the Avvogaria di Comun, Cerberus, f. 18ʳ, the law of September 1299, the earliest recorded on the subject, is in a different hand from the other entries.

81 The text of the motion of 11 September 1298 in Pilosus, f. 211 reads: 'Capta fuit pars quod consilium continens de Consilio Maiori fiendo sit deinceps sicut est modo.' The words after 'Capta fuit pars quod' are illegible except by ultra-violet rays and Cessi's edition, *Deliberazioni*, III, p. 418n, reads there 'ordo' instead of 'consilium continens,' but the reading given above and obtained by ultra-violet light is the same as that given in Giovanni Antonio Muazzo, 'Del governo antico della Repubblica di Venezia: Discorso historico politico,' Civico, MS Cicogna 2000, pp. 53-4.

82 The words 'sit deinceps sicut est modo' used in 1298 might be taken to imply permanent membership, but they refer to the procedure specified in February 1297, not to the membership. On 30 September 1299 it was voted that 'dictum consilium super electione maioris consilii debeat ad huc durare sicut ipsum continet.' ASV, Avvogaria di Comun, Deliberazioni del Maggior Consiglio, Cerberus, f. 18. Copies of a similar resolution dated February 1299 are given in Muazzo (Cicogna 2000) ff. 53-4, and in a collection of copies of laws passed during the dogeship of Pietro Gradenigo in Museo Civico-Correr, Gradenigo collection, busta 112. Tentori, *Saggio*, v, f. 185-6, says he found such laws for both 30 September 1298 and 30 September 1299. In 1300 and 1301 the great council passed motions confirming the membership lists for the great council approved by the *Quarantia*. That of 15 October 1301 reads: 'C.F.P. quod illi sint firmi sicut probati essent in festo Santi Michaelis ...' ASV, Avvogaria di Comun, Deliberazioni del Maggior Consiglio, Liber Magnus, f. 15.

83 On continued yearly ballotting to determine membership, see Besta, *Nuovo archivio venuto*, n. s., XIV (1897), p. 221, and Tentori, *Saggio*, v, pp. 158-67, 180-6, and the chronicles cited above, note 4. Tentori argued convincingly by references to books of the *Quarantia*, now lost, that all the names of members for the next year were voted on each year by the *Quarantia*, that there was not yet any permanent membership. But while all

those already members and still living were included in the list examined
each year by the *Quarantia*, only the new names added presented real
issues; the re-election was a mere formality. Practically speaking, a member once in was locked in. That the voting of the complete list was dis-
pensed with in 1436, because it was a superfluous formality and because
assembling all those to be voted in was considered a health hazard in time
of plague, is reported by Tentori, *Saggio*, v, pp. 191-2.
84 ASV, Avvogaria di Comun, Deliberazioni del Maggior Consiglio, Cerberus,
f. 18
85 *Ibid.*, Magnus et Capricornus, f. 6, new numbering
86 Muazzo, Cicogna 2000, ff. 58, 63, 67. Muazzo, in arguing for the great antiquity of all the Venetian nobility, maintained that the reform of 1297 did
not open the way to any men who did not have distinguished Venetian ancestors, that it was understood that the electors in choosing men not members of the outgoing council would choose only those whose ancestors had
held office. As far as the wording of the laws is concerned, that is quite possible. The reason for thinking some men of new families were added lies in
the statements of the chronicles cited at the beginning of this article. In a
law cited in Muazzo, Cicogna 2000, p. 70, a member who must have a majority in the *Quarantia* is called *hominem novum*. But this probably means
merely a new member and implies nothing about ancestry for passages in
a law of 1307 (quoted on the same page) refer to similar persons as 'illi
qui dabuntur ad eligendum de novo de Majoris Consilio.'
87 See above, note 78
88 *Deliberazioni*, III, p. 446; ASV, Maggior Consiglio, Deliberazioni, Liber
Pilosus, f. 222ᵛ; Muazzo, Cicogna 2000, p. 59; Besta, *Nuovo archivio
veneto*, n.s. XIV (1897), 219, dates this law in 1297
89 Giovanni Fiastri, 'L'assemblea del popolo a Venezia come organo constitu-
zionale dello State,' *Nuovo archivio veneto*, n.s., XXV (1913), 340-80
90 Cracco, *Società e stato*, pp. 240-1, describes how he imagines the Venetian
general assembly to have been rigged in 1268. That time it was planned
against the Tiepoleschi, but on another occasion it might be tried in their
favour.
91 This point was emphasized in the fourteenth century by Bartolus in his
favourable comment on the Venetian constitution, in his *Tractatus de regimine civitatis*, par. 15-19, 22, see Lane, *Venice and History*, p. 305.
92 Besta, *Nuovo archivio veneto*, n.s., XIV, (1897), 218-20
93 *Ibid.*, p. 219. Although Tentori, *Saggio*, I, pp. 143-4, agrees in regard to the
requirements for admission *per grazia*, he maintains that the electors continued to function until 1319, although only to nominate new members
whose fathers or forefathers had been in the council.
94 Muazzo, Cicogna 2000, ff. 61-2, noted the indirect approach embodied in
these laws.
95 Kretschmayr, *Geschichte von Venedig*, II, p. 75
96 *Ibid.* The age requirement and the arrangements for admitting at the age
of twenty those who drew the gold balls from the urn were specified in
1319. Sandi, *Principi di storia civile*, II, I, pp. 15-17.

97 ASV, Capitolare dei consoli dei mercanti, cap. 112; Avvogaria di Comun, Deliberazioni del Maggior Consiglio, Magnus, ff. 7, 8

98 *Ibid., Magnus,* f. 53ʳ⁻ᵛ. I am much indebted to Francis-Xavier Leduc for communicating to me the results of his researches into Venetian commercial administration in this period. He shows that the *Provveditori* were part of a general protectionist movement.

99 *Cassiere della bolla ducale, Grazie,* I, paragraph 400

100 *Ibid.,* paragraph 400, mentions that the *Provveditori* had been considering fifty-five years necessary. In the mid-thirteenth century, in contrast, the rules required only ten years, and there were many special grants by the great council. *Deliberazioni,* II, p. 145 and *passim.* A ducal bull of 1268 granting Venetian citizenship to a Jew, David of Negroponte, is mentioned by Pompeo Molmenti, *Storia, di Venezia nella vita privata* (Bergamo 1925-7), I, p. 79. Other special grants also are mentioned by Silvano Borsari, *Studi sulle colonie veneziane in Romanie nel xiii secolo* (Naples 1966), p. 123n.

101 Avvogaria di Comun, Deliberazioni del Maggior Consiglio, Magnus, f. 10ᵛ. The law was vague concerning the trading rights of those allowed to continue to live in Venice after having done so for ten years, saying only 'possint morari Veneciis sicut possunt aliis veneti,' but these laws seem to be the basis for the distinction later called that of *cittadini de intus,* who had rights of trade only within the city, and *cittadini de extra,* who could export and import as Venetians, Molmenti, *Storia di Venezia.* I, p. 72.

102 ASV, Provveditori di Comun, reg. I, ff. 6ᵗ, 8ʳ, 11; R. Predelli, *Liber commemoriali registi* (in Deputazione Veneta di Storia Patria, *Monumenti storici,* serie 1, [Venice 1876], I), Lib. 1, paras. 250, 270, 276, and *passim.*

103 Avvogaria di Comun, Deliberazioni del Maggior Consiglio, Magnus, f. 7ᵗ; *Le deliberazioni del consiglio dei rogati (Senato), Serie mixtorum, I,* eds. R. Cessi and P. Sambin (Deputazione di Storia Patria per le Venezie, *Monumenti storici,* n.s., xv [Venice 1960]), pp. 95-6.

104 Avvogaria di Comun, Deliberazioni del Maggior Consiglio, Magnus 12ᵗ; Provveditori di Comune, reg. I. f. 11ʳ

105 Roberto Cessi, 'L "Officium de Navigantibus" e i sistemi della politica commerciale veneziana nel secolo xiv,' in *idem, Politica e economica di Venezia nel Trecento,* (Storia et letteratura, xl [Rome 1952]), pp. 23-61, and in *Nuovo archivio veneto,* n.s., xxxii (1916).

106 Senato Misti, reg. 15-6 *copia,* f. 128 (2 March 1333)

107 ASV, Libri Commemoriali, reg. 2, ff. 7-8; and in *Diplomatorium Veneto-Levantinum, 1300-1350,* ed. Georg M. Thomas (*Monumenti storici,* publ. deputazione Veneta di Storia Patria, serie 1, v, [Venice 1880]), p. 104. Other references to Marco Minoto, in *Libri Commemoriali,* I, Lib. I, no. 329; Lib. II, nos. 172, 182, 269, 349; Lib. III, nos. 57, 89, show that he was a galley commander in 1307-8, at Constantinople in 1319, 1320, and 1322, *bailo* and *capitano* at Negroponte in 1326, and *Provveditore di Comun* in 1324.

108 Nicolai Rubinstein, 'The Beginnings of Political Thought in Florence,' *Journal of the Warburg and Courtauld Institute,* v (1942), 198 ff.

Biondo, Sabellico,
and the beginnings of Venetian
official historiography

Felix Gilbert

The 'Venetian myth' has unusual strength and durability; the first task of a historian of Venice usually is to correct erroneous views and assumptions rooted in legends about the Venetian past.

The longevity of the Venetian myth is not surprising. In this city, born of the marriage of sea and stone, of Byzantium and Rome, crowded into a narrow space and ruling over a large empire, constantly threatened and constantly saved, miracles and superhuman feats seem to provide a more appropriate explanation for the course of events than do rational criteria and ordinary human psychology.

There is still another, perhaps more potent, reason for the persistence of the Venetian myth. The myth is deeply ingrained in those magnificent tomes which the Venetians, perhaps conscious that they were the last heirs of a vanishing splendour, produced in the eighteenth century: Agostini's *Notizie*, Foscarini's *Della letteratura Veneziana*, the ten volumes *Degli istorici delle cose Veneziane*, Quirini's *Tiara et purpura Veneta*, and Zeno's *Dissertazioni Vossiane*.[1] These volumes in parchment with lovely engravings are persuasive advocates of the Venetian myth.

Finally, there are practical reasons for the influence of these eighteenth-century writers upon later scholarship. The Venetian archives have been damaged by a number of great fires[2] and these eighteenth-century volumes used documents which are no longer available to us. However, the manner in which the writers of the eighteenth century presented this material was intended to confirm and justify the traditional mythical story of the Venetian past.

In the following I shall try to reduce to its bare facts an episode of Venetian intellectual history which has been frequently discussed but has remained vague and shadowy: the story of the beginnings of Venetian official historiography.[3] I might perhaps add that two of the humanist historians who have a crucial role in this study – namely Flavio Biondo and Sabellico – have been discussed in the work of the scholar to whom this volume is dedicated, in Ferguson's *Renaissance in Historical Thought*.[4]

The story of the beginnings of Venetian official historiography is confused and obscure and, in order to clarify it, it is necessary to re-examine three intricate problems and to question the opinions which writers of the past have expressed on this issue.

The first problem is whether in the middle of the fifteenth century the Venetians planned to create the special position of an official historiographer: what kind of job did Lodovico Foscarini offer to Flavio Biondo in his letter of July 1462? Secondly, did Sabellico later in the century occupy the position of a public historiographer and is it justifiable to count his work as the first in the series of official histories? Thirdly, if the position of an official historiographer existed, why did ten years elapse after Sabellico's death before a successor, in the person of Andrea Navagero, was appointed?

There are reasons why the plan of creating the position of an official historiographer has been ascribed to Lodovico Foscarini.[5] Foscarini had great interest in humanistic studies. He was close to the most prominent patrons of humanism and of humanists among the Venetian patricians. Moreover, Foscarini was a disciple of Francesco Barbaro, the outstanding figure of early Venetian humanism,[6] and he was an intimate friend of Bernardo Giustiniani, a light in Venetian intellectual life in the later part of the quattrocento.[7] Foscarini served as Venetian ambassador in Rome where he frequented the humanist circles at the papal court; in particular he was in contact with Bessarion.[8] It seems more than a coincidence that, soon after Foscarini became procuratore di San Marco, a plan to house Bessarion's books in a new building on the Piazzetta was adopted and a vacant lectureship for humanities in the school of San Marco was filled.[9]

It is equally certain that Foscarini took particular interest in historical studies and made great efforts to induce humanist scholars to embark on the composition of a history of Venice.[10] He urged Porcellio to continue writing commentaries on contemporary events because they would inform posterity about the great men of former years.[11] Moreover, knowledge of Venetian history would be most useful to the senate for reaching the right political decisions. Foscarini's particular concern was the writing of the history of his own time which he regarded as more instructive than the history of previous centuries. Reports about events in the remote past could easily be falsified and arouse distrust; but people believed reports about recent events. In another letter to his friend, Girolamo da Ponte,[12] Foscarini called the reading of histories his favourite recreation; he complained that he lacked books on Venetian history whereas he possessed many books on the history of other peoples. He therefore asked da Ponte to send him his manuscript of Lorenzo de Monacis' Venetian history. The letter[13] with which Foscarini then returned this manuscript was a eulogy of history. Like most of his contemporaries, Foscarini regarded the time of Rome's greatness as the high point of history, but he emphasized that people were still full of admiration for the Romans because their deeds had been preserved in histories composed by great writers. Foscarini was proud to read what Lorenzo de Monacis had written about the achievements of the Venetians in the past; knowledge of such exemplary behaviour was necessary in order to maintain the great Venetian tradition of selfless service to the fatherland. The chief purpose of knowledge of the past was to inspire people with a desire for true glory.

Foscarini held all the usual humanist views about history. History provided examples which served to generate moral strength and political wisdom. The historian alone can assure that the great deeds of the past are not forgotten. Like other rulers or governments in the Renaissance, Foscarini was eager to see the activities of the great men of his city immortalized in a history written by a humanist.

But did Foscarini go further and envisage the creation of a position which committed its holder to one exclusive task, that of writing a history of Venice? This is the interpretation which usually is given to the letter which Foscarini wrote to Biondo in July 1462.[14] It is assumed that with this letter Foscarini offered Biondo the position of public historiographer of Venice. However, an exact analysis of Foscarini's letter to Biondo will show that this is an erroneous interpretation.

Foscarini and Biondo met first in 1459 at the congress in Mantua which Foscarini attended as Venetian ambassador.[15] Foscarini expressed a wish to have a history of Venice written by a humanist, and Biondo showed interest in undertaking the task. When, in July 1462, Foscarini wrote to Biondo, he was anxious to find out whether Biondo was still attracted by such an idea.[16] However, he had first to explain why the discussions which they had had three years before in Mantua had had no practical results.[17] After his return from Mantua to Venice in January 1460, Foscarini had taken up the matter with members of the senate. But he was informed that other humanists – Perleo, Mario Filelfo, George of Trebizond – were likewise attracted by such a project. A public competition among these scholars would have been necessary and Foscarini had felt that he had no right to expose Biondo to a competition which might end with a rebuff. But by 1462 the situation had changed. George of Trebizond and Mario Filelfo were away and Perleo had lost interest. Now there was an opportunity to realize the plans they had discussed in Mantua. Foscarini's term as governor in Friuli was near its end and he would soon return to Venice.[18] If Biondo was still willing to undertake the writing of a history of Venice Foscarini would do whatever he could to further Biondo's work and to see him established 'in amplissimo locupletissimorum ac maximorum scribentium gradu.'

Foscarini's letter did not give an exact description of the position which Foscarini had in mind for Biondo. But some conclusion might be drawn from Foscarini's explanation of why in 1460, after his return from the congress of Mantua, his efforts on behalf of Biondo had been unsuccessful. It seems highly significant that the three competitors whom Foscarini mentioned – Perleo, Mario Filelfo, George of Trebizond – all were connected with the school of San Marco.

The most renowned intellectual centre under Venetian control was outside Venice: the university of Padua. But at the beginning of the fifteenth century a school with a lectureship for the teaching of logic and philosophy was established in Venice itself, near the Rialto.[19] It was soon realized both that instruction in these traditional subjects did not satisfy the intellectual curiosity of those interested in the development of humanistic studies, and that the school at the Rialto did not fulfil the needs of Venetian government service. Thus, in 1443, another school was established in Venice, this time near San Marco; its lecturer received a salary from the government and was obliged to train young men for service in the chancellery. He was also expected to lecture in the humanities before a public audience.

At the time of Foscarini's negotiations with Biondo the lecturer at the school of San Marco was Perleo, one of the names mentioned by Foscarini in his letter to Biondo. Perleo had been appointed in 1457;[20] it was realized at the time, however, that it was difficult for one lecturer to fulfil the purposes for which the school of San Marco was established: to train candidates for service in the chancellery and to make Venice a centre for humanistic studies. Thus, the Venetian government decided to create a second lectureship at the school of San Marco, and the first appointment to this second lectureship was made in March 1460; that means that the appointment followed immediately upon Foscarini's return from the congress at Mantua. Thus, when Foscarini and Biondo were discussing Biondo's future literary plans in Mantua, preparations for the establishment of a second lectureship at the school of San Marco must have been far advanced. In March 1460 this newly created second lectureship was given to Mario Filelfo, another of the names mentioned by Foscarini to Biondo.[21] The decree of appointment stated that Filelfo was obliged 'legere cotidie duas dignas lectiones publice, unam scilicet in poetica, alteram in arte oratorica aut in historia.' However, Mario Filelfo's tenure of this position was brief; he left Venice after a few months. On 4 October 1460 he was succeeded by George of Trebizond, the third name mentioned in Foscarini's letter.[22] George of Trebizond too kept this position for only a short period; in 1462 he settled in Rome. Thus in July 1462, when Foscarini wrote to Biondo, one of the lectureships at the school of San Marco was vacant and Perleo, the other lecturer, was ill and close to death.[23]

To sum up: both times that Foscarini discussed with Biondo the possibility of his settling in Venice—in 1459 as well as in 1462—the position of a lecturer at the school of San Marco was vacant. Obviously this was the position which Foscarini had in mind for Biondo; he wished to see Biondo as lecturer in Venice because he expected that part of his literary activities there would be concerned with a history of Venice.

Biondo actually began to write such a history, probably in order to strengthen his chances for obtaining a lectureship at San Marco.[24] However, his work remained a fragment and it can no longer be ascertained whether he abandoned this project because Foscarini's efforts on his behalf had again run into obstacles, or whether Biondo's death in the summer of 1463 interrupted the writing of the history of Venice as it frustrated Foscarini's plans. The second lectureship at the school of San Marco remained vacant for another five years.

This interpretation of the nature of Foscarini's offer to Biondo is confirmed when we examine the second problem: that of Sabellico's official position. It is generally assumed that he received a salary from the government for his work on the history of Venice.[25] But Sabellico was actually a government-paid lecturer at the school of San Marco. This aspect of Sabellico's activities in Venice is generally overlooked.[26] And there are reasons for this oversight. The decree which appointed Navagero as public historiographer characterized him as a successor to Sabellico[27] and, since Navagero was primarily an official historiographer and had no contacts with the school of San Marco, it was assumed that Sabellico had held the same position. Moreover, while in most cases the decrees of appointment to lectureships in the schools of the Rialto and of San Marco are still extant, Sabellico's decree of appointment has not been found.[28] Nevertheless, there is documentary proof of Sabellico's appointment to a lectureship at the school of San Marco.

On 29 July 1505, the Venetian senate decreed that, because of his advancing years, Sabellico, who 'in urbe nostra humanitatis studia publice per viginta fere annos professus sit' be relieved of the burden of teaching but should continue to receive his full salary.[29] This statement permits the conclusion that Sabellico's salaried teaching activities in Venice began in the middle of the 1480s. Sabellico had come to Venice in 1485 to present to the doge and the senate his thirty-three books 'rerum

Venetarum ab urbe condita' which he had written in Verona. That his reward was the lectureship at the school of San Marco is confirmed by another document which gives some indication of Sabellico's functions in the school. Between 1462, when Foscarini tried to secure a position for Biondo, and 1485, when Sabellico came to Venice, the teaching staff at the school of San Marco had entirely changed. Perleo's chair was filled first by Filippo di Federighini and then, from 1466 on, by Benedetto Brognolo. The other lectureship had remained vacant until 1468 when Merula was appointed because he had distinguished himself teaching Greek and Latin, 'poesi et historia.'[30] In 1485 Merula moved to Milan to write the history of the Visconti and his place was taken by Giorgio Valla.[31] Valla died at the beginning of the year 1500. Then it was officially announced that Sabellico ought to be considered to hold by right and by merit the 'primum locum.'[32] The meaning of this announcement was elucidated by another official statement, issued four weeks later,[33] which stated that because Sabellico had been given Valla's place and was offering lectures in the mornings on Latin literature, his former functions should be taken over by Giovanni Baptista Scytha. In the mornings Scytha was to teach candidates for jobs in the chancellery; if he wanted to give lectures of a more general character to a larger audience they ought to be offered in the afternoons. Since Scytha was to take Sabellico's place, it can be assumed that before Valla's death Sabellico's primary function was to train candidates for jobs in the chancellery but that he also gave public lectures in the humanities.[34]

Thus, in the fifteenth century Venice was not paying a scholar so that he could give all his time to the writing of a history of Venice: Venice had no official historiographer. In these matters the Venetian attitude was not different from that of other rulers or governments. Literary services were rewarded by a job; it was expected that those who held these publicly paid jobs would, in addition to the duties which their job required, embark on literary activities which would enhance the reputation of the ruler or the government by which they were paid.

Once it is realized that the position of an official historiographer did not exist in the quattrocento but that the literary activities of a lecturer at the school of San Marco might include the writing of history, the answer may have been found to the third question: why ten years passed between the death of Sabellico and the appointment of Navagero. The answer might lie in the developments at the school of San Marco.

There were frequent changes in the staff of the school in the first

decade of the cinquecento; the story is a rather confusing one.[35] At the
beginning of the century there were three publicly paid lecturers at the
school of San Marco.[36] There was the chair originally established in 1443
which was now held by Benedetto Brognolo, one of whose chief functions
was the training of candidates for jobs in the chancellery. Then Sabellico
served in a position which until 1500 had been occupied by Giorgio Valla,
while Scytha had been moved into the position previously held by Sabellico. Scytha's tenure was brief and precarious. In 1500 he lost his job,
and it is not clear whether this occurred because his appointment was regarded from the outset as temporary or because his performances as lecturer were found to be unsatisfactory.[37] In any case he was replaced by
Gregory Amaseo, a better-known man with influential patrons.[38] But
Amaseo also had enemies and they used the argument that his appointment was illegal because it had not been preceded by a public competition;
hence, Amaseo was dismissed and replaced by Maserio.[39] A few years
later, in 1507, Maserio was the only lecturer teaching at the school of San
Marco: Sabellico had died in 1506; Brognolo had died some years earlier,
in 1502, and his successor, Leonico, left Venice for Rome in 1506.[40] The
shrinking of the teaching staff worried the Venetian senate enough that it
appealed to scholars to apply for these lectureships. This appeal was issued in December 1508[41] but it met with no response because it coincided
with the darkening of the political horizon. The league of Cambrai was
concluded in December 1508, and the war waged by this powerful coali-
tion against Venice made it an uninviting place. As a result of the war the
school of San Marco almost ceased to function because in the summer of
1509 Maserio disappeared. He had worked not only as teacher and scholar
but also as astrologer, and it was his bad luck to become a false prophet:
he prognosticated a complete victory for Venice after a short war. With
his reputation destroyed he fled;[42] in this crisis the government resorted
to an emergency solution and asked Hieronimo Calvo and Mario Becichemo to undertake the training of candidates for the chancellery.[43] As
soon as the war clouds were lifted the Council of Ten issued a decree to
re-establish the school of San Marco and appointed two lecturers: Gregory
Amaseo and Marco Musuro. In the decree announcing these appointments[44] Greek instruction was entrusted to Musuro and Latin instruction
to Amaseo; the latter received the additional assignment 'to write history.'[45] As in previous times one of the lecturers was expected to devote
the time left over from his teaching duties to the writing of history. In
short, there was no real lacuna between Sabellico's death and Navagero's

appointment; as soon as circumstances permitted, the government tried to recreate the situation which had existed in Sabellico's time.

Nevertheless, this is not the end of the story. The appointment of Musuro and Amaseo by the Council of Ten encountered hostility in the *Pregadi*. As in the case of Amaseo's appointment ten years earlier, the opponents claimed that the appointments were illegal because no public competition had taken place. The Council of Ten was forced to give in; the decree of appointment was withdrawn and the public competition for the two lectureships was opened. Musuro had no opponents and was elected lecturer in Greek, but Amaseo had several competitors and was defeated. Raphael Regio received the second lectureship.[46]

Musuro's position was characterized as a lectureship in Greek. Regio was a lecturer in humanities, but his chief duty was to instruct in Latin. These functions corresponded to Musuro's and Regio's scholarly interests: the former was an editor of Greek texts; the latter was chiefly interested in Latin literature. Thus, a division of labour between the lectureships at the school of San Marco had taken place: the lecturers now were specialists in particular fields of classical knowledge. Indeed, Musuro and Regio were philologists rather than *rhetores*.[47] This transformation in the character of the lectureships of the school of San Marco made it impossible to expect that its lecturers would concern themselves with the writing of modern history. The connection which in the past had existed between lecturing at San Marco and the composition of a Venetian history was severed. If the Venetian government wanted its actions and achievements immortalized in a work of history, a new independent position would have to be created. This was the situation which brought about the appointment of Navagero as official historiographer.

This story might give the impression that the establishment of the position of an official historiographer in Venice occurred almost accidentally, that it was caused by the quirks of institutional contingencies and personality factors. This would be a misunderstanding. The separation of work in Venetian history from instruction at the school of San Marco was a reflection of the emergence of new conceptions of humanistic studies and of history – conceptions which widened the divergence between the developments in the two fields. In other words, it was the change of concepts which brought about the developments which we have outlined and it might be appropriate to make a few suggestions which might help to throw light on these broader aspects of our study.

The school of San Marco was established to create in Venice a centre for the humanistic studies which were eagerly cultivated by the rulers and governments of other Italian states. Clearly, at the beginning the patrons of humanism among the Venetian patricians took great interest in the school and determined its appointments. Such enthusiasts for humanism were Lodovico Foscarini, whom we have found active in the affairs of the school of San Marco; Domenico Grimani; Francesco Barbaro,[48] to whose favour George of Trebizond owed his lectureship at San Marco; and Bernardo Giustiniani to whom Mario Filelfo owed his appointment.[49] All these Venetian patricians were primarily interested in attracting to Venice a humanist of great reputation. The decrees of appointments to the school of San Marco indicate that general excellence in poetry, rhetoric, grammar, and history was required[50] and this demand for an all-round distinction in the *bonae artes* was reflected in the characterization of these lecturers as *rhetores*.[51]

But the Venetian patricians who decided on the school of San Marco were, as well, foremost politicians, and political influence played its role in selecting lecturers. Political considerations are evident in both of Amaseo's appointments, in 1500 and 1512. In 1500 the French Ambassador appeared before the Senate and made a speech praising Amaseo.[52] The political reasons for his appointment in 1512 were revealed by Amaseo himself in his memoirs.[53] He had assisted Savorgnano in Friuli when Venice was fighting there against King Maximilian and when Amaseo came to Venice the doge promised him *motu proprio* 'la lettura de humanità de Venetia.' Amaseo believed he had an additional claim on the position because his ancestors had been partisans of Venice in Udine and he was deeply indignant when his appointment was annulled and an open competition for the position was called.

But who were the people who opposed Amaseo's appointments and insisted on public competition for the vacant lectureships at San Marco, who successfully resisted appointments which smacked of personal or political favouritism? We hear that in November 1503 a group of young scholarly gentlemen appeared before the government and demanded the appointment of Maserio in Amaseo's place.[54] In 1512 the decision of the Council of Ten ran into opposition in the *Pregadi*, and it might be suggested that the same young gentlemen who had demonstrated in 1503 — now either members of the *Pregadi* or with influence on relations and friends in the *Pregadi* — played their role in determining the senate to reject the appointments and to hold a public competition. The concerns of

the men who emerged victoriously from this competition give some indication of the interest and intentions of this opposition group. Regio was
an editor of Ovid, Quintilian, and Cicero and made the funeral speech
after the death of Aldus Manutius; Musuro was one of Aldus' most reliable collaborators, and most famous Greek expert, the editor of Aldus'
Plato edition.[55] With these two appointments, the lectureships at the
school of San Marco had become a chair for Greek and a chair for Latin.

By the end of the fifteenth and the beginnings of the sixteenth centuries Venice had become the recognized European centre for the revival
of classical literature through the activities of its printers, particularly
Aldus Manutius whose most famous enterprise was his Greek press.[56]
Aldus embarked on publishing authentic texts of Greek and Latin authors
in volumes economical enough to be bought by a large public; and this
project was favoured not only by many Venetian patricians but also by
several young Venetian nobles – Paolo Canale, Pietro Bembo, Vincenzo
Quirini, Andrea Navagero – who were active collaborators. Partnership
in the Venetian patriciate secured to this group a powerful voice when
questions of schools and of intellectual life had to be decided by the government. Obviously this group had an interest in having in the school of
San Marco lecturers who might co-operate in the enterprises of Aldus and
of other printers and who would be able to train future editors of Greek
and Roman texts. Material considerations probably were also involved in
making the *Pregadi* amenable to the urgings of this group: book production and printing shops represented a valuable economic asset. Thus, the
men who gravitated towards the Aldine Academy must probably be considered the moving force in shifting the tasks of the lecturers at the school
of San Marco from rhetoric and humanities to Greek and Latin philology.

The severance of the tie between the functions of the school of San
Marco and the task of writing a history of Venice was the result not only
of the increasingly philological orientation of humanist studies. Notions
about the service which history could render were also shifting.

Foscarini viewed history chiefly as a part of rhetoric. He believed that
the historian ought to illuminate the achievements of good men, coura-
geous men, and wise men.[57] If these tasks were not undertaken and merit
were to go unrewarded, men would lack guidance which the examples of
great men could give. To Foscarini the writings on the *viri illustres* must
have seemed patterns of good history; they should be presented in a decorous style to engrave the reported deeds on the mind of the reader. This
view of the function of the historian was determined by the Aristotelian

thesis that history and poetry are closely related and fulfil the same task
by different methods. This was the prevailing view in the quattrocento,[58]
and accounts for the fact that the decrees appointing the lecturers at the
school of San Marco stated that they were expected to teach poetry and
history. Even Sabellico's history with its comparisons between the greatness of Rome and the greatness of Venice, fitted the scheme, although his
pedestrian style hardly fulfils the ideals of humanist historiography.

There are indications that, with the beginning of the sixteenth century,
this rhetorical concept of history began to lose appeal in Venice. It is
significant that in the announcement of 1512, proposing Amaseo as lecturer at the school of San Marco, the commission to write history appears
as an afterthought, quite apart from the description of his other duties.[59]
Actually, at this time several writers were occupied with composing histories of recent events. They sought permission to study the registries of
the chancellery and received it 'pro pleniore rerum veritate, quae in
historia pars est potentissima.'[60]

A pragmatic concept of history began to develop: clarification of the
causal connection between historical events became the purpose of historical investigation. The discussion of Navagero's appointment gives
some indication of this change of approach. Sanuto viewed this appointment with some disgust[61] because he considered the humanist training of
Navagero insufficient preparation. In Sanuto's opinion the appointment
ought to have gone to Andrea Mocenigo who knew how to deal with contemporary events because he had almost finished a history of the league
of Cambrai; he had used the registers of the chancellery for this purpose.
Navagero's decree of appointment was written by the head of the Venetian
chancellery, and it shows the appropriate decorous commonplaces.[62] Only
elegantly and eloquently written histories, it is said, can assure that the
great deeds and men of the present would be known by posterity. But the
introduction to the decree also employed arguments of a practical political nature. Practical politics requires the maintenance of a high reputation because reputation frequently can achieve more than force. There
was, it is further stated, a particular need for the continuation of Sabellico's history because the last few years had been full of deeds worth
remembering – never, since the foundation of the city, had such great
things been accomplished in so short a time.

This sentence of the decree alludes to the events which produced a
heightened and more pragmatic interest in history. In Florence the revolutionary upheaval brought about by the invasion of Charles VIII in 1494

had raised new questions about the forces working in history and had stimulated historical inquiry to discover the causes for the disaster which had overtaken the city. Pragmatic treatments of history took their place beside the rhetorical histories of the humanists and began to supplant them. For a while – for almost fifteen years – Venice remained somewhat distant from the events which occurred in Italy after the French invasion. But, with its desperate struggle for existence against the league of Cambrai, Venice, too, became conscious of the need to study the past in order to secure a future; the Venetians too discovered the usefulness of history as a guide in practical politics.

Thus, the philological emphasis in humanistic studies coincided with a new pragmatic interest in history aroused by the events of the recent past. These developments formed the intellectual background for the creation of the special position of an official historiographer in Venice. But when history was placed in the context of politics rather than in that of literature a foreign humanist could no longer be commissioned to write Venetian history. This had to be entrusted to a man who knew the working of Venetian politics: to a member of the Venetian ruling group. It is characteristic of the succession of Venetian official historiographers that, beginning with Navagero, they all were Venetian patricians. Navagero's appointment did not represent, as the Venetian myth wants it, the continuation of a tradition reaching far back into the past; it arose from a new and unique situation and signified the beginning of a new trend. Navagero must be regarded as the first official historiographer of Venice.

NOTES

1 Giovanni degli Agostini, *Notizie istorico-critiche intorno la vita, e le opere degli scrittori Viniziani* (Venezia 1752, 1754) ; Marco Foscarini, *Della letteratura Veneziana libri otto* (Padova 1752) ; *Degli istorici delle cose Veneziane i quali hanno scritto per pubblico decreto* (Venezia 1718-22) ; Angelo Maria Quirini, *Tiara et purpura Veneta ab anno 1379 ad annum 1759 serenissimae reipublicae Venetae a Civitate Brixiae dicata* (Brescia 1761) ; Apostolo Zeno, *Dissertazioni Vossiane, cioè giunte e osservazioni intorno agli storici Italiani che hanno scritto Latinamente* (Venezia 1752-3).

2 See Andrea da Mosto, *L'Archivio di stato di Venezia* (Bibliothèque des 'Annales Institutorum,' v, Roma 1937), i, p. 3

3 For a recent treatment of this issue, see Caetano Cozzi, 'Cultura, politica e religione nella "Pubblica Storiografia" Veneziana del '500,' *Bollettino dell' Istituto di storia della società e dello stato Veneziano*, v-vi (1963-4),

215-94. Cozzi's presentation of the facts is extremely useful, but I do not fully agree with the interpretative aspects of his essay.

4 Wallace K. Ferguson, *The Renaissance in Historical Thought* (Cambridge, Mass., 1948), pp. 12-17

5 A description of Foscarini's life can be found in Agostini, *Notizie istorico-critiche*, I, 45-107; for a more recent discussion, see G.B. Picotti, 'Le Lettere di Lodovico Foscarini,' *L'Ateneo Veneto*, XXXII, 1 (1909), 21-49. Picotti directs attention to Foscarini's humanistic correspondence and describes the codex in which it is preserved. I have used a copy of this codex preserved in the Biblioteca Comunale of Treviso.

6 See Percy Gothein, *Francesco Barbaro* (Berlin 1932), pp. 301-4

7 See Treviso, Biblioteca Comunale, cod. 85, nos. 198, 199, 249, 282 (letters by Foscarini to Bernardo Giustiniani), hereinafter cod. 85; on Giustiniani, see P.H. Labalme, *Bernardo Giustiniani: A Venetian of the Quattrocento* (Rome 1969)

8 For a document which shows Foscarini and Bessarion working together, see *Libri commemoriali* (R. Deputazione Veneta, *Monumenti storici*, serie I, vol. x), v, 198-200

9 See *La Civiltà Veneziana del quattrocento* (ed. Fondazione Giorgio Cini, Firenze 1957), p. 224

10 Other Venetians made similar efforts, see Giovanni Zippel, 'Lorenzo Valla e le origini della storiografia Umanista a Venezia,' *Rinascimento*, VII (1957), 93-133

11 Cod. 85, no. 84, *De laudibus poetae scribentis istorias*: 'Proderit etiam maxime ad bene consulendum et persuadendum Senatui Veneto istoriarum suarum cognitio, nam etsi rationes plurimum possint, exempla maxime movent nostororum presentium temporum.'

12 Cod. 85, no. 160

13 Cod. 85, no. 186, *De laudibus Laurentii Monachi et optimis antiquorum Venetorum moribus*. On Lorenzo de Monacis, see Mario Poppi, 'Ricerche sulla vita e cultura del Notaio e Cronista Lorenzo de Monacis, Cancelliere Cretese,' *Studi Veneziani*, IX (1967), 153-86

14 Cod. 85, no. 204, written July 1462. Parts of this letter have been published, first by Agostini, *Notizie istorico-critiche*, I, 76-7, and by Marco Foscarini, *Della letteratura*, pp. 230-1, and recently by R. Fubini in the article 'Flavio Biondo' in the *Dizionario biografico degli Italiani* (hereinafter DBI). But since these authors assume that Foscarini had the creation of the position of an official historiographer in mind, and since none of these authors gives the full text of Foscarini's letter, I shall quote the passages of this letter on which I base my interpretation which differs from that of these authors.

15 On Foscarini's role in Mantua and the data of his stay there, see G.B. Picotti, *La Dieta di Mantova e la politica de' Veneziani* (R. Deputazione Veneta, *Miscellanea di storia Veneta*, serie III, vol. IV, Venezia 1912)

16 'Tempus postquam ex Mantua discessimus nobis tacendi visum fuit, nunc loquendi futurum arbitramur. Ideo tibi im primis cujus doctrinae dicta

facta consilia facultatesque dedicavi, studia nostra polliceor, si Venetis rebus posteritati commendandis quae olim fuerat, tibi mens est.'

17 'Cum primum ex legatione Venetias applicavi, coepi nostrorum Senatorum mentes perquirere et ipsis persuadere quod cum integerrimo patre Hieronimo Barbadico mecumque sentirent, quos diversorum studiorum cognovimus, quia aderant Georgius Trapesundeus, Petrus Perleo, Marius Philelphus miles qui certatim et gratis se pulcherrimo muneri offerebant. Noluimus publice edictum de industria tua eligenda proponere ne concurrentibus multis neglectam Senatus Venetus operam tuam haberet, quam non suspirasset habendam. Interim Forum Julii meae fidei commendatum est quo tempore cesserunt Georgius et Marius; Petrus tepescere videtur. Quapropter ego in dies magis et magis ascendor, et tempus perficiendorum votorum nostrorum advenisse censeo ...'

18 'Quas ob res volui meam ad te opinionem deferre quoniam designato successore nostro prope diem in patriam nobis redeundum est, ubi omnia faciam quae te velle arbitrabor et honori tuo accedere intellexero. Semper desideriis tuis praesto ero. Nulla res quae gravissimos patronos huius causae interdum remorata est, me deterrebit; quid possim in tanta re publica nescio vel verius me parum posse scio. Hoc tamen tibi suadeas vellim: majoribus officiis dignitati coeptisque tuis favebo ... Ego si auctoritate aut gratia tantum potero quantum te velle arbitror, desiderium quod jam diu parturiebat effundam, et te in amplissimo locupletissimorum ac maximorum scribentium gradu constituemus ...'

19 For the following, see Bruno Nardi, 'Letteratura e cultura Veneziana del Quattrocento,' *Civiltà Veneziana del quattrocento,* pp. 101-45

20 On Perleo and his appointment see also Giuseppe Pavanello, *Un maestro del quattrocento (Giovanni Aurelio Augurello)* (Venezia 1905), p. 4

21 The decree appointing Mario Filelfo is printed in Castellani, 'Documenti veneziani inediti relativi a Francesco e Mario Filelfo,' *Archivio storico Italiano,* XVII (1896), 370. For the intrigues involving Mario Filelfo, Perleo, and George of Trebizond, see Guillaume Favre, *Mélanges d'histoire littéraire* (Genève 1856), I, pp. 90-3, and Arnaldo della Torre, *Di Antonio Vinciguerra e delle sue satire* (Rocca S. Casciano 1902), pp. 16 ff.; a documented story of these rivalries can be found in Ferdinando Gabotto, 'Un nuovo contributo alla storia dell' Umanesimo Ligure,' *Atti della Società Ligure di storia patria,* XXIV (1892), 79 ff.

22 For Trebizond's appointment, see the brief notice in Malipiero, 'Annali Veneti,' *Archivio storico Italiano,* VII, 2 (1844), 653. The decree appointing George of Trebizond was published in an appendix to the article by Giorgio Castellani, 'Giorgio da Trebisonda, maestro di eloquenza a Vicenza e a Vinegia,' *Nuovo archivio veneto,* XI (1896), 139-41. The decree stated that Trebizond received this appointment because he had dedicated his translation of Plato's *Laws* to the Venetian senate; Trebizond, in the introduction to this translation, maintained that the Venetian constitution was the realization of the Platonic idea. See my article 'The Venetian Constitu-

tion in Florentine Political Thought,' *Florentine Studies*, ed. Nicolai Rubinstein (London 1968), p. 469.

23 See Gabotto, '*Un nuovo contributo,*' p. 62; Perleo died early in 1463

24 Flavio Biondo, *Scritti inediti e rari*, ed. Bartolomeo Nogara *(Studi e Testi*, XLVII [Roma 1927]), pp. 77-89; for speculations why Biondo's work remained a fragment, see *ibid.*, p. clviii-clxi, and Fubini in his article on Biondo in DBI

25 Such statements have behind them the authority of Eduard Fueter, *Geschichte der neueren Historiographie* (München 1925), p. 30

26 Despite the clear statement in Sabellico's biography by Apostolo Zeno which precedes the publication of Sabellico's Venetian history in *Degli istorici delle cose Veneziane*, I, p. xxxix: 'Venetias igitur appulit ea tantum de causa, ut humaniores literas publice traderet ...'

27 'Essendo adonque ... Marco Antonio Sabellico, da poi scripte et reducte in historia per decreto publico et cum publico premio le cose de la Republica nostra fin al tempo de la guerra de Ferrara, manchato da questa vita ...' The decree was published by Pennato in *Archivio Veneto*, III (1872), 256-7; a further link between Sabellico and Navagero was that they were both custodians of the books left to Venice by Bessarion, but it is erroneous to assume that this job was the justification for their salaries.

28 I searched in the Venetian Archivio di Stato in vain, and I was told that many others had been equally unsuccessful.

29 Published in Sabellico's *Vita* by Apostolo Zeno, *Degli istorici delle cose Veneziane*, I, pp. lvii-lviii

30 Merula's decree of appointment was published by Segarizzi, 'Cenni sulle Scuole Pubbliche a Venezia,' *Istituto Veneto*, LXXV, 1 (1915-16), 651. Merula was expected to write a history of Venice, according to Sabellico; see his letter, printed in Sabellicus, *Opera* (Basilea 1560), IV, p. 450: 'Noluisset credo ab aliis scribi, quae ipse aut noluit scribere, aut non potuit.'

31 His decree of appointment was published by Francesco Foffano, 'Marco Musuro Professore di Greco a Padova ed a Venezia,' *Nuovo archivio veneto*, III (1892), 472; the decree called Giorgio Valla 'non solum in humanitate scientificum sed etiam in philosophia et in metaphysica praestantem optimis moribus et exemplari vita ornatum.'

32 'Sit ille qui primum obtineat locum, quem jure meritoque obtinere debeat.' see Marino Sanuto, *Diarii*, ed. Rinaldo Fulin *et al.* (Venezia 1879-1903), III, c. 136.

33 Sanuto, *Diarii*, III, c. 178

34 An allusion to this activity might be found in a letter by Sabellicus, *Opera*, IV, p. 400: 'Frequentat domum meam nobilium adulescentulorum coetus ingens, qui dant matutinis horis mihi operam, suntque plerique senatorum filii.'

35 Pavanello, *Un maestro del quattrocento*, pp. 23-5, gives the main facts although the description which I give seems to me less speculative and more correct. Nevertheless it is astonishing that this most useful book by Pavanello is rarely mentioned or quoted.

36 The situation at the beginning of the sixteenth century is well described by Sanuto, *Chronichetta*, ed. R. Fulin (Venezia 1880), pp. 50 ff.

37 Sanuto, *Diarii*, III, c. 249, calls Scytha 'non ben grato a li scolari'

38 On Amaseo, see the article in DBI

39 The crucial document can be found in Sanuto, *Diarii*, V, cc. 437-8, where it is stated that Amaseo's appointment was made 'contra consuetudinem huius civitatis nostrae, quae est quod, antequam huiusmodi lecturae conferrantur, fiat periculum plurium competitorum qui postea balotari debeant in hoc Consilio ut eruditior deligatur ...' For these events, see also Sanuto, *Diarii*, V, cc. 228, 333, 433, 592, 599.

40 On Leonico's appointment, see the decree published by Foffano, 'Marco Musuro,' 471, and Sanuto, *Diarii*, VI, c. 117. On his withdrawal from Venice, see Sanuto, *Diarii*, VI, c. 433.

41 Printed in Foffano, 'Marco Musuro,' 471, but see also Sanuto, *Diarii*, VII, c. 682; the lecturer was required to instruct in the *studia humanitatis* and to prepare young men for a career in the chancellery.

42 Sanuto, *Diarii*, VIII, c. 384

43 See Sanuto, *Diarii*, XII, c. 296; Cecil Clough, the author of the article on Mario Becichemo in the DBI, is in error when he writes that Becichemo lectured in Venice from 1509 to 1517. Sanuto's report makes clear that Becichemo's and Calvo's employment was not a regular appointment but an emergency measure, and this is then confirmed by the decree of appointments in 1512 (see below, note 44), which said that the lectureships at the school of San Marco had been vacant for three years. The decree stated that 'ab urbe condita' it had been a praiseworthy institution to have 'semper in civitate publico stipendio literarum professores utriusque linguae eruditione praestantes ... Verum triennium iam labitur quod omnis publica lectura ... omissa est.'

44 Dated 23 January 1512, published by Foffano, 'Marco Musuro,' 473-4

45 'qui D. Gregorius teneatur historiam scribere.'

46 The facts are lengthily reported by Sanuto, *Diarii*, XIII, cc. 406-7, 485-6. Regio's name had frequently appeared among the candidates for lectureships at San Marco.

47 The reference to the 'professores utriusque linguae' in the decree quoted above in note 43 is a characteristic reflection of this new trend. See also Marcantonio Michiel's Diary, Venice, Biblioteca Correr, MSS Cicogna, cod. 2848, f. 8ᵛ: 'Fu eletto alla lettura Grecha M. Marco Musuro et alla Latina M. Rafael Regio.'

48 See Deno John Geanakoplos, *Greek Scholars in Venice* (Cambridge, Mass., 1962), p. 30

49 See Francesco Filelfo's letter to Bernardo Giustiniani of 1460, printed in Philelphus, *Opera* (Venice 1502), p. 115

50 For this see the decrees of appointment of Filelfo (above, note 21), of George of Trebizond (above, note 22), and of Merula (above, note 30)

51 As in the decree appointing Merula: '... quia oratoria facultas rebus publicis maxime necessaria est, constituit dominatio nostra pro eruditione im-

primis juvenum patriciorum et aliorum civium nostrorum publico salario in hac civitate duos rhetores ...'

52 On the intervention of the French ambassador in favour of Amaseo, see Sanuto, *Diarii*, III, c. 249. The ambassador had his reasons: Amaseo had written a pro-French vaticinium, dedicated to the French ambassador.

53 See the *Diarii Udinesi* (R. Deputazione Veneta, *Monumenti Storici*, vol. XI, serie III), I, p. 539

54 See Sanuto, *Diarii*, v, c. 333, but it ought to be mentioned that Maserio's appointment also had a political aspect; in the decree of his appointment it is mentioned that 'de statu nostro optime meruit cum esset apud apostolicum legatum in Hongaria.' See Sanuto, *Diarii*, v, c. 592.

55 On Musuro, Geanakoplos, *Greek Scholars*, chap. 5, pp. 111-66, although the description given on pp. 143 ff. about the situation at the school of San Marco is not quite correct. For Regio placing the Romans above the Greeks, see his speech *De laudibus eloquentiae* (Venice 1492). The tendency of making a sharp separation between a chair for Greek and a chair for Latin might be found first in the decree of Leonico's appointment of 1504, published by Foffano, 'Marco Musuro,' p. 471: '... qui elegendus teneatur etiam legere in hac Urbe nostra Auctores graecos per commodam lectionem.' Perhaps it should be added that Musuro's successor (since 1518), the Graecist Victor Faustus, and Regio's successor (since 1520) the Latinist Battista Egnazio, were both close to Aldus.

56 On the Venetian Greek press and the significance of Greek studies in Venice, see Geanakoplos, *Greek Scholars*, pp. 279 ff.

57 From Foscarini's letter to Biondo: 'Tria sunt hominum genera, quae per te illustrari cupio et tu nec mihi negare pro tua pietate, nec ipsis deesse pro tua virtute debes: Optimos scilicet fortes et sapientes. Optimis enim viris, qui per sanctimoniam ex vita nostra demigraverunt, major gloria debetur quam templis auratis quae tu tanta religione colis. Pro fortissimorum laude arma litteraria non minus capescenda arbitror quam illi militaribus usi sint strenue in patriae salute defendenda. Sapientium vero vitae et mores ornandi sunt, quoniam omnibus institutionibus anteponuntur.'

58 For a detailed discussion of the 'theory and practice of history in the fifteenth century' and the rise of a more pragmatic concept of history, see my book *Machiavelli and Guicciardini* (Princeton 1965), particularly chaps. 5 and 6.

59 See above, note 45

60 On 20 August 1515, Sanuto received permission to 'videre libros, litteras et scripturas Cancellariae ... pro pleniore rerum veritate, quae in historia pars est potentissima.' This decree is printed in 'Documenti per servire alla storia della tipografia Veneziana,' *Archivio Veneto*, XXIII (1882), 184. I am taking up the question of the use of archives by Renaissance historians in another context.

61 See Sanuto, *Diarii*, XXI, cc. 484-5

62 For a full text of the decree, see *Archivio Veneto*, III (1872), 256-7, but the salient passages have been frequently reprinted, most recently by Cozzi,

'Cultura, politica e religione,' 225-6; on pp. 222 ff., Cozzi gives an interesting analysis of the various possible candidates for the position of an official
historiographer; see also his recent article, 'Marin Sanudo il Giovane:
dalla cronaca alla storia,' *Rivista storica Italiana*, LXXX (1968), 297-314.
In general Cozzi seems to me slightly to underestimate the novel element
in the creation of this position. Of course, the first two appointees – Navagero and Bembo – were humanists, but they were also men experienced in
political affairs. Thus, the creation of an official historiographer is a sign
of a break with the rhetorical humanist tradition.

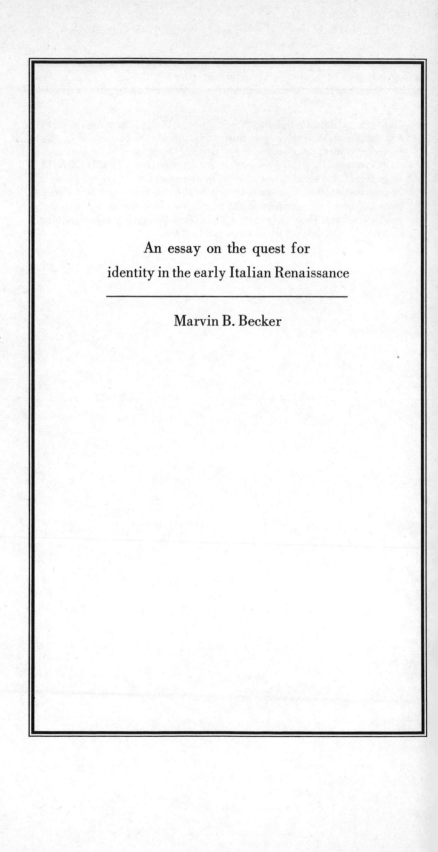

An essay on the quest for
identity in the early Italian Renaissance

Marvin B. Becker

Post-Enlightenment European romanticism and modern scholarship have lavished sympathy upon the nobility and northern European clergy of the later Middle Ages. Such tender concern has been amply justified by the many hard-won historical insights achieved over the last century and a half. Perhaps the best example of this solicitude has been evinced by Professor Gerhart Ladner in his recent study of alienation and order in the late medieval world.[1] Here the reader is made to experience many of the stresses and strains of a culture that would proclaim an adherence to both the order of this world and the justice of the next. As Ladner and others have shown, the Dantean metaphor of the pilgrim lost in the dark forest has become a symbol of medieval estrangement. Jacques Le Goff reaches similar conclusions although viewing medieval society from the colder vantage point of modern anthropology à la Claude Levi-Straus. He sees late medieval culture as the locale for the assertion of spiritual doubt and Christian guilt at the expense of the hardy, less reflective values of an older military chivalry. This is particularly in evidence when reading late medieval romances where conflicting loyalties to God, the *patria*, and *la donna* created splits in personality and divisions in the psyche. Lately, George Duby has been studying the tensions in twelfth- and thirteenth-century society caused by familial aggression and the brutalization required to survive the hard career of knight errantry, while R. Nelli has indicated the explosive, often damaging, quality of medieval eroticism.[2] Arno Borst has contrasted the ideals of knighthood with its reality; for him the twelfth and thirteenth centuries witnessed a noble social stratum caught between lordship and service, living in a world of 'Utopian exaggeration.'[3] This world of lost or, at least, muted causes seldom fails to evoke an empathy; the language of historical narrative employed by modern scholars is replete with metaphors that would place this suffering world in the most affectionate light: sunset, twilight, and autumn are but a few.

If Ladner, Kantorowicz, and especially Oberman and Leff are correct in their assessments of the psychological tensions and intellectual ambiguities in late medieval culture, then more than empathy for northern Europeans is called for. Eugenio Garin and Charles Trinkaus have indicated the extent to which Italians were involved in the tense nominalist controversies of the early fourteenth century.[4] The awesome notion of the 'absolute power of God' disturbed theologians and scientists alike. The hopeful expectation that an easy synthesis might be constructed between the promptings of faith and the teachings of reason was gravely disappointed. Doubt was soon cast on the possibility of maintaining a scientific base for theological inquiry. Criticism of prevailing epistemologies reflected the influence of the new and disconcerting insights of Duns Scotus and William of Ockham. Facile generalizations rendered by thirteenth-century Aristotelians convinced of man's educability came under criticism. Indeed, any sustained appreciation for the spiritual matrix of early Italian humanism would necessarily include a ready acknowledgment that Petrarch, Coluccio Salutati, Poggio Bracciolini, Marsiglio Ficino, and others responded to that philosophic and psychological dilemma characteristic of the autumnal northern Middle Ages. Like their contemporaries they sought answers in Christian scepticism and fideism and, while rejecting particular intellectual forms and even the language of discourse, they continued to harbour similar doubts.

Our purpose might reasonably be to consider the seemingly sturdy bourgeoisie of early Renaissance Italy with the same sympathy as is regularly extended to their northern confrères. Prey to the insecurities of late medieval culture, these sons of north Italy still struggled to uphold the structures and values of a public world. Should not their expenditure of energy in business and politics, against a background of religious anxiety, merit our deepest regard? A reading of the private correspondence of the fourteenth-century merchant Francesco Datini, or the sixteenth-century artist Michelangelo, reveals the spiritual and metaphysical travail of an Italian bourgeois attempting to effect a safe Christian passage through the menacing seas of this life.

During the thirteenth century, northern Italy does differ from most of Europe in that the alternative of a civic culture is more readily available to a large segment of the population. Indeed, public education, the notarial arts, rhetorical training, and political careers are attractive possibilities for a people caught up in a commercial and urban revolution. In fact, newer scientific and scholastic developments do not immediately make the same inroads in the south as in the north. A forceful defence of the position that the triumph of civic education in Italy well antedated the coming of thirteenth-century northern philosophy could be advanced. It is a commonplace of intellectual history to suggest that scholastic thought did not flower so early in the south as in the north.[5]

What is striking in the city-state milieu of Italy has not been underscored sufficiently. At first blush it would appear that the north is more replete with tension and philosophic controversy. This generalization, if extended through the fourteenth century, appears still more convincing. The sense of tragedy north of the Alps is accompanied by a high degree of alienation. Most punishing of all to the traditional sense of identity of the intellectual were the anguished theological inquiries and interminable religious allegorizing. Endlessly, the unknowability of God was proclaimed and his arbitrary and capricious power celebrated by despairing prophets.

At the outset the Italian burgher seems so much less troubled and yet he, too, was not without the ingredients for, in modern parlance, a first-rate identity crisis. By the thirteenth century so many of his traditional ego supports were in process of deterioration. His landscape of socially defined roles was cluttered, while his schema of ceremonial identities was utterly confused. Chivalric codes were not likely to produce responsible leaders capable of performing the humdrum tasks of government. Extensive violence among magnates indicated that an education in courtesy seldom produced a minimal respect for burgher law. Messianic visions and erotic poetry contributed little to the maintenance of what contemporary documents euphemistically referred to as 'the peaceful and tranquil condition of the *civitas*.' Instead they agitated the public conscience and increased disaffection among the various orders of medieval society.[6] From two different vantage points the *polis* was seen as repressive and fatally compromised. Town law was as little sympathetic to the code of adultery as it was to the eschatology that fed the aspirations for justice of a working class. Yet the burghers themselves were torn: they too harboured deep sympathy for a society that would live in tune with the rule of love that prevailed when Christ and his apostles trod the earth.

The conscience of medieval townsmen of north Italy was beset by enervating conflict: On the one hand, they proclaimed the benefits of an open society with its insistence upon the nobility of deeds, while on the other they boasted pride of lineage. Similarly, they rhapsodized upon the *topoi* of work and thrift, while despising the *gente nuova* who subscribed so wholeheartedly to these virtues. Their psyches were flushed with patriotic impulse and yet they entertained monumental suspicions against aggrandizing and expansionist foreign policy: Did not the people won in wars of conquest frequently carry the dread taint of treason in their blood? Although committed to doctrines of municipal expansion, the native-born citizen saw certain of the subject population damned simply because they were alleged to be the progeny of Roman conspirators and traitors. Moreover, while announcing the virtues of popular education and vernacular culture, this self-same citizenry continued to harbour abiding prejudice against the immigrant and his sons, whose successful acculturation in a new urban milieu was the highest tribute to be paid their *polis*.[7]

Their own society, measured against Christian perfection, was found corrupt and disordered. At work was a contest between a traditional hierarchical vision and a more horizontal view of social groupings. No cadre of their society appeared to be performing in accord with a vertical conception wherein *magnates et potentes* were animated by true civic concerns.[8] Indeed, the scale was sometimes in process of being overturned, for prudence and historical experience instructed burghers to look to the upper echelons of society for the names of those seeking to betray the *polis*. Seldom did kings, princes, and knights perform politically in conformity with their proclaimed ideals. Burgher literature, which is after all our best source for these attitudes, expressed its deepest dismay when pope and prelate behaved at variance with sacred Christian principle. Soon this distress was converted to humour, thereby becoming bearable, as the novella thrived on the play of false religious identities. The reader stood forewarned always to keep in mind that those seeming to be most at home in the ceremonial orbit of the church were instead despicable strangers to the teachings of Christ. This was a prize sample of social wisdom; bourgeois literature from Boccaccio through Aretino prospered by reiterating the theme of social roles and ascribed rank.

This popular and colourful literature throbbed with a dominant message: Those attempting to navigate the treacherous waters of the social world should remember that religious signs and group identities are always misleading and, if they desire safe harbour, they would be wise to discount the religious world of appearances. Medieval poets constructed high tragedy from this spiritual disarray while still believing that *renovatio* (renewal) of temporal and spiritual realms was imminent. To be 'cast down' in this world might be the beginnings of spiritual rebirth: Did not Dante's pilgrim have to descend to the depths of hell before commencing his sacred ascent? The core of proverbial wisdom in the quattrocento emanated from a commitment to the literary observation that those without friends, political influence, or wealth were fated for destruction. Not a Poggio Bracciolini, Giovanni Cavalcanti, or Machiavelli expressed anything but absolute confidence in the irrevocable decline of the solitary voyager. And yet, against this could be juxtaposed another abiding piety voiced by chroniclers, diarists, and letter writers who lavished further

sympathy upon a beleaguered bourgeoisie. For a very different reason
the world was ever-menacing: Those most dependent upon wealth or influence would soon be cast down by the wheel of *fortuna*. Conventional
morality functioned in this way to augment tension and make passage
through this life precarious.

The prevalent idea of how to confront these harsh realities was expressed by Boccaccio's celebration of wit, Sacchetti's apotheosis of nig-
gardly prudence, and Machiavelli's hosannas to *virtù*.[9] There was also
that enormous civic legacy of the humanists – Salutati, Bruni, Poggio,
and the rest – which stood as a stunning tribute to the need for repression
of the citizen's own irrational proclivities in favour of the ordered *polis*
circumscribed by law.[10] In any case, this literature is characterized by an
intense appreciation of the threat that the political, social, and economic
world of the times posed to the always vulnerable individual. The motif
of human frailty was elevated to a poetic ideal by Petrarch and a metho-
dological construct by Machiavelli. For civic humanists such as Salutati
and Bruni, all who ruled must acknowledge this fragility. By the early
quattrocento, so sensitive had philosophy and literature become to the
plight of the earth-bound voyager that they furnished him with a bifur-
cated code which recognized that the highest standards prevailing in the
realm of personal ethics could not possibly be realized by the most virtuous of men in the public world. These secular counsels were constantly
being advanced to men whose Christian anxieties were never quieted.

We also observe the weakening of confidence in those ritual bonds
fixing loyalty and affection between men. Feudal ties of obligation had
not been firm in north Italy for more than a century. Italy remained as
the single great territory unable to produce a chivalric epic. Instead she
was to borrow from France a poetry epitomizing ideal courtly relationships. The indigenous vernacular poetry of very recent origin voicing
trust in the social force of *amicitia* and *amore* was losing its élan by the
early trecento. For Dante and his circle the secrets of the 'gentle heart'
could be understood only by a spiritual élite. *Amore* was directed toward
the Virgin herself, while Christ became lord of courtesy; most of the
contemporary world, however, was condemned to live without hope in an
inferno.

Traditional concepts of loyalty and a high spiritualization of love
did little to form the intimate world of men or tame anti-social behaviour.
Dante, Boccaccio, Sacchetti, and other literati saw the contemporary
scene as the locale for aggression, seldom restricted by moral bonds or ties

of friendship. Major chroniclers, from Matteo Villani and Stefani to Giovanni Cavalcanti, instructed their Florentine compatriots that traditional allegiances were valueless in troubled times; to rely upon the medieval staples of friendship and fidelity was to be a victim of *fortuna*. The motors of communal society were seen as naked self-interest and quest for power. New generalizations of historical interpretation were emerging, not the least of these being man's insatiable capacity to inflict harm on others without incurring divine wrath. The moral stance of the chronicler stood at variance with the cruel ethos he felt surrounding him. His historical metaphor was now drawn from the language of disease and pestilence. A century before Machiavelli images of bestiality and nature-run-rampant were historiographical coin.

In cultural historical terms, what occurred was not that there was less *amicitia* and *amore* in society, but rather that neither was to be celebrated programmatically, elevated to the level of an ideal or employed as a tool for understanding. The middle of the trecento witnessed the last of the great Tuscan poets of the 'sweet new style'; the Petrarchan lyric soon took over with its insistence upon the evanescence of friendship and love. Indeed, human emotions were characterized by this very impermanence and ideals never served as a bridge to God. A sense of subjectivity was evidenced so that the poet observed his feelings about objects rather than the thing in itself.

Love was a disease for the Petrarchan but, unlike the medieval man, he was condemned to seek no cure.[11] The chroniclers did discover pockets of isolated virtue inhabited by valorous men responsive to the promptings of *amicitia* and *amore;* but death, piteous and ineffectual, was generally their historical reward. By the second quarter of the quattrocento, Poggio and even Bruni voiced doubts concerning the modest possibility of sustaining the human community. The all-too-familiar literary motif of hypocrisy was firmly installed in humanistic political discourse. Renaissance prose writers had become staunch expositors of a comic view depicting men as bound together by their addiction to vice. Sometimes this view was extended to include a tragic dialectic between aristocratic ideals and burgher realities. Fantasy offered some release with visions of women who combined the virtues of burgher fidelity with aristocratic passion, in a Renaissance counterpart of the unwieldy *Playboy* philosophy.[12]

More relevant, but less charming, is a stricter impulse detectable in public policy formulated over the second half of the trecento. Gone were so many of the hortatory frescoes adorning walls in the town-council

halls of north Italy.[13] Likewise, appeals by government to the good nature of the citizens were diminishing. Peace officials for making voluntary
treaties among feuding families, communal-sponsored religious ceremonies staged to produce domestic accord, and even the ritual of exchang-
ing the kiss of peace gave way before the onset of more coercive public
policies. Judicial dispensation and remission of fines also dwindled.
Artistic styles became more controlled and geometric, while rhetorical
modes were standardized. The world of the *polis* was more commanding
and the classical revival added monumentality and durability to the
milieu.[14]

As the individual in the novella stood isolated and less able to rely on
traditional supports, there followed a withering away of comforting
political ideology. That 'demystification of politics' described by Ernst
Kantorowicz is well in process.[15] Neither citizen nor *polis* could hope to
take a sure reading of political longitude by siting on either of those
twin stars in the medieval firmament – empire or papacy. The structure
of north Italian chronicles illustrates the problems of attempting to sub-
sume recent historical experience under traditional medieval schema.[16]

Classical historiographical style comes to the fore with its abiding
sense of distance from the recent past. Imitation of Roman writers was accompanied by this feeling of disjunction from the historical universals of
the late Middle Ages. History became the record of participation in a public world whose temporal bounds were set by presently shared political experience. Politics was viewed as a brutal struggle for office and advantage
conducted by men to whom the principles of Ghibellinism and Guelfism
were at best anachronisms and at worst pious frauds.[17] Old political
nomenclature was disvalued; only when such terms could be translated
into patriotic, civic rhetoric did they retain even a shade of their former
meaning. The language of political discourse in the council halls of Florence displayed a remoteness from Christian metaphor and medieval
political cosmology. Over the fourteenth century there was a decline in
the messianic tradition and a lessening of confidence in the efficacy of
Christian agencies for moral regeneration.

The erosion of the play of the sacred in the north Italian public world
paralleled the decline of traditional ego supports for the individual. As
the *polis* was loosened from the universal frame, the individual was likewise deprived of facets of his ascribed identity. The north Italian towns-
man was required to confront a society which had limited sympathy for
the prevailing business ethic. Further, the solace a burgher might receive

from membership in an extended family (*consorteria*) was on the wane. Even his security formerly gained from activities in the family business was being dissipated. Capitalism was becoming more impersonal; holding companies were being formed as the more intimate business structures of an older world receded. Wealth tended to be liquid so that estates were readily divisible and family fortunes not so durable. Patrimony and ancestral property were easily alienable; as a result fewer clan holdings survived intact over the generations. Primogeniture was not so prevalent, more usually all heirs shared equally in bequests. Common living quarters, joint ownership of property, clan fortifications, familial codes of honour, councils of the *consorteria*, all these were in decline in late medieval Florence.[18]

The burgher now stood in greater isolation than ever before. Separate households and the idea of privacy were displacing the heightened sociability of the extended family with its communal style of life. In Florence strict enforcement of law served to weaken the *consorteria*, while factious politics and the differential effects of economic trends militated against the old solidarity.[19] Once the medieval *polis* had been throbbing with expressions of that associative impulse characteristic of communal society. Guild, confraternity, tower society, Guelf and Ghibelline parties, and other institutions acted to relieve individual isolation. Day-to-day co-operation in the councils of the *consorteria* and neighbourhood militia prompted social cohesion. Lacking ample bureaucratic structure, the medieval *polis* relied upon grass roots political and social action. The effective associative structures of the late medieval world would bear out that quality in life-style aptly termed *Stufenkosmos* by the German historian Heinrich Miteis.[20]

The creative impulse toward co-operative forms in religious and secular life is certainly not the hallmark of the Renaissance. Instead, political systems became more unitary and bureaucracy more commanding; the effect was to dull corporate energies and enthusiasms. Voluntary societies of knights, foot-soldiers, castle guards, and other similar groups were superseded by mercenaries. Guild courts and the tribunal of the merchants lost pre-eminence as state courts came to dominate. Procedures at law were formalized while tax structures were regularized. The citizen could not easily draw strength and support from that myriad of quasi-public bodies once so effective in their operation.

There is also an accompanying decline of burgher confidence in the efficacy of collectivized concepts of honour, loyalty, and *carità*. These ideals tended to become personalized, and the early humanists, Petrarch, Boccaccio, and Salutati, minimized the possibility of their group implementation. Petrarch spoke to a broad audience when denying the existence of any overriding concern for the salvation of others. His neglect of the concept of *carità* was paralleled in the many bourgeois diaries and memorials whose emphasis was consistently upon the prudential.

When Petrarch entertained the traditional metaphor of 'the ladder of virtues' it was only to affirm the reality of the lower two rungs (the political and purgatorial) for the men of this world. Even among the seemingly most ascetic of Christians the supreme virtues did not prevail. The weakening of abstract and generalized concepts of virtue led many in Petrarch's generation to posit secularized models and *exempla* from history; these would serve better to encourage the Christian to the good life. Indeed, one of the most prominent features of this new culture was to underscore the phenomenal and finite (that is, the historical) rather than the wisdom of the transcendent and philosophy of the infinite. This is merely a highblown way of stating that at a time when ceremonial identity, ritual ties, and sacramental bonds were cast in doubt, early humanism and Florentine burgher culture were colonizing the outer rim of the mind with a novel mode of historical consciousness.[21]

By the late trecento what was being celebrated in Florence was not the informal and abstract ties between men, but 'the chain of law.' Whereas the individual had been separated from many associative and corporative imperatives, he was now liable to severe restraints. Free in one sense (with all the attendant anxieties), he now lived in a *polis* where public power became increasingly commanding. Here a dissent must be registered against the Burckhardtian view that the emergence of the individual was exclusively a process whereby north Italians were released from older restraints and ascetic norms to follow the impulses of an unbridled ego. This interpretation does not stress sufficiently the new pressures (social, political, and economic) to which the Renaissance citizen was liable. While it is true that the constraints of a corporate society were dissipated, the new repressive power of the Renaissance state was more than ample to shape and batter human egos. The law could be and was readily enforced against the *maiores et potentes* of Florence, beginning in the 1340s.[22] The strict containment of an obstreperous nobility and the domination of rural feudatories was no less significant. At the level of everyday citizen life the authority of the territorial state was still more telling. Conformity to the dictates of public law was no longer a fact to which a citizen might be persuaded, rather it was the *sine qua non* of Florentine republican experience.

The citizen ego under novel compulsions, stripped of many ancient props, and separated from the comforting hierarchy of a medieval cosmos with its attendant sociability, proved highly adaptable. The emotional history of the early Florentine Renaissance was characterized by a quest for new ego supports. The principal thrust of the new humanism paralleled this emotional surge: from Petrarch through Salutati, Bruni, and Poggio, we observe a resolute and surprisingly consistent defence of the claims of the human ego. Gradually, customary contempt for the 'active life' was challenged. Human desire for fame and renown was legitimized. Wealth and human industry were now regarded as both aids and tokens of virtue. This celebration of ambition and acquisitiveness was done in the name of religious and political ideals. As with Petrarch, sometimes the religious impulse verged upon the blasphemous: Scipio's elevation to the level of deity in the *Africa* is a case in point. Boccaccio's rendering of the Prometheus legend is so civic in tone that the author cannot imagine that the gods would have punished this mythic figure for bringing man the indispensable element for civilization.[23]

For the Florentine, structuring of ego could best be achieved through firm identification with the emerging Renaissance *polis*. This *polis* was beginning to assume an organic character in the minds of the citizenry by the late trecento. Its life and vitality were to be reckoned not in years but rather in centuries. Unconsciously, the grammar in the discussion of its nature changes; now 'the commune' does thus and thus (*fa cosi*). Equally durable were the glory and rewards to be won in its service. The compensations of the public world were boldly proclaimed in the new civic art of the early quattrocento. Nor was it necessary to find moral justification for acts of conquest and the building of empire. In the medieval view wealth and armed aggression by the *polis* were sure to incur God's wrath. Now, the capture of Pisa or even the defeat of papal troops is taken as the harbinger of God's election of the republic. Florentines writing in the vernacular in the late trecento enjoined *lo stato* to effect a *renovatio* of the Christian world; the narrow politics of the city state had assumed a redemptive quality. *Lo stato* was sacrosanct, and the citizen, although emancipated from medieval collective notions and ascetic restraints, was expected to be a loyal if not subservient denizen of the *polis*.[24]

Identity was to be gained, not by contesting imperatives of the public world as in the time of Dante, but by conforming to them. In the late Middle Ages. when connections between things spiritual and political were firm, the individual dared withstand the injunctions of a civil order. Further, the public world did not yet have such extensive coercive authority. Again, while the individual was liberated, in the Burckhardtian sense, from certain constraints, the *polis* with its lures and power could better serve as an agency of repression and thereby structure citizen ego.

A survey of the abundant evidence from Florentine last wills and testaments shows a sizable increase in the number of civic bequests. Pious works, grants to hospitals, donations for support of orphans, dowries for poor girls, and even funds for construction of the first foundling home in Europe: these are the causes to which the civic-minded subscribed. The character of early Renaissance Christianity is imbued with a feeling for community; the ascetic, contemplative, and penitential are in recession as the values of an activist Christianity become more apparent. The content and form of sermons delivered by leading Tuscan clerics at this time are evidence of a response to this new life-style. Renowned figures like Fra Giovanni Dominici, San Bernardino of Siena, and San Antonino of Florence tirelessly emphasized citizen obligation toward their *polis*. San Antonino advised Florentines to bequeath their shares of government stock to the city; San Bernardino was eloquent in his defence of the active Christian life; Fra Giovanni denied the possibility of returning to the days of pristine purity when Christ and his apostles walked the earth. Instead of pursuing chimeras by seeking a return to 'il primo stato della chiesa,' men must follow 'la più onesta usanza della patria.'[25]

Even the more ascetic of the Tuscan clergy will show intense sympathy with the perils confronting men of state embarking upon 'an earthly pilgrimage.' The Vallombrosan, Giovanni dalle Celle, writing to influential Florentine politicians and businessmen in the 1370s and 1380s, was to demonstrate deep appreciation of the plight of *veri Cristiani* dedicated to their *polis*.[26] The Augustinian, Luigi Marsili, intellectual heir of Petrarch, was to proffer consolation to public men at a time when the *polis* warred against the church. A programmatic difference emerged wherein leading clerics sought to reconcile the public and private worlds of an activist citizenry. Interestingly enough, the ideal figure portrayed by cleric and civic-minded artists is the Christian patriot. Correspondent of both dalle Celle and Marsili, Guido del Palagio is as much the symbol of his political generation as Donatello's statue of David is of the next.[27] Religion and art combined to produce a new breed of men, the civic prophets – the Joshuas and St Georges who populated the streets of Florence in the early quattrocento. Was Abraham less beloved by God because he chose to follow the ways of this world? asks Coluccio Salutati. A younger contemporary, Bruni, also to become chancellor of Florence, displayed particular compassion when describing the tribulations of public men and the difficulties of political decision. Rhetoric and a new oratorical style assumed much of their character as a consequence of this new awareness. Part Christian, part patriot, the public man will be depicted as reverent toward law and social usage; his character will be forged in daily confrontation with the thousand ills secular life is heir to. Heeding the Ciceronian maxim to stand in line and fight resolutely, he presents a very different figure from the untamed egoist constructed by Burckhardtians as typical of the Renaissance.[28]

Humanists and clerics revealed a sympathy for the pious businessman-politician of the early quattrocento. Already, for at least a generation, a defence of the dignity of his world was seen in chronicles. It was the merchant, not the knight, who made the city great; wealth accumulated by the commercial class shall serve as 'blood and sinew' of the republic. There was also a stout defence for marriage and the family when Salutati contradicted Petrarch's views.[29] Pervasive throughout society was an elevation of the pleasures of life in the nuclear family. Again we can see this as a response to the loss of previous emotional supports. More intimate bonds of affection challenged courtly ideals, allegiance to *consorteria*, and medieval, aristocratic eroticism. Like the civic world which conferred fame upon the individual, the nuclear family became a quintessential element of man's *humanitas*. The social phenomenon, brilliantly depicted by Philippe Ariès for the France of later times, has its beginnings in north Italy in the early Renaissance. The family was the focus of man's moral life, and women and children served to sustain and enrich the earthly pilgrimage.[30] Here lie the origins of new educational ideas, especially in the treatment of the young: Children were to be kept at home; parents were to oversee their education; the cruelty of the medieval apprentice system was scorned. Wives were no longer idealized in chivalric fashion but were depicted as partner and helpmate. The frailty of children was to be the source of tenderness, while the wishes of daughters must not be ignored when selecting a spouse for them. Treatises on domestic management proliferated, while household concerns were raised to a science.

The individual emerged from the corporate and associative world of the late Middle Ages bereft of traditional supports. The prototype of the modern family would in part sustain him. Increased security provided by the Renaissance state made it easier for the individual to survive without depending upon the power of the extended family. With the break-up of the *consorteria* separate households were established and the idea of privacy challenged commitments to the wider sociability of the declining medieval world. This stands as something of the price men must pay for alienation from the protracted sustaining values of an older society.

What is dominant is an exteriorization of perspective, whereby character and action are viewed from the vantage point of the public world. This angle of vision became more commanding as the extent of civic identification was amplified. There remained, however, deeper psychological needs not so easily satisfied. While some among the humanists assured the citizenry that a harmonious way was open to all who would love that larger human family, 'il santo e buono Comune,' the cost of repression was high. When Bruni decided to write a biography of Dante, he picked up Boccaccio's earlier work on the subject only to find the *Vita* full of sighs and bathed in the sweet elixer of love. Bruni preferred to stress the civic Dante, politician and warrior, whereas Boccaccio had portrayed the man of passion. Medieval strategies for gaining knowledge of the interior world grew apace during the late Middle Ages: scholastic psychology, introspective devices in chivalric literature, metaphysical poetry, and the rest all contributed. During the early quattrocento, the pull of the public world was so intense, and humanists so anxious to proffer support to the beleaguered ego, that a gulf between the cultivated civic persona and the deepest recesses of interiority developed.

What was in process of being colonized in the human mind was the rim of consciousness visible to society and the psychic centre ministered to by the ceremonial and liturgical. The culture was all too anxious to furnish justification for the civic persona as well as consolation to the unquiet centre. The obligation to make viable connections between rim and core was not encouraged by early humanism. Petrarchism, so popular among north Italians, established mobility of ego as an operational principle. The human condition is, then, precisely defined by its failure to sustain ideals and commitments. Further, the psyche is depicted as being circumscribed by its own laws that render much of religious and ethical philosophy useless. The lyricism of the Renaissance became a noble stance in the face of inevitable loss. Renaissance poetry could be constructed from discouraging antitheses such as love and hate, youth and old age, thus demonstrating the evanescence of all things human. A depth psychology could not be readily formulated to connect these polarities of human experience. Italian prose employed a behaviouristic psychology whereby character was revealed through actions and there was little temptation to delve into the recesses of the human mind. Clearly, the cosmic view of antiquity becomes most entertaining and comfortable, for it alone described man's fate and charted his knowable personality. Significantly, the tragic mode was most alien to Renaissance dramatic art. Finally, in humanist historiography it is the phenomenological and limited that was championed against the transcendent and infinite. Renaissance historians rejected the grand quest for the noumenal more thoroughly than they did any other intellectual activity.

A new taste for the gaudy in religious ceremony accompanied the accentuation of styles and forms in civic life. What is suggested here is that the origins of the baroque can be found in the early Renaissance. In order to believe in the public world it was becoming necessary to exaggerate and aggrandize its qualities. Intellectuals were perhaps too tender and solicitous in their desire to provide justification for the newly acquired ego props. Moreover, their fideism and contempt for metaphysics and theology helped to encourage a separation between the deep centre of irrational yearning and the rim of cultivated ego.

In the north of Europe neither public world nor civic Christianity served to structure personality. Moreover, the extended sociability and chivalric ethos of medieval times managed to sustain the individual ego. Metaphysics, theology, and pietism readily acknowledged mystical alternatives; hence guilt and expiation were at the level of consciousness. The northern intellectual may have suffered more but he continued to maintain an awareness of evil and sin. His world witnessed the gradual recession of medieval magic (sacramental bonds, ritual ties, and ceremonial identities) ; therefore, the irrational was omnipresent, luring him to seek deeper understanding of its equivalent in himself. His sensibilities were becoming protestant: the colonization of the rim of the mind (the public world) would not be so extensive; his energies served to clear new pathways between the outer and inner worlds.

NOTES

* This is a slightly expanded version of a paper given at the annual meeting of the American Historical Association held in Toronto, Canada, in December of 1967. The theme of this paper, the quest for identity in the Renais-

sance public world, will be more fully explicated in a volume being prepared on Florentine cultural history in the trecento and quattrocento. No
attempt will be made here to footnote this paper generously, since this
task is more appropriate to the book. At present, my purpose is to offer
only an essay that might be useful for provoking further inquiry. The ego
psychology employed here is highly simplistic and owes little to Eric
Erickson; indeed, it is commonsensical. Without being irreverent, I should
like to suggest that this holds true for Erickson's own historical writing
and that Freudian theory is really seldom essential for making the crucial
deductions.

1 'Homo Viator: Medieval Ideas on Alienation and Order,' *Speculum*, XLII
(1967), 233-59, with extensive bibliography. Against the autumnal language regularly employed by historians to describe the ethos of the somber
north in the fourteenth and fifteenth centuries, are juxtaposed the imagery
of spring, youth, and joy utilized to characterize the culture of Renaissance Italy. Such a vocabulary is misleading in the extreme, since it mis-
represents the very documents upon which its metaphoric thesis is constructed. Cf. A. Chastel, 'Melancholia in the Sonnets of Lorenzo de'
Medici,' *Journal of the Warburg and Courtauld Institutes*, VIII (1945),
61-7; E. Walser, *Gesammelte Studien zur Geistesgeschichte der Renaissance* (Bâle 1932), pp. 116 ff.

2 Jacques Le Goff, *La Civilisation de l'occident médiéval* (Paris 1964);
Georges Duby, 'Dans la France du Nord-Ouest; au XIIᵉ siècle: les "jeunes"
dans la société aristocratique,' *Annales Economies-Sociétés-Civilisations*,
XIX (1964), 835-46; R. Nelli, *Spiritualité de l'hérésie: le catharisme* (Toulouse 1953), and especially *L'érotique des troubadours* (Toulouse 1963).

3 Arno Borst, 'Das Rittertum im Hoch-Mittel Alter-Idee und Wirklichkeit,'
Saeculum, X, (1959), 213-31

4 E.H. Kantorowicz, 'Mysteries of State: An Absolutist Concept and its Late
Medieval Origins,' *The Harvard Theological Review*, XLVIII (1955), 71 ff.,
and *Selected Studies* (Locust Valley, N.Y., 1965); H. Oberman, 'Some
Notes on the Theology of Nominalism,' *The Harvard Theological Review*,
LIII (1960), 47-75; G. Leff, *Gregory of Rimini, Tradition and Innovation
in the Fourteenth Century* (New York 1961); C. Trinkaus, 'The Problem
of Free Will in the Renaissance and Reformation,' *Journal of the History
of Ideas*, X (1949), 51-62, and his soon to be published manuscript, 'In Our
Image and Likeness: Humanity and Divinity in Italian Thought.'

5 Cf. P.O. Kristeller, *Eight Philosophers of the Italian Renaissance* (Stan-
ford 1964), as well as his many other studies, in which this problem is
carefully analyzed. Indeed, the commonplace observation that north Italian culture in the late Middle Ages was essentially occupied with practical
questions and political matters appears to be readily defensible. History,
medicine, legal studies, and rhetoric dominated the culture and seldom
was there ample hospitality for sustained metaphysical and theological
inquiry. I shall attempt to survey these developments, or their absence, in
a forthcoming study on medieval historiography. For a negative evaluation of Latin literature, with its excessive interest in history and contem-

porary events, see A. Monteverdi, *Studi e saggi sulla letteratura italiana dei primi secoli* (Milan-Naples 1954), pp. 3-14.

6 M. Becker, *Florence in Transition* (Baltimore 1967), I, pp. 30-44

7 M. Becker, 'Florentine Popular Government (1343-1348),' *Proceedings of the American Philosophical Society*, CVI (1962), 360-82

8 Becker, *Florence in Transition*, II, pp. 134-49

9 Most valuable for Boccaccio studies is V. Branca's monograph, *Boccaccio medievale* (Florence 1956) ; see also E. Li Gotti, *Franco Sacchetti, uomo 'discolo e grosso'* (Florence 1940), a particularly notable study. For an analysis of Machiavelli's imagery, especially germane for this problem, see F. Chiappelli's *Studi sul linguaggio del Machiavelli* (Florence 1962), pp. 88 ff.

10 Of Hans Baron's numerous works on the theme of civic humanism, see *The Crisis of the Early Italian Renaissance* (Princeton 1955), 2 vols.

11 Likewise, *amore* did not serve as a civilizing force for Petrarch and his followers. Late medieval Italian poetry is characterized by substantial emphasis upon the socializing aspects of love and courtesy. Significant for the later history of the Renaissance is the fact that the *cri de coeur* of Petrarch is muted; the aristocratic repression of the cinquecento makes musicality and harmony the hallmarks of Petrarchism. Giorgio Santangello, in his *Il Petrarchismo del Bembo e di altri poeti del '500* (Palermo 1962), p. 23, speaks of the poet's 'sentimento della caducità delle cose umana' as being coupled with his notion of style. This style, which Santangello considers to be 'the most intimate and profound aspect *dell' anima del Rinascimento,'* would seek a synthesis of 'umanità e poesia.' Such a synthesis will enable man to triumph over 'la discordia delle cose' and gain 'il mondo sereno della armonia.' Petrarch's poetry, unlike that of his more scholastically minded forebears, did not present an abstract conception of human nature as fixed and immutable. As has been suggested by numerous commentators, the poet's own shifting emotions are accorded primacy; these are projected to the reader through the play of antithesis and assonance, as well as the fabrication of technical difficulties.

12 See G. Preti's introduction to Castiglione's *Il libro del Cortegiano* (Turin 1960), where he considers this and other relevant ambiguities. The writings of Leon Battista Alberti also reveal deep conflict on this score. See J. Gadol's review of a new edition of Alberti texts in *Renaissance Quarterly*, XX (1967), 484.

13 N. Rubinstein, 'Political Ideas in Sienese Art: The Frescoes by Ambrogio Lorenzetti and Taddeo di Bartolo in the Palazzo Pubblico,' *Journal of the Warburg and Courtauld Institutes*, XXI (1958), 179-207.

14 For Brunelleschi and Alberti, mathematics conferred a quality of indestructibility and eternity upon the world, while through geometric figures the divine mind spoke. G. Fasoli, 'La nuova spazialità,' *Leonardo: saggi e richerche* (Rome 1954), pp. 293-311; G. Argan, *Brunelleschi* (Milan 1955). In mural painting we observe that Piero della Francesca, Domenico Veneziano, and Castagno lowered the horizon line in order to increase the monumentality of the figure. Cf. also L. Alberti's *On Painting*, trans. J.R.

Spencer (London 1956), p. 110. I wish to thank Professor Nancy Struever for allowing me to read her penetrating dissertation on Florentine rhetoric and politics.

15 Cf. note 4 above and also *The King's Two Bodies* (Princeton 1957), pp. 173-231. Further discussion is found in Michael Wilks, *The Problem of Sovereignty in the Later Middle Ages* (Cambridge 1963), and Walter Ullmann, *Principles of Government and Politics in the Middle Ages* (London 1961).

16 Becker, *Florence in Transition*, ii, pp. 43-9

17 In the early quattrocento the influential Dominican, Giovanni Dominici, instructed his Florentine audience that 'niuno partigiano va in paradiso ... non essere guelfo ne ghibellino.' Cf. *Regola del governo di cura familiare*, ed. Donato Salvi (Florence 1860), p. 76. Even so staunch a champion of the *Parte Guelfa* as Lapo da Castiglionchio could only furnish bizarre etymology for the old political idiom. Writing in the early fifteenth century, the historian Gregorio Dati advised his readers that to many the origins of the terms 'Guelf' and 'Ghibelline' seem naught but 'favole'; this is not to be marvelled at, for many things have names for which one cannot assign reasons because they have insignificant and lowly beginnings. On Lapo, see R. Davidsohn, 'Tre orazioni di Lapo da Castiglionchio, *Archivio storico Italiano*, xx (1897), 225-46. Cf. also Dati, *L'Istoria di Firenze dal 1380 al 1405*, ed. L. Pratesi (Norcia 1904).

18 A general assessment of differences between developments in the north and south of Europe during the late Middle Ages might run thus: In the north, from the thirteenth century on, there was a marked tendency to replace the institutions of an individualistic feudal era, characterized by arrangements between vassal and lord, with corporate structures. Guilds, universities, leagues of clerics and nobles, parliaments, estates, and business partnership were of course on the rise. In the Italian cities, on the other hand, the flowering of corporatism was over by the late thirteenth century. The impulse had not been so strongly contested by powerful feudatories or checked by secular rulers. The southerner, then, lived in a society where neither corporate nor familial bonds were so supportive.

19 Especially useful for this essential, but neglected, question is R. Goldthwaite, *Four Florentine Families* (Princeton 1969).

20 *Der Staat des hohen Mittelalters* (2nd ed. Weimar 1944)

21 See the special number of *Archivio di filosofia* (Padua 1966) devoted to the problems of consciousness and demystification. On the desacralization of nature, see the monumental work of Pierre Duhem, *Le Système du monde de Platon à Copernic* (Paris 1913-17). Here we observe a critique of traditional symbolism serving as a necessary prolegomenon to the rise of a new science: Natural phenomena are considered not as God himself, but rather as his creation. On emerging Renaissance historical consciousness, see E. Cassirer, *The Individual and the Cosmos in Renaissance Philosophy*, trans. M. Domandi (New York 1964), pp. 42 ff.

22 M. Becker, 'A Study in Political Failure: The Florentine Magnates, 1280-1343,' *Mediaeval Studies*, xxvii (1965), 246-308. Coluccio Salutati extols

the 'legum catena' which bound the city together, existing over and above
the ties of kinship, friendship, and even parentage. *Epistolario*, ed. F.
Novati (Rome 1891-1911), I, p. 21. Cf. also Salutati's 'Invectiva' in *Prosa-
tori latini del quattrocento*, ed. E. Garin (Milan 1952), p. 32.

23 G. Boccaccio, *Genealogiae deorum gentilium libri*, ed. V. Romano (Bari
1951), IV, 4

24 Gregorio Dati, after speaking of the well-ordered *polis*, says that the *concordia* is so great, and the melody which emanates so sweet, that the saints
in heaven are moved to love the city and defend it from whomever would
seek to disturb its peaceful and tranquil condition. Cf. *L'Istoria di Firenze*,
p. 171. Giovanni Cavalcanti addresses his fellow Florentines, praising
them for subduing the obdurate nobility and conquering the foreigners
resident in their land. The citizenry have unseated depraved tyrants and
each man can well be compared to Hercules. Indeed, this is the very
essence of the commune – that multitude of brave men living under one
law. Is it not so, then, that anyone rebelling against the 'civile reggimento'
or harming the commune in any way is like a husband who cuts off 'i testi-
coli per dispetto alla moglie'? *I storie fiorentine* (Florence 1839), III, 2.
One of the telling differences between trecento chroniclers and their quattrocento counterparts stems from a general failure of the latter to create a
base for individual dissent, and even opposition, to the imperatives of the
state.

25 Giovanni Dominici, *Regola del governo*, p. 136: 'Ora so bene posto che
volesse di ridurre il primo stato della chiesa ne' tuoi nati, non potresti.
Pure attendi, seguitando la più onestà usanza della patria.' On this and
related themes, see Christian Bec's valuable study, *Les Marchands écri-
vans à Florence, 1375-1434* (The Hague 1967). His treatment of San
Antonino and San Bernardino begins on page 255; his discussion of their
views on civic duty is particularly illuminating.

26. F. Tocco, 'I Fraticelli,' *Archivio storico Italiano*, XXXV (1905), 348. *Lettere del Beato Giovanni dalle Celle monaco Vallombrosano e d'altri*, ed.
B. Sorio (Rome 1845)

27 Becker, *Florence in Transition*, II, pp. 60-2

28 In the late quattrocento the Ciceronian ideal tends to become less muscular
and civic; *humanitas* is more frequently equated with that elegance and
refinement of culture which allows the Florentine merchant to vie socially
with the chivalrous nobility of the north of Europe. Cf. K. Borinski, *Die
Antike in Poetik und Kunsttheorie* (Leipzig 1914), I, pp. 108 ff.

29 Not only did Salutati defend the institution of marriage from his beloved
Petrarch's harsh judgments, but he repeatedly opted for the word 'maritus'
and not 'uxorius.' His love for children became one of the most touching
themes of his finest epistles. Cf. V. Rossi, *Il Quattrocento* (Milan 1933),
p. 131.

30 E. Panofsky, in his *Early Netherlandish Painting* (Cambridge, Mass.,
1953), pp. 22-3, discusses the numerous iconographic motifs of an in-
tensely emotive domesticity originating in the northern Italian early Renaissance.

Notes on the word *stato*
in Florence before Machiavelli

Nicolai Rubinstein

The first noun in Machiavelli's *Il principe* is *stato*,[1] and it occurs 113 times in the rest of this short work.[2] Did he use it with the meaning the term 'state' acquired in the modern political vocabulary? There is wide agreement that he did so only in some cases, and that he used *stato* in a variety of meanings which, if at all, only touch on certain aspects of the modern notion of state. Several attempts have been made to classify these different meanings, which however cannot always absolve Machiavelli from the accusation of terminological inconsistency.[3] Thus Hexter has pointed out that Machiavelli uses *stato* in *Il principe* predominantly in an 'exploitative' sense, that is, as an object and not as a subject of political power.[4] However, there are instances, especially in the *Discorsi*, where he uses it to denote régime, or constitution,[5] or a political organization having the power to act and command.[6]

Machiavelli was not alone in his time in using *stato* in this varying and flexible manner; according to Chabod, the oscillations in its meaning in the political vocabulary of the first half of the sixteenth century reflect the formation of the modern state.[7] They may, however, also reflect Florentine usage in the fifteenth century. In view of the careful analysis devoted to the meaning of *stato* in Machiavelli's *Il principe*, and of the importance such analyses may have for the interpretation of that work, it is a matter of surprise that so little attention has been paid to Machiavelli's linguistic background. Gaines Post's fundamental researches on *status* in medieval Europe,[8] while mainly concerned with northern Europe, also throw fresh light on the role of legal terminology in the early Italian usage of the term,[9] but stop short of the fifteenth century; Condorelli's and Ercole's studies on the use of *stato* by Machiavelli, though based on the correct assumption that it has to be examined in the context of the changing meanings of the word in late medieval Italy, rely mainly on evidence from the fourteenth and sixteenth centuries.[10] The following notes, which are in no way designed to be conclusive, might help to see Machiavelli's usage of *stato* in a Florentine perspective, and thus make a small contribution to the history of the notion of the state.

We may begin with a usage the Florentines had in common with other European countries, and whose long pedigree can be traced back to ancient Rome: *status* as public welfare or prosperous condition of kingdom or church.[11] The legists contributed to defining this concept,[12] and lawyers, who played a prominent role in the public life of the Italian city states, no doubt helped to diffuse it. It would be worth investigating the influence on the political and legal vocabulary of the medieval Italian communes of Ulpian's definition: 'Publicum ius est quod ad statum rei Romanae spectat' (D.1, 1, 1, 2) and of the glossators' theory of public utility which was largely based on it.[13] In the fifteenth century, *stato* was commonly used in Florence with this meaning,[14] especially in connexion with violations of the security or welfare of the commune. On political grounds, official documents would motivate condemnations to exile or imprisonment, as having been made *pro negotiis* or *occasione status*;[15] citizens who suffered them would be described as *condannati per istato*.[16] In one instance, a law listing the names of citizens exiled because of 'conspirationis ... contra statum civitatis Florentie,' is summarized, in the margin of the register in which it is entered, as giving 'nomina exbannitorum pro statu,' which shows that *status* could be used as equivalent of *status civitatis*.[17] This, in its turn, corresponds to the *status regni* as used in medieval England,[18] and ultimately to the *status rei Romanae* of the *Digest*.

   Stato could also mean constitution, or form of government. In his commentary on Aristotle's *Politics*, St Thomas Aquinas paraphrases William of Moerbeke's *aristocratia, oligarchia,* and *democratia,* as *status paucorum, status optimatum* and *status popularis*.[19] In this, he may have followed classical Roman usage,[20] and thus revived a term which, having once formed part of the political vocabulary of antiquity, could once more serve its purpose when the rise of the free cities had created similar constitutional types.[21] At the same time, Aquinas evidently equates *status* with κράτος; accordingly, 'paucorum status est quando dominantur politiae illi qui abundant in divitiis.'[22] As we shall see presently, this equation of *status* with *dominatio* by a social group was to play a significant role in the political vocabulary of Renaissance Florence. As for *status* as constitution, Dante's 'Tra tirannia si vive e stato franco'[23] shows that, by the beginning of the fourteenth century, the Italian form of the word was currently used in this sense. Fourteenth-century Florentines described their form of government as *popolare stato* or *popularis status*,[24] and so does Leonardo Bruni who, like Aquinas, translates δημοκρατί in *Politics*, III, 6, 1 and 2, as *popularis status*[25] in his brief analysis of the Florentine constitution of about 1413.[26] But while Aristotle classifies democracy as one of the 'perverted' forms of government, Bruni considers the *popularis status* one of the three *speties legittimae*. It is not difficult to discover the reason for this, at first sight surprising, interpretation of Aristotle: Bruni was adapting the vocabulary of the *Politics* to current Florentine usage.[27] In doing so, he could have appealed to the authority of Bartolus of Sassoferrato, who in his *De regimine principum* gives contemporary equivalents of the Aristotelian types of constitutions: 'nomina secundum praesens tempus congruentius inseremus.'[28] In his commentary on the *Politics*, Donato Acciaiuoli is evidently faced by the same problem as Bruni. In enumerating the good constitutions, he includes the *popularis status* among them, although immediately afterwards he quotes Bruni's translation which renders 'corruption of polity into democracy' as 'labes' from the 'respublica in popularem statum.'[29] If *status popularis* could thus be used to describe the traditional 'popular régime' of Florence, *status optimatum* could similarly be used to describe the aristocratic one of Venice.[30]

The humanist contribution to the semantics of *status, stato,* was certainly significant, but it was hardly decisive: if classical texts offered abundant evidence of *status* as a political term, current Florentine usage provided similar meanings of *stato*. This also applied to the notion of constitutional change. Salutati, who uses *status* several times in his *De tyranno*,[31] quotes from Macrobius: 'Qui presentem statum civitatis mutari non optat et civis et vir bonus est,'[32] and Bruni describes, in his *Historiae Florentini populi*, the reforms of the Ciompi revolt of 1378 as 'status reipublicae mutationem.'[33] But, as early as the first half of the fourteenth century, Giovanni Villani had called the constitutional reform of the ordinances of justice of 1293 a *mutazione di stato*.[34]

Aristotle defines a constitution as the organization of magistracies, and especially the highest ones, in a state.[35] William of Moerbeke translates: 'Est autem politia ordo civitatis aliorum principatuum, et maxime dominantis omnium ... in democraticis quidem dominans populus, pauci autem e contrario in oligarchiis.'[36] St Thomas comments that a constitution is 'ordinatio civitatis quantum ad omnes principatus qui sunt in civitate, sed praecipue quantum ad maximum principatum, qui dominatur omnibus aliis principatibus.'[37] Bruni translates in a manner which is not only more faithful to Aristotle, but also relevant to conditions in an Italian city state: 'Est autem res pub. ordinatio civitatis et circa magistratus alios, et maxime circa id quod summam in civitate habeat auctoritatem et sit principalissimum ... in populari quidem populus, in paucorum vero potentia [pauci].'[38] He thus distinguishes clearly between government and the groups of individuals controlling it. The Aristotelian 'democracy' and 'aristocracy,' as translated by him with *status popularis* and *status optimatum*, could consequently be defined, in institutional terms, as different forms of government, and also, as well, in terms of effective power, as different kinds of organization of supreme political control by social classes. *Status*, defined by 'what has the supreme power in the state,' comes close to the meaning with which *stato* was widely used in fifteenth-century Florence. This may be illustrated by the use of the word in contemporary criticisms of involvement in political life.[39]

These criticisms, which contrast the troubles of public activity with the benefits of private life, are directed less against public life as such than against its manifestation in the power structure of the state. This is described as *stato*, and distinguished from the *comune* or *città* or *repubblica*. Thus the author of the version of Alberti's *Della famiglia*, who goes under the name of Agnolo Pandolfini, distinguishes between *stato* and *comune*: 'come si può arricchire dello stato, se non col rubare il Comune?'[40] In the *Della famiglia*, the condemnation of participation in the *stato* by the *staterecci* by one speaker, is qualified by another who considers service of the *repubblica* a duty of good citizens;[41] in the version ascribed to Pandolfini, the contrast between these two views is sharpened by being put forward by the same speaker: 'Those who do not want to sit in the highest magistracies to conduct public affairs for the sake of self-aggrandizement and in order to lord it over others are to be praised as good and true citizens,'[42] but it is again blurred when the same speaker is requested to give a 'regola nel desiderare lo stato, nel vivere pubblico.'[43] Giovanni Rucellai, who almost literally excerpts this work in his counsels to his sons, concludes by advising them 'a lasciare lo stato a chi piace.' But, as he himself admits later on, when he was writing this he was 'non accetto ma sospetto allo stato.'[44] In 1461 Giovanni Rucellai was finally accepted into the Medici *stato* after twenty-seven years in the political wilderness.[45]

This distinction between *stato* and 'state' recalls the earlier contrasts between the commune and such powerful corporations as the Guelph party within it – corporations which practically constituted states within the state.[46] However, in fifeenth-century Florentine usage, the *stato* was not identical with any *organized* group, although such groups could dominate the *stato* and determine its character. Giovanni di Paolo Morelli, writing at the beginning of the century, puts it aptly when he defines *statuali* as 'chi tiene e possiede il palagio e la signoria,' that is, who is in control of government.[47] When Stefani speaks of 'una parte de' Fiorentini trovandosi nello stato,'[48] or when, in 1447, Alessandra Macinghi-Strozzi explains that the Parenti had 'un poco di stato,' because the head of the family had recently held one of the three highest offices of the commune,[49] they refer to the participation of these citizens in the power structure of the state, that is, in the control of the government and of the higher ranks of the administration. The same is true of such expressions as *avere lo stato*[50] and *governare lo stato*.[51]

The position of political power or influence which participation in the *stato* brought with it could in its turn be described as *stato* in a manner common to later medieval usage in western Europe.[52] But it could also mean, in a more generic sense, political rights, so that *torre lo stato, perdere lo stato*, could stand for loss of a position within the ruling group, or, in a general sense, of the right to hold public office.[53] In this wider sense, *stato* comes at times to mean the governmental and administrative machinery of the state as a whole, so that Matteo Villani could speak of 'reggere e governare lo stato della repubblica,' and Stefani could describe the institution of the priorate in 1282 as being devised to 'reggere lo stato di Firenze.'[54]

There was only a short step from *stato* as power structure of the state to *stato* as dominant régime. Stefani describes the ascendancy of the Ricci and Albizzi after 1371 as 'lo stato delli Ricci e Albizi;'[55] the 'oligarchical' régime of the early fifteenth century could equally be described as *stato*.[56] But it was not until the establishment of the Medici régime that this became, in Florence, the prevailing meaning of the term as applied to internal politics. Hence, when Lorenzo de' Medici states, in a famous passage of his *Ricordi*, on his 'succession' that 'a Firenze si può mal vivere senza lo stato,'[57] he wants to say that as a prominent citizen one cannot live well without participating in the power structure of the state. Only four years before this event, attempts had been made by the opposition against the Medici to 'dirizzare lo stato,' that is, to reform the *stato*;[58] but their defeat had only confirmed the transformation of the *stato* of Florence into the Medici régime. By the time Vespasiano da Bisticci was writing of Cosimo that 'conosceva la difficultà ch'era a tenere uno stato,'[59] the *stato* which had been established by Cosimo had for a long time been *il presente stato*, or, briefly, *lo stato*: its opponents the *nimici* or *sospetti dello stato*, its members or supporters the *uomini* or *cittadini dello stato*;[80] legislation was passed to secure and strengthen it.[61] Yet there remained the earlier distinction between *stato* and *città*, régime and state. Thus Lorenzo de' Medici writes, in the passage of his *Ricordi* from which we have quoted,[62] that on the death of his father 'there came to our house *i principali della città e dello stato* to urge me to take charge *della città e dello stato*, as my father and my grandfather had done'; and a reform scheme of 1484 recommends, for the 'buono essere del presente stato' and the 'buono ghoverno della città,' 'that all those things which are necessary for the *stato* and for the security of the citizens, so that they can pursue their business affairs, be carried out speedily.'[63]

What was Lorenzo's place in, or relationship to, the Medicean *stato*? Benedetto Dei, in analyzing its stratification, lists him as the first of its *cittadini principali*;[64] but the Milanese orator, Filippo Sacramoro, describes the constitutional reform which took place in 1480 after the end of the Pazzi war as 'restauramento de questo stato et del Magnifico Laur.o,'[65] and Francesco Guicciardini writes, circa 1508, of the same reform, that the *Balìa* 'rilegorono e rifermorono lo stato con più grandezza e stabilità di Lorenzo.'[66] However much Lorenzo owed this ascendancy to the *stato*, the régime, his personal power is distinguished from that of the *stato*, just as the *stato* is distinguished from the state, the *città*. Nowhere is this threefold distinction, between Lorenzo, the *stato*, and the *città*, as well as their interrelation, formulated more lucidly than in a letter the Florentine chancellor wrote to him in 1480 on the eve of the peace with Naples. From that peace, and from Lorenzo's understanding with the king, Bartolomeo Scala says, will result security 'a voi et allo stato che è congiunto con voi et alla città che [è] congiunta collo stato' – 'for you and the régime which is joined to you and for the state which is joined to the régime.'[67] But Lorenzo could also be seen as taking part, as the first of its leading citizens, in the *stato* – a view to which Lorenzo himself, who more than once stressed his position as private citizen, might subscribe, at least officially.[68] It was natural enough that the Florentines, with their keen interest in social classification, should try to analyze the structure of the Medici régime. In 1472 Benedetto Dei provides one such attempt, when he distinguishes the *principali dello stato*, headed by Lorenzo de' Medici and Tommaso Soderini, from its second and third group (*schiera*), to be followed by its rearguard (*retroguardo*).[69] The concept of the *stato* as a social unit was bound to lead, in its turn, to its being invested with a collective personality – so that Giovanni Rucellai could say that he had been 'suspect to the *stato*'[70] and Piero Guicciardini could speak of citizens of lowly origin who were 'carezzati dallo stato.'[71]

By the time the Medici fell from power, in 1494, the theoretical concept of *stato* as constitution had lost most of its original meaning by the transformation of the power structure of Florence into the Medici régime:

it was hardly realistic to continue describing the Florentine constitution as *status popularis*,[72] and when Vespasiano da Bisticci speaks of the 'mutazione dello istato' of 1434, he refers to a change of the dominant régime, not of the constitution of the city.[73] Once the Medici régime was replaced by the new republican form of government, it was tempting to see the *mutazione dello stato* in constitutional terms, as one from the *stato de' Medici*, or *di Piero*, which was now being described as a tyranny,[74] to the *stato*, *or* governo, *popolare*.[75] But Francesco Guicciardini came closer to the meaning *stato* had acquired in fifteenth-century Florence when, some eighteen years after the fall of the republican régime in 1512, he defined the contrast between the Medici régime and the republican government not as one between two different *stati* or constitutions, but as one between government 'a uso di stato' and government 'a uso di libertà.'[76]

Guicciardini's use of *stato* was wide enough to embrace such different forms of government as the Medici régime and the absolute rule of Italian despots. So was fifteenth-century usage in Italy at large.[77] It was customary to describe, for instance, the rule of the Sforza as their *stato*, or as *stato di Milano*.[78] In diplomatic documents, the *stato* of a ruler might be distinguished from his lands and subjects;[79] but the term could also be used in a geographic sense for his territorial dominions.[80] In fact, in the case of despotic states, *stato* as political régime could be considered practically equivalent to *stato* as dominion.[81] In either sense, there was a tendency, in diplomatic relations, to equate despotic states with republics: thus Ercole d'Este promised, in 1478, to assist the 'stato di Milano o di Firenze' in case of war;[82] later Guicciardini describes, in his *Storie fiorentine*, the alliance between Florence and Milan as 'coniunzione … tra l'uno e l'altro stato.'[83] In 1454, the Italian league, which was joined by republics as well as by princes, was concluded 'ad tutelam et conservationem statuum et dominiorum' of the signatories, or, more briefly, 'ad conservationem et defensionem statuum ipsarum partium,'[84] *status* and *dominium* being evidently considered, for all practical purposes, one and the same thing. While preserving traditional distinctions, diplomatic usage thus comes close to the modern notion of state in so far as it refers to a combination of political power and territorial dominion. In Florence too, it was possible to use *stato* exclusively in the latter sense, as when Giovanni Villani divides the *stato* of Florence into city, *contado*, and *distretto*,[85] or when Guicciardini speaks, *circa* 1508, of Pisa as belonging to 'lo stato nostro.'[86] In Florence, such usage was at variance with that of *stato* as power structure or régime; in the despotic states, this distinction was blurred, since both the internal régime and the territory were 'held' by the signore, as his dominions. Thus when Machiavelli, in the opening sentence of *Il principe*, speaks pleonastically of 'tutti gli stati, tutti e' dominii che hanno avuto e hanno imperio sopra gli uomini,'[87] he may be following diplomatic usage in identifying *stati* with dominions whose acquisition and preservation by princes is the chief subject of the work.[88] Conversely, when, in the proem of the *Discorsi*, he criticizes princes and republics for not heeding the example of the ancients 'nello ordinare le republiche, nel mantenere li stati, nel governare e' regni,' he clearly uses *stato* with the meaning of constitution or régime:[89] it is with the fatal decline of 'simple' constitutions, or *stati*, and the survival of 'mixed' ones, that the second chapter deals.[90] Thus, when we read, in the letter in which he announces the composition of his *De principatibus*, that he had been studying the 'arte dello stato' ever since entering the service of the republican government in 1498,[91] we cannot fail to notice the shades of meaning which *stato* derived from having formed, for so long a time, part of the political vocabulary of his city.

NOTES

1 *Il principe*, 1: 'Tutti gli stati, tutti e' dominii che hanno avuto e hanno imperio sopra gli uomini, sono stati e sono o republiche o principati.' References to *Il principe* and the *Discorsi* arc to the edition of G. Mazzoni and M. Casella in Machiavelli, *Tutte le opere* (Florence 1929).

2 J.H. Hexter, '*Il principe* and *lo stato*,' *Studies in the Renaissance*, IV (1957), 113-35 (117)

3 See O. Condorelli, 'Per la storia del nome "Stato" (il nome "Stato" in Machiavelli),' *Archivio Giuridico*, LXXXIX (1923), 223-35, and XC (1923), 77-112; F. Ercole, *La politica di Machiavelli* (Rome 1926), chap. 2: 'Lo Stato nel pensiero di Machiavelli'; F. Chabod, 'Alcune questioni di terminologia: stato, nazione, patria nel linguaggio del cinquecento,' in *L'idea di nazione* (Bari 1961; paperback edition 1967); H. de Vries, *Essai sur la terminologie constitutionelle de Machiavel ('Il Principe')* ('s Gravenhage 1957); Hexter, '*Il principe*.' F. Chiappelli, on the other hand, believes that in 75% of the cases in which Machiavelli uses *stato* in the *Prince*, he uses the term 'in tutta la sua maturità' (*Studi sul linguaggio del Machiavelli* [Florence 1952], p. 68).

4 Hexter, '*Il principe*,' pp. 119 ff.

5 See below, p. 321

6 For examples, see the studies by Condorelli, Ercole, Chabod, and de Vries, note 3 above

7 Chabod, 'Alcune questioni,' paperback ed., p. 153; see also Condorelli, 'Per la storia,' xc, 107 ff.

8 Gaines Post, *Studies in Medieval Legal Thought* (Princeton 1964), chaps. 5 to 8

9 *Ibid.*, pp. 336 ff.

10 Note 3 above

11 Condorelli, 'Per la storia,' xc, 78-81

12 See Post, *Studies*, p. 269 ff.

13 *Ibid.*, pp. 316-17, 335; see also L. Martines, *Lawyers and Statecraft in Renaissance Florence* (Princeton 1968), p. 440, on the argument from *utilitas publica* used by Florentine lawyers in the fifteenth century

14 Matteo Palmieri, *Della vita civile*, ed. F. Battaglia (Bologna 1944), p. 110: 'Lo stato e fermamento di ogni republica è posto nell' unione civile.' The notion is spelled out in such passages as in the proem of the *Statuto del podestà* of 1325, ed. R. Caggese (Florence 1921), p. 1: 'ad honorem et salutem et bonum statum Communis et populi civitatis et districtus Florentie.' In 1460 the councils decided to extend the special powers *(balìa)* of the eight of ward, on the grounds that 'quando habet baliam ... plus operatur ad conservationem boni et pacifici status et libertatis civitatis Florentie' (Archivio di Stato, Florence [hereinafter ASF], Provvisioni, 151, ff. 77ᵛ-78ʳ.

15 See e.g. ASF, Balìe, 25, f. 127ᵛ (30 December 1434) : 'Condemnationes ... pro negotiis status'; Balìe, 26, f. 24ᵛ: condemnations 'pro occasione status'; Balìe, 27, f. 217ᵛ (13 March 1454) : 'confinati ... occasione status.'

16 Giovanni Cambi, *Istorie*, in *Delizie degli eruditi toscani*, ed. I. di San Luigi (Florence 1785). xx, p. 205

17 ASF, Balìe, 18, f. 68ᵛ (5 February 1381)

18 See Post, *Studies*, pp. 310 ff.

19 *In libros politicorum Aristotelis expositio*, ed. R.M. Spiazzi (Turin 1951), p. 139 (nos. 393-5). See also E.H. Kantorowicz, *The King's Two Bodies* (Princeton 1957), p. 271, n. 235, and Post, *Studies*, pp. 345 ff.

20 See E. Köstermann, ' "Status" als politischer Terminus in der Antike,' *Rheinisches Museum*, LXXXVI (1937), 227-8; W. Suerbaum, *Vom antiken zum frühmittelalterlichen Staatsbegriff* (Münster 1961), p. 17

21 Post, *Studies*, pp. 336 ff., considers the legists' interpretation of *status* as magistracy another source of the new constitutional usage of *status*. However, Aquinas appears to have been primarily responsible for the revived use of *status* for constitution.

22 *In libros politicorum*, p. 139 (no. 395)

23 *Inferno*, XXVII, 54

24 E.g., Giovanni Villani, *Cronica*, ed. I. Moutier (Florence 1823), XII, 19; Marchionne di Coppo Stefani, *Cronaca fiorentina*, ed. N. Rodolico, in L. Muratori, *Rerum italicarum scriptores* (new edition), XXI, 1 (Città di

Castello 1903 ff.), 216, rubrica 594; for *popularis status*, see e.g. G. Brucker, *Florentine Politics and Society, 1343-1378* (Princeton 1962), p. 252,
n. 23 (1372)
25 *Opera Aristotelis* (Venice 1496), f. 275ʳ
26 Letter to Emperor Sigismund, ed. H. Baron, *Humanistic and Political
Literature in Florence and Venice at the Beginning of the Quattrocento*
(Cambridge, Mass., 1955), p. 182: 'Aut populus ipse regit; que speties
a Grecis democratia, a nostris vero popularis status nominatur.'
27 Elsewhere, he correctly distinguished *respublica* (polity) from *popularis
status* (democracy) as a 'legitimate' constitution from its 'perverted' counterpart: *Epistolae*, ed. L. Mehus (Florence 1741), ii, pp. 105-6. See also
N. Rubinstein, 'Florentine Constitutionalism and Medici Ascendancy in
the fifteenth century,' in *Florentine Studies*, ed. N. Rubinstein (London
1968), p. 447.
28 In *Opera* (Basel 1588), v, pp. 417, 420. He calls the *regimen ad populum*
'magis Dei quam hominum regimen.' In antiquity, the Roman republic
lived under it, and, in his own day, Perugia (p. 419). Bartolus, who incidentally does not use *status* for 'constitution,' equates the *regimen ad
populum* of contemporary Italy not with democracy, but with polity *(regimen politicum)*, that is, with one of Aristotle's good constitutions, and
describes the Florentine constitution as an aristocracy.
29 *In Aristotelis libros octo politicorum* (Venice 1566), ff. 88ʳ, 90ʳ
30 *Consulta* of 14 November 1465, ed. G. Pampaloni, 'Fermenti di riforme
democratiche nelle consulte della Repubblica Fiorentina,' *Archivio storico
Italiano*, cxix (1961), 261
31 *Il trattato 'De tyranno' e lettere scelte*, ed. F. Ercole (Bologna 1942), ii,
21, p. 19: 'statum ... legitimum institutum ... perturbare'; iv, 14, p. 32: 'rei
publice status' = 'wellbeing'
32 *Ibid.*, iv, 8, p. 30. Macrobius, *Saturnalia*, ii, iv, 18
33 *Historiarum Florentini populi libri* xii, ed. E. Santini, in L. Muratori,
Rerum Italicarum scriptores (new edition), xix, 3 (Città di Castello
1914-26), 224
34 *Cronica*, viii, 1. See also vii, 79: 'mutazioni dello stato della città'; xii, 72;
'e fu quasi uno cominciamento di rivolgimento di stato'
35 *Politics*, iii, 6, 1
36 St Thomas, *In libros politicorum*, p. 135 (no. 245)
37 *Ibid.*, p. 136 (no. 385)
38 *Historiarum Florentini populi*, 224
39 See Leon Battista Alberti, *I primi tre libri della famiglia*, ed. F.C. Pelle-
grini and R. Spongano (Florence 1946), pp. 273-9, and *Giovanni Rucellai ed il suo Zibaldone, I:* 'Il Zibaldone quaresimale,' ed. A. Perosa (London 1960), pp. 39-43
40 Agnolo Pandolfini, *Trattato del governo della famiglia* (Pistoia 1827),
p. 104
41 Alberti, *I primi tre libri*, p. 281

42 Pandolfini, *Trattato del governo*, p. 111: 'Chi si mette a voler sedere ne'
    priori magistrati per guidare le cose pubbliche, non con sua voluntà, non
    a sua utilità, non a sua maggioria ... costui è da essere lodato, ed è buono,
    e vero cittadino.'
43 *Ibid.*, p. 112
44 *Giovanni Rucellai*, pp. 42, 122
45 *Ibid.*, p. 122: '... sono stato non accetto ma sospetto allo stato anni 27, cioè
    dal 1434 al 1461.' In 1466 his son Bernardo married Piero di Cosimo's
    daughter Nannina (*ibid.*, p. 28)
46 See Brucker, *Florentine Politics*, pp. 99 ff.
47 Giovanni Morelli, *Ricordi*, ed. V. Branca (Florence 1956), pp. 274, 275.
    Elsewhere he speaks of rich and long-established citizens who are 'nello
    istato' (p. 264). Cf. Alberti, *I primi tre libri*, p. 273. In this context, the
    meaning of *stato* comes close to that of *reggimento*, another term of the
    Florentine political vocabulary which would deserve a special study. Cf.
    e.g. Morelli, *Ricordi*, p. 430: 'Questi isquittini furono contro alla volontà
    di molti sono nel reggimento, e spezialmente contro alla volontà delle
    famiglie.' Martines, *Lawyers and Statecraft*, p. 205, defines *reggimento*
    as 'the dominant group *in* government — a concert of the most powerful
    families.'
48 Stefani, *Cronaca fiorentina*, p. 192, rubrica 550
49 Alessandra Macinghi-Strozzi, *Lettere di una gentildonna fiorentina* ..., ed.
    C. Guasti (Florence 1877), p. 3
50 E.g. Stefani, *Cronaca fiorentina*, p. 158, rubrica 446: 'la grandigia de'
    cittadini, che avieno lo stato ...'
51 Vespasiano da Bisticci, *Vite di uomini illustri del secolo XV*, ed. P. d'An-
    cona and E. Aeschlimann (Milan 1951), p. 410: 'quegli che governano gli
    stati.'
52 See e.g. the *consulta* of 1372, quoted by Brucker, *Florentine Politics*, p.
    252, n.23: 'cives ... habentes statum in civitate.' Lorenzo de' Medici con-
    sidered, in his *Ricordi*, the vast expenditure of his family 'esser gran lume
    allo stato nostro' (ed. W. Roscoe, *The Life of Lorenzo de' Medici called
    the Magnificent* [2nd ed. London 1796], I, appendix, p. 29). Vespasiano
    da Bisticci, *Vite*, p. 475: the ruling group ('chi governava') was trying to
    'assicurare lo stato loro'; Piero Parenti, *Storia fiorentina*, in J. Schnitzer,
    Quellen und Forschungen zur Geschichte Savonarolas (Leipzig 1910), IV,
    30-1 (on the reform of 23 December 1494): the new electoral method was
    introduced 'per rendere lo stato alla nobilità, la quale per molte factesi per
    lo adrieto revolutioni perduto lo havea, et ne' populani ... ridocto s'era.'
    Examples could be easily multiplied. On *status*, estate, *état*, etc., as rank,
    exalted position, etc., see e.g. H.C. Dowdall, 'The word "State," ' *Law
    Quarterly Review*, XXXIX (1923), 103 ff.
53 'E principali [si dolevano] d'avere lo stato perso' (Parenti, in Schnitzer, p.
    8) exemplifies the first meaning, 'torre lo stato ... per via d'ammunirgli,'
    i.e. by depriving of political rights (Vespasiano da Bisticci, *Vite*, p. 397),
    the latter meaning.

54 Matteo Villani, *Cronica*, IV, 69; Stefani, *Cronaca fiorentina*, p. 57, rubrica 157

55 Stefani, *Cronaca fiorentina*, p. 283, rubrica 734

56 See e.g. the poem ascribed to Niccolò da Uzzano, in *Archivio storico Italiano*, IV, 1 (1943), 297-300. The poem is addressed to the Florentine patricians and concludes (p. 300): 'Il vostro stato sarà tutto pesto/Da quella nuova gente che traligna.' Cf. Condorelli, 'Per la storia,' XC, p. 85, on '*stato* nel senso di parte o parte al potere.' Already Burckhardt had said (*The Civilization of the Renaissance*, tr. S.G.C. Middlemore [London 1944], p. 2, n. 2) that 'the rulers and their dependants were together called "lo stato".' However, in Florentine political terminology, *stato* had a wider meaning.

57 Roscoe, *The Life of Lorenzo, loc. cit.*

58 Macinghi-Strozzi, *Lettere*, p. 512

59 Vespasiano da Bisticci, *Vite*, p. 417

60 *Ibid.*, p. 478: 'questi dello stato'; Piero Guicciardini, on the electoral scrutiny of 1484, in N. Rubinstein, *The Government of Florence under the Medici, 1434-1494* (Oxford 1966), pp. 319, 323: 'sospecti allo stato,' 'casa nimica dello stato,' 'uomini dabene grandi dello stato.'

61 Filippo Sacramoro to the duke and duchess of Milan, 27 April 1478 (Archivio di Stato, Milan, Potenze Estere, Firenze, 299): 'provisione per stabilimento et fermezza di Laur.o et di questo stato.'

62 See n. 52 above

63 G. Pampaloni, ed., 'Progetto di riforma alla Costituzione complitato da un seguace di Lorenzo il Magnifico,' *Archivio storico Italiano*, CXIII (1955), 264: 'che tutte quelle cose, le quali per lo stato sono necessarie et per la sicurtà de' cittadini, acciochè possino arditamente exercitarsi ne loro traffichi, si faccino tra brieve tempo.'

64 See n. 69 below

65 To the duke and duchess of Milan, 11 April 1480 (Archivio di Stato, Milan, Potenze Estere, Firenze, 299); see also note 61 above

66 Francesco Guicciardini, *Storie fiorentine*, ed. R. Palmarocchi (Bari 1931), p. 54

67 5 January 1480, ASF, Mediceo avanti il Principato, XXXIV, 412. I should like to thank Mrs Alison Brown for drawing my attention to this passage.

68 See Rubinstein, *The Government of Florence*, pp. 226-8

69 *Cronaca*, ASF, manoscritti, 119, f.35ᵛ

70 *Giovanni Rucellai*, p. 42

71 Rubinstein, *The Government of Florence*, p. 319. On the notion of personality in Machiavelli's use of *stato*, see Ercole, *La politica*, p. 78, and De Vries, *Essai sur la terminologie*, pp. 79-81 (such personification 'regarde surtout les hommes qui y appartiennent').

72 As early as c. 1439, Bruni had described it as a mixed constitution: see Rubinstein, 'Florentine Constitutionalism,' pp. 447-8.

73 Vespasiano da Bisticci, *Vite*, p. 395

74 See Rubinstein, *The Government of Florence*, p. 218

75 Cf. e.g. F. Guicciardini, *Storie fiorentine*, pp. 98, 99, 208
76 Francesco Guicciardini, *Ricordi*, ed. R. Spongano (Florence 1951), p. 25
     (*ricordo* 21). In the first version of this *ricordo* (pp. 25-6), he has, instead,
     'secondo gli ordini di uno stato stretto,' and 'secondo gli ordini della
     libertà.'
77 The use of the word *stato* outside Florence would require a special study;
     the following observations are merely designed to point to additional
     meanings of *stato* which fifteenth-century Florentines had in common with
     other Italians.
78 E.g. Vespasiano da Bisticci, *Vite*, pp. 193, 199. Once more, examples could
     easily be multiplied.
79 See e.g. the treaty between Francesco Sforza and Federigo da Montefeltro
     of 31 August 1450, in J. Dumont, *Corps universel diplomatique* (Amster-
     dam 1726), III, pt. 1, 179-80; Francesco Sforza takes under his protection
     'el stato, citade, terre, castelle, homini, subditi ...' of Federigo da Monte-
     feltro. The different shades of meaning of *stato* as applied to despotic
     states is well illustrated by a Florentine diplomatic memorandum of 1479
     dealing with the question of a possible return of the exiled Sforza brothers
     to Milan (Biblioteca Nazionale, Florence, Fondo Ginori-Conti, 29, 237) :
     'mettendo in stato questi fratelli' (*stato* as position of political power) ;
     'o obterrano pacificamente tutto ... o quello stato si smembrerà in più
     parti' (*stato* as territory, dominions) ; they will have to defeat the 'stato
     che regge' (*stato* as régime, i.e. the Sforza *stato* which was ruled at that
     time by Bona of Savoy with the help of Cecco Simonetta, Francesco
     Sforza's former secretary).
80 E.g. Vespasiano da Bisticci, *Vite*, p. 192: 'gli tolse grande parte dello stato
     suo.'
81 This aspect of the semantics of *stato* would well deserve separate
     treatment.
82 Additional articles to Ercole's *condotta*, ASF Riformagioni, Atti pubblici,
     10 Settembre 1478: 'quando decti stati, o qualunche d'essi, cioè stato de
     Milano o di Firenze, havesse guerra ...'
83 Guicciardini, *Storie fiorentine*, p. 28
84 Dumont, *Corps universel diplomatique*, III, pt. 1, 221
85 Villani, *Cronica*, II, 655
86 Guicciardini, *Storie fiorentine*, p. 113
87 *Il principe*, 1
88 See Dowdall, 'The word "State",' pp. 110-11: since *stato* was used in many
     senses, and not all *stati* were dominions, 'it would be necessary to define
     the sense in which *stato* was used.'
89 I cannot follow Chabod's interpretation ('Alcune questioni,' p. 150) of
     stati, in this passage, as dominions.
90 Cf. *Discorsi*, I, 2: Lycurgus 'fece uno stato che durò più che ottocento
     anni.'
91 10 December 1513, in Machiavelli, *Lettere*, ed. F. Gaeta (Milan 1961),
     p. 305. Cf. pp. 239-40 (9 April 1513) : 'non sapendo ragionare né dell'arte
     della seta, né dell' arte della lana ... e' mi conviene ragionare dello stato.'

Bonds, coercion, and fear:
Henry VII and the peerage

J. R. Lander

One of the main themes of English history has been the increasing degree of control attained by government over society. Historians have all too often assumed that the monarchy achieved such increased control by frontal attacks on the power of the aristocracy; the two main points of attack, widely separated in time, are considered to have been Henry II's assault on the feudal courts of the lords through the development of royal courts staffed by a judicial bureaucracy and Henry VII's repression of the nobility in favour of middle-class servants. Both conceptions are somewhat tarnished. It is now generally recognized that, in meeting contemporary demands for justice, Henry II had no idea of destroying the courts of his tenants-in-chief. To have done so would have been to deny great and powerful men their just rights. Moreover, in a turbulent, undisciplined society, attacks upon any institutions which helped to maintain public order would have been dangerously unrealistic. Henry II introduced new instruments which offered supplements and more efficient alternatives to the old. The royal courts of justice ultimately replaced the feudal courts because these feudal courts withered away, gradually becoming incompetent to serve the needs of a society where feudal relationships and land tenures became too tangled and complicated for baronial courts to deal with. More immediately, however, as Glanvill's great legal treatise makes amply clear, the royal court could be expected to strengthen feudal justice by advising barons on the treatment of difficult cases which sub-tenants brought to their own courts.[1] Henry VII was no more consciously revolutionary than Henry II had been. The first Tudor continued to rely on the aristocracy in government and yet, at the same time, attempted to control them by methods which, although short-lived, are, in themselves, interesting.

All late medieval and early modern societies lived in fear that their inadequate institutions would fail to hold the terribly thin line between order and chaos.[2] English society had proved quite incapable of producing an effective bureaucracy (even had Henry VII found the money to pay it, which he could not). In the thirteenth century enquiry after enquiry had revealed an almost sempiternal corruption of local government. The sheriffs' offices were notorious from at least the early part of the fourteenth century and from its very inception experienced judges like Sir Geoffrey Scrope (d. 1340) had looked upon the system of justices of the peace with justifiable doubts about its probable efficiency.[3] Since many of the justices of the peace were corrupt and violent themselves, they had failed to improve the standard of law and order in any notable way.[4] Moreover, control of the countryside at the village level was far less adequate than it afterwards became. Even in the 1520s (if a recent investigation of Buckinghamshire and Rutland can be accepted as typical) probably only one village in five had a resident squire whereas by 1680 more than two out of three had one.[5]

In these conditions the king could not possibly ignore, much less suppress, any class of men who could assist in maintaining public order and the defence of the realm. Indeed, contemporary statements show that nobody at the time was so wildly eccentric as to harbour the slightest idea of suppressing the nobility. Contemporary writing of all kinds constantly stressed their power and with equal constancy stressed the need for upholding it. Even violence and disloyalty could not destroy the nobleman's essential role in society. In 1459 an anonymous pamphlet, the *Somnium vigilantis*, could even argue, though it is true that the author in the end rejected the argument, that the utter destruction of the Yorkist lords, outrageous and treasonable though their actions had been, would harm the realm far more than the injury which their earlier offences had already inflicted upon it. Considering (so the pamphlet runs) that the realm was surrounded by enemies on every side 'it were more need for to procure to have more heads and lords for the tuition and defence of the same than for to depose and destroy any of them ...'[6] In draft sermons written for delivery to parliament in 1483, Bishop John Russell described nobility as 'virtue and ancient riches,' went on to compare the nobles themselves to firm rocks in an unstable sea, and averred 'the politic rule of every realm standeth in them; they like Moses and Aaron approach the king, the commons stand afar off.' Their quarrels were to be settled by the king, other men's affairs in the ordinary courts of law. Finally, in at least two different passages, William Caxton described the government of the realm as, more or less, a co-operative effort between the king and the nobles.[8]

Impressive as the development of English governmental and legal institutions had been during the high Middle Ages, in practice these institutions had always been defective. Their working, to a great extent, depended upon the local support of the aristocracy. In October 1453 Henry VI (or his council) reminded Lord Egremont that the king had made him a baron, not for any past services 'but for the trust and trowing that we had of the good service ye should do to us in time coming, in especial in keeping of the rest and peace of our land and in letting of all that should mowe be to the contrary.'[9] Sir John Fortescue thought the aristocracy the most influential group of people in the country,[10] and even William

Worcester, who vehemently deplored the declining martial spirit of the
nobility and gentry[11] and their preoccupation with estate management
and legal matters, admitted that they should concern themselves with civil
affairs to the extent of 'maintaining' the justices and other royal officers in
carrying out their duties.[12]

The influence of noblemen followed naturally enough from their
wealth and territorial power. As Dr G. A. Holmes has pointed out, the
English were highly realistic about status. In the fourteenth century no
man was elevated to an earldom unless he had built up, or unless the king
granted him, an inheritance sufficient to maintain the dignity.[13] A poor
nobleman was almost a contradiction in terms.[14] The same held true in the
fifteenth and early sixteenth centuries, though deliberate endowment by
the king then became less frequent.[15] Moreover, contemporary feeling
that government was naturally better in the hands of the rich who, almost
from the mere fact of their wealth, were less openly corrupt and self-
seeking than other people, also re-inforced the position of the aristocracy.[16]

Although Tudor England showed most of the characteristics common
to Renaissance states elsewhere it was with a difference, for such traits
were there less extreme in degree. Its smaller area and the peculiar development of both the monarchy and feudal institutions had given England
greater unity. Although dialects were so divergent still that people from
different parts of the country found difficulty in understanding each other
and as late as 1497 Cornishmen rose in revolt rather than pay taxes to
defend the remote inhabitants of the north against the Scots, regional
feeling never combined with the discontents and ambitions of the nobility.
In England noble estates had always been scattered over many counties.
Moreover, as an intelligent Venetian envoy remarked in the same year as
the Cornish revolt, the nobility possessed no fortresses[17] and only very
limited judicial powers. He claimed, indeed, that by continental standards they were hardly nobles at all, merely rich gentlemen in possession
of great quantities of land.[18] Such conditions meant that, even when
granted royal offices in districts where their estates lay, no single great
family ruled a compact block of territory combining all the coercive
powers of landowner, military commander, and judge. Therefore, no
single family could rely for its own enhancement on attracting strong
feelings of provincial separatism. There was nothing in England to compare with what Shakespeare so rightly called France's 'almost kingly
dukedoms.' Even though the greater peers showed intense jealousy of any

encroachment upon their local spheres of influence, they never, even during Henry VI's minority, attempted formally to parcel out the country amongst themselves like the Scottish nobles during the minority of James IV.[19]

Yet, in spite of their somewhat weak position, as compared with other aristocratic groups, the English peers were still the natural leaders, the natural disciplinarians of their local communities.[20] No king could govern unsupported by their wealth and prestige. Even in the late sixteenth century the local lord, knight, or even esquire, set the tone of his district and, for example, the survival of catholicism and the development of puritanism depended to a marked degree upon their influence and protection.[21] Ideally, therefore, a higher standard of behaviour should prevail amongst such people,[22] partly to set an example to lesser folk, partly because when powerful nobles quarrelled their neighbours and clients tended to be drawn into the disputes and whole districts might be disturbed by affrays and riots.[23]

In practice, of course, such a system was often, by modern standards, rank with self-seeking, oppression, and injustice. To make the system work the king had to enforce sufficient control over powerful men to keep their activities within decent bounds. In the imaginary exhortation from God to a monarch at the end of Dudley's *Tree of Commonwealth* the deity is made to say:

> Thou hast kept the temporal subjects in a loving dread, and hast not suffered them, nor the mightiest of them, to oppress the poor, nor yet woldes not suffer thine own servants to extort or wring any other of my people, thy subjects, nor hast not suffered the nobles of thy realm, nor any other of thy subjects [so] to run at a riot as to punish or revenge their own quarrels.[24]

If the king himself were spotless, setting his nobles an example which they faithfully followed, what a realm there would be![25]

Self-help had been endemic in medieval life: even the administration of the law itself had always been a violent matter although the growing sophistication of society had tended somewhat to reduce its worst excesses. Royal harryings of the countryside – which, in late Anglo-Saxon days, kings had from time to time deliberately commanded in the name of discipline – were past long since and the seizure of estates by force, though by no means unknown, was far less common than it had been in Anglo-Norman days. Moreover, reform of the law of distress under

Edward I had made more peaceable the relationship between landlord and tenant.[26] Nevertheless, the still deplorably weak sanctions of the criminal law and the confused obsolescence of the law of real property worked against improvement[27] and, unfortunately, the nobility upon whom so much depended were probably no less violent and corrupt than any other group of people. From time to time the king or the royal council found it necessary to remind them of the need for higher standards of conduct. In 1425 and 1430 the nobility agreed not to take to violence to settle their own quarrels[28] and in 1426, 1461, and 1485 they were either forbidden to receive or maintain criminals or had sworn oaths against so doing.[29] However, self-help and the oppression of lesser men tended to go on as before.

Late medieval and early modern kings could not suppress the nobility. To govern at all they were forced to sustain it and yet, at the same time, to control it. Such a policy meant, amongst other things, the maintenance of aristocratic numbers. The great mortality of individual noblemen during the Wars of the Roses did not abnormally reduce the number of aristocratic houses. Aristocratic mortality had always been extremely high, so high that during the fourteenth and fifteenth centuries about one-quarter of the peerage families died out in the male line about every twenty-five years.[30] Only the custom of allowing men who married the heiresses of peers to assume their titles[31] and the practice of deliberate new creations kept up their numbers. Though the earliest example dates from 1397, the creation of parliamentary baronies by royal letters patent first became established in the mid-fifteenth century when Henry VI and his advisers began, quite consciously, to create new peers to support the throne and its occupants during times of political stress.[32] The practice continued well into the sixteenth century. Just after Henry VIII's death a patent issued in favour of John, viscount Lisle, stated quite clearly that Henry had intended to ennoble and endow certain of his councillors and servants in order to *strengthen his nobility*.[33]

At the same time many historians have noted that the early Tudor nobles were more cautious and more docile than their ancestors had been, though the contrast with those of the mid-fifteenth century has probably been too strongly drawn. The late K. B. McFarlane suggested that the nobility had long memories of the consequences of violence and treason and, possibly, had become more tractable following the quarrels and disastrous confiscations of estates during the reigns of Richard II and Henry IV.[34] I have myself suggested elsewhere the possibility of a failure of nerve and a disinclination to take responsibility during both the minority and the personal rule of Henry vi.[35] Certainly the reluctance of the peers to follow Richard, duke of York, into treason in the 1450s and their even greater reluctance to support the earl of Warwick in the late 1460s disposes of any idea that the aristocracy were unusually turbulent and treacherous during the Wars of the Roses.[36]

This already existing caution was undoubtedly strengthened in two ways during the second half of the fifteenth century: from 1459 onwards by parliamentary attainders for treason, and by the wide extension under Henry vii of a system of bonds and recognizances.

It is now proposed to investigate the effect of this combination of attainder and financial sanction on the attitude of the nobility. First of all, the most extreme form of control – attainders. Parliamentary attainders, though originally intended as confiscatory measures against political opponents, came, in the end, especially under Henry vii, to operate as a sanction for good behaviour. During Henry vii's reign, nine peers were attainted. Of these attainders three were permanent,[37] six were ultimately reversed, five by Henry himself, one after his death.[38] Only one of these five reversals, that of Walter Devereux, Lord Ferrers, in favour of his son John in 1489, shows no special features. Pardon and restitution of property were apparently complete in their case. All other attainted families suffered from considerable reservations imposed on reversal.

In July 1486 John, Lord Zouche, produced securities in 2,000 marks to be of good behaviour and a few days later the king granted him a pardon under the great seal for his offences. Ostensibly the pardon also restored his lands but, unless Henry changed his mind after the pardon had been issued, this must be interpreted as permission merely to *acquire* his property again by some means or other, for when parliament formally reversed the attainder in 1489 the reversal did not extend to the estates confiscated under the original attainder act of 1485. In 1489 Zouche was permitted to inherit only the lands of his grandmother, Elizabeth, the wife of Lord Scrope of Bolton. A further act of 1495 allowed the return of his own paternal lands – at a very considerable price. In November, Zouche sold two manors to Sir Reynold Bray for £1,000 (a figure undoubtedly far below their real value), 'since Sir Reynold helped to obtain grace for Sir John from his liege lord to repeal the attainder and recover his land.' The acts also protected the interests of Giles, Lord Daubeney and his heirs in certain properties which had been granted to them.[39] Other Zouche estates which the king had granted to three prominent courtiers, Sir John Savage, Sir Richard Edgecombe, and Sir Robert Willoughby, were still in the hands of their descendants in 1523.

John, Lord Fitzwater, was attainted in 1495 and later executed after attempting to escape from imprisonment in Calais. Restitution cost his son Robert very dear. In July 1505 he bound himself to pay the king £5,000, obviously the price for the reversal of the attainder under letters patent the following November. Robert Fitzwater paid the king at least £2,000 under the agreement. These were immense sums for a family which probably ranked amongst the poorer barons.[40] Even so, he did not obtain complete restitution of his father's property, for grants were made from it in 1506 and in 1509 he took, at an annual rent of £100, the manors of Hampnell and Disse in Norfolk, which had been part of the paternal estate.

John de la Pole, earl of Lincoln, slain fighting for Lambert Simnel at the battle of Stoke, was attainted during the lifetime of his father, John de la Pole, duke of Suffolk. After the father's death, the younger brother, Edmund, in return for a payment of £5,000 and the surrender of the dukedom, was allotted certain lands and manors as though his brother had never been attainted and the title of earl of Suffolk only. Edmund himself was later attainted in 1504 and this second attainder was never reversed.

The story of the Howards is perhaps the most intriguing of all. John Howard, duke of Norfolk, and his son Thomas, earl of Surrey, were both attainted for their support of Richard III at the battle of Bosworth. The father had been slain on the battlefield and rumours spread that the king intended to execute the son. Instead Surrey remained a prisoner in the Tower of London until January 1489 when he was released after taking an oath of allegiance. From then onwards he served Henry VII and his son faithfully for nineteen long years as soldier, ambassador, councillor, and administrator, gradually and only gradually, receiving back sections of his property. First in 1489 he was restored to the title of earl of Surrey, the lands of his wife's inheritance, and lands which he might inherit from ancestors other than his father and lands which the king had granted to the earl of Oxford and Lord Daubeney. From 1492 onwards more of his estates were restored and, after his victory over the Scots at Flodden Field in 1513, Henry VIII gave him back the dukedom of Norfolk. Even so, however, he never recovered all the Howard estates.[41]

So one noble family was eliminated by attainder, another after considerable reduction in property and rank was also finally eliminated in the male line. One, and only one, apparently achieved complete restitution. Three suffered more or less severe losses.[42] The example of such severity would certainly not be lost on the rest of the aristocracy.[43]

The second method of discipline and control (if so it may be called) lay in bonds and recognizances: a terrifying system of suspended penalties.[44] A few years ago Mr K. B. McFarlane again remarked upon a change which came over the nature of the entries in the close rolls of the chancery especially in Henry VII's later years. He pointed out that after 1500 over one-third of the entries in the close rolls consist of recognizances in favour of the king and that over fifty of them bear the condition that those entering such recognizances should keep their allegiance to Henry VII and his heirs. Plausibly assuming that many more recognizances which merely acknowledge a debt to the king were imposed with the same intention in mind, Mr McFarlane suggested that the king was so suspicious of those who surrounded him that 'the point had almost been reached where it could be said that Henry VII governed by recognizance.' In this he was neither 'medieval' nor 'modern' but *sui generis*. The possibility that the difference in the entries (and therefore any theory built upon it) may be due to an order of December 1499 tightening up the procedure for enrolment cannot be entirely ruled out,[45] but this is unlikely for, as far as the nobility was concerned, the number of recognizances taken did not increase until 1502.

Before discussing the application of this system it may be well to say something of its origins. Apart from somewhat similar methods used from time to time in earlier centuries but by then probably forgotten,[46] bonds and recognizances were part of normal methods of estate management during the fifteenth century. Dishonesty and corruption were endemic in all administration, both royal and private. Methods of criminal procedure against defaulting officials being inefficient in the extreme, it was standard practice on many estates to demand the production of bonds carrying a heavy financial penalty, and of mainpernors or guarantors, as a condition of appointment for officials.[47] Mainprises were also usually taken from customs officials. Similarly, bonds and recognizances were extremely common amongst private people in such matters as binding them to keep the peace towards each other, guaranteeing the execution of family settlements, commercial transactions, arbitrations over land disputes, and many other matters. Bonds and recognizances were in fact very much a part of the normal texture of late medieval life.

At government level, to go no further back, they were common enough

all through the fifteenth century, covering most of the matters for which
Henry VII exacted them and even some for which he did not.[48] In the 1470s
their use in some areas may have become more systematic, particularly
in the marches of Wales. At the great sessions held at Newport in 1476
recognizances were taken from seventy-two people, mostly for 100 marks,
but from some for up to 500 marks. Most men from whom they were
taken had not been charged with any crime and Mr T. B. Pugh has suggested that the recognizances were taken because the crown demanded
them, and that the system may well have been a quite recent development,
perhaps the result of discussions between the marcher lords and the prince
of Wales' council at Ludlow shortly before.[49] Whether this surmise be
true or not, Henry VII early adopted this system for the marches and it
continued in force until the reforms of Thomas Cromwell in the 1530s.[50]

The nobility were accustomed to give and take bonds and recognizances on ordinary matters of business both amongst themselves and with
lesser men. The Lancastrian kings had also demanded financial guarantees
from them for various purposes. However, the first Lancastrian, Henry IV,
can hardly be said to have used such methods as a form of discipline
against the nobility itself. During his reign thirteen nobles (including one
widow) gave mainprises in chancery. All but one were guarantees for
keeping the peace given on behalf of lesser men. One involved the custody
of a royal ward.[51] The most important, and probably the only one of any
political significance (though even this is doubtful) was a recognizance
for 10,000 marks in 1409 from the earl of Arundel to keep the peace
towards his uncle, the archbishop of Canterbury.[52]

At the beginning of Henry V's reign such matters took on a more
political turn. In November 1413 the earl of Arundel, the earl of March,
the earl marshal, Lord Roos, and Lord Morley each gave a recognizance
for 10,000 marks and Lords Talbot, Willoughby, Clinton, Haryngton, and
Ferrers of Chartley, each gave one of £4,000 'to be of good behaviour
towards the king and people.'[53] Later in the reign Lady Burgavenny gave
a mainprise of £2,000 for her appearance before the council, and another
of £1,200 not to harm Nicholas Burdet or any other people and four commoners also gave mainprises for her good behaviour in this matter.[54] Also
five peers gave mainprises for the good behaviour of other men, including
one peer, Lord Poynyngs, who was also bound in 1,000 marks himself.[55]
Thus under Henry V fifteen peers and a peeress were under some form of
financial obligation to the crown, ten for their own actions, five for those
of other men.

During Henry VI's minority sixteen peers found themselves in similar situations though no recognizance at this time seems to have borne any particular political significance.[56]

The same kind of thing continued during the period of Henry VI's personal rule. Between 1437 and the beginning of 1458 twenty-two peers were at various times under bonds and recognizances.[57] Particularly notable are a series of bonds and recognizances imposed upon John Mowbray, duke of Norfolk, the nephew of Richard, duke of York, and one of his political associates. Even by the standards of his own day John Mowbray was an exceptional ruffian and he was twice, in 1440 and in 1448, imprisoned for violent conduct.[58] In July 1440 Norfolk gave a recognizance for 10,000 marks that he would remain in the royal household until he found security to keep the peace towards people in general and towards John Haydon in particular. This was cancelled as Norfolk fulfilled the condition. In December the duke was in trouble again, giving another recognizance for £500 that he and certain other people would pay a fine (to be settled apparently by negotiation) for the improper disposal of certain lands without a royal licence. This too was cancelled. Then in 1443 the earl of Stafford, Lord Fauconberg, Lord Latimer, and Lord Willoughby gave a mainprise of £500 in chancery for Norfolk and Norfolk himself under 'a pain of £2,000' undertook to appear in person before the king and council in the quinzaine of Easter to answer certain charges against him, and in the meantime not to molest Sir Robert Wingfield, his household, servants, and tenants. The council put his dispute with Wingfield to arbitration. It appeared that Norfolk had attacked and ransacked Wingfield's house at Letheringham, for which the arbitrators ordered him to pay 3,500 marks compensation, and also made certain other dispositions.[59] Even this was not the end of Norfolk's violent course. In December 1453 he gave another enormous recognizance, this time for £12,000 to appear in chancery on the Monday of the first week in Lent and in the meantime to refrain from harming Alice, duchess of Suffolk.[60]

During the same period the duke of Exeter, the earl of Northumberland, and Lord Grey of Codnor were all, at some time, placed under recognizances to keep the peace.[61] So were the earl of Devon and Lord Bonvile during their notorious quarrels in the south-west.[62] It seems that the king and council were at this time using such instruments to quell the growing recalcitrance of, and the personal feuds between magnates which, as Dr R. L. Storey has shown,[63] preceded the Wars of the Roses.

In 1458 and 1459 recognizances took on a more directly political note.

A great council, held from 29 January to the fourth week of March 1458, tried to patch up the differences between the king and the families who supported him on the one side and Richard, duke of York, and his supporters, the Nevilles, on the other. Various arrangements were agreed upon to settle the personal and political feuds of all the great families concerned and after the agreements were sealed on 24 March the participants ostentatiously displayed their reconciliation in a grand procession to St Paul's.[64] More practically, the day before the king had taken recognizances making a grand total of £68,666 13s. 4d. that they would abide by the awards from the duke of York, the earls of Salisbury and Warwick, the dowager duchess and the duke of Somerset, the earl and countess of Northumberland and Lord Clifford.[65] Six other peers also gave recognizances during these years.[66]

Under the Yorkists the use of recognizances continued as before, though for almost all purposes except routine administrative matters they were few in number. Under Edward IV only two groups, involving six peers and a peeress, were of any high political significance. In 1470, on the same day as Henry Percy, earl of Northumberland, (still under attainder) was released from imprisonment in the Tower of London, he guaranteed his allegiance and his appearance before the king in chancery at a certain date by a bond in £5,000, supported by a joint bond in £3,000 from the bishop of Ely, the earls of Arundel and Kent, and Lord Ferrers.[67] In March 1473 the countess of Oxford, whose husband had been, and still was, actively engaged in treason,[68] gave a bond in £3,000, supported by bonds of £2,000 each by the earl of Essex and Lord Howard (and others by commoners) that she would appear daily before the king in council at Easter next, and within three days after due warning given her, answer certain matters pending against her until she was dismissed.[69] Other bonds concerning seven noblemen dealt with legal arbitrations and the keeping of the peace and one guaranteed the sale of certain estates to the king.[70]

Considering the brevity of his reign, bonds and recognizances were more frequent under Richard III than under Edward. Only seven, however, affected noblemen.[71] Surprisingly enough, in view of the political tensions of Richard's reign, none of these directly dealt with the question of allegiance, although bonds for this purpose were certainly taken from commoners.[72]

So, in the course of twenty-four years some twenty nobles (including one woman, the countess of Oxford) were placed under bonds or recognizances of some kind, ten for themselves, ten on behalf of other people.

In addition, Edward IV attainted sixteen peers and Richard III another four,[73] thus making a total of thirty under some form of direct discipline themselves and ten more on behalf of others. By 1485 the nobility were thoroughly accustomed to sanctions on their behaviour which involved financial penalties and the forfeiture of estates.

From the point of view of the nobility, matters changed considerably for the worse under Henry VII. During the Yorkist period about two-thirds of the titled families of England were, at some time or other, under the discipline of either attainders or recognizances. Between 1485 and 1509 the proportion rose to slightly more than four-fifths. Although in comparison with the Yorkists Henry inflicted few attainders on them, his conditions for reversal became more severe[74] and, as we shall see, his employment of bonds and recognizances became much more intensive and much more stringent than even the numbers so far quoted might indicate. As before, evidence of these instruments comes mainly from the close rolls of chancery, though a seventeenth-century copy of Edmund Dudley's notebook in the British Museum adds to the numbers.[75] The same notebook, together with Sir John Heron's payments book as treasurer of the chamber for the years 1505 to 1509, containing a list of the bonds and recognizances which passed through Heron's hands,[76] also provides a good deal more detail about their operation. An investigation of other sources would undoubtedly reveal more details of particular cases, but it is most likely that it would not materially alter the observations now offered.

Things did not change rapidly. Judging from the close rolls, between Henry's accession and the end of 1499 eleven peers gave bonds and recognizances varying in amount from £100 to £10,000.[77] Even then, in spite of the order of December 1499, earlier mentioned,[78] for the enrolment of bonds and recognizances, numbers did not rise immediately. There was, in fact, only one more before the beginning of 1502.[79] From then onwards, however, the close rolls show an immense increase, no less than twenty-seven peers giving bonds and recognizances between that date and the end of the reign.[80] To these can be added another nine for which evidence is provided from Dudley's notebook and Heron's payments book.[81]

It would be tedious to go into the details of these bonds and recognizances in great numbers. A random selection must suffice to show their purpose and conditions. In December 1485 Viscount Beaumont gave a bond payable at Christmas for his good behaviour.[82] In the same month the earl of Westmorland gave the king the custody and marriage of

Ralph, his son and heir, guaranteeing the grant with bonds totalling 1,000 marks.[83] In 1504 the earl of Northumberland and the archbishop of York each gave a bond of £2,000 to keep the peace towards each other.[84] In 1505 Lord Clifford gave a recognizance for £2,000 that he would keep the peace both for himself, his servants, tenants, and 'part-takers' towards Roger Tempest of Broughton and endeavour within forty days to bring before the king and his council 'such as were present at the late pulling down of Roger's place and house at Broughton.'[85] In August 1506 the duke of Buckingham entered into an obligation to pay the king 300 marks 'for the king's gracious favour in the recovering of the 800 marks assessed upon the tenants of Brecknock.'[86] In 1508 Lord Willoughby de Broke gave a recognizance for 1,000 marks, the condition being payment of £2,000 within two months of warning given by the king's letters missive or privy seal.[87]

These examples so far quoted are what may be called 'simple' recognizances, that is, they affected nobody but the single person concerned. Other types (what one might call 'composite' recognizances) involved several, or even a great many, people. In such cases one man's misbehaviour or failure to fulfil specified conditions could bring other people into financial peril. In 1500 Lord Grey of Powys, Richard ap Thomas, and Richard Pole gave a recognizance for £100, Master John Tolley another for 100 marks, and Sir William Sandys and Sir Hugh Vaughan jointly a third, also for 100 marks, that Pole would be true in his allegiance as constable of Harlech castle, that Pole would also pay any debts due to the king by prisoners permitted to escape and various heavy fines (the amounts are specified) for any escapes of prisoners incarcerated for murder, rape, or felony.[88] In 1504 Thomas Wyndham of Felbrigge, Norfolk, gave a recognizance for £2,000, supported by another for the same amount given jointly by the earl of Essex and the earl of Kent, guaranteeing that Wyndham would find sufficient security before Pentecost next for keeping his allegiance, appearing when required before the king and council, paying 2,000 marks by instalments, or else surrendering to imprisonment in the Tower of London.[89]

One of the most complicated of all these transactions concerns William Blount, Lord Mountjoy, the student and later the patron of Erasmus, the companion of the child, Prince Henry, who had served in the army against Perkin Warbeck in 1497. In May 1503 he was appointed keeper of Hammes castle, one of the subsidiary fortresses of Calais. His indentures, besides laying down his duties and various other arrangements, stipulated that he should give a recognizance of 10,000 marks himself and find guarantors in a similar sum that he would keep the castle safely and surely to the king's use, deliver it up when required in writing under the great or privy seal, appear personally before the king and council upon reasonable warning under any of the king's seals and keep his allegiance.[90] Mountjoy duly gave his recognizance for 10,000 marks but his guarantors put up recognizances totalling only 8,180 marks. There were, however, no less than twenty-eight of them, including five other peers, the earl of Shrewsbury, viscount Lisle and Lords Burgavenny, Hastings, and Strange; Mountjoy himself had to put up yet another recognizance for £1,000 to find substitutes in the event of death and for allowing the castle treasurer £200 from the local revenues towards the cost of repairs.[91] Mountjoy did, in fact, later find four replacements, including the earl of Arundel, the earl of Kent, and the marquess of Dorset.[92] Nor were these the only recognizances in which Mountjoy was involved: there were at least another twenty-one in which he was at various times concerned.[93]

Although some of these bonds and recognizances were small and remained in force for limited periods only, others could have been ruinous, for they involved immense sums of money and even, in some cases, put part, or all, of a nobleman's estates within the king's grasp. An examination of four of the greatest cases will show the nature and extent of the perils threatening the families concerned and the way in which the system operated. The cases chosen for study are those of the earl of Northumberland, the marquess of Dorset, Lord Burgavenny, and the earl of Kent.

Henry Percy v, the earl of Northumberland, first gave a recognizance for £2,000 in 1504 in the course of his quarrel with the archbishop of York.[94] Four years later, in 1506, with others, he gave a recognizance in £200 for the payment of a debt of £100 to the king by his probable relation, William Percy, and in 1507 another of £100 as a guarantor for the safe-keeping of Castle Cornet, Guernsey, by Richard Weston and the same year replaced the earl of Kent in £200 for Sir Nicholas Vaux as keeper of Guisnes.[95] All this, however, was very small beer compared with difficulties in which the earl was already involved. In 1505 he was condemned to pay the enormous sum of £10,000 for 'ravishing' Elizabeth Hastings, a royal ward, that is, interfering in some way with royal rights of wardship. The king suspended the fine 'during his pleasure,' when the earl agreed that he and four others would enter into a recognizance of 6,000 marks to pay 3,000 marks in annual instalments of 500 marks each Candlemas.[96]

In November 1507 this arrangement (which may not, in fact, have come into effect), was changed. On the tenth of the month the earl gave a recognizance of £5,000 payable at the king's pleasure.[97] Another recognizance made ten days later stiffened conditions by making the money payable the same day.[98] Even worse, according to an entry dated 13 November in Sir John Heron's payments book the earl had levied a fine to put certain of his estates into the hands of feoffees to the king's use until £5,000 of his fine had been paid by half-yearly instalments of 500 marks:[99] moreover, payment of the remaining £5,000 of the fine was still to hang at the king's pleasure.[100] It has not been possible to trace payments under these arrangements. Even if the feoffees paid the instalments as they became due, however, the earl could not have lost more than £1,000. In this he was fortunate in the king's death, for Henry VIII, on his accession in 1509, cancelled all the outstanding recognizances. Thus, as Dr Bean has remarked on these transactions, 'if the earl did suffer financially from the crown's policy, his losses in the event were much less than those threatened by the agreements he was forced to make. Nevertheless, the harshness of the terms, and the fact that some of his estates were temporarily in the crown's hands, emphasize the threatening and humiliating nature of the situation in which he was placed.'[101]

If the king's treatment of the earl of Northumberland is considered humiliating, there are hardly words left to describe his dealings with Thomas Grey, marquess of Dorset, thirteen years earlier. Thomas Grey, the eldest son of Edward IV's queen, Elizabeth Wydeville, by her first husband, Sir John Grey of Groby, had been created marquess of Dorset by his stepfather in 1475. Under Richard III he joined in Buckingham's rebellion, on its failure fled to Henry of Richmond in Brittany, and in his absence was attainted. In Brittany his conduct was somewhat twofaced and, apparently despairing of Richmond's success, he prepared to return to England and make his peace with Richard. Richmond, however, sent a messenger to him and persuaded him to abandon the idea. During Richmond's invasion, Dorset and John Bourchier were left behind in Paris as surety for a loan. Presumably as a result of his duplicity in Brittany, to achieve the reversal of his attainder he had to renounce all grants which Edward IV had made to him other than those associated with his creation as marquess of Dorset, and in particular to repudiate any agreements concerning property which had belonged to Henry, duke of Exeter, and the wardship, marriage, and custody of Edward, earl of Warwick.[102] This hard bargaining may well have rankled deeply. Henry, perhaps suspecting Dorset's resentment, seems never to have trusted him again. In 1487 he fell under suspicion of complicity with Lambert Simnel, was imprisoned in the Tower of London, but was restored to favour after the battle of Stoke (16 June 1487).[103]

Dorset took part in the expedition against the French in 1492, but on 4 June, just before the fleet sailed, the king and the marquess entered into a very interesting indenture,[104] which ran that if the marquess would find sureties and demean himself loyally the king would admit him to favour and grant him letters of pardon. The cost of the royal forgiveness (whatever offence he may have committed) and the royal favour turns out to have been very high indeed. Dorset was forced to make a lawful estate in fee simple to twelve trustees named in the indentury of '*all* castles, honours, manors, lands, rents and services, whereof he or Cecily his wife is seised, or any other persons to his use or by recovery,' saving only two manors in Essex which were to be left in the hands of their farmers to the use of the marquess and marchioness and for the performance of the marquess' last will.[105] Then follow a number of extremely stringent conditions. If Dorset did not in future offend the king 'nor do misprision to the king's person, but disclose such treason to his highness in writing, and the parts be proved and the plotters convicted' the trustees should be seised to the king's use in the lands. If, however, the marquess was taken prisoner overseas, sufficient manors might be sold to pay for his ransom. The marquess was in addition to 'labour' to place all his and his wife's remaining lands in Lancashire 'or elsewhere' under the same conditions. All these arrangements were to be ratified in the next parliament and this was, in fact, done in the parliament of 1495.[106] The indenture (and the act of parliament) continue that if the marquess remained innocent of any of the specified offences during his lifetime, after his decease the arrangement should be void and his heir would be allowed to inherit according to the normal course of the law.

Even now Henry had not finished. Dorset had also to grant to the king the wardship and marriage of Thomas, his son and heir, 'to be found in the king's service at the cost of the marquess.' The marquess was also to pay the king £1,000 if the boy was redelivered to him unmarried under the age of nineteen.

Dorset himself gave a recognizance for £1,000 for the performance of all this and also undertook to find 'sureties of divers persons bound in recognizances of £10,000,' and to be prepared, if necessary, to replace any of them with others at three-weeks' notice.[107] Dorset had, in fact, already found fifty-five people, including the earl of Kent, viscount Lisle, Lord Grey of Codnor, and Lord Grey of Wilton, to put up mainprises totalling £9,225.[108] In February 1495 another peer, Lord de la Warre, gave a bond of 500 marks for Dorset's loyalty during life.[109]

As with many other of Henry VII's arrangements, this was a disposition *in terrorem*, probably only partially carried through. Had the terms of the agreement of 1492, confirmed in 1495, been fully executed, the unfortunate marquess of Dorset would have been left without an acre to his name except for the manors of Stobbyng and Fairested in Essex. He was not, however, completely denuded of income, and, possibly, not even of land. In 1495 he was still in possession of an annuity of £35 granted to him on his creation as marquess in 1475,[110] and in 1495 certain offices which he held were exempted from the act of resumption covering the principality and other estates held by the prince of Wales.[111] Moreover, in September 1492 he sold three manors in Kent to the archbishop of Canterbury for £120.[112] It is possible that he was granted an income from the estates which he had made over to the trustees or that he was allowed to retain at least part of them.[113] Dorset seems in the end to have satisfied the king of his loyalty, for the arrangement was ended some time before August 1499, possibly, though unlikely, as early as May 1496.[114]

Dorset continued loyal and took part against the Cornish rebels in 1497. He died in 1501. Yet, even after such harsh sanctions against him, his son may possibly have dabbled in treason, for under the year 1508 the *Chronicle of Calais* states 'the Lord Marquess Dorset and the Lord William of Devonshire, which were both of kin to the late Queen Elizabeth[115] and her blood,' after being imprisoned in the Tower of London 'a great season' were brought to Calais and were there 'kept prisoners as long as King Henry VII lived and should have been put to death if he had lived longer.'[116]

As far as sums of money were involved, during the whole reign the most extreme case involving a peer was that of George Neville, Lord Burgavenny. In the Michaelmas term 1507 the court of King's Bench fined Burgavenny the grand total of £70,650 for unlawfully retaining 471 men below the rank of knight or squire.[117] This was a fine which no one at the time could possibly have paid, so now bargaining began. On 5 November twenty-six people and institutions entered into recognizances totalling £3,233 6s. 8d. that Burgavenny would be the king's true liegeman for life.[118] On 23 December he himself gave a recognizance for £5,000 to be true to his allegiance and to find substitutes for any of his recognitors whom, before the utas of the purification next, the king or any of his councillors should deem insufficient,[119] and the following day gave a second recognizance for 5,000 marks not to enter the shires of Kent, Surrey, Sussex, and Hampshire at any time during his life without the king's licence.[120]

The details of all Henry's dealings with Burgavenny seem to be incomplete, for in an indenture also dated 24 December Burgavenny admitted that he was indebted to the king in £100,000 'or thereabouts' for unlawful retainers. He also admitted in this indenture that the execution and levy of the debt was clearly due, both in law and conscience, and that the king might attach his body, keep him in prison and take all the issues of his lands until the whole sum was paid. The king, however, was gracious enough to eschew the full severity of the law and accepted instead, as parcel of the debt, the sum of £5,000 payable in instalments over ten years at Candlemas.[121]

So in the end Lord Burgavenny got away with the prospect of losing £500 a year for ten years. The recognizances and the indenture were in this case all cancelled during the first year of Henry VIII's reign.[122] So Burgavenny probably paid no more than £1,000.[123] We do not know what Burgavenny's income was. In 1436 his grandparents were assessed for an income tax at £667, but this certainly did not represent the total income of their estates.[124] At this time, however, the conventional figure for the income of a baron was £1,000 a year. A few had more, some had a good deal less. Whatever Burgavenny's income was, the prospect of losing a very large proportion of it for a whole decade was a sufficiently shattering blow in a society where ostentatious display was a considerable factor in maintaining a man's prestige. And, moreover, the shadow of absolute ruin hung over him for two years.[125]

After all this, it seems somewhat ironical that in 1510 he was granted in reversion for life the constableship of Dover castle and the wardenship of the Cinque ports and in 1512, in preparation for the king's invasion of France, Henry VIII issued Burgavenny a licence 'to retain as many men as he can get in Kent, Sussex and Surrey and elsewhere ... and he shall give them badges, tokens or liveries as he thinks convenient.'[126]

There are numerous references in the close rolls to the exceedingly involved affairs of Richard Grey, third earl of Kent, who succeeded to the earldom in 1503, and whose father in his will had expressed the fear that 'he will not thrive but will be a waster.'[127] Traditionally he is held to have dissipated his estates by gambling and the king certainly took advantage of his difficulties. At the time he inherited, his father owed the king 'certain moneys' for the payment of which a number of manors had

been specially enfeoffed.[128] In 1506 Earl Richard owed the king
£1,683 6s. 8d.[129] For this, under a recognizance of 4,000 marks, he had
to make 'surety of lands' worth 500 marks a year from which payments
by half-yearly instalments of 200 marks could be made until the debt
was cleared off; moreover, he was to make an estate, described as 'freely
offered' of lands worth £100 a year to the use of himself and his heirs
male with remainder in default to the king and his heirs.[130] The following
year he sold a manor to Sir John Huse for 300 marks in return for a life
annuity of £42 which was to be used for the payments of his debts to the
king.[131] Eleven weeks before this particular arrangement was made the
earl had also given an indenture stating that he still owed the king £1,800
of earlier debts (viz. those of his father and other sums due for livery of
his lands) plus the earlier recognizance of 4,000 marks.[132] The indenture
went on to state that the earl could not pay these sums 'without in manner
his utter undoing.' The king therefore, 'consented' (a distinct euphemism
in the circumstances) to a recovery being made against him, by Edmund
Dudley and others, of 10,000 acres of land, 4,000 of meadow, 4,000 of
woodland, and a rent of £120 in lordships in Wales and Shropshire. The
king was to take the issues and profits of these lands to the annual value
of £216, together with the profits of various other manors bringing up the
total to £300 a year, until £1,800 had been paid. If the earl was still alive
when this debt was settled, he in turn was to receive the annual rent of
£212 from the Welsh lands and the rest were to be handed back to him.
Not, however, to his heirs, who would suffer most under this arrangement
for all the lands named in the recovery to Dudley and the other feoffees
were to revert to the king and his heirs forever after the earl's death.[133]

Then, in August of the following year, 1507, the king forced a recognizance of £10,000 from the wretched peer that he would make no sale,
lease, or any other grant of land, that he would grant no office or annuity
nor sell growing timber on his estates without the king's consent in
writing under his sign manual or one of his seals. Under the same recognizance he suffered the humiliation of having a royal servant placed in
charge of his household,[134] whose activities he was not to meddle with, or
hinder, in any way. The earl himself was to appear once a day in the
royal household and not to depart without licence in writing 'except for
eight days in each quarter to be taken at his liberty.'[135] How much of the
estate was left at the end of Henry VII's reign it is impossible to say but
when the spendthrift earl died in 1523 it was so wasted that Henry Grey,
his half-brother and heir, never assumed the title 'by reason of his slender

estate' and his descendants were not summoned to parliament again until 1572.[136]

All in all, as the result of these activities, out of sixty-two peerage families[137] in existence between 1485 and 1509, a total of forty-six or forty-seven were for some part of Henry's reign at the king's mercy. Seven were under attainder, thirty-six, of whom five were also heavily fined, gave bonds and recognizances, another was probably also fined,[138] and three more were at some time under subpoenas which carried financial penalties. Only sixteen (possibly only fifteen) remained free of these financial threats.[139]

As we have seen, the system was by no means new. Attainders had been prominent enough in late Lancastrian and Yorkist times and bonds and recognizances were part of the normal discipline and the normal hazards of fifteenth-century life. Never before, however, had any monarch developed the disciplinary use of such financial instruments to so systematic and involved a degree. The mere numbers of families, great as they were, give only an inadequate idea of the complications and dangers which this intensified system brought with it. Under the Yorkists only a single peer, Lord Ferrers of Chartley, gave more than one recognizance.[140] Under Henry VII the number giving more than one rose to twenty-three, eleven gave five or more, two (Edward Sutton, Lord Dudley, and Lord Dacre) as many as twelve, and Lord Mountjoy twenty-three. Moreover, as noted earlier, many of the peers concerned gave bonds, recognizances, and mainprises for the good behaviour and the contracts of other noblemen, and, for that matter, a great many commoners too, as well as for their own. John Talbot, fourth earl of Shrewsbury, for example, besides giving the king recognizances totalling £466 13s. 4d. on his own behalf, between 1505 and 1507 stood guarantor for Lord Mountjoy in the sum of £500 and up to the end of the reign was jointly endangered with five different groups of people in sums totalling over £5,000.[141] There thus developed in the later years of Henry VII's reign an immensely tangled, complicated series of relationships in which a majority of the peerage were legally and financially in the king's power and at his mercy, so that in effect people were set under heavy penalties to guarantee the honesty and loyalty of their fellows. The system was so extensive that it must have created an atmosphere of chronic watchfulness, suspicion, and fear.

Polydore Vergil, who was in England during the later part of Henry's reign, had a very good idea of the king's motives. In his account of the year 1502, a date which exactly coincides with the remarkable increase in the number of recognizances enrolled on the close rolls, he remarked that Henry VII 'began to treat his people with more harshness and severity than had been his custom in order (as the king himself asserted) to ensure that they remained more thoroughly and entirely in obedience to him,' although people in general attributed his motives to greed. Vergil went on to allege that the king wished to keep his subjects obedient through fear, that he inflicted heavy financial penalties thinking that they derived from great wealth the courage to commit offences, and that his policy of financial terror was eminently successful.[142] Vergil's opinion (which Edward Hall exactly followed,[143] and Sir Robert Cotton and Sir Francis Bacon, as usual, exaggerated) deserves respect, for although the fragmentary and limited sources still available allow no calculation of the income which the king derived from these methods, it is most probable, as Professor Dietz surmised, that except for the fines levied on the Cornish rebels of 1497, the returns from fines, recognizances, and pardons sold was not great.[144]

Side by side with such financial sanctions as these, Henry VII's strictness in enforcing his feudal rights is notorious and, although there is no space to discuss such matters here, the king's transactions in the land market with various noble families also reinforce the impression of harshness and deserve investigation. So does the question of the sale of justice and payments for royal favours in legal cases:[145] a question which had been difficult and contentious all through the Middle Ages.[146] As usual, the whole atmosphere was probably made far worse by the corruption of the royal agents.[147]

To sum up, as remarked earlier, status and wealth went hand in hand, at this time. As the monarchy possessed little coercive power at its direct command, it was forced to rely on the rich, that is, the titled nobility and the greater gentry, to keep order in the countryside and to provide the bulk of the military forces both to suppress revolt at home and to wage its campaigns overseas. Far from destroying the peerage it was, therefore, essential to maintain its numbers. Periods of political tension, significantly enough, saw not only attainders but the greatest number of new creations. In their own interest kings had either to endow new peers or to promote men already rich enough to sustain the dignity. Between the late fourteenth century and the Reformation they generally preferred the latter course.[148] The later part of the fifteenth century and the first three decades of the sixteenth century was a period of remarkable stability for noble property. From 1450 onwards political miscalculation was the only conspicuous cause for loss of property. Neither land nor money was granted to the peerage in any great degree. On the other hand, theories of their economic decline appear to have been greatly exaggerated. As in any other age, reckless incapacity might ruin an individual – like the third Grey earl of Kent – or estates – like those of the Percies or the dukes of Buckingham – might suffer from poor administration or over-exploitation during periods of attainder or during minorities. Otherwise no peer is known to have been in more than temporary difficulties. The greater lords who fought in the Wars of the Roses were all richer than their grandfathers had been.

Though history, of course, never crudely repeats itself, various writers have noted a marked tendency in the Yorkists and early Tudors to by-pass ancient institutions which had become formalized, cumbersome, and over-rigid, and to adopt more directly personal forms of government which bear a very close resemblance to the practices of earlier times. An increased reliance on revenue from the crown lands was one of these methods; so was financial administration through the chamber rather than the exchequer and Dr J. G. Bellamy has described Edward IV's judicial methods as a return, at least in part, to the peripatetic tradition of Angevin kingship.[149] The arbitrary element in medieval English kingship was always strong. The king, as well as being the fount of that justice and discipline which flowed through the law courts, still exercised justice, tinged with favour, through his own will, especially upon his richer subjects. Great landed fortunes, and the power which they carried with them, could be profoundly affected by the royal favour or displeasure and the success of government still depended upon keeping a balance between the powerful. Indeed, the powerful expected the king to arbitrate fairly in their quarrels rather than to have to take their disputes to the law courts like ordinary men.[150]

Given this centuries-old tradition, direct interference in the affairs of the great can hardly, of itself, be considered new or unusual. Although many of Henry VII's actions may seem to us the very negation of justice, we should at least bear in mind that his conduct was less violent than that of many earlier kings. A good deal of the violence of the Anglo-Norman period is now attributed to the fact that William the Conqueror and his sons refused even to recognize the hereditary tenure of many estates.[151]

King John had compelled men to seal deeds allowing him to seize their
lands at his pleasure and he had imposed enormous fines upon his
tenants-in-chief, manipulating the huge resulting debts for political purposes.[152] Recently Mr K. B. McFarlane excoriated Edward I's treatment
of his earls, his violent 'arrangement' of escheats which, on very flimsy
pretexts, deprived a number of great families of wide inheritances for
the benefit of the royal house and its members.[153] It may also be stressed
that the somewhat evil reputation of Henry VII which has come down to
posterity owes more to contemporary and near-contemporary denunciation of his greed rather than to comments on the disciplinary aspects of
his policy. In spite of its evil reputation the fifteenth century was no more
violent than earlier times – indeed, it may have been rather less so. Certainly Edward IV and Henry VII were in some ways extremely cautious in
their relations with their subjects in general[154] and Henry VII's dealings
with the nobility had at least a conventional background both in political
tradition and in the way in which the king and the great lords themselves
dealt with their own estate officials and dependents and in the way in
which government was carried on in Wales and the marches.

As James Harrington wrote in the middle of the seventeenth century,
monarchy could be of two kinds, 'the one by arms, the other by a nobility'
and added 'a monarchy, divested of its nobility, has no refuge under
heaven but an army.'[155] Henry had no army. As his taxation policy, like
that of Edward IV, was principally aimed at avoiding discontent amongst
large numbers of his subjects, he could not afford to maintain one.
Foreign visitors noted with continual surprise how small the English
military forces were.[156] Henry, therefore, could do no other than rely
upon his nobility. In the north of England, the marches against Scotland
were still a frontier and, as Mr M. E. James has pointed out, a frontier
at this time was not a neat line of barbed wire fence, but a march many
miles deep, given over to endemic violence.[157] Although Henry experi-
mented with the abolition of aristocratic wardens of the marches[158] he
was soon forced to resort once again to the appointment of powerful
noblemen.[159] The famous council in the north (if indeed it had anything
more than a sporadic existence under Henry VII) was only a limited
success and, even in the late 1530s when Henry VIII and Thomas Cromwell
deprived the Percy earl of Northumberland of all his power and most
of his estates, they replaced him in office by a former Percy client, Thomas
Wharton, endowed from the Percy lands and suitably ennobled for the
purpose: a man belonging to the same landed society as the magnates. It

was only after 1570 that the power of the Percies and other great northern families finally passed to civil servants from London.[160]

Even in less abnormal areas the king exercised insufficient power through his own officials. Therefore, as Professor S. T. Bindoff once wrote, 'the keystone of the many arched temple of the Tudor peace were the noblemen and gentlemen of the kingdom ... The problem before Henry VII was how to suppress the magnates' abuse of power while preserving the power itself. He could no more do without a ruling class than he could do with a class that refused to be ruled.'[161]

If also, as Professor MacCaffery has remarked, for fifty-five years after Henry VII's accession the Tudors succeeded in keeping the greater aristocracy cowed,[162] this success was due in part to the fact that they gave the aristocracy no great cause for political and social offence. As long as the king was not actively evil or politically stupid they had no particular wish to dominate the central government: they cared far more for the maintenance of their inheritances and their local influence. In part Henry VII's oppressive disciplinary measures (which, after all, affected their conduct rather than their powers), exercised, in varying degrees, against at least three-quarters of the titled families of the kingdom, were all the more effective because the disturbing political experiences of a century and more had probably left the greater and more ancient families in a cautious mood.[163] Though far from being without precedent, the degree to which Henry VII took the use of bonds and recognizances was so extreme that, as Mr McFarlane wrote, during the last few years of his reign it produced a form of government that was indeed *sui generis*.

Henry VIII at once eased the system as part of a general reaction against the harsher aspects of his father's rule. The Venetian ambassador reported the new king's liberality,[164] and Lord Mountjoy wrote to Erasmus just after the arrest of Empson and Dudley that 'All England is in ecstasies. Extortion is put down, liberality is the order of the day.'[165] However, Henry, or his advisers, mixed his popular gestures with considerable financial caution. When granting a more comprehensive general pardon than the one which his father had issued just before his death, the new king included the reservation 'for all things except debts.'[166] With something of a flourish, to demonstrate 'how favourable and benevolent sovereign lord we have been unto divers our nobles and other our subjects' he merely *respited*, not pardoned, 'divers recognizances and other weighty matters drawn by our special commandment out of divers books signed with the hand of our dearest father' concerning fifty people, including ten aristocrats (three of them women).[167] As late as 1512, Thomas Lucas, Sir James Hobart (Henry VII's attorney), and the late king's executors were ordered to investigate debts due to the crown upon recognizances, obligations, recoveries, and deeds of feofment, long respited by the executors.[168] Such discrimination was, after all, to be expected, for a majority of bonds and obligations had always been made for purposes recognized as legal and just. For a decade and more the chamber went on collecting money in settlement of recognizances made under Henry VII and the practice of collecting the king's debts and dues in instalments by means of obligations continued, only to fall into disuse during Henry VIII's later years: and even then it was revived under Mary.[169]

Nevertheless, Henry VIII cancelled at least forty-five recognizances during the first year of his reign and one hundred and thirty more over the next five years.[170] In fifty-one cases the recognizances were stated to have been unjustly extorted.[171] Henry seems to have been as careful in dealing with recognizances taken from peers as with those of lesser men. A number concerning what might be called normal debts and contracts were allowed to stand,[172] at least, no record of their cancellation appears to have been made. However, Henry reduced the use of the system *in terrorem* over peers to minute proportions, though he did not discard it completely.[173] The ruinous sanctions hanging over Lord Burgavenny and their humiliating conditions of payment were cancelled.[174] So was the earl of Northumberland's fine of £10,000.[175] Henry cancelled bonds and recognizances affecting ten other peers during the first year of his reign.[176] In two cases the recognizances were stated to have been unjustly taken.[177] Even some of the land which Empson and Dudley had questionably wrung from peers for the crown was restored.[178] Henry VII himself had, of course, cancelled many other recognizances at various times, so, by the middle of 1510, possibly nine peers at the most remained bound for other than normal debts or mainprises (generally small in amount) for the good conduct of themselves and other men in office.[179]

The reasons for this new policy can be a matter only of opinion. Professor F. C. Dietz, writing nearly fifty years ago, thought that 'The stern justice of Henry VII's day was no longer needed to ensure respect for the laws.'[180] Since Dietz wrote, however, others have shown that the repression of lawlessness and violence was a much less rapid phenomenon than his generation held it to be: that its occurrence was the result, not so much of action taken by Henry VII, as of a more gradual process extending over most of the sixteenth century.[181] It is far more probable that, by the end of the reign, Henry VII's ruthless methods were producing a dangerous backlash of resentment,[182] and that his son's immediate, though by no means precipitate or incautious, relaxation of his methods was an avowed policy of appeasement to soften the resentment and anger of those aggrieved by the potentially ruinous fines and recognizances hanging over them – and the most important and dangerous of the aggrieved were the resentful nobility.

NOTES

1 'The lord himself can place his court into the court of the lord king, so that he may have the advice and agreement of the lord king's court touching the matter in doubt. And this lord king owes his barons as a matter of right ... But when a baron's doubts are resolved in the lord king's court he can return with his plea and determine it in his own court.' Glanvill, *De legibus et consuetudinibus regni Anglie*, ed. G. E. Woodbine (New Haven 1932), II, p. 123, quoted from D.M. Stenton, *English Justice between the Norman Conquest and the Great Charter* (Memoirs of the American Philosophical Society, vol. 60, 1964), p. 78.

2 See J.R. Lander, *Conflict and Stability in Fifteenth Century England* (London 1969), chap. 7

3 M. McKisack, *The Fourteenth Century* (Oxford 1959), pp. 201-2

4 For the sixteenth century, see F.W. Brooks, *The Council in the North* (revised ed., Historical Association, general ser., no. 25, 1966)

5 J. Cornwall, 'The Early Tudor Gentry,' *Economic History Review*, XVII (1964-5), 459-61; L. Stone, 'Social Mobility in England, 1500-1700,' *Past and Present*, 33 (1966), p. 52

6 J.P. Gilson, 'A Defence of the Proscription of the Yorkists in 1459.' *English Historical Review* (hereinafter EHR), XXVI (1911), 515. The Yorkist lords themselves stressed the same point in a letter sent to Henry VI at Ludlow in 1459, commenting on the action of their enemies who had shown '... ne any tenderness to the noble blood of this land such as serve to the tuition and defence thereof, ne not weighing the loss of your true liegemen of your said realm.' *An English Chronicle of the Reigns of Richard II, Henry IV, Henry V and Henry VI*, ed. J.S. Davies (Camden Society, Old Series, LXIV, 1856), p. 82. I have modernized spelling and punctuation in all quotations in this article.

7 *Grants, Etc., From the Crown During the Reign of Edward the Fifth*, ed. J.G. Nichols (Camden Society, Old Series, LX, 1854), pp. xxxix-lxiii

8 'And therefore my right redoubted lord I pray almighty god to save the king our sovereign lord, to give him grace to issue as a king, to abound in all virtues, to be assisted with all other his lords in such wise that his noble realm of England may prosper, abound in virtues, and that sin may be eschewed, justice kept, the realm defended, good men rewarded, male-

factors punished, the idle people to be put to labour, *that he with the nobles of his realm may reign gloriously.' The Prologues and Epilogues of William Caxton*, ed. W.J.B. Crotch (Early English Text Society 1928), pp. 14-16, see also p. 81.

9 *Proceedings and Ordinances of the Privy Council of England*, ed. Sir H. Nicolas (London 1834-7), VI, p. 161

10 '... the might of the land *after* the might of the great lords thereof standeth most in the king's officers.' *The Governance of England*, ed. C. Plummer (Oxford 1885), pp. 150-1

11 So, incidentally, did Caxton.

12 *The Boke of Noblesse*, ed. J.G. Nichols (Roxburghe Club 1860), pp. 77-8. See also Edmund Dudley, *The Tree of Commonwealth*, ed. D.M. Brodie (Cambridge 1948), pp. 44-5, 66. For Dudley the functions of the nobility entailed the duty of 'true defence,' that is, the protection of the poor from injury and the defence of the king. Instances can be multiplied almost indefinitely, e.g., 'For so much as the great surety, defence, honour and the politic governance of this noble realm standeth and oweth to be in the noble persons, born of high blood, and exalted to high estate and power ...' (creation of the duke of York) *Rotuli parliamentorum* (hereinafter *Rot. parl.*), VI, 168. In 1497 Raymundo de Raymundis, commenting on the Cornish rebellion, Perkin Warbeck, and the Scottish attack, wrote, 'Everything favours the king, especially an immense treasure, and because all the nobles of the realm know the royal wisdom and either fear him or bear him an extra-ordinary affection ... and *the state of the realm is in the hands of the nobles not of the people.' Calendar of State Papers and Manuscripts existing in the Archives and Collections of Milan*, ed. and trans. A.B. Hinds (London 1912), I, p. 325. See also *ibid.*, pp. 316-17.

13 G.A. Holmes, *The Estates of the Higher Nobility in Fourteenth-Century England* (Cambridge 1957), pp. 4-5.

14 In 1478 George Neville was degraded from the dukedom of Bedford, ostensibly on grounds of poverty. *Rot. parl.*, VI, 173. Also, see below, p. 345-7 for the case of the earl of Kent.

15 See below, p. 348-9

16 See Lander, *Conflict and Stability*, chap. 7

17 This seems to be true except for a few castles in the northern marches. Fifteenth-century 'castles' were built as comfortable residences, not fortresses, and by this time most of the older private castles, even in Wales and the marches, were so dilapidated that they were probably indefensible. See B.H. St. J. O'Neil, *Castles and Cannon* (Oxford 1960), pp. 1-64; J.R. Lander, *The Wars of the Roses* (London 1965), intro.; T.B. Pugh, *The Marcher Lordships of South Wales, 1415-1536* (Board of Celtic Studies, University of Wales History and Law Series, no. xx, 1963), p. 247.

18 *A Relation, or Rather a True Account of the Island of England*, ed. and trans. C.A. Sneyd (Camden Society, Old Series XXXVII, 1847), p. 37

19 R.L. Mackie, *King James IV of Scotland* (Edinburgh and London, 1958), pp. 50-1

20 L. Stone, *The Crisis of the Aristocracy, 1559-1641* (Oxford 1965), chap. 5
21 J. Bossy, 'The Character of Elizabethan Catholicism,' *Past and Present*, 21 (1962), 39-59; J. Hurstfield, *The Elizabethan Nation* (London 1964), p. 30
22 As the household ordinances of November 1454 state, 'In so much as faith and truth and liegance compelleth every subject to do all that in him is for the honour, estate and welfare of his sovereign lord – it must natheless be thought and understand that lords and such as be called to be councillors with a prince must more tenderly take to heart those things wherein resteth his renown, honour, worship and politique rule of his land and ease of his people.' *Proceedings and Ordinances*, VI, 220.
23 See the observations, made in 1504, upon a quarrel between the earl of Northumberland and the archbishop of York: '... considering that they both were men of great honour and authority many enormities might and were like thereupon to ensue. Wherefore the king's highness then and there commanded my Lord Chancellor to show unto them on his behalf that for as much as they both being men of honour and such persons as the King's grace had chiefly committed to governing and authority in the parts of the north his highness would not otherwise take it but as a great fault in them both and that it should rather have been to both their honours to have given good example to other men than to have been of such demeanour ...' *Select Cases in the Council of Henry VIII*, ed C.G. Bayne and W.H. Dunham Jr. (Seldon Society 1958), pp. 41-2.
24 Dudley, *The Tree of Commonwealth*, p. 103
25 *Ibid.*, p. 39
26 T.F.T. Plucknett, *The Legislation of Edward I* (Oxford 1949), chap. 3
27 See J.R. Lander, *The Wars of the Roses* (London 1965), pp. 25-6, and the references there given
28 *Proceedings and Ordinances*, III, 174-7; IV, 36; *Rot. parl.*, V, 407
29 *Proceedings and Ordinances*, III, 217-18; *Rot. parl.*, V. 408, 487-8; VI, 287-8
30 K.B. McFarlane, 'The Wars of the Roses, '*Proceedings of the British Academy*, L (1964), 115-16. The tendency continued. Between 1485 and 1547, twenty-eight out of fifty-five families (fifty-six peers) were extinguished in the male line, only twenty-seven remaining. H. Miller, 'The Early Tudor Peerage, 1485-1547,' *Bulletin of the Institute of Historical Research*, XXIV (1951), 88-91.
31 Between 1439 and 1504, twenty-one peerages were continued in this way.
32 Lander, *Conflict and Stability*, p. 174. In the difficult years between 1447 and 1450 there were no less than fifteen new creations, in 1460 and 1461 nine, followed by another four between 1464 and 1470. Henry VII added only five: significantly enough, all but two during the first three years of his reign. See J.E. Powell and K. Wallis, *The House of Lords in the Middle Ages* (London 1968), chaps. 25-9. In the period of calm between 1509 and 1527 his son created only seven. In the years of strain between 1529 and 1547 the number of new creations rose to eighteen. This tendency was at

least as important as the ferocious attainders which, temporarily in most
cases, permanently in a few, deprived peerage families of their wealth and
position. Excluding members of the royal families, thirty-four peers were
attainted between 1459 and 1504. Nine were attainted and executed. All
but five (viz 84%) were ultimately restored between 1536 and 1540. J.R.
Lander, 'Attainder and Forfeiture, 1453-1509,' *The Historical Journal*, IV
(1961), 119-51; H. Miller, *'The Early Tudor Peerage*, p. 89.

33 *Calendar of Patent Rolls* (hereinafter *Cal. Pat. R.*), *1547-1548*, p. 252
34 McFarlane, 'The Wars of the Roses,' 119. One of the most constant themes
of the later Middle Ages (as probably earlier too) was fear for property.
After the extensive treason trials, executions, and confiscations of estates
under Edward II, Edward III had restored a feeling of security to the landed classes by gradually returning forfeited property and by conceding in
1352 a statute which narrowly restricted the definition of treason. Richard
II's confiscations, particularly his withholding of the great Lancastrian inheritance from Henry of Derby in 1399, had revived these terrors. For his
reign in general, see C.D. Ross, 'Forfeiture for Treason in the Reign of
Richard II,' EHR, LXXI (1956), 560-75. During the 1450s Richard of York
constantly harped on these fears in his propaganda against the court (e.g.
see his letter to the citizens of Shrewsbury in 1452; *Original Letters Illustrative of English History*, ed. H. Ellis [London 1824], I, 11-13) and it may
well be that the threat to property in the attainders of 1459 brought over
to York a number of peers who had hitherto declined to support him.
Davies, *An English Chronicle*, pp. 79-80.
35 Lander, *Conflict and Stability*, chap. 3
36 J.R. Lander, 'Marriage and Politics in the Fifteenth Century,' *Bulletin of
the Institute of Historical Research*, XXXVI (1963), 122-7, 147-8
37 John de la Pole, earl of Lincoln, Edmund de la Pole, earl of Suffolk, and
Francis, viscount Lovell.
38 Lord Audley, attainted 1497. The reversal of 1514 in favour of his son John
was, like Henry VII's reversals (see below), incomplete. It exempted
grants made from the estates to Lord Dudley and others.
39 The act states that Zouche might take over any of these reserved properties only if he could persuade the grantees to sell them.
40 The family income is unknown but in 1433 the marriage of the Fitzwater
heiress and the keeping of her lands had been sold 'for the comparatively
small sum of £533.' T.B. Pugh and C.D. Ross, 'The English Baronage and
the Income Tax of 1436,' *Bulletin of the Institute of Historical Research*,
XXVI (1953), 19.
41 In effect Surrey recovered the hereditary estates of the Howards and that
part of the Mowbray estates of the duchy of Norfolk to which his family
was entitled as co-heirs, which the king had not already granted away. The
king, by certain legal concessions, made it easier for him to negotiate with
the grantees to buy them back. Surrey, however, never recovered the immense grants from the crown lands which had enriched his family under
Richard III.

42 As also a fourth, the Audley family, restored under Henry VIII. See above, note 38.

43 For a more detailed account and evidence for these attainders, see J.R. Lander, 'Attainder and Forfeiture, 1453 to 1509,' *The Historical Journal*, IV (1961), 133 ff.

44 The legal, technical differences between obligations, bonds, recognizances and mainprises are irrelevant to this study. The crucial point is that they all involved promises or guarantees under financial penalties.

45 EHR, LXXXI (1966), 153-5. McFarlane allowed the possibility that the difference in the entries from 1500 onwards may be somewhat misleading owing to a tightening up of procedural methods, but on the whole discounted this factor. The order of December 1499 alleged that, owing to the negligence of the royal officers, recognizances 'in cases of high treason or misprision of the king's majesty by his subjects or strangers' had failed to be enrolled and laid down heavy penalties for failure to enrol within eight days. *(Cal. Pat. R., 1485-1500*, no. 1199). Mr. McFarlane argued that the royal officers 'as a precaution ... decided thereafter to enrol all recognizances to which this order might conceivably apply.' Many, in fact, seem to fall somewhat outside the regulation. McFarlane's argument is strengthened by the fact that chroniclers noted a more rigid attitude on Henry's part shortly after this time. See below, pp. 347-8.

46 See below, pp. 349-50

47 E.g., in the marcher lordships of the Stafford dukes of Buckingham the steward and other officers had to give recognizances as guarantees of good conduct and they were liable to forfeit large sums of money if they defaulted. When Thomas Vaughan of Hergest (d. 1469) was appointed receiver of the lordship of Brecon in 1451 he had to find at least six mainpernors with freehold estates in England, each of whom was bound in the sum of 2,000 marks, and at least six other mainpernors bound jointly and severally in a further 2,000 marks in the ducal exchequer at Brecon. Pugh, *The Marcher Lordships*, p. 246 and n. 2. For the duchy of Lancaster and the Burgavenny estates see R.R. Davies, 'Baronial Accounts, Incomes and Arrears in the Later Middle Ages,' *Economic History Review*, 2nd ser., XXI (1968), 221 and n. 7, 227, n. 6. For examples on the crown lands see *Calendar of Fine* Rolls, 1471-1485, nos. 48-57, 61-71 and many others.

48 Eg., not to sue in foreign courts, to serve the king faithfully in the French wars. *Calendar of Close Rolls* (hereinafter *Cal. Close R.) 1419-22*, pp. 38-9, 44, 66.

49 Pugh, *The Marcher Lordships*, pp. 29-30

50 See *ibid.*, and T.B. Pugh, 'The Indenture for the Marches between Henry VII and Edward Stafford (1477-1521), Duke of Buckingham,' EHR, LXXI (1956), 436-41

51 *Cal. Close R., 1399-1402*, pp. 93, 413; *1402-5*, pp. 506-7, 516-17; *1405-9*, pp. 134(2), 370, 525 (Arundel)

52 A similar recognizance was also taken from the archbishop. Uncle and nephew had apparently been on bad terms since 1405 and the earl had

become a political ally of his uncle's rivals, the Beauforts. *Dictionary of National Biography* (hereinafter DNB), VII, 101-2.

53 *Cal. Close R., 1413-19*, pp. 97-99
54 *Ibid.*, p. 500
55 *Ibid.*, pp. 451, 515; *1419-22*, p. 63. Figures given in the text do not exactly tally as one peer, Lord Clinton, was involved in two of these transactions. Non-nobles also gave mainprises for the good behaviour of Lady Lestraunge and the countess of Arundel, *1413-19*, pp. 458, 459, and two citizens of London gave recognizances that the duke of Exeter should content the king for the value of the goods taken from a Genoese carrack wrecked off the Devonshire coast, *1419-22*, p. 38.
56 The duke of Gloucester, the duchess of Clarence, the earls of Huntingdon, Northumberland, Ormond, Oxford, Salisbury, Stafford, Westmorland. Joan Beaufort, Countess of Westmorland, Lords Daker, Fauconberg, Fitzhugh, Greystoke, Grey of Ruthyn, and Talbot. *Cal. Close R., 1422-9*, pp. 53, 58-59, 66, 69, 132, 259, 277, 325, 342, 343, 448; *1429-35*, pp. 67, 125, 190-1, 322, 346-7, 348, 351, 359; *1435-41*, pp. 102, 157-8. The most interesting are those taken in the course of the notorious quarrel about the Westmorland inheritance which continued for well over a decade. (See E.F. Jacob, *The Fifteenth Century, 1399-1485* [Oxford 1961], pp. 321-3). Several of these guarantee repayment of a loan which Humphrey of Gloucester had taken from the royal treasury and that of 1432 in which Richard of York had to find friends sufficient to put up ten recognizances of 100 marks each as security for payment by the duke, within five years, by two instalments each year of 1,000 marks demanded for livery of his lands.
57 The dukes of Buckingham, Exeter, and Norfolk, the earls of Devon, Northumberland, Oxford, Salisbury, Westmorland, and Wiltshire, Lords Berners, Bonvile, Camoys, Clinton, Fauconberg, Grey of Codnor, Grey of Ruthyn, Grey of Wilton, Latimer, Roos, Rougemont, Welles, Willoughby. *Cal. Close R., 1435-41*, pp. 178-9, 239, 276, 279, 381, 384, 388, 446, 471; *1441-7*, pp. 144, 149, 196, 460; *1447-54*, pp. 398, 476, 512; *1454-61*, pp. 44, 109, 171, 173, 227.
58 In the cases of John Heydon and Robert Wingfield mentioned below. R.L. Storey, *The End of the House of Lancaster* (London 1966), pp. 79, 226-7.
59 *Ibid.*, pp. 226-7
60 See note 57 above
61 Storey, *The End of the House of Lancaster, ibid.*
62 *Ibid.*, and J.R. Lander, 'Henry VI and the Duke of York's second protectorate,' in *Bulletin of the John Rylands Library*, XLIII (1960), 59 ff.
63 Storey, *The End of the House of Lancaster*, chaps. 5-9
64 Sir J.H. Ramsay, *Lancaster and York* (Oxford 1892), II, pp. 208-9
65 *Cal. Close R., 1454-61*, pp. 292-3. Three more recognizances totalling £9,333 6s. 8d. were taken from minor members of the Percy family. *Ibid.*, p. 293.
66 In May 1458, William Neville, Lord Fauconberg, and the duke of Bucking-

ham, the earl of Warwick and Viscount Bourchier on Fauconberg's behalf. In April 1459 the duke of Exeter and Lord Roos on Exeter's behalf. *Cal. Close R. 1454-61*, pp. 287-8, 350. These do not seem to have had the same political significance.

67 *Cal. Close R., 1468-76*, nos. 403, 404

68 DNB, xx, 240-1

69 *Cal. Close R., 1468-76*, no. 1103

70 In 1468 the earl of Shrewsbury, and Lords Dudley and Mountjoy gave a joint recognizance for £1,000 binding the earl not to molest certain jurors and to keep the peace towards Henry, Lord Grey. Lord Grey, Lord Hastings, and a squire, Thomas Wyngfield, gave a similar guarantee regarding the earl. In 1472 Lord Stanley gave a bond in 3,000 marks to abide by the award of arbitrators chosen by the king in his quarrel with Sir James Harrington; in 1476 Edward, Lord Burgavenny, gave a bond in 4,000 marks to appear in chancery on the morrow of All Hallows and not to molest William Culpepyr of Aylesford, and in 1478 his son, George, Lord Burgavenny, gave a bond of £4,000 guaranteeing the sale of estates to the king. *Cal Close R., 1468-76*, nos. 93, 94, 403, 900, 1103; *1476-85*, nos. 44, 407.

71 Three concerned land transactions. John, duke of Suffolk, together with four commoners, gave a bond in 2,000 marks, for John Wyngfield, concerning the transfer to the king of some of the property of the late duke of Norfolk; John, Lord Audley, a bond for £5,000, also concerning the transfer of property to the king; William Berkeley, earl of Nottingham, a bond in £10,000 concerning the very complicated transfer to the king of the inheritance of the Mowbray dukes of Norfolk, of whom he was one of the co-heirs. Four others were imposed for good behaviour: 1,000 marks on viscount Lisle to remain within a mile of London and generally keep the peace; a bond in £1,000 from Lord Ferrers to keep the peace towards the abbey of Waltham, and a bond given by Lord Stourton for the good behaviour of Sir William Berkeley which is known only from a reference to the payment of part of it. *Cal. Close R., 1476-85*, nos. 1184, 1218, 1225, 1317, 1412, 1423.

72 *Cal. Close R., 1476-85*, nos. 1194, 1242, 1243, 1244, 1245, 1258, 1259, 1417, 1456

73 Lander, 'Attainder and Forfeiture,' p. 149

74 See above, pp. 333-5. The eighteen reversals of Yorkist attainders (four under Edward IV, the rest in 1485) appear to have been unconditional, except for that of Dorset in 1485.

75 BM, MS Lansdowne, 127 (hereinafter BM, L, 127), covering the period of 9 September 1504, to 28 May 1508. A special list of obligations taken by Dudley for 21 Henry VII is also contained in BM, MS Harleian 1877, f. 47.

76 Public Record Office (hereinafter PRO), Exchequer treasury of receipt, miscellaneous books, E 36/214. In the back part of this book Heron kept careful lists of all the obligations and recognizances in his hands from

1505 to 1509. These lists were from time to time annotated by the king. They also give a fuller description of the bonds, etc., than is to be found in the receipt books. See F.C. Dietz, *English Government Finance, 1485-1558* (University of Illinois Studies in the Social Sciences, IX, 1920), p. 33.

77 *Cal. Close R., 1485-1500*, nos. 52, 82, 616, 618, 753, 894, 942, 973, 974, 1008, 1056, 1060. The earls of Westmorland and Devon, viscount Beaumont, Lord Grey of Wilton, and Charles Somerset, Lord Herbert, each gave a recognizance on his own behalf; in a similar way Lord Burgh gave two. The marquess of Dorset, the earls of Devon and Kent, viscount Lisle, Lords Burgh, Grey of Codnor, Grey of Wilton, and Willoughby de Broke gave them on behalf of others. They covered such varied matters as feudal custody and marriage, rents, the safekeeping of royal castles, good behaviour in office and appearance before the king at specified dates.

78 See note 45 above

79 *Cal. Close R., 1485-1500*, no. 1222, 20 July 1500, concerning Edward, Lord Dudley. No condition was specified.

80 *Cal. Close R., 1500-9*, nos. 131, 226, 228, 290, 304, 331, 332, 347, 361, 377, 408, 415, 423, 428, 459, 499, 518, 543, 549, 550, 599, 602, 605, 609, 622, 635, 658, 669, 675, 686, 705, 756, 773, 798, 814, 818, 821, 822, 825, 851, 904, 955, 963. The peers concerned (some being involved in several bonds and recognizances) were: the duke of Buckingham, the marquess of Dorset, the earls of Arundel, Derby, Essex, Kent, Shrewsbury, and Surrey, viscount Lisle, Lords Burgavenny, Clifford, Conyers, Darcy, Dacre of Gilsland, Daubeney, Edward Sutton, Lord Dudley, Grey of Powys, Hastings, Mountjoy, Seyntmount, Stourton, Scrope of Upsall, de la Warre, Willoughby de Broke, Willoughby of Eresby, and Lady Hungerford.

81 BM, L, 127, r. 4, 16d, 20r, 43r, 48d; PRO E 36/214, pp. 256, 381, 445, 472, 491, 492, 499; Lords Berners, Dacre of the South, FitzWarren, Grey of Ruthyn, Ogle, Scrope of Bolton, Herbert (Charles Somerset), and Lady Arundel

82 *Cal. Close R., 1485-1500*, no. 52

83 *Ibid.*, no. 82

84 Bayne and Dunham, *Select Cases*, pp. 41-2, 44

85 *Cal. Close R., 1500-9*, no. 499

86 BM, L, 127, m. 29d; PRO E 36/214, p. 502

87 *Cal. Close R., 1500-9*, no. 955 (xii)

88 *Ibid.*, no. 377 (xii)

89 *Ibid.*, no. 332. For other recognizances involving seventeen more people in Wyndham's affairs, see *ibid.*, nos. 361, 419, 579, 741.

90 *Ibid.*, no. 226

91 *Ibid.*, no. 228

92 *Ibid.*, nos. 290, 428, 756. Henry VIII cancelled all these recognizances on 3 November 1509 but at the same time took another recognizance of £10,000 from Mountjoy whom he had re-appointed on 6 October. *Letters and Papers Foreign and Domestic of the Reign of Henry VIII, preserved in the Public Record Office, the British Museum, and elsewhere* (I, cata-

logued by J.S. Brewer, 2nd ed. R.H. Brodie, 1920; ii-iv, catalogued by J.S.
Brewer, 1864-72), i, no. 257 (5) ; see also no. 257 (4).

93 Seven for £100 each jointly with Sir Thomas Greisley and Sir John Mont-
gomery for payment of 100 marks at each of seven terms down to Pentecost, 1505. They were then cancelled when, presumably, the debts had
been paid; eleven for 240 marks each together with Sir William Say,
Robert Newport, and Thomas Periunt for various payments totalling
2,300 marks down to Christmas 1511, when they were then cancelled; in
1507 he gave a recognizance of £100 for Sir Richard Carew who had become keeper of Calais under terms rather similar (but considerably less
onerous) to his own tenures at Hammes. *Cal. Close R., 1500-9*, nos. 228,
549, 773; pro, e 36/214, p. 395. For two other small ones, see e 36/214,
pp. 409, 463.

94 See above, p. 340

95 *Cal. Close R., 1500-9*, nos. 602, 675(i), 767

96 W.C. Richardson, *Tudor Chamber Administration 1485-1547* (Baton
Rouge 1952), p. 150; J.M.W. Bean, *The Estates of the Percy Family,
1416-1537* (Oxford 1958), p. 143; pro, e 36/214, p. 474, 1 October 1505.
Another entry mentions ravishment of the king's ward 'and other retainers,' *ibid.*, p. 479, 6 December 1505.

97 pro, e 36/214, p. 403

98 *Cal. Close R., 1500-9*, no. 821 (i)

99 pro, e 36/214, p. 530. See also *ibid.*, p. 403. Bean, *The Estates*, p. 143

100 bm, l 127, p. 50.d. The net value of the Percy estates c. 1523 was something under £3,900. Bean, *The Estates*, p. 140.

101 Bean, *The Estates, loc. cit.*

102 *Rot. parl.*, vi, 315-6. Dorset's first wife had been Anne Holland, daughter
and heiress of the last Holland duke of Exeter. There had been complicated property settlements at the time of the marriage.

103 dnb, viii, pp. 644-5

104 *Cal. Close R., 1485-1500*, no. 612

105 The indenture details the property as two manors in Lincolnshire, two
manors and a pasture in Leicestershire, and all lands in Kent, London, and
Coventry.

106 *Rot. parl.*, vi, 472-3. This act makes it clear that the remaining lands had,
in fact, by this time been placed in the hands of the trustees.

107 *Cal. Close R., 1485-1500*, no. 612, '... after due notice given by the king he
will after three weeks cause other persons to be bound to the king by recognizances so that his highness or his heirs may discharge the executors.'

108 *Cal. Close R., 1485-1500*, no. 618. All these arrangements must have been
under discussion for some time for the fifty-five 'mainprised for the loyalty
of Dorset' on 19 and 22 May, a fortnight before the indenture was enrolled.

109 *Cal. Close R., 1485-1500*, no. 836

110 *Reports from the Lord's Committees touching the Dignity of a Peer of the
Realm* (London 1829), v, pp. 402-3. In 1495 the act assigning revenues for
the expenses of the royal household was not to be prejudicial to Dorset

'touching any annuity granted to the said marquess, in, of, or upon the creation of him into Marquess Dorset.' *Rot. parl.*, VI, 502.

111 Exempted 'for any office to him by my Lord Prince given by his Letters
Patents.' *Rot. parl.*, VI, 466.

112 *Cal. Close R., 1485-1500*, no. 650

113 It is just possible that in spite of their apparently comprehensive language
the indenture and the act of parliament did not, after all, cover all Dorset's
estates. The act of parliament states 'except such manors, lands and tene-
ments, rents, reversions and services, as be excepted and forprised in the
said indentures ...' This may possibly indicate that some property was exempted in the second arrangement concerning the lands not immediately
enfeoffed in 1492.

114 In May 1496 Dorset was able to make a marriage contract for his daughter, Elizabeth, which involved the payment of 1,000 marks. *Cal. Close R.,
1485-1500*, no. 945. The original indenture of 1492 has a note appended in
a schedule stating that it was vacated by a writ signed by John Blythe,
keeper of the chancery rolls. Unfortunately the note is undated but Blythe
died in August 1499. (See J. Le Neve, *Fasti Ecclesiae Anglicanae 1300-
1541*, III, Salisbury diocese, compiled by J.M. Horne [London 1963], p. 3.)
The arrangement may possibly have been cancelled in September 1496
when nine men, including the earl of Devon, put up mainprises for Dorset's
allegiance totalling £2,766 13s. 4d., *Cal. Close R., 1485-1500*, no. 972.
These new arrangements do not mention the indentures of 1492 so that
these men were not substitutes for earlier guarantors. So this seems to be
the most likely point for the replacement of one set of arrangements by
another less severe.

115 Henry VII's wife died in 1503.

116 *The Chronicle of Calais*, ed. J.G. Nichols (Camden Society, Old Series,
XXXV, 1846), p. 6. In April 1509 Dorset had been excepted by name from
the general pardon, but in July he was brought back from Calais and in
August he was pardoned and granted the office of forester of Sawsey for-
est, Northants. *Letters and Papers*, I, nos. 11 (10), 104, 158 (49), (75). In
September the lieutenant of Calais stated that he could not have made ends
meet but for the money he had received for Dorset's board and lodging.
Letters and Papers, I, 170.

117 Bayne and Dunham, *Select Cases*, pp. cxxi-cxxii; W.H. Dunham, Jr, 'Lord
Hastings' Indentured Retainers, 1461-1483,' *Transactions of the Connec-
ticut Academy of Arts and Sciences*, XXXIX, (1955), pp. 103-4

118 *Cal. Close R., 1500-9*, no. 825(i)

119 *Ibid.*, no. 825(ii)

120 *Ibid.*, no. 825(iii)

121 *Ibid.*, no. 825 (iv) ; BM, L 127, p. 53^r notes the delivery, on Lord Burgavenny's behalf, of the various documents concerned.

122 *Ibid.*

123 The first instalment due was paid at Candlemas 1508 in ready money. BM,
L 127, p. 55^r, dated 12 February.

124 H.L. Gray, 'Incomes from Land in England in 1436,' EHR, XLIX (1934), 617. This seriously understates their income. Underassessment was considerable (see T.B. Pugh and C.D. Ross, 'The English Baronage and the Income Tax of 1436,' *Bulletin of the Institute of Historical Research*, XXVI [1953], 1-28. There was a dowager alive at the time, whose income was apparently not included, nor did this particular tax cover Welsh estates. In 1559 the *gross* rental of the estates was between £2,000 and £2,999 *p.a.* (L. Stone, *The Crisis*, p. 760), but by this time very considerable additional estates had fallen in from the Beauchamp family. *The Complete Peerage* hereafter CP), ed. V. Gibbs and others (1910-59), I, pp. 27-34.

125 Although this is not made explicit in the main indenture, Sir John Heron's book states that Burgavenny, over and above the £5,000 agreed upon, was still obliged to pay the residue of the acknowledged debt at the king's pleasure, PRO, E 36/214, p. 535.

126 *Letters and Papers*, I, 632(4), 1356(16)

127 CP, VII, 169

128 *Cal. Close R., 1500-9*, no. 473. By the time of the second earl's death he still owed 2,500 marks (apparently for a wardship) of which the king now pardoned £1,000; *ibid.* no. 482. See also BM, L 127, p. 6d; PRO, E 36/214, p. 466.

129 Made up of £750 for livery of his lands, 1,000 marks remaining for the wardship of Elizabeth Trussell and 400 marks for livery of his mother's lands.

130 *Cal. Close R., 1500-9*, no. 553; BM, L 127, p. 27d

131 *Cal. Close R., 1500-9*, no. 724. This apparently replaced the slightly earlier sale of the reversion of the manor (together with other lands). *Ibid.*, no. 702.

132 Here incorrectly stated as £4,000.

133 *Cal. Close R., 1500-9*, no. 765; BM, L 127, pp. 32d, 44r

134 Apparently Sir William Gascoigne was put in charge of the household, for an entry of 10 August 1507 in Dudley's notebook records repayment of £43 6s. 8d. which the king had advanced to Gascoigne for the charges of the earl's household. BM, L 127, p. 47r.

135 *Cal. Close R., 1500-9*, no. 797

136 CP, VII, 169-71

137 The parliamentary peerage was, in fact, somewhat smaller than this figure suggests as not all these families were members of it at the same time; e.g. John, Lord Cheyne, was made a baron in 1487 and his peerage became extinct on his death without heirs in 1499 and the barony of Dinham, created in 1467, died out in 1501. I have excluded (a) two foreign families, that of Louis de Gruthuyse, earls of Winchester between 1472 and 1500, and Philibert de Chandée, earl of Bath from 1486, (b) members of the Plantagenet and Tudor royal families who held peerages.

138 Lord Beauchamp of Powicke, though his identification is somewhat doubtful.

139 Earl Ryvers, the earls of Huntingdon, Stafford, and Westmorland,

viscount Welles, Lords Cheyne, Cobham, Dinham, Egremont, Fitzhugh, Welles and Willoughby (Richard Hastings), Latimer, Lumley, Morley, Rochford, and Roos. See also note 138 above.

140 Two recognizances were taken from the Burgavenny family, but one each from father and son during the time each held the barony.

141 *Cal. Close R., 1500-9*, nos. 599, 904; PRO, E 36/214, pp. 392, 402, 403, 493, 495. See also the petition which Lord Dacre presented to Henry VIII in 1509 for discharge from recognizances, alleging (1) that bonds in 2,000 marks had been wrongfully taken for the keeping of Herbottle castle from Sir George Tailboys and still retained after Dacre had been discharged from keeping that office, (2) for £500 in which he was bound for keeping the peace against Lord Greystoke and for his own and others' appearance in the Star chamber, (3) £200 of which he was bound jointly with others, allegedly wrongly forfeited, (4) a recognizance of 3,000 marks wrongly transformed by Empson and Dudley into a debt payable at Michaelmas and (5) of 1,000 marks (600 of which had been paid) in which he had been bound with George, Lord Fitzhugh, for his mother Dame Mabel Dacre accused of (wrongfully, it is alleged), and imprisoned for ravishing a royal ward. Another entry reveals that he had also given a recognizance for 1,000 marks jointly with Sir Edward Musgrave, *Letters and Papers*, I, nos. 131, 132 (50). For the original indenture with Musgrave, see *Cal. Close R., 1500-9*, no. 582; for no. (3) above, *ibid.*, no. 315. See also, *ibid.*, no. 818. For six more recognizances in which Dacre was bound see *ibid.*, nos. 543 and 601. The grand total of recognizances for Dacre from various sources reaches at least *twelve*.

142 '... all people, in terror of losing their wealth, at once began to behave themselves and (as the saying goes) to withdraw into their shells.' In discussing the actions of Empson and Dudley, Vergil added 'they proceeded not against the poor but the wealthy churchmen, rich magnates, even the intimates of the king himself, and any and every individual of fortune' and '... the king claimed that he tolerated these exactions of set plan, in order thereby to maintain the population in obedience.' *The Anglica Historia of Polydore Vergil, A.D. 1485-1537*, ed and trans. D. Hay (Camden Society, 3rd series, LXXIV, 1950), pp. 126-31. It is interesting to note that in 1541 Henry VIII 'graciously remarked that he had an evil people to rule and promised that he would make them so poor that they would never be able to rebel again.' J.J. Scarisbrick, *Henry VIII* (London 1968), p. 428.

143 Though he was slightly more inclined to give Henry the benefit of the doubt on the question of greed. E. Hall, *Chronicle* (London 1809), pp. 499, 502-3.

144 At least up to Michaelmas 1505, when Heron's receipt book ends, Dietz, *English Government Finance*, p. 34. Payments 'by obligation' begin to appear in the chamber records in 1493, and towards the end of the reign, together with similar payments 'by recognizance,' they became very important, though, of course, only a minority were from peers. In the year, Michaelmas 1504 to Michaelmas 1505, Dietz states that £34,999 was received in this way. Unfortunately most of the entries are brief and do not

specify the cause. Elsewhere Dietz implies that it was 'bonds of various sorts' together with jewels, plate, and loans that made up the bulk of the immense fortune Henry VII is alleged to have left at his death. *Ibid.*, pp. 33, 87. For serious doubts about the extent of this fortune, see B.P. Wolffe, 'Henry VII's Land Revenues and Chamber Finance,' EHR, LXXIX (1964), 253-4.

145 E.g., see Bayne and Dunham, *Select Cases*, pp. xxxix and BM, L 127/34ʳ, 37ʳ, 55ʳ

146 W. Stubbs, *The Constitutional History of England* (Oxford 1873-8), II, pp. 636-7, J.C. Holt, *Magna Carta* (Cambridge 1965), p. 226

147 As noted earlier (see above, pp. 333 ff.) courtiers and officials made considerable gains at the expense of unfortunate peers suing for the reversal of their attainders. Dudley, a poor man in the mid-1490s before he entered the royal service, died possessed of lands in thirteen counties and goods worth £5,000. Many years after his death he was accused of forgery. It should be remembered, however, that few people at this time were over-scrupulous about forgery if it suited their own interests and accusations of corruption after the death of powerful men were common enough. Sir Robert Plumpton accused Empson of trying to dispossess him of his lands for the benefit of the heirs general of his father, Sir William Plumpton, to one of whom Empson planned to marry his daughter, Brodie, *Dudley: The Tree of Commonwealth*, p. 10; Dietz, *English Government Finance*, pp. 46-47; *The Plumpton Correspondence*, ed. T. Stapleton (Camden Society, Old Series, IV, 1839), pp. cii ff.

148 See above, p. 330

149 J.G. Bellamy, 'Justice under the Yorkist Kings,' *American Journal of Legal History*, IX (1965), 135-55

150 See above, p. 329

151 R.H.C. Davis, 'What happened in Stephen's reign,' *History*, XLIX (1968), 1-12; *King Stephen* (London 1967), pp. 6, 8-10, 14, 24-25, 41, 53, 121 ff.

152 S. Painter, *The Reign of King John* (Baltimore 1949), chap. 2 and pp. 110 ff.

153 K.B. McFarlane, 'Had Edward I a "policy" towards the earls?' *History*, L (1965), 145-49

154 E.g., in their demands for taxation.

155 J. Harrington, 'Oceana,' in *Ideal Commonwealths*, ed. H. Morley (New York 1901), pp. 203, 223

156 E.g., *Calendar of State Papers, Milan*, I, 324

157 M.E. James, *Change and Continuity in the Tudor North: the Rise of Thomas, Lord Wharton* (St. Anthony's Hall, Borthwick Papers, no. 27, York, 1965), p. 3

158 R.L. Storey, 'The Wardens of the Marches of England towards Scotland,' EHR, LXXII (1957), 608-9, 615

159 *Rot. Scot.* (London 1814-19), II, pp. 470-1, 484-5. Even when lieutenants, not wardens, were appointed they were generally magnates. *Ibid.*, 472-3, 479, 486, 501-2, 515, 519.

160 M.E. James, *Change and Continuity*, p. 39

161 S.T. Bindoff, *Tudor England* (London 1950), p. 53
162 W.T. MacCaffery, 'England, the Crown and the New Aristocracy,' *Past and Present*, xxx (1965), 52-64
163 See above, pp. 332-3
164 Dietz, *English Government Finance*, p. 49; *Calendar of State Papers, Venetian*, i, ed. R. Brown (London 1864), pp. 942, 945
165 *Opus Epistolarum Des. Erasmi Roterodami*, ed. P.S. Allen *et al.* (Oxford 1906-58), i, no. 215
166 *Letters and Papers*, i, no. 11 (i)
167 *Ibid.*, i, no. 309
168 *Ibid.*, i, no. 1493. They were provided with the names of 49 people under recognizances and 125 owing other kinds of debts. Their instructions also gave them scope to include other people not named.
169 Dietz, *English Government Finance*, pp. 49-50; Richardson, *Tudor Chamber Administration*, p. 145
170 These figures are calculated from the calendar of *Letters and Papers*. They are certainly incomplete as other cancellations, not found here, are entered after the original recognizances on the close rolls of Henry vii's reign.
171 E.g., '... were made without any cause reasonable or lawful, and that the parties recognizing the same were without ground or matter of truth, by the undue means of certain of the learned council of our said late father thereunto driven, contrary to law, reason and good conscience, to the manifest charge and peril of the soul of our said late father ...' *Letters and Papers*, i, no. 448. See also nos. 651 (7) ; 731 (7), (20) ; 749 (16) ; 804 (9) ; 1123 (45) ; 1524 (38).
172 From the earls of Essex, Kent, Northumberland, and Westmorland, Lords Berkeley, Darcy, de la Warre, Mountjoy, Scrope of Upsall, and Willoughby.
173 Recognizances of this kind affecting the earl of Kent and Lords Burgh, Clifford, Darcy, and Daubeney, seem to be uncancelled. Possibly also recognizances from Lords de la Warre, Grey of Powys, and Willoughby come into this class. Henry viii obviously made some distinction between recognizances for good behaviour in office and those of a more directly coercive nature. Recognizances taken from Lord Mountjoy by Henry vii were cancelled, those for Hammes castle in 1 Henry viii. *Cal. Close R., 1500-9*, nos. 226, 228, 290, 428, 756. At the same time, however, he was forced to give a new recognizance for £10,000 for Hammes and another for 1,000 marks concerning victual money for Calais. *Letters and Papers*, i, no. 257 (4), (5). Other recognizances of Mountjoy's were cancelled at various times, one as late as 4 Henry viii. *Cal. Close R., 1500-9*, nos. 549, 955 (xiv). Henry viii also made Mountjoy find sureties as master of the Mint and give recognizances for various other purposes. *Letters and Papers*, i, nos. 110 (2) ; 2578 (80).
174 See above, p. 345
175 See above, p. 342. But a recognizance given in 1506 on behalf of Richard

Weston for the safe-keeping of Castle Cornet, Guernsey, stood. *Cal. Close R., 1500-9,* no. 765.

176 The earls of Arundel, Buckingham, Kent, and Shrewsbury, the marquess of Dorset, Lords Dacre, de la Warre, Hasting, Mountjoy, Somerset. Not all the recognizances affecting Kent and Mountjoy (see note 174 above) were, however, cancelled.

177 Lords Daubeney and Mountjoy; *Letters and Papers,* i, nos. 749 (24), 1524 (38)

178 E.g., to Lord Darcy and his wife. Dietz, *English Government Finance,* p. 49; *Letters and Papers,* i, nos. 132 (115); 289 (5).

179 See notes 172 and 173 above

180 Dietz, *English Government Finance,* p. 49

181 E.g., L. Stone, *The Crisis,* chap. 5

182 This is also the opinion of Dr. P.B. Wolffe on Henry vii's financial practices generally. See 'Henry vii's Land Revenues and Chamber Finance,' EHR, LXXIX (1964), 252-4, and *Yorkist and Early Tudor Government* (Historical Association, 1966), pp. 18-20.

Incitement to violence?
English divines on the theme of war,
1578 to 1631*

J. R. Hale

Elizabethan England was an unmilitaristic country where armies were raised with the greatest difficulty;[1] the civil wars, however, were fought by men who took up arms with a sharply contrasting, if not general, alacrity, and the pulpit, during this same period, had an enormous influence on public opinion.[2] This essay takes these two well-established generalizations and, through a survey of sermons and devotional works which concentrate on justifying war, suggests one possible link between them.[3] It attempts to do this first by considering this literature as a whole and showing how remarkably thorough and enthusiastic a defence of war it contained, and, secondly, by reviewing it chronologically, and drawing attention to the way in which puritanism, by its characteristic use of military imagery to describe the conflict between good and evil, could have encouraged individuals to see their cause as one justifying a recourse to arms.

We could not, of course, expect to hear pacifist views expressed from Elizabethan, Jacobean, or Caroline pulpits. Erasmian pacifism had faded away, leaving hardly more than the tag 'Dulce bellum inexpertis' behind it – and that was used to emphasize the seriousness, not the unchristian nature, of war;[4] anabaptist pacifism lingered only as a bogey; quaker pacifism was yet to come. All the strains which mingled in English theology supported the rightness of military service in a just cause. Catholic teaching, based on Aquinas, licensed the clergy to support a just war by every means in their power short of actually fighting;[5] Luther had pointed out that 'war is as necessary as eating, drinking or any other business' and that once war had been formally declared 'the hand that bears the sword is as such no longer man's, but God's, and not man it is, but God who hangs, breaks on the wheel, beheads, strangles';[6] Calvin 'repeatedly said that no consideration could be paid to humanity when the honour of God was at stake.'[7]

The English contributors to the secular literature of war which swelled so considerably from the mid-sixteenth century took it for granted that their subject-matter would be pleasing to God. 'For God,' wrote Roger Ascham in his treatise on archery, 'is well pleased with wyse and wittie feates of warre.'[8] Geoffrey Gates, an experienced soldier, begged his countrymen 'be wise ... and acquainte your selves with armes, both corporal and spiritual, that you may at all times and in all cases be compleate Iraelites ready for the fielde.'[9] It was God, William Neade, inventor of a combination bow and pike, pointed out, who first 'set his bow in the cloud' after the flood 'and afterward it pleased God to inspire men with such wisdom and policy to imitate and make materiall bowes.'[10] If preachers like Adams and Gouge used 'The Lord is a man of war' as their text, so did Edward Cooke in *The Character of Warre ... contayning many usefull directions for musters and armes* (1626) and William Barriffe placed a verse from psalm 144, 'Blessed be the Lord my strength which teacheth my hands to warre, and my fingers to fight,' on the title page of his *Military Discipline, or, the Young Artillery Man* (1635).

No convention suggested that laymen should keep clear of the theological aspects of war or that clerics should not dabble with the practical side of the subject. John Norden, the greatest topographer of his time and a surveyor of crown lands and forests, was also one of the most copious and popular devotional authors of his day: his *Pensive Man's Practice* (1584) went through more than forty impressions by 1627. His *Progress of Piety* (1596) was followed in the next year by *The Mirror of Honor*, in which he glorified the military profession to the extent of equating the good warrior with the good man and the bad man with the coward, who 'may be truly sayd to be an incarnate infernall spirit.'[11] Against the background of threatened Spanish revenge for the Cadiz expedition – and dedicated to its leader, the earl of Essex – the book warned 'every militarie man, to whom especially I bend my speech' that sinful behaviour would lead 'to the destruction and overthrowe of all godly discipline in warre' and put the country in peril.[12] In 1602 the discipline of God's own troops, the Hebrews, was described by Lodowick Lloyd, sergeant at arms to the queen and an author who hitherto had restricted himself to doggerel verse and jejeune historical compilations. Called *The Stratagems of Jerusalem*, it began with the uncompromising statement that 'the whole Bible is a book of the battles of the Lord.' If, to these works by a part-time devotional writer and an author whose interests were otherwise entirely secular, we add a purely practical guide to warfare written by a dean of Exeter and royal chaplain, the concern of the pulpit with war is robbed of its element of surprise. In his *The Practice, Proceedings and Lawes of Armes* (1593), Dean Matthew Sutcliffe swiftly dispersed any doubts about the morality of his topic. 'It is needless (as I suppose) to dispute whether it be lawfull, either for Christian princes to make warres, or for Christians to serve in warres. Those that think it unlawfull, as men devoyd of iugement in religion and state, are declared long since to be both heretical and phrenetical persons.'

It should also perhaps be pointed out that there was nothing specifically English about the ready acceptance of war as part of God's plan. In

1574 Henry Grantham translated Girolamo Cataneo's *Most breif tables to knowe redily howe manye ranckes of footemen armed with corslettes, as unarmed, go to the making of a iust battayle*, in which, speaking of war, Cataneo says that 'whosoever behaveth himself honorablie in the exercise thereof, representeth nothing more than the true image of the most great and omnipotent God.' In the Armada year came a Huguenot view, *A short Apologie for Christian Souldiours*, translated from the French of Hubert Languet, and in 1591 John Eliot translated the Huguenot pastor Bertrand de Loque's *Deux Traitez, l'un de la Guerre, l'autre du Duel* (Lyon 1589), commending the book as 'setting downe the ancient rules of warre, grounded on God's holy word,' a description warranted by an elaborate introduction in which de Loque points out that men may fight not only 'because God hath so expressly commanded' but 'because Jesus Christ and his disciples have allowed the warre.'[13] As far as military literature was concerned, in English or in translation, the accordance of war to the word of God, in both the Old and New Testaments, was taken for granted – always subject to the caveat that 'warres are not to be taken in hand but in case of necessity.'[14]

The number of books on war and justifying war (again, both native works and translations) mounted steadily towards the civil wars[15] but, in a period when readers can rarely be identified, and the numbers of copies printed of each edition is, in almost all cases, unknown, the influence of books on public opinion is impossible to calculate. With sermons we are on firmer ground. This essay is based, it is true, on printed works, but each sermon had been delivered before a congregation, and, in the case of the Paul's Cross sermons[16] (Gosson, Hacket, Hampton, Stockwood, White), those preached in the key London parishes of St Stephen's Coleman Street (Davenport), St Andrew's Holborne (Everarde), St Anne's Blackfriars (Gouge), or before the monarch (Field) were assured of a large and, if John Manningham is at all representative, thoughtful auditory.[17] The sermon (the puritan sermon, at least) was intended not only as a crucial part of divine service but as the focus of a discussion in the homes of those who heard or read it. And, finally, it can be assumed that the subject-matter of printed sermons was representative of delivered, but unprinted, sermons in a sense far more meaningful than the suggestion that each printed book represents the drift of others mouldering in bottom drawers. Rejected (or suppressed) manuscripts are read by few: sermons, in a time when church attendance was compulsory, were heard by many. 360,000 has been suggested as the minimum number of sermons delivered between 1600 and 1640.[18] As the number of parishes remained unchanged in the period with which I am dealing (c1580–c1630) we can assume that of the minimum of 450,000 sermons delivered, a significant number, a *really* significant number, echoed the endorsement of military violence which is the common denominator of the works with which we are concerned.[19]

The fear of censorship or official disapproval hardly complicates this assumption. Peter Heylyn's comment in his *Cyprianus Anglicus* (1668) that Elizabeth 'used to tune the pulpits' was a fair one. From 1565 preaching was by licence only, and new incumbents had to swear 'I shall not preach, or publicly interpret, but only read that which is appointed by public authority, without special licence of the bishop under his seal.'[20] Licences were reviewed again in 1606, and by the articles of 1622 preachers were sternly warned against dealing with matters of state or with 'the deep points of predestination, election, reprobation or of the universality, efficacy, resistibility or irresistibility of God's grace.' They were to 'confine themselves to those two heads of faith and good life which are the subject of the ancient sermons and homilies.'[21] But war was one of the subjects of the ancient sermons and homilies; from Henry VIII's reign the state had sponsored appeals to Englishmen to take up arms against its enemies[22] and the chief non-doctrinal theme of the Elizabethan homilies was that of the subject's duty to defend the monarch against all threats, domestic and foreign.[23] Article 37 of the articles of religion stated clearly that 'it is lawful for Christian men, at the commandment of the magistrate, to wear weapons, and serve in the wars.' Provided that the impression was given that arms could only be borne against enemies of the state, the theme of war was safe from the tuning of pulpits or the censorship of the press. Five of the pro-war sermons discussed below were preached at Paul's Cross, where sermons 'were almost official Government pronouncements.'[24]

Lastly, the clergy were directly involved in the organization of military service. Armour, powder, and shot were stored in their churches, announcements about musters made from their pulpits, musters themselves were on occasion held in churchyards or even in the church itself. They were instructed to encourage their parishioners to contribute financially and in person to war and were themselves taxed for military purposes, being expected, according to the value of their livings, to provide money, men, or arms. When Whitgift called on the clergy through the bishops to contribute generously in the Armada year, Robert Wood, vicar of Shephall, went up to London and brought a caliver. 'I promise you,' he wrote, the demand 'could not have come to me in a worse time for I was bare of money, yet the Queen's Majesty must and shall be served.'[25] In general the clergy were grudging with their own contributions but willing to scold others into sacrifice. Roger Hacket, preaching at Paul's Cross on 14 February 1590 against the citizens' indifference to national defence, took his text from Judges 5:23: 'Curse ye Meroz, sayeth the Angel of the Lord, and in cursing curse the inhabitants thereof, because they come not to help the Lorde, to helpe the Lorde against the mighty.' We are dealing with a period when the feudal army had virtually disappeared, when mercenaries were, with good reason, distrusted, and when an effective permanent army was not yet in being. The clergy were needed, as never before or since, to goad men to take arms and to combat pacifism as well as to fulfil their more enduring functions: to equate patriotic with just causes, to bless soldiers and their weapons,[26] and to give spiritual comfort in the field. Their works provide a telling conspectus of what Englishmen were told by their pastors, from Paul's Cross to country church, to think about war.

The first concern of the church was to identify the enemies of England with the enemies of the Lord. 'Concerning Gog,' said Edmond Harris, 'looke Ezekiel 38 and 39, and there you shall see that Gog is called the Prince of Mesech and Tuball: by which Tuball are understood the Italians and Spaniards ... by Mesech the Turke.'[27] These are the enemies of the true servants of the faith; after quoting Deuteronomy 32, 41, and 42, 'I will execute vengeaunce on myne enemies (saith the Lord) and will reward them that hate me. I will make myne arrowes dronke with their blood,' he points out that this last remark especially should 'not bee lightly overpassed by us, considering the bowe and the arrowe are weapons of defence wherewith the Lorde hath armed our nation above the rest.' Hampton warned about the horrors that would follow if men did not take up the bow. He reminded his congregation of the Spaniards' behaviour toward the unarmed natives of the new world: 'Yea, they did not only feed their doggs but also themselves with men's flesh.' 'Unlesse our soveraigne be supplied,' he pointed out, you will 'see your wives ravished before your faces, your friends slain, your children murdered, your infants dashed against the stones or broached on the picke, and all the land made nothing but the shambles of Castillian and Ignatian butchers.'

After identifying the enemy and cataloguing the atrocities which may

be expected to follow if he is permitted to land, the church played the fife
to the recruiting officer's drum. The enemy seeks our blood, said Hacket;
it is useless to rely on allies or on mercenaries. When Saul called on the
people, 'they came, they hired not other, but they came in person ... But
nowe, my brethren, when your rulers do call and countrie require, do
you come?' He put the constitutional issue squarely to his congregation.
'For as in a clocke or watch all the wheeles shoulde goe when the maister
wheele doth moove, and if any stay the same putteth all out of frame and
must be mended, even soe in publicke states and civill governements, if
the prince doe moove as the cheefe commaunder and master wheele, the
people shoulde followe, and if any stay and trouble the whole, the same
is to bee mended, and forced to his due and timely order ... since the
prince representeth here the person of God, and is his vicegerent upon
earth, hee ought to teeach the people, if they will not learne, that he
beareth not, as the Apostle speaketh, the sworde in vaine."

When volunteers did come forward, they must drill and exercise con-
scientiously. 'Have we practised anie feats of armes whereby we may be
ennabled to meete a Spaniard in the field?' asked E.R. 'Let us exercise the
same daily, and continue in this forewardnes of service ... For although
the Lord watcheth for his Israel, yet must not Israel snort securely.' The
preachers roundly condemned any civil commotions that might blunt the
war effort. 'The Lord knit the knot of peace,' said Thomas White, 'and
make it fast from slypping and breaking, that being at quiet in our bow-
elles from sedition at home, we maye be stronger in body to resyst all
forraigne powers abroad.' Mutiny, too, was soundly thrashed. One of the
most chronic grievances among the troops was the irregular appearance
of their pay. Be content, don't grumble about these delays, warned the
author of *A Spiritual Chaine*. Don't let it be said that 'no longer plentie,
no longer dutie; no longer pay, no longer Prince.' He went on, somewhat
optimistically: 'A holy souldier will say thus in time of his governours
disabilitie to pay wages: I serve a good Lord, even the Lord Jesus Christ,
who hath promised not to leave us nor forsake us. He will pay you and
me our wages, good captaine.' Nor must the soldier listen to subversive
suggestions that the monarch's cause is not such as to justify a war. They
must 'iudge lovingly of ther Prince ... and rest fully persuaded that the
cause is good ... and then our gracious God, who seeth his holy purpose,
will take this good hope conceived of his deputie in good part ... Beware
then of false whisperings, which many times bring disobedient murmur-
ings. Gods Vice-regent must not be denied aide, no, nor so much as grudged

at, upon surmises and rumors.' Or, as Bachiler put it more crisply in a
sermon to troops on active service, 'Another wicked thing is murmuring
and mutining in the campe – see this taken notice of in those rebels
(Numbers, 16, 1, 2, 3, 11), which was to be punished with death (Joshua,
1, 18).' And to support these armies in the field, and to provide for defence at home, the pulpit co-operated with the government by asking
their congregations for cash contributions, as in E.R.'s 'Wee must forget
our old vaine of sparing and begin to open our bags ... Shall we reserve
in our coffers as it were swords to cut our owne throats?' 'There is a
thing called *nervus Belli,*' William Hampton declared, 'without which
warre cannot subsist ... for unless our soveraigne be supplied, that some
course may speedily be taken for our defence, wee shall have neither
lands, nor rents, nor money, nor corne, nor wives, nor children, nor anything else in safety, but all will fall into our enemies' hands.' The same
message was forcibly put in 1626 by Thomas Barnes. 'Never had Chal-
dean greater cause to fight with Moab, than wee with Rome ... Fit purses
for contribution must now stand open, fit persons for execution are now
called upon ... Gird your swords therefore upon your thighes, O you
valiant ones, and ride on with courage and renowne. Our Iehosophat
summons against this Moab; what ranke, what degree amongst the gentry,
amongst the commonalty of his dominions may not account it their glory
to have an hand in this enterprise?'

The church could not preach war without feeling some tremors of
unease, and commonly cleared its conscience by liberal abuse of the one
recalcitrant sect. When threatened by war, said Thomas White, we must
not 'tempt God in refusing lawfull meanes, as Anabaptistes that wyll
weare no weapons.' Preaching at Paul's Cross, John Stockwood deplored
'the furie of the Anabaptistes, which, contrary to the scriptures, do teache
that it is unlawfull for the magistrate to use the swords.' As late as 1626
Barnes set himself to combat 'that fantasticall conceit of the Anabap-
tisticall sect that it is not lawfull for true Christians to make warre.'
Gouge spoke for clergy of all shades of opinion with his forthright declaration that 'warre is a kind of execution of publique justice and a
means of maintaining right ... and though by their [soldiers'] valour
much bloud may be shed, yet they need not be any more daunted thereat
than iudges, iuries, executioners and other ministers of iustice for putting
many malefactors to death.'

Moreover, the divines sought, in the words of one of them, 'to prove
that warre was a blessing.' War, in the first place, could be a social good,

a moral cleanser, God's scourge for vice. Peace led to laxity, to foul or at best indolent behaviour. War purified, energized. Peace corrupted, war restored. As Scott put it: 'All the beggerly nations of the world became rich and potent by raysing of warre, and were diminished and consumed to nothing by the corruption of peace and bewitching of pleasure.' In the second place, war brought a country fame and prestige while peace brought obscurity and scorn. What has made England 'famous and illustrious to forreigne Nations?': the warlike exploits of Cavendish, Drake, Essex, and Mountjoy. Show therefore, cried Hacket, 'That you carry in you the courage of the auncient English, whose glory was to rule, not to be ruled.' Is war too risky? asked Scott. Why, look at the Dutch, and 'whether warre hath been a blessing unto them iudge for your selves, considering they have augmented their fame and renown abroad, and increased their wealth and territories at home.' War, again, was honourable, and warriors honourable men. As the author of *A Spiritual Chaine* pointed out, 'we perceive that all people of understanding despise a coward and respect a man of valour, whence it is that the name of a dastard is a base by-word of great reproach. And hence also it comes that they who are to be chosen to offices of any eminencie in the weale publike, one speciall qualitie regarded in them is (according to Ioshua's counsell) that they be men of courage.' In the third place, war was justified by God's action and teaching. In *The Bible-Battells* Bernard neatly brought together the most frequently quoted Old Testament examples.

Some, as the Anabaptists, hold it not lawfull for Christians under the Gospell to make warre, but such are but dreamers, for God is pleased to be called a man of Warre (Exodus 15, 3). He hath given commandment to his people sometimes to fight (Numbers 31, 3; 1 Samuel 15, 3; Deuteronomy 2, 24). Hee made lawes for direction to them when they went to warre (Deuteronomy 20, 10, 15). Holy men of eminent place and graces have made warre, as did Abraham, Ioshua, David and others (Genesis 14). God would send his spirit upon them to encourage them to the warre, as he did upon Gideon, Ehud, Sampson, as wee may read in the book of Iudges. God raised up some prophets to comfort and set forward his people to warre (Judges 4, 2; Chronicles 14, 15). God taught David to play the part of a valiant captaine and souldier (Psalms 144, 1 and 18, 39, 40). In batell, when his people rested upon him and cryed to him, he did help them and made them conquerors (1 Chronicles 5, 20).

Most clerical authors were content to justify war out of the Old Testament, using these and comparable passages. But a few asked with Barnes, 'how stands this with that counsell of our Saviour: Love your enemies, bless them that curse you, pray for them that persecute you?' Bernard was one of those who accepted the challenge and, again, brought together the most frequently quoted texts.

> Our Prince of peace telleth us of warrs, and is pleased to be set out as a captaine of an host riding on horse back and subduing his enemies, and making a slaughter of them. Hereby shewing that his Church shall have warrs, and he will take their part and helpe to subdue their enemies, as he hath often done and yet will doe (Matthew 24; Revelations 19 and 17). When the souldiers asked Iohn Baptist what they should doe? Hee did not will them to forsake their calling, but to be content with their wages, as allowing the calling but reforming the abuse (Luke 3, 14). We find religious soldiers in the New Testament; the religious centurion, Cornelius, a Captain and a soldier fearing God that waited on him (Matthew 8, 8, 10; Acts 10, 1, 2, 3, 4, 7). Saint Paul maketh it a fruit of faith to be valiant in battle. If the lawfulness of warre had been out of date under the gospell, the Apostle would have left that out, as now no fruit of faith (Hebrews 11, 34). God hath now appointed kings to use the sword, not only to punish offenders under them, but also to defend their subjects from violence and wrong at home and abroad (Romans 13, 4). The Lord in calling the Gentiles to the gospell made choice in the first place to begin with one of this calling before another: even a Captaine called Cornelius.

And Bernard added another point which was common to the European pro-war literature: 'We must know that the gospell taketh not away the law of nature to defend ourselves by forcible meanes against violent enemies.' Furthering the case for a militant New Testament, Barnes commented on Isaiah's prophecy 'of the times of the gospell in the New Testament that when he said "They shall beate their swords into plow-shears": the Anabaptists allege that "therefore Christians may not make warre now under the gospell." I answer, the scope of the prophet there is not to forbid magistrates a necessary warre against the enemies of their lives, and Gods cause, but to shew what peace should be betwixt the Iewes and the Gentiles by the preaching of the gospell.' And the case was clinched by the author of *A Spiritual Chaine* with the syllogism: Christ took man's nature upon him; man is a warrior; therefore Christ is a man of war. 'As He took mens nature upon him, so taketh He mens' names unto him; they men of warre, He a man of warre.'

Indifference, let alone pacifism, was treachery. Harward took up his pen in defence of the military profession 'for that England hath (I doubt) many seditious malcontents which, being wearie of their own welfare, doe repine against those meanes whereby our prosperity is preserved.' So strong, indeed, was the defence of war that the eulogists of peace were few and cautious. It is with a characteristically tentative remark that Thomas Adams opened his *Eirenopolis: the Citie of Peace* (1622) : 'Peace take it with all its faults, is better then warre.' He hazarded a full-scale portrait. 'Peace is a fair virgin ... she hath a smiling looke ... snowy armes, soft as downe, and whiter than the swannes feathers ... her bowels are full of pitty,' etc., but later in the book he was at pains to point out that 'I am no Anabaptist, nor Libertine, to deny the magistracie or lawfulness of authoritie ... The Lord himself hath appoynted tribunals, and no law, no love.'

Like their secular counterparts, religious writers pointed out that fighting could only be approved if it were in a just war, that is, a war waged in a just cause, with righteous intent, and at the command of a lawful authority. It must be 'necessary' in the sense of defending oneself or succouring an ally or co-religionist. Religious writers, however, with the help of holy writ, could extend the scope of the just war concept beyond its use by secular writers, who were bound by a narrower legalistic approach. Besides, as Sutcliffe noted, 'if the unjustice of the warres be not notorious, the subject is bound to pay and serve, and the guilt shall be laide to his charge that commandeth him to serve.' The Old Testament illustrated specific points such as the notion that a neutral can be attacked if he hinders an army crossing his territory; Gosson pointed out that 'when Amelec had vexed the Israelites as they went out of Egypt, and smote the hindmost of them, God commanded them to revenge it, and to roote out the remembrance of Amelec from under heaven.' It also provided a general sanction for foreign conquest, for 'warres have beene justly made by Israel, God's people, at God's command to subdue nations and to possesse their kingdomes as they did the kingdomes of Canaan and inherited them.' Every aggressor could persuade himself that his cause was just, and it is not surprising that the pulpit devoted itself to reassurances like Gosson's 'you shall find the warres of the enemie in the Indies, in Portingale, in Grenada, in the Low Countries, in France, and against

us to be uncharitable and uniust ... Looke upon your owne warres another
while, you shal find them to be very charitable and iust.'

The Bible also provided precedents for most of the implements and
customs of war. Practice with the bow and arrow was recommended from
the pulpit usually by reference to King David's worthies. Gunpowder
appeared too late to be mentioned in the Bible, but more than one preacher pointed out that, 'as St. Paul gives a Christian in his welfare the whole
armour of God; a sword to offend, a shield to defend, so in this kind of
[modern] Warre, we must improve all things whatsoever the bowels or
face of the earth can affoord for our defence.' Thus, though gunpowder
was invented with the Devil's aid, 'seeing the fierie disposition of our
enemies use this as all others to our annoyance, why may wee not snatch
these weapons out of madde mens hands, and turn them into their owne
bosomes?' As for the employment of subterfuge and terrorism, why, in a
good cause, the Christian might follow his instincts. So long as the issue of
a war was in doubt, said Gosson, 'al the meanes are lawful that are requisite
to the attaining of the victory; sleights, shifts, stratagems, burning, wasting, spoiling, undermining, battery, blows and bloud. I will give you one
example in Scripture for al, Ioshua 8. In the taking of Ai there is a
stratageme, an ambush laide behind the cittie, an assault given before
it, semblance of flight by retiring to draw the enemy out, the city fierd, the
enemy enclosed and then slaughtered before and behind.' As for loot, so
long again as the cause is just, soldiers, Bernard comforted, may take
what they find, for 'God allowed Israel to take what they did win in thier
iust wars.'

There was considerable difference of opinion about how far the presence of evil-living soldiers spoiled an army's chances of success. Preachers were agreed that soldiers should behave in an orderly and Christian
way. 'It is thought of some wicked person,' Harris told his congregation
of recruits, 'that to have a payre of dice in the one hand and a whore in
the other, this is souldierlike, but wo unto such.' And it was pointed out
that such behaviour not only imperilled the immortal soul of the individual but, by undermining the discipline of the army, lessened its
chances of victory. In real life, however, the good man was likely to be
the snug, prosperous man who had no intention of trusting his fortune to
the wars. Precept and practice were neatly bridged by Thomas Barnes'
thesis that God can use unworthy instruments to good ends. 'It is as lawfull a thing to presse the bad for military service in times of warre,' he
claimed, 'as to employ the good, yea, in the ordinary service of common

souldiers. I doubt not it may stand as well with true piety as state-policy
to spend the worst first, and spare the best to the last extremity ... Warre
in it self is a punishment for sinne ... who better to taste it, than the lewd-
est men, that most deserve it?' He went on to suggest that war can frighten
a bad man into a more virtuous state of mind. This being so, 'it were a
thousand pities he should not see the pikes, nor be sent to the field. I
speake this the rather that I may incite such as have the office of pressing
in these needfull times committed unto them to be careful to cleanse the
city and rid the country as much as may be of those straggling vagrants,
loytering fellowes and lewd livers (so they be fit for service) which doe
so swarme amongst us.'

As far as the use of prayer was concerned, the attitude was one of
trusting God and keeping the powder dry. In the pulpit's opinion victories were won in heaven but prepared on earth. The Armada had been
scattered by the protestant wind. 'Not an angell, but God himselfe had a
favourable eye towards us, and an holy hand over us,' John Prime told
an Oxford congregation, and 'hee was as much with us as ever with any
nation, when, notwithstanding all their crakes and famous Dons and
doutie adventeres, huge shippes all to be-swathed with gables and printed
vauntes, we lost by them, who are now sent home a wrong way, neither
man, nor ship, nor boat, nor mast of ship.' In 1626, however, the official
Forme of prayer, necessary to be used in these dangerous times of Warre,
issued by the king's printer, while it acknowledged that 'victory is absolutely in the will and power of God,' and that an essential prelude to victory was fasting, prayer, and repentance, went on to ask 'but are men
spirits only? Are they to fight their battels onely with spirituall armour?
No; for were not that to tempt God, in neglecting the good meanes ordained by him for that end? Verely, politique preparations are God's
ordinance, and have ever beene used by his good servants.' Thomas Scott
reported a good practical prayer from the Low Countries in 1624. God's
aid should be begged against the enemy, that He should 'lay open their
plots, discover their devises, weaken their armes and overthrow their inventions, confound their councells, and consume their numbers.' Lest
prayers of this sort, addressed to the God whose son had said 'Love your
enemies ... pray for them which despitefully use you' should puzzle the
conscience, the matter was cleared up by Bachiler. 'We are to know then,'
he pointed out, 'that we must pray for *our* enemies, but against *God's*
enemies ... We may lawfully pray against their designes though not
against their persons ... or we may pray against their persons indefinitely,

though not particularly ... or lastly, we may pray against their persons in particular, conditionally, though not absolutely; first, we are to pray for their conversion, and then if maliciously and wilfully they persist in their obstinacy, in the second place for their confusion. This was David's method.' As with the weapons and customs of war, the pulpit was able to justify the warrior's darker instincts with only the most general of qualifications; if the cause were just, in fact, then no holds need be barred – providing, that is, that discipline did not suffer. Christian and heathen were at one on this point; the priest at the provost marshal's elbow. 'There is nothing displeasing to God, but sinne,' Bernard wrote. 'As Moses exhorted Israel and as Aurelianus the Emperor said to his Generall in a military epistle of his, if thou be a tribune, yea, if thou wilt live, keepe back the souldiers hands from doing evill.'

Bernard's book was designed to support a biblical example with a classical one, to show that the Bible was comparable in value as a source of military information to the popular classical texts of, for example, Vegetius, Frontinus, and Caesar. 'Most that delight to reade, or almost all so delighted, do spend their time in perusing over humane stories, and do highly extoll the histories of the warres of heathen commanders ... but doe lightly price the scriptures' historie of warres, the right art militarie indeed, which was commanded to bee penned by that great man of warre (as Moses stileth him) the only cheife and highest commander, whose name is the Lord of Hosts.' The idea of using the Bible as a military handbook, lessons reflecting the ideas of a greater warrior than any the Greeks or Romans could name, was not original to Bernard. His book had been preceded by Alexander Leighton's *Speculum Belli Sacri* (1624), in which he said, 'I have applied the generall rules warranted by the Word to the particular necessity of our present times.' Though he gave more information of a practical kind in chapters like 'The oppugnation of a hold,' 'The ordering of the Battell,' 'The fight itself,' Leighton brought the Bible alongside the classical literature on war without suggesting that it could replace it. Bernard, however, was at pains to rebut the view that biblical wars were no longer relevant in the modern world. Basic considerations like the choice and training of soldiers, their discipline and morale, were unaffected by changing fashions in armament. The problem of supply, the ordering of a march, or a camp – all matters to which he devoted a chapter – were subject to little change through the ages. He too did not suggest that the Bible should take the place of Vegetius, but that it should be added to the shelf of classical texts as a work of equal practical value

and higher authority. Though his points were all buttressed by biblical
illustrations he drew on a wide range of ancient and contemporary
authors as well; his remarks on discipline, for instance, were supported
by references to Moses, Alexander, Severus, and the Turks who, thanks to
their superior discipline, 'have mightily prevailed against us Christians,
who may be ashamed of our over-much loosenes herein.'

It was not only in formal treatises that attention was drawn to the
value of the Bible as a military text. Preaching in 1618, John Everarde
said that some misguided persons had tried to explain away those passages in holy writ which referred to God as the lord of hosts, Christ as the
captain of the lord's army, angels as soldiers, by suggesting that 'simili-
tudes in the book of God be sometime drawne *a rebus non amandis*, from
evill things, and applyed unto those that are good.' But, he went on in a
characteristically puritan style, 'what neede wee strive so much to expresse and wring iuyce from symbolicall divinitie, which seldom concludes, when waters sufficient to quench our greatest thirst of knowledge
do so plenteously gush from the rocke of the Word?' Are the scriptures not
as exact 'in the affaires of the army as in the businesse of the sanctuary?
Will you see *modum indicendi bellum*, a prescript form of denouncing
warre? ... see Deuteronomy 20, 10; will you see *delectum militis*, the
choice of souldiers? see Exodus 17, 9; will you see *sacramentum militare*,
the oath of obedience from a souldiour to his captaine? see Ioshua 1, 16,
17; will you see colonells and captaines? looke Numbers 31, 14.' And so
he proceeds, for 'the sounding of an all'arme, Numbers 10, 5, 6; the order
of a camp, Numbers 2; a march, who have the van and who the riere,
Numbers 10, 14 etc; a councell of warre, ib. 4; a city besieged, Ioshua 6;
a city releeved, Ioshua 10, 9; an ambush, Ioshua 8, 9; a prey taken, 1
Samuel 30; the spoile divided, Numbers 31, 27. But what, should I stand
wearying you with repetition of watches, spies, battels, skirmishes, defeats, supplies, strategems and six hundred things of like nature, whereunto the blessed spirit hath every where in scripture given not only approbation, but direction?'

The preachers who, like Everarde, were invited to speak to the military associations, identified themselves openly, almost ardently, with the
military interests of their auditors, and it is in their sermons that the
church's attitude to war appears most explicitly martial. 'I doe openly
acknowledge and publickely professe,' cried William Gouge, preaching
to the Artillery company of London, 'that my heart is set upon your Artillery company. I love it, I admire it, I honour it, I praise God for it.'

Samuel Buggs, addressing the company who practised arms in the Military garden at Coventry, explained his martial tone by pointing out that his intention was to 'imitate a son of the prophet Azaziah the sonne of Obed, who encouraged the valiant Asa, and gave him some directions how to fight the Lord's battailes,' while Leech was clearly tempted to jump down from the pulpit and shoulder a pike himself among the members of the London Artillery garden who formed his congregation. 'I wish I could add reall encouragements to those verball that I give you,' he mourned, and returning to the theme towards the end of his sermon, he said that 'we for our parts, we that are of poore Levie's tribe, we will helpe you what we can too ... If you fight for us, we will pray for you.' In these perilous times, he said, how could a man resist a longing to take arms? 'Shall he live like a luskish Sidonian, or like an effeminated Sybarite, languishing in ease and raveling out his time in courtship and dalliance? Shall he doe nothing but sit singing and sonnetting among ladies and gentlewomen, or perhaps stretch his armes now and then at shittlecock or billiards?' It is in keeping with the stirring tone and militant imagery of these sermons that Buggs announced the end of his with the words 'But now time compels me to sound a retreat.'

'In peace prepare for war.' This was an obvious theme for these sermons, and it was given vigorous treatment. 'I know prayers are good weapons,' admitted Thomas Adams, who was also addressing the members of the London Artillery garden, 'and Exodus 17 – there was more speed made to victorie by lifting up of Moses' hands than of Ioshua's sword ... But is it enough to bend the knee, without stirring the hand? Shall warre march against us with thundering steps and shall we only assemble our selves in the temples, lie prostrate on the pavements, lift up our hands and eyes to heaven, and not our weapons against our enemies? Shal we beat the aire with our voices, and not their bosomes with our swords? Only knock our own breasts, and not knock their heads? Sure, a religious conscience never taught a man to neglect his life, his libertie, his estate, his peace.' The sermons praised Solomon, the ideal ruler: a lover of peace but the supervisor of formidable preparation for war. They held up as a dread example the fate of the inhabitants of Laish, 'a people that were quiet and secure' and were exterminated for their indolence by the Danites. John Davenport took as his text 2 Samuel 1: 18 'Also he bade them teach the children of Iudah the use of the Bow,' and commented 'It is a care well beseeming kings, to provide that their subiects be instructed and trained up in military exercises.'

The preachers to the military companies took especial pains in tackling the texts which would seem to imply a condemnation of warlike activity. As Everarde said, recurring to a familiar stumbling block, 'Tis true, it was once prophesied of the dayes that were then to come ... They shall breake their swords into plough-shares, and their speares into sithes. But take away ... the cover of the letter, and you shall finde there no prohibition of the use of weapons and lawful war, much lesse of the due preparation there unto, but onely a sweet and gracious promise of unity and spiritual concord between them who are ... of the household of faith, and know themselves to be brethren by grace.' And, turning to the New Testament, Davenport explained that 'though the end of Christ his coming was to reconcile things in heaven and things on earth ... yet so long as Satan workes in the children of disobedience, and so long as any remnant of sinne is in the heart of any, there will be a necessity and lawfulnesse of war, and of this care to prepare for it.' It is not to be expected that, speaking to such an audience, a divine would hesitate to commend the use of guns and gunpowder. God gave animals horns and tusks to defend themselves, said Davenport, 'but unto Man, God hath given reason and understanding, which is in stead of all these, whereby he is able not only to espie meanes of escape from dangers, but he can take from every creature upon earth, yea from within the bowels of the earth, what may serve for his use and benefit.'

Whatever the danger and drudgery involved, whatever the weapons that had to be handled, the military career was a glorious one, and glorious too was the preparation for it. Buggs told his congregation 'You have entered now one of the two professions which are the onely life and lustre of true gentrie.' Go on, then! 'Tread all oppositions and encumbrances under your feete, and spurne with the heeles of contempt the base and faeculent vulgar, whose muddie braines and dull spirits neither can conceive nor dare attempt to high designs.' Go on, urged Gouge, 'The time would faile mee to speake in particular of Ioshua, Gedeon, Ieptha, David, Iehosophat, Hezekiah, Iosiah and other like worthies, royall persons, that were trained up in the artillery profession.' It was no easy thing to be a soldier, the demands of the calling were high. 'Many honourable parts and endowments are requisite to make a man expert in the artillery profession,' Gouge flattered his audience by going on to say, 'as soundnesse of iudgement, sharpenesse of wit, quicknesse of conceit, stoutnesse and courage of mind, undauntednesse in danger, discretion mixed with passion, prudence, patience, ability and agility of body, and of the severall

parts thereof, with the like; all which doe demonstrate that the function
whereunto they are required is an honourable function.' On him everything depends, however important, however trivial. Without him who
would protect the monarch, the church? Without him, asked Adams, 'who
should keepe the foggie epicure in his soft chaire after a full meale fast
asleepe? Who should maintaine the nice ladie in her caroch, whirling
through the popular streets?'

The military sermons were ceremonial occasions, attended by important civic dignitaries, and the frequency with which the preachers request
money suggests that the officials of the companies put a word in their ear
beforehand. 'Oh, you Londoners!' cried Adams reproachfully. 'You re-
searve one bagge for pride, another for belly-cheare, another for lust, yet
another for contention and sutes in law ... You then, that have the places
of government in this honourable citie, offer willingly your hands, your
purses, your selves to this noble exercise.' Leech acknowledged that some
of the city worthies before him would not cut very likely figures on the
parade ground themselves, but they should at least enable others to
shoulder pike and musket there. 'You therefore that cannot be souldiers,
make souldiers!'

From this kaleidoscopic treatment of our sources we can see how rich
and how various was the defence of war offered by the church. If we now
look more analytically, one point stands out very clearly: the preponderance of puritans among these militant divines, especially in the seventeenth century. Thomas White (?1550-1624), vicar of St Dunstan-in-the-
West, London, when he preached at Paul's Cross, was to become successively canon of Christ Church, Oxford, and of Windsor; orthodox in the
main, his outcry against superstitious observances, delicate living, Sab-
bath-breaking, and the theatres has led him to be labelled as a puritan.[28]
John Stockwood (d. 1610), minister of Battle in Sussex and headmaster
of Tonbridge grammar school at the time of his sermon, has also been
called a puritan.[29] John Prime (1550-96), rector of Adderbury, Oxford-
shire, appears to have been orthodox; about 'E.R.' and Edmond Harris
I have no information. Roger Hacket (1559-1621), rector of North
Crawley in Buckingham, was orthodox and so, in all probability, was
Simon Harward (fl. 1572-1614), chaplain of New College, Oxford, and
later vicar of Banstead. I can see nothing of the puritan in the work of
Matthew Sutcliffe (c.1550-1629) who in 1593 was dean of Exeter and
one of the queen's chaplains. Stephen Gosson, who as vicar of Sandridge

in Hertfordshire had come forward with a caliver in the Armada year, held the living of Great Wigborough in Essex when he preached *The Trumpet of Warre*. Puritanical in his onslaught on the theatres (*The Schoole of Abuse*, 1579) and women's indecent fashions, in theology and politics he was a thoroughly establishment figure.[30]

From 1617, the date of *The Souldiours Honor*, the balance changes. Thomas Adams (c.1580 – c.1660) held the preachership of St Gregory's under St Paul's Cathedral; one of the best known from a literary point of view, of seventeenth-century divines, 'almost any sermon exhibits Adams' mastery of all the popular resources of the City and Puritan preacher.'[31] John Everarde (1575?-1650?), reader from about 1618 at St Martin's-in-the-Fields, was so often in and out of prison for meddling with state affairs that James I is reported to have said 'What is this Dr. Ever-out? His name shall be Never-out.' Strongly influenced by Tauler and the *Theologia Germanica*,[32] his highly individual puritanism led to a charge of heresy in 1636 and three years later he was deprived of his benefice. I know nothing about John Leech, but his being chosen as preacher by the Artillery company suggests (for reasons we shall see shortly) that he was a puritan. Samuel Buggs, 'minister of the word of God in Coventrie' was a puritan.[33] *A Spiritual Chaine* is a puritan work. Alexander Leighton (1568-1649), critic of the queen and rabid anti-episcopalian, has been described as a puritan 'of the narrowest type.' In 1630 he was convicted of sedition, degraded from orders, had his nose slit and was imprisoned for ten years. Thomas Scott (1580?-1626), appointed a chaplain to James I in 1616, left England after publishing a tract against the projected marriage of Prince Charles with the Spanish infanta and became preacher to the English garrison at Utrecht. A puritan. According to the life prefixed to his commentary on Hebrews,[34] William Gouge was counted as 'an Arch-Puritan' while a fellow of Kings. Rector of St Anne's Blackfriars from 1608, he was a member of the puritan society of the Feofees of Impropriations.[35] One of the best known of moderate puritans, 'it was said of him that "when the godly Christians of those times came out of the Country into London, they thought not their businesse done unlesse they had been at Blackfriars lecture." '[36] Thomas Barnes, 'preacher of God's word at Much-Waltham in Essex' was a puritan.[37] I am not sure about William Hampton. In 1628 Theophilus Field (1574-1636) was bishop of St Davids and moved without a breath of theological scandal to the see of Hereford in 1635. John Davenport (1597-

1670) was, like Gouge, a member of the society of Feoffces and (again, like Gouge) a member of the group of London clergymen who created a fund for the relief of the distressed protestants of the Palatinate. Vicar of St Stephens, Coleman Street, from 1624 till 1633 when he resigned his living and emigrated to New England, Davenport was one of the most prominent puritan divines in London. Samuel Bachiler is known to me only through this sermon; from this he appears to have been chaplain to the English forces at Gorcum in the Netherlands and, as his *Campe Royall* is prefaced by lines from Thomas Scott, he was probably a puritan. About Richard Bernard's puritanism there is no doubt. Bernard (1568-1641) was suspended from his living at Worksop in Nottinghamshire (where he wrote his treatise on preaching, *The Faithfull Shepheard* [1607]) for his separatist ideas, but settled down under an indulgent diocesan as vicar of Batcombe to produce a long array of writings, the best known being his *Isle of Man or Proceedings in Manshire* (1627), an allegory faintly anticipating Bunyan's *Pilgrim's Progress.*

With this subject matter, and these men in mind, it is worth looking again, I think, at some familiar royalist comments on the outbreak of civil war. 'There are monuments enough,' wrote Clarendon, 'in the seditious sermons at that time printed and, in the memories of men, of others not printed, of such wresting and perverting scripture to the odious purposes of the preacher, that pious men will not look over without trembling ... There was one who, from the 48th chap. of the Prophet Jeremiah and the 10th verse, "Cursed be he that keepeth back his sword from bloud," reproved those who gave any quarter to the King's soldiers.'[38] John Hacket was of the opinion that the country had been 'preach't into disorder by Presbyterian divines' and that 'church-men are the most dangerous instruments to turn male-contents into sword-men.[39] According to Clement Walker it was the divines on both sides who 'inflamed the people to the rage of battell, as the elephant is inraged at the sight of red.[40] Finally, writing at closer quarters to the early stages of the conflagration, 'Mercurius Civicus' declared that 'the truth is, brother Rusticus, these military preparations had affected little, had not the fire been given from the pulpit.'[41]

Now these are biased opinions, and they refer with especial force to the period 1641-2. Before the breakdown of the censorship, printed works by divines had not preached rebellion; they did no more, I am suggesting, than habituate their auditors to the use of violence in a cause they believed just, a cause which, even within the tuning of pulpits and censorship of the press, could let 'Spaniards' blur into 'Antichrist' and 'Antichrist' become the forces inhibiting the practice of right worship.[42]

Mercurius Civicus does, however, reach back in another passage to the period of conditioning with which we are dealing. 'You may well remember,' he points out to his friend in the country, 'when the Puritans here did as much abominate the Military Yard or Artillery Garden as Paris Garden itself; they would not mingle with the prophane. But, at last, when it was instilled into them that the blessed reformation intended could not be effected save by the sword, these places were instantly filled with few or none but men of that faction ... so that when any prime commanders dyed, new men were elected wholly devoted to that faction.'[43]

The members of the Artillery company who practised in the Artillery garden were not all puritans; some became prominent on the royalist side in the civil wars.[44] But, on the evidence of the works under discussion here, the puritan connection was very strong. The puritan author of *A Spiritual Chaine* dedicated his book 'to those patterne captaines (so I call them who are leaders by their godly example) of the Artillery and Militarie in the Citie of London,' and he is unstinting in his approbation of 'the training up of the citie's valiant men, yea, youths, nay very children in feates of armes (being first taught to feare their God, and to be armed against, and fight against, Satan).'[45] This is a puritan addressing fellow spirits. Thomas Scott, referring to the Artillery company, would hardly have used this prayer before men to whose doctrine he was unsympathetic: 'Blesse, O Lord, we intreat, their new inventions of warre, and make them skilfull and full of knowledge, that all the world may know that Thou conductest our armies.'[46] Gouge was surely speaking to a significant number of co-religionists among his congregation of amateur soldiers: 'I say vacant houres cannot better be spent than in the Artillery Garden, and in the practise of martial discipline there exercised.'[47] The company, of course, chose their own preachers: Adams, Everarde, Gouge, and Davenport were all prominent puritans. Leech was possibly one. When Captain Henry Waller died in 1631 another well-known puritan, George Hughes, lecturer at All Hallows, Bread Street, was invited to preach at his funeral.[48] Following the example of Leech, who had told his congregation that he was 'your fellow-souldier in the battailes of our Lord Iesu,' Hughes referred to himself as 'your hearty orator and fellow-souldier in Christ's artillery.' Judging from the evidence of printed sermons, the Artillery company was told that the practice of arms was pleasing to the Lord and that the interest of lay worshipper and minister were identical – and it was told these things in tones of uncommon fervour. It is not without interest that Gouge said 'me thinkes that it is more then meete that everie citie and corporation, if not every towne and village throughout the land should have an Artillery Garden, and that the great populous cities, especially London, should have as many Artillery Gardens as it hath wards, and that publique allowances should bee afforded to such as willingly offer themselves to these military exercises.'[49] It is intriguing that Davenport referred approvingly to the example given by his congregation for 'as Paul speaks to the Romanes, "Your zeal hath provoked many" – as may be seene in Coventry, Chester, Bristow, Norwich, besides other places, who not only have raised up like companies in imitation of yours, but also have been guided therein by some of your followers and instructed by some of your schollers.'[50] But we cannot assume that there was a militant puritan plot to reach out from the Artillery garden in order to preach the country into disorder.

We must bear in mind an old strain in pulpit oratory: the praise of healthy open-air occupations (especially if they could be of service to the country) as against the tavern recreations – dice, cards, and so forth. Latimer regretted in a sermon of 1549 that 'now we have taken up whoring in taverns instead of shooting in the fields.'[51] A good proportion of our divines not only praised war but scourged vain pleasures and pastimes. To give examples merely from the extremes of our period, Stockwood asked a Paul's Cross congregation 'Wyll not a fylthie playe wyth the blast of a trumpette sooner call thyther a thousand than an houres tolling of a bell bring to the sermon a hundred?'[52] and Davenport, speaking of the activities of the Artillery garden, begged his audience 'abandon your caroling, dicing, chambring, wantonnesse, dalliance, scurrilous discoursing and vaine revelling out of time, to frequent these exercises.'[53] A petition to the privy council from Derby to have an artillery ground of its own referred, indeed, to 'some able persons of the younger sort who are willing for exercise sake and to avoid resorts to tavernes and ale houses and other improfitable employments ... to bestow that time to trayning, which by many of them is spent in idleness.'[54]

And yet, surely there is more in the enthusiasm, the military glee we have been watching than a 'puritanical' hand-clapping at the thought of men being kept away from vain shows and idle temptations? There is no need to emphasize the importance of preaching to puritans of all degrees of rigour, nor to stress the opportunities given by the lectureship system, the tolerance of certain bishops, and the protection of powerful men to the expression of their views. It is, however, worth emphasizing how frequently the puritan preacher likened himself to a military leader. 'The generall that for his proper gains,' wrote Richard Stock, a staunch puritan, and George Hughes' predecessor at All Hallows, 'or private respects shall admit captains and colonels and marshals for the leading of severall bands, which have no skill in war and martiall affaires, are not able to lead their bands and to go in and out before them, can never answer it to their prince if it be known that this is the cause why the battel succeeds so badly.'[55] All Christians are soldiers, wrote John Downame, 'but especially this courage and care is required of God's ministers, unto which is required not onely that they be valorous in fighting the Lord's battails, but also prudent and skilfull in the militarie discipline, that they may be able to teach and traine others in these feates of armes and how to use their valure, strength and weapons to their best advantage, seeing that they are called of God not to be common souldiers but captaines and leaders of his holy armies.'[56]

Every puritan would have agreed with John Traske that 'the maine or chiefe practice of preaching is to wrestle and fight with, yea, to overcome all opposition.'[57] Every puritan would have nodded agreement with Broade when, after pointing out that the scriptures likened Christians to soldiers and the resistance to evil to a battle, he went on 'this then being an usuall allegorie in the scriptures, if I shall continue it in handling of this text [Ephes. 6: 11: "Put on the whole armour of God ..."] it will not I hope seeme strange to any – unless happily themselves be strangers to God's word.'[58] But he might have been unaware how far, as the seventeenth century proceeded, the preachers were going to introduce the terminology of contemporary wars. 'Even children as soone as they be borne,' said Leech, 'they have presently their names put into the checkrowle and receive from their captain their press-money in their baptism.'[59] Watch your tongues, admonished Field, for 'the portcullis of the teeth and the counter-scarfe of the lips are not sufficient to keep in this unruly member.'[60] It was, of course, a time of wars, and of wars which were, or could be regarded as, wars of religion, with 'the proud race of Ottoman, now advancing his moony standards in Polonia'[61] and, more pertinently, with protestants being oppressed in the Palatinate, in France, and in the Low Countries, a time when puritan divines were agitated by the crown's flirtations with the Spanish-catholic bogey.

But the alertness to real wars on the continent, the experience of men like Bachiler and Scott who served as chaplains to the forces overseas, the relationship of ministers to the mock or trial wars of the Artillery garden were important, I would suggest, largely because these things enriched and made more strident a vocabulary of militancy that was, in any case, a part of puritan devotion, and had been so under Elizabeth. The wayfaring-warfaring theme in puritan literature has been described with great force, and delicacy, by Haller.[62] Man fared on his way toward God, and he needed God's armour to protect him from Satan's assaults and stratagems on his road. The difference between real war and allegorical war, the combat of the soul with sin, was clear, or should have been clear. 'In all our affayres of our outward warfare, Lord grant us grace especially to be zealous in our inward combate against sinne and wickeness,' ran part of the prayer[63] Harward wrote for seamen on active service. But already, in this prayer, there is what must have seemed to the ordinary man a confusing identity of terms between the nature of the inward and the outward battle.

In Downame's *The Christian Warfare* the emphasis is all the time on spiritual combat with spiritual weapons, but the language is so concrete that the image of real warfare is present with a modish insistence that runs the risk of occluding the image of spiritual warfare. The secular military literature was full of references to soldiers who found shotproof armour too heavy. Speaking of God's armour, Downame says that it is not enough 'that we put on one piece of the armour and, like young soldiers, leave off the next for ligh[t]nes sake.' Another secular theme was the difficulty of preventing troops from scattering in search of food or loot. 'We must keep us in God's armie and campe, the Church militant,' Downame wrote. 'For as those stragling souldiers who depart from the armie and range abroad to forraige or get some bootie are easily vanquished by their enemies, so those who depart and make an apostasie from God's Church ... are easily overthrowne, falling into Satan's ambushments.' He goes to unusual lengths to give his allegorical images a realistic cladding. Speaking of the girdle of virtue, he points out that 'the word here signifieth a broad studded belt used in wars in ancient times, wherewith the ioints of the breast-plate and that armor which defended the belly, loines and thighes were covered.' Practice was needed in the use of the sword of the spirit, for 'if a man have this two edged sword of God's word and have no skill to rule it, he will strike flat-long and not cut.'[64]

The divines were not unaware of the possibility of confusion. *A Spiritual Chaine* covers two themes: it urges upon the reader the legitimacy of fighting in just wars in thoroughly down-to-earth terms (there is a woodcut of an infantryman on the title-page),[65] and it encourages him to meditate on the purpose of his spiritual armour: Truth the girdle, Righteousness the breastplate, Peace the shoes, Faith the shield, Salvation the helmet, the Word the sword. Attempting to make the distinction clear between these themes, the author explains that:

> the heavenly armour of a soldier was in truth and substance before the earthly (howsoever for our weake capacitie the spiritual armour was afterwards made plaine to us by the corporall), so as according to a supernaturall sence, the bodily armour may be said to take dominion of the armour of the spirit, and the corporall combat dominion also of that spirituall combat which the children of God have with Satan and his children. For why? The armour of armours belonging to this combate (even the armour of God) was before any corporall combat could be used.[66]

This somewhat cloudy explanation was the more necessary for the turning away by puritan divines from the 'four senses' explanation of the significance of Holy Writ and their concentration at once on seeking a literal meaning and on writing and speaking in a style which was as graphic and immediate as possible. In urging warfaring wayfarers 'to repaire the breaches which Satan made, to fortifie their holds where they are weake, to trie their weapons in better manner'[67] the temptation of the style was to introduce contemporary military jargon, to keep abreast, as it were, of the news, and the consequence of the method was a playing up of the militancy of the Bible, because the battles recorded there lent themselves to literal interpretation, and a playing down of the 'pacifist' passages because they did not. Thus Gouge, faced by Isaiah's prophecy about swords being beaten into ploughshares and spears into pruning hooks – after a deluge of texts justifying war – comments: 'these and such-like propheticall phrases are somewhat hyperbolicall. They expresse that intire amity that should be betwixt true Christians and the alteration of their nature by the spirit of Grace ... to which purpose tend those other high transcendent hyperbolicall phrases of the prophet Isay.'[68] This is from a commentary on Exodus dedicated to the earl of Warwick because 'your lordship is known to be a man of warre,' written by the author of a work on spiritual warfare,[69] an author who justified torture in a case of 'requiting like for like: as the Israelites dealt with Adonibezek, whose thumbs and great toes they cut off, for so had he done to threescore and ten kings before' with the caution: 'what thou doest against thine enemies do in love. Love their persons though thou hate their practices.'[70] The border-line between inner and outward warfare was there, but it must have been increasingly difficult for puritan congregations to keep it in mind.

Alongside the 'orthodox' endorsement of war (typified towards the end of our period by Field) there was, then, a growing volume of puritan writing and preaching which not only justified war with increasing urgency, but which spoke of the soul's struggle against evil in terms which appeared to endorse the notion of fighting against the forces of Antichrist in real earnest. Against this background there is nothing surprising about a minister who, like Edmund Calamy, could urge parliament to bring in a Scottish army and (in the same year, 1643) publish a booklet justifying military service by describing the nature of the 'inner man that is a fit souldier to fight the Lord's battles.'[71] Nor is it surprising that parliamentary leaders should come to justify their militancy in terms not of a constitutional struggle but of a crusade.[72] And it has been the purpose of this essay to suggest that, if it was uncharacteristic that a generation of Englishmen fell to settling their differences by violence, a study of the theme of war in the age's only mass medium goes some way to reducing the element of surprise in the greatest anomaly in English history.

APPENDIX

SERMONS AND OTHER WORKS BY CLERICS
LARGELY OR ENTIRELY DEVOTED TO JUSTIFYING WAR

1578 T[homas] W[hite]
A Sermon preached at Pawles Crosse on Sunday the ninth of December 1576
[1578] John Stockwood
A Sermon preached at Paules Crosse on Bartholmew day, being the 24. of August 1578
1588 John Prime
The Consolations of David, breefly applied to Queene Elizabeth, in a Sermon preached in Oxford the 17. of November (Oxford) 1588 E.R.

Two Fruitfull Exercises: a Christian Discourse upon the 16. and 17.
verses of the 16. chapter of Judges ...
1588 Edmond Harris
A Sermon preached at Brocket Hall before the Right Worshipfull
Sir John Brocket and other Gentlemen there assembled
for the Trayning of Souldiers
1591 R[oger] H[acket]
A Sermon needful for these times ... Preached at Paules Crosse
the 14. of Feb. 1590
1592 Simon Harward
The Solace for the Souldier and Saylour ...
[1598] Stephen Gosson
The Trumpet of Warre. A Sermon preached at Paules Crosse the
seventh of Maie 1598
1617 Thomas Adams
The Souldiours Honour. Wherein by divers inferences and gradations
it is evinced that the profession is iust, necessarie and honourable; to be
practised of some men, praised of all men ... Preached to the worthy
Companie of Gentlemen that exercise in the Artillerie Garden
1618 John Everarde
The Arriereban. A Sermon preached to the company of the Military
Yarde, at St. Andrewes Church in Holborne on St. Iames his day last
1619 John Leech
The Trayne Souldier. A Sermon preached before the worthy Society of
the Captaynes and Gentlemen that exercise Armes in the Artillery Garden,
at Saint Andrew-Undershaft in London, April 20. 1619
1622 Samuel Buggs
Miles Mediterraneus. The Mid-land Souldier. A Sermon preached in the
audience (and published at the request) of the worthie Company of
Practizers in the Military Garden in the well governed City of Coventry
1622 Anon.
A Spiritual Chaine and Armour of choice for Sion Souldiers
1624 [Alexander Leighton]
Speculum belli sacri: or the lookingglasse of the holy war, wherein is
discovered the evil of war, the good of war, the guide of war. In the last
of these I give a scantling of the Christian tackticks, from the levying of
the Souldier to the sounding of the Retrait ...
1624 [Thomas Scott]
The Belgick Souldier ... or, Warre was a Blessing [Dort]
1626 William Gouge

*The Dignitie of Chivalrie; set forth in a Sermon preached before the
Artillery Company of London, Iune xiij, 1626*
1626 [Thomas Barnes]
Vox Belli, or an Alarum to Warre
1627 William Hampton
*A Proclamation of Warre from the Lord of Hosts, or England's warning
by Israel's ruin ... Delivered in a Sermon at Paul's Cross
Iuly the 23. 1626*
1628 T[heophilus] F[ield]
*A Watch-Word, or the Allarme, or a good Take Heed. A Sermon preached
at White-Hall in the open preaching place the last Lent before
King Charles*
1629 John Davenport
*A Royall Edict for military Exercises, published in a Sermon preached
to the Captaines and Gentlemen that exercise Armes in the Artillery
Garden at their General Meeting*
1629 Samuel Bachiler
The Campe Royall ... preached in the Army at the Leaguer
1629 Richard Bernard
*The Bible-Battells, or the Sacred Art Military. For the rightly waging
of Warre according to Holy Writ*
1631 William Gouge
*The Churches Conquest over the Sword: set out on Exod. Chap. XVII
verse VIII &c. to the end*
(This is the separate title-page of the last section of the three-part work,
Gods three Arrowes: Plague, Famine, Sword, in three Treatises,
to which a new edition of *The Dignitie of Chivalrie* is appended
with continuous pagination.)

NOTES

* I am grateful to Mr Christopher Hill for reading the manuscript of this
article. Arguments and inferences and any errors that may remain are, of
course, my own responsibility.
1 Lindsay Boynton, *The Elizabethan Militia* (London 1967) and C.G.
Cruickshank, *Elizabeth's Army* (2nd ed. London 1966) *passim*
2 'It is hardly possible to exaggerate the importance of the sermon in the
seventeenth-century world.' D. Bush, *English Literature in the earlier
Seventeenth Century* (Oxford 1945), p. 296. 'Surely the time has come for
historians to turn their attention to the pulpits, which, as Macaulay said

long ago, were "to a large proportion of the population what the periodi-
cal press now is".' G. Davies, 'English political sermons (1600-1640),'
Huntington Library Quarterly (Oct. 1939), p. 2. (The analogy today
would be with television – and the inconclusive debate about the connection between violent programmes and violent behaviour warns us to caution when dealing with a period beyond the reach of sociological investigation.) Also, Christopher Hill, *Puritanism and Revolution* (London 1962),
p. 269.

3 See appendix, pp. 393-4. As the purpose of this essay is no more than to
raise an issue, I have not moved into the most crucial decade of all, 1631-
41, which demands a far more thorough analysis than I can attempt here.
When I wrote this essay I had not seen Michael Walzer's *The Revolution
of the Saints* (Harvard 1965). He anticipates (pp. 277-8 and 290-1) two
of the points developed in the following pages: the increasingly concrete
nature of the imagery used in puritan sermons, which might have led to a
blurring of the distinction between spiritual and physical warfare, and the
suggestion that there can have been a connection between militant imagery
and militant behaviour. I can only hope that my treatment of these themes
appears in the guise of substantiation rather than of supererogation.

4 As in Adams, pp. 24-5. (Citation by author only is a reference to the
works listed in the appendix.)

5 *Summa, q.* XL, *a.* II

6 *Ob Kriegsleute auch in seligem Stande sein können* (1526). H. Bender,
'The pacifism of the sixteenth-century Anabaptists,' *Mennonite Quarterly
Review* XXX (1959), 7-8

7 Roland H. Bainton, *Christian Attitudes to War and Peace* (London 1961),
p. 145

8 *Toxophilus* (1545), ed. E. Arber (London 1868), p. 70. (In quotations,
original spelling is retained, but capitalization and punctuation is modernized.)

9 *The Defence of Militarie Profession* (London 1579), p. 62

10 *The Double-armed Man* (1625), f. B3ʳ

11 John Norden, *The Mirror of Honor* (1597), p. 48

12 *Ibid.*, p. 69

13 *Discourses of War and Single Combat*, f. A2ʳ⁻ᵛ and 1-2

14 John Denison, *Beati pacifici: The Blessednes of Peace-makers* (1620),
p. 11

15 M.J.D. Cockle, *A Bibliography of English Military Books up to 1642*
(London 1900). The supplements of T.M. Spaulding, *Proceedings of the
Bibliographical Society of America* (1940), 186 ff., and J.R. Hale, *ibid.*,
137 ff., are but respectful flourishes on this admirable work.

16 For their importance, see M. Maclure, *The Paul's Cross Sermons, 1534-
1642* (Toronto 1958)

17 *The Diary of John Manningham*, ed. J. Bruce, *Camden Society*, XCIX
(1868) contains careful notes on sermons attended in 1602-3

18 This is a 'meagre allowance'; G. Davies. 'English political sermons,' 1.
Meagre indeed; London clergymen commonly preached twice on Sundays

and on Wednesdays as well. Davies' figure is based on one sermon per parish per *year*.

19 A computerized theme-check of sermons, 1550-1642, would be of great value to the study of public opinion, especially if coupled with an analysis of the texts cited and of imagery.

20 Christopher Hill, *Society and Puritanism* (London 1964), p. 34

21 Henry Gee and W.J. Hardy, *Documents Illustrative of English Church History* (London 1896), pp. 516-17. According to Thomas Fuller, James was 'informed that it was high time to apply some cure to the pulpits, as sick of a sermon-surfeit' and that the effect of the articles was to 'cut off half the preaching in England ... at one blow.' *The Church History of Britain*, ed. James Nichols (London 1868), III, pp. 355, 358.

22 E.g., Richard Morison, *An Exhortation to styr all Englyshe Men to the Defence of theyr Contreye* (1538)

23 *Certayne Sermons appoynted by the Queenes Maiestie, to be declared and read, by all Parsons, Vicars and Curates, every Sunday and Holyday in theyr Churches* (1559)

24 Hill, *Society and Puritanism*, p. 35

25 This quotation, and the preceding facts are taken from Boynton, *The Elizabethan Militia*, p. 36, and *passim*.

26 As Davenport did with a prayer printed at the end of his sermon.

27 To avoid a surfeit of footnotes, references are not given in this section. All quotations are from works listed in the appendix, unless a new reference is made in the text.

28 J.W. Blench, *Preaching in England in the late Fifteenth and Sixteenth Centuries* (Oxford 1964), p. 170. Unless references are given, biographical information is from DNB.

29 Blench, *Preaching in England*, p. 169

30 W. Ringler, *Stephen Gosson: A Biographical and Critical Study* (Princeton 1942), *passim*. C.S. Lewis pointed out that 'in his sermon, *The Trumpet of Warre*, he quotes Aquinas and Cajetan.' *English Literature in the Sixteenth Century* (Oxford 1954), p. 395.

31 Bush, *English Literature in the earlier Seventeenth Century*, p. 398

32 Rufus M. Jones, *Spiritual Reformers in the Sixteenth and Seventeenth Centuries* (London 1914), pp. 207 ff.

33 Not so much on the evidence of *Miles Mediterraneus* as on that of another sermon, *Davids Strait. A sermon preached at Pauls-Cross July 8, 1621* (1622) ; e.g., p. 7, 'Indeed, in God's eternal predestination and election, no man ought to enquire; as why Iacob is loved and Esau hated, because the potter may doe with the clay as he listeth.'

34 Published posthumously, in 1655, three parts in one volume. On Hebrews 7: 1, Gouge comments: 'This giveth a plain proof both of the lawfulnesse of war and also of slaying enemies in war.' A similar point is made *à propos* 11: 33.

35 Valerie Pearl, *London and the Outbreak of the Puritan Revolution* (London 1961) ; see her index for Gouge and Davenport

36 W. Haller, *The Rise of Puritanism* (New York 1938), p. 68

37 To judge mainly from his *The Gales of Grace; or the Spiritual Wind: Wherein the Mysterie of Sanctification is opened and handled* (1622)
38 *The History of the Rebellion and Civil Wars in England, begun in the year 1641* (Oxford 1720), II, pt. i, 22-3
39 *Scrinia Reserata: a memorial offer'd to the great deservings of John Williams, D.D.* (1692), II, p. 139
40 Theodorus Verax [Clement Walker], *The Mysterie of the two Iuntos, Presbyterian and Independent* (1647), p. 3. My attention was directed to these three passages by E.W. Kirby, 'Sermons before the Commons, 1640-42,' *American Historical Review*, XLIV (1938-9), 528n.
41 *A Letter from Mercurius Civicus to Mercurius Rusticus* (1643), ed. Walter Scott, *Somers Tracts*, IV (1965), 583
42 E.g., Harward's 'Antichristian Catholics,' meaning Spaniards, *The Solace for the Souldier and Saylour*, f. C2ᵛ
43 *A Letter*, 582
44 Pearl, *London and the Outbreak of the Puritan Revolution*, pp. 170-3
45 *A Spiritual Chaine*, f. A2ʳ
46 Scott, *The Belgick Souldier*, f. F2ʳ
47 Gouge, *The Dignitie of Chivalrie*, p. 19
48 *The Saints Losse and Lamentation* (1632)
49 P. 46
50 Davenport, *A Royall Edict*, pp. 14-15
51 For this reference, and a development of this theme, see Sir John Smythe, *Certain Discourses Military*, ed. J.R. Hale (Cornell 1964), pp. xlii ff.
52 *A Sermon preached at Paules Crosse on Bartholomew Day*; Blench, *Preaching in England*, p. 306
53 Davenport, *A Royall Edict*, p. 18
54 *Acts of the Privy Council*, 14 September 1622, p. 30
55 *A learned and very useful Commentary upon the whole Prophecy of Malachy*. This was published posthumously in 1642, in 2 parts, edited by Samuel Torshell. Stock died in 1626 (II, p. 49). The work was dedicated to (among others) Captain John Venn of the Artillery company.
56 *The Conflict between the Flesh and the Spirit. Or the last part of the Christian Warfare* (1618) f.2ᵛ (the dedication to Francis Bacon)
57 *The Power of Preaching* (1623)
58 T. Broade, *A Christians Warre* (1613), p. 2. Referring to its publication, Broade said that his 'sermon ... is pressed forth to war, as thou seest. God grant it may stoutly fight the Lord's battles' (f. H5ᵛ)
59 Leech, *The Trayne Souldier*, p. 41-2
60 Field, *A Watch-Word*, p. 20
61 Buggs, *Davids Strait*, p. 5. Dedicating *Vox Belli* to Sir Horatio Vere, Barnes says that he hopes 'what I have written may prevaile to provoke them whom it concernes to a readinesse to succour the distressed church in forreine parts.' And Scott, after running through a list of religious wars – Hus, Zizka, Luther, 'then stood Geneva on their guard, then Denmark, Norway, Sweden, England, Scotland' – asks 'if it be thus, was not warre a

blessing, and hath not religion beene propagated by that meanes?' (f.
B2ᵛ – 3ʳ).

62 Haller, *The Rise of Puritanism*, in the chapter 'The Rhetoric of the Spirit'
63 Harward, *The Solace for the Souldier and Saylour*, f. G3ʳ
64 First printed 1604, I used the edition of 1612, pp. 47, 49, 51, 64
65 All the more down-to-earth for not being shown in allegorical company, as was the soldier on the 1634 title-page of Downame's *The Christian Warfare*
66 *A Spiritual Chaine*, pp. 4-5
67 William Jemmatt, *A Spirituall Trumpet exciting and preparing to the Christian Warfare* (1624), p. 195. The first edition is 1623. The work is dedicated 'To all the Lord's captains and souldiers.' Jemmatt, a puritan, was at that time 'preacher of God's word at Lechlade in Gloucestershire.'
68 *The Churches Conquest*, p. 211
69 *The Whole-Armour of God: or the Spirituall Furniture which God hath provided to keepe safe every Christian Souldier from all the Assaults of Satan* (1616)
70 Tonge, *The Churches Conquest*, p. 296
71 *The Souldiers Pocket Bible, containing the most (if not all) those places contained in Holy Scripture which doe shew the qualifications of his inner man that is a fit souldier to fight the Lords battels both before the fight, in the fight and after the fight*; see Harold Willoughby, *Soldiers' Bibles through three Centuries* (Chicago 1944), esp. pp. 3 ff.
72 R.H. Bainton, 'Congregationalism: from the Just War to the Crusade in the Puritan Revolution,' *Andover Newton Theological School Bulletin* (April 1943)

PRINCIPAL WRITINGS OF
WALLACE K. FERGUSON

In compiling this bibliography we have not listed the considerable number of book reviews and minor notes which Professor Ferguson has written. The listing is chronological.

'The Place of Jansenism in French History,' *The Journal of Religion* VII (1927), 16-42

'The Attitude of Erasmus toward Toleration,' *Persecution and Liberty: Essays in Honor of George Lincoln Burr* (The Century Co., New York, 1931), pp. 171-82

Erasmi Opuscula: A Supplement to the Opera Omnia (Martinus Nijhoff, The Hague, 1933)

'An Unpublished Letter of John Colet, Dean of St. Paul's,' *American Historical Review*, XXXIX (1934), 696-9

A Survey of European Civilization, Vol. I (vol. II by Geoffrey Bruun), (Houghton Mifflin Co., Boston, 1936; 2nd revised ed., 1947; 3rd revised ed., 1958; 4th revised ed., 1969; Swedish translation, Tidens Forlag, Stockholm, 1938)

'Humanist Views of the Renaissance,' *American Historical Review*, XLV (1939), 1-28

The Renaissance (Henry Holt & Co., New York, 1940; revised ed., 1969)

'Jacob Burckhardt's Interpretation of the Renaissance,' *Quarterly Bulletin of the Polish Institute of Arts and Sciences in America* (Jan., 1943), pp. 1-14

The Renaissance in Historical Thought: Five Centuries of Interpretation (Houghton Mifflin Co., Boston, 1948; French translation, Payot, Paris, 1950; Italian translation, Il Mulino, Bologna, 1969)

'The Interpretation of the Renaissance: Suggestions for a Synthesis,' *Journal of the History of Ideas*, XII (1951), 483-95

'The Church in a Changing World: A Contribution to the Interpretation of the Renaissance,' *American Historical Review*, LIX (1953), 1-18

'Toward the Modern State,' *The Renaissance, A Symposium* (Metropolitan Museum of Art, New York, 1953), pp. 1-16; republished as *The Renaissance, Six Essays* (Harper Torchbooks, 1962), pp. 1-27

'Renaissance Tendencies in the Religious Thought of Erasmus,' *Journal of the History of Ideas*, XV (1954), 499-508

'The Revival of Classical Antiquity or the First Century of Humanism: A Reappraisal,' *Report of the Annual Meeting of the Canadian Historical Association* (1957), pp. 13-30

'The Interpretation of Humanism: The Contributions of Hans Baron,' *Journal of the History of Ideas*, XIX (1958), 14-25

'The Reinterpretation of the Renaissance,' *Facets of the Renaissance*: The Arensberg Lectures, 1956 (University of Southern California Press, Los Angeles, 1959; republished, Harper Torchbooks, 1963), pp. 1-18

'Recent Trends in the Economic Historiography of the Renaissance,' *Studies in the Renaissance*, VII (1960), 7-26

'Some Problems of Historiography: Presidential Address,' *Report of the Annual Meeting of the Canadian Historical Association*, 1961, pp. 1-12

Europe in Transition, 1300-1520 (Houghton Mifflin Co., Boston, 1962)

Renaissance Studies (University of Western Ontario Studies in the Humanities, 1963; republished, Harper Torchbooks, 1970)

Erasmus and Christian Humanism, The Smith History Lecture (University of St. Thomas, Houston, 1963)

Introduction to Alfred von Martin, *Sociology of the Renaissance* (Harper Torchbooks, 1963), pp. v-xiv

Introduction to J. C. L. de Sismondi, *A History of the Italian Republics* (Anchor Books, Doubleday & Co., New York, 1966), pp. v-xxi

This book

was designed by

ALLAN FLEMING

with the assistance of

ELLEN HUTCHISON

and was printed by

University of

Toronto

Press